DATE DUE			

THE

ANNUAL REGISTER

Vol. 236

ANNUAL REGISTER ADVISORY BOARD

Rex Features

Peace and War

[*Top*] Washington, 25 July: Applauded by President Clinton, King Husain of Jordan and Prime Minister Rabin of Israel shake hands on their historic peace declaration. [*Bottom*] Grozny, mid-December: The Russian offensive against the rebel republic of Chechenya meets fierce resistance from Chechen fighters.

Rex Features

Progress and Regression

[*Top*] Calais. 6 May: Queen Elizabeth and President Mitterrand of France open the Channel Tunnel, providing the first fixed link between Britain and the European continent. [*Bottom*] Goma, Zaïre, late July: The millions of refugees from the blood-letting in Rwanda include thousands of orphaned children.

THE
ANNUAL REGISTER

A Record of World Events
1994

Edited by
ALAN J. DAY

assisted by
VERENA HOFFMAN

FIRST EDITED IN 1758
BY EDMUND BURKE

STOCKTON

THE ANNUAL REGISTER 1994
Published by Cartermill International Limited, Maple House,
149 Tottenham Court Road, London, W1P 9LL, United Kingdom

ISBN 1-86067-015-6 (Cartermill)

Co-published in the United States and Canada by Stockton Press,
49 West 24th Street, New York, NY 10010-3206, USA

ISBN 1-56159-138-6 (Stockton)

Library of Congress Catalog Card Number: 4-17979

British Library Cataloguing in Publication Data
The Annual Register—1994
  1. History—Periodicals
  909.82'8'05   D410

ISBN 1-86067-015-6

Set in Times Roman by
THE MIDLANDS BOOK TYPESETTING COMPANY, LOUGHBOROUGH
Printed and bound in Great Britain by
BPC WHEATONS LTD, EXETER

CONTENTS

CONTRIBUTORS

CZECH AND SLOVAK REPUBLICS	**Jan Obrman,** Senior Research Analyst, RFE/RL, Prague
	Sharon Fisher, Research Analyst, Open Media Research Institute (OMRI), Prague
HUNGARY	**George Schöpflin,** Joint Lecturer in East European Political Institutions, London School of Economics and School of Slavonic and East European Studies, University of London
ROMANIA	**Gabriel Partos,** Eastern European Analyst, BBC World Service
BULGARIA	**Stephen Ashley,** MA, DPhil, Senior Talks Writer, BBC World Service
FORMER YUGOSLAVIA	**John B. Allcock,** MA, PhD, Head of Research Unit in South-East European Studies, University of Bradford
ALBANIA	**Richard Crampton,** PhD, University Lecturer in East European History and Fellow of St Edmund Hall, Oxford
RUSSIA, BELORUSSIA, UKRAINE, MOLDOVA AND CAUCASIA	**Stephen White,** PhD, Professor of Politics, University of Glasgow
BALTIC REPUBLICS	**John Hiden,** Professor of Modern European History and Director, Baltic Research Unit, University of Bradford

PART IV

USA	**Neil A. Wynn,** MA, PhD, Reader in History and American Studies, University of Glamorgan
CANADA	**David M.L. Farr,** Professor Emeritus of History, Carleton University, Ottawa
LATIN AMERICA	**Peter Calvert,** AM, MA, PhD, Professor of Comparative and International Politics, University of Southampton
THE CARIBBEAN	**Ciarán Ó Maoláin,** BA, Research Fellow, Centre for the Study of Conflict, University of Ulster; writer on Caribbean, Latin American and Pacific affairs

PART V

ISRAEL	**Joel Peters,,** BSc, PhD, Lecturer in International Relations, University of Reading
ARAB WORLD, EGYPT, JORDAN, SYRIA, LEBANON, IRAQ	**Christopher Gandy,** Formerly UK Diplomatic Service; writer on Middle Eastern affairs
SAUDI ARABIA, YEMEN	**R.M. Burrell,** Lecturer in the Contemporary History of the Near and Middle East, School of Oriental and African Studies, University of London
ARAB STATES OF THE GULF	**George Joffé,** Deputy Director, Geopolitics and International Boundaries Research Centre, School of Oriental and African Studies, University of London
SUDAN	**Ahmed al-Shahi,** DPhil, Lecturer in Social Anthropology, Department of Social Policy, University of Newcastle-upon-Tyne
LIBYA, TUNISIA, ALGERIA, MOROCCO, WESTERN SAHARA	**R. I. Lawless,** PhD, Emeritus Reader in Modern Middle Eastern Studies, University of Durham

PART VI

ETHIOPIA, SOMALIA, DJIBOUTI	**Christopher Clapham**, MA, DPhil, Professor of Politics and International Relations, University of Lancaster
KENYA, TANZANIA, UGANDA	**William Tordoff**, MA, PhD, Emeritus Professor of Government, University of Manchester
GHANA	**D.G. Austin** (see Pt. III, Malta)
NIGERIA	**Guy Arnold**, Freelance writer specializing in Africa and North-South affairs
SIERRA LEONE, THE GAMBIA, LIBERIA	**Arnold Hughes**, BA, Director, Centre of West African Studies, The University of Birmingham
CHAPTER 3 (SENEGAL to EQUATORIAL GUINEA)	**Kaye Whiteman**, Editor-in-Chief, *West Africa*

PART VII

CHAPTER 1 (ZAÏRE TO ANGOLA)	**Robin Hallett**, MA, Writer and lecturer on African affairs
ZAMBIA, MALAWI	**Robin Hallett** (see above)
ZIMBABWE	**R. W. Baldock**, BA, PhD, Senior Editor, Yale University Press; writer on African affairs
NAMIBIA, BOTSWANA, LESOTHO, SWAZILAND, SOUTH AFRICA	**Greg Mills**, MA, PhD, Director of Studies, South African Institute of International Affairs, Johannesburg

PART VIII

IRAN	**Keith McLachlan**, BA, PhD, Professor of Geography, Director, Geopolitics and International Boundaries Research Centre, School of Oriental and African Studies, University of London
AFGHANISTAN, INDIA, BANGLADESH, NEPAL, BHUTAN	**Peter Lyon**, BSc(Econ), PhD, Reader in International Relations and Academic Secretary, Institute of Commonwealth Studies, University of London; Editor, *The Round Table*
CENTRAL ASIAN REPUBLICS	**Shirin Akiner**, PhD, Director, Central Asia Research Forum, School of Oriental and African Studies, University of London
PAKISTAN	**David Taylor**, Senior Lecturer in Politics with reference to South Asia, School of Oriental and African Studies, University of London
SRI LANKA	**Charles Gunawardena**, former Director of Information, Commonwealth Secretariat, London
SEYCHELLES, MAURITIUS, MALDIVES	**Harry Drost**, Writer on European and Third World affairs
MADAGASCAR AND COMOROS	**Kaye Whiteman** (see Pt. VI, Ch. 3)

PART IX

MYANMAR (BURMA), INDONESIA, PHILIPPINES	**Raymond L. Bryant**, PhD, Lecturer in Geography, King's College, London
THAILAND, VIETNAM, CAMBODIA, LAOS	**Jonathan Rigg**, PhD, Lecturer in South-East Asian Geography, University of Durham

MALAYSIA, BRUNEI, SINGAPORE   **Michael Leifer,** BA, PhD, Professor of International Relations, London School of Economics and Political Science

CHINA, TAIWAN, HONG KONG   **Robert F. Ash,** MSc(Econ), PhD, Director, Contemporary China Institute and Senior Lecturer in Economics, School of Oriental and African Studies, University of London

JAPAN   **I.H. Nish,** Emeritus Professor of International History, London School of Economics and Political Science

SOUTH AND NORTH KOREA   **James H. Grayson,** PhD, Director, Centre for Korean Studies, University of Sheffield

MONGOLIA   **Alan Sanders,** FIL, Lecturer in Mongolian Studies, School of Oriental and African Studies, University of London

PART X

AUSTRALIA   **James Jupp,** MSc (Econ), PhD, FASSA, Director, Centre for Immigration and Multicultural Studies, Australian National University, Canberra

PAPUA NEW GUINEA   **Norman MacQueen,** Reader in International Relations, University of Sunderland

NEW ZEALAND, PACIFIC ISLAND STATES   **Roderic Alley,** PhD, School of Political Science and Public Administration, Victoria University of Wellington

PART XI

UNITED NATIONS   **Sam Daws,** MA, Consultant on UN Affairs, New College, Oxford

COMMONWEALTH   **Derek Ingram,** Consultant Editor of *Gemini News Service*; author and writer on the Commonwealth

EUROPEAN UNION   **Michael Berendt,** Expert on affairs of the European Union

OECD, EFTA   **Roger East,** Editor of *Keesing's Record of World Events*; founder and director of CIRCA Research and Reference Information

NON–ALIGNED MOVEMENT AND DEVELOPING COUNTRIES   **Peter Willetts,** PhD, Reader in International Relations, The City University, London

CONFERENCE ON SECURITY AND COOPERATION IN EUROPE   **Adrian G.V. Hyde-Price,** BSc(Econ), PhD, Lecturer, Department of Politics, University of Southampton

EUROPEAN BANK FOR RECONSTRUCTION AND DEVELOPMENT   **Michael Kaser,** MA, DLitt, DSocSc, Emeritus Fellow of St Antony's College, Oxford, and Honorary Professor, University of Birmingham

COUNCIL OF EUROPE   **Colin Lee,** MA, Secretary to UK delegation to Parliamentary Assembly of the Council of Europe

NORDIC AND BALTIC COOPERATION   **Hilary Allen** (see Pt. II, Nordic Countries)

AFRICAN CONFERENCES AND ORGANIZATIONS   **Kaye Whiteman** (see Pt. VI, Ch. 3)

CONTRIBUTORS

SOUTH ASIAN ASSOCIATION FOR REGIONAL COOPERATION	**Peter Lyon** (see Pt. VIII, Afghanistan, etc.)
ASIA-PACIFIC ORGANIZATIONS	**D.J. Sagar,** Regional Editor, *Keesing's Record of World Events;* director, CIRCA Research and Reference Information
SOUTH PACIFIC COOPERATION	**Roderic Alley** (see Pt. X, New Zealand, etc.)
AMERICAN ORGANIZATIONS	**Peter Calvert** (see Pt. IV, Latin America)
CARIBBEAN ORGANIZATIONS	**Ciarán Ó Maoláin** (see Pt. IV, Caribbean)

PART XII
DEFENCE, DISARMAMENT AND SECURITY

Phil Williams, PhD, Professor of Security Studies, Graduate School of Public and International Affairs, University of Pittsburgh
Robert E. Mullings, Graduate School of Public and International Affairs, University of Pittsburgh

PART XIII
RELIGION

Geoffrey Parrinder, MA, PhD, DD, Emeritus Professor of the Comparative Study of Religions, University of London

PART XIV
MEDICAL, SCIENTIFIC AND INDUSTRIAL RESEARCH
INFORMATION TECHNOLOGY

ENVIRONMENT

Martin Redfern, Deputy Science Editor, BBC World Service
David Powell, A director of Electronic Publishing Services Ltd; editor, *EP Journal*
Lloyd Timberlake, Senior Fellow, International Institute for Environment and Development

PART XV
INTERNATIONAL LAW

EUROPEAN COMMUNITY LAW

LAW IN THE UK

LAW IN THE USA

Christine Gray, MA, PhD, Fellow in Law, St Hilda's College, Oxford
N. March Hunnings, LLM, PhD, Editor, *Encyclopedia of European Union Laws: Constitutional Texts*
David Ibbetson, MA, PhD, Fellow and Tutor in Law, Magdalen College, Oxford
Robert J. Spjut, ID, LLM, Member of the State Bars of California and Florida

PART XVI
OPERA

MUSIC

BALLET/DANCE

Charles Osborne, Author; opera critic, *The Jewish Chronicle*
Francis Routh, Composer and author; founder director of the Redcliffe Concerts
Jane Pritchard, Archivist, Rambert Dance Company and English National Ballet

THEATRE	**Jeremy Kingston,** Theatre critic, *The Times*
CINEMA	**Derek Malcolm,** Film critic, *The Guardian*
TV & RADIO	**Raymond Snoddy,** Media correspondent, *The Financial Times*
ART	**David Cohen,** MA (Courtauld), Art historian and critic, contributor to national press and fine art journals
ARCHITECTURE	**Paul Finch,** Editor, *The Architects' Journal*
LITERATURE	**Alastair Niven,** Literature director of the Arts Council of England

PART XVII
| SPORT | **Tony Pawson,** OBE, Sports writer, *The Observer*; cricket, football and fly-fishing international |

PART XVIII
| THE INTERNATIONAL ECONOMY | **Victor Keegan,** Assistant Editor, *The Guardian* |
| STATISTICS | **Sue Sparks,** Former member of the Statistical Department, *The Financial Times* |

PART XX
| OBITUARY | **H. V. Hodson,** Former editor of *The Annual Register*; editor, *The Sunday Times*, 1950–61; Provost of Ditchley Foundation, 1961-71 |
| MAPS | MJL **Graphics,** N. Yorks, YO14 9BE |

ACKNOWLEDGEMENTS

THE Advisory Board again gratefully acknowledges its debt to a number of institutions for their help with sources, references and documents, notably the NATO Information Service, Brussels, and the Israeli embassy, London. Acknowledgement is also due to the principal sources for the national data sections (showing the situation as at end-1994 unless otherwise stated), namely *Keesing's Record of World Events* (Cartermill), *People in Power* (CIRCA), *World Development Report* (OUP for the World Bank) and the *Financial Times*. The Board and the bodies which nominate its members disclaim responsibility for any opinions expressed or the accuracy of facts recorded in this volume.

ABBREVIATIONS

ACC	Arab Cooperation Council
ACP	African, Caribbean and Pacific states associated with EEC
AfDB	African Development Bank
AID	Agency for International Development
AIDS	Acquired Immune Deficiency Syndrome
AMU	Arab Maghreb Union
ANZUS	Australia-New Zealand-USA Security Treaty
APEC	Asia–Pacific Economic Cooperation
AR	Annual Register
ASEAN	Association of South-East Asian Nations
CARICOM	Caribbean Common Market
CEEAC	Economic Community of Central African States
CIS	Commonwealth of Independent States
CSCE	Conference on Security and Cooperation in Europe
Cwth.	Commonwealth
EBRD	European Bank for Reconstruction and Development
EC	European Community
ECO	Economic Cooperation Organization
ECOWAS	Economic Community of West African States
ECU	European Currency Unit
EEA	European Economic Area
EFTA	European Free Trade Association
EMS	European Monetary System
ERM	Exchange Rate Mechanism
ESCAP	Economic and Social Commission for Asia and the Pacific (UN)
EU	European Union
FAO	Food and Agriculture Organization
G–7	Group of Seven
GATT	General Agreement on Tariffs and Trade
GCC	Gulf Cooperation Council
GDP/GNP	Gross Domestic/National Product
IAEA	International Atomic Energy Agency
IBRD	International Bank for Reconstruction and Development
ICO	Islamic Conference Organization
IDA	International Development Association
ILO	International Labour Organization
IMF	International Monetary Fund
IRA	Irish Republican Army
MTO	Multilateral Trade Organization
NAFTA	North American Free Trade Agreement
NAM	Non-Aligned Movement
NATO	North Atlantic Treaty Organization
OAS	Organization of American States
OAU	Oganization of African Unity
OECD	Organization for Economic Cooperation and Development
OPEC (OAPEC)	Organization of (Arab) Petroleum Exporting Countries
PLO	Palestine Liberation Organization
SAARC	South Asian Association for Regional Cooperation
SADC	Southern African Development Community
START	Strategic Arms Reduction Treaty
UN	United Nations
UNCTAD	United National Conference on Trade and Development
UNDP	United Nations Development Programme
UNESCO	United Nations Educational, Scientific and Cultural Organization
UNHCR	United Nations High Commission for Refugees
UNICEF	United Nations Children's Fund
WEU	Western European Union
WHO	World Health Organization

PREFACE

LOYAL readers will notice that this 236th volume marks the end of the long connexion between the AR and the Longman publishing house. The latter ceased to exist as such at the end of 1994. Its operations were distributed among various subsidiaries of parent company Pearson plc, the AR and other Longman current affairs reference titles coming under the imprint of Cartermill International. It is therefore worth recalling, at this moment of transition, the AR's publishing history over nearly two-and-a-half centuries of continuous publication.

The founding publisher of the AR in 1758 was Robert Dodsley, bookseller, poet, playwright and friend of Dr Johnson. He commissioned the 29-year-old Edmund Burke (for a fee of £100) to collect and compile material for a 500–page volume covering the year's significant events, to be published by Lady Day 1759. The AR quickly established itself (some early volumes running to as many as nine editions), and Burke remained editor until 1788. The Dodsley family connexion ended with the death of James Dodsley in 1790, after which the AR became a 'trade book' with many publishing partners. The Longman publishing house (itself founded in 1724) took a share from 1805 and in the course of the nineteenth century became the managing AR publisher. A major reorganization of the volume's content from 1863 established genuinely worldwide coverage of the year's events, with the focus on political and economic affairs.

The AR 'share publishing' arrangement, with what was then called Longmans Green becoming the dominant partner from 1889, survived well into the twentieth century. Not until after World War II were the other partners finally bought out by Longmans Green, which in 1947 set up a prestigious Advisory Board to assist the editor. Longmans Green changed its name to Longmans in 1959 and to Longman in 1969, forming part of what became the Pearson media and entertainment conglomerate. But the direct AR–Longman relationship was to end in 1994, having by then lasted nearly 190 years. Under a restructuring of Pearson's publishing activities, and of Longman in particular, the AR and other Longman reference/professional titles were transferred to Cartermill International, an existing Pearson subsidiary specializing in information dissemination through new technology. At the same time, Cartermill itself became part of a newly-formed company, Pearson Professional, bringing together various other related publishing activities.

The change in publishing imprint signals no change in the ethos and purposes of the AR, and the guiding role of the Advisory Board has been retained. The present volume, like its predecessors, chronicles the political and economic events of the year in all countries of the world, as well as the progress or otherwise of the major inter-governmental organizations. It also provides expert surveys of the year's developments in other areas of human activity, including the law, the sciences, the arts and sport, as well as comprehensive tables of economic and social data and reference texts of the year's important documents.

EXTRACTS FROM PAST VOLUMES

200 years ago

1794. *Downfall of Robespierre.* [27 October, Paris] Robespierre, deeply sensible of his danger, endeavoured to obtain a hearing, and had mounted the tribune for that purpose; but as soon as he was perceived there, he was universally assailed with the cry of Down with him. You shall not speak, said a member—the blood of Danton is upon your head; it flows into your throat, it chokes you.

150 years ago

1844. *Dispute over Post Office.* [House of Commons, 14 June] Sir James Graham said that the Post Office Act of 1837, which consolidated previous laws, contained a provision which permitted the Secretaries of State to empower the Post Office authorities to open letters. Under that power, he had given a warrant, no longer in existence, to open the letters of one of the petitioners [who included Mazzini], whom he refused to name. Sir James Graham declined to give any further explanation. Mr Wallace, Mr Hume, Dr Bowring, and some other members on the Liberal side, took up the subject with much warmth, and denounced the proceeding as despotic and unjustifiable.

100 years ago

1894. *Chicago Railway Strike.* Traffic was blocked for several days on many of the great lines leading into Chicago, beginning on 26 June. Then came a time of incendiarism and violence, which led to the calling out of the United States troops. Hitherto no soldiers had been sent to the State of Illinois except at the request of the State authorities. President Cleveland issued a proclamation (8 July) announcing that a part of the army of the United States would be employed in that State to enforce law and order, and remove obstructions to the United States mails caused by the stoppage of traffic on the railways.

50 years ago

1944. *German Flying-bomb Assault on Britain.* [House of Commons, 6 July] With regard to the actual scale of the attack, Mr Churchill said that between 100 and 150 flying bombs, each weighing about one ton, were being discharged daily. A very large proportion of these had either failed to cross the Channel or had been shot down and destroyed by various methods—batteries, aircraft and balloons—which had been very rapidly placed in position. The weather had been unfavourable to them in this operation also; nevertheless, their success had been considerable. They had brought so many down that so far it had taken on the average one bomb to kill one person.

ANNUAL REGISTER

FOR THE YEAR 1994

EDITORIAL
THE PROCESS OF PEACE

THERE was a moment, quite late in the past year, when a pacific tide seemed to be running across the world, and winning 1994 distinction as a year of peace-making. In the Middle East, under the 1993 pact which gained its signatories the Nobel Peace Prize, Israel had passed qualified self-rule to the Palestinians in Gaza and the West Bank, had signed a peace treaty with Jordan and was edging towards a settlement with Syria. In Ireland, the Downing Street Declaration of the previous December had led both the IRA and militant loyalist factions to forego violent action, if not permanently at least indefinitely. The bloody conflicts in former Yugoslavia, though still continuing, had been reduced in scale, and a number of areas, once victims of mass slaughter and destruction, had been restored to order and relative calm. South Africa had changed from apartheid to multiracial democracy with miraculous amity and good order. The death of Kim Il Sung had nourished hopes of lessened strain in the relations between North and South Korea. In several other zones of violence in the world—Angola, for instance—weariness of war had heightened hopes of peace.

Then the storm clouds massed. Violent incidents exploded in Israel and Palestinian territory: it was no gain for peace if Arab-Jewish conflict was matched by deadly violence between Yassir Arafat's PLO and the irreconcilables of Hamas. A political crisis in Dublin seemingly stopped the clock of advance to peace in Ireland. Western forces in the Gulf area went on war alert as Iraq mounted a menacing army movement southward towards Kuwait. Moscow threatened separatist Chechenya with war to the death. Bosnian Serb obduracy, together with the USA's defection from enforcing the arms embargo, raised fears that the UN/NATO presence would be driven to a bitter choice between withdrawal and participation in the war, and that humanitarian aid itself, dependent as it was on UNPROFOR's impartial protection, would have to end.

Had the flame of peace, then, been no more than the flicker of a wasting candle? To answer that question requires a more discriminating look at the nature of the several wars and warlike violence, and threats of war, that disfigured the global scene. Some were international—Korea, for instance, or Israel's relations with hostile neighbours, or Iraq's unextinguished ambition—but most were internal to nation states (including Ireland, where two nation states were at one in coping with a common menace to their peace), many being historically the product of emergence from the rule of European empires, which released old tribal, religious and other communal enmities. These last were the most genocidal of all, and also the most difficult to heal. Half a century had passed since decolonization began: as long again might be needed before the conflicting communities could be reconciled—or separated—in a stable, peaceful order.

A similar time-scale opens ahead for other causes of violence: in Ireland, until the incompatibles of all-Irish nationalism and Ulster separatism can be permanently reconciled in a peaceful democratic frame; in the Middle East, until the same can happen between the rival aspirations of Jews and Arabs. Pacification of Israel's frontiers with Egypt, Syria, Jordan and Lebanon are a vital phase of the process to peace, but not its essence. Two terrible wars in this century were needed to drive Europe to sink its divisions in a union of nations, even now sharply divided on its own future form. Seventy years of communist grip in the Russian empire ended abruptly, but another lifetime will probably pass before democracy, economic freedom and the rule of law become secure in that vast area, which never knew them in its past history. In the present bellicose disputes already cited, and in others round the world, aspiring to stable peace means thinking in terms of many decades of effort, advances and setbacks.

The strife in former Yugoslavia compounds ethnic conflicts, which can be reconciled only after a long period of time, with war between self-assertive states, which can be arrested by ceasefires based on territorial compromise. The long-term reconciliation cannot begin until the fighting stops, but without progress on the inter-community front any such armistice is bound to be fragile. The vile strategy of 'ethnic cleansing'—a crime not unknown elsewhere in the world in 1994—has left the communal map somewhat less confused but has stirred revengeful hatreds which jeopardize the long-term processes of peace.

So unremitting did the war (or wars) continue to be that the peace-making efforts of the international community, though persistent, as persistently failed. The active policy of the United Nations, and of the major powers, rightly concentrated on limited and achievable ends; to prevent the war from spreading beyond ex-Yugoslavia's frontiers, to avoid being drawn into it in a partisan way, to mitigate its lethal violence by a leaky arms embargo, to give humantiarian relief to its victims, with the aid of international protective forces, and to keep alive the struggle for peaceful settlements. Although at the end of 1994 peace seemed as far off as ever, the record in terms of those aims deserved more praise than it was commonly given. If, however, the dire circumstances then prevailing had forced a reversal of policy, including the withdrawal of all UN forces, the probable end of humanitarian relief convoys, and intensification of the war after a lifting of the arms embargo, then indeed the critics would have been justified in calling the UN's efforts a humiliating failure. That prospect was fortunately deferred, but it did imply a need for a radical review of the UN's peace-keeping function by its members, especially those of the Security Council.

The UN's role is, to say the least, ambiguous. It is an association of sovereign states, to whose defence against aggression its members are pledged, but it has no military arm or enforcement means of its own. If its Security Council calls for any action this can be effected only by such members of the association as choose to comply, with forces or non-military policies of their own. (In the Balkans, NATO was indispensable for the organization and command of UN forces.) Its past record is patchy and inconsistent, ranging from all-out war in defence of Kuwait against Iraq to abstention from any measures against Israel for its condemned seizure and continued occupation of neighbouring territories. On this showing, the UN might be described as little more than a whitewashing cover for the policies of the major powers. Such a judgment is not altogether fair. UN intervention gave a moral force to lines of action which would otherwise have had only the appeal of national interest; many nations have taken part, both in non-military sanctions and in military campaigns under the UN banner, who would not so have acted from national interest alone.

A second limitation of the UN's peace-making authority is that it has no constitutional mandate to intervene in disputes, however violent, within nation states. If it does act in such cases, its legitimate objectives can only be, as they were in ex-Yugoslavia, to prevent the conflict from becoming international, to restrain its military violence, to render humanitarian aid, and to promote peaceful settlement by diplomatic means.

One notion advanced for strengthening the UN's power and authority is that it should be furnished with a standing force, composed of contingents from many members and presumably of all arms, ever ready to stand between combatants if war should threaten, to protect humanitarian relief if war should start, to establish and defend neutral-ized zones, and to take any other forceful action decided upon by the Security Council. This idea raises complex questions about command structure—the most essential and minimum ingredient—national contri-butions, location, training, rotation of personnel and *matériel*, and many other aspects, but it also encounters a fundamental issue.

The UN was created to uphold peace, not to engage in war. War against war may sometimes be necessary, but it does not itself make peace. Under UN direction, successful wars were fought in Korea and the Gulf, but they did not scotch the continued threat to peace in those regions. Peace-making is a political exercise. All concerted military action has to be guided and controlled by political aims. In human ailments, surgery may be the needed short-term cure, but recovery and future health depend upon long-term treatment and care, in which the patient plays as great a role as the surgeon or physician. Making and defending peace is not a one-off exercise but a continuous process.

Therein is summed up the story of peace and war in the past year. The ups and downs should be judged less in terms of immediate success or failure than in those of advance or retreat in an unremitting campaign. Peace itself is not a climax but a journey. In Ireland, in the Middle East, the efforts of those directly and indirectly concerned have been rightly called 'the peace process'. The attainment of peace, whether seen as the ending or the prevention of war, is not a moment of success but a long haul to calm bellicose emotions, to remedy causes and to reconcile rival ambitions. In that light, 1994, despite its alarms, can still be seen as a hopeful year for the process of peace.

London, January 1995

I UNITED KINGDOM

CAPITAL: London   AREA: 244,100 sq km   POPULATION: 57,800,000 ('92)
OFFICIAL LANGUAGE: English (also Welsh in Wales)
POLITICAL SYSTEM: parliamentary democracy
HEAD OF STATE: Queen Elizabeth II (since Feb '52)
RULING PARTY: Conservative Party (since May '79)
HEAD OF GOVERNMENT: John Major, Prime Minister (since Nov '90)
PRINCIPAL MINISTERS: Douglas Hurd (foreign & Commonwealth affairs), Kenneth
   Clarke (Exchequer), Michael Howard (home affairs), Lord Mackay of Clashfern
   (Lord Chancellor), Malcolm Rifkind (defence), Michael Heseltine (trade &
   industry), John Selwyn Gummer (environment) (*for full list see* XIX.5)
INTERNATIONAL ALIGNMENT: NATO, OECD, EU, G-7, Cwth.
CURRENCY: pound sterling (end-'94 £1=US$1.56)   GNP PER CAPITA: US$17,790 ('92)
MAIN EXPORT EARNERS: machinery & transport equipment, mineral fuels & lubricants,
   manufactured goods, chemicals, financial services, tourism

1. 'BACK TO BASICS' OR 'BACKS TO THE WALL'?

THE government began the year with the divisive Maastricht debate
behind it, drawing encouragement from figures which suggested a
continuing if patchy economic recovery. Any complacency, however,
was immediately shattered. Shadows were cast over the Prime Minister's
'back to basics' campaign—launched at the Conservative Party conference in October 1993 (see AR 1993, p. 25)—when several Tory
politicians were caught up in controversy or scandals relating to family
or business matters in the first nine days of 1994. Two junior ministers
and a parliamentary private secretary resigned. Mr Major faced further
charges of indecisive leadership both on the broad issue itself, and for
failing to dismiss his Environment Minister (Tim Yeo), who resigned
on 5 January over an extra-marital affair but only after he had lost the
support of his constituency party. Right-wingers urged Mr Major to act
firmly to 'stop the rot'. Lord Archer, a former deputy party chairman,
admitted that the government had been 'thrown off course'. Parallels
were drawn with the Profumo affair, which had damaged a Tory ministry
in 1963 (see AR 1963, pp. 23-7, 33-4).

   Some cabinet ministers had been laying particular emphasis on the
importance of stable, two-parent families, and many Tory MPs and
activists argued that the party must not be open to the charge of
applying double standards—preaching family values on the one hand
while proving all too fallible within its own ranks. As MPs returned
to the House of Commons on 11 January after the recess, Edward
Leigh, a former Trade Minister, accused Mr Major of retreating under
fire. In his view 'back to basics', *pace* the Prime Minister, did extend
to personal morality. Amid further claims of disunity in the cabinet,
two newspapers reported that Mr Major had threatened to 'crucify'

right-wing ministers. The Prime Minister's Office denounced this as a 'malicious fiction', while the chairman of the 1922 Committee of Conservative backbenchers stated that there were suspicions that one or two newspapers were intent on destroying the government. *The Sun, Daily Mail* and *Sunday Times* were the leaders of this assault. Speculation revived once more as to how long Mr Major could survive as Prime Minister.

In speeches on 6 and 21 January, Mr Major insisted that he had not launched 'a crusade about personal morality'. His prime interest lay in the 'basics' relating to education, economic policy and the fight against crime. Government policies should be based on 'the common-sense values of the British people' and the encouragement of individual responsibility. *The Times*, however, was among those voices which joined the Labour leader in declaring that the government had got itself into 'a hopeless muddle'.

After a four-year investigation into Westminster council (frequently acclaimed by Tory ministers as a prime example of good management among local authorities), an independent auditor on 13 January accused it of a 'disgraceful, unlawful and improper' vote-rigging scandal. Basically, the council was said to have adopted a slanted housing policy in eight marginal constituencies in the 1980s in order to increase potential Tory voters at the expense of Labour and at a cost of £21 million to local tax-payers. Mr Major replied to Labour charges of a corrupt 'homes-for-votes' policy by promising to condemn any such activities if and when the case was fully proven. On 15 January it was revealed that a second Tory council, Wandsworth, was also under scrutiny by financial watchdogs.

Yet another scandal led to the resignation of a ministerial aide on 12 February. A *Sunday Telegraph* poll showed that a majority viewed the government as 'very sleazy and disreputable'. There was other evidence that the 'back-to-basics' policy was failing to impress the public, a majority of whom reportedly thought that it should include personal morality. More excitement followed on 13 March when the Chief of the Defence Staff, Air Marshal Sir Peter Harding, resigned following press revelations of an affair with the ex-wife of a former (Conservative) junior defence minister.

Imminent tax increases (put at £12.50 a week for the average family) began to steal the headlines from the middle of January. This alarmed Tory backbenchers even more than the various scandals. The Treasury itself conceded that from April most families (except those earning around £100,000) would be paying a higher percentage of their incomes in tax (of all types) than under the last Labour government. Many MPs were unimpressed by the Chancellor's claim that taxes would always be lower under the Tories than under Labour or the Liberal Democrats, and that in real terms average tax-payers would still be better off (by about 30 per cent) than in 1979. He was bluntly told by many Tories that the tax trend had to be reversed as soon as possible, in particular by cuts in government spending.

On 8 February the Institute for Fiscal Studies published detailed figures for actual and projected taxation trends between 1985 and 1995. They showed that increases in indirect taxation had been particularly damaging to the poorest families. Overall taxation was expected to equal 38.5 per cent of the whole economy in 1998–99, more than under any Labour government. One Tory MP likened the biggest peace-time tax increases in British history to 'a long walk to the scaffold'. Later government figures released in mid-July underlined the considerable redistribution of wealth which had occurred in favour of the rich since 1979. One-in-three children were living in poverty, and 59 per cent of single parents were similarly placed. The income of the poorest 10 per had fallen by 17 per cent since 1979, while that of the richest 10 per cent had risen by 62 per cent. Average incomes had grown by 36 per cent over the same period (and old-age pensions by 56 per cent), according to the Social Security Secretary.

Other crises and rumours continued to batter Tory morale. On 1 February Mr Major had to rebuff a three-man delegation of Tory MPs which tried to press for a cabinet reshuffle to increase right-wing representation. It was an inept move and had not been authorized by the 92 Group, which the trio claimed to represent. But the fact that the attempt was made seemed to suggest that almost anything was becoming possible. Further evidence of weakening Tory morale and organization was provided by news that the party was resorting to drastic cost-cutting to reduce its large financial deficit. Both John Smith, the Labour leader, and his party were riding high in the polls. There were particularly alarming signs of disaffection among middle-class Tory voters in the south of England, with Labour edging ahead (39 to 31 per cent) by the end of January. The Liberal Democrats, at 20 per cent, trailed the Tories by only eight points nationally. Such was the dismay and disarray in Tory ranks that Mr Major addressed the 1922 Committee on 3 February and bluntly told backbench MPs that the 'sniping' had to stop.

On the same day, the government announced pay rises of up to 3 per cent for more than a million public sector workers, but insisted on self-financing through increased efficiency. On 6 February Mr Smith launched Labour's *Business Plan for Britain*, which promised investment in industry, training and skills. Some of his party, however, regretted the lack of detail, or complained that there was nothing to excite people to vote Labour. Three days later Bryan Gould announced his intention to retire from British politics and to return to his native New Zealand. A leading Labour figure in the later 1980s, he had suffered a series of defeats in his efforts to promote more radical ideas and had been a distant runner-up to Mr Smith in the 1992 Labour leadership contest. Mr Gould believed that a future Labour government was unlikely to be one which he could serve or support with 'great enthusiasm'.

The President of the Board of Trade (and Trade and Industry Secretary), Michael Heseltine, claimed on 19 January that his Deregulation and Contracting Out Bill provided 'the biggest bonfire of controls' in modern times, and that businesses would benefit to the tune of hundreds of millions of pounds. The bill was given a second reading by the Commons on 8 February. Some peers, however, expressed the fear that ministers were seeking too much discretion to repeal or amend legislation without reference to parliament, and that the interests of consumers might suffer.

The government clearly hoped that it had put an end to the long-running battle with teachers over the National Curriculum when on 5 January the Education Secretary accepted the recommendations of the Dearing Report in full. These envisaged a scaling-down of the curriculum, with special attention being concentrated on three core subjects, namely English, maths and science. The new structure would begin in September 1995, and there were plans to add new vocational courses at a later date. Teachers would be given more freedom and would be less burdened with the running of elaborate tests. In September a new Education Secretary (Gillian Shephard had replaced the much-criticized John Patten in the summer ministerial reshuffle) acted on her promise to let teachers 'get on with the job' by delaying league tables based on the testing (by external examiners) of 11–year-olds until 1996.

On 12 January Lord Howe launched a bitter attack on the 'arms to Iraq' inquiry (see AR 1992, pp. 30–1), accusing its chairman, Lord Justice Scott, and its counsel, Presiley Baxendale, of acting as 'detective, inquisitor, advocate and judge'. He complained that the guidelines for the inquiry were being broken. Downing Street rejected a Labour demand that the government dissociate itself from Lord Howe's criticisms; he was, it declared, speaking for himself. On 17 January it was the turn of Mr Major to appear before the inquiry—the first time a serving Prime Minister had been called before a member of the judiciary to account publicly for the execution of government policy. Mr Major insisted that at no time during his tenure of three cabinet posts had he been involved in the 'consideration, amendment or interpretation' of the export guidelines introduced in 1984. He also said that a 'massive trawl' of Whitehall documents had found no evidence that he had been advised of a change in the guidelines or that ministers had breached them. The impression given was (at the very least) one of confusion at the heart of government. Robin Cook for Labour insisted that Mr Major had left himself open to the charge that he was not in control.

Mr Heseltine was interviewed by the Scott inquiry on 28 February. He disclosed that in 1991 he had initially refused to sign a 'public interest immunity' (PII) certificate—sometimes referred to as a 'gagging order'—in the Matrix Churchill trial because he had not wanted to appear to be part of a ministerial cover-up. He had thought that the case for releasing Whitehall documents to assist the defendants had been 'overwhelming'. However, the Attorney-General, Sir Nicholas Lyell, had insisted that it was Mr Heseltine's duty to sign the PII. In the end, he had signed a 'watered down' certificate, only to be told later that there was not always a duty to sign. Sir Nicholas denied that he had given inconsistent advice. For Labour, Mr Cook said that Mr Heseltine was the first minister to admit to a 'cover-up', and claimed that the Scott inquiry was turning into a rout for the government.

On 4 March Mr Smith fiercely condemned the government's record on crime. Not only did it have no strategy, he said, but other policies (such as cuts to the urban and youth programmes) were aggravating the problem. All three parties were making this an issue in the forthcoming local elections. In a series of Commons votes on 21 February, another attempt to bring back the death penalty was defeated, while the legal age of consent for private homosexual acts was reduced from 21 to 18 years (following the defeat of a proposal to establish parity with heterosexuals at 16).

The degree to which British legislation could be affected by European Union (EU) laws was highlighted on 3 March when the House of Lords ruled that certain aspects of UK employment protection legislation relating to unfair dismissal and redundancy payments were in conflict with European law in that they discriminated against part-time workers (80 per cent of whom were women). Under the ruling, those with two years service were entitled to better job protection. The Employment Secretary accepted the change on 20 December, but warned that jobs might be lost.

The government was also in conflict with the great majority of its European partners on the subject of changes to the voting rules of the Council of Ministers in the context of the prospective enlargement of the EU. Currently, two large states plus one small one could block certain types of legislation with 23 votes out of 76. Britain wished to preserve the 23-vote blocking power, against those who favoured 27 out of a new total vote of 90. Ministers were caught between the fear of isolation in the EU and a revolt by Tory 'Euro-sceptics' at home. There were also fears of 'socialism by the back door' in the form of future EU legislation reversing post-1979 domestic reforms.

British demands prompted the Danes on 15 March to warn that stalemate could put EU enlargement at risk. Mr Major told the Commons on the same day that he favoured enlargement, but he also wanted to ensure 'democratic legitimacy and the rights of minorities in Europe'. A week later, anxious to satisfy Tory Euro-sceptics even at the risk of alarming pro-Europeans, he added that 'We aren't going to do what the Labour Party do, which is to say "yes" to everything that comes out of Europe without any critical examination.' He branded the Labour leader as 'Monsieur Oui, the poodle of Brussels', contending that, if the EU voting dispute delayed enlargement, this would be due to the 'inflexible and doctrinaire line' of two members in particular (later identified as the Netherlands and Belgium).

Such strong words, however, prompted a sharp response from Brussels. On 27 March Britain was asked for an answer within 48 hours to a proposal whereby, following EU enlargement, a minority of between 23 and 26 Council votes could not be overruled without a 'reasonable delay' for further discussion. Spain, Britain's sole initial supporter, consented to this compromise. Accordingly, after a 90-minute discussion on 29 March, the British cabinet decided to accept the advice of the Foreign Secretary, Douglas Hurd, that the deal was the best that could be obtained in the circumstances. Four ministers were reported to have voiced serious reservations.

Numerous Tory backbenchers sat in glum dismay as they listened to Mr Major's explanation to the Commons. Mr Major claimed that the voting system would be reviewed in 1996 by the EU Inter-Governmental Conference and that the European Commission had made concessions to Britain on social law-making. This was immediately denied by the Commission's president, Jacques Delors, and was followed by further claims and counter-claims by the British government and the Commission. In the Commons, Mr Smith spoke of a humiliating government climbdown. It was widely felt that Mr Major had erred by threatening a strong stand only to back down a week later. More questions were asked about his future as leader, and there were even calls for his resignation from three of the most disaffected Tory bachbenchers. However, amid much talk of a leadership challenge in the autumn, many influential figures rallied behind the Prime Minister over the Easter weekend (2–3 April).

The government's strategy on community care was attacked on 19 April by a committee of MPs, who claimed that mentally ill patients were being discharged (and left to fend for themselves) to make room for others in a worse condition. This followed charges (emphatically denied by the Prime Minister) that under-funding of the National Health Service (NHS) was leading to rationing of treatment for some over-65s.

The first women priests of the Church of England were ordained in Bristol Cathedral on 12 March amid continuing controversy among the clergy (see Pt. XIII). The Princess Royal was appointed a Lady of the Garter in April, her public and charity work having earned her the reputation of being the hardest-working member of the royal family.

2.   MID-TERM ELECTION DISASTERS

GOVERNMENT preparations for the European Parliament elections in June began in earnest in March, with both Mr Major and Mr Hurd on 7 March expressing their determination to uphold the British veto on major EU decisions. Mr Hurd argued that it was necessary to perfect the Maastricht arrangements before proceeding to the next stage of the EU's development. Sir Edward Heath complained that the government's position was too negative. Mr Major tried to dampen down speculation over his leadership prospects by stating that he would stay on even if his party did badly in the elections; but it was clear that many were determined to treat the European as well as the forthcoming local polls as a referendum on the Prime Minister and the government.

In the run-up to the local elections in May, the Tories were confronted not only by dismal reports from the opinion polls but also by continuing confusion inside their own ranks. Thus on 1 May the then Chief Secretary to the Treasury, Michael Portillo, bluntly opposed British agreement to a European single currency. Two days later, under pressure from the Prime Minister, Mr Portillo explained that he fully accepted the government's position, namely that this was a question to be decided by parliament at some point in the future, if it had to be decided at all. Meanwhile, David Evans, a member of the 1922 Committee's executive, was calling upon Mr Major to sack several 'incompetent' ministers to restore public confidence in what Labour was describing as a 'clapped-out' government. 'Unofficial' canvassing to prepare for a leadership contest was said to be taking place.

There was apparently sufficient concern in Downing Street for the Prime Minister to intervene personally in the preparation of the Conservative Euro-election manifesto (then in the hands of a committee chaired by Mr Hurd) to try give it a more vigorous and populist flavour. Foreign Office 'polysyllables' were replaced by much plain 'Anglo-Saxon' language. The manifesto also attacked the opposition parties for proposing European policies harmful to Britain. The Tories wanted a wider, decentralized, free enterprise and competitive Europe.

Tory prospects were not helped by the April tax increases. It was estimated that the economy overall had returned to its pre-recession peak, but manufacturing output remained 4 per cent below its previous maximum. The official March unemployment figure of 2,720,000 (9.7 per cent of the registered labour force) was the lowest for almost two years, though controversy continued to surround the accuracy of the total, which many put at nearer 4 million. Much of the reported fall in the jobless was credited to the growth in part-time work. Certainly the fear of unemployment remained strong. Significantly, Britain qualified for £1,700 million over three years from the new Euro-fund set up to assist the poorest regions of the EU. Parts of London, the Midlands, the North of England, Scotland and Wales were among the eligible regions. Whatever the real state of the economic recovery, it was not enough to generate a sense of confidence and well-being among large numbers of people from most sections of society.

The local elections on 5 May confirmed the worst Tory fears. Over 5,000 seats were at stake, usually those last contested in 1990. The Tories secured the same share of the votes as the Liberal Democrats (27 per cent), but suffered a net loss of 429 seats and slipped to third place in numbers of councillors. They had been particularly vulnerable in London, where they retained overall control of only four boroughs compared with 11 before the polling. The capital had been badly hit by a recession for the first time for many years. *The Times* supported Labour's call on 14 April for a new overall authority, arguing that London was the only Western capital city without a representative body to speak on its behalf on urban planning, transport and the environment.

Labour, with 42 per cent of the overall local election vote, might have been expected to do even better given the massive unpopularity of the government. It was true, however, that the party managed to improve on its very good performance in the 1990 elections, achieving a net gain of four councils and 88 extra seats. The Liberal Democrats increased their share of councils to 19, a net rise of nine, and registered a net gain of 388 seats, performing particularly well in much of southern England. The Tories were left with only 15 councils, their 18 defeats including such traditional bastions of power as Ealing, Harrow, Winchester and even Tunbridge Wells. Tory MPs with comfortable majorities began to share the apprehensions of colleagues whose seats were more obviously at risk.

Mr Major admitted that his party had suffered 'a poor result', but said that it was no use whinging. By 9 May Tory dissension had shifted to the question of a possible referendum on the introduction of a single European currency. Norman Lamont (the ex-Chancellor of the Exchequer) went further by suggesting that one should be held in response to any further 'significant' erosion of British sovereignty. Along with some other Tories, he also argued that a referendum might (as with Labour in 1975) be a way to resolve the party's divisions on Europe. The Liberal Democrat leader, Paddy Ashdown, agreed that public opinion should be tested by a general election or a referendum before any more fundamental changes were implemented in the relationship between Britain and Europe. On 10 May Mr Smith pressed the Prime Minister fiercely on the subject of Tory divisions and a referendum. Mr Major reiterated his scepticism concerning the latter, adding that in any case it was not a question which needed to be resolved before the EU Inter-Governmental Conference in 1996. 'No one expects', he said, 'that this parliament is going to be asked to decide on a single

European currency. . . . Even if I wished to, I could not bind a future parliament.' On the same day, Mr Major offered an assurance that he would veto any further moves towards a federal Europe at the next Maastricht-style summit.

The sudden death of John Smith on 12 May meant that for the second time in 31 years the Labour Party had been robbed of a leader who was seemingly bringing it to the threshold of power (see XX: Obituary). One of the most moving tributes came from the Prime Minister, who spoke of 'the waste of a remarkable political talent . . . and of a man who in all his actions retained the human touch'. Others praised Mr Smith as an outstanding parliamentarian and recalled his skilful handling of the Scottish devolution issue in 1979. As leader of the Labour Party, he had successfully resolved the one-member-one-vote issue and had built upon the work of his predecessor to project a more reassuring image to the voters. His successor was soon embarking on even more radical changes than had seemed likely under Mr Smith (see below).

Mr Major rounded off the Scottish Conservative Party conference on 13 May with a demand that he be judged on his performance over the whole of the current parliament. He also sought backing for his vision of Europe—'a people's Europe' that was not 'the remote preserve of a circle of planners', but one which addressed the concerns of ordinary people and was not unnecessarily intrusive. 'Europe', he said, 'is absolutely fundamental to this country's interest.' Without Europe, Britain would be 'a little country in a lost world'. On the domestic front, he reiterated that the government's main targets were crime, education and the economy.

The inter-party truce caused by Mr Smith's death began to crumble as early as 15 May, while Labour's decision to postpone its leadership election until after the European polling failed to stop manoeuvring between various factions within the party. Tony Blair quickly emerged as the front-runner and was assisted by the withdrawal from the contest on 1 June of Gordon Brown, a fellow modernizer and close friend. Only a year before, Mr Brown would have been a leading contender, but his popularity had declined after he had taken a number of controversial decisions as shadow Chancellor to try to shake off Labour's image as the high-tax, high-spending party. His decision greatly strengthened the modernizers and was expected to place Mr Brown in a powerful position at the start of any Blair-led government.

The Euro-election campaign began on 23 May. Mr Major, desperate to persuade disillusioned Tories to come out and vote, insisted that this was an election 'which does matter'. He claimed that the plans of the opposition parties would destroy parliamentary sovereignty in Britain by the creation of a 'stagnant socialist swamp' in Europe. His government was not anti-European, but it would never sign away its veto. Labour and Liberal Democrat spokesmen retorted that the government was failing British workers by leaving the country on the fringe of Europe. They also set out to exploit Tory divisions and to highlight the government's failures on the domestic front, including the 'highest tax increases in history', the alleged decline of the health service and the rise in crime. On 16 May the Metropolitan Police Commissioner had announced new measures relating to the wider use of firearms and the introduction of American-style batons. The police, he said, were entitled to better protection in dangerous situations.

On 31 May the Prime Minister called for a new multi-speed, multi-layered Europe in which Britain would be free to make its own policy on social and currency questions. The European Commission, he said, should not be involved in defence policy, adding that enforced conformity was 'a socialist way of thinking'. Britain must retain its veto but had also to be at the heart of Europe. Margaret Beckett (Labour's acting leader) responded on 1 June that such an approach would confine Britain to 'the bicycle lane' and condemn the nation to silence in the EU. Lord Tebbit (a former Tory minister and party chairman), however, applauded the Prime Minister's move towards the Euro-sceptics, describing it as the best reason yet for voting Conservative. Mr Major dismissed as 'trivial' any suggestions that a flexible EU would mean the creation of leagues in which states would be placed according to their degree of importance. He added on 7 June that a 20-member EU would fall apart unless it became less rigid. He also said that people who stayed at home on election day should not complain if a socialist majority at Strasbourg called for more spending, taxes and controls.

Five by-elections were also held on 9 June, four in Labour-held seats and one for the Eastleigh seat, whose Tory MP, Stephen Milligan had died in sensational circumstances on 7 February. In the Eastleigh contest a Tory majority of nearly 18,000 was turned into a victory for the Liberal Democrat candidate, who recorded a 9,239-vote lead over the Labour candidate (the Tory being relegated to third place). Labour easily held Barking, Bradford South, Dagenham and Newham North-East, all on very low turnouts, the Liberal Democrats twice coming second. Labour hoped that its good performance in Eastleigh was further proof of its reviving credibility among key voters in the south.

The Tories were relieved to find that the Euro-election results on the same day were not quite so bad as they had feared. Suggestions had been made that, if fewer than 10 seats were won, Mr Major's position would be untenable, whereas more than 15 would buy him time. In fact, with 28 per cent of the vote, the Tories won 18 of the 87 UK seats compared with 32 out of 81 in 1989. This was their worst national electoral performance of the century, yet it might so easily have been even more catastrophic, 15 seats being won by Conservative candidates by tiny margins. One senior official commented that the party had come within 12,000 votes of 'disaster'. Seats were lost to Labour in such 'true-blue' territory as East Anglia, Essex, Kent, Bedfordshire and Hertfordshire. Although the

Tories were injured by tactical voting in favour of Labour and the Liberal Democrats, they were also saved in some seats by the splitting of the vote among fringe parties as well as their main opponents. Devon and Plymouth East, for instance, was retained with no more than a 700-vote majority over the Liberal Democrats, in a constituency where a candidate calling himself a 'Literal Democrat' won no less than 10,000 votes.

Although the result appeared to have bought time for Mr Major as Prime Minister, it did nothing to lessen party in-fighting. Sir Edward Heath called for the sacking of the 'anti-European' cabinet ministers, while Euro-sceptics on the right demanded a stonger anti-Brussels line and the addition of more of their number to the cabinet. Mr Major retorted that he would act in his own time on the subject of a ministerial reshuffle, while on Europe he reiterated his faith in what he described as 'a middle way, a practical way'. His party, however, seemed no nearer agreement on this or several other major issues. Allied-Lyons, one of the party's biggest corporate donors, chose this moment to announce that it was suspending its contributions, thereby adding to the already serious Tory Party funding problems.

Labour, meanwhile, had won 44 per cent of the vote and had raised its share of the 87 Euro-seats to 62 (an increase of 17 compared with the 1989 elections), although it lost Scotland North-East to the Nationalists (see I.6). There was further confirmation of the party's reviving fortunes in the south, where it secured a promising 25 per cent of the vote. Indeed, its performance as a whole caused Mr Major to argue that the country had returned to 'the politics of real choice. . . . The only alternative to a Conservative government is a Labour government.' The Liberal Democrats' vote was a disappointing 17 per cent (compared with 27 per cent in the May council elections), although the party won its first two Euro-seats, both in south-west England. The party polled strongly in the south as a whole, its 31 per cent share being only 5 per cent less than the Tory share. Some Liberal Democrats, however, were already fearful that Labour under the leadership of Mr Blair might come to be regarded as an electable social democratic party.

The overall turnout was a disappointing 36.1 per cent, although Britain lost its status among EU members as the least-interested in Euro-elections, this accolade passing jointly to the Netherlands and Portugal (see II.1.v; II.3.ii). There were particularly strong variations in England: in some areas participation was no more than 25–30 per cent, but returns of 41–47 per cent were registered in the south-west, where Tories and Liberal Democrats battled for supremacy. The relative lack of enthusiasm elsewhere could be variously interpreted as evidence of a general lack of interest in Europe, or as a protest by profoundly discontented Tories who might still be won back by the government. At the same time, the actual verdict of those voting could be seen as evidence of a real sea-change in the thinking of the electorate. A MORI poll for the *Sunday Times* of 26 June suggested widespread disillusionment with government polices among white-collar workers, especially in the 35–54 age group. Worries abounded over unemployment, higher taxes, the moral fabric of society, education, and opportunities for the young. A large minority was critical of the effects of the free-market reforms, while few believed that the recession was over. The *Sunday Times* commented: 'Britain's middle classes have never had it so bad.' Meanwhile, on 15 June the Chancellor of the Exchequer, Kenneth Clarke, had set out to reassure the City that the government would take no risks in its economic policies in a bid to win back voters. He insisted that taxes would be cut only when it was safe to do so, and that the battle against inflation would continue. He was determined to avoid the previous errors which had upset previous periods of growth.

The struggle for the Labour leadership began in earnest after the Euro-elections, with Mrs Beckett and John Prescott running for the posts both of leader (against Mr Blair) and of deputy leader (against each other). Mrs Beckett made a strong bid for left-wing support, favouring the return of secondary picketing and a wholesale repeal of Tory trade union legislation. She also opposed further party constitutional changes for the time being. Two big unions declined to recommend any candidate in the contest, whereas members of the Transport and General Workers' Union were encouraged to support Mrs Beckett. The majority of party members, however, regarded strong identification with the unions as a vote loser.

Mr Blair, in contrast, preferred to talk of revising the existing union laws rather than total repeal. He promised on 24 May to rebuild the 'social fabric of society', arguing that unfettered liberalism was producing 'an atomized, uncaring, rootless society'. He called for an updated version of citizenship with stress on duties as well as rights. In his election statement on 23 June he offered a vision of a left-of-centre party which would modernize industry, the welfare state and the education system. The statement was designed to reassure voters that he was 'anti-poverty' but not 'anti-wealth' or 'anti-opportunity'. He wished to give a 'modern expression' to Labour's traditional values. He was careful, however, to sidestep specific policy detail, leading the Tory Party chairman to claim that the statement was 'not so much the vision thing as the vacuum thing'. On 13 July Mr Blair directed his attention to the 'insecure majority', stressing that welfare should be based on reducing state dependency rather than raising benefits. He wanted 'a nation at work, not on benefit'. Reforms were needed to make it worthwhile for the poor to seek work by the elimination of poverty traps.

Mr Prescott, in his election manifesto of 4 July, put great emphasis on full employment and called upon Labour to create a commission to set 'achievable' employment targets. He also demanded a fairer distribution of wealth, work and power in the country; but, significantly, he made no reference to spending commitments, the unions or public ownership. A journalist commented that he had taken on the style of a patrician in place of that of a pugnacious MP. On 5 July Mr Blair took the strongest pro-European stance of the three candidates. He also argued that Labour should learn from Margaret Thatcher by putting forward a clearly-defined set of ideas. In addition, he sought to win over Liberal Democrats by stressing the degree to which modern social democracy provided common ground. *The Observer* on 17 July gave its blessing to a Blair–Prescott team, arguing that together they would give Labour what it most needed—the ability to persuade voters that it had changed without casting off its fundamental values. 'Labour must keep that vision thing', said the newspaper.

Mr Blair duly won a convincing victory, with 57 per cent of the electoral college vote against 24.1 per cent for Mr Prescott and 18.9 per cent for Mrs Beckett. Proclaimed leader on 21 July (at the age of 41 he was Labour's youngest ever), Mr Blair declared in his victory speech that he wanted a future in which 'there is no corner of Britain where we shield our eyes in shame'. Mr Prescott won 56.5 per cent of the vote in the race for the deputy leadership against Mrs Beckett. The latter might perhaps have retained this post had she not simultaneously made a bid for the leadership, but her left-wing views cost her votes in any case. The party wished to be seen to be marching into a new era. Mr Blair had gone furthest among the candidates in accepting the principles of market competition. At the same time, he had stressed their limitations and had shown interest in social responsibility, community, and other things which made up the intermediate ground between the state and the market.

On 6 May the Channel Tunnel was officially opened by the Queen and President Mitterrand of France. This was an extraordinary engineering achievement, but worries continued over the high costs (the latest estimate stood at £3,000 million) and the building of a satisfactory 68-mile rail link from Folkestone to London to lessen the glaring speed disparities between trains in Britain and France. The Queen, in her speech on the occasion of this formal recognition of a British land link with Europe, diplomatically observed that Britain and France had experienced many ups and downs in their relations, but she was confident that French élan and British pragmatism formed 'a highly successful combination'.

3.   THE 'BATTLE FOR MIDDLE ENGLAND' COMMENCES

MR Major greatly improved his standing with some Conservative MPs by his performance at the Corfu EU summit of 24–25 June. The main question was the designation of a successor to M. Delors as head of the European Commission (see also XI.3). The British team found itself increasingly isolated in its opposition to the Belgian candidate, Prime Minister Jean-Luc Dehaene. Mr Major argued that Mr Dehaene, of the Flemish Christian People's Party, represented 'the tradition of big government and interventionism' and that he was 'not quite in touch' with new trends in Europe. He also complained that Germany and France had pushed the Belgian's candidature without proper discussion with other EU states. Although Mr Major's recourse to Britain's veto was widely condemned, not all the reactions in Europe were hostile. Thus, while a commentator in the French newspaper *Le Figaro* declared that de Gaulle had been right to keep Britain out of the European Community, Mr Major was not without friends in France.

Mr Major's action delighted Tory Euro-sceptics at home, and the Prime Minister was given his warmest welcome for some time from Tory backbenchers on his next appearance in the Commons. Sir Edward Heath, however, publicly expressed dismay, and some other Tory pro-Europeans were privately uneasy. Mrs Beckett claimed that Britain had been relegated to the EU sidelines, and that Mr Major was 'a prisoner of his Euro-sceptics'. Mr Ashdown said that long-term national interests had been sacrificed in order to appease the Tory right.

Many Tories hoped that the Corfu episode would help to heal party divisions, it being noted that Lady Thatcher had praised Mr Major's action. However, continuing differences were apparent when Mr Hurd and Mr Heseltine quickly distanced themselves from a statement of support for a single European currency issued by Mr Clarke. The EU leaders agreed unanimously on 15 July that the Prime Minister of Luxembourg, Jacques Santer, should be the new Commission president. Despite claims that M. Santer had the same vision of Europe as M. Dehaene, Mr Major insisted that there were important differences. Some observers thought the main effect would be the exercise of more influence by European commissioners from the strongest EU members.

Meanwhile, on 23 June the government's White Paper on pension reforms in light of the Maxwell scandal (see AR 1991, p. 35) promised changes in the regulation of the industry, but added that these could not come into effect before April 1997. Many MPs and unions described the proposals as totally inadequate, whereas employers feared higher costs as a result of new requirements concerning minimum solvency levels. During the year many salesmen and pension companies were attacked for having persuaded numerous people to switch from company to private pension schemes, with disastrous financial results. Some mistakes were admitted and recompense promised. Claims were inevitably made that this was another example of the indiscriminate way in which Thatcherite free market policies had been pursued in the 1980s.

The Health Secretary unveiled the first of the hospital performance league tables on 29 June, claiming that these provided a basis for competition by comparison. Medical organizations and opposition speakers criticized the tables as flawed and misleading, although a spokesman for hospital managers thought that they were a step in the right direction. The provision of accurate data clearly remained a problem. At the annual conference of the British Medical Association (BMA) in early July, bitter attacks were made on the government's introduction of the competition culture into the NHS. The BMA council chairman spoke of demoralization among staff, and claimed that treatment was becoming a lottery. A little earlier, the Bishop of Birmingham had described the reforms as 'un-Christian' because patients were being treated like consumers.

Prince Charles, in an unusually revealing television royal documentary, spoke on 29 June of the problems in his private life. He made an admission of adultery after his marriage to Princess Diana had broken down, but also protested against media intrusion. There was no question of a divorce at this time, said the heir to the throne, but if one took place he did not see it as an obstacle to his succession. On his position as head of the Church of England, he said that he would prefer to be the 'defender of faith' and not just of the Anglican faith (see also Pt. XIII). He was impressed by Germany's use of national service for civil as well as military purposes, and thought it might help to promote self-discipline in the young. In a broadly sympathetic leader the following day, *The Times* showed particular interest in the loosening of the ties between the monarchy and the Church.

Mr Major gave full government backing to Prince Charles's claim that a divorce would not prevent him from becoming king, and it also seemed that the Prince was winning considerable public support. The Archbishop of York, however, warned that any loosening of the links between Church and state might cause the whole British constitution to 'unravel'. Prince Charles said later that his recent remarks did not imply any support for disestablishment of the Church of England or any change to the coronation oath. The government, meanwhile, was addressing the subject of religion in schools. Multi-faith teaching was approved on 5 July, although it was decided that Christianity should predominate except in schools where most children were of another faith.

Lady Thatcher made a strong plea on 8 July against further defence economies. Arguing that efficient and mobile forces were essential to deal with unexpected emergencies, she described such forces as Britain's greatest asset. This was followed on 14 July by the announcement of cuts of 18,700 service and civilian defence personnel over the next three years. The RAF was identified as the main sufferer, being earmarked to lose 11 per cent of its manpower. The Defence Secretary, Malcolm Rifkind, insisted that the £750 million cuts were not aimed at front-line fighting strength. New frigates and nuclear-powered submarines, an extra 259 Challenger–2 tanks and the modernization of Tornado bombers were promised. The option of buying American Tomahawk cruise missiles (to be carried by submarines) was to be examined. Most of the RAF cuts would be caused by the transfer of much aircraft maintenance to private contractors. Adverse reaction to the plans included the expression of doubts by experts as to whether, after the cuts, Britain would be able to provide forces on the scale deployed in the Gulf in 1991. There were also complaints that the cuts were driven by financial rather than long-term strategic considerations.

A government White Paper, *Continuity and Change* (13 July), outlined proposals for a leaner and more businesslike civil service among its upper echelons. It anticipated 50,000 job losses over the next four years and contained a commitment to greater movement between Whitehall and the private sector. But even some Tories joined Labour critics who warned of possible threats to the ethos of the civil service and its almost unparalleled reputation for integrity.

The much-anticipated cabinet reshuffle took place on 20 July and proved to be less radical than many had expected. The biggest surprise was the appointment of Armed Forces Minister, Jeremy Hanley, to the party chairmanship with the onerous task of getting the party into shape for the next general election. Four cabinet ministers left the government, namely Mr Patten, who was replaced as Education Secretary by Gillian Shephard; John MacGregor, whose Transport portfolio went to Brian Mawhinney; Peter Brooke, who was succeeded as National Heritage Secretary by Stephen Dorrell; and Lord Wakeham, who was replaced as Lord Privy Seal and Leader of the House of Lords by Lord Cranborne. Mr Waldegrave moved to Agriculture, while Mr Hunt as Chancellor of the Duchy of Lancaster was to be much involved in cabinet committees and behind-the-scenes organization. Right-wing Tories welcomed the appointment of Mr Portillo as Employment Secretary and Jonathan Aitken as Chief Secretary to the Treasury. Here was further evidence of the Prime Minister's desire to keep a balance between the two wings of his party.

Parliament broke up with the polls showing no signs of a Tory revival. Ostensibly, Labour was at least twice as popular as the government. Mr Major's personal ratings were lower than any Prime Minister's since regular polling began in the 1940s. There was growing evidence of popular confidence in Labour's policies, though only on education had the approval factor reached 40 per cent. Labour strategists were on their guard against any feelings of over-confidence. Mr Blair told the shadow cabinet on 15 September that they could not rely on the government losing the next election. He wanted Labour to prove that it could run the economy better than the Tories, and in other ways to be seen as a party prepared for government; hence his discreet stance on certain controversial issues.

Already on 24 July Mr Blair had criticized single mothers who had chosen to have children outside stable relationships. Although they were a tiny minority, he insisted that a two-parent family was a vital component of a stable society. Overall he was intent upon making the family a prime issue for Labour at the expense of the Tories. Two days later he promised strong action to improve education in Britain. There would be no wholesale changes of current policies, but grant-maintained schools would be returned to local authority control. On the same day, Mr Major highlighted his main differences with Mr Blair by continuing to call for less government, and by reaffirming his commitment to more private ownership, more private involvement and investment in public activities, and more individual choice in areas ranging from education to pensions.

At the end of July the former Labour leader, Neil Kinnock, was named as Britain's new (junior) European commissioner. His wife Glenys had recently been elected as the MEP for South Wales East. Mr Kinnock's support for the EU's social chapter caused concern among some Tories. At the same time, a complicated row erupted over Mr Portillo's handling of new EU legislation. The minister claimed that the new laws threatened government preferential treatment of firms employing disabled people under the 'priority suppliers' scheme. European officials insisted that the government had not asked for an opt-out from the legislation and that they would not have forced the government to scrap the scheme. A Labour MEP blamed Mr Portillo's 'right-wing dogma' and anti-Europeanism for actions which damaged the interests of numerous disabled workers. The British government also opted out from Commission directives on works councils and, at the end of September, on three-month paternity leave. Labour spokesmen again attacked Mr Portillo for depriving British workers of important rights. A ruling by the European Court of Justice on 28 September gave millions of part-time workers (mostly women) the right to join their employers' pension schemes.

The search for an end to the troubles in Northern Ireland reached a possible turning-point on 31 August with the IRA's announcement of a cessation of hostilities (see I.8; XIX.3). Earlier in the year, the IRA had threatened further violence unless the government made concessions over the Downing Street Declaration of December 1993 (see AR 1993, pp. 572-4). On 9 March it made the first of three unsuccessful mortar attacks on Heathrow airport, and subsequently caused further disruption at Gatwick. On 19 May the government, while standing firm on its demand for an end to the violence, offered a last chance (though without a deadline) to Sinn Féin to join talks on the constitutional future of Ulster. Sinn Féin replied on 26 July that, while there was as yet no blueprint for talks, important steps had been taken in the peace process.

Meanwhile, it was estimated that Britain was subsidizing Northern Ireland to the tune of £4,000 million a year, more than a quarter of this being devoted to security. On 2 June 25 senior counter-terrorist personnel died with four RAF crewmen in a helicopter crash on a hillside in the Mull of Kintyre. The loss of so many highly-experienced officials was a serious blow to the security services in Northern Ireland.

The IRA announced a 'complete' cessation of hostilities from midnight on 31 August. Mr Major said that this development was 'a very great chance for peace', but added that Sinn Féin could not expect to join in talks until it was absolutely clear that the ceasefire was 'permanent'. Mr Blair expressed similar reservations. On 1 September the Sinn Féin leader, Gerry Adams, pointed to the views expressed in Dublin and Washington that the ceasefire was 'permanent', saying that these were correct. Given the distrust of many Ulster Protestants—fears which were shared by Tories such as Lord Tebbit and Mr Lamont—Mr Major once again found himself walking a political tightrope. On 16 September he announced that any political settlement that was finally negotiated would have to receive majority support in a special referendum by the people of Northern Ireland. On 13 October the loyalist paramilitary groups also announced a ceasefire. This was followed on 21 October by a pledge from Mr Major that he would open initial talks with Sinn Féin before Christmas.

There was widespread Tory dismay when Mr Clarke raised interest rates by half a point (to 5.75 per cent) on 12 September. Shortly afterwards it was announced that the inflation rate had edged up 2.4 per cent in August. The interest rate move persuaded some observers that the government was prepared to delay the next election until 1997 as it strove to demonstrate its ability to deliver sustained economic growth. Labour's response was cautious. The shadow chancellor, Mr Brown, emphasized the supply-side weaknesses in the British economy, claiming that both the industrial base and new investment were too small, so that growth could soon generate inflationary pressures. Labour, he said, was devising plans for sustained expansion with, for instance, more emphasis on investment and training skills. Growth had to go hand in hand with, or even precede, increases in consumer demand. Mr Blair stressed the party's commitment to 'fair' taxation.

The question of British economic competitiveness was the cause of much debate throughout the year, featuring divisions of opinion among businessmen as well as ministers. The latter were split between the pure free-market believers led by Mr Portillo and the rather more activist approach of the Department of Trade and Industry under Mr Heseltine. A leaked letter from Mr Portillo to Mr Heseltine (written in early August) revealed differences of opinion over government support to industry. The Confederation of British Industry (CBI) favoured Mr Heseltine, whereas the Institute of Directors called for tax cuts as the best way to help industry. Howard Davies, director-general of the CBI, complained on 8 September about the Treasury's short-term economic policies and its lack of enthusiasm for the *Competitiveness* White Paper produced by the DTI and published on 24 May.

This document admitted that it would be 'an enormous task to correct over 100 years of relative decline'. Much of it drew together or built upon existing policies such as the efforts to reduce the number of government regulations affecting industry, while an attempt was made to inject additional money and life into the training programmes for those who had left school at 16. Earlier, in February, the Institute of Directors had complained that Britain was suffering from an 'enterprise deficit' among middling and small businesses. On the other hand, an inquiry led by the chairman of IBM concluded that there was 'a strong correlation between the countries with the highest emphasis on individualism and the poorest economic performance over the last ten years'. Meanwhile, some businessmen were showing at least an academic interest in Labour's outline of its economic thinking.

At the Trades Union Congress (TUC) conference in Blackpool in September, a campaign for full employment was put forward as the 'big idea' to win the next election for Labour. But a demand on 6 September to repeal all the employment laws enacted since 1979 was overwhelmingly defeated. Mr Blair, when questioned about the railway signalmen's series of one- and two-day strikes since 15 June in a pay dispute with Railtrack, stressed the need to depoliticize the issue. He favoured recourse to arbitration (ACAS did indeed help to bring the dispute to an end on 30 September). On the relations of a future Labour government with the unions, Mr Blair spoke of 'fairness, not favours'. Any union reservations, however, were tempered by the desire not to damage Labour's prospects at the next election. Sections of the movement continued to show much interest in EU employment law and similar measures in the hope of outflanking Tory union laws. M. Delors had addressed the TUC in London at the end of August. Some union leaders were also looking for ways to increase the movement's appeal to middle-class employees, conscious of the fact that union members formed a minority of the workforce as a whole.

At their party conference in Brighton on 18–22 September, the Liberal Democrats were still trying to come to terms with the soaring popularity of Labour under Mr Blair as well as with their own internal dissensions. Earlier, on 3 August, three of the four founder members of the former Social Democratic Party had urged the Liberal Democrats to establish closer links with Labour. They and others continued to argue on the same lines in Brighton, only to encounter opposition, especially from those involved in local politics, who pointed to 400 election gains in the last year. Divisions on other subjects surfaced at the conference, votes being carried against the platform on the subject of a minimum wage and the decriminalization of cannabis. There was even a debate on the abolition of the monarchy. Mr Ashdown, in his keynote speech on 22 September, warned activists that they could damage the party by sending out the wrong signals. He also indicated that the Liberal Democrats no longer stood equidistant between the two larger parties, and said that he was ready to make 'common cause' with Labour while demanding a commitment to proportional representation in return. Labour, however, was not interested in a deal when it seemed possible that the Liberal Democrats might be marginalized at the national level.

At the end of September Mr Blair and Mr Brown did their best to reassure the Labour left wing that there would be tough tax moves against the 'something-for-nothing élite'; at the same time, they tried to bury Labour's 'tax, spend and borrow' image. A Labour government would reward merit and hard work. The polls, meanwhile, continued to give Labour support of 50 per cent or more, though doubts persisted concerning its ability to run the economy better than the Tories.

The Labour Party conference was held in Blackpool on 2-7 October. Some union leaders pressed the leadership for detailed commitments on full employment and the minimum wage, John Edmonds of the GMB calling for 'some concrete with the rhetoric'. But Mr Brown warned against setting 'targets that could not be met'. On the question of the minimum wage, Mr Blair said that it would work provided it was 'sensibly introduced'. Two left-wing MPs were unexpectedly chosen to sit on Labour's national executive committee, which was still dominated by Blair loyalists nevertheless. In his first speech as party leader (on 4 October), Mr Blair astounded the conference by announcing his intention to rewrite the 76-year-old party constitution (including, by implication, Clause IV with its commitment to public ownership). Mr Blair said he believed not in the socialism of Marx or in state control but 'in a strong and decent community with principles and standards and common aims and values'. This was the sort of society, he added, in which the individual did best.

The implicit attack on Clause IV was denounced by members of the Labour left, Mr Scargill describing it as 'heretical'. Mr Blair, he said, represented the Tory Party Mark 2. Nevertheless, the initial impression was that Clause IV would—without much difficulty for Mr Blair—eventually share the fate of unilateralism and anti-Europeanism and effectively disappear from the Labour programme. On the other hand, a conference vote on 6 October, on a standard resolution that attracted attention because of the Blair bombshell, narrowly supported (by 50.9 to 49. 1 per cent) the party's longstanding commitment to nationalization. Its passage had been preceded by an impassioned debate, which included some sharp attacks on Mr Blair by members of the old left who insisted that their form of socialism was far from dead. There were also critics who took a more pragmatic view. They thought that Mr Blair had acted too precipitately, and that with more preparation a majority could have been secured. Several big unions had been mandated to support Clause IV, but given time might have swung the vote the other way. As it was, the unions had voted narrowly in support of Mr Blair, whereas constituency parties had been more supportive of Clause IV. Some saw the vote as a salutary warning that the party should be treated with more sensitivity. Mr Blair was unrepentant and said that it would have no effect on the review of the party constitution. Party officials similarly played down a conference vote to scrap Trident and make further defence cuts.

In his speech of 4 October, Mr Blair also warned his party of the need for caution. 'Hope is not born of false promises; disillusion is.' He reaffirmed his commitment to a dynamic market economy based on partnership between the public and private sectors. Many of his listeners seemed unsure as to what these references to 'solidarity', 'partnership', 'common aims and values', and 'the one-nation party' really meant, and how they fitted in with the party's traditional aspirations. But Mr Blair was intent on wooing 'middle- and lower-income Britain', which he said had been betrayed by the Tories. In a radio interview he went so far as to say that with a strong and growing economy Labour would be able 'to spend more wisely and to reduce the burden of tax on middle-income families'. Mr Prescott rounded off the conference with a highly effective barnstorming speech. He promised that the new constitution would 'stand solid as the rock of our socialist convictions for the next century', asserting that public ownership remained a fundamental part of socialist faith. He also launched a campaign to boost party membership (currently under 300,000) to half a million by the next election. Despite reports that some senior figures were among those taken aback by the pace of change being set by Mr Blair, it was widely agreed that this had been a highly successful conference both for the party and for its new leader.

The Tories assembled in Brighton amid news that their party membership had probably dropped below half a million, a decline of two-thirds since 1975 and one which had been accelerating since 1984. Constituency leaders blamed the government's uncertain and accident-prone performance together with the impression of greed and 'sleaze' at the centre. Such economic recovery as had taken place had not generated a 'feel-good' factor. Indeed Mr Hanley, the new party chairman, had earlier coined the phrase 'a voteless recovery' to describe the current political climate. Unemployment was still increasing among the professional classes, although some comfort was drawn from evidence that new jobs were being found fastest in the typical Tory constituencies. Unemployment as a whole was its lowest for four years (according to the official figures) while annual inflation at 2 per cent was the lowest since November 1967. The polls, however, continued to suggest record desertions from the Tories to Labour among professional and managerial people.

Lord Tebbit on 11 October demanded that the Prime Minister should make it clear that he opposed a single European currency, but stopped short of supporting Mr Lamont, who suggested that a withdrawal from the EU must be treated as a possibility. Other Euro-sceptics were also vocal at the Tory conference, though perhaps not to the same extent as during the battle over Maastricht. Mr Hurd defended government policy: the federalist blueprint had a 'faded' look, he said. But Mr Portillo on 12 October launched a fierce attack on the 'crackpot schemes' emanating from Brussels. Mr Heseltine later fought back, arguing that to turn aside from, or to opt out from, Europe 'would be the most abject surrender of our national interests'. On the basis of the length and intensity of the applause, Mr Portillo was reckoned the clear winner. Other influential members of the right were also highly critical of the EU, demanding that the party shift away from the political middle ground and put 'clear blue water' between Conservative and Labour. Home Secretary Michael Howard, for instance, insisted that politics was 'not about splitting the difference'. On the same day, the Social Security Secretary, Peter Lilley, unveiled a new scheme of 'back-to-work' bonuses to encourage people to move from part-time to full-time work. But it was Mr Portillo who had dominated the day, and who was again described as 'the unchallenged standard-bearer of the right'.

Mr Clarke and Lord Howe led a counter-attack the following day. Lord Howe warned that Labour might develop into an attractive and effective centrist party. This could challenge the Tory political dominance which 'we have come almost to take for granted'. To wrap oneself in the Union Jack against the EU, he argued, would 'simply be a prelude to burial at sea in clear blue water somewhere out in the mid-Atlantic'. Mr Clarke won reluctant backing from the conference that tax cuts had to take second place to restoring public finances ravaged by the recession. Despite the many mishaps at the beginning of the year, Mr Major's speech on the final day was well, if not rapturously, received. He spoke modestly but confidently as if he felt that the worst was behind him. He stressed that, while he did not disparage the 'vision thing', he put more trust in actions based on realism and common sense. At the next election both main parties might be 'talking Tory language', but only one would mean it. The content of the speech showed that he was bidding as strongly as Labour for the centre ground—despite the excitement generated by the party's right wing during the conference. This was most evident in his total rejection of claims that he intended to dismantle the NHS (a remark which won the biggest applause of the afternoon). He also promised a period of consolidation in education.

Mr Major stated his belief that it was possible to double living standards in a generation. This raised some eyebrows among economic historians, since growth had averaged around 2.25 per cent a year since 1945 (and only 1.7 per cent since 1979). Although Mr Major did not mention the 'sleaze factor' in his speech, he ordered Mr Hunt, the cabinet's new trouble-shooter, to head a ministerial drive against corruption and waste, instances of which had been reported by the Commons public accounts committee as well as by the media. Meanwhile, despite Mr Major's determined bid for 'middle England' with centrist policies, it was evident that the party was still far from united over how this was to be done and over the way forward in general.

4. MORE TORY TROUBLES

MR Major barely had time to draw breath after the Tory Party conference before the question of 'sleaze' was reopened. One junior minister, Tim Smith, resigned on 20 October following allegations that he had been paid to ask questions in parliament. Neil Hamilton, a junior industry minister, also left the government five days later for the same reason, protesting that he was the victim of 'foully motivated rumour and a media witch-hunt'. His friends criticized the government's handling of the matter. Mr Blair had earlier asserted that the government was 'becoming tainted' and had demanded precise definitions of proper behaviour in public life, citing the cases of ex-ministers who joined the boards of companies which they had helped to privatize. Many Tories shared his concern. Mr Major responded on 25 October by establishing a high-powered and permanent committee to uphold standards in public life. But Mr Blair feared that the creation of the committee was being used to sweep specific allegations 'from the public view'. It was announced on 28 October that the new body would be chaired by Lord Nolan.

Two other ministers and one of the Tory Party's deputy chairmen also became the focus of media attention. Particular interest centred on whether part of a Paris hotel bill incurred by Mr Aitken (Chief Secretary to the Treasury) had been paid by a London-based Egyptian businessman, Mohamed al-Fayed, who owned the hotel in question. Mr al-Fayed, who had given the story to *The Guardian* newspaper, later challenged the minister's version of what had happened. But outrage was growing in the Commons over the methods employed by *The Guardian*, notably its production of a forged fax to the hotel bearing Mr Aitken's name and written on House of Commons notepaper. On 2 November MPs voted overwhelmingly for the editor's conduct to be investigated by the Commons privileges committee. Lord Nolan, the chairman of the new committee on standards in public life, said he believed that these had declined over the last 30 years and that this was becoming a matter of concern to the public. The *Sunday Times* affirmed that the 'sleaze train' had been around Westminster too long, adding: 'Mr Major must derail it—forever.' In a Commons speech on 31 Ocober, Sir Edward Heath said that much had to be done to regain public confidence in the government. In the last week of October nearly 50 MPs declared free gifts and foreign trips dating back to the New Year. But Labour failed in its bid on 31 October to secure Commons agreement that the House privileges committee should hold the 'cash-for-questions' hearings in public.

The government suffered further embarrassments on 9–10 November when the Home Secretary was accused of abusing his powers by failing to refer an alteration in compensation for victims of violent crime to parliament, while the Foreign Secretary was said to have acted unlawfully in the Pergau Dam affair (see I.5). On 3 November, moreover, a handful of Tory MPs forced the government to abandon its proposals to privatize the Post Office (PO). The PO chairman said that 'crippling uncertainty' faced the service and agreed with Mr Heseltine (the minister responsible) that it needed private capital and commercial freedom if it was to remain competitive. Some right-wingers protested at further evidence of government weakness and lack of direction, but Mr Heseltine refused to be downcast by the outcome.

As the Queen arrived in Moscow on 17 October for the first visit by a British monarch to Russia, speculation intensified back home over the future of the Prince and Princess of Wales after the publication of extracts from two forthcoming books. Politicians and churchmen debated the constitutional implications of a divorce, some Tory MPs also arguing that this would ultimately prove less damaging to the monarchy than the current state of affairs.

On 19 October details of the first moves to streamline the civil service were announced. The Treasury was to lose about a third of its top posts. This was followed by a White Paper on 24 October which put the idea of 'workfare' at the heart of government action to get the long-term unemployed back to work. Unemployment benefit and income support would be replaced by a 'jobseeker's allowance' for retraining or community work. On the same day the 'social justice commission' set up by John Smith as Labour leader in 1992 published its report called *Strategies for National Renewal*. Mr Blair, while welcoming the report, said that a future Labour government would pick and choose among the recommendations, which the commission itself expected would require a 15-year implementation period. The report, though described as prescribing 'the biggest shake-up in welfare for 50 years', was not a second Beveridge Report (1942); rather, it was a pragmatic and eclectic attempt to adjust welfare to modern needs. The reforms were to be self-financing, by means of higher taxation of the richest, contributions from graduates to the cost of their studies and getting more people back to work. Welfare provision was to be directed to those most in need.

The Queen's Speech on 16 November lacked any radical new proposals, its emphasis being on consolidation and on fine-tuning previous reforms. The government's aim was clearly to try to establish a reputation for competent government and economic progress before the next election. Peace in Northern Ireland and the protection of British interests in Europe were also stressed, and retirement for women as well as men at 65 was to take effect in 2020. But the main excitement of the day was centred on the Prime Minister's warning to Tory Euro-sceptics that he would seek a dissolution of parliament if there was a successful revolt against the 'essentials' of a bill to increase Britain's financial contribution to the EU. Mr Blair thought that matters had come to a pretty pass if the government could carry through its policies only by threatening its own demise.

On 22 November the Euro-sceptics launched a campaign to persuade Mr Major to drop the general election threat, which was described as a 'constitutional outrage'. On the following day Mr Clarke insisted that the threat had the full backing of the cabinet. But questions continued to be asked as to why, rather than resorting to this 'suicide pact', Mr Major had not chosen to await the outcome of the debate and then demanded a vote of confidence in the event of a government defeat. The rebels continued to utter dire threats of their own, although they failed in their bid to oust Sir Marcus Fox from the chairmanship of the 1922 committee. The party's vice-chairman, Patrick Nicholls, resigned after writing a newspaper article in which he bitterly attacked the French and Germans and expressed his regret that Britain was in the EU. On 24 November Mr Blair described the Tories as an 'ill-disciplined rabble, incapable of governing the country'. A MORI poll claimed that the public (by ratios of more than two to one) was now crediting Labour with having the best policies as well as the best team.

The debate on the controversial EU finance bill on 28 November was a bruising, ill-tempered affair among the Tories. Mr Lamont, although declining to lead a challenge to Mr Major as leader, repeated that consideration of withdrawal from the EU must remain an option. Mr Clarke uncompromisingly attacked the sceptics, insisting that the cost of membership was a price worth paying on both political and economic grounds. Despite warnings that they would lose the Conservative whip, seven Tory rebels abstained in the crucial vote, which saw the government prevail by 330 votes to 303 with the help of the Ulster Unionists. Another Tory abstained on a separate vote, while a ninth later resigned the whip on his own initiative. The withdrawal of the whip from the nine, which meant that the government was technically reduced to minority status, represented a sharp break from past Tory treatment of rebels. One political correspondent, Anthony Howard, later went so far as to claim that it had 'destroyed a whole libertarian parliamentary tradition'.

Attention now turned to the budget. It was clear that the economy was continuing to recover. Overall growth had exceeded the predictions made at the start of the year, while inflation remained low. Business investment, however, had shown only a 2 per cent increase in 1994. Some economists, taking account of long-term trends, noted that capital stock had grown by only 5 per cent since 1979 compared with a 40 per cent rise in consumer spending. Some estimates suggested that to achieve and maintain a growth rate of 3 per cent, the next five years would require capital stock to increase at twice the rate achieved in any quinquennial period since 1945. Inward investment would help, but only if it occurred on a larger scale than ever.

The motor and electronics industries had already been profoundly influenced by foreign companies. Rover (the last British-owned mass car producer) had been taken over by BMW of Germany earlier in the year. Fears lest this might adversely affect Honda's investment in Rover were subsequently allayed. Rolls Royce announced in December that BMW would be providing its next generation of engines. There were now eight world-class car firms in Britain, more than in any other EU state (although none was British owned). In mid-October it was reported that the South Korean industrial giant Samsung, encouraged by British government grants and a loan to the tune of £58 million, intended to invest on a large scale in Cleveland, one of the nation's unemployment blackspots.

Cabinet meetings between 8 and 10 November reached agreement on cuts in projected government spending for the financial year 1995/96. It was broadly accepted that only significant tax reductions in the following years might prevent defeat at the next election; however, ministers resisted backbench calls for cuts in the forthcoming budget. On 8 November the Chancellor announced a major expansion of the government's 'private finance initiative' that was intended to reduce public borrowing. The Treasury would not approve further public capital projects unless and until private finance options had been explored. Meanwhile, a social survey which appeared on 16 November suggested that there was little public interest in tax cuts and a strong demand for more welfare spending.

Mr Clarke submitted a cautious budget to the Commons on 29 November. He described his first objective as the attainment of 'sustainable growth'; but there was also an unspoken detemination to prepare the way for tax cuts in time for the next election. Public expenditure was to be reduced by £24,000 million over the next three years, it being hoped that government accounts would be in the black by 1998/99. Tax changes for the most part were modest, but people with mortgages would enjoy less tax relief. The Chancellor persisted with controversial increases in VAT on domestic fuel (see AR 1993, pp. 11, 29), though with additional compensatory payments to pensioners, nearly three million of whom would also benefit from increased tax allowances. A package of measures was promised to get more of the long-term unemployed back to work. Mr Clarke insisted that 'we must prevent the emergence of a deprived underclass excluded from the opportunity to work'. Other changes were designed to help small businesses.

Apart from the vexed question of the further increase in VAT on domestic fuel, Tory backbenchers seemed reasonably content. Mr Blair said that this would be known as the 'VAT-on-fuel budget', while the tax changes for the average family were the equivalent of a 7p rise in the standard rate of income tax. He also reminded the House of the verdict of the Institute for Fiscal Studies that tax changes over the last ten years had worsened the position of the poorest 40 per cent of the population and given only slight help to another 20 per cent. The IFS itself reported on 30 November that middle-income earners would be hardest hit by the budget. A subsequent announcement by the Social Security Secretary of cuts in state help to the unemployed with home mortgages threatened to add to the pain. The IFS described the new incentives offered to the unemployed to take jobs as too small, while Labour criticized cuts in the training programme. The Institute of Directors said that the budget had only 'tinkered with the real needs of business'.

The VAT issue exploded on 6 December when, despite massive efforts by the whips and ministers, seven Tories (with a further eight abstaining) joined the opposition parties to defeat the government by 319 votes to 311. Mr Clarke immediately dropped the 9.5 per cent increase, which would have yielded just over £1,000 million to the Treasury in the coming year. Earlier in the debate, Mr Blair had said that pensioners could freeze in their homes as the government sought to create the financial conditions for tax cuts in 1995. After the high drama of the vote, both Labour and Liberal Democrat spokesmen insisted that the government was 'discredited' and 'out of touch' with the people. Mr Clarke, amid cries of 'resign', tried to reassure nervous City markets with a pledge that the existing targets for government borrowing would be met.

The Chancellor returned to the Commons on 8 December with a new package to replace the lost VAT revenue. He announced that the elderly would receive £15 a year less in pension payments as a result of the VAT defeat, while most of the lost revenue would be recovered by tax increases on petrol, tobacco and alcohol. Mr Brown accused the government of punishing pensioners for its own mistakes and raising the tax bill of the average family by £875 per year since the election. Mr Clarke retorted that any complaints over the changes should be laid at the door of Labour and the Tory rebels. He subsequently castigated the 'ill-informed Latin American machinations' of the latter. But he also appeared to imply that the two-stage VAT legacy from his predecessor, Mr Lamont, had been a loser from the start. There were many other suggestions that the government had been saved from an act of folly. Mr Clarke's pugnacity received some praise amid media discussion of a 'collective insanity' permeating the Tory Party and a loss of authority by the Prime Minister.

A half-point rise in base rates (to 6.25 per cent) on 7 December had been defended as a move against inflationary pressures, though the actual timing was probably influenced by fears of City disquiet following the VAT débâcle. On 8 December the governor of the Bank of England claimed that a lower PSBR would not by itself justify pre-election cuts. If warranted, he might seek to offset tax cuts with increases in interest rates. The rate rise on 7 December pleased financial markets but not businessmen and building societies. Fears were expressed that the recovery might be stalled by such action, especially as higher interest rates might make British exports more expensive.

Mr Major himself on 8 December declared that he would continue to do what was right regardless of critics and rebels. There was no promise of an early return of the whip to the Tory rebels, although he would still describe them as 'Conservatives' and hoped that they would judge future issues on their merits. At a European Council summit on 9 December, the Prime Minister called for an all-out battle against fraud in the EU, which was a leading demand among Euro-sceptics. Two days later, Mr Portillo urged Mr Major to become more of a Euro-sceptic to end the 'terrible rift' in the Tory Party. At the same time, he criticized those who had lost the whip as being guilty of 'self-indulgence' and warned that party unity could not be restored by appeasing them. He also disclosed that a referendum on the future of the EU was not his first choice as a means of trying to heal the party's wounds. Mr Major, however, told the Commons on 12 December that circumstances at some point might make a referendum appropriate. There were also indications from some leading Labour Party figures that they were warming to the possibility of a referendum.

In general, Mr Blair was proving less of a Euro-enthusiast than his predecessor. His main priority was the development of a strategy to win the votes of 'middle England', or what he described as the 'mainstream majority'. Unlike some of his party, he was clearly more intent on modifying than reversing Tory legislation since 1979, and in searching for ways to improve efficiency in government and the public services and thereby avoiding tax increases. Meanwhile, Labour's shadow home secretary, Jack Straw, called for a monarchy based on the Scandinavian model and more in accord with the movement towards a classless society.

The names of the first eight rail routes to be privatized were announced on 14 December. Some cuts in services were likely, although the Transport Secretary promised further subsidies for certain lines on social grounds. He had stated earlier, on 24 November, that Railtrack would be sold off in the lifetime of the present parliament. This was widely interpreted as an intention to raise money for tax cuts before the next election, and also as a political move to offset the failure of the bid to privatize the Post Office. The government itself had long admitted that rail privatization was the most complex of such programmes. But at the end of December it was at least able to announce the completion of the controversial privatization of British Coal (see AR 1993, pp. 11-12, 27).

Questions of traffic congestion and new road building attracted further attention during the year. The Transport Secretary on 26 October had dismissed recommendations of a Royal Commission that the £19,000 million current road construction programme be halved, and the funds diverted to improve public transport, and that petrol prices should be doubled within ten years to help relieve congestion and pollution. Another report followed in December which claimed that new roads led to increases in traffic rather than less congestion. The minister promised a review of road policies.

The Tories suffered a crushing defeat in the Dudley by-election on 15 December, a majority of 5,789 being turned into a Labour majority of 20,694. The 29 per cent Conservative-to-Labour swing was the biggest since 1935. On the same day, the government came under fire over plans by British Gas to cut showroom staff pay by 16 per cent shortly after a 75 per cent salary increase had been given to its top executive. The Home Secretary spurned calls for his own resignation on 19 December after the publication of the Woodcock Report into the escape of armed IRA prisoners from Whitemoor gaol in September.

In the newspaper circulation war, *The Times* and the *Sunday Times* continued to gain ground at the expense of other quality newspapers, on the strength of a tough price-cutting campaign initiated in mid-1993. *The Independent* and its Sunday sister paper were taken over by the Mirror Group in March. A government White Paper on 6 July announced that the BBC's charter would be renewed for ten years from 1997 and that the licence fee would continue until at least the year 2001 (see also XVI.1.vi). The BBC was also urged to develop a wide range of commercial radio and TV channels at home and abroad. The government's decision was seen as a triumph for the management reforms effected under the direction of John Birt, the BBC director-general. There were hopes that the BBC would become a leading multi-media international enterprise.

It was a long and bruising year for Mr Major and his party. A senior minister was reported as saying: 'We've got to sort ourselves out, or John is going to go down like Arthur Balfour.' (The latter's

Conservative government had split from 1903 over tariff reform versus free trade and the party had been routed in the 1906 election.) Quite apart from the question of the economy, it was widely believed that the Conservatives were doomed unless they could demonstrate real unity and a firm sense of direction. MORI reported on 22–23 December that the government was more unpopular than any recorded in the history of opinion polls. Similarly, there was more public discontent with performance on economic policy than at any time since 1979.

Ministers pointed in vain to a significant number of encouraging economic trends. Unemployment had fallen below 2.5 million by the end of the year and had been accompanied by an upsurge in full-time jobs. The PSBR (at under £20,000 million for the first seven months of the year) represented a drop of more than a quarter compared with the same period in 1993. The economy was growing at around 4 per cent a year. The current account in the third quarter was in surplus for the first time since the beginning of 1987. Financial commentators welcomed the surge in exports over imports, helped by larger markets in the United States and by a revival of demand in Europe. A closing of the trade gap, rather than a sharp rise in consumer demand at home, was exactly the sort of economic recovery the experts had been recommending. For much of the year, exports increased almost twice as quickly as imports.

It was clear, however, that the general public was much more conscious of living standards being squeezed by higher taxes, and of the weak housing market, than of the proclaimed economic recovery. Falling unemployment was not accompanied by a comparable sense of job security. Although the question of the true levels of employment and unemployment remained a statistical nightmare, the seriousness of the plight of the long-term unemployed was not in doubt. These numbered around 1.5 million (or 60 per cent of the total without work). It was clear that, despite the economic upturn, the government still had much to do before it could hope to improve its standing with the public.

5.   INTERNATIONAL AFFAIRS

BRITAIN supported NATO's formal invitation to the Central and East European states to join the Partnership for Peace plan put forward by the United States (see IV.1; XII.2; XIX.1). On 10 January Mr Major listed Poland, Hungary and the Czech Republic as having 'a strong claim to membership' of NATO as rapidly developing democracies, although the Foreign Secretary added that much remained to be done before they could be admitted as full members. During the year the government continued to agonize over British involvement in Bosnia as part of the UN peace-keeping force (see III.1.vi; XI.1). The killing on

5 February of 68 people in Sarajevo was followed by intensive NATO talks, during which pressure from the United States and France brought reluctant agreement from London on 9 February to a NATO ultimatum which threatened air strikes unless the Bosnian Serbs withdrew their artillery from around the city within ten days. The following day, the Foreign Secretary told the Commons that Bosnia had become 'a crucial test for the Atlantic Alliance'. The proposed measures were not simply punitive but were designed to improve the situation around Sarajevo. His cautious approach won the backing of many Tories who had formerly opposed any direct military involvement.

Much of the support was based primarily on the belief that a damaging split within NATO had to be prevented. The Prime Minister and Foreign Secretary visited Moscow on 15–17 February at a time of much Russian resentment over the NATO air threats in Bosnia. Little was revealed concerning the talks, but a Russian mission to Pale soon afterwards helped to organize the ensuing ceasefire around Sarajevo. The Moscow talks also brought agreement that British and Russian missiles would no longer be targeted against each other.

During a short visit to Latvia on 16 February, Mr Hurd assured all three Baltic states that the West saw their independence as irreversible and that they could look to the West for trade and security ties. A visit by Mr Major and Mr Hurd to Washington on 28 February–1 March was an opportunity for some fence-mending by both sides. Anglo-American relations had been strained by President Clinton's decision to admit the Sinn Féin president for a two-day visit to the United States at the end of January, during which Mr Adams had gained much useful publicity. Progress was claimed on future policy towards Bosnia, Russia and the implementation of the recent GATT agreement. Mr Major laid strong emphasis on the need to back Mr Yeltsin and to bring about cooperation between Russia and NATO. There was also American backing for British policy in Hong Kong. Mr Major spoke of a 'partnership of shared interests and instincts'.

The first weeks in March brought a further shift in British policy towards Bosnia. Ministers and service chiefs were increasingly persuaded by the success in Sarajevo of the British UN commander, General Rose, that more progress might be possible; they therefore pressed strongly for further UN troop deployments. It was announced on 10 March that Britain would send an extra 900 troops (making 3,200 in all). Mr Rifkind explained the change of mind as a response to new conditions and the chance of a real peace. But he was still unable to secure American ground involvement in Bosnia, while incidents around Goražde in April caused the death of a British soldier and the loss of a British fighter aircraft. Mr Rifkind insisted that UN forces were not deployed to alter the military balance and cautioned that the 'messy' Bosnian war could not be 'sorted out in some neat, clinical way'. On 18 April the French and British Foreign Ministers agreed that the 'Goražde débâcle' would mean no change in policy; they also complained that no less than three separate outside groupings were trying to broker a peace, with attendant confusion. NATO issued a further warning to the Bosnian Serbs on 22 April, Mr Hurd stating that they must accept a total exclusion zone around Goražde or face the consequences. On 13 May the NATO Foreign Ministers agreed in Geneva to back a confederation of ethnically 'pure' communities, a plan which would leave the Serbs with about half of Bosnia. Mr Hurd assented to the proposal but seemed to expect it to fail.

At the Group of Seven (G-7) summit in Naples early in July there were indications that, in the absence of an early peace in Bosnia, the British would reluctantly agree to the lifting of the arms embargo on the Bosnian Muslims. This would almost inevitably lead to the withdrawal of British troops from their peace-keeping mission, since their position would become impossible if the fighting intensified. On 13 July Mr Hurd (again in company with his French counterpart) bluntly warned the Bosnian Serbs that a rejection of the latest peace plan would be 'a choice for war and disaster' on their part. Cooperation over Bosnia was the most obvious example of what appeared to be a warmer relationship between Britain and France in 1994.

Fierce fighting around Bihać provoked action by NATO aircraft (some of them British) late in November. But the limitations of such action soon became apparent, while American hostility towards the Bosnian Serbs further increased fears in London for the safety of British troops. Claims by Mr Hurd that differences over NATO's role in Bosnia had been eased at a meeting on 1 December failed to dispel the concern. Thus on 5 December Mr Major and Mr Rifkind again warned that a withdrawal of British troops was a 'serious possibility' if the situation continued to deteriorate. On the same day, at the Budapest summit of the Conference on Security and Cooperation in Europe (see XI.5.i), Mr Major said that the enlargement of NATO should proceed cautiously and without deadlines. Meanwhile, tensions increased between the United States and Russia, as President Yeltsin warned that the inclusion of East European states in NATO might mean that a 'cold peace' replaced the cold war (see also III.2.i).

During the year there was increasing talk in Europe (fuelled in part by the frustrations generated by the confusion surrounding Western and UN responses to the Bosnian question) of the need for a common EU defence policy. Hopes were expressed that Britain would move towards an integrated defence system which was not dependent on the United States. The Queen's Speech to parliament on 16 November, however, merely included a promise that the government would assist with the adaptation of NATO 'to allow it to play a wider role in protecting stabillity throughout Europe'.

In Hong Kong, Governor Patten's controversial electoral reform package was finally approved in July by a narrow margin (see IX.2.iii). China unsurprisingly responded on 31 August by announcing its intention to end the democratic experiment when it took control in 1997. A seven-month dispute with Malaysia began in February 1994 after a series of British newspaper reports had accused the government of Mahathir Mohamad of corruption (see IX.1.iii). Under scrutiny, too, were British ministerial promises of aid in the building of the Pergau Dam as part of the negotiations for an arms deal in 1988. Labour accused ministers of a cover-up and corruption. Mr Hurd admitted to the Commons foreign affairs select committee on 2 March 1994 that there had been an 'incorrect entanglement' between arms sales and aid in 1988, but claimed that the mistake had been corrected within three months. In November the High Court ruled that the Foreign Secretary had acted unlawfully when in July 1991 he had authorised £234 million in aid for the Pergau project. A Malaysian ban on public contracts with British companies had been lifted two months earlier.

In October extra British forces were sent to the Gulf in response to Iraqi deployments near the Kuwaiti border (see V.2.vi; V.3.iii). Earlier in the year, Mr Hurd had said that the question of the sovereignty of the Falklands/Malvinas had been settled in 1982. Nevertheless, the islanders were still troubled by a visit to Argentina by the Duke of York in December and by the possible long-term implications of oil surveys around the islands.

6. SCOTLAND

THE second reading of the Local Government Bill (Scotland) on 17 January, whereby 28 single-tier councils were to replace the 65 regional and distict councils, provoked Labour and Scottish National Party (SNP) charges of gerrymandering against the government. The Secretary of State for Scotland, Ian Lang, rejected the charges and said that the objective was to introduce a less expensive and more accountable system. Labour retorted that the new system would concentrate more power in the Scottish Office. The Liberal Democrats insisted that it was 'profoundly anti-democratic'. Criticism also came from the unions (which feared job losses) and from the Convention of Scottish Local Authorities.

Early in the year there were complaints from SNP leaders that the government had handed Sinn Féin an olive branch in Northern Ireland while disregarding the constitutional demands of nationalists in Scotland. Gordon Wilson, a former SNP leader, spoke of corruption and decline among the British élite, forecasting that 'radical change' was only 'a matter of time'. Delegates at the SNP's 60th anniversary conference in Inverness (21–24 September) protested that there had been talk of a referendum for Ulster but not for Scotland: self-determination could not be arranged on a pick-and-choose basis.

Land reform was another prominent issue at the SNP conference, many attacks being made on the current activities of the big estates. It was resolved that limits should be put on the size of deer herds. Overall, the SNP was intent on developing the image of a mainstream but radical party. It was attacking the Labour Party while trying to attract Labour voters. There were hopes that Mr Blair's anxiety to woo voters in the south of England would strengthen the appeal of the SNP's emphasis on social issues north of the border.

Labour was running well ahead of all its rivals in the polls at the time of its Scottish conference in March, while the Tories were struggling to stay in double figures. The shadow Scottish secretary, George Robertson, insisted the newly-named Scottish Labour Party had a distinct identity within the British party. Only Labour could rid Scotland of the Tories. The party, however, appeared to face a bitter battle over the pace at which equal representation for men and women in local council wards would be implemented. In October Mr Blair promised that a Labour government, in its first year, would 'legislate for a strong Scottish parliament'. In contrast, Tory leaders, during their party conference, unequivocally defended the Union and warned of increased taxes if a separate parliament were created.

A council-run poll in Strathclyde found 97 per cent of respondents (in a 71 per cent return) opposed to current government plans for water reorganization. The Secretary of State dismissed the referendum as 'meaningless', but the Chief Secretary to the Treasury conceded on 22 April that things should be 'done differently in different places'. Privatization was ruled out in Scotland 'absolutely'. Even so, the local elections on 5 May were a disaster for the Tories, given contentious issues such as water, changes in local government, VAT on domestic fuel, taxes and the economy in general. Their share of the poll, at 14 per cent, was about half that of the SNP, which finished 14 points behind Labour and made a net gain of 19 seats. No party managed to win outright control of a new council, but the SNP displaced Labour as the largest single party in Tayside, while the Liberal Democrats did the same in Grampian. The Liberal Democrats doubled the number of their councillors (to 61) and pulled well ahead of the Tories.

The Euro-elections in June saw the SNP capture Scotland North-East from Labour, with a majority of more than 31,000, and retain the Highlands and Islands. It ran second to Labour in five out of the other six Scottish constituencies. With nearly 33 per cent of the total vote (an increase of one-sixth in actual votes since 1989), this was the party's best ever performance. The average turnout in each constituency, however, was only 38 per cent.

The Monklands East by-election caused by the death of John Smith (see I.2; and XX: Obituary) precipitated a crisis in Labour ranks, as controversy mounted over alleged misconduct by the Labour-run local council. The charges included disproportionate spending in Catholic Coatbridge compared with Protestant Airdrie. The Labour candidate promised to look into the charges (already dubbed 'Monklandsgate'). The election on 29 June saw the majority won by Mr Smith in 1992 spectacularly slashed, from 16,000 to just 1,640 more than the SNP. This was a two-horse race, the other candidates being left with barely 5 per cent of the vote. The Scottish Office promised action if evidence of council misconduct was forthcoming. Meanwhile, Labour leaders were anxious to find ways to reverse the undoubted surge in support for the SNP, not least by putting an end to the confusion in the ranks of the party in Monklands.

There was some disappointment in the Highlands when Norway voted against EU membership in November. It had been hoped that the interests of all the northern regions of Europe might have been strengthened in Brussels had the whole of Scandinavia become part of the EU. Existing forms of cooperation with Norway, however, were expected to continue.

The state of the Scottish economy was open to various interpretations. Eight consecutive quarters of economic growth gave rise in October to reports of improving business confidence. Union leaders, however, noted with some concern that the unemployment figures in November had fallen back into line with the British average (8.7 per cent). Nearly half the population lived in development areas, although Scotland was reckoned to be the fourth wealthiest region in the UK. The strongest sectors in the economy were finance, oil and electronics, but the rest of the manufacturing sector had declined by 14 per cent since 1990. Scotland also lagged behind England in the creation of new small and middle-sized businesses. Tourism, a major employer, was facing problems.

In the first eight months of 1994 it was estimated that foreign companies were planning to provide over 4,000 new jobs. IBM assigned the production of the next generation of high-powered personal computers to its Greenock plant—an important signal of confidence at a time when IBM was planning to shed 40,000 workers worldwide. The Japanese electronic giant, NEC, promised a second silicon chip plant in Livingstone, where the existing plant had achieved record levels of productivity. Although low oil prices led to significant job losses in BP and Highland Fabricators, hopes of big new developments were raised by the government's go-ahead in November to the first oilfield to the west of the Shetland Islands. In addition, new cost-saving techniques had turned the Britannia gas field (one of the largest in the North Sea) into a commercial proposition.

The closure of the Rosyth naval base and the Edinburgh headquarters of British Gas, coupled with Tesco's takeover of Scotland's Wm. Low supermarket chain, entailed significant job losses. Decommissioning began in April of the important fast-breeder nuclear reactor at Dounreay in Caithness, after 40 years of research and development.

Record rainfall in Strathclyde on 10–11 December caused three deaths and widespread flooding and chaos. Paisley was among the worst-affected areas.

7. WALES

THE long-term task of rebuilding the Welsh economy saw some progress during the year, but there were also some obvious setbacks. The Secretary of State for Wales, John Redwood, could boast in October that manufacturing output in Wales had risen by 9.3 per cent during the previous 12 months and that the unemployment rate was falling. But the year also saw the closure of the Dairy Crest factory at Whitland, Dyfed, the rundown of the Raytheon jet factory at Broughton, Clwyd, and substantial job losses at the British Steel Tinplate works at Trostre and Ebbw Vale, all of which were particularly damaging to local economies.

Government statistics showed that Welsh income per head remained the lowest in Britain, while it was reported that Wales had the highest proportion of workers earning below the European Union's decency threshold of pay: almost 40 per cent of the workforce earned less than £212 a week. The president of the European Investment Bank, Sir Brian Unwin, stated in October that 'by European standards Wales is still one of the least prosperous areas'. Yet the bank showed its confidence in Wales's economic future by signing loan agreements totalling £65 million with Welsh Water and South Glamorgan County Council.

The economy of west Wales was boosted when the final part of the M4, a 3.2–mile elevated motorway at Baglan, was opened by the Secretary of State in December. However, grave disquiet was expressed over the increasingly high tolls charged for crossing the Severn Bridge, in light of evidence that lorries were reverting to alternative routes, unsuitable for heavy traffic, to avoid paying tolls.

Controversy surrounding the activities of the Welsh Development Agency (WDA) continued, and many of the responsibilities of the Development Board for Rural Wales (DBRW) were transferred to other authorities, including the WDA. The appointment of a Monaco-based businessman and former Conservative Party fund-raiser, David Rowe-Beddoe, to chair the DBRW as well as the WDA led to further complaints that Tory placemen were being used to push through unpopular government policies. In May the former director of corporate services at the WDA alleged that millions of pounds of money had been channelled through the WDA into key marginal constituencies in Mid-Wales. However, the following month saw some praise for the work of the agency in a National Audit Office report, which stated that the clearance of 13,000 acres of derelict land by the WDA had been one of Britain's outstanding success stories of the last 30 years.

The unpopularity of the Conservative government in Wales was reflected in the results of the European elections held in June. Labour won all five Welsh seats with 58 per cent of the total vote, but of greater significance was the collapse of the Conservatives to third place behind Plaid Cymru, which polled particularly well in the North Wales and the Mid and West Wales seats. By comparison with the 1992 general election result, the percentage vote for the Conservatives had been halved, while Plaid Cymru's vote had more than doubled.

The following month saw the long-serving Minister of State for Wales, Sir Wyn Roberts, announce his retirement. He was replaced by the right-wing MP for Clwyd North-West, Rod Richards. Whereas Sir Wyn had been a moderating influence in the Welsh Office, it was expected that the uncompromising views of the abrasive Mr Richards would stir up fresh controversies. True to form, in December Mr Richards's abusive comments about Labour councillors, whom he described as 'short, fat, slimy and fundamentally corrupt', caused acute embarrassment to the Secretary of State and led to a public apology.

Education was constantly in the news during the year. In January Mr Redwood attacked the under-achievement of Welsh school-children but his attempts to encourage schools to 'opt out' from local authority control were consistently rebuffed by parents. In the summer Wales's best-ever A-level results were recorded, the 85 per cent pass rate being higher than the British average (excluding Scotland). On the other hand, Welsh school league tables also revealed a high rate of absenteeism.

In April, unlike its counterpart in England, the governing body of the Church in Wales voted against the ordination of women, although in September a more liberal attitude was evident in its decision to reconsider its ban on divorcees remarrying in church. Meanwhile, in July, the Presbyterian Church put forward a £10 million plan to replace a third of the denomination's 977 chapels with more than 6,000 affordable homes. It was argued that this was a sensible response to dwindling congregations and rising maintenance costs, a related hope being that church-sharing with other denominations would provide a more practical way forward. In October delegates at a conference called by the Free Church Council of Wales voted in favour of a single non-conformist church for Wales.

In June, following what was believed to be Britain's biggest criminal case involving child abuse, five men were convicted at Swansea Crown Court of belonging to a paedophile ring in south-west Wales. Six others were acquitted amid claims that witnesses had been pressured to give evidence by social workers. Also in court during the summer was Eddie Browning of Cwmparc, Rhondda, who was freed by the Court of Appeal five years after his conviction for the notorious murder of Marie Wilks on the M50 in June 1988.

The 25th anniversary of the investiture of the Prince of Wales was greeted with general indifference by the Welsh public. Opinion polls showed declining support for the Prince. Even hard-line Welsh nationalists saw little need to protest at the low-key celebrations held at Caernarfon on 1 July.

It was announced in September that a prestigious competition to design a new £43 million opera house on Cardiff Bay had been won by the Iraqi-born architect, Zaha Hadid; by the end of the year, however, widespread criticism of her design and fears that the Millenium Fund would not support the scheme led to alternative proposals being considered (see also XVI.2.ii). One of the more unusual events of the year was the nomination for an Oscar of the Welsh-language film, *Hedd Wyn*. Largely ignored by London-based critics, the film's success gave a timely boost to the nation's burgeoning film industry (see XVI.1.vi).

8.   NORTHERN IRELAND

THE year was one of two parts, the watershed being the historic cessation of hostilities announcements by the IRA and the loyalist paramilitaries on 31 August and 13 October respectively (see XIX.3). Once achieved, the ceasefire opened the prospect of 'normality' and a new layer of preliminary talks leading to all-inclusive negotiations. The existence of bilateral party talks, at times with the Prime Minister, the London–Dublin ministerial discussions on a new framework document on North-South relations and the general meetings of the Anglo-Irish Inter-Governmental Council (AIIC) placed increased demands on the political process. However, just when progress seemed likely, an internal crisis in the Irish Republic in November, leading to the fall of the Fianna Fáil/Labour coalition (see II.1.vii), provided a hiatus in development. The political developments were accompanied by positive improvements in local economic prospects.

The first eight months of the year were spent trying to achieve a cessation of violence on the basis of the Downing Street Declaration of December 1993 (see AR 1993, pp. 44, 572–4). Local parties were rapidly forced to declare their attitude to it, but Sinn Féin resisted the political pressure by two tactics. First, it went into a formal process of consultation within the broader republican movement and held a series of 'peace commissions' throughout Ireland. While the views of individuals were known earlier, the formal negative response was not given until 24 July at a special conference in Letterkenny, Co. Donegal. Second, Sinn Féin regularly asked for 'clarification' of the document, pointing to differences between the British and Irish interpretations. The London government refused at first to respond, because of the risk of being drawn into direct negotiation on the declaration. However, a more open approach by Dublin, the removal of the broadcasting ban on Sinn Féin in the Republic and the granting by President Clinton of a US visa to its leader, Gerry Adams, led to a change. Speeches by NIO ministers began to offer insights into new institutions for a future Northern Ireland. It was to no avail initially: on 13 March the IRA offered a ceasefire in return for direct negotiations with the UK government but on different terms from the declaration. To show its sincerity, it declared a unilateral three-day ceasefire on 5–8 April. The tactic of seeking clarification formally ended on 19 May when the UK government published its response to 20 detailed questions from Sinn Féin, submitted through the Department of Foreign Affairs in Dublin.

The reaction of the republican movement at the special Letterkenny conference on 24 July was an official rejection of the Downing Street Declaration. It recognized this document as a 'step in the right direction' but condemned what it called the 'Unionist veto' (the principle of consent) to constitutional change. Just over a month later, an IRA message to RTE (the Irish broadcasting corporation) said that there would be a complete cessation of military operations from 31 August. The message saluted IRA activists over 25 years and reiterated its commitment to republican objectives, again rejecting the declaration as a solution.

The IRA decision was welcomed for the relief from murder and the political potential that it represented. It raised important questions for the loyalist campaign of violence, the broadcasting ban, security deployment and the weapons issue. On the political level, there was scepticism as well as optimism. The UK government was cautious, seeking use of the word 'permanent' rather than 'complete' with reference to the ceasefire. Irish nationalist politicians, such as the then Dublin Prime Minister, Albert Reynolds, and the leader of the Social Democratic and Labour Party (SDLP), John Hume, were more optimistic and sure that the ceasefire was genuine. This produced the historic three-way handshake between Mr Reynolds, Mr Hume and Mr Adams in Dublin on 6 September and a statement about a 'new era in which we are totally and absolutely committed to democratic and peaceful methods of resolving our political problems'. The US view was also optimistic and Mr Adams went on his second visit (from 24 September to 10 October), during which the ban on official contacts with Sinn Féin was lifted.

UK caution was determined by the responsibilities of government but it was also influenced by Unionist fears that a deal had been done to produce the ceasefire. On 7 September there was a confrontation between Dr Ian Paisley (leader of the Democratic Unionists) and Prime Minister Major at Number 10. During a visit to Northern Ireland on 16 September, Mr Major announced several measures to contribute to the peace process, namely the opening of ten border roads, the ending of the broadcasting ban on proscribed organizations and the pledge of a referendum in the province on the outcome of talks. He continued to insist on 'permanence' of the ceasefire as a condition for Sinn Féin entering into 'talks about talks'.

The loyalist ceasefire from 13 October was described as 'permanent' so long as all nationalist/republican violence had ended; it also expressed 'abject and true remorse' for the suffering that had been caused. Mr Major was again cautious, using similar phrases in his reactions to those used earlier. The Irish government's more radical reaction involved the announcement of the end of the state of emergency in the Republic (in existence since 1939) and the revoking of the Emergency Provisions Act of 1976. Maintaining his direct involvement, Mr Major paid a further visit to Northern Ireland on 24 October and said that he would make the 'working assumption' that the IRA ceasefire was intended to be permanent and that preliminary talks with Sinn Féin could begin before Christmas. He promised the opening of all border roads, the end of exclusion orders and a review of the role of the army. He also proposed a Northern Ireland Assembly, promised a referendum on any final deal and called an investment conference for December.

Despite the absence of the Unionists, the opening of the Forum for Peace and Reconciliation in Dublin on 28 October placed the focus on the conditions for sustaining peace and moving forward to all-inclusive talks. A month after the loyalist ceasefire, Mr Major said in London that talks with representatives of loyalist paramilitaries would begin before Christmas. Two days later, in the debate on the Queen's Speech, he insisted that in the exploratory dialogue the decommissioning of arms would be 'utterly important'.

The process was not all smooth. The IRA's murder of a postal worker in a robbery at Newry sorting office on 10 November reopened the 'permanence' issue and raised the problem of splinter groups, as did the discovery of a semtex bomb in Enniskillen on 19 December. The fall of the coalition government in Dublin on 17 November, and the four-week interval before it was replaced by a Fine Gael/Labour/Democratic Left coalition, created something of a hiatus. A claim by the outgoing Prime Minister, Mr Reynolds, on 17 December that all-Ireland bodies with executive powers and changes in Articles 2 and 3 of the Irish constitution and in the Government of Ireland Act 1920 had been agreed, created controversy, annoyed Unionists and provoked doubts about his motives.

There was impatience for progress. For example, a meeting between Mr Hume and Mr Adams on 30 November resulted in a joint statement calling for 'inclusive negotiations . . . without further delay'. But the UK government proceeded as planned to open preliminary talks with Sinn Féin (beginning on 9 and 20 December) and with the loyalists (at Stormont on 15 December). These positive images of political and economic activity were heightened when the new Irish Prime Minister, John Bruton, met Mr Major in London on 19 December. On his return to Dublin, Mr Bruton briefly met Mr Adams, who had described Fine Gael policy as based on a 'flawed analysis' but took some comfort from the promise of continuity in Irish government policy and the continued presence of Dick Spring as Deputy Prime Minister.

At the end of the year a sense of progress was in the air. Preliminary talks had opened with Sinn Féin and the loyalists, creating the possibility of substantive inclusive talks in 1995. In a further joint statement on 20 December, Mr Hume and Mr Adams set their agenda as demilitarization, action against discrimination and an amnesty for 'political' prisoners. Although significant republican groups, such as the Irish National Liberation Army (INLA) and Republican Sinn Féin (RSF), had not committed themselves to the political path, there was optimism that politics was replacing violence.

Politics had continued at other levels during the year. Michael Ancram renewed his bilateral discussions with the constitutional parties and at times representatives of these met the Prime Minister. While the Ulster Unionist Party (UUP) remained non-hostile, the Democratic Unionists were noticeably critical of Mr Major's approach. The British and Irish governments began work on a new framework document for North-South relations in March and the local parties began to publish their blueprints for the future. One substantive change occurred at Westminster in the shape of a decision on 9 March to create a Commons select committee on Northern Ireland affairs; it was constituted with 13 members on 28 March and met under the chairmanship of Sir James Kilfedder on 14 April. In light of the unchanged underlying situation, the emergency legislation was renewed in March and May, while direct rule was continued for another year from June. Two Northern Ireland junior ministers were affected by London scandals, one being promoted in January to replace confessed adulterer Tim Yeo as Environment Minister and the other, Tim Smith, resigning over the 'cash for questions' affair in October (see I.4).

The total of 60 deaths due to violence in 1994 was the lowest of any year since 1970, with the exception of 1985. The total was helped by the respective ceasefires which virtually removed the last four months from the calculations. The earlier part of the year had been little different from 1993. Only eight people had died in the first three months, but from April to August 50 were killed. Indeed, the yearly total would have been significantly higher but for the exclusion of the 29 security and other personnel who died in the helicopter crash on the Mull of Kintyre in June. Over the year, five members of the security forces (three RUC, two army) were killed by republican paramilitaries, who also killed 19 civilians. Loyalist paramilitaries were responsible for 36 deaths, the third consecutive year in which they committed more murders than the republicans. The security forces were responsible for no deaths in 1994.

The IRA's terrorist campaign in Britain had reopened at the end of January, not with the 'blockbuster' bombs of 1993 but with fire bombs in central London shops. The most significant attack was the mortar assaults on Heathrow airport on 9–13 March. While none of the mortars exploded, the potential was frightening. Other attacks, such as those on the railway station and track at Stevenage in June and the bicycle bombs in Bognor Regis and Brighton in August, paled in contrast. Apart from the Heathrow attacks, IRA activity was much reduced, in part due to increased security precautions, discovery of materials, arrests and convictions.

There was a strong improvement in the Northern Ireland economy in 1994. It was marked by significant investment by existing and new companies, by infrastructural and educational projects, by improved company profits and by a buoyant retail sector which, after the ceasefires, gave the main towns a boom Christmas by accommodating a surge of cross-border shoppers. The establishment of a Habitat store and the prospective arrival of Sainsbury's were indicative of the new climate. Unemployment fell regularly during the year, from 102,409 (13.7 per cent) in January to 90,074 (12.2 per cent) in December, the lowest level for 13 years. The number employed was at an all-time high, the government being especially pleased with an increase in the manufacturing sector.

The changing economic situation was reflected in a fall in the number of bankruptcies, the first since 1986, and in the increased profitability of business. The banks declared record profits and local companies announced over £100 million in new investment. Following the ceasefire announcements, various Northern Ireland departments hoped to benefit from an estimated potential saving of £180 million a year on security. There was also the promise of additional resources being allocated by the European Union and the International Fund for Ireland to underpin the peace process. A special investment conference, called by Mr Major in December, yielded considerable interest and initial pledges of investment totalling £75 million. A similar conference to be convened by President Clinton in Washington in May 1995 was expected to stimulate renewed US investment.

II WESTERN, CENTRAL AND SOUTHERN EUROPE

1. GERMANY—FRANCE—ITALY—BELGIUM—THE NETHERLANDS— LUXEMBOURG—IRELAND

i. GERMANY

CAPITAL: Berlin AREA: 357,000 sq km POPULATION: 80,600,000 ('92)
OFFICIAL LANGUAGE: German POLITICAL SYSTEM: federal parliamentary democracy
HEAD OF STATE: President Roman Herzog (since July '94)
RULING PARTIES: Christian Democratic Union (CDU), Christian Social Union (CSU) &
Free Democratic Party (FDP)
HEAD OF GOVERNMENT: Helmut Kohl (CDU), Federal Chancellor (since Oct '82)
PRINCIPAL MINISTERS: Klaus Kinkel (FDP/foreign affairs), Günter Rexrodt (FDP/
economics), Friedrich Böhl (CDU/head of chancery), Manfred Kanther
(CDU/interior), Sabine Leutheusser-Schnarrenberger (FDP/justice), Theo Waigel
(CSU/finance), Volker Rühe (CDU/defence), Norbert Blüm (CDU/labour & social
affairs)
INTERNATIONAL ALIGNMENT: NATO, OECD, EU, G-7
CURRENCY: Deutschmark (end-'94 £1=DM2.43, US$1=DM1.55)
GNP PER CAPITA: US$23,030 ('92)
MAIN EXPORT EARNERS: machinery & transport equipment, manufactures, chemicals

IT was a year of 20 electoral contests in Germany: eight *Landtag* (state parliament) elections; the European Parliament elections; a presidential election; nine municipal elections; and finally, and most importantly, the Bundestag (federal lower house) elections on 16 October. At the start of 1994, Chancellor Kohl's 1990 promise of 'unification without tears' seemed to be ending in tears without proper unification. The economy was stagnating and the future of the German economic model was clouded with doubt. Germany's leaders, and the population as a whole, seemed dispirited and lacking in self-confidence, weary of struggling to set right the problems of a time so out of joint, in a cyclical economic downturn. Reduced social benefits, real wage cuts and rising unemployment had produced disillusionment with, and deep electoral unpopularity for, the coalition government of the Christian Democratic/Social Union (CDU/CSU) and the Free Democrats (FDP).

By the end of the year all this had changed remarkably. The one political figure whose optimism never faltered was Chancellor Kohl. The CDU's electoral strategy leading up to the October general elections centred on him and his vision of a united Germany in a united Europe—in Thomas Mann's phrase, 'a European Germany, not a German Europe'. As Elke Tonscheidt, a party official, described the CDU campaign: 'The first strategy was to regard Germany as one country . . . . The second strategy was the Chancellor himself. . . , it was his personality we were selling in both west and east Germany.'

The recession had officially come to an end in December 1993; thereafter the economy moved forward with increasing momentum. Economic growth was 2.5 per cent in Germany as a whole in 1994. The economy confounded its critics by showing a greater capacity for evolutionary adaptation than the critics of its much-derided rigidities had appreciated. The profitability of west German industry increased by no less than 150 per cent in 1994, to DM 50,000 million, and unit labour costs fell by 1.2 per cent after a 3.6 per cent rise in 1993. In the eastern *Länder*, after deep recession in 1992–93, output took off in 1994, assisted by favourable developments in ex-communist Eastern Europe.

In May the tide of electoral opinion turned decisively in favour of Chancellor Kohl's government, which was returned to power in October, though with a reduced majority. In a turnout of 79.1 per cent, the results for the new 672-seat Bundestag were as follows (comparable figures for 1990, when there were 662 seats, being shown in parentheses):

	seats	% of votes
Christian Democratic Union (CDU)	244(268)	34.2 (36.7)
Christian Social Union (CSU)	50 (51)	7.3 (7.1)
Free Democratic Party (FDP)	47 (79)	6.9 (11.0)
Social Democratic Party (SPD)	252(239)	36.4 (33.5)
Greens/Alliance 90	49 (8)	7.3 (5.1)
Party of Democratic Socialism (PDS)	30 (17)	4.4 (2.4)

As in previous elections, the fact that 328 Bundestag seats were filled by candidates directly elected in constituencies meant that the other 'half' of the seats filled on the basis of the proportional vote of the parties had to be increased by 'supra-proportional' mandates to achieve overall proportionality in the results. Whereas the 12th Bundestag elected in 1990 had 656 seats plus six 'supra-proportional' members, the 13th Bundestag elected in 1994 consisted of 656 plus 16 seats. Without these additional seats, the majority of Chancellor Kohl's coalition over all other parties would have been only two rather than the ten-seat margin actually achieved.

The crucial feature of the outcome was the FDP's success in surmounting the 5 per cent barrier to representation, contrary to many predictions and despite a string of electoral failures earlier in the year (see below). Also noteworthy was the achievement of the unified Greens in crossing the 5 per cent threshold; in the 1990 federal elections, only the eastern Greens, as part of Alliance 90, had won seats. As expected, the far-right Republicans, beset by internal divisions, failed to win representation, taking only 1.9 per cent of the vote as against 2.1 per cent in 1990. Following the election, the new Bundestag re-elected Herr Kohl as Chancellor on 15 November by 338 votes to 333. In his new cabinet the number of posts was reduced to 16, the CDU providing nine ministers, the CSU four and the FDP three.

The Bundestag results demonstrated the great truth that oppositions do not win elections: governments lose them, by losing self-confidence or the confidence of the electorate. However, although the opposition Social Democrats (SPD) failed to depose the Kohl government, their steady advance in the year's *Landtag* elections gave the party a clear majority in the Bundesrat (the federal upper house). In light of that chamber's important role in the legislative process, the consequence was that the re-elected CDU/CSU-FDP government found itself in a *de facto* grand coalition with the SPD. The broad consensual politics characteristic of the German political landscape over the past 40 years therefore seemed set to become even more pronounced.

The great unresolved question remained: when and how would the two Germanies become one, both economically and psychologically? At times in the past four years it had seemed that the problems of unification were institutionalizing themselves. The existing western parties had experienced difficulties in putting down roots in the new eastern *Länder*, so that one legacy of unification was east-west voter fragmentation and an attendant threat to stable coalition government. For example, the (ex-communist) Party of Democratic Socialism (PDS) demonstrated its localized support by securing 17.6 per cent of the vote in the eastern *Länder*, compared with less that 1 per cent in the west. The PDS achieved Bundestag representation of 30 seats because it secured four 'direct' mandates (i.e. constituency seats won outright on a simple majority of first votes), three such seats being required for a party with less than 5 per cent of second votes to be eligible for proportional seats. As essentially a regional party that had abandoned marxism, the PDS was expected to experience eroding support as the east was drawn into the German mainstream, although full normalization was likely to take time.

As regards the east German economy, the formal winding-up of the Treuhandanstalt trust agency on 31 December 1994 marked the end of the initial phase of privatization, restructuring and closures which had followed the currency union of the two Germanies on 1 July 1990. The number of people in jobs in the east had fallen from 8.8 to 6.3 million since 1990 and unemployment remained as high as 45 per cent in isolated pockets. However, for the first time since June 1991, the eastern total of unemployed fell below one million in 1994, the average rate of unemployment falling to 13 per cent by year's end. Productivity in manufacturing remained at 40 per cent of west German levels, while wages were only 20 per cent lower than western levels. Financial transfers from the west totalled DM 175,000 million in 1994, equivalent to 4.7 per cent of the west German GDP and 47 per cent of the east German GDP. The rate of economic growth in the east during 1994 was 8.5 per cent higher than in 1993, the great bulk of this activity being in infrastructure and construction.

The basic strategy of the government was to pour developmental resources into the eastern *Länder* in the hope that the rest of the economy would eventually ignite. This approach was thought likely to succeed in the long run, but was imperilled in the shorter term by the lack of belief of east German citizens both in themselves and in their future. The latest statistics showed that birth and marriage rates in the east were half the west German levels, having fallen by 55 and 65 per cent respectively since unification. Against this background, there was general agreement that a revival in the morale of the east Germans was a necessary condition of full economic and social integration.

Chancellor Kohl recognized this problem when he sponsored an east German candidate for the federal presidency on the expiry of Richard von Weizsäcker's second term of office in May. Herr Weizsäcker had established an exceptional reputation as President, so that finding a successor of comparable stature was always going to be difficult. Herr Kohl's initial choice of Saxony's CDU justice minister, Steffen Heitmann, had proved to be a misjudgment because of his outspoken right-wing views (see AR 1993, p. 49). There were strong arguments subsequently for a consensus candidate in the person of Johannes Rau, the SPD minister-president of North Rhine-Westphalia and former Chancellor-candidate, who enjoyed widespread public respect. However, notwithstanding the presidency's non-political role, Herr Kohl's instinct for political power precluded the SPD being allowed a free run at such a prestigious office. The CDU's second choice fell on Roman Herzog, president of the Federal Constitutional Court, who had also held political office at state level. In the Federal Assembly convened in Berlin on 23 May, voting went along party lines, Herr Herzog being elected on the third ballot by 696 votes to 605 for Herr Rau. Although not as well-known as his predecessor or Herr Rau, and lacking their weight as a factor for integration, President Herzog nevertheless brought great personal distinction to the office and quickly proved himself to be a sure-footed head of state.

Elections on 12 June for the 99 German seats in the European Parliament (up from 81) proved to be a qualified success for Chancellor Kohl and a serious setback for the SPD. With an aggregate 38.8 per cent of the vote (and 47 seats), the CDU/CSU alliance was down on its 1990 federal election share but narrowly ahead of its 1989 Euro-election percentage. In contrast, the SPD managed only 32.2 per cent (and 40 seats), a decline compared with both 1990 and 1989. The qualification for the government was the failure of the FDP to surmount the 5 per cent barrier this time, whereas the Greens made a strong showing to win 10.1 per cent of the vote and 12 seats. There was accordingly much speculation at that stage that a 'red–green' alliance would be the most dangerous threat to Chancellor Kohl in the October federal elections.

The European results highlighted the fact that Chancellor Kohl's coalition difficulties stemmed mainly from the problems of the FDP, which had been in coalition with the CDU/CSU at federal level since 1982. In order to maintain a distinctive profile, the FDP had formed coalitions with the SPD at *Land* level—for example, in the Saarland and Lower Saxony—while remaining in the federal government with the CDU/CSU. This trick worked as long as the party secured more than 5 per cent of vote and thus won parliamentary seats. In the *Landtag* elections of 1994, however, the FDP failed to win representation in all eight contests and also experienced a haemorrhaging of its support at municipal level. By October the only *Land* government to which it still belonged was that of Bremen, so that it had come to be described as 'a general staff without an army'. In the federal contest, the FDP scraped back into the Bundestag with 6.9 per cent in the proportional vote, but this share was thought to include a significant number of CDU voters who had cast their first vote for their own party candidate and their additional party vote for the FDP. The FDP chairman, Klaus Kinkel, survived a challenge to his leadership at a hostile special party congress at Gera in December; but his future looked as uncertain as that of his party, with obvious implications for the survival of the federal coalition.

Increasing doubts were expressed during 1994 about the future of Germany as a centre of manufacturing industry and about the continued viability of its social market economy. The latter had traditionally laid emphasis on corporate and social consensus, featuring investment rather than distribution of profits, a limited role for equity markets, retention of a large semi-public sector and a high degree of employment protection. All these features, critics claimed, were indications of senescence—evidence that the system needed to be revitalized by injections of privatization, deregulation and the cult of shareholder value. The collapse of the Schneider group in April, following closely on the huge losses in the Metallgesellschaft group in November 1993, were regarded by some as symptomatic of the failure of the German pattern of corporate governance. The decision of Mercedes-Benz in December to site a new factory for the production of the Swatchmobile car at Hambach in France was a setback to German employment hopes. On the other hand, the accelerating economic recovery of 1994 encouraged those who argued that the future of social market institutions lay in their evolutionary adaptation rather than in their abandonment in favour some supposedly more virile system of stock market capitalism.

Germany's presidency of the European Union (EU) in the second half of 1994 culminated in the Essen summit in December, at which the first steps towards extending the EU eastwards were agreed (see XI.3).

Increased domestic scepticism about the Maastricht Treaty made the slower progress of European integration convenient for the government, although Herr Kohl remained publicly committed to economic and monetary union. As regards Germany's international role, the removal of constitutional obstacles to the deployment of German forces outside the NATO area in peace-keeping roles did not lead to the assumption of wider responsibilities. The Federal Constitutional Court had ruled that an affirmative vote in the Bundestag was a prerequisite for such deployment, and this inevitably had a muting effect. Nevertheless, the longer-term challenge for Germany was clearly to find ways of adapting to its undoubted political leadership in the centre of Europe.

ii. FRANCE

CAPITAL: Paris   AREA: 544,000 sq km   POPULATION: 57,400,000 ('92)
OFFICIAL LANGUAGE: French   POLITICAL SYSTEM: presidential parliamentary democracy
HEAD OF STATE & GOVERNMENT: President François Mitterrand (since May '81)
RULING PARTIES: Socialist Party (PS) holds presidency; government is centre-right coalition of the Rally for the Republic (RPR) and the multi-party Union for French Democracy (UDF)
PRINCIPAL MINISTERS: Edouard Balladur (RPR/Prime Minister), Alain Juppé (RPR/foreign affairs), Edmond Alphandéry (UDF/economy), Nicolas Sarkozy (RPR/budget), François Léotard (UDF/defence), Charles Pasqua (RPR/interior), Pierre Méhaignerie (UDF/justice), Simone Veil (social affairs & health)
INTERNATIONAL ALIGNMENT: NATO, OECD, EU, G-7, Francophonie
CURRENCY: franc (end-'94 £1=F8.35, US$1=F5.34)
GNP PER CAPITA: US$22,260 ('92)
MAIN EXPORT EARNERS: machinery & transport equipment, manufactures, chemicals, food & beverages, tourism

THE founder of the Fifth Republic, Charles de Gaulle, detested self-serving politicians who neglected the national interest. Despite this legacy, politics in 1994 seemed endlessly preoccupied with scandal and jockeying for position in the run-up to the 1995 presidential election. For much of the year the Prime Minister, Edouard Balladur, fresh from success in the December 1993 GATT negotiations, was the favourite to win the presidency on the first ballot. However, legislation allowing local authorities to make capital grants to church schools stirred furious opposition from defenders of the secular tradition. First M. Balladur conceded an extra F 2,500 million for the state sector; then the Constitutional Council ruled that his scheme was unconstitutional. A 250,000–strong rally in Paris sought to revitalize a French left demoralized by defeat in the previous spring's legislative elections (see AR 1993, p. 52). In February, despite the allocation of F 300 million in emergency aid, protests by fishermen against cheap imports from outside the European Union (EU) turned to violence. Demonstrations by miners against pit closures and strikes by public service workers followed.

The most serious protests came over a proposal that young people in their first job should be paid only 80 per cent of the minimum wage. Demonstrations in many towns, some degenerating into violent clashes with the police, forced a climb-down. M. Balladur's preferred response to such situations was to promise consultation, as he did over education and with the young. Some saw him as weak or indecisive, but he remained popular. The cantonal elections in March showed some recovery by the left-wing parties, but also gave the government cause for modest satisfaction. The European elections in June were a sterner test. The joint government list of the Rally for the Republic (RPR) and the Union for French Democracy (UDF) was challenged in particular by the 'Other Europe' list headed by Philippe de Villiers, combining traditionalist right-wing values with the conviction that the EU posed a threat to French interests and identity. Also in serious contention was the extreme-right National Front (FN), while the once-dominant Socialists came under challenge on the centre-left from the list of the Left Radical Movement (MRG).

The actual campaign was dominated by domestic concerns, although a 'Sarajevo' list opposing government policy on Bosnia captured much media attention before half withdrawing. On a 53.7 per cent turnout, the results gave the RPR-UDF alliance 25.6 per cent of the vote and 28 of the 87 French seats, well ahead of the Socialists, who managed only 14.5 per cent and 15 seats. An impressive third place was taken by the Other Europe (12.3 per cent and 13 seats), just ahead of the MRG's Radical Energy list (12.0 per cent and 13 seats). The FN won 11 seats with 10.5 per cent of the vote (two points down on its 1993 showing) and the Communists took the other seven seats (with 6.9 per cent). The other 14 lists presented all failed to achieve the 5 per cent minimum required for representation.

If the government's performance was simply mediocre, the Socialists' was disastrous and immediately fatal to Michel Rocard's presidential ambitions; he resigned as party first secretary and was replaced by Henri Emmanuelli. Jaded, offering little that was new, the Socialists suffered from the Sarajevo diversion and also lost votes to Jean-Pierre Chevènement's Alternative Politics initiative (2.5 per cent) and, more especially, to Bernard Tapie's Radical Energy list. M. Tapie's appeal seemed to be unaffected by multiple allegations of fraud and corruption against him. The Communists, led by the unknown Robert Hue, who had replaced the veteran Georges Marchais in January, experienced a further fall in popular support. The warring ecologists presented two separate lists but neither got near the 5 per cent threshold, so that the movement lost all nine seats won in 1989. Over half the votes went to maverick, marginal or extreme groups—telling evidence of voter disaffection.

This phenomenon had several causes: slow economic recovery, intractable social problems and continuing revelations about political corruption. The Tapie saga ran throughout the year, ending with him bankrupt and awaiting trial. In February a National Assembly deputy, Yann Piat, was murdered in southern France, apparently because of what she might have revealed about corruption. Three ministers had to resign after being indicted. The mayors of several large cities faced charges, as did several members of parliament, senior officials and prominent industrialists. All major parties were in some degree involved, but the newer revelations predominantly concerned government supporters. The politicians felt that they were being unfairly stigmatized for the failings of a few. Nevertheless, they felt compelled to enact various anti-corruption measures, including a ban on company political contributions, a reduction of permitted election expenditure and a requirement that parliamentarians and certain officials should disclose their assets. Whether these would be more effective than previous measures remained to be seen.

Corruption was not the only blight on politics. In September the former Socialist Prime Minister, Laurent Fabius, and two colleagues faced the controversial charge of 'complicity in poisoning' over the transmission of AIDS by blood transfusions to haemophiliacs in 1985. In April Paul Touvier, a senior member of the wartime collaborationist Milice organization, who had so far escaped justice thanks to political and clerical complicities, was sentenced to life imprisonment over the killing of seven Jewish hostages in 1944. The trial stirred painful reflection on France's wartime experience. The debate was fuelled when a new biography of François Mitterrand disclosed a closer involvement with the Vichy regime than had been generally known, as well as his long friendship with an official (subsequently assassinated) who should have stood trial for his role in the deportation of Jews. Many Socialist loyalists were shocked. In contrast, the revelation that M. Mitterrand had a 20-year-old illegitimate daughter stirred only criticism of press intrusion into a private matter. The President's health was a further cause of political uncertainty: a second operation for prostate cancer and related chemotherapy left him much weakened, although determined to see his term through to its end in May 1995.

Meanwhile, there were strains within the governing coalition, as the presidential ambitions of Jacques Chirac, the RPR secretary-general, were threatened by the greater popularity of M. Balladur. In 1994 the latter refused to reveal his hand, while increasingly behaving as a candidate-in-waiting. A fall-off in the Prime Minister's fortunes after the summer resulted in the tag of favourite being appended to Jacques Delors (a Socialist), who had served two terms as president of the

European Commission and who was untarnished by scandal. Briefly, the French left scented an unimagined victory—only to have its hopes dashed when M. Delors declined to stand on grounds of age and the difficulty of securing a parliamentary majority to support a further Socialist presidency. Devastated, the Socialists began the search for what was likely to be a sacrificial candidate. It seemed, therefore, that the chief presidential protagonists would be M. Chirac and M. Balladur, with all the frustration for the left and dangers of division for the right that this implied.

M. Balladur's aim was to reduce unemployment by one million over five years, while maintaining the strong franc and meeting the criteria for European monetary union. His claims in August of a 'strong recovery' were borne out by a 3 per cent increase in GDP over the year and a 4.7 per cent expansion of industrial production. Inflation (1.6 per cent) was the lowest in the EU, average income rose by 2.3 per cent and overseas trade was in healthy surplus. On the other hand, the Bourse had a poor year, falling 17 per cent, while unemployment, having reached a record 3,426,000 in January, remained obstinately over 12 per cent. Described as 'strict' by the responsible RPR minister, Nicolas Sarkozy, the 1995 budget presented in September provided for a 4.7 per cent increase in taxation, while expenditure was to rise by 1.9 per cent. A targeted reduction of the budget deficit to F 274,600 million (3.5 per cent of GDP) assumed growth of 3.1 per cent and receipts of some F 55,000 million from privatization. The budget draft also included some creative accounting which was later disallowed by the Constitutional Council. Education, welfare, justice, local authorities and overseas France were favoured in the proposals; social housing, defence and culture lost ground.

The privatization programme continued with the full disposal of Elf-Acquitaine and the UAP insurance group and a partial sale of Renault. The Bull computer company was prepared for 51 per cent privatization, receiving F 11,100 million in government aid. Air France implemented a rescue package that involved 5,000 job losses, a three-year wage freeze and a capital injection of F 20,000 million to prepare it for privatization.

Security remained a major preoccupation. The RPR Interior Minister, Charles Pasqua, continued his tough line on law and order, particularly against illegal immigrants and incipient Islamic fundamentalist activism. He scored a major success in August when the wanted international terrorist, Illich Ramírez Sánchez ('Carlos the Jackal'), was arrested in Sudan on a French intelligence tip-off and flown to Paris to face trial on murder charges (see also V.4.i). Concern at the spread of fundamentalist sentiments also led the Education Minister, François Bayrou (UDF), to ban school pupils from displaying 'ostentatious religious signs'—in practice, Muslim headscarves—on the grounds that they were incompatible with the secular basis of state education. He also unveiled a 'new contract' for schools containing 150 proposals affecting every level from primary to adult education, including curricula, the teaching week, professional training and evening courses. The plan was well received, but so modestly funded that it was doubtful how far it would be implemented. Similar scepticism met the 100 proposals for youth arising from a consultation exercise launched by M. Balladur after the demonstrations in March.

FOREIGN AFFAIRS AND DEFENCE. The most divisive issue was Europe. The mainstream parties proclaimed their commitment to a close relationship with Germany, although anxieties about German dominance often lay just below the surface. Some doubted the wisdom of extending the European Union (EU) without first deepening it. However, greater popular scepticism about Europe was reflected both in support for politicians and groups hostile to the Maastricht Treaty and in the way presidential hopefuls blurred their positions to avoid alienating support across widening fault-lines on the EU.

The trend towards a rapprochement with NATO continued. In February a White Paper advocated that France should participate in NATO-run peace-keeping operations, while in September François Léotard became the first French ministerial representative to attend a NATO Defence Ministers' conference since the withdrawal of France from the integrated command structure in 1966. France continued to be the leading supplier of UN 'blue helmet' forces in ex-Yugoslavia, although dissatisfaction with lack of political progress led to the numbers being reduced from a peak of 7,520 to about 5,000.

In January France withdrew support for the CFA franc used in ex-French Africa, causing a 50 per cent devaluation (see VI.3; XI.6.i). This was widely seen as signifying a measure of disengagement from the former colonies, with which the Balladur government had no sentimental links. However, France also wrote off everything owed by the poorest CFA countries and half of what was owed by the better off. France was inevitably involved in the Rwandan tragedy (see VII.1.ii), sending 2,000 troops in June to establish a 'safe zone', despite the new Kigali government's suspicions arising from earlier French involvement in training and equipping the Rwandan army. The operation was successful and the force was withdrawn in August. France was slow to approve EU aid, seeking to use such approval as a lever to encourage the formation of a Hutu-Tutsi coalition government.

The civil war in Algeria (see V.4.iv) was the greatest external preoccupation in 1994. After a series of murders of French nationals, the hijack of a French airliner at Algiers airport in December ended in all four hijackers being killed by French security forces at Marseilles airport. This was followed in Algeria by the revenge murder of four priests, three of them French. Apart from anxiety about Algeria itself, where France had extensive interests and many ties, the government feared contagion of the rest of North Africa and France itself, whether by fundamentalist activism among the population of North African origin or by an influx of refugees. Though officially neutral, it uneasily tilted towards the Algerian government by supplying combat-related equipment.

The defence White Paper reflected the need for fresh thinking after the Cold War and the 1990–91 Gulf confict, the latter having displayed France's limited capacity for high-tech non-nuclear warfare. It argued that the primacy of nuclear deterrence should remain, but that greater emphasis was needed on mobile conventional forces and international cooperation in weapons development. In April the defence equipment review deferred a decision on new nuclear missiles until 1997, proposing that conventional weaponry would have priority in expenditure of F 613,000 million during 1995–2000, representing a real increase of 0.5 per cent a year. The army would have 227,000 men in eight divisions, with 792 tanks and 405 artillery pieces. The air force would have 20 squadrons of combat aircraft and the navy 100 ships. There would be a new generation of nuclear submarines, a long-range cruise missile and a standing foreign intervention force with a 4,000-mile capability. Experience suggested, however, that it would be financially difficult to sustain so many programmes. Discussions were subsequently initiated with several countries for joint weapons development.

OVERSEAS DEPARTMENTS AND TERRITORIES. When the government agreed that French Polynesia would receive F 2,420 million in aid over four years in compensation for the effects of the continued moratorium on nuclear tests, the president of the territorial assembly, Gaston Flosse, warned that this might not quieten local demands for independence (see also X.2.ii). Independence likewise remained an issue in New Caledonia, where the main pro-independence Kanak movement demanded the 'updating' of the 1988 law providing for a referendum on the territory's future. Visiting Mayotte in November, M. Balladur promised that the islanders would be consulted about their future before the year 2000. In the Caribbean overseas departments, separatist agitation subsided, not least because of greater EU protection for locally-produced bananas. In June the government approved measures to stimulate employment in the overseas departments, where it remained much higher than in metropolitan France. Corruption was also a problem: during 1994 politicians or officials were either convicted of, or were facing, corruption charges in Réunion, French Polynesia, New Caledonia, French Guiana and Guadeloupe.

iii. ITALY

CAPITAL: Rome   AREA: 301,000 sq km   POPULATION: 57,800,000 ('92)
OFFICIAL LANGUAGE: Italian   POLITICAL SYSTEM: parliamentary democracy
HEAD OF STATE: President Oscar Luigi Scalfaro (since May '92)
RULING PARTIES: caretaker coalition of Forza Italia (FI), Northern League (LN),
    National Alliance (AN), Christian Democratic Centre (CCD), Union of the
    Democratic Centre (UCD) and Panella List/Radical Party (PR)
HEAD OF GOVERNMENT: Silvio Berlusconi (FI), Prime Minister (since May '94,
    caretaker from Dec '94)
PRINCIPAL MINISTERS: Giuseppe Tatarella (AN/deputy premier), Roberto Maroni
    (LN/deputy premier, interior), Antonio Marino (FI/foreign affairs), Cesare Previti
    (FI/defence), Alfredo Biondi (FI/justice), Lamberto Dini (non-party/treasury),
    Giancarlo Pagliarini (LN/budget), Giulio Tremonti (non-party/finance)
INTERNATIONAL ALIGNMENT: NATO, OECD, G-7, EU
CURRENCY: lira (end-'94 £1=Lit2,538, US$1=Lit1,622)
GNP PER CAPITA: US$20,460 ('92)
MAIN EXPORT EARNERS: machinery & transport equipment, manufactures, chemicals,
    agricultural products, tourism

ITALY'S political crisis entered a new phase in 1994 but showed no sign
of drawing to a close. By the end of the year the extraordinary rise
to power of media tycoon Silvio Berlusconi and his new Forza Italia
party had gone into reverse, amid uncertainty as to whether he offered
a long-term solution or was a symptom of a persisting gap in political
authority.

On 13 January the then non-party Prime Minister, Carlo Azeglio
Ciampi, resigned after securing parliamentary approval of a new electoral system involving a large measure of 'first-past-the-post' (see AR
1993, p. 59). The partial abandonment of proportional representation,
together with the low public standing of parties whose involvement in
corruption had been revealed to be systematic, ensured that preparations
for general elections in March were marked by a number of novelties,
including the formation of alliances between parties. On the left, matters
were relatively straightforward. In early February a Progressive Alliance
(AP) was formed consisting of eight components: the ex-communist
Democratic Party of the Left (PDS), the Socialist Party (PSI) and
a splinter PSI group, the hardline Communist Refoundation Party,
the Greens, the anti-Mafia La Rete party, the liberal-left Democratic
Alliance and the left-Catholic Social Christians. On the centre-right,
alliance formation was more complex. The once-dominant Christian
Democrats, who in January decided to become the Italian Popular
Party (PPI), refused to ally with the federalist Northern League (LN)
and eventually opted to stand jointly with the Pact for Italy list headed
by the political reform campaigner, Mario Segni.

On the right, the LN at first refused to ally with the National Alliance
(AN), the front organization of the neo-fascist Italian Social Movement
(MSI), which had scored well in local elections in Rome and Naples in
November 1993 (see AR 1993, pp. 60–1). There was therefore a real

risk that victory would be handed on a plate to the ostensibly more united left. It was this possibility which induced Signor Berlusconi to enter the political fray, at the head of a new movement called Forza Italia, founded in January using the resources of his Fininvest empire. As an entrepreneur with interests in broadcasting, construction, publishing, sport, the retail sector and insurance, he had more to fear than most from a left that was promising, among other things, to introduce strict anti-trust legislation into the private television sector. Using the charisma that derived from his associations with consumerism, television and football, Signor Berlusconi overcame the divisions on the right by reaching separate electoral agreements with the LN and the AN, respectively designated the Freedom Alliance and the Good Government Alliance. Places in Forza Italia's lists were also allocated to right-wing former Christian Democrats and Liberals and to the Reformist grouping headed by Marco Pannella of the Radical Party.

Signor Berlusconi dominated the campaign with promises of lower taxes and a million new jobs and warnings that, if 'the communists' took power, the country would be plunged into penury and illiberalism. In response, the AP parties attacked the Forza Italia leader for his irresponsible policies and sought to demolish his image as a 'new man' by pointing out that he owed his dominant position in commercial television to his close association with the disgraced former PSI leader, Bettino Craxi. They also criticized him for refusing to submit himself to newspaper and television interviews or to engage in regular debates with his opponents. These attacks proved to be ineffective, however. After two years of political scandal and four of economic recession, many Italians were ready to believe the promise of redemption and prosperity that Signor Berlusconi offered.

Held on 26–27 March and involving the renewal of both the Chamber of Deputies and the Senate, the elections resulted in the right-wing bloc winning an aggregate 43 per cent share of the proportional vote, against 34.4 per cent for the AP (the left's worst result since 1948) and only 15.7 per cent for the centrists. Because three-quarters of the seats in both houses were directly elected, the right-wing parties obtained a 100-seat overall majority in the 630-member Chamber and fell only narrowly short of an overall majority in the 315-member Senate. Within the right-wing bloc, Forza Italia obtained 21 per cent of the vote, while the AN and the LN scored 13.5 and 8.4 per cent respectively. Within the AP, in contrast, only the PDS (20.4 per cent) and Communist Refoundation (6 per cent) achieved the 4 per cent minimum required to obtain proportional seats in the new parliament, the once powerful Socialists being reduced to a humiliating 2.2 per cent. Squeezed between the two blocs, the PPI and the Segni group obtained 11.1 and 4.6 per cent respectively.

Because of post-election internecine conflict on the right, it took Signor Berlusconi 40 days to form his first administration. Several of the new Prime Minister's business associates secured key posts, including Antonio Martino (Foreign Affairs) and Cesare Previti (Defence), while the Treasury and Finance ministries went respectively to the 'technicians' Lamberto Dini and Giulio Tremonti (the latter elected on the Segni list). A striking number of politicians 'recycled' from the old parties also secured portfolios. Among these, the former Socialist, Giuliano Ferrara, became Minister for Relations with Parliament; the former Christian Democrat, Clemente Mastella, was appointed to the Labour Ministry; and the former Liberals, Alfredo Biondi and Raffaele Costa, obtained the Justice and Health portfolios respectively. The League won the Interior Ministry for Roberto Maroni, while AN members took Culture, Posts, Agriculture and Transport.

From the beginning, two features of the new government rendered it controversial not only at home but also abroad. First, the inclusion of the AN in the coalition meant that for the first time since 1945 members of a party associated with the dictatorial regimes of the inter-war period held posts in the government of a country belonging to the European Union. The Prime Minister insisted that there were no fascist ministers in his cabinet, meaning by this that none had personally been associated with Mussolini's rule. However, the efforts of Gianfranco Fini, the AN leader, to turn his party into a formation of the moderate right were undermined by his own references to Mussolini as a great statesman. These remarks induced the European Parliament to adopt a resolution expressing opposition to the inclusion of fascists in the governments of member states.

Second, there was much disquiet over the concentration of economic and political power in Signor Berlusconi's hands. He had resigned as president of his Fininvest group in January but President Scalfaro and most commentators agreed that a clearer separation from his business interests was required to avoid conflicts of interest. In the absence of any formal legal or constitutional provisions in this regard, the Prime Minister was himself allowed to appoint three 'wise men' to study possible solutions to the problem. Their final recommendation, presented at the end of September, was the creation of an Italian-style 'blind trust' under which the Prime Minister would place his business interests under the control of an administrator approved by parliament. This solution was accepted by the government (at least in theory: by the end of the year no bill had been tabled), but it was not deemed satisfactory by critics. In their view, only two solutions were possible: either that the businesses should be sold or that Signor Berlusconi should resign.

Meanwhile, the Italian elections to the European Parliament on 12 June had confirmed the ascendancy of the right. Forza Italia was by far the strongest individual party, winning 27 of the 87 Italian seats (with 30.6 per cent of the vote), while the AN took 11, the Northern

League six and the Pannella list two. On the left, the PDS obtained 16 seats (with 19.1 per cent), Communist Refoundation five, the Greens three, the Socialists two and La Rete one. In the centre, the PPI won only eight seats (with 10 per cent of the vote), the Segni list three and the Republicans, Democratic Socialists and South Tyrol People's Party one each.

In light of the economic progress achieved by his two predecessors, it was expected that Signor Berlusconi would continue efforts to reduce the national debt and reorganize the public sector. However, the new government appeared unable or unwilling to pursue economic rigour effectively or consistently. The situation was complicated by disputes within the coalition over various policy issues, notably Signor Berlusconi's pledge not to raise taxes. The Finance Bill, prepared in a hurried fashion, penalized the lower-paid by concentrating spending cuts in the areas of pensions and health care. This gave rise to massive public protest, which culminated in an enormous national demonstration organized by the trade unions in Rome on 12 November. Faced with the prospect of strikes, the government watered down the measures. This negatively affected business and international confidence, which was further shaken by the failure to proceed rapidly with extensive privatization. In consequence, the lira fell on the international exchanges, as did the share index of the Milan stock exchange. Moreover, the national debt remained above the target of 135–140,000,000 million lire.

Two questions dominated the government's agenda. The first was the consolidation of its own power. Taking office after more than 40 years of Christian Democratic dominance, the parties of the right were concerned to establish their authority within the state. Following the resignation of Romano Prodi as president of the IRI state industrial holding company in June, the government forced the resignation of the non-party board which had been appointed just a year earlier to depoliticize and reorganize the RAI broadcasting corporation. A tame new board replaced the directors of RAI's three networks and of their respective news departments with its own nominees (several of whom currently worked for Fininvest or the Berlusconi-controlled publisher Mondadori). Similar developments occurred in the press sector and there were even attempts to interfere with appointments to senior posts in the Bank of Italy (traditionally an independent institution), although these provoked a stern rebuke from President Scalfaro. It was notable that the bulk of positions were filled by Forza Italia and AN nominees, whereas the Northern League, to its increasing chagrin, was systematically excluded.

The continuing anti-corruption investigations by Milanese magistrates provided the government with its second concern. By the start of 1994, the inquiries into the activities of the old parties had run their full course, although few trials had yet been held. The investigations were therefore directed into new areas, namely the largely public banking sector, which had traditionally been under strict political control, and the financial police, who were revealed to have taken bribes in return for closing an eye to irregular accounting practices. The latter inquiries involved significant sectors of the Milanese economy, including many of the top names in the fashion industry. Aware that there was a real risk of inflicting damage on the economy, the investigating magistrates, led by Antonio Di Pietro, appealed to the politicians to find a solution. Instead, the government intervened to alleviate the position of those charged with bribery offences, adopting a decree in July that ended preventive detention and made provision for plea-bargaining. A public outcry forced the withdrawal of the measure.

Of great concern to Signor Berlusconi and his allies was the interest that the magistrates showed in Fininvest. Members of the government, including the Prime Minister himself, frequently attacked the judiciary and an inspection was ordered by the Justice Ministry into the legitimacy of inquiries concerning Fininvest. When the head of the Milan Procurator's Office, Francesco Saverio Borrelli, suggested in early October that the Prime Minister might be placed under investigation, pandemonium broke out. However, the campaign of intimidation failed to stave off the inevitable: on 22 November Signor Berlusconi received a summons to appear before the magistrates in connection with their inquiries into the financial police. While the Prime Minister protested his innocence, Signor Di Pietro sensationally resigned from the magistrature, claiming that conditions had deteriorated to the point where he could no longer carry out his functions with the necessary degree of calm and anonymity.

Although this was the first time since the beginning of the anti-corruption investigations that a serving head of government had been placed under investigation, Signor Berlusconi believed at that stage that he would not be compelled to resign. This calculation proved to be erroneous for two reasons. On the one hand, the main opposition parties, the PDS and the PPI, began to assert themselves under new leaders and also to cooperate against the Berlusconi government. Second, the Northern League, which had always been a restless partner and which had grown ever-more frustrated with the lack of progress on privatization and federalism, withdrew from the majority and tabled a no-confidence motion together with the opposition. Faced with what he did not hesistate to label the 'betrayal' of an ally, Signor Berlusconi resigned a week before Christmas to avoid defeat in parliament. At the end of the year it was unclear whether it would be possible to form a new government or whether Italians would be called to the polls for the third time in as many years.

iv. BELGIUM

CAPITAL: Brussels AREA: 30,500 sq km POPULATION: 10,000,000 ('92)
OFFICIAL LANGUAGES: French & Flemish
POLITICAL SYSTEM: parliamentary democracy, devolved structure based on language
  communities
HEAD OF STATE: King Albert II (since Aug '93)
RULING PARTIES: Christian People's Party (CVP/Flemish), Christian Social Party
  (PSC/Walloon), Socialist Party (SP/Flemish) & Socialist Party (PS/Walloon)
HEAD OF GOVERNMENT: Jean-Luc Dehaene (CVP) Prime Minister (since March
  '92)
PRINCIPAL MINISTERS: Frank Vandenbroucke (SP/Deputy Premier, foreign affairs),
  Melchior Wathelet (PSC/Deputy Premier, justice, economic affairs), Herman Van
  Rompuy (CVP/deputy premier, budget), Philippe Maystadt (PSC/finance), Frank di
  Rupo (PS/Deputy Premier, communications, public enterprises), Philippe Maystadt
  (PSC/finance), Robert Urbain (PS/foreign trade, European affairs), Johan Vande
  Lanotte (SP/interior), Karel Pinxten (CVP/defence)
INTERNATIONAL ALIGNMENT: NATO, OECD, EU, Benelux, Francophonie
CURRENCY: franc (end-'94 £1=BF49.80, US$1=BF31.83)
GNP PER CAPITA: US$20,880 ('92)
MAIN EXPORT EARNERS: machinery & transport equipment, manufactures, chemicals,
  agricultural products

The Agusta scandal, or 'three Guys affair', over allegations of bribes
paid by a military helicopter supplier to the Walloon Socialist Party
(PS) proved serious enough to cause the resignation of three of the
most senior leaders of the party. Guy Coême (a federal Deputy
Prime Minister as well as Minister for Communications and Public
Enterprises), Guy Spitaels (minister-president of the interim Walloon
administration) and Guy Mathot (Walloon minister of the interior)
all resigned on 21 January in order to contest the allegations. As
well as destabilizing the four-party federal coalition government of
the Flemish Christian People's Party (CVP), the Walloon Christian
Social Party (PSC), the PS and the Flemish Socialists (SP), the scandal
revealed a deep-seated power struggle within the PS, whose credibility
with the electorate sagged. Replacements for the departed ministers
maintained the existing political power balance in both the federal
and the Walloon governments. That the PSC was not immune from
scandal was demonstrated by the resignation in March of the mayor
of Brussels, Michel Demaret, following alleged corruption in allocating
public contracts and the publication of an interview in which he had
criticized the Pope and questioned the integrity of lawyers.

The results of the European Parliament elections on 12 June unsurprisingly showed voters' support swinging away from the coalition
parties, especially from the PS, to the right-wing Flemish and Walloon
Liberals. The CVP won four of the 25 Belgian seats (down one), the
PSC retained two (on a lower vote share) and the PS and SP each won
three (down two in each case), while the two Liberal parties both went
up from two to three seats. It was also notable that both Flemish and
Walloon parties of the far right gained ground strongly, the Flemish Bloc
winning two seats and the National Front (modelled on the French party

of the same name) one, while the more moderate Flemish Volksunie retained one seat but lost votes. The other two seats were shared by the two Green parties, the Flemish Agalev and the Walloon Ecolo. In the Brussels region the French-speaking Democratic Front, in an electoral alliance with the French-speaking Liberals, was successful in persuading voters to support federal unity, and particularly ties between Brussels and Wallonia, against possible future encroachment by an independent Flanders, in which Brussels would be an island.

Much the same pattern of results occurred in the local and provincial elections held in October. In both Flanders and Wallonia, parties of the extreme right improved their position strongly compared with the previous municipal elections in 1988. Although these parties did not gain control of any significant municipality, the Flemish Bloc became the largest single party in Antwerp, the biggest commune in the country, threatening the position of the local ruling coalition.

In the external sphere, the despatch of additional Belgian troops to Rwanda in early April, following the killing of 10 Belgian UN soldiers in an upsurge of massive inter-ethnic slaughter (see VII.1.ii), proved to be dramatically unsuccessful. The withdrawal of all Belgian forces later the same month marked the end of an era, being the final abandonment by the Belgian government of any pretension to a special relationship with its former colony. More positively, the Belgian Deputy Prime Minister and Foreign Minister, Willy Claes (SP), was appointed as the new secretary-general of NATO in September (see also XII.2) and was succeeded in the federal cabinet by Frank Vandenbroucke, hitherto SP president. In a simultaneous change, Louis Tobback was replaced as Interior Minister by his chef de cabinet, Johan Vande Lanotte, having decided to devote himself to his newly-acquired post as mayor of Leuven/Louvain (also becoming the new SP president). But Belgium was saved from having to find a new Prime Minister when the Franco-German nomination of Jean-Luc Dehaene (CVP) as the next president of the European Commission was vetoed by Britain on the grounds that he was too much of a European federalist (see I.3; XI.3).

The economy improved as the year progressed. Tax revenue rose, enabling the government to put together a July budget which continued austerity in government spending, although without the need for any further tax increases, and was intended to meet the official target of of 3.6 per cent of GDP for the net government financing requirement in 1995. This was generally considered to be an acceptable progression toward the European Union's convergence criterion of a maximum of 3 per cent of GDP for the central government deficit. The Prime Minister told parliament at the start of the new session on 20 September that official policy would emphasize job creation rather than transfers to personal consumption. On employment, he made it clear that a pay freeze would be implemented in 1995/96 and that there would be reduction of the working week in order to create jobs, although work-sharing agreements would be encouraged at individual employer level.

As the economy moved into a phase of greater stability, the National Bank was able progressively, and very gradually, to lower the central interest rate. Indicators for industrial output showed a clear recovery, but investment continued to fall and most companies had plenty of spare productive capacity. Consumer spending declined, influenced by high unemployment and a decline in real average monthly earnings. Overall, it was clear that the economy had improved considerably but that the business recovery was patchy and not yet broadly based.

v.   THE NETHERLANDS

CAPITAL: Amsterdam   AREA: 37,000 sq km   POPULATION: 15,200,000 ('92)
OFFICIAL LANGUAGE: Dutch   POLITICAL SYSTEM: parliamentary democracy
HEAD OF STATE: Queen Beatrix (since April '80)
RULING PARTIES: Labour Party (PvdA), People's Party for Freedom and Democracy
   (VVD) & Democrats 66 (D66)
HEAD OF GOVERNMENT: Wim Kok (PvdA), Prime Minister (since Aug '94)
PRINCIPAL MINISTERS: Hans Dijkstal (VVD/Deputy Premier, home affairs), Hans van
   Mierlo (D66/Deputy Premier, foreign affairs), Gerrit Zalm (VVD/finance), G.J.
   Wijers (D66/economic affairs), Joris Voorhoeve (VVD/defence), Winnie Sorgdrager
   (D66/justice)
INTERNATIONAL ALIGNMENT: NATO, OECD, EU, Benelux
CURRENCY: guilder (end-'94 £1=f2.71, US$1=f1.74)
GNP PER CAPITA: US$20,480 ('92)
MAIN EXPORT EARNERS: oil & gas, machinery & transport equipment, chemicals,
   agricultural products

THE evidence of the public opinion polls during the period leading up to the 3 May general elections suggested that both the Christian Democrats (CDA) and the Labour Party (PvdA), which formed the outgoing coalition government, were losing popular support. A key factor arousing much hostility was the projected reform of social security payments, in particular the CDA's proposal for a freeze on old-age pensions; the departure of Ruud Lubbers, the popular CDA Prime Minister who had held office for 12 years, also had its effect. It was clear, as well, that a significant proportion of the electorate considered the coalition parties to be soft on immigration, an increasingly divisive social issue.

The results of the elections, in which there was a 78 per cent turnout, did indeed prove bad for the two government parties. The CDA lost a third of its support, its representation in Second Chamber dropping from 54 seats to only 34, while the PvdA lost 12 seats, although it tally of 37 left it as the largest party in lower house. The winners included the right-wing liberal People's Party for Freedom and Democracy (VVD), which gained nine seats for a total of 31, while centrist Democrats 66 (D66) doubled their representation to 24 seats. Reflecting dissatisfaction on the part of pensioners, two new parties representing their interests—the General League of the Elderly (AOV) and the Union 55+—together won seven seats. Other changes were small, though it was notable that the Greens, expected to do well, lost a seat and that the anti-immigrant Centre Democrats (CD), against predictions, gained only two additional seats (against one previously) with no more than 2.5 per cent of the total vote.

The election results meant that no combination of two parties commanded a majority in the Second Chamber, making a three-party coalition inevitable. With the CDA and its policies having been clearly rejected, the party reconciled itself to being in opposition for the first time since 1917. In the event, after protracted negotiations, the PvdA, the VVD and D66 joined uneasily in a new coalition government, which took office on 22 August under former trade union leader Wim Kok of the PvdA.

The new government's economic policies included a four-year programme of spending cuts, to include substantial reductions in social security and defence expenditure (the latter decision causing the resignation of the Chief of Staff of the Armed Forces). It was significant, however, that in the short term planned cuts in social security would be modest, the tougher and more fundamental reductions being deferred for two years, to the disappointment of the VVD. The budget presented on 20 September in effect set the same level of current deficit as in 1994, although the overall deficit, including special items, was expected to be much higher, implying more borrowing and possible interest rate increases. The budget was widely criticized as lacking the necessary rigour to reduce the public deficit.

Attracting a turnout of only 35.6 per cent (the joint lowest, with Portugal, among the European Union member states), the elections to the European Parliament on 9 June produced a better result for the CDA, which retained ten of the 31 Dutch seats (up from 25 previously), while the PvdA retained eight. The VVD doubled its representation to six seats on an appreciably higher vote, while D66 actually doubled its vote share and won four seats (up three). A Calvinist confessional alliance took two seats (up one) and the Greens one (down one), while the two pensioners' parties did not put up candidates.

Signs early in the year that economic growth was quickening were confirmed by trends in the main indicators. Growth in business investment accelerated to an annual rate of 3.5 per cent by mid-year, when government capital spending was rising by 4 per cent, and industrial production began to recover, led by strong export demand. On the other hand, consumer confidence remained low, rising unemployment and concerns about government spending cuts being among the causes. An important development for Dutch business in 1994 was the privatization of the state-owned post and telecommunications group, KPN, involving the Netherlands' largest-ever share issue. It was also announced that, unless the stock exchange and the companion association of listed companies themselves produced the necessary measures, the government intended to introduce radical legislation to end Dutch companies' ability to use existing regulations to make themselves virtually immune from hostile takeover bids.

vi. LUXEMBOURG

CAPITAL: Luxembourg   AREA: 3,000 sq km   POPULATION: 392,000 ('92)
OFFICIAL LANGUAGE: Letzeburgish   POLITICAL SYSTEM: parliamentary democracy
HEAD OF STATE: Grand Duke Jean (since Nov '64)
RULING PARTIES: Christian Social People's Party (PCS) & Luxembourg Socialist
    Workers' Party (LSAP)
HEAD OF GOVERNMENT: Jacques Santer (PCS), Prime Minister (since July '84), due to
    be succeeded by Jean-Claude Juncker (PCS) in Jan '95
PRINCIPAL MINISTERS: Jacques Poos (LSAP/Deputy Premier, foreign affairs),
    Jean Spautz (PCS/interior), Jean-Claude Juncker (PCS/finance, labour), Robert
    Goebbels (LSAP/economy, public works)
INTERNATIONAL ALIGNMENT: NATO, OECD, EU, Benelux, Francophonie
CURRENCY: Luxembourg franc (end-'94 £1=LF49.80, US$1=LF31.83)
GNP PER CAPITA: US$35,160 ('92)
MAIN EXPORT EARNERS: basic manufactures, machinery & transport equipment,
    tourism, financial services

THERE was a low-key campaign leading up to the general election on 12 June. The coalition government made up of the Christian Social People's Party (PCS) and the Socialist Workers' Party (LSAP), which had held office for ten years, fought on its record of successful economic policies which had mitigated the worst effects of the European business recession. The results showed minimal changes: both the coalition parties lost one seat but retained a commanding majority of 38 seats out of 60 seats in the Chamber of Deputies. Of the other parties, the Democrats (DP) won 12 seats (a gain of one), the Greens five (up one) and a pensioners' party now called the Action Committee for Democracy and Justice five (up one), while the Communists lost their only seat. Elections to the European Parliament, held on the same day, produced proportionately similar results, the PCS and LSAP each winning two seats and the DP and Greens one each.

The new government, which took office on 13 July, was virtually indistinguishable from its predecessor. Its policies, too, were effectively unchanged, continuing to emphasize opposition to any European Union (EU) measures that would erode Luxembourg's banking secrecy laws and thus undermine its position as a major international banking centre.

The new budget, unusually, provided for a deficit, but nevertheless looked conservative and prudent by EU standards.

The appointment of the Prime Minister, Jacques Santer (PCS), as president of the European Commission (see XI.3) foreshadowed his departure from the government in January 1995. In a non-controversial transition, the PCS Minister of Finance, Jean-Claude Juncker, was nominated as the new Prime Minister, and it was assumed that there would be no changes in policies.

It was a better year for the economy. The rate of inflation fell to a little over 2 per cent. Industrial production improved steadily and by mid-year was 5 per cent higher than a year earlier; even the steel industry, still the dominant sector, recovered from a depressed first six months, and output of crude steel was running over 6 per cent higher in the third quarter than in the same period of the previous year.

vii. REPUBLIC OF IRELAND

CAPITAL: Dublin   AREA: 70,280 sq km   POPULATION: 3,500,000 ('92)
OFFICIAL LANGUAGES: Irish and English   POLITICAL SYSTEM: parliamentary democracy
HEAD OF STATE: President Mary Robinson (since Dec '90)
RULING PARTIES: coalition of Fine Gael (FG), Labour Party (LP) and Democratic Left (DL)
HEAD OF GOVERNMENT: John Bruton (FG), Prime Minister/Taoiseach (since Dec '94)
PRINCIPAL MINISTERS: Dick Spring (LP/Deputy Prime Minister, foreign affairs), Ruairi Quinn (LP/finance), Nora Owen (FG/justice), Richard Bruton (FG/employment & enterprise), Brendan Howlin (LP/environment)
INTERNATIONAL ALIGNMENT: neutral, OECD, EU
CURRENCY: punt (end-'94 £1=IR£1.01, US$1=IR£0.65)
GNP PER CAPITA: US$12,210 ('92)
MAIN EXPORT EARNERS: tourism, machinery & electronic equipment, agricultural products

THE Downing Street Declaration on Northern Ireland, signed in December 1993 by the Taoiseach (Prime Minister), Albert Reynolds, and the British Prime Minister, John Major (see AR 1993, pp. 69, 572-4), dominated political activity for much of the year. Mr Reynolds set about urging Sinn Féin (SF) to advise the IRA to proclaim a ceasefire. He took a number of conciliatory steps, clarifying aspects of the declaration in response to SF requests and lifting the ban on interviews with SF spokesmen by broadcasting services in the Republic. The mild disapproval which these measures drew from the British government was matched by similar expressions of Irish dissatisfaction with supposedly intransigent British attitudes.

How far the two governments were in genuine disagreement was matter for conjecture: British anxiety to assuage Unionist suspicions was understood in Dublin, so that the approaches of the two heads of government looked very like a twin-pronged strategy to bring the extreme elements of both Northern Ireland communities into the peace process. However, British protests over a visit to the United States in January by the SF president, Gerry Adams, which Mr Reynolds had facilitated by a personal plea to President Clinton, together with continuing loyalist violence in the North and IRA bomb attacks on Heathrow airport in March, dampened popular expectations until the IRA announced a complete cessation of violence on 31 August (see I.8; XIX.3).

The ceasefire was unanimously welcomed in the Republic, where British doubts over whether it was meant to be permanent were not shared. Mr Reynolds was much praised for using his influence with President Clinton and Northern nationalists to create the prospect of rapid economic and political progress as a 'peace dividend' if violence were ended. In the wake of the ceasefire, he set up a Forum for Peace and Reconciliation, as envisaged in the Downing Street Declaration, to identify common ground between the different Irish traditions. All political parties on the island were invited to take part, including Sinn Féin. Much publicity surrounded the arrival of Mr Adams in Dublin for meetings with the Taoiseach and to attend the Forum. However, the Unionist parties refused to take part, so that the Alliance Party was the only non-nationalist group from Northern Ireland to participate in the Forum's deliberations, which began in November.

In parallel with these events, a more shadowy search for common ground was undertaken by the Irish and British governments, the aim being to agree a 'framework document' on the future of Northern Ireland. It was hoped thereby to instil life into the moribund three-strand talks involving the two governments and the Northern parties. According to unconfirmed reports before the year's end, difficulties concerning the Irish constitutional claim to jurisdiction over Northern Ireland and the British Government of Ireland Act of 1920 (which secured Northern Ireland's status within the United Kingdom) were being slowly overcome.

Meanwhile, a political crisis had erupted in the Republic. The coalition of Mr Reynolds's Fianna Fáil (FF) and the Labour Party, led by the Foreign Minister, Dick Spring, came under severe strain. By early summer it was clear that Labour's popular support had dwindled because of the party's association with FF policies such as a so-called 'amnesty' for tax evaders (in fact, a remission of much of the tax due), an extension of the tax on residential property and various schemes for the privatization of state assets. Labour's vote slumped at the European Parliament elections in June. Although the party retained its one seat in Dublin, the electorate rejected the candidate most favoured by Mr Spring. The success of the Green Party, which headed the poll in the capital and also won in the adjacent Leinster constituency, was seen less as an endorsement of environmental concerns than as a rebuke to

Labour. Of the other 12 Irish seats, seven went to the Fianna Fáil, four to Fine Gael (then the main opposition party) and one to an independent candidate.

In the circumstances, pressure mounted on Mr Spring to demonstrate that Labour had not abandoned its distinctive policies. He clashed with Mr Reynolds in August over the report of a tribunal investigating irregularities in the beef industry. The following month tension was exacerbated when the Taoiseach insisted that the Attorney-General, Harry Whelehan, should be appointed president of the High Court—a judicial office second only to that of Chief Justice. Mr Spring opposed the nomination, arguing that Mr Whelehan was insufficiently liberal. Enigmatic statements, leaks to the media and an attempted reconciliation followed, until in October a new factor arose. It transpired that warrants for the extradition of a Roman Catholic priest to stand trial in Northern Ireland for paedophile offences had been delayed in the Attorney-General's office; the priest had meanwhile voluntarily returned to Northern Ireland, been found guilty and gaoled. Mr Spring invoked this episode to justify further stalling on the promotion of the Attorney-General, but Mr Reynolds pressed ahead with the appointment nonetheless. The outcome, following a rapid succession of statements, revelations and resignations, was that the government collapsed on 15 November and that Mr Reynolds was replaced as FF leader by Bertie Ahern, the outgoing Finance Minister.

Following abortive efforts to reconstruct the FF-Labour alliance under Mr Ahern's leadership, a new coalition was negotiated between the relatively conservative Fine Gael, Labour and the Democratic Left (a smaller socialist party). The new government took office on 15 December with the Fine Gael leader, John Bruton, as Taoiseach and Mr Spring back at his former post as Foreign Minister. This was the first time in the history of the Republic that an administration had been changed through a realignment of parties rather than by a general election—a development seen as a logical reflection of the Irish system of proportional representation and also as a step towards closer conformity with the European norm.

Mr Bruton, aged 47, was a highly experienced politician from the social democratic wing of his party. With a background in economics, law and farming, he had served in a number of ministries in the 1970s and 1980s, twice holding the key portfolio of Finance. A palpable earnestness of purpose left him at a disadvantage vis-à-vis more charismatic leaders such as Mr Spring and kept his ratings down in the opinion polls, to such an extent that an attempt had been made within Fine Gael earlier in the year to remove him from the leadership. His determined and successful resistance to this challenge had won admiration from hardened political observers. Widespread goodwill, even from FF sources, greeted his election as Taoiseach: most commentators judged him the ideal head of government for the 'right-left' coalition, despite previous differences between himself and Mr Spring.

The Republic's economy fared well in 1994. Inflation remained at about 2 per cent, one of the lowest levels in the European Union (EU). Although industrial relations problems arose from cost-cutting exercises in a number of companies (notably the state-owned Irish Steel and the Team Aer Lingus aircraft maintenance firm), overall employment grew steadily—not least in the volatile electronics industry, in which a number of factory closures had taken place the previous year. Tourism, which had long been adversely affected by the Northern troubles, recorded a boost of 11 per cent in earnings for 1994. By December the current budget was in surplus, with tax revenue exceeding spending for the first time since 1967. Whether the Bruton government would be able to maintain the near-miracle of non- inflationary economic growth, while meeting demands for tax reductions and sundry social reforms, remained to be seen, but the availability of substantial EU development funds promised further progress in 1995. Among the many indicators of confidence in business circles was the purchase by the Irish paper and packaging group, Jefferson Smurfit, of the French manufacturer in the same field, Celulose du Pin, a subsidiary of St Gobain, for IR£683 million: the acquisition made Smurfits one of the ten largest paper companies in the world.

The Roman Catholic Church suffered serious damage to its image in Ireland in 1994. The affair of the paedophile priest was only one among several highly-publicized cases in which priests or religious brothers were found guilty of sexual offences or involvement in relationships forbidden to celibate clergy. People were able to accept with adult understanding that the clergy harboured their share of delinquents, like any other segment of society, but were distressed to learn that the church authorities had responded to the problem in grossly inappropriate ways, such as moving the offenders from place to place, thereby unintentionally facilitating the commission of further offences. The bishops admitted the mistakes of the past and set up advisory bodies to guide them on the correct approach for the future, but it could scarcely be doubted that their credibility in taking a public stance on moral issues had been severely dented.

The sporting highlight of the year was the Republic of Ireland's participation in the World Cup football finals (see also Pt. XVII). Thousands of supporters travelled to the United States, were elated by the Irish victory against Italy but dejected by the dismissal of their team in the second round by Holland. In athletics, Sonia O'Sullivan won Ireland's first gold medal in the European Championships, with a record run in the 3,000 metres, and also set a world record for the 2,000 metres at Edinburgh. Less international acclaim accrued to Ireland in the arts in 1994 than in recent years, although the momentum was well maintained, especially in the theatre. Brian Friel's new play, *Molly Sweeney*, was enthusiastically received, as were new productions of Frank Fitzgibbon's *Observe the Sons of Ulster Marching to the Somme* and J. M. Synge's classic *The Well of the Saints*.

2. DENMARK—ICELAND—NORWAY—SWEDEN—FINLAND—AUSTRIA—SWITZERLAND—EUROPEAN MINI-STATES

i. DENMARK

CAPITAL: Copenhagen   AREA: 43,000 sq km   POPULATION: 5,200,000 ('92)
OFFICIAL LANGUAGE: Danish   POLITICAL SYSTEM: parliamentary democracy
HEAD OF STATE: Queen Margrethe II (since Jan '72)
RULING PARTIES: coalition of Social Democrats (SD), Venstre Liberals (V) & Centre Democrats (CD)
HEAD OF GOVERNMENT: Poul Nyrup Rasmussen (SD), Prime Minister (since Jan '93)
PRINCIPAL MINISTERS: Niels Helveg Peterson (V/foreign affairs), Mimi Stilling Jakobsen (CD/industry), Mogens Lykketoft (SD/finance), Marianne Jelved (V/economic affairs), Bjoern Westh (SD/justice), Hans Haekkerup (SD/defence), Birthe Weiss (SD/interior)
INTERNATIONAL ALIGNMENT: NATO, OECD, EU, Nordic Council
CURRENCY: krone (end-'94 £1=DKr9.52, US$1=DKr6.09)
GNP PER CAPITA: US$26,000 ('92)
MAIN EXPORT EARNERS: agricultural produce, machinery & transport equipment, manufactures

ON 28 January the Prime Minister, Poul Nyrup Rasmussen of the Social Democratic Party (SDP), undertook a government reshuffle designed to strengthen the Centre Democrats (CD), a key component in his four-party centre-left coalition. Public opinion polls showed that the CD was in danger of failing to cross the 2 per cent threshold for parliamentary representation in the elections due before the end of the year. The reshuffle had the unforeseen consequence that the government lost its one-seat overall majority in the Folketing when the new CD Social Affairs Minister, Bente Juncker, was forced to resign on 11 February for having made serious unfounded accusations against a political opponent. She left the party on 28 February to sit as an independent, so that the coalition's committed parliamentary support fell to 89 seats out of 179.

The Supreme Court trial of the former Justice Minister, Erik Ninn-Hansen, opened on 7 March. He was accused of violating laws governing ministerial conduct and foreigners' rights. The charges arose from decisions made between September 1987 and January 1989 when, it was alleged, Mr Ninn-Hansen had ordered a halt to the processing of applications from Tamil refugees for permission to bring their families to Denmark from Sri Lanka. The trial was still in progress at year's end as a result of delays caused by the defendant's ill-health.

In a low turnout of 52 per cent, the European Parliament elections on 9 June resulted in the SDP slipping from four to three seats and both CD seats being lost, whereas the Radical Liberals (also in the ruling coalition) won their first European seat. The opposition Venstre Liberals and Conservatives each gained one seat (winning four and three respectively), the former Conservative Prime Minister, Poul Schlüter, obtaining the largest personal vote and becoming one of the parliament's vice-chairmen. Of the other five seats, four went to formations opposed to Danish membership of the European Union (EU), which took over a quarter of the vote, and one to the 'Euro-sceptic' Socialist People's Party (SPP).

By summer Denmark's economy was responding to the government's 1993 fiscal stimulus with strong growth, while inflation and short-term interest rates were low. On the other hand, the budget deficit had risen to 5 per cent of GDP and long-term interest rates were relatively high. Unemployment was still nearly 13 per cent of the workforce, despite higher growth and job-creation measures, including a job-rotation scheme introduced in January. The draft budget presented on 24 August foresaw a smaller deficit in 1995, the aim being to maintain Denmark's position as a core EU member, to hold down inflation and to reduce long-term interest rates.

Mr Rasmussen called the general election for 21 September. In a turnout of 84 per cent, the results were as follows (1990 figures in brackets):

	seats	% of votes
Social Democrats	62 (69)	34.6 (37.4)
Venstre Liberals	42 (29)	23.3 (15.8)
Conservatives	27 (30)	15.0 (16.0)
Socialist People's Party	13 (15)	7.3 (8.3)
Progress Party	11 (12)	6.4 (6.3)
Radical Liberals	8 (7)	4.6 (3.5)
Centre Democrats	5 (9)	2.8 (5.1)
Christian People's Party	0 (4)	1.8 (2.3)
Unity List	6 (0)	3.1 (1.7)
independents	1 (0)	1.0 (3.6)
Greenland/Faroes	4 (4)	

The principal victors were the Venstre Liberals led by Uffe Ellemann-Jensen (the former Foreign Minister), whereas the Conservatives lost ground. On the left, the SPP's losses were interpreted as voter punishment for its frequent support for the Rasmussen coalition and for its acceptance of the 1992 'national compromise' which led to Denmark's belated acceptance of the EU's Maastricht Treaty in May 1993 (see AR 1993, p. 70). In contrast, the anti-EU Unity List made its début in the Folketing. Within the government parties, SDP losses were less than had been predicted, the Radical Liberals improved slightly and the CD retained a parliamentary presence (albeit reduced), but the Christian People's Party's failed to achieve the 2 per cent minimum. Accordingly, Mr Rasmussen was reappointed Prime Minister on 21 September at the head of a minority three-party coalition commanding 76 of the 179 seats.

In early November the SDP Taxation Minister, Ove Stavad, resigned from the government after accepting responsibility for a controversial rescue of a bank in his constituency in 1993; he was replaced by a party colleague. Later in November the government secured parliamentary approval for its 1995 budget measures, attracting support from the Liberal and Conservative parties.

Elections to the Faroe Islands' Lagting (parliament) were held on 7 July against a background of deep economic crisis. The poll was called when the coalition of Social Democrats, Republicans and Independence Party lost its majority in May. The outcome was a coalition of the Unity Party, Social Democrats, Workers' Front and Independence Party.

ii. ICELAND

CAPITAL: Reykjavík   AREA: 103,000 sq km   POPULATION: 261,000 ('92)
OFFICIAL LANGUAGE: Icelandic   POLITICAL SYSTEM: parliamentary democracy
HEAD OF STATE: President Vigdís Finnbogadóttir (since Aug '80)
RULING PARTIES: Independence (IP) & Social Democratic (SDP) parties
HEAD OF GOVERNMENT: David Oddsson (IP), Prime Minister (since April '91)
PRINCIPAL MINISTERS: Jón Baldvin Hannibalsson (SDP/foreign affairs), Fridrik Sophuson (IP/finance), Thorsteinn Pálsson (IP/fisheries, justice, ecclesiastical affairs), Sighvatur Björgvinsson (SDP/industry & commerce)
INTERNATIONAL ALIGNMENT: NATO, OECD, EFTA/EEA, Nordic Council
CURRENCY: króna (end-'94 £1=ISK107.27, US$1=ISK68.59)
GNP PER CAPITA: US$23,880 ('92)
MAIN EXPORT EARNERS: fish & fish products, tourism

ON 4 January Iceland and the United States signed a joint defence statement covering the period 1994–96. This reaffirmed their 1951 bilateral defence agreement, in particular the continued presence of US forces at the Keflavík base, although with a reduced number of US fighter aircraft.

In March the conclusion of entry negotiations between the European Union (EU) and Finland, Norway and Sweden (Iceland's three Nordic partners in the EFTA/EEA grouping) led to an increasingly open debate about possible Icelandic EU membership. Prominent among those pressing the advantages of membership was the Social Democratic (SDP) Foreign Minister, Jón Baldvin Hannibalsson. He argued that Norway's fisheries agreement demonstrated the EU's flexibility on this vital issue and warned of Iceland's political isolation within Europe and the Nordic area. These arguments were rejected by the Prime Minister,

David Oddsson, and the Fisheries Minister, Thorsteinn Pálsson, both of the Independence Party (IP). While not excluding membership at some future date in changed circumstances, they argued that Iceland's economic interests were adequately protected by the EEA agreement (which had entered formally into force on 1 January); any additional benefits from membership, they argued, would not compensate for the loss of sovereignty over Iceland's fishing grounds, the economic foundation of the country's independence.

Both sides of the debate were agreed that the immediate task was to renegotiate the EEA agreement, setting Iceland's relations with the EU on a bilateral basis. In July Mr Oddsson met the European Commission president to initiate these negotiations. Earlier, at the SDP conference in June, the party had voted in favour of negotiations to clarify the terms on which Iceland could join the EU. A public opinion survey showed that a majority of Icelanders favoured membership. However, the Norwegian electorate's rejection of membership on 28 November was generally considered to have removed the economic urgency of the issue. Norway's decision meant that Iceland's chief Nordic competitor in Europe's seafood market would remain outside the EU and, therefore, that Icelanders would not face disadvantage in a vital export market.

Icelandic-Norwegian disagreements over Icelandic fishing in the Barents Sea continued throughout 1994 (see AR 1993, pp. 72–3). In April the Norwegian and Russian governments addressed separate notes to Mr Oddsson urging him to stop Icelandic vessels fishing in the area jointly administered by them in the Barents Sea. Mr Oddsson replied that the Icelandic government had no legal powers to do so. Sharper conflicts were caused by Icelandic fishing within the Svalbard (Spitzbergen) 200-mile protection zone. In March the government announced its intention to accede to the 1920 Svalbard Treaty. Norway, however, still refused to grant Iceland fishing quotas in the zone, its coastguard vessels forcibly ejecting or arresting Icelandic boats during the summer. On 26 September Iceland formally protested to Norway over the arrest of the vessel *Björgulfur*. On 1 October Mr Oddsson announced that, if Norway refused to grant access to Svalbard waters, Iceland would take its case to the International Court of Justice. Bilateral negotiations opened on 11 October but had reached no conclusion by the end of the year.

On 29 April the leader of the Progressive Party (PP), Steingrímur Hermannsson, resigned to become head of the central bank and was succeeded by Halldór Ásgrímsson. In local elections on 28 May the coalition parties both lost some support. In Reykjavík the IP lost to a combined list of the SDP, the PP, the People's Alliance and the Women's Alliance. Equally significant for the national elections due in April 1995 was the resignation of Jóhanna Sigurdardóttir from the SDP on 16 September, following her unsuccessful challenge to

Hannibalsson for the party leadership in June. One of Iceland's most popular politicians, she was expected to launch her own list, drawing support from the centre and left-wing parties.

Iceland's seven-year recession ended in 1994 with growth of 2 per cent. The visible trade balance was positive, while inflation and interest rates were low. The 1994/95 budget presented on 1 October forecast a deficit of 1.5 per cent of GDP (half the previous year's level) on the strength of expanding economic activity and spending cuts. However, unemployment at some 3 per cent of the labour force was still high by Icelandic standards.

On 17 June Iceland celebrated the 50th anniversary of the foundation of the Republic with a ceremony at the Thingvellir national shrine attended by all the Nordic heads of state. On 1 December President Vigdís Finnbogadóttir opened the new National Library building in Reykjavík.

iii. NORWAY

CAPITAL: Oslo   AREA: 324,000 sq km   POPULATION: 4,300,000 ('92)
OFFICIAL LANGUAGE: Norwegian   POLITICAL SYSTEM: parliamentary democracy
HEAD OF STATE: King Harald V (since Jan '91)
RULING PARTY: Labour Party (minority government)
HEAD OF GOVERNMENT: Gro Harlem Brundtland, Prime Minister (since Nov '90)
PRINCIPAL MINISTERS: Bjoern Tore Godal (foreign affairs), Gunnar Berge (local government & labour), Sigbjørn Johnsen (finance), Jens Stoltenberg (industry & energy), Joergen Kosmo (defence), Grete Faremo (justice), Jan Henry T. Olsen (fisheries)
INTERNATIONAL ALIGNMENT: NATO, OECD, EFTA/EEA, Nordic Council
CURRENCY: krone (end-'94 £1=NKr10.58, US$1=NKr6.76)
GNP PER CAPITA: US$25,820 ('92)
MAIN EXPORT EARNERS: oil & gas, machinery & transport equipment, manufactures, chemicals, fish

NORWEGIAN public debate and politics were dominated throughout 1994 by the issue of membership of the European Union (EU), which was not decided until the end of November, when the people voted against joining.

The year began with a heavy blow to Mrs Brundtland's minority Labour government in the premature death on 13 January of the Foreign Minister, Johan Joergen Holst, who in 1993 had brokered the Israeli-Palestinian framework agreement. He was succeeded on 24 January by Bjoern Tore Godal, who as Trade Minister was leading Norway's EU membership negotiations. These were subsequently concluded on 16 March, over two weeks after those of the other three applicants. Agreement had been delayed by Norway's refusal to grant the EU larger fishing quotas than those already conceded in the European Economic

Area (EEA) agreement—a key issue as regards the government's hope of winning the referendum on membership. The accession treaty maintained Norway's control over fish resources in northern waters until 1998, after which Norway's strict fisheries management regime would be the basis on which Brussels would take decisions on catch quotas there. Oslo also retained effective control of its petroleum resources, while generous Arctic subsidies and transitional payments would help Norway's heavily-subsidized agricultural sector to adjust to the EU's lower prices. Jan Henry T. Olsen, the Fisheries Minister, declared himself satisfied and ready to recommend membership.

The Conservatives, at their congress on 8–10 April, voted over-whelmingly in favour of membership. The Progress Party, meeting a week later, postponed a decision on membership but, in an important political development, split into two wings; of these, the more liberal faction left the party and its four members of parliament formed a Group of Independents. On 25 May this group prevented the fall of Mrs Brundtland's government on a no-confidence motion against the Finance Minister, arguing that Norway would be ill-served by political instability and a minority anti-EU government led by the Centre Party. In mid-June the Storting voted to hold Norway's referendum on 28 November, after the consultations in Finland (16 October) and Sweden (13 November). On 19 June the Labour Party conference voted in favour of EU membership by 197 votes to 93.

In contrast to the campaigns in Finland and Sweden, the debate in oil-rich Norway took place against a background of national prosperity and rising living standards. The balance of payments was strong and growth steady, while inflation, interest rates, wage settlements and unemployment were all low. There were longer-term worries, in par-ticular declining petroleum reserves and low investment levels—anxi-eties which underlay the economic case for EU membership. But these did not significantly lessen the sense of prosperity, which in turn weakened the impact of such arguments, especially as the EEA agreement had already given Norway much of the immediate economic benefits of membership.

EU membership was supported by most of the Labour leadership, by the Conservatives, and by industry and business. Their main arguments were political: Norway should participate in developing Europe's post-Cold War political and security structures and have a voice in the institutions where key decisions would be made. The entry of Norway along with Sweden and Finland, it was argued, would retain the cohesion of the Nordic bloc. As regards economic issues, the pro-EU side contended that national control of key natural resources—petroleum, fish and agriculture—was assured by the accession agreement.

Opposition to membership came from the organizations representing fishermen and farmers, from the Centre, Christian People's, Liberal and Socialist Left parties, and from much of the population of rural, especially northern, Norway. They all feared a loss of national sovereignty and control of natural resources, as well as the erosion of democratic institutions, the welfare state and Norway's egalitarian society. Opponents argued that NATO guaranteed Norway's security, while Norway's role in the Middle East peace settlement demonstrated the benefits of an independent foreign policy. On 22 September the Norwegian trade union congress rejected its leadership's recommendation to support membership.

The consistently substantial 'no' majority shown by opinion polls in Norway narrowed significantly in the wake of the Finnish and Swedish votes in favour of EU accession. However, although these verdicts gave a late boost to Norway's 'yes' campaign, the actual result on 28 November was a clear rejection of membership by 52.2 to 47.8 per cent. The verdict was a severe political defeat for Mrs Brundtland, although, unlike the Labour Prime Minister at the time of Norway's previous rejection of membership in 1972, she had never linked the continued existence of her government to a 'yes' vote. Indeed, she argued that Norway now required political and economic stability in order to face the serious situation created by this second rejection of EU membership. She said that a priority would be to negotiate satisfactory adjustments to the EEA Treaty now that it applied only to Norway, Iceland and Liechtenstein.

iv. SWEDEN

CAPITAL: Stockholm   AREA: 450,000 sq km   POPULATION: 8,700,000 ('92)
OFFICIAL LANGUAGE: Swedish   POLITICAL SYSTEM: parliamentary democracy
HEAD OF STATE: King Carl XVI Gustav (since Sept '73)
RULING PARTY: Social Democratic Labour Party
HEAD OF GOVERNMENT: Ingvar Carlsson, Prime Minister (since Sept '94)
PRINCIPAL MINISTERS: Mona Sahlin (deputy premier, equality issues), Laila Freivalds
    (justice), Lena Hjelm-Wallén (foreign affairs), Thage G. Peterson (defence),
    Göran Persson (finance), Sten Heckscher (industry & commerce)
INTERNATIONAL ALIGNMENT: neutral, OECD, EU, Nordic Council
CURRENCY: krona (end-'94 £1=skr11.83, US$1=skr7.43)
GNP PER CAPITA: US$27,010 ('92)
MAIN EXPORT EARNERS: machinery & transport equipment, timber and wood
    products, iron & steel, tourism

THREE closely-related issues occupied Sweden in 1994: the serious state of public finances; the September general election, which would decide the policies applied to address this problem; and the November referendum on European Union (EU) membership, in which Swedish voters had to take what was widely regarded as their most important decision of the post-war period.

Carl Bildt's minority centre-right coalition survived until the election despite a series of setbacks. First, it lost the external support of part of the populist New Democracy (ND) party when the latter split following Count Ian Wachtmeister's resignation as chairman on 5 February. Second, the Centre Party (CP) chairman, Olof Johansson, resigned as Environment and Natural Resources Minister on 16 June in protest against the government's final approval of construction of the bridge and tunnel link across the Öresund Sound between Sweden and Denmark. One group of ND deputies continued to support the government, while a replacement CP minister was appointed to succeed Mr Johansson. Meanwhile, the government had successfully concluded Sweden's entry negotiations with the EU in early March (the accession treaty being signed on 24 June) and had also signed the Partnership for Peace agreement with NATO on 9 May (see XII.2; XIX.1).

By summer the parties had lined up for the two autumn polls. In the general election campaign, the then opposition Social Democrats, with a solid lead in the polls, faced a less than united ruling coalition, one of whose four parties, the Liberals, announced their readiness to form a post-election coalition with the Social Democrats. The centre-right parties stood for pro-market reforms, deregulation and privatization as the answers to Sweden's structural problems; the Social Democrats for retaining a leaner version of the welfare state model they had created. On the EU issue, by contrast, the majority of Social Democratic leaders joined the coalition parties, business and industry in supporting membership, facing a strong anti-EU coalition led by a significant minority of Social Democrats and by the Green and (ex-communist) Left parties. Pro-EU campaigners argued that membership was vital for Sweden's economic recovery and influence in post-Cold War Europe. Those opposed argued that EU membership would erode Sweden's independence as well as its neutrality, welfare state and impressive achievements in social and sexual equality.

Social Democratic leader Ingvar Carlsson, whose activists and voters were deeply split on the EU question, insisted that the general election should be fought on domestic questions and that the European debate should be postponed until the referendum. The election issues were unemployment, public sector finances and the future of the welfare state. Despite a surge in export-led growth starting in late 1993 and the government's spending cuts and market reforms, the 1993/94 budget deficit was some 13 per cent of GDP. Total public sector debt was forecast to reach 90 per cent of GDP by 1995, while the consequent very high long-term interest rates posed a danger to investment and growth. The situation was dramatized on 1 July when the insurance company Skandia announced a halt to the purchase of government bonds pending convincing steps to curb the public debt. By late summer a broad consensus had developed behind the goal of stabilizing total debt by 1998.

The Social Democrats, the Greens and the Left Party all made significant gains in the general election on 18 September, the results of which were as follows (1991 figures in brackets):

	seats	% of votes
Social Democrats	161(138)	45.2 (37.6)
Moderates	80 (80)	22.4 (21.9)
Centre Party	27 (31)	7.7 (8.5)
Liberals	26 (33)	7.2 (9.1)
Left Party	22 (16)	6.2 (4.5)
Greens	18 (0)	5.0 (3.4)
Christian Democrats	15 (26)	4.1 (7.1)
New Democracy	0 (25)	1.2 (6.7)
Others	0 (0)	1.0 (1.2)

In the strong swing to the left, the Moderates were the only party of the government coalition to hold all their seats. Women played a prominent role in the election, particularly in leading and supporting the Left and Green parties. In the new Riksdag, 41 per cent of the seats were held by women (against 33 per cent in 1991). Women also took half the posts in Mr Carlsson's new minority Social Democratic government appointed on 7 October.

Attention then shifted to the EU referendum. Mr Carlsson conducted a low-key, conciliatory campaign designed to avoid splitting his party, while winning over doubters. He had included two prominent anti-Europeans in his government, a strategy that was much criticized by some pro-EU campaigners. It was vindicated when, in the voting on 13 November, EU membership was approved by 52.2 to 46.9 per cent of the electorate in a turnout of 82.4 per cent (0.9 per cent of the ballots being blank). Surveys indicated that among Social Democratic voters the majority in favour was 55 to 43 per cent. As in Finland (see II.2.v) and later (more decisively) in Norway (see II.2.iii), most of rural Sweden voted against, while the southern urban centres were overwhelmingly in favour. On 23 November parliamentary approval was given, by a large majority, to the constitutional changes enabling Sweden to become an EU member as from 1 January 1995.

On 28 September Sweden suffered its worst human disaster of modern times when some 450 Swedes were among over 900 passengers and crew who drowned when the Estonian-owned ferry ship *Estonia* capsized and sank in a storm in the Baltic Sea (see III.2.ii).

v. FINLAND

CAPITAL: Helsinki AREA: 338,000 sq km POPULATION: 5,000,000 ('92)
OFFICIAL LANGUAGES: Finnish & Swedish POLITICAL SYSTEM: presidential democracy
HEAD OF STATE: President Martti Ahtisaari (since Feb '94)
RULING PARTIES: Centre Party (KESK), National Coalition Party (KOK) & Swedish
  People's Party (SFP)
HEAD OF GOVERNMENT: Esko Aho (KESK), Prime Minister (since April '91)
PRINCIPAL MINISTERS: Heikki Haavisto (KESK/foreign affairs), Mauri Pekkarinen
  (KESK/interior), Anneli Jäätteenmäki (KESK/justice), Jan Erik Enestam
  (SFP/defence), Iiro Viinanen (KOK/finance)
INTERNATIONAL ALIGNMENT: neutral, OECD, EU, Nordic Council
CURRENCY: markka (end-'94 £1=Fmk7.42, US$1=Fmk4.74)
GNP PER CAPITA: US$21,970 ('92)
MAIN EXPORT EARNERS: timber & wood products, manufactures, machinery &
  transport equipment, tourism

IN Finland's first direct presidential elections, held in two rounds on 16 January and 6 February, the four front-runners in the first round were Martti Ahtisaari (Social Democrat) with 25.9 per cent, Elisabeth Rehn (Swedish People's Party) with 22.0 per cent, Paavo Väyrynen (Centre Party) with 19.5 per cent and Raimo Ilaskivi (National Coalition Party/Conservative) with 15.2 per cent. The surprise was the late surge of support for Mrs Rehn, the Defence Minister in the incumbent centre-right coalition government and an ethnic Swede. Personally popular despite belonging to an unpopular government, Mrs Rehn went forward to the run-off vote against Mr Ahtisaari, agreeing with him on the desirability of European Union (EU) membership but diverging from him on domestic economic policy (an area of very limited presidential powers). Mr Ahtisaari emerged the victor with 53.9 per cent of the vote, against 46.1 per cent for Mrs Rehn, on a turnout of 82.3 per cent. Previously a career diplomat, Mr Ahtisaari took office on 1 March, succeeding Mauno Koivisto (also a Social Democrat), who had served two six-year terms.

The presidential inauguration coincided with the successful conclusion of Finland's EU membership negotiations. The most controversial and politically sensitive aspects were the terms for Finland's highly-subsidized agricultural sector, whose interests were represented by the Centre Party, the leading component in the four-party centre-right coalition. The EU had rejected Finland's original demand that the whole sector be treated as a special Nordic category under the CAP and had insisted on an immediate lifting of import controls and alignment of Finnish farm prices to EU levels (on average 40 per cent lower). Finland was permitted to provide income support over a five-year transitional period. In addition, 85 per cent of Finnish agriculture qualified for extra subsidies under 'less favourable area' provisions, while 56 per cent also qualified for additional special subsidies for the Arctic region.

These terms were accepted by the Conservatives and by the opposition Social Democrats, while the Centre Party made its approval conditional on a generous farm support package being agreed. Prime Minister Esko Aho (of the Centre Party) initially proposed that the Finnish referendum should be held on the same day as Sweden's, but both the President and Conservatives disagreed. The eventual decision, announced on 27 May, was that Finland would vote on 16 October, as the first of the three Nordic applicants in a sequence which, EU supporters hoped, would carry first Finland, then Sweden and finally Norway into membership. Also announced was a farm support package amounting to Fmk 5,500 million a year, supplemented by the transitional subsidies.

Pertti Salolainen, the Foreign Trade Minister, resigned as Conservative chairman on 3 June after being criticized for failing to link the farm support package to tax cuts. On 18 June the Centre Party approved Mr Aho's handling of the EU issue but linked its final acceptance of membership to prior parliamentary passage of the farm support package. The anti-EU Finnish Christian Union withdrew from the government coalition on 20 June, reducing its parliamentary base to 108 out of 200 seats. On 3 September the farmers' central organization unanimously rejected EU membership, while on 15 September Mr Aho proposed that final parliamentary ratification of accession should be delayed until after the Swedish referendum on 13 November.

One cause of the controversy surrounding the size of the farm support package was the serious state of Finland's public finances after a three-year recession during which the economy had shrunk by 15 per cent and unemployment had risen to 20 per cent. During 1994 the public sector debt rose to 70 per cent of GDP (from 15 per cent in 1991) and the budget deficit was running at 10 per cent of GDP. Despite a low-inflation, export-led return to growth in 1994, the debt was forecast to rise to some 90 per cent of GDP before it stabilized. The 1995 budget, published on 19 August, continued the government's policy of spending cuts and high taxation, providing for a small reduction in expenditure in real terms despite Fmk 10,000 million in extra spending associated with EU membership. On 30 September a special presidential commission on unemployment headed by Matti Pekkanen reported that a reduction in unemployment to 8 per cent of the labour force by the year 2000 would require annual growth of 5 per cent. The Pekkanen Report's many recommendations for achieving this target looked set to provide the economic agenda for the 1995 election.

The result of the Finnish referendum on 16 October, in a turnout of 70.8 per cent, was a decisive 56.9 per cent majority in favour of membership, with 43.1 per cent against. The outcome was decided by the large 'yes' majority in the populous southern urban areas; north of a line through Tampere most Finns voted 'no'. In a separate vote on 20 November, the Aaland Islands (part of Finland but inhabited by ethnic Swedes enjoying local autonomy) recorded a 74 per cent majority in favour of membership. Meanwhile, following Sweden's pro-EU vote on 13 November (see II.2.iv), the Finnish parliament gave its final ratification of EU membership on 18 November by 152 votes to 45.

vi.   AUSTRIA

CAPITAL: Vienna   AREA: 84,000 sq km   POPULATION: 7,900,000 ('92)
OFFICIAL LANGUAGE: German   POLITICAL SYSTEM: federal parliamentary democracy
HEAD OF STATE: Federal President Thomas Klestil (since Aug '92)
RULING PARTIES: Social Democratic (SPÖ) & People's (ÖVP) parties
HEAD OF GOVERNMENT: Franz Vranitzky (SPÖ) Federal Chancellor (since June '86)
PRINCIPAL MINISTERS: Erhard Busek (ÖVP/Vice-Chancellor, education & culture),
   Aloïs Mock (ÖVP/foreign affairs), Ferdinand Lacina (SPÖ/finance), Wolfgang
   Schüssel (ÖVP/economic affairs), Franz Löschnack (SPÖ/interior), Werner
   Fasslabend (ÖVP/defence), Nikolaus Michalek (non-party/justice)
INTERNATIONAL ALIGNMENT: neutral, OECD, EFTA/EEA
CURRENCY: schilling (end-'94 £1=Sch17.06, US$1=Sch10.91)
GNP PER CAPITA: US$22,380 ('92)
MAIN EXPORT EARNERS: basic manufactures, machinery & transport equipment,
   chemicals, tourism

IN 1994 Austrians twice startled the political establishment by voting decisively for change: first with an unexpectedly positive vote in favour of European Union (EU) membership in a national referendum held on 12 June; second, by inflicting unprecedentedly sharp reverses on the governing parties in the national elections of 9 October. Both the Social Democrats (SPÖ) and the People's Party (ÖVP) recorded their lowest election scores since 1945, their combined parliamentary majority dropping below two-thirds. This represented a major political upheaval for Austria, even though the 'grand coalition' of the SPÖ and the ÖVP continued as before.

EU entry negotiations concluded on 1 March after a marathon three-day negotiating session, having achieved acceptable compromises on the difficult issues of agriculture, transit traffic and foreign ownership of second homes in Austria. The deal, seen as a triumph for the pertinacity and commitment of the Foreign Minister, Dr Aloïs Mock, was overwhelmingly endorsed by parliament in early May. But initial euphoria among EU supporters had swiftly given way to anxiety about the effect on Austrian voters of strong criticisms from the Greens and from Jörg Haider, leader of the radical right-wing Freedom Party (FPÖ). In the event, all nine Austrian provinces voted in favour on 12 June and, in a high turnout of 81 per cent, 66.39 per cent of the electorate voted for and 33.61 per cent against membership. Austria signed its accession treaty at Corfu on 24 June and, with EU entry scheduled for 1 January 1995, deposited its ratification document in Rome on 24 November. The same month, 21 parliamentarians were nominated to represent Austria in the European Parliament, while the Agriculture Minister, Franz Fischler, was named as Austria's first

European commissioner, being subsequently allocated the agriculture portfolio in the new Commission.

The national election results in October were effectively foreshadowed by those of three provincial polls held on 13 March in Salzburg, Tyrol and Carinthia. All three were primarily dominated by local issues and local personalities, but conflicting views about the EU accession package were also aired, and dissatisfaction with the federal coalition clearly remained strong. In all three provinces the SPÖ did badly, the ÖVP vote held up better than expected and the FPÖ improved its position, while the Green parties performed well in Salzburg and Tyrol. The broadly similar outcome of the federal contest on 9 October, in which there was a 78.1 per cent turnout, was as follows (original 1990 figures in parentheses):

	seats	% of votes
Social Democratic Party (SPÖ)	65 (80)	35.2 (42.8)
People's Party (ÖVP)	52 (60)	27.7 (32.1)
Freedom Party (FPÖ)	42 (33)	22.6 (16.6)
Greens	13 (10)	7.0 (4.8)
Liberal Forum (LF)	11 (–)	5.7 (–)

Although the press portrayed Dr Haider's success as a sharp rightward shift in Austrian politics, the increased vote for the left-of-centre Greens and the Liberal Forum (formed by FPÖ moderates in 1993—see AR 1993, p. 79) was in fact greater than that achieved by the FPÖ. Nonetheless, the FPÖ was now within striking distance of supplanting the ÖVP as Austria's main right-wing party, an achievement which lent credibility to Dr Haider's ambition to take over as federal Chancellor in 1998. His offer of parliamentary support for an ÖVP minority government, provided that Erhard Busek stepped down as party leader, was promptly rejected, the SPÖ and ÖVP preferring to enter into talks to renew the 'grand coalition'. Since Chancellor Vranitzky personally was judged to be the main loser in the elections, the ÖVP was able to drive a harder bargain than usual, having lost less electoral support than the SPÖ. After five weeks of negotiations, a coalition agreement was signed and a new government sworn in on 29 November. The SPÖ and the ÖVP had ten cabinet portfolios each, the Ministry of Justice being held as before by an independent.

The process of coalition negotiation was to some extent eased by a marked improvement in Austria's economic performance during 1994. Estimated real growth in GDP reached 2.8 per cent, although annual unemployment and inflation rates remained relatively high at approximately 6.5 and 3 per cent respectively. However, in light of the estimated budget deficit for 1994 of Sch 100,000 million (due to rise sharply from 1995 as a result of EU budgetary contributions), the ÖVP was able to insist on substantial cuts in public spending. The financial programme presented to parliament on 30 November envisaged savings of Sch 250,000 million over four years. The prospect of cuts in family allowances, welfare benefits and a wide range of social programmes and government subsidies brought vigorous protests from trade unions, white-collar workers and other interest groups. Chancellor Vranitzky argued that cuts in public spending were required to secure a sound financial base for Austria's future, pledging that the fight against tax evasion and abuse of social benefits would be stepped up and substantial numbers of new jobs and dwellings created.

The prospect of EU entry brought some adjustments in foreign policy. The government confirmed that Austria would retain its neutrality, but decided on 13 December to apply for observer status in the Western European Union (WEU). It had previously been announced that Austria would also participate in NATO's Partnership for Peace (see XII.2; XIX.1), in the form of joint humanitarian and peace-keeping actions and disaster relief. On the ex-Yugoslavia conflict, however, Austria was intermittently out of step with EU governments, arguing that the arms embargo on Bosnia should be lifted. Relations with Eastern Europe flourished, featuring increased trade, a 25 per cent increase in Austrian investment over 1993 and substantial injections of aid. On 13–15 November President Klestil paid a state visit to Israel, the first by an Austrian President, declaring that 'we cannot change the past, but we can fashion the future'. That promise was backed up by the passing in July of a law setting up a national fund of Sch 3–4,000 million to compensate Austrian victims of nazism, and by further gaol terms imposed on right-wing extremists in August and October.

vii. SWITZERLAND

CAPITAL: Berne   AREA: 41,300 sq km   POPULATION: 6,940,000 ('93)
OFFICIAL LANGUAGES: German, French, Italian & Rhaeto-Romanic
POLITICAL SYSTEM: federal canton-based democracy
RULING PARTIES: Christian Democratic People's (CVP), Radical Democratic (FDP), Social Democratic (SPS) & Swiss People's (SVP) parties
HEAD OF STATE & GOVERNMENT: Otto Stich (SPS), 1994 President of Federal Council and Finance Minister
OTHER MINISTERS: Flavio Cotti (CVP/foreign affairs), Ruth Dreifuss (SPS/interior), Jean-Pascal Delamuraz (FDP/economy), Arnold Koller (CVP/justice), Adolf Ogi (SVP/communications & energy), Kaspar Villiger (FDP/defence)
INTERNATIONAL ALIGNMENT: neutral, OECD, EFTA
CURRENCY: Swiss franc (end-'94 £1=SwF2.05, US$1=SwF1.31)
GNP PER CAPITA: US$36,440 ('92)
MAIN EXPORT EARNERS: financial services, machinery, chemicals, tourism

PROBLEMS with the European integration process remained at the top of the list of Swiss political concerns in 1994. In light of the decision of three fellow members of the European Free Trade Association

(EFTA)—Sweden, Austria and Finland—to join the European Union (EU) from the start of 1995, the isolation of Switzerland became even more obvious. In order to limit the negative effects which might arise from the Swiss rejection of membership of the European Economic Area (EEA) in December 1992 (see AR 1992, p. 81), the Federal Council (government) in 1993 had intensified its pleas in Brussels for the opening of negotiations on new bilateral treaty arrangements between the EU and Switzerland (see AR 1993, p. 82).

These bilateral talks at last started in 1994, covering Swiss participation in EU research programmes, reciprocal access to labour markets, a partial liberalization of the Swiss agricultural market, non-discriminatory conditions for public contracts and the mutual recognition of technical regulations and standards. The EU authorities declared that agreements on single issues would not be available and that a negative Swiss decision on one would negate them all—a stipulation of potentially crucial importance. The fear of unrestricted immigration had been one of the major reasons for the Swiss rejection of the EEA Treaty. The still-rising proportion of foreigners living in Switzerland (18 per cent of regular residents plus a further 4 per cent made up by asylum-seekers and workers on short-term contracts) remained one of the most delicate issues in internal politics.

The Brussels Commission was unwilling to put the question of Swiss participation in a deregulated aviation market on the agenda, even though this was one of Switzerland's major concerns and had been promised by EU authorities in 1993 when a ten-year agreement on transit through the Alps had been signed. But the EU could cite a good reason for this postponement: in a referendum on 20 February Swiss citizens had approved an initiative which enjoined that within ten years all transportation of goods through the Alps should be transferred from road to railway. This initiative had been launched by ecologists and had been backed by the Social Democrats (SPS) and the Greens. The federal government and a majority of parliamentary deputies were opposed to the proposal, not because of its basic aim but because of its absolute nature and because of likely negative reactions from neighbouring states and the EU. Such reactions came very promptly and were rather harsh, the decision being judged to be a violation of the spirit of the EU-Swiss transit agreement by the EU authorities. The latter accordingly asked for detailed explanations as to how the Swiss government intended to execute the new constitutional amendment without discriminatory measures against heavy road traffic in general and EU transport enterprises in particular. They also informed the Federal Council that, until a satisfactory answer was given to this question, talks concerning the integration of Switzerland into a deregulated aviation market could not be initiated.

The year saw another severe setback for the government's aspiration to bring about Switzerland's closer integration into international institutions and agreements. In a referendum on 12 June, the citizens vetoed a parliamentary decision that armed Swiss troops could be deployed on UN peace-keeping missions (although non-combat troops, such as sanitary detachments, would continue to be available). On the other hand, ratification of the December 1993 GATT agreement (involving the creation of the new World Trade Organization) encountered no significant obstacles in the Swiss parliament: almost everybody agreed on the importance of free trade for a small nation that depended so heavily on exports of goods and services. Swiss farmers, who stood to suffer financial losses from the opening-up of agricultural markets, were placated by the promise of higher subsidies (although these would not be production-related). At the end of the year, however, it was still uncertain whether a popular vote would be initiated on the question: some dissident farmers and fundamentalist ecologists who opposed the GATT agreement had started to collect the 50,000 signatures required for the holding of a referendum.

The precarious state of the public finances remained a major concern. The federal deficit for 1994 reached SwF 7,000 million and the forecast for 1995 was only slightly less. With a view to curbing over-expenditure, parliament adopted an amendment to the constitution which required that new government spending should be approved by absolute majorities of both houses. On the other hand, the general economic situation improved in 1994. For the first year since 1991 there was positive growth (GNP expanding by 1.75 per cent), with small beneficial effects on the labour market. By the end of the year the number of unemployed had fallen from 184,000 at end-1993 to 165,000, representing 4.5 per cent of the registered workforce. The annual inflation rate dropped to 0.4 per cent by the end of 1994.

Two important decisions were taken in the field of social policy. The first was a reform of the health insurance system, approved in a popular vote on 4 December in spite of opposition from some insurance companies. On the same day, however, Swiss citizens rejected by a large majority an SPS initiative which proposed that the existing system of individual (but obligatory) insurance contracts should be replaced by public health insurance, financed by taxes on income. The second decision concerned the public old-age pensions scheme. After deliberations which had gone on for several years, the Swiss parliament approved a reform involving substantial improvements for women, notably in that full account would be taken of years spent in the bringing-up of their own children. The resultant costs were to be covered by a gradual rise of the age of retirement for women from 62 to 64 years (compared with 65 for men). This decision provoked angry protests from some women's organizations and from the political left, including the SPS, which collected the necessary signatures for the issue to be put to a referendum in 1995.

A number of laws intended to help in the fight against new forms of crime were voted either by parliament or by the citizens in 1994. There was no objection to tougher measures against money laundering, organized crime and computer fraud. But intense controversy arose over new draft regulations directed against non-resident foreigners who were convicted of minor offences such as dealing in small amounts of drugs. The government proposed to give judges the option of placing such persons in custody for up to nine months if their expulsion from Switzerland could not be ordered immediately because their true identity had not been finally established. The measures were fiercely attacked by the left, on the grounds that they might also be used against asylum-seekers whose request had been rejected and who were trying to evade expulsion. On 4 December, however, a large majority of the citizens approved the new law in a referendum.

The Radical Democrat Defence Minister, Kaspar Villiger, was elected to the annually-rotating post of President of the Federal Council for 1995.

viii. EUROPEAN MINI-STATES

Andorra
CAPITAL: Andorra la Vella   AREA: 460 sq km   POPULATION: 61,000 ('92)
OFFICIAL LANGUAGE: Catalan   POLITICAL SYSTEM: parliamentary democracy
HEADS OF STATE: President Mitterrand of France & Bishop Joan Martí Alanis of Urgel (co-princes)
HEAD OF GOVERNMENT: Marc Forne, President of Executive Council (since Dec '94)
CURRENCY: French franc & Spanish peseta
MAIN EXPORT EARNERS: tourism, banking, smuggling

Holy See (Vatican)
CAPITAL: Vatican City   AREA: 0.44 sq km   POPULATION: 742 ('93)
OFFICIAL LANGUAGES: Italian & Latin   POLITICAL SYSTEM: theocracy
HEAD OF STATE: Pope John Paul II (since '78)
HEAD OF GOVERNMENT: Cardinal Angelo Sodano, Secretary of State (since Dec '90)
CURRENCY: Vatican lira (pegged to Italian lira)

Liechtenstein
CAPITAL: Vaduz   AREA: 160 sq km   POPULATION: 30,000 ('92)
OFFICIAL LANGUAGE: German   POLITICAL SYSTEM: parliamentary democracy
HEAD OF STATE: Prince Hans Adam II (since Nov '89)
RULING PARTIES: Patriotic Union (VU) & Progressive Citizens' Party (FBP)
HEAD OF GOVERNMENT: Mario Frick(VU), Prime Minister (since Dec '93)
CURRENCY: Swiss franc   GNP PER CAPITA: US$36,440 ('92 est.)
MAIN EXPORT EARNERS: manufactured goods, tourism, financial services

Monaco

CAPITAL: Monaco-Ville   AREA: 1.95 sq km   POPULATION: 28,000 ('91)
OFFICIAL LANGUAGE: French   POLITICAL SYSTEM: constitutional monarchy
HEAD OF STATE: Prince Rainier III (since '49)
HEAD OF GOVERNMENT: Paul Dijoud, Minister of State (since Dec '94)
CURRENCY: French franc
MAIN EXPORT EARNERS: tourism, financial services

San Marino

CAPITAL: San Marino   AREA: 60.5 sq km   POPULATION: 23,000 ('92)
OFFICIAL LANGUAGE: Italian   POLITICAL SYSTEM: parliamentary democracy
HEADS OF STATE & GOVERNMENT: Captains-Regent Renzo Ghiotti & Luciano Ciavatta
(Oct '94–March '95)
RULING PARTIES: Christian Democratic & Socialist parties
CURRENCY: Italian lira
MAIN EXPORT EARNERS: tourism, agricultural products, postage stamps

DURING 1994 Liechtenstein sought to adjust to the changing European political scene, as the European Economic Area (EEA) came into force on 1 January and the European Union (EU) was expanded a year later to include neighbouring Austria as well as Finland and Sweden. At the end of 1994 there were changes of government in both Andorra and Monaco. The Vatican opened up diplomatic relations with both Jordan and Israel.

In LIECHTENSTEIN, even though the principality had voted in a referendum in favour of participating in the EEA in December 1992 (see AR 1992, pp. 85, 418), the EEA did not come into effect for the principality on 1 January. This was because Switzerland, with which Liechtenstein maintained a customs union, had voted against participating in the EEA. It was expected, however, that negotiations during 1994 would result in Liechtenstein joining the EEA from 1 May 1995. In a speech at the opening of parliament on 9 February, Prince Hans Adam II said that the monarch should remain head of state only for as long as this was the wish of the people. As a result, he proposed that the constitution should be amended to allow for the possibility of a vote of no-confidence against the monarch and for the possible abolition of the monarchy.

In ANDORRA, Oscar Ribas Reig was sworn in on 3 February as President of the Executive Council (prime minister) of a government comprising members of his National Democratic Grouping (AND) and independents, following the general election on 12 December 1993 (see AR 1993, p. 86). The final results of that contest had given AND eight of the 28 seats in the General Council of the Valleys, the Liberal Union (UL) five, New Democracy (ND) five, the National Andorran Coalition and the National Democratic Initiative two each, and independents and others six. However, the Ribas Reig government fell in November when five ND deputies withdrew their support for the 1995 budget. On 21 December the lawyer Marc Forne, of the centre-right UL, was sworn in as head of government. Meanwhile, Andorra had joined the Council of Europe as its 33rd member on 10 November, its adhesion leaving only Monaco and the Holy See as non-members among sovereign west European states.

In MONACO, Prince Rainier III (71) underwent heart surgery on 25 November, this prompting speculation in the French magazine *Paris Match* that he might abdicate in 1995 in favour of his son, Prince Albert. Indeed, on 2 December Prince Albert stood in for his father when Paul Dijoud was sworn in as Minister of State (prime minister). M. Dijoud, a French diplomat who had been ambassador to Mexico, replaced Jacques Dupont, who had held the post since 1991. As was customary, M. Dijoud was among a list of three individuals proposed for the Monegasque premiership by the French government. Earlier, in October, the principality had signed an agreement with France aimed at coordinating the fight against money laundering. The accord required banks, insurance companies and bureaux de change to hand over bank account and transaction details where these were suspicious.

In SAN MARINO, the coalition of the Christian Democrats and Socialists, which had been re-elected in the May 1993 general election (see AR 1993, p. 86), continued in office throughout the year. The tiny Republic featured in the international headlines in May when the Brazilian racing driver, Ayrton Senna, was killed during the San Marino Grand Prix (see Pt. XVII; XX: Obituary).

During 1994 the HOLY SEE (Vatican) established diplomatic relations with Jordan on 3 March and with Israel on 15 June, the latter as envisaged in an agreement concluded in December 1993 (see AR 1993, pp. 86–7; 208). At the beginning of September, Pope John Paul II announced that the Vatican also wished to establish official relations with representatives of the Palestinian people. Amid some concerns for his health, the 74–year-old Pope did not undertake as many foreign visits as in previous years and postponed a planned visit to the United States until 1995. He nevertheless went to Zagreb (Croatia) on 10–11 September but cancelled a planned visit to Sarajevo because of the risks involved.

At the UN's third International Conference on Population and Development in Cairo on 5–13 September, the Vatican found itself in an unlikely alliance with traditionalist Muslim states on issues such as birth control and divorce (see also Pt. XIII). Its representatives opposed draft provisions which were seen as legitimizing abortion and extra-marital sex, but these were nevertheless included in the Programme of Action endorsed at the end of the conference by a majority of delegates (see XI.1). The Pope's conservative theological views were also evident in an apostolic letter issued on 30 May which restated his view that women should not be ordained as priests. On 26–27 November he invested 30 new cardinals, increasing the number of cardinals entitled to elect a new Supreme Pontiff to 120 (the maximum permitted). Some media reports saw the appointments as a move by the Pope to ensure that the College of Cardinals elected a traditionally-minded successor when he died.

3. SPAIN—PORTUGAL—GIBRALTAR—MALTA—GREECE—CYPRUS—
TURKEY

i. SPAIN

CAPITAL: Madrid   AREA: 505,000 sq km   POPULATION: 39,100,000 ('92)
OFFICIAL LANGUAGE: Spanish   POLITICAL SYSTEM: parliamentary democracy
HEAD OF STATE: King Juan Carlos (since Nov '75)
RULING PARTY: Spanish Socialist Workers' Party (PSOE)
HEAD OF GOVERNMENT: Felipe González, Prime Minister (since Nov '82)
PRINCIPAL MINISTERS: Narcís Serra Serra (Deputy Premier), Julián García Vargas
     (defence), Antonio Asunción Hernández (interior), Javier Solana Madariaga
     (foreign affairs), Pedro Solbes Mira (economy & finance), Juan Alberto Belloch
     Juive (justice)
INTERNATIONAL ALIGNMENT: NATO, OECD, EU
CURRENCY: peseta (end-'94 £1=Ptas205.94, US$1=Ptas131.63)
GNP PER CAPITA: US$13,970 ('92)
MAIN EXPORT EARNERS: tourism, transport equipment, agricultural products, minerals
     & base metals

ALTHOUGH Prime Minister Felipe González looked forward to the Spanish presidency of the European Union (EU) in the second half of 1995, it was clear by the end of 1994 that his long tenure of power at the head of successive governments formed by the Socialist Workers' Party (PSOE) was coming to an end. Spain's severest post-war economic recession and a string of political scandals, together with a growing desire for change after 13 years of PSOE rule, had undermined Sr González's appeal.

In the European Parliament elections held on 12 June, just a year after general elections had returned the PSOE for a fourth successive term (see AR 1993, pp. 89–90), albeit without an overall majority, the conservative Popular Party (PP) obtained 7,450,000 votes on a 64 per cent turnout against 5,720,000 won by the PSOE. The PP had 28 members in the 64-strong Spanish contingent to the new European Parliament, up from 15 in the outgoing Strasbourg legislature (which had 60 Spanish members), while the PSOE returned 22 members, down from 27. The other seats went to the Communist-led United Left (IU), which improved from four to nine seats, the Catalan nationalist Convergence and Union (CiU), which went up from two to three seats, and the Basque-led Nationalist Coalition (up one to two seats). With opinion polls showing a ten-point PP lead over the PSOE, the principal opposition party, led by José María Aznar, was expected to make sweeping gains in municipal and regional elections scheduled for May 1995.

The waning fortunes of the PSOE, and the rise of the PP, were underlined in the 23 October polling for the 75-member Basque parliament. The elections returned the Basque Nationalist Party (PNV) as the dominant political group in the region with an unchanged tally of 22 seats. The Basque wing of the PSOE returned 12 members, four less than in the 1990 Basque elections, and the PP won 11 seats (against six in 1990). After long-drawn negotiations, José Antonio Ardanza, the Lehendakari (Basque prime minister), announced a coalition government formed by his own PNV, the Socialists and Basque Solidarity (EA), a PNV splinter group which had returned eight members to the Basque parliament.

Sr González's credibility came under fire on 29 April when Luis Roldán, the former head of the 70,000-strong paramilitary Civil Guard, went into hiding to escape a legal probe into large amounts of money that he had allegedly embezzled. The disappearance of Sr Roldán marked the start of a series of serious corruption allegations that dogged the Prime Minister throughout the year. The government was rocked again in 4 May when Sr Vicente Alberó, the Agriculture Minister, resigned following allegations of tax evasion and when Mariano Rubio, the former governor of the Bank of Spain, was indicted in connection with a share-pushing scandal. Sr Rubio was remanded in custody during May, together with his stockbroker, Manuel de la Concha, a former president of the Madrid stock exchange. The public perception that a lax administration was responsible for a scandal-ridden society heightend as some of those who had made fortunes during the economic boom of late 1980s were disgraced. On 18 October Javier de la Rosa, who had led a major investment strategy in Spain on behalf of the Kuwait Investment Office (KIO), was arested on charges of fraud, while Mario Conde, the former head of the Banco Español de Crédito (Banesto) banking group was imprisoned on similar counts on 23 December. Sr de la Rosa had been dismissed by the KIO in 1992 and Sr Conde had been ousted from Banesto in December 1993 by the Bank of Spain after an inspection had revealed that the group had grossly overvalued its assets. The fall of the two financiers, both of them national celebrities, shook public confidence and prompted comparisons between Spain and Italy.

However, the most damaging scandal to envelop the government broke out on 19 December when three former senior security officers, including Julián Sancristobal (a PSOE stalwart and former head of national security), were held on remand in connection with allegations that they had run a shadowy 'death squad' in an underground war against the Basque separatist ETA organization in the mid-1980s. They were indicted on charges of kidnapping, attempted murder and misuse of public funds as part of a widening judicial investigation into government involvement in the so-called Grupos Antiterroristas de Liberación (GAL), which had claimed 26 victims in south-west France, then an ETA safe-haven area, between 1983 and 1986. The charges followed detailed confessions to an investigating judge by two former Bilbao police officers who had been sentenced in 1991 for their role in the recruitment of mercenaries to form the GAL death squads.

What emerged in the complex 'dirty war' case was evidence of considerable corruption in the Interior Ministry, including widescale embezzlement of public funds by senior officials. Suspicion that the government had lost control of the ministry had first surfaced when Sr Roldán went into hiding to avoid prosecution. In an attempt to stem growing criticism of his administration, Sr González had in May asked the Justice Minister, Juan Alberto Belloch, to take on the Interior Ministry as well. In the months that followed Sr Belloch carried out a large-scale purge of the police force, replacing more than 40 senior officers, although Sr Roldán remained at large at the end of the year.

The scandals raised the prospect of political instability, as the PP joined with the IU in calling on Sr González either to resign or to set a date for early elections. The Prime Minister, however, insisted that he would remain in power and serve out a full four-year term (until the summer of 1997) because he had the necessary parliamentary backing to continue in government. This support was provided mainly by the CiU led by Jordi Pujol, president of Catalonia's regional government, the Generalitat. The 17 CiU members in the 350-member Madrid Congress of Deputies worked closely with the 159 PSOE deputies to ensure an overall government majority on key questions such as the 1995 budget, which successfully completed its parliamentary passage on 30 December.

Catalan support did not spare the government from considerable money market pressure, which brought the peseta to an historic low against the Deutschmark at end-1994 and forced the Bank of Spain to prepare to intervene in order the prevent the currency's expulsion from the exchange rate mechanism of the European Monetary System. In addition to doubts over the scandal-battered government's ability to remain in power, the markets were penalizing what was viewed as a high inflation rate of 4.3 per cent in 1994 and an excessive budget deficit (of 6.7 per cent of GDP). There were also doubts about the government's ability to sustain economic recovery (evidenced by a 2 per cent GDP growth rate in 1994) while reducing inflation and the budget deficit in order to meet the convergence criteria for economic and monetary union as laid down by the EU's Maastricht Treaty. Against this background, ministers were at work at the end of the year on a mini-budget in order to ensure that the target of reducing the budget deficit to a maximum of 5.9 per cent of GDP in 1995 would be met. In May the government, backed by the Catalan nationalists, had reformed domestic labour market regulations, viewed as restrictive by employers, and further reforms were planned in 1995 to liberalize hiring and firing rules.

As 1994 ended, Sr González was aiming to remain in power by demonstrating that he was serious about cleaning up corruption and by taking all the appropriate measure to revive the economy. It was not clear, however, how many new scandals remained as skeletons in the PSOE cupboard, ready to be resurrected by the increasingly hostile domestic media. Nor was it clear how soon the incipient economic recovery would filter through to society at large. Although registered unemployment fell by 150,000 during 1994, the jobless total on 31 December stood at some 2,500,000, representing 16.5 per cent of the working population. In light of such negative factors, many observers believed that the key political question was not whether Sr Aznar of the PP would replace Sr González but when the change-over would take place.

ii.   PORTUGAL

CAPITAL: Lisbon   AREA: 92,000 sq km   POPULATION: 9,800,000 ('92)
OFFICIAL LANGUAGE: Portuguese
POLITICAL SYSTEM: presidential/parliamentary democracy
HEAD OF STATE: President Mário Soares (since March '86)
RULING PARTY: Social Democratic Party (PSD)
HEAD OF GOVERNMENT: Aníbal Cavaco Silva, Prime Minister (since Nov '85)
PRINCIPAL MINISTERS: Joaquim Fernando Nogueira (presidency, defence), Eduardo
    Catroga (finance), Manuel Dias Loureiro (home affairs), José M. Durão Barroso
    (foreign affairs), Alvaro Laborinho Lúcio (justice)
INTERNATIONAL ALIGNMENT: NATO, OECD, EU
CURRENCY: escudo (end-'94 £1=Esc249.07, US$1=Esc159.20)
GNP PER CAPITA: US$8,615 ('93)
MAIN EXPORT EARNERS: tourism, basic manufactures, textiles, agricultural products

THE year started ominously with a public debate, entitled 'Portugal—What Future?', sponsored by none other than President Mário Soares, founder and former leader of the opposition Socialist Party (PS). The promotion of such a debate might have seemed surprising to a casual visitor to Portugal, who could not fail to be impressed by the evident signs of modernization throughout the country, epitomized by the move of the ancient Bolsa de Valores (the Lisbon stock exchange) from its eighteenth-century arched building into a state-of-the-art financial centre in the expanding outskirts of the capital. The reality was that since Portugal in 1986 joined what was then the European Community, now the Union (EU), social and economic expectations had risen faster than available resources, creating widespread anti-government resentment in a country where the old rich and the new affluent were still a small minority. The debate was therefore tacitly designed to create a forum for criticism of the twice-elected government of the (centre-right) Social Democratic Party (PSD) and of Prime Minister Cavaco Silva personally. The latter's rise and decline in popularity over the past decade had close parallels with the experience of other EU governments, notably the Socialists in Spain and the Conservatives in Britain, under the impact of increasingly internationalized economic conditions and factors.

The promotion of the debate drew prompt support from the Communist Party and quickly developed into a left-versus-right issue, although it also generated controversy amongst PS leaders. Some of the latter expressed concern that President Soares appeared to be exceeding his constitutional role of non-partisan arbiter and to be assuming the mantle of opposition leader; others feared that the 'cohabitation' dispute apparent between President and Prime Minister since late 1993 (see AR 1993, p. 92) might prove obstructive to normal government. Moreover, the dispute had tacitly become personalized, giving the impression that President Soares, in his second and final term, was trying to reassert his power at the expense of the Prime Minister and in favour of the party he had founded in 1972 while still in exile. Curiously enough, Dr Soares himself, when Prime Minister of a PS-led government in the early 1980s, had been the loser in an animated 'cohabitation' clash with the then President, Ramalho Eanes.

In such 'cohabitation' disputes, given the President's limited and non-executive powers, the Prime Minister tended to be at a considerable disadvantage, because the responsibilities (and opprobrium) of governance fell exclusively on the ruling party. By all empirical accounts, against a background of recession and stringent curbs in social and public spending (including a substantial cut in the allocation to the President's office for 1995), the last few years had been particularly difficult for the government. Data published by the National Statistical Institute showed that in 1993 Portugal had, for the first time in recent history, registered a negative GDP growth rate of 1.3 per cent, experiencing falls in both domestic demand and exports (of 9.5 and 5 per cent respectively). In the same year, the average monthly salary was only Esc 108,000 (£410), while the state's old-age and disability basic pensions were no higher than Esc 30,000 (£118). Such statistics added to popular disenchantment and anxiety over the prospects of a speedy recovery from recession.

Coinciding with the opening of the debate on Portugal's future, the trial took place of a fraud case involving funds of the hard-pressed Health Ministry. It resulted in the imprisonment of Secretary of State Costa Freire and of an outside contractor who was a brother of the Health Minister, Leonor Beleza, who was herself eventually obliged to resign. The debate proceeded with inter-party controversies over EU issues of federalism versus anti-federalism, becoming a feature of the campaigning for the Portuguese elections to the European Parliament on 12 June. These also provoked intense rivalries within the main parties, as was the case with the PS when experienced EU parliamentary veterans such as João Cravinho were superseded at the top of the candidates' list by João Soares, son of the President and a rising politician in his own right. In the event, the results put the SP (34.8 per cent) marginally ahead of the PSD (34.4 per cent), the two main parties respectively winning ten and nine of the 25 seats alloted to Portugal, while the Democratic Social Centre and the Communist-led Unified Democratic Coalition won three each. The record 64 per cent rate of abstentions (joint highest with the Netherlands) seemed to show that the Portuguese electorate, like those of other member countries, regarded Euro-elections as a rather meaningless contest between pre-chosen party candidates.

In speeches and occasional exclusive newspaper interviews, President Soares talked of 'false stability' and of growing public frustration and resentment at the 'dictatorship of majorities'. This assessment was vindicated by a wave of public protest actions during 1994, starting with student demonstrations and boycotts against increased fees and reforms in schools, and leading on to protests by factory workers in the industrial centre of Marinha Grande and elsewhere against long delays in the payment of wages. Another significant feature of the year was a mass protest of unprecedented proportions against a steep increase in the tolls for cars and lorries crossing the suspension bridge over the River Tagus in southern Portugal. The toll increase, apparently designed to provide funds for a much-needed alternative bridge between Sacavem and Montijo further inland, was proposed by the Minister of Public Works, Ferreira do Amaral, who badly under-estimated the likely public reaction. The ensuing spontaneous mass blocking of the entrances to the bridge by thousands of cars and lorries not only provided an entertaining anti-government show on television but was also a striking example of 'people power': the protests resulted in the cancellation of the toll increases and a government decision to seek funds for the new bridge elsewhere.

Towards the end of the year it became clear that recovery from recession was proceeding more slowly than previously anticipated. While inflation was under control, the rate of unemployment rose to 7 per cent, particularly affecting first-time job seekers. Sr Cavaco Silva's government also appeared to be vulnerable to speculation arising from unfounded but recurrent devaluation rumours, as the escudo reverted to a downward trend. The fact that in neighbouring Spain the peseta, and the economy generally, were in even worse shape (see II.3.i) offered little consolation to the Portuguese. On the contrary, this only reinforced the fear that, despite the influx of considerable EU 'cohesion' funds since 1986, the Iberian countries would continue to lag behind EU average social and economic standards for the foreseeable future.

In the foreign policy arena, the appointment in November of a Portuguese diplomat, José Cutileiro, as secretary-general of the Western

European Union, was a rare example of Portugal making an impact. The long-running dispute with Indonesia over East Timor (see also IX.1.vi) had an emotional significance in Portugal out of proportion to the territory's importance or to what the Portuguese governmemt could do at a distance of over 10,000 miles. The territory was again in the news in November when a flare-up of agitation and protest was timed to coincide with an Asia-Pacific economic summit in Indonesia (see XI.6.iii). But regular meetings between Portuguese Foreign Minister Durão Barroso and his Indonesian counterpart showed little sense of urgency. All in all, from the Portuguese point of view, the indications were that, even after the celebration in 1998 of the 500th anniversary of the arrival of Vasco da Gama in India and the peaceful reversion of Macao to China in 1999, East Timor might still remain an unfinished postscript to the end of the Portuguese empire.

Lisbon's relations with the PALOP grouping—the five 'African Countries of Official Portuguese Language'—varied from amicable routine to coldness, the latter state applying particularly to relations with Angola (see also VII.1.vi). The Angolan President, José Eduardo dos Santos, voiced his displeasure with President Soares for the latter's alleged sympathy with the defeated Unita leader, Jonas Savimbi, and with Portuguese interference in Angolan internal affairs. At the end of the year, during the investiture in Maputo of President Chissano of Mozambique in December (see VII.1.v), President dos Santos met the Portuguese Foreign Minister but pointedly avoided even a courtesy encounter with President Soares. As for Mozambique, Portugal's relations with its former colony remained good, although there was some concern in Lisbon that the end of apartheid and the democratization of South Africa would hasten the 'anglicization' of its Portuguese-speaking neighbour.

A major diplomatic setback for Portugal was the cancellation of a scheduled summit conference of leaders of lusophone countries in Lisbon, at which it had been intended to institutionalize cultural relations between Portuguese-speaking countries. The meeting had to be postponed when President Itamar Franco of Brazil (containing over 80 per cent of the world's Portuguese speakers) was unable to travel to Portugal because of the death of a close relative. The timing of the summit, with both Angola and Mozambique still involved in civil wars or difficult peace negotiations, was clearly not judicious; but it was noted that President dos Santos seemed particularly eager to cancel his own trip to Lisbon.

Towards the end of the year, President Soares appeared to be winning the 'cohabitation' dispute when Prime Minister Cavaco Silva on 16 December indicated his intention to resign in 1995. Portugal therefore seemed likely to be spared the upheaval of a presidential decision to call early elections, although uncertainty and party anxieties remained strong. In that the 'cohabitation' arguments had become personalized into a political contest between two men of different generations, and of contrasting styles and temperaments, the Prime Minister's resignation announcement was seen by many as more a tactical move than a gesture of surrender. Whereas President Soares was 70 years old and due to conclude his tenure of office in 1996, Sr Cavaco Silva was still only 55 and well-placed to mount a challenge for the presidency (for which his resignation from the premiership and PSD leadership was a constitutional requirement). The next two years were therefore expected to be politically more animated than the last two, although it remained to be seen whether they would be more productive economically.

iii.   GIBRALTAR

CAPITAL: Gibraltar   AREA: 6.5 sq km   POPULATION: 32,000 ('92)
OFFICIAL LANGUAGE: English   POLITICAL STATUS: UK dependency, democracy
HEAD OF STATE: Queen Elizabeth II   GOVERNOR: Field Marshal Sir John Chapple
RULING PARTY: Socialist Labour Party (SLP)
HEAD OF GOVERNMENT: Joe Bossano, Chief Minister (since March '88)

THE longstanding dispute between Spain and the United Kingdom over the British crown colony of Gibraltar reached a new level in the run-up to bilateral talks held in London on 20 December at the level of Foreign Ministers. In the weeks prior to the talks, a rigorous system of frontier double-checks was imposed by the Madrid government on the isthmus linking the Rock with Spain.

The move was justified by the Spanish authorities on the grounds that Gibraltar had become an important centre for drug-trafficking (in addition to the colony's traditional cigarette-smuggling trade) and a focal point for laundering the proceeds from narcotics and other illicit activities. It was criticized by Gibraltar's Chief Minister, Joe Bossano, and also by the UK government as a device to squeeze the colony's economy. During the six-week period that the double checks lasted, long queues formed at the border crossing and turnover at the duty-free shops in Gibraltar fell dramatically.

The London talks between Douglas Hurd and Javier Solana appeared to defuse the diplomatic confrontation by creating a joint consultative commission with a brief to promote cooperation between Spain and the UK on drug-trafficking in the Gibraltar area. Its creation was hailed by Spanish officials as a concession by London that allowed Madrid a greater say over the Rock's affairs, but Mr Hurd was careful to restate the British government's commitment to respect the wishes of the people of Gibraltar over any change in the colony's sovereignty status.

While maintaining his opposition to the Spanish-UK talks and his refusal to participate, Mr Bossano issued a conciliatory statement after the London meeting which expressed his government's wish to work in 'close cooperation' with Britain and also in 'harmony with its neighbour'. The Gibraltarian leader had nevertheless made clear his preference for the Rock's self-determination during a Gibraltar National Day rally on 10 September, despite the fact that this option, implying that neither London nor Madrid would exercise control, had been ruled out by both the British and the Spanish governments.

Indeed, a feature of the increasingly complex Gibraltar dispute was the growing mistrust colouring the relationship between Whitehall and Mr Bossano's government. On 3 August the colony's Attorney-General, John Blackburn Gittings (appointed by Whitehall to advise the Gibraltar administration), resigned citing a difference of views between himself and Gibraltar's governor. His resignation brought to the surface a simmering row over what Mr Bossano saw as increasing interference from London that hampered Gibraltar's efforts to establish itself as an off-shore banking centre. The UK Treasury, however, continued to insist on close supervision of Gibraltar's financial affairs in the context of British responsibility for the local implementation of European Union directives.

iv. MALTA

CAPITAL: Valletta   AREA: 316 sq km   POPULATION: 360,000 ('92)
OFFICIAL LANGUAGES: Maltese, English   POLITICAL SYSTEM: parliamentary democracy
HEAD OF STATE: President Ugo Mifsud Bonnici (since April '94)
RULING PARTY: Nationalist Party (NP)
HEAD OF GOVERNMENT: Edward Fenech Adami, Prime Minister (since May '87)
PRINCIPAL MINISTERS: Guido De Marco (Deputy Prime Minister, foreign affairs),
    Louis Galea (home affairs), John Dalli (finance), Joseph Fenech (justice)
INTERNATIONAL ALIGNMENT: neutral, NAM, Cwth.
CURRENCY: lira (end-'94 £1=Lm0.58, US$1=Lm0.37)
GNP PER CAPITA: US$7,280 ('91)
MAIN EXPORT EARNERS: tourism, manufactured goods, machinery

DR Ugo Mifsud Bonnici, previously Minister of Education and Home Affairs and a former leader of the ruling Nationalist Party (NP), was sworn in for a five-year term as President on 4 April in succession to Vincent Tabone. He was the fifth person to hold the office since Malta became a republic in 1974.

The year was marked by a number of protests. Hunting restrictions adopted in October 1993 (see AR 1993, p. 96) were rigorously enforced and led to sporadic incidents of violence. Unrest on economic questions focused on the proposed introduction of value-added tax (VAT) in January 1996 following the parliamentary passage of relevant legislation in July. Strikes by union members and shop-owners culminated in a general strike on 24 October, organized by the 43,000-strong General

Workers' Union and supported by the opposition Malta Labour Party. On a happier note, it was announced in September that Malta dockyards would merge with Malta ship-building, workers in both industries being awarded a 20 per cent pay increase. During the same month, Air Malta took delivery of its first medium-range airliner.

Poor weather in February once again disturbed the annual carnival. April saw the heaviest rainfall since records began. Torrential rain also led to widespread flooding in October after 100 mm of rain fell during a violent five-hour storm. Figures released during the year showed that, for the first time, British tourists had numbered less than 50 per cent of the total in 1993.

Political squabbles enlivened the year. In July the Agriculture Minister, Lawrence Gatt, resigned after a corruption commission had reported that he was responsible for irregularities within his ministry. The Prime Minister, Edward Fenech Adami, offered to resign in October when the employment commission ruled that he had discriminated politically against a candidate for the directorship of a government-appointed body. The President declined to accept his offer. In October the opposition also moved a no-confidence motion against the Justice Minister, Joseph Fenech, after the release from prison, under a presidential pardon, of a Portuguese national who was a convicted drug-trafficker.

The UK Foreign Secretary, Douglas Hurd, visited Malta in January and reiterated his support for Malta's application for full membership of the European Union. Other visitors included the Israeli Foreign Minister, Shimon Peres (in August), and President Mário Soares of Portugal (in October). While still in office, President Tabone paid state visits to Albania and Hungary in February. The Prime Minister visited China in June and Washington in September. Dr Adami also attended the Budapest summit of the Conference on Security and Cooperation in Europe in December (see XI.5.i).

The former acting President, Paul Xuereb, died on 6 September.

v.   GREECE

CAPITAL: Athens   AREA: 132,000 sq km   POPULATION: 10,300,000 ('92)
OFFICIAL LANGUAGE: Greek   POLITICAL SYSTEM: parliamentary democracy
HEAD OF STATE: President Konstantinos Karamanlis (since May '90)
RULING PARTY: Pan-Hellenic Socialist Movement (PASOK)
HEAD OF GOVERNMENT: Andreas Papandreou, Prime Minister (since Oct '93)
PRINCIPAL MINISTERS: Andonios Livanis (Deputy Prime Minister), Karolos Papoulias (foreign affairs), Gerasimos Arsenis (defence), Georgios Kouvelakis (justice), Kostas Skandalidis (interior), Ioannis Papandoniou (economy), Alexandros Papadopoulos (finance), Kostas Simitis (industry & commerce)
INTERNATIONAL ALIGNMENT: NATO, OECD, EU
CURRENCY: drachma (end-'94 £1=Dr376.42, US$1=Dr240.60)
GNP PER CAPITA: US$7,290 ('92)
MAIN EXPORT EARNERS: tourism, merchant marine, textiles, agricultural products

QUESTIONS of foreign policy, and in particular the country's relations with its immediate neighbours, dominated the political scene in Greece in 1994. The recognition of Macedonia by the United States, despite intensive pressure by the powerful Greek-American lobby, prompted a massive protest rally outside the US consulate in Thessaloniki in mid-February. This was followed on 16 February by the imposition of a trade embargo against Macedonia, intended to register Greece's displeasure at what it viewed as the appropriation of the name of Macedonia, at what were seen as irredentist aspirations in the Macedonian constitution and at the adoption of the 16-pointed star of Vergina as the Macedonian national symbol. The move provoked a strong reaction from Greece's European Union (EU) partners, the European Commission declaring the embargo to be in violation of European trade law. However, the European Court of Justice, in an interim ruling of 29 June pending the hearing of the case in 1996, did not find that there were grounds for an immediate injunction requiring that the embargo be lifted (see also XI.3; XV.1.ii).

If relations with Macedonia were bad throughout the year, those with Albania were even more charged (see also III.1.vii). In February the killing of two Albanian conscripts near the border led to Albanian allegations, subsequently retracted, of official Greek involvement. The incident was the catalyst for a serious deterioration in relations between the two countries, with Athens making continual complaints of alleged Albanian persecution of the substantial Greek minority in south Albania and of restrictions on the religious freedom of Orthodox Christians. This war of words culminated in the arrest in May of six prominent members of Omonia, the main Greek minority organization in Albania. At their subsequent trial, five of the six received prison sentences of between six and eight years for treasonable advocacy of the secession of 'Northern Epirus' to Greece and the illegal possession of weapons. A number of Greek journalists covering the trial were expelled. Greece retaliated by the mass round-up and deportation of tens of thousands of illegal Albanian immigrants, whose earnings in Greece were a significant prop to the Albanian economy. In turn, Albania claimed that its diplomats in Greece were subject to harassment. The release of one of the five convicted ethnic Greeks in December did little to appease Greek anger over the case.

Relations with Turkey also remained tense throughout the year and reached a particularly critical stage in the weeks before the 1982 UN Convention on the Law of the Sea was due to come into force in mid-November (see also II.3.vii). This gave rise to Turkish fears that Greece would extend its territorial waters from six to 12 miles, thereby, on account of the multiplicity of Greece's islands, establishing control of much of the Aegean. Turkey made it clear that such an extension would be regarded as a *casus belli*. Against a background of naval and air exercises by both countries, President Clinton wrote to the Turkish President and Prime Minister to the effect that Greece had no immediate intention of extending its territorial waters. The Greek authorities for their part made it clear that Greece reserved the right to to make such an extension in the future.

Athens–Ankara relations were placed under further strain by Greece's veto in December of proposals for a customs union between the EU and Turkey and by the Greek parliament's proclamation of 19 May as a day of remembrance for the alleged Turkish genocide of several hundred thousand Greeks from Pontos on the Black Sea in the 1920s. Further tension was occasioned by the holding of bilateral Greek and Greek Cypriot military manoeuvres in October under the terms of a 'unified defence doctrine' agreed between the two countries in June (see also II.3.vi).

In elections to the European Parliament held on 12 June, the ruling Pan-Hellenic Socialist Movement (PASOK) won 10 of the 25 Greek seats with 37.6 per cent of the vote, seven percentage points lower than in the 1993 national elections (see AR 1993, p. 97). The opposition New Democracy (ND) secured nine seats with 32.7 per cent, as against 39 per cent in 1993. The smaller opposition parties all performed better than in 1993. The right-wing Political Spring, headed by Antonis Samaras (a defector from ND), almost doubled its share of the vote to 8.7 per cent and won two seats. The orthodox Communist Party of Greece, with 6.3 per cent, also secured two seats, while the broadly Euro-communist Alliance of the Left and Progressive Forces, which had narrowly failed to achieve representation in the national parliament in 1993, likewise obtained a 6.3 per cent share and two seats. During the European election campaign, an attempt was made to assassinate three Communist candidates.

In local elections held on 16 and 23 October, ND scored a striking success in the Athens mayoral contest when the relatively-unknown Dimitrios Avramopoulos inflicted a significant defeat on the high-profile PASOK candidate, Theodoros Pangalos, who had resigned as Minister of Transport to contest the election. PASOK's control of the majority of municipalities was, however, left largely intact.

Both main parties, PASOK and ND, were beset by internal tensions, resignations and expulsions in 1994. In December, Anastasios Peponis resigned as Minister to the Prime Minister in protest against PASOK's willingness to take on additional workers in the already-bloated public sector. In September, Andreas Andrianopoulos (a former Industry and Commerce Minister) and Mikhalis Papakonstantinou (a critic of Greece's intransigent line over Macedonia) were expelled from ND. In the same month, the Greek parliament voted to indict the former ND Prime Minister, Konstantinos Mitsotakis, on the charge of having received bribes in connection with the sale of a state-owned cement company to an Italian firm. Two other former ND ministers were indicted on charges of breach of trust. For good measure, Mr Mitsotakis was also accused of authorizing the phone-tapping of political opponents and with the illegal acquisition of antiquities.

The PASOK government, which had been a severe critic of ND privatization plans, announced in November that it was to privatize 25 per cent of the national telecommunications concern OTE. This move met with strong opposition from the trade union movement and from a small group of PASOK deputies. The decision to lift exchange control regulations prompted a short-lived drachma crisis in May.

Terrorism continued to be a major problem. The elusive '17 November' terrorist group claimed responsibility for the shooting in January of Mikhail Vranopoulos, the former head of the National Bank, and for the assassination in July of a Turkish diplomat, Omer Haluk Sipahioglu. Subsequent bomb attacks on Rhodes, in which tourists were injured, were seen as reprisals for the assassination. '17 November' also planned an unsuccessful attack on the British aircraft-carrier *Ark Royal* in April and was one of two organizations claiming responsibility for the attack in September on a police bus which resulted in one death and 11 injuries.

Legislation initiated by the Minister of Public Order, Stelios Papathemelis, to curb Greece's traditionally exuberant nightlife gave rise to numerous police raids but was partly rescinded in the interests of the country's important tourist industry.

The death in March of Melina Mercouri, the rather larger-than-life actress who became a PASOK deputy and Minister of Culture, was marked by a massive public funeral (see XX: Obituary). A redoubtable opponent of the 1967–74 military dictatorship, she had latterly campaigned strenuously for the return to Greece of the Elgin Marbles, housed in the British Museum in London. After her death, the Melina Mercouri Foundation was established to continue the campaign.

In April the Greek parliament passed a law stripping ex-King Constantine II of his citizenship and nationalizing the remaining royal properties. The ex-monarch declared that he would explore all legal avenues to secure the rescinding of the decree.

vi. CYPRUS

CAPITAL: Nicosia AREA: 9,250 sq km POPULATION: 735,000 ('94 est.)
POLITICAL SYSTEM: separate presidential democracies in Greek area and in Turkish
    Republic of Northern Cyprus (recognized only by Turkey)
HEAD OF STATE & GOVERNMENT: President Glafkos Clerides (since Feb '93);
    Rauf Denktash has been President of Turkish area since Feb '75
PRINCIPAL MINISTERS: (Greek Cyprus) Alexandros Michaelides (foreign affairs),
    Christodoulos Christodoulou (finance), Dinos Michaelides (interior), Costas
    Eliades (defence), Alexandros Evangelou (justice & public order)
INTERNATIONAL ALIGNMENT: (Greek Cyprus) NAM, Cwth.
CURRENCY: Cyprus pound (end-'94 £1=£0.74, US$1=£0.48)
GNP PER CAPITA: (Republic) US$12,510, (TRNC) US$1,152 ('94 est.)
MAIN EXPORT EARNERS: tourism, textiles, agricultural products

IN the 30th year of the UN's involvement in Cyprus, its efforts to broker a constitutional settlement between the Greek and Turkish Cypriot communities reached deadlock. The fragile truce, which the UN Force in Cyprus (UNFICYP) had helped to maintain since the island was divided in 1974, began to fray as each community stepped up its military preparedness and began to engage in sabre-rattling. At the heart of the impasse was the demand by the Turkish Cypriot leader, Rauf Denktash, for recognition of the sovereignty of the self-proclaimed Turkish Republic of Northern Cyprus (TRNC) prior to a confederal settlement. This ran counter to the UN's continued acceptance of the principle espoused by the Greek Cypriots that the Republic of Cyprus should be a federal state with one sovereignty and one international personality.

The last comprehensive approach to the problem—the 100-point Set of Ideas tabled by the UN Secretary-General Boutros-Ghali—had been shelved in 1993 after the election of the conservative Glafkos Clerides as Greek Cypriot President (see AR 1993, pp. 99-100). To sustain the negotiating momentum, a package of confidence-building measures (CBMs) had been proposed, envisaging in particular that the Varosha tourist district of the east-coast port of Famagusta (currently in the TRNC) and Nicosia international airport should be reopened under UN administration. Such moves would have meant that some 15,000 Greek Cypriots regained their former homes, in exchange for a partial lifting of the communications embargo on the Turkish Cypriots. However, the CBMs idea foundered on repeated demands by the Turkish Cypriots for amendments which would have afforded the TRNC a form of international recognition.

After UN experts' reports had demonstrated that the CBMs would provide the TRNC with 'tens of millions of dollars' of international aid and a 20 per cent annual increase in gross domestic product, an effort to resurrect negotiations was undertaken early in 1994 (see also XI.1). The Secretary-General's special representative, Joe Clark, and his resident deputy, Gustave Feissel, made strenuous efforts, but the commitment of the disputants was desultory. The method used was proximity talks, in which the UN officials met separately with President Clerides and Dr Denktash to establish possible compromises on each side's demands and objections. The Turkish Cypriots advanced an ever-increasing list of detailed demands, each of which nibbled at the recognition issue, until finally the Greek Cypriots said that a UN summary of respective positions dated 21 March contained all the concessions they were prepared to make.

An exhaustive report to the UN Security Council by Dr Boutros-Ghali dated 30 May argued in detail the merits of the CBMs and, in a breach of precedent, put the blame for the failure of the negotiations on 'a lack of political will on the Turkish Cypriot side'. He offered the Security

Council five options, in descending order of extremity: (i) withdrawal of UNFICYP (which had been on Cyprus since March 1964, at a cost to date of some $2,250 million); (ii) adoption of 'coercive measures' against Turkey and the Turkish Cypriots for failing to abide by UN resolutions; (iii) a return to matters of substance such as those in the Set of Ideas; (iv) Security Council renewal of his mandate to pursue in-depth consultations on 'far-reaching options'; and (v) a further effort to obtain agreement on the CBMs.

The Security Council renewed the mandate of UNFICYP until December 1994 and began working its way backwards through the options. Efforts in June by Mr Feissel extracted further concessions from the Turkish Cypriots on the CBMs, although with the proviso that the 21 March document should be rewritten. Conveying the Greek Cypriot rejection of this proviso, President Clerides in July wrote to the Security Council urging it to address the essentials, which he itemized as demilitarization of the island; the future of the Turkish mainland settlers (numbering 90,000 according to Greek Cypriot estimates); and basic constitutional structures and their guarantee. These issues, said President Clerides, should now be considered by a fullscale international conference on the future of Cyprus. At the end of July the Security Council passed Resolution 939, which did not call for an international conference but urged the Secretary-General to engage in wider talks with the guarantor powers (Greece, Turkey and the United Kingdom) and with the member states of the Council, particularly the five permanent members.

During 1994 the Greek Cypriot government continued to press its 1990 application for full membership of the European Union (EU) for Cyprus, which had become an associate member in 1973, a year before the division of the island. The Brussels Commission, in its opinion issued in 1993, had said that, while Cyprus qualified on economic grounds, the application could not be considered for the time being because of the political division of the island. The TRNC administration strenuously opposed the application, insisting that Cyprus should not become a member until Turkey did, otherwise the Greek Cypriots would achieve a form of *enosis* (union) with Greece (already an EU member). The Turkish Cypriots also cited treaty agreements whereby Cyprus was precluded from joining international organizations of which both Greece and Turkey were not members.

Holding the EU presidency during the first half of 1994, Greece managed to secure a commitment at the Corfu summit in June that Cyprus would be included in the next enlargement process following the Inter-Governmental Conference scheduled for 1996. The EU's decision infuriated the Turkish Cypriots, their anger being compounded when the European Court ruled on 5 July that EU countries could no longer import goods from the TRNC unless they were accompanied by documentation from the recognized government of the island (see also XV.1.ii). This combination of events precipitated the passage through the TRNC assembly in August of a resolution which argued that the Turkish Cypriots' sovereign rights as co-founders of the state of Cyprus had been flouted by the unilateral Greek Cypriot application for EU membership and warned that, if the application were accepted, the TRNC would 'integrate' economically with mainland Turkey. The resolution also repealed previous TRNC assembly declarations that a Cypriot federation was the only basis for an eventual settlement.

During the latter half of 1994, the Greek Cypriots launched a major diplomatic offensive seeking an early date for the commencement of formal EU entry negotiations. They were supported by Greece, which on 19 December again vetoed the inauguration of an EU-Turkey customs union until such time as a date had been set, to the annoyance of some other EU members. The French government (which was due to assume the EU presidency for the first half of 1995) warned that, if the Greek veto was not withdrawn, the Cypriot membership application was unlikely to progress.

The Greek government of the Pan-Hellenic Socialist Movement elected in October 1993 moved quickly to implement a new defence strategy embracing Cyprus (see also II.3.v). In March it signed a series of defence cooperation agreements with the Greek Cypriot government, including one to provide air and naval cover in the event of hostilities. In October this was given practical demonstration when Greek warplanes carried out mock bombing raids over south-coast cities during Greek Cypriot military exercises. The Greek Cypriot government announced its intention to increase the strength of the National Guard by a third, to 15,000 personnel, and to transform it into a semi-professional force by offering five-year contracts to non-commissioned officers, who would be trained in the operation of its increasingly large arsenal of sophisticated modern weaponry. The Greek Cypriots maintained that this arsenal was purely defensive, designed to hold any further Turkish advance long enough to mobilize international diplomatic intervention. The Turkish Cypriots contended that, with air cover, the Greek Cypriots would also be able to mobilize reserves of 80,000. According to UN sources in 1994, the Turkish military presence in the TRNC had recently been reinforced to 30,000 men and 300 tanks. In June, and again in October, the Greek Cypriot government protested to the UN about violations of Cypriot airspace by Turkish fighter aircraft.

In his semi-annual report to the UN Security Council on 12 December requesting an extension of the UNFICYP mandate for a further six months, Dr Boutros-Ghali noted pointedly that there was '. . . only a ceasefire. . . not peace' in Cyprus and that 'in the absence of progress towards a settlement between the two sides, the overall situation remains subject to sudden tensions, generated by events outside the island as well

as within'. He added that the rate at which both sides were increasing
their armaments was 'a cause of serious concern'.

vii. TURKEY

CAPITAL: Ankara   AREA: 779,000 sq km   POPULATION: 59,200,000 ('92)
OFFICIAL LANGUAGE: Turkish   POLITICAL SYSTEM: parliamentary democracy
HEAD OF STATE: President Süleyman Demirel (since May '93)
RULING PARTIES: True Path Party (DYP) & Social Democratic Populists (SHP)
HEAD OF GOVERNMENT: Tansu Çiller (DYP), Prime Minister (since June '93)
PRINCIPAL MINISTERS: Murat Karayalçin (SHP/Deputy Prime Minister & foreign
    affairs), Mehmet Mogultay (SHP/justice), Mehmet Gölhan (DYP/defence), Nahit
    Menteşe (DYP/interior), Ismet Atilla (DYP/finance)
INTERNATIONAL ALIGNMENT: NATO, OECD, ICO, ECO
CURRENCY: lira (end-'94 £1=LT60,546.3, US$1=LT38,700.1)
GNP PER CAPITA: US$1,910 ('92)
MAIN EXPORT EARNERS: textiles, iron & steel, agricultural products, tourism

THE coalition government of the centre-right True Path Party (DYP)
and the centre-left Social Democratic Populist Party (SHP) was forced
to curb government over-spending, which had fuelled a consumer boom
in 1993 (see AR 1993, pp. 105-6). But while the Prime Minister, Tansu
Çiller of the DYP, took the first steps to put the economy on a sound
footing, her reliance on Turkish nationalist sentiment prevented any
progress towards a solution of the problem posed by the disaffection
of the country's large Kurdish minority.

Mme Çiller's tactic of delaying austerity measures until after the local
government elections on 27 March led to the collapse of the national
currency (the lira) at the end of January. She then sought to profit
from the indignation felt by the ethnic Turkish majority at the terrorist
campaign waged by the Kurdish nationalist Kurdistan Workers' Party
(PKK) and supported the lifting of the parliamentary immunity of
radical Kurdish members of parliament on 2 March. Seven members
and one former member of the Democracy Party (DEP), which had
voiced Kurdish nationalist demands, were arrested and tried by the
state security court in Ankara; six other DEP deputies escaped to
Europe; and the party was dissolved by the Constitutional Court on
16 June. On 8 December five of the Kurdish deputies—including the
DEP leader, Hatip Dicle, and Leyla Zana, wife of the former mayor of
Diyarbakir (chief city of the Kurdish-speaking area)—were sentenced
to 15 years in prison and one to seven-and-a-half years, while two given
lesser sentences were released, account having been taken of the time
they had spent in detention.

The sentences (which were subject to appeal) drew widespread
criticism in the West, particularly within the European Union (EU).
The European Parliament voted to suspend the work of the joint

EU-Turkish parliamentary commission, and the US State Department expressed its concern. The action against the DEP was one reason for the failure of the European Council to endorse the framework agreement negotiated by the Commission for the implementation of the customs union due to come into force at the end of 1995 under the terms of the association agreement between the EU and Turkey. However, it was the Greek refusal to drop its opposition to the customs union with Turkey unless the Council committed itself to a timetable for full membership negotiations with Cyprus that prevented the EU-Turkey association council from taking any decision on the customs union at its meeting in Brussels on 19 December (see also II.3.vi).

Military operations against the PKK were pursued vigorously in the Kurdish-speaking areas, as the security forces attempted to clear rebels from the mountains north of Iraq, the Ağridağ (Mount Ararat) massif on the Iranian frontier, and the Tunceli (Dersim) mountains (west of Erzurum), where the murder of a number of schoolteachers by the PKK led to the forced evacuation and destruction of Kurdish villages by the military in the closing months of the year. On several occasions, Turkish ground forces crossed into Iraqi Kurdistan, while Turkish aircraft bombed PKK targets in the area. In spite of fears that the presence of allied aircraft, as part of the Provide Comfort operation to deter an Iraqi attack on the Kurds, encouraged Kurdish nationalists on the Turkish side of the frontier, the Ankara parliament twice extended the permission for these aircraft to be stationed on Turkish territory.

PKK terrorism, and retaliation by shadowy Turkish nationalist groups, spilled over into the rest of the country. The PKK killed six army cadets and wounded another 60 by exploding a bomb at a suburban railway station near Istanbul on 11 March. It also targeted tourist resorts in Istanbul and the Aegean coast. Turkish nationalists killed persons associated with the DEP and bombed its offices and publications sympathetic to it. The government claimed that some 4,000 Kurdish rebels were killed and 750 captured during the year, and attributed some 1,000 civilian deaths to the PKK. Official promises of economic help for the Kurdish areas and of wider democratic freedoms for the whole country produced no results by the end of the year. However, the cause of wider democratization found an increasing number of advocates, particularly in the ranks of the New Democracy Movement, founded in December by Cem Boyner, the young ex-president of the Turkish Industrialists' and Businessmen's Association.

The decision of the DEP to boycott the local polls swelled the vote of the Welfare Party (RP), a formation of Islamist inspiration. On 27 March the RP received 19 per cent of the total vote, winning control of the metropolitan municipalities of Ankara and Istanbul and of most cities in the Kurdish areas. Mme Çiller's DYP came first in the countrywide count, although its share of the poll fell to 22 per cent (from 27 per cent in the 1991 parliamentary elections). The mainstream opposition Motherland Party (ANAP), founded by the late President Turgut Özal and now led by Mesut Yilmaz, came second with 21 per cent (down from 24 per cent), while the vote of the SHP fell from 21 to 13 per cent.

Factionalism within SHP obstructed effective government action. On 5 August the SHP leader and Deputy Prime Minister, Murat Karayalçin, changed the party's ministerial team, replacing Foreign Minister Hikmet Çetin (an ethnic Kurd) by Mümtaz Soysal, a noted left-wing nationalist and a critic of the government's privatization plans. Professor Soysal agreed to drop his opposition to privatization in exchange for an extension of free speech. On 24 November parliament finally approved a framework law for privatizing loss-making public enterprises. Four days later Professor Soysal resigned after disagreeing with the Prime Minister on Foreign Ministry appointments, and before the government could fulfil its promise to liberalize the current anti-terrorist law. The foreign affairs portfolio was taken over by Mr Karayalçin.

The austerity programme, finally put in place on 5 April and supported by a stand-by credit agreement negotiated with the IMF, reduced civil service salaries, farm subsidies and other government expenditure in real terms, while increasing the prices of goods and services produced by the public sector and levying one-off taxes on assets. Combined with the devaluation of the lira (from under LT 15,000 to over LT 38,000 to the US dollar), the programme had the effect of restraining imports (which fell by 23 per cent to US$16,000 million in the first nine months of the year) and increasing exports (by 16 per cent, to US$12,000 million), thus allowing the external current account to move into credit. Foreign reserves increased in spite of the repayment of US$6,000 million of foreign debt. But so did inflation, as urban consumer prices rose by 125 per cent by the end of the year. In December an IMF team returned to Ankara to discuss the government's programme for 1995, amid fears of a slackening of the government's resolve to balance the budget.

Austerity led to a record drop in economic activity. GNP, which had risen by 7.6 per cent in the 1993 boom year, increased by another 3.5 per cent in the first quarter of 1994 but then fell by 10.3 per cent in the second quarter and by 8.6 per cent in the third quarter. However, while cutbacks slowed down investment on public works, the motorway from the Bulgarian frontier to Istanbul was completed, as was the first of two tunnels drawing water from the new Atatürk dam/lake on the Euphrates to irrigate the Harran plain north of the Syrian border.

Hampered by domestic political and economic difficulties, Turkish diplomacy battled nevertheless to maintain profitable links with the West and to defend the interests of Turkish Cypriots, Bosnian Muslims and Azeris and other Muslims in the former Soviet Union. A summit meeting of the leaders of the Turkic republics was held in Istanbul on 18 October and was followed by a visit by President Süleyman

Demirel to Turkmenistan (see also VIII.1.iii). Prime Minister Çiller went to Sarajevo on 2 February and in June a Turkish contingent joined the UNPROFOR force in Bosnia (see III.1.vi). Mme Çiller's visit to Washington in April was concerned largely with Turkey's search for foreign funds. Relations with Greece were strained, particularly when the Foreign Ministry was in the hands of Professor Soysal, who had earlier acted as adviser to Rauf Denktash, the leader of the Turkish Cypriot community. When the UN Law of the Sea Convention came into force in November, Turkey threatened to resist any Greek attempt to extend its territorial waters in the Aegean (see also II.3.v). Rival naval manoeuvres were held in contiguous areas of the sea, but there were no serious clashes.

III EASTERN EUROPE

1. POLAND—CZECHOSLOVAKIA—HUNGARY—ROMANIA— BULGARIA—FORMER YUGOSLAVIA—ALBANIA

i. POLAND

CAPITAL: Warsaw   AREA: 313,000 sq km ('90)   POPULATION: 38,400,000 ('92)
OFFICIAL LANGUAGE: Polish   POLITICAL SYSTEM: presidential democracy
HEAD OF STATE: President Lech Walesa (since Dec '90)
RULING PARTIES: Democratic Left Alliance (SLD) & Polish Peasant Party (PSL) head
coalition
PRINCIPAL MINISTERS: Waldemar Pawlak (PSL/Prime Minister), Grzegorz Kolodko
(ind./Deputy Premier, finance), Aleksander Luczak (PSL/Deputy Premier, state
administration & education), Wlodzimierz Cimoszewicz (SLD/Deputy Premier,
social policy & justice), Andrzej Olechowski (ind./foreign affairs), Andrzej
Milczanowski (ind./internal affairs)
CURRENCY: zloty (end-'94 £1=Zl.38,126.9, US$1=Zl.24,370.0)
GNP PER CAPITA: US$1,910 ('92)
MAIN EXPORT EARNERS: engineering equipment, coal, metals, agricultural produce

IT was a frustrating year in which potential benefits of economic growth
were jeopardized by the government's negative approach to Western
integration and by endless wrangling and mutual insults between the
government of former communists and the presidency of Lech Walesa,
which made both increasingly unpopular. Premature posturing of rivals
in a presidential race not due to be decided until the end of 1995 was
regarded with indifference by a general public primarily concerned with
economic performance.

The political initiative was held by the coalition government of former
communists and their supporters formed in October 1993 (see AR 1993,
p. 108–9). Its two partners, the Democratic Left Alliance (SLD) led by
Aleksander Kwasniewski and the Polish Peasant Party (PSL) led by
Waldemar Pawlak, who was also Prime Minister, pledged to remain in
coalition until the 1997 legislative elections. They promised to sustain
the gains of the earlier 'shock therapy' through tough monetary controls
and a tight 'fiscal discipline', including employment of 20,000 new
tax-inspectors.

This package was enshrined in a budget approved by the Sejm (lower
house of parliament) on 5 March by 289 votes to 155, with 27 abstentions.
Its growth target (4.5 per cent over the year) was exceeded in the
succeeding months, but so was that for inflation (23 per cent), which
was driven up by increases of up to 33 per cent in the price of food and
services. However, the ratio of budget deficit to GDP (4.2 per cent)
remained within IMF guidelines, enabling Poland to obtain further
significant reductions in its international debts. Debt to the London

Club (of some 300 commercial banks) was reduced by almost half on 10 March, and this was followed by a Paris Club (inter-governmental debt) reduction of a further 20 per cent in addition to the 30 per cent agreed in April 1991. The IMF itself confirmed its standby arrangement of some SDR 476 million (about US$500 million) for Poland, part of which was taken up immediately.

The domestic outcome was less positive. Despite paying lip-service to the idea of privatization, known officially as 'ownership transformation', Mr Pawlak did all he could to stall the process. On 22 September the minister concerned made this accusation in public, and President Walesa added his voice to the condemnation. The Prime Minister retorted that sell-offs of state property were giving foreign companies excessive influence in Poland, but reluctantly agreed on 19 October that a further 444 enterprises would be sold into private ownership.

Control over top state appointments was hotly contested. On 16 April the President threatened to dissolve the Sejm unless the coalition abandoned plans to abolish the presidential veto over governmental posts. After a noisy crisis (which was increasingly the pattern in Polish politics), the confrontation was resolved by an agreement to draft a new constitution in which the respective powers of parliament and the President would be properly enunciated. In the meantime, it was made clear that there would be no retrospective justice. The governing coalition rejected a proposal to screen state officials for evidence of collaboration with the secret police during the communist period. On 19 August two former secret service generals were acquitted of aiding and abetting the murderers of the pro-Solidarity priest, Jerzy Popieluszko, ten years earlier (see AR 1984, p. 116).

Political recriminations came to a head in mid-October when the Sejm rejected a request by President Walesa for the dismissal of the Defence Minister, Admiral (retd.) Piotr Kolodziejczyk. It passed a resolution by 305 votes to 18, with 22 abstentions, appealing to the President to desist from 'anti-democratic' interventions. He replied on television that, faced with so incapable a government coalition, the country needed a strong President to 'bring order' to Poland. In turn, the Justice Minister denounced Foreign Minister Andrzej Olechowski (appointed and supported by President Walesa) for breaching 'anti-corruption' legislation by receiving a second salary. Mr Olechowski, a Western-oriented economist, declared that his additional earnings from membership of the supervisory board of the Savings Bank were not illegal. Nonetheless, he handed over to the Deputy Foreign Minister, pending a constitutional ruling.

Admiral Kolodziejczyk was dismissed by the President on 10 November, whereupon he publicly denounced Mr Walesa's proposal to subordinate the General Staff to himself as being incompatible with civilian parliamentary control of the military. The country remained without

Ministers of Defence and Foreign Affairs for some months—a state of affairs seen by many as indicating the ascendancy of those who sought to replace the Brussels–Washington orientation in foreign and defence policy with a Bratislava–Moscow axis. It was also highly prejudicial to Poland's official aspiration to become a member of the Western Alliance.

Poland had signed NATO's Partnership for Peace plan on 2 February (see XII.2; XIX.1). In May, moreover, Poland had been admitted as one of nine 'associate' partners of the Western European Union (WEU), with the (non-voting) right to attend weekly WEU meetings and to contribute to humanitarian and peace-keeping operations. President Clinton of the USA, speaking in Warsaw on 7 July, failed to set out a time-table for Poland and other ex-communist states to become NATO members. But this disappointment was partly mitigated by Poland's participation in joint NATO exercises in the autumn. A second step forward in foreign relations was the signature of a treaty of friendship and cooperation with Lithuania on 26 April, renouncing mutual territorial claims and guaranteeing the rights of minorities. Relations with Russia remained frosty, as indicated by the cancellation of the Russian Prime Minister's scheduled visit to Warsaw in November.

On 1 July the Sejm voted to postpone ratification of a concordat with the Vatican until after the adoption of a new constitution. President Walesa responded by condemning the government for seeking 're-communization' and vetoed legislation to liberalize the existing strict anti-abortion law. After the Primate of Poland had declared that the Catholic Church was 'under attack', the Sejm gave way and withdrew the abortion bill in September.

The minority parties attempted to regroup after their electoral debacle in 1993. On 23 April the third largest grouping, the Democratic Union (UD) led by former Prime Minister Hanna Suchocka, merged with the pro-market Congress of Liberal Democrats (KLD) to form the Freedom Union (UW), chaired by Tadeusz Mazowiecki, the first post-communist Prime Minister. The divided right—whose various groupings polled some 15 per cent in total in 1993, although all failed to reach the 5 per cent threshold required to enter parliament—came together to form a Covenant for Poland (PdP). A significant role was played in parliament by the Labour Union (UP), a socialist-oriented grouping composed of former Solidarity leaders and intellectuals. But all the evidence was that many Poles regarded party politics as irrelevant to their immediate problems.

New features of public life included the building of a Warsaw metro (first announced in 1950); the advent of a Catholic broadcasting station (Radio Maria); new currency denominations under which, with effect from 1 January 1995, four zeros were removed (i.e. 10,000 old zloty = 1 new zloty); and ubiquitous mobile telephones. Less attractive aspects of modernity included a growth of pornography and a rising incidence of mafia-style attacks on 'unprotected' shops and restaurants. Labour unrest was minimal, although in late April half a million workers protested at an additional tax (*neopopiwek*) on state enterprises which awarded inflationary wage increases. The protests ended on 11 May when the Solidarity national commission abandoned plans for a general strike. Nonetheless, many workers and their families continued to endure considerable hardships.

No new popular champion emerged in 1994, so that the 1995 presidential race remained wide open. Lech Walesa continued to be a formidable political operator, able to call on the historical memories still powerful with the older generation. Mr Kwasniewski of the SLD skilfully distanced himself from the PSL's distaste for privatization and refused to be drawn into the constitutional debates. He remained President Walesa's most plausible opponent.

ii.   CZECH REPUBLIC AND SLOVAKIA

Czech Republic

CAPITAL: Prague   AREA: 30,450 sq km   POPULATION: 10,300,000 ('93)
OFFICIAL LANGUAGE: Czech   POLITICAL SYSTEM: parliamentary democracy
HEAD OF STATE: President Václav Havel (since Jan '93)
RULING PARTIES: coalition of Civic Democratic Party (ODS), Christian Democratic
    Union–Czech People's Party (KDU-CSL), Christian Democratic Party (KDS) & Civic
    Democratic Alliance (ODA)
PRINCIPAL MINISTERS: Václav Klaus (ODS/Prime Minister), Ivan Kocarnik (ODS/Deputy
    Premier, finance), Josef Lux (KDU-CSL/Deputy Premier, agriculture), Jan
    Kalvoda (ODA/Deputy Premier), Josef Zieleniec (ODS/foreign affairs), Jan Ruml
    (ODS/interior), Jiří Novák (ODS/justice), Vilem Holan (ind./defence)
CURRENCY: koruna (end-'94 £1=K43.61, US$1=K27.88)
GNP PER CAPITA: US$2,500 ('93 est.)

Slovakia

CAPITAL: Bratislava   AREA: 18,930 sq km   POPULATION: 5,300,000 ('93)
OFFICIAL LANGUAGE: Slovak   POLITICAL SYSTEM: parliamentary democracy
HEAD OF STATE: President Michal Kováč (since Feb '93)
RULING PARTIES: coalition of Movement for a Democratic Slovakia (HZDS),
    Association of Slovak Workers (ZRS) & Slovak National Party (SNS)
PRINCIPAL MINISTERS: Vladimir Mečiar (HZDS/Prime Minister), Katarina Tóthová
    (HZDS/Deputy Premier), Sergej Koslik (HZDS/Deputy Premier, finance), Jozef
    Kalman (ZRS/Deputy Premier), Juraj Schenk (HZDS/foreign affairs), Jan Ducky
    (HZDS/economy), Ludovit Hudek (HZDS/interior), Jozef Liscak (ZRS/justice), Jan
    Sitek (SNS/defence)
CURRENCY: koruna (end-'94 £1=K48.62, US$1=K31.07)
GNP PER CAPITA: US$1,500 ('93 est.)

THE CZECH REPUBLIC remained politically and economically stable throughout 1994, with few signs of social unrest or even public dissatisfaction. The single most important political event was the local elections held on 18–19 November. While independent candidates won almost

50 per cent of the seats in municipal councils, the Civic Democratic Party (ODS) of Prime Minister Václav Klaus took more than 25 per cent of the popular vote. Opinion polls throughout the year confirmed that the ODS remained particularly strong in larger cities, while its coalition partner, the Christian Democratic Union–Czech People's Party (KDU-CSL), gained ground in the countryside. But despite this remarkable degree of stability in a generally unstable region, the political elite of the country was split on a variety of issues, ranging from the administrative structure of the country to the restitution of church property confiscated under communist rule.

Among these issues was the question of how, if at all, to set up the second chamber of the Czech parliament, the Senate. The Czech constitution clearly called for the creation of a Senate, but the lower chamber had voted down all proposals to establish it in 1993. In early 1994 the government reached a consensus with the opposition that the Senate should be elected in November. However, a draft Senate electoral law submitted by the government in February was vigorously opposed by junior coalition parties, who argued that the law would favour the ODS and ensure it a landslide victory. Amid squabbling within the coalition, parliament failed to adopt the draft law in June, making the ultimate fate of the Senate even more uncertain.

Plans for a decentralization of the Czech Republic, also prescribed by the constitution, remained inconclusive. A draft law, submitted by the ODS-dominated government, stipulating the division of the Republic into 17 regions, was turned down not only by the opposition but also by the ODS's coalition partners. Critics of the plan maintained that such small units would be too weak to stand up to the central government and that the law was thus counter-productive. The decentralization debate therefore continued into 1995.

Another contentious issue that seriously strained relations between the coalition partners was the restitution of Catholic Church and Jewish property. While the coalition failed to find a solution to the question of whether to restore church property, it succeeded in reaching an agreement on Jewish property. Although in early February parliament rejected a law that would have provided for the return of confiscated property to Jewish communities, Mr Klaus decided to return state-owned property by government decree. In April, over the government's objections, parliament passed an amendment to the restitution law, inserting a provision for the return of confiscated property owned by municipalities.

US President Clinton's Prague meeting with Central European leaders in January was the single most outstanding foreign policy event of the year. It was overshadowed by ongoing disagreements between the Czech Republic and its Visegrad Group partners (Poland, Hungary and Slovakia) over whether these countries should make united approaches to the West, or whether they should seek individually to join Western political, cultural, economic and security institutions. The Czech refusal to cooperate with its neighbours in this respect was illustrated by the fact that the Czech Defence Minister declined an invitation from President Walesa of Poland to hold consultative talks prior to Mr Clinton's visit. Although a visit by President Havel to Budapest in November and one to Warsaw by Foreign Minister Josef Zieleniec in October helped to improve Czech relations with both countries, Prague's repeated refusals to coordinate policies vis-à-vis NATO and the European Union with the other Visegrad countries continued to have a cooling effect. The Czechs instead insisted that relations with the Visegrad countries should focus on such practical matters as trade within the framework of the Central European Free Trade Agreement.

Relations with Slovakia were affected by the political turmoil in that country (see below). Leaders of both nations made some progress on issues such as the division of former federal property and improving cross-border cooperation; but Mr Klaus's lack of support for the Slovak government of Jozef Moravcik, which replaced the government of Vladimir Mečiar in March, angered some Slovak politicians and media. Relations with Austria were soured early in the year by angry exchanges between the two countries' leaders over Czech plans to complete a nuclear power plant in Temelin. Austria opposed the project on environmental and safety grounds.

Czech-German relations were generally good in 1994, culminating in the signing of a repatriation treaty which Germany had long sought. But there were also problems. The unwillingness of Czech politicians to deal with the issue of some three million Sudeten Germans who were expelled from Czechoslovakia after World War II continued to burden bilateral relations. An attack by xenophobic Czech right-wing extremists on a group of Germans during a commemoration of victims of the Nazis at the site of the former Terezin concentration camp on 30 July provoked public outrage in Germany, as did the fatal shooting of two German tourists by Czech police in the autumn.

Early admission to NATO remained high on the Czech Republic's agenda. The country joined NATO's Partnership for Peace programme (see XII.2; XIX.1), although the reluctance of Western politicians to offer full membership prompted some criticism by Czech politicians. Mr Klaus announced in October that the Czech Republic would officially apply for full European Union membership in 1996 and told the Czech parliament in December that EU membership was the country's most important foreign policy objective.

The highly-acclaimed voucher privatization programme was basically completed by the end of 1994. Since a majority of Czechs decided against investing directly, investment funds became the country's largest shareholders. In December over 80 per cent of Czech firms, with a total value exceeding K 900,000 million, had been privatized. But the successes of the programme were overshadowed by a number of corruption scandals.

Other economic developments appeared promising. The country's GDP grew by about 3 per cent in 1994, fuelled not only by booming exports but also partly by the growth of industrial production, which increased for the first time since 1989. The annual inflation rate decreased to about 11 per cent and unemployment remained low at 3.5 per cent. Not only did the country produce a small budget surplus, but also the hard currency reserves of the Czech National Bank increased to about $5,800 million. Wage controls were maintained throughout the year, with two main effects: inflation was kept down and foreign investment was attracted by low labour costs. Although direct foreign investment was only some $600 million in 1994, there were large capital inflows in the form of direct lending to Czech firms by foreign banks ($1,200 million) and investment by foreigners on the Prague stock exchange. Capital inflows began to create inflationary pressures, prompting the government to complain that the Czech Republic already had enough foreign investment.

Developments in the banking and financial sectors were generally considered as positive, although a number of smaller banks collapsed due to liberal licensing and supervision regulations. Parliament acted quickly to adopt new laws introducing tighter controls and a system of state insurance of individual deposits at the largest Czech banks. The Prague stock exchange performed relatively well at the beginning of the year, but the value of many stocks began to decline in the spring—a trend that had not been arrested at year's end.

Czech exports again increased in 1994 (by some 7 per cent in the first nine months), although in comparison with 1993 the rate of growth slowed down, owing mainly to a decline in trade with Slovakia. Some 40 per cent of exports went to Germany, the main source of foreign capital. In general, exports to the West continued to grow at the expense of exports to the former Soviet-bloc countries. However, imports continued to grow even faster than exports, causing a trade deficit of about $40 million.

For SLOVAKIA, it was a year of change and uncertainty on the political front, as Slovaks went to the polls three times and three different governments held office.

Prime Minister Mečiar's fragile parliamentary majority was destroyed on 3 February, when a breakaway Slovak National Party (SNS) faction united with the opposition against the government's proposals for amendments to the large-scale privatization law, claiming they would lead to a concentration of power in the hands of Mr Mečiar. As the parliamentary crisis deepened, then Foreign Minister Jozef Moravcik and Deputy Prime Minister Roman Kováč initiated the formation of a new faction within Mr Mečiar's party, the Movement for a Democratic Slovakia (HZDS). On 11 March, after urging from President Michal Kováč, Mr Moravcik's faction, along with two other HZDS and SNS breakaway parties, joined the right-of-centre Christian Democratic Movement (KDH) and the post-communist Party of the Democratic Left (SDL) in passing a vote of no-confidence in the Mečiar government. Five days later the President installed a new cabinet, which required tacit support from the ethnic Hungarian parties for a parliamentary majority. The HZDS and the remaining members of the SNS, whose new leaders transformed it into an extreme nationalist party, formed the opposition.

The new coalition government, headed by Mr Moravcik, immediately set out to revamp Slovakia's struggling economy and to improve its image abroad. Although the next parliamentary elections were not due until June 1996, the SDL persuaded its coalition partners to vote for an early contest—a motion which was also supported by the HZDS and SNS. Public opinion polls suggested that, although the HZDS would win the most votes of any party, the left-right coalition would maintain a parliamentary majority. However, a lavish election campaign helped the HZDS and its ally, the tiny Peasant Party (PP), to win an unexpectedly high 34.96 per cent of the vote and 61 of the 150 parliamentary seats in the balloting on 30 September–1 October. The Common Choice bloc, a four-party leftist coalition centred on the SDL, won only 18 seats, followed by the ethnic Hungarian coalition and the KDH with 17 seats each. Mr Moravcik's centrist Democratic Union of Slovakia (DUS), which combined the three HZDS and SNS breakaway parties, won only 15 seats, while the far-left Association of Slovak Workers (ZRS) took 13 seats and the SNS nine.

Both Mr Moravcik and Mr Mečiar needed the help of the 13 ZRS deputies to gain the majority necessary to form a government. After a series of coalition talks, during which Mr Mečiar alienated the leadership of most other parties by his unwillingness to compromise and by his attacks on President Kováč, in early December the ZRS finally agreed to participate in a new Mečiar-led cabinet, a coalition agreement between the HZDS, PP, SNS and ZRS being signed on 11 December. Two days later the government was installed with Mr Mečiar as Prime Minister, his deputies including HZDS members Katerina Tóthová and Sergej Kozlik (who was also appointed Finance Minister) and ZRS member Jozef Kalman. The HZDS took 12 posts in the 18-member cabinet, compared with two for the SNS and four for the ZRS.

Even before the coalition was formed, the four parties had joined forces in parliament to make sweeping changes in privatization procedures and in the leadership of key organizations. Such personnel changes continued after the government's installation, including the replacement of the Attorney-General, the top officials at the Supreme

Supervisory Office, all ministerial state secretaries and the directors of 27 district offices. Changes in the media included the replacement of the directors and board members of Slovak Radio and Television as well as the reinstatement of the previous director of the state news agency, TASR. In further privatization changes, all direct-sale projects passed by the Moravcik cabinet after 6 September were cancelled, decision-making powers were transferred from the government to the National Property Fund and the fund's leadership was replaced.

On the broader economic front, Slovakia registered an unexpected turnaround. Although most observers had expected the economy to stagnate at best in 1994, GDP growth was expected to reach 4.2 per cent for the year as a whole. By September the unemployment rate had fallen to 14.5 per cent, down from 15.2 per cent in January, while inflation fell from an annual rate of 25.1 per cent in 1993 to just over 13 per cent in 1994. Slovakia's foreign trade picture also improved significantly in 1994. A 10 per cent import surcharge introduced by the Mečiar government in March had a particularly strong effect on Slovak-Czech trade, and Slovakia soon started running a large surplus with the Czech Republic, to the benefit not only of Slovakia's overall trade balance but also of its state budget income. Despite these positive signs, foreign investment remained relatively low in Slovakia.

A major success of the Moravcik government was the securing of foreign loans to support Slovakia's economic stabilization. After the cabinet passed stricter measures to control the budget deficit, an IMF loan of $263 million was approved in July, followed by loans from the G-24 countries and the European Union (EU). The budget restrictions were apparently effective; after the Moravcik government's final session on 12 December, the deficit was down to only K 9,000 million, despite original predictions for a K 14,000 million deficit at year's end.

By the time the registration period for the second wave of privatizations closed in November, almost 3.5 million Slovaks (over 90 per cent of those eligible to participate) and 166 investment funds had registered, even though Mr Mečiar had threatened during his election campaign to cancel the programme. Property worth over K 60,000 million was earmarked to be sold, and the first round was scheduled to start on 15 December. On 14 December, however, Mr Kozlik decided to delay the second wave, claiming insufficient preparation, and the list of offered firms was put under review. Meanwhile, the choice of ZRS member Peter Bisak for the post of Privatization Minister was not a positive sign, as his party was basically opposed to privatization. This was demonstrated by its support for a referendum, held on 22 October, asking Slovaks whether a law should be passed requiring participants in privatization to disclose the source of their funds. Although the referendum failed because under 20 per cent of the electorate participated, supporters of the proposal could draw comfort from the fact that parliament had passed a similar law in August applying to future projects.

In terms of foreign policy, Slovakia remained committed to closer ties with the West, particularly with the EU and NATO. The country signed NATO's Partnership for Peace agreement in February (see XII.2; XIX.1) and planned to apply for EU membership in 1995. Although Mr Moravcik's government strengthened links with Europe, many observers expected relations to worsen under the new Mečiar administration. On 23 November the EU political committee issued a *démarche* to Slovakia, expressing concern about the post-election political situation and noting that future relations depended on the new government's policies. However, the appointments of HZDS member Juraj Schenk (a university professor without international experience) as Foreign Minister and of SNS member Jan Sitek as Defence Minister gave rise to further doubt of to Slovakia's intentions.

Meanwhile, bilateral relations with Hungary, which were largely tied to minority issues, got off to a bad start in 1994 when an assembly of ethnic Hungarians living in southern Slovakia met on 8 January to discuss possible territorial autonomy. Although the situation improved under the Moravcik cabinet, thanks to the passage of two laws giving minorities more rights, bilateral relations were widely expected to deteriorate once again under Mr Mečiar's new government.

iii.   HUNGARY

CAPITAL: Budapest   AREA: 93,000 sq km   POPULATION: 10,300,000 ('92)
OFFICIAL LANGUAGE: Hungarian   POLITICAL SYSTEM: parliamentary democracy
HEAD OF STATE: President Arpád Göncz (since Aug '90)
RULING PARTIES: Hungarian Socialist Party (MSP) heads coalition with Alliance of
   Free Democrats (SDS)
HEAD OF GOVERNMENT: Gyula Horn (MSP), Prime Minister (since July '94)
PRINCIPAL MINISTERS: Gábor Kuncze (SDS/Deputy Prime Minister, interior), László
   Kovács (MSP/foreign affairs), László Békesi (MSP/finance), György Keleti
   (MSP/defence), Pál Vastagh (MSP/justice)
CURRENCY: forint (end-'94 £1=Ft177.02, US$1=Ft113.15)
GNP PER CAPITA: US$2,970 ('92)
MAIN EXPORT EARNERS: machinery & transport equipment, agricultural products,
   basic manufactures

HUNGARY underwent a major political change in 1994. The centre-right coalition led by the Hungarian Democratic Forum (MDF) was very severely defeated by the left, which was able to form a new coalition commanding a two-thirds majority and thus in a position to introduce constitutional changes.

Under Hungary's highly complex electoral law (described by some as the most complex system in Europe), the elections were held in two rounds of voting in single member seats on 8 and 29 May. The Hungarian

Socialist Party (MSP) gained an absolute majority, taking 54 per cent of the poll and 209 of the 386 seats in the unicameral National Assembly, while the centre-left Alliance of Free Democrats (SDS) became the second-largest party, polling 18 per cent and winning 70 seats. These two formations eventually put together a coalition agreement. The outgoing government parties were in disarray, the MDF falling from 42 per cent in 1990 to under 10 per cent this time and retaining only 37 seats, while the Independent Smallholders slipped to 37 seats and the Christian Democrats managed only 22. The Federation of Young Democrats also had a disappointing election, winning only 20 seats.

The election outcome highlighted the fact that the Hungarian political system was showing signs of both stability and instability. It was stable in that the 1990 Assembly was the first post-communist parliament to serve a full term and that the party system itself showed remarkable continuity: the same six parties elected in 1990 won almost all the seats in 1994. On the other hand, the massive voting shifts between these six parties indicated that Hungarian society was expressing significant dissatisfaction both with the outgoing government and with the system itself.

The accession to power of the MSP, which had been put together from various elements of the communist party that had ceded power four years previously, was viewed with dismay by some, who feared that the practices of communism would be revived. In reality, the success of the MSP was attributable to a complex of factors. In the first place, the election result was the verdict of Hungarian voters on what they regarded as the incompetence and corruption of the MDF-led government. This coalition had been increasingly perceived as amateurish, bungling and unconcerned with the needs of the average Hungarian. Crucially, it was seen as incapable of running the economy, in that living standards were sliding and privatization was not producing greater prosperity (not least because it was moving at a snail's pace). The government was also condemned as morally unfit to be in office in the light of the burgeoning corruption over which it presided, while many voters were alienated by the MDF's nationalist rhetoric.

The MSP, on the other hand, benefited from the nostalgia factor—memories that during the final years of the communist era the population had lived adequately and with a much higher sense of security than currently. The Socialists, now espousing democratic socialism but nevertheless the legatees or successors of communism, were felt to be capable of bringing back 'the good old days'. The party was very effective in conveying an image of competence—that it had considerable expertise at its disposal and that the amateurishness of its predecessors would be replaced by a modern, professional government. Finally, the MSP was also the beneficiary of disenchantment with the nationalist sloganeering of the centre-right government. Many people felt that, while the fate of ethnic Hungarians in neighbouring Slovakia, Romania and Serbia was important, it should not be the key issue of government policy, as it appeared to be with the MDF in power. In fact, contrary to much Western comment, Hungarian public opinion was increasingly neutral on the question of the ethnic Hungarians and was irritated that the government seemed to be paying more attention to non-citizens of Hungary than to its citizens. That the extreme rightist party led by MDF dissident István Csurka performed very badly at the polls (taking only 1.3 per cent) was a clear indicator of the low level of concern aroused by nationalist issues.

The overwhelming success of the MSP posed something of a problem for the party leadership. The new Prime Minister, Gyula Horn, and his prospective ministerial team came mainly from the reform wing of the old communist party. They were therefore uncertain of the loyalty of some MSP deputies when government spending cuts came on the agenda. These were seen as inevitable, given the country's very serious foreign indebtedness, but there was concern that a group of left-wing MSP deputies would not support the government if cuts were introduced. Against this background, the MSP entered into post-election negotiations with the SDS with a view to establishing a broader parliamentary base. After several weeks of negotiation, it put together a seemingly solid coalition, both parties being prepared to make concessions and both gaining something from the agreement.

The MSP leadership gained the assurance that with SDS support it would be able to enact its programme, notwithstanding the presence of MSP dissidents in the parliamentary party. In addition, the Free Democrats were seen as giving the MSP-led government a degree of international respectability, in light of doubts as to how the West would react to a communist successor party commanding an absolute majority. Furthermore, the formation of a coalition with a two-thirds majority would allow the government to introduce structural changes to the political system. Hungary still had no new post-communist constitution, only a heavily-amended version of the communist text, which was felt by many to be unsatisfactory. The coalition was therefore determined to oversee the formulation of a new one, a process that was thought likely to take about two years to complete. There were also plans to amend the electoral law by simplifying it. The Free Democrats, for their part, entered the coalition because they wanted experience in office.

However, once in office, the MSP–SDS coalition seemed to become curiously torpid. Despite promises of action and professionalism, not to mention the urgency of the economic situation, very little was done during the new government's first six months in office. In particular, reform of the economic infrastructure, especially the banking system, was not tackled with the energy that had been expected. This was seen as potentially dangerous by expert opinion, which held that without substantial improvement the government could easily find itself in a major balance-of-payments crisis. Hungary's debt service ratio—the proportion of export earnings spent on servicing and repaying debts—was already one of the highest in Europe.

In the foreign policy sphere, the new government suffered from bad luck. Unlike its predecessor, it was eager to come to an early accommodation with its neighbours on ethnic Hungarian and other issues. But it found itself facing much more difficult negotiating partners in both Slovakia and Romania, where nationalist forces were in the ascendancy (see III.1.ii; III.1.iv). Hungary also achieved little in its relations with the West in 1994. In common with other post-communist states, it signed up for NATO's Partnership for Peace programme (see XII.2; XIX.1) but did not obtain appreciably greater international security thereby. As far as the European Union (EU) was concerned, Hungary aspired to speedy full membership but in 1994 had to be content with the decision of the EU's Essen summit in December that 'priority' would be given to preparing for the accession of the associated central and eastern European countries (see also XI.3).

Local government elections held as the year ended confirmed the dominance of the MSP. Although the majority of those elected as mayors were independents, the MSP gained about a third of all elected councillors, while the SDS candidate was re-elected as mayor of Budapest.

iv. ROMANIA

CAPITAL: Bucharest AREA: 237,500 sq km POPULATION: 22,700,000 ('92)
OFFICIAL LANGUAGE: Romanian POLITICAL SYSTEM: presidential democracy
RULING PARTIES: coalition of Party of Social Democracy of Romania (PSDR), Party of Romanian National Unity (PRNU) & independents
HEAD OF STATE & GOVERNMENT: President Ion Iliescu (since Dec '89)
PRINCIPAL MINISTERS: Nicolae Văcăroiu (PSDR/Prime Minister), Teodor Viorel Meleşcanu (ind./foreign affairs), Gheorghe Tinca (ind./defence), Iosif Gavril Chiuzbaian (ind./justice), Ioan Doru Tărăcilă (PSDR/interior), Florin Georghescu (ind./finance), Dumitru Popescu (PSDR/industry), Valeriu Tabără (PRNU/agriculture)
CURRENCY: leu (end-'94 £1=L2,776.00, US$1=1,774.37)
GNP PER CAPITA: US$1,130 ('92)
MAIN EXPORT EARNERS: oil, raw materials & metals, machinery & transport equipment, chemicals, tourism

FOR the Romanian leadership, the year brought a realization that the policy drift of previous years could not continue. In economic affairs this new-found awareness led to greater financial discipline and, in general, to a more pronounced commitment to market-oriented reforms—though not much of that commitment was translated into practice. In politics the governing Party of Social Democracy of Romania (PSDR) finally acquired a coalition partner, albeit in the form of the radical right-wing Party of Romanian National Unity (PRNU). That placed further strain on the often tense relations between the Romanian authorities and the ethnic minorities, particularly the Hungarians. Further afield, the marked progress Romania had made in the previous year in forging closer ties with the West (see AR 1993, p. 120) continued apace during 1994.

The year was punctuated by cabinet reshuffles and failed attempts by the opposition to pass motions of no-confidence in the government. Prime Minister Nicolae Văcăroiu's first reshuffle, which took place in March, was designed in part to get rid of unpopular ministers. He also wanted to bolster Romania's improving international image by replacing the generals serving as Ministers of Defence and Interior with civilians, to show that Romania was espousing Western democratic practices.

A further reshuffle in August was motivated more by domestic party political considerations. It brought two PRNU politicians, Adrian Turicu and Valeriu Tabără, into the government as Ministers of, respectively, Telecommunications and Agriculture. The PRNU had extracted an undertaking from the PSDR in February that its members would be offered cabinet posts. That was the price for the PRNU's continued support for Mr Văcăroiu's minority government of PSDR ministers (predominantly ex-communist officials) and independent technocrats. However, concern that bringing the ultra-nationalist PRNU into government would damage his country's image abroad prompted the Prime Minister to delay the implementation of the accord until the late summer. There were also suggestions that he felt that the PRNU had been weakened by its close links with the dubious banking practices of the Caritas company, which collapsed in May.

Even after the formation of the coalition, the government remained dependent on the continued backing of two other parliamentary groups, namely the right-wing Greater Romania Party and the neo-communist Socialist Labour Party. Thanks to their support, it had survived a vote of no-confidence in June which the opposition Democratic Convention of Romania (DCR) had proposed over the government's failure to tackle economic mismanagement and corruption. Another no-confidence motion—the sixth against the government in two years—was defeated in December. Earlier in the year, the opposition had also launched an unprecedented move to impeach President Ion Iliescu, on the grounds that he had violated the independence of the judiciary. This followed his advice to officials in one area to ignore a local court ruling on the restitution of property until parliament had passed the relevant legislation. Parliament defeated the impeachment move in July, after the Constitutional Court had already ruled that there were no grounds for such proceedings.

The failure of the opposition's repeated challenges to the government reflected its own internal divisions. The 18-party DCR remained a broad umbrella organization lacking internal coherence. Yet the opposition's attempts to topple those in the executive were not taking place in a political vacuum. Several opinion polls confirmed the growing unpopularity of President Iliescu and Prime Minister Văcăriou, each of them receiving the approval of only a little over a quarter of respondents.

The slide in the government's popularity came in spite of marked improvement in some economic indicators. The budget deficit was curbed, the leu gained in strength and, most importantly for ordinary Romanians, the annual rate of inflation was reduced from close to 300 per cent at the end of 1993 to around 75 per cent a year later. Success in the battle against inflation was helped by a tighter monetary policy, new taxes and greater restraint on government spending. These policies had been demanded by the IMF, which had also called for a more liberal foreign exchange system along the lines of the one introduced in April. In return, the IMF began to disburse its promised US$720 million support for Romania's reform and stabilization programme.

Greater financial discipline pleased the IMF, but—with the exception of lower inflation—the government's achievements had little direct impact on most people's everyday lives. Romanians' living standards remained among the lowest in Europe, some 20 per cent of the population being classified as living in extreme poverty. In spite of a bumper 1994 grain harvest of 19 million tonnes (about 25 per cent up on the previous year), some 60 per cent of the average family budget still went on food. The average monthly pay of 170,000 lei (about US$95 at the end-year exchange rate) was barely enough to purchase four pairs of shoes. Although social and industrial unrest remained at a level well below what was seen in the early 1990s, there were several rounds of protest demonstrations and strikes during the year.

In spite of some other economic reforms, there was little progress in Romania on privatization—regarded as one of the benchmarks of change in ex-communist Europe. The State Ownership Fund sold off around 1,000 mostly small companies, less than half the projected number due for privatization in 1994. As a result, Romania continued to trail behind most other ex-communist countries in the pace of privatization and was nowhere near the target of having 50 per cent of the economy in private hands by end-1994 as set by Mircea Coşea, the Minister of Economic Reform.

Relations between the authorities and the ethnic Hungarian minority came under increased strain on several occasions. In the early summer thousands of Hungarian protesters surrounded a statue in Cluj (Transylvania) of King Mathias—the fifteenth-century ruler who was a symbol of Hungary's past glory—in a successful bid to prevent its removal to make way for an archaeological excavation. The row over the statue coincided with the passage through the Chamber of Deputies of a bill which curbed the prospects for Hungarian-language education, particularly at university level. The Hungarian Democratic Union of Romania collected half a million signatures in support of its demand for more widespread use of Hungarian in education and other language concessions. Romanian leaders rejected these appeals. Instead, in November a new law was passed with provision for up to three years' imprisonment for persons found guilty of flying the flag or singing the national anthem of another state.

In spite of these developments, the traditionally poor state of Hungarian-Romanian relations did not worsen in 1994, mainly because Hungary's new government headed by the (ex-communist) Socialists adopted a less confrontational style than its more nationalist predecessor (see III.1.iii). In September Teodor Melescanu became the first Romanian Foreign Minister since the 1989 revolution to visit Hungary. But negotiations on a new bilateral treaty made little progress. Hungary continued to insist that it would not sign the document and give further guarantees of its acceptance of current inter-state borders unless Romania agreed to include in the wording the protection of national minority rights as stipulated in international covenants.

Another treaty, with Russia, was held up by Romanian demands that it should include a reference to 'overcoming the consequences' of the Molotov-Ribbentrop Pact of 1939—a wording suggesting that Romania had a right to recover Bessarabia and Northern Bukovina (annexed by the USSR in 1940 and now in independent Moldova and Ukraine respectively). Indeed, Romanian hopes for eventual union with mostly Romanian-inhabited Moldova suffered a series of setbacks in the first half of the year (see also III.2.i). Moldova's pro-independence forces won a convincing election victory over the movement favouring unification with Romania, after which Moldova joined the Russian-led Commonwealth of Independent States (CIS) and its new parliament voted to define the country's language as 'Moldovan' rather than Romanian. These events prompted Romanian opposition figures and the media to accuse Moldova's leaders of committing 'treason'. Government officials adopted a more restrained tone, but politicians of all hues reiterated that these developments would not alter Bucharest's long-term aim of reunification with Moldova.

Romania managed to maintain good relations with all the Balkan states, while expressing uneasiness about Moscow's renewed assertiveness in the region. The Romanian role as a stabilizing factor—and as a potential mediator among several Balkan states—strengthened the trend among Western countries to upgrade their relations with Bucharest after their caution in the early 1990s, when they had shown concern about Romania's human rights record. During the year, President Iliescu paid visits to Paris, Washington and London. On his visit to France in April, he received assurances that the European Union would treat Romania in the same way as other former communist countries further to the north. In September the United States renewed for another year the most-favoured-nation trading status it had restored to Romania in 1993.

The most prestigious event in the Romanian political calendar came in April when Bucharest played host to the Crans-Montana Forum. This conference, attended by six Presidents and a dozen Prime Ministers or their deputies, helped to improve Romania's international standing by displaying once again Romania's tradition of bringing adversaries together, whether from the Middle East or the Balkans.

v. BULGARIA

CAPITAL: Sofia   AREA: 110,000 sq km   POPULATION: 8,470,000 ('92)
OFFICIAL LANGUAGE: Bulgarian   POLITICAL SYSTEM: parliamentary democracy
HEAD OF STATE: President Zhelyu Zhelev (since Aug '90)
RULING PARTY: Bulgarian Socialist Party (BSP) won Dec '94 elections
PRINCIPAL MINISTERS: (non-party caretaker government at end-'94) Reneta Indzhova
   (Prime Minister), Ivaylo Trifonov (Deputy Prime Minister), Nikola Vasilev
   (Deputy Prime Minister), Hristina Vucheva (Deputy Prime Minister, finance),
   Ivan Stanchov (foreign affairs), Boyko Noev (defence), Chavdar Chervenkov
   (interior), Teodor Chipov (justice)
CURRENCY: lev (end-'94 £1=L103.22, US$1=L65.98)
GNP PER CAPITA: US$1,330 ('92)
MAIN EXPORT EARNERS: minerals & chemicals, agricultural produce, machinery,
   tourism

THE emphatic victory of the (ex-communist) Bulgarian Socialist Party (BSP) in a general election on 18 December offered the prospect of the first stable government since the end of one-party dictatorship in 1990. The BSP won 43.5 per cent of vote in a respectable turnout of 75 per cent of the electorate. Translated into seats, this gave the ex-communists 125 in the 240-member National Assembly, or a majority of ten over four opposition parties. The BSP's success owed much to its targeting of economic discontent, but there was also an element of personal triumph for the 35-year-old party leader, Zhan Videnov, who at the year's end seemed likely to be named Prime Minister of a one-party Socialist government early in 1995.

Although its vote declined to just over 23 per cent, the Union of Democratic Forces (UDF) consolidated its place as the main opposition grouping, winning 69 seats. The third party in the outgoing parliament, the (ethnic Turkish) Movement for Rights and Freedoms (MRF) under Ahmed Dogan, similarly lost a third of its support and dropped to 15 seats but seemed relieved to have beaten off two breakaway pro-Muslim parties. The result deprived the MRF of its role as the political 'kingmaker', following its crucial parliamentary backing for both the 1991–92 UDF government and the successor 'national responsibility' cabinet formed in December 1992 (see AR 1992, p. 121). The election returned two new groups to parliament: the People's Union (allying the Agrarian Union of Anastasia Moser with the ex-UDF Democratic Party of Stefan Savov) and the Bulgarian Business Bloc of George Ganchev, which garnered a sizeable protest vote.

Both newcomers made overtures to the UDF, which underwent a post-election change of leadership on 29 December when ex-Finance Minister Ivan Kostov replaced Filip Dimitrov, the former Prime Minister. In pre-election rifts in the UDF, Mr Savov's Democratic Party had broken away in the summer and the Radical Democrats had threatened to follow. The divisions were triggered by a centralization of decision-making in the UDF national coordinating council at the expense of constituent organizations. The UDF had also suffered from having spent the first half of the year as an uninfluential opposition, moving its fifth, sixth and seventh no-confidence motions against the non-party government of Professor Lyuben Berov. It had boycotted the National Assembly after 31 May.

Despite reshuffling his cabinet and producing a new three-month programme in May, Mr Berov was burdened by illness and achieved little. He underwent heart by-pass surgery in March and contracted hepatitis in April. The root of his government's weakness was its lack of committed parliamentary support and its dependence on behind-the-scenes dealing with the BSP. President Zhelyu Zhelev officially withdrew his support on 2 April and the Deputy Prime Minister and Trade Minister, Valentin Karabashev, resigned on 28 April. On 18 May the National Assembly rejected a list of ministerial changes, forcing Mr Berov to wait for ten days to win a majority for his economic rescue package.

Informed opinion suggested that Mr Berov genuinely wanted reforms but was blocked by ministerial backers of the so-called Group of Thirteen (G-13), an informal association of private business enterprises derived from the former communist bureaucracy. It was said that the G-13 had a vested interest in letting central authority erode and in blocking fullscale privatization. Another sign of government weakness was that taxes went uncollected. Inflation reached an annual rate of 121.9 per cent, after speculation undermined the value of the lev in the spring. Industrial production revived in some sectors, but insufficiently to restart GDP growth, so that unemployment rose to almost 20 per cent. By the end of Mr Berov's premiership, according to government statistics, just 38 per cent of land was in private hands. So unsuccessful was the agricultural sector that the BSP proposed reviving state-led cooperatives. Kiril Tsochev was named Deputy Premier and Trade Minister on 15 June; but on 2 September Mr Berov resigned. The BSP and the UDF agreed that there should be an early election and successfully opposed efforts by the President to sponsor a new 'cabinet of experts' under former the Defence Minister, Dimitur Ludzhev.

The many government failures eroded public morale, especially among the young. Living standards tumbled, some shortages reappeared and a national health crisis worsened; but the protests were few. The introduction of value-added tax in April triggered isolated strikes and about 800,000 workers backed a warning stoppage called by the CITUB trade union confederation on 4 May. In December a chronic water shortage and the first-ever complete shutdown of the Kozloduy nuclear power plant underlined the decay of the economic infrastructure. A media obsession was the growth of crime—from trivial domestic violence to the emergence of a mafia in the economy and the administration. After a mysterious shoot-out between rival corrupt factions within the Sofia police in January, President Zhelev called publicly for the restoration of the death penalty. However, on 1 August he controversially pardoned the last communist Prime Minister, Georgi Atanasov, who had been gaoled for embezzlement in 1992 (see AR 1992, p. 121).

Combating the mafia was the declared priority of the caretaker Premier, Reneta Indzhova, whom Dr Zhelev appointed on 18 October to oversee the general election. Mrs Indzhova was a former head of the privatization agency, which had announced a Czech-style voucher scheme on 28 June but had managed to sell off only 35 of the country's 3,000 large and medium-sized industrial enterprises by the end of 1994. The caretaker government clamped down on semi-legal security firms—the so-called 'wrestlers'—many of which operated protection rackets. Mrs Indzhova also dismissed about 4,000 allegedly corrupt state officials, coming under attack from the BSP as a result.

Mr Berov's government concluded deals with the Paris and London Clubs of Western banks to reschedule Bulgarian debts, amounting to $9,600 million. The agreements followed a new stand-by credit from the IMF, as well as a systemic transformation facility and a third credit for debt-rescheduling. Bulgarian politicians complained about the economic burden of the UN embargo on Federal Yugoslavia (see III.1.vi) and the government sought to develop close relations with the new Macedonian republic. However, a visit to Sofia by President Kiro Gligorov in February was marred by the re-emergence of historic disputes over the linguistic and national identity of Macedonia.

vi. STATES EMERGING FROM THE FORMER YUGOSLAV FEDERATION

Bosnia–Hercegovina

CAPITAL: Sarajevo AREA: 51,129 sq km POPULATION: 4,383,000 ('92)
OFFICIAL LANGUAGE: Serbo-Croat POLITICAL SYSTEM: republic, divided by civil war
RULING PARTY: Party of Democratic Action
HEADS OF STATE & GOVERNMENT: President Alija Izetbegović (Bosnia-Hercegovina),
President Krešimir Zubak (Federation of Bosnia-Hercegovina)
CURRENCY: dinar
GNP PER CAPITA: US$3,590 ('90 est.)

Croatia

CAPITAL: Zagreb AREA: 56,538 sq km POPULATION: 4,789,000 ('92)
OFFICIAL LANGUAGE: Croatian POLITICAL SYSTEM: republic
RULING PARTY: Croatian Democratic Union
HEAD OF STATE & GOVERNMENT: President Franjo Tudjman
CURRENCY: kuna (end-'94 £1=K8.81, US$1=K5.63)
GNP PER CAPITA: US$7,500 ('92 est.)

Macedonia

CAPITAL: Skopje AREA: 25,713 sq km POPULATION: 1,936,877 ('94)
OFFICIAL LANGUAGE: Macedonian POLITICAL SYSTEM: republic
RULING PARTY: Alliance for Macedonia
HEAD OF STATE & GOVERNMENT: President Kiro Gligorov
CURRENCY: denar
GNP PER CAPITA: US$3,330 ('90 est.)

Slovenia

CAPITAL: Ljubljana AREA: 20,251 sq km POPULATION: 2,000,000 ('92)
OFFICIAL LANGUAGE: Slovene POLITICAL SYSTEM: republic
RULING PARTY: Liberal Democracy of Slovenia heads coalition
HEAD OF STATE & GOVERNMENT: President Milan Kučan
CURRENCY: tolar (end-'94 £1=T200.35, US$1=T128.06)
GNP PER CAPITA: US$6,540 ('92)

Federal Republic of Yugoslavia (FRY)

CONSTITUENTS: Montenegro (13,812 sq km), Serbia (88,316 sq km)
CAPITAL: Belgrade AREA: 102,128 sq km POPULATION: 10,597,000 ('92)
OFFICIAL LANGUAGE: Serbo-Croat
POLITICAL SYSTEM: federation of republics
RULING PARTIES: Socialist Party of Serbia heads coalition in Serbia, Democratic Party
of Socialists of Montenegro in Montenegro
HEAD OF STATE & GOVERNMENT: President Zoran Lilić
LEADERS OF CONSTITUENT REPUBLICS: President Slobodan Milošević (Serbia) &
President Momir Bulatović (Montenegro)
CURRENCY: new dinar

BOSNIA-HERCEGOVINA. Political developments in Bosnia-Hercegovina were dominated by the problems of maintaining internal solidarity within the warring sides. Cooperation between Croat and Presidential/Muslim forces gradually strengthened through the year, largely as the result of sustained pressure from the major powers. Disagreements between the Bosnian Serb leadership and the Federal Republic of Yugoslavia, over the appropriate response to a further internationally-negotiated plan for the region, tested the solidarity of Serb forces.

A crucial development in the cementing of a Croat/Muslim alliance came on 23 February, when a general ceasefire between the two sides was negotiated in Zagreb. A significant pre-condition of this was the resignation on 8 February of Mate Boban, the hardline leader of the Croat secessionist 'republic of Herceg-Bosna' (see AR 1992, p. 124). Talks began on 26 February in Washington directed towards the elaboration of a wider constitutional framework to unite the two sides. The conclusion of negotiations in March produced a proposal for the territory controlled by parties to the agreement to be divided into eight 'cantons': four with Muslim majorities, two with Croat majorities and two (Mostar and Travnik) with no overall majority. The new state, designated the Bosnian Federation of Muslims and Croats, was headed by a Croat President (Krešimir Zubak) with a Muslim Prime Minister (Haris Silajdžić), who ratified the final agreement in Geneva on 14 May. President Franjo Tudjman of Croatia paid a visit to Sarajevo on 14 June, emphasizing his support for the venture.

Doubts about the longer-term stability of the new federation hinged upon the lack of progress in developing joint institutions, including a unified military command, and the prevailing lack of clarity over the territory to be included within it. One of the most serious difficulties obstructing cooperation between the two sides was removed when the city of Mostar was placed under European Union (EU) administration on 23 July. Fighting between Croats and Muslims continued sporadically in several locations in central Bosnia to the end of September, particularly where Croat extremist forces refused to abandon their commitment to an independent 'Herceg-Bosna'. Reports of sniping in the Mostar region persisted into October.

Another general ceasefire was signed for Bosnia-Hercegovina on 8 June, although this collapsed after less than a month, on the opening of a major Muslim/Croat offensive against the Bosnian Serbs. The political hopes of the Muslim/Croat forces were raised by a series of military successes, especially in central Bosnia, which were interpreted as meaning that delay in reaching a settlement would place them in a more advantageous negotiating position. Evidence accumulated during the summer of the effectiveness of Bosnian evasion of the arms embargo.

Serious fighting broke out in late July in the Bihać region of north-western Bosnia, between presidential forces and dissident Muslim forces loyal to the local political magnate, Fihret Abdić, who was unwilling to accept the new federation. The Bihać pocket fell to the Bosnian army in August, precipitating a serious refugee problem when supporters of Mr Abdić tried to flee into the neighbouring Serbian 'Krajina republic'. During October significant territorial gains were made by the Bosnian army east of Bihać, at the expense of the Bosnian Serbs. During November, however, the position was dramatically reversed, when delay in the onset of winter, poor coordination between Muslim and Croat forces and the intervention of a well-armed Serb force from the Krajina compelled the Bosnian army to withdraw towards Bihać. The position subsequently stabilized as a result of threatened international intervention in support of the UN-designated 'safe area' of Bihać and the effective support of Croatian forces.

CROATIA. The war as it affected Croatia appeared to have been placed into cold storage when, on 19 January, a joint declaration was issued by Croatian and Yugoslav representatives inaugurating a 'process of normalization'. Expectations of possible moves towards the easing of relations between the Croatian government and the separatist Serb enclaves known as the 'republic of Serbian Krajina' (RSK) were also raised by the victory of the Socialist Party of Serbia (SPS), led by Milan Martić, in elections to the RSK assembly (the SPS in the Krajina being closely associated with its Serbian counterpart). Following protracted diplomacy by Russian special envoy Vitaly Churkin, a ceasefire came into effect on 4 April, involving the creation of a demilitarized buffer zone between the two sides. However, these conciliatory moves did not satisfy the more liberal wing of President Tudjman's Croatian Democratic Union (CDU), which split during April, largely over the conduct of the war in Bosnia-Hercegovina. The speakers of the two houses of the Assembly, Stipe Mesić and Josip Manolić, left to set up their own Croatian Independent Democrats (CID). The resulting bitter disagreements over the management of Assembly business resulted in an opposition boycott lasting until mid-September. President Tudjman's need to retain the support of the moderate centre of his party was evident in his disciplining of some extreme right-wing members, especially the Osijek party boss, Branimir Glavaš. Even so, the secession of the CID left the CDU with a more clearly articulated nationalistic stance.

President Tudjman's declared willingness to negotiate with the Krajina Serbs aroused considerable anger on the part of refugees from the region, who on 1 July began a blockade of the delivery of supplies by the UN Protection Force in Former Yugoslavia (UNPROFOR). This precipitated a period of ambiguity in Croatian goverment dealings with the Krajina Serbs. On the one hand, negotiations were concluded re-establishing some service links, including (on 2 December) the reopening of a stretch of the formerly severed main road through Sector West. On the other hand, calls were issued with growing insistence for more decisive action by the UN to return these areas to Croatian control, under threat of suspension of the UN mandate. The informal blockade was finally lifted on 1 August.

On 23 September the lower house of the Sabor (Croatian parliament) voted to terminate the existing UNPROFOR mandate, setting strong terms for its renewal. President Tudjman presented these to the UN

General Assembly on 28 September. In spite of widespread speculation that the Zagreb government's position was a tactical bluff, UNPROFOR was asked to begin planning its withdrawal following the expiry of its current mandate on 20 January 1995.

Croatia introduced a new currency called the kuna on 30 May. Although the designation actually harked back to a medieval unit of exchange, it was pointed out by parties advocating a less strident nationalism that the wartime fascist Croatian state had adopted the same name for its currency. A significant feature of the Croatian economic scene in 1994 was an intensification of trade links with Iran. On the home front, the forcible conscription on 5 January of Viktor Ivančić, chief editor of the satirical weekly *Feral Tribune*, sharpened controversy over allegations of growing state censorship of the communications media in Croatia. Pope John Paul II visited Zagreb on 10–11 September, bringing a message of reconciliation and forgiveness.

FEDERAL REPUBLIC OF YUGOSLAVIA. Following the elections to the Serbian National Assembly in December 1993 (see AR 1993, p. 129), conflict persisted over the formation of a new government. On 22 February Mirko Marjanović was appointed as Prime Minister, leading a coalition government composed of the Socialist Party of Serbia (SPS) and New Democracy (ND), the latter deserting the opposition DEPOS bloc which it had hitherto supported. Serbian politics throughout the year were dominated by divisions over President Milošević's accommodationist stance towards an internationally-brokered settlement in Bosnia, in particular over his decision to impose economic sanctions on the Bosnian Serbs, in return for the easing of UN sanctions against the Yugoslav federation. In the economic sphere, a new dinar was launched on 24 January, its value being initially pegged to the Deutschmark. The fruit of planning by former World Bank economist Dragoslav Avramović (current president of the Yugoslav National Bank), the currency reform brought to an end two years of hyper-inflation (see AR 1993, p. 130).

Serbian moves to integrate the mainly ethnic Albanian province of Kosovo into the Serbian state continued throughout the year. On 23 February the authorities enforced the closure of the Academy of Sciences of the former autonomous province. A government-sponsored programme of resettlement of Serbs in the region, together with constant and heavy pressure by the police and military, made for constant tension between the two communities. The Trepča mines remained closed throughout the year; and largely because of the strength of the private sector, economic leverage remained in Albanian hands. Informal and secret talks between representatives of the Serbian government and the Democratic League of Kosovo (DLK) were reported to have taken place in May, brokered by the more accommodationist Montenegrins. Trials in September of ethnic Albanians and of Muslims from the Sandžak region of south-western Serbia, on charges of secessionist activity, underlined the sensitivity of inter-ethnic relations.

Despite the narrowness of his parliamentary majority, President Milošević demonstrated his effective control over Serbian politics on 28 April by abolishing the paramilitary Chetnik organization, associated with Vojislav Šešelj's ultra-nationalist Serbian Radical Party (SRP). Following violent exchanges in the Assembly in May, Mr Šešelj was sentenced to a brief term of imprisonment in September, this development being followed by a split in the SRP. On 15 September a reconstructed federal cabinet was announced, with the aim of enhancing government efficiency.

MACEDONIA. The deteriorating relations between Macedonia and its southern neighbour took a turn for the worse on 16 February when the Greek Prime Minister, Andreas Papandreou, announced further trade sanctions, in an attempt to prevent the use of the name 'Macedonia' by the former Yugoslav republic (see also II.3.v). The sanctions were a response to the recognition of the republic by both Russia and the USA, which was accompanied by the granting of loans totalling some $97 million, intended to support reform and stabilization, by the IMF and the World Bank. The Greek action was condemned as being contrary to EU law by the Brussels Commission. However, in an interim ruling on 29 June, the European Court of Justice declined to grant the Commission's application for an injunction ordering Greece to lift the sanctions (see also XI.3; XV.1.ii).

The internal politics of Macedonia continued to be preoccupied with relations between Slav Macedonians and the Albanian minority in the west of the republic. At its congress on 12–13 February, the Party of Democratic Prosperity (PDP)—the main Albanian formation—split into accommodationist and radical wings. The split came hard on the heels of the arrest of ten Albanians (including a deputy minister) on charges of organizing armed insurrection (see AR 1993, p. 128) and served to focus attention on the growing Albanian radical voice. Following the conviction of the accused on 10 June, the PDP (hitherto a member of the governing coalition) initiated a parliamentary boycott.

Controversy also surrounded the holding of a new census, which was partly intended to answer the accusation that the 1991 census had underestimated significantly the size of ethnic minorities in the republic. The count, repeatedly threatened by talk of an Albanian boycott, eventually took place between 21 June and 10 July and found that 23 per cent of the population were of Albanian ethnicity. This figure, although higher than that for 1991 (21 per cent), still met with the charge that it underestimated Albanian numbers by excluding recent migrants from Kosovo. Tension between Macedonia and Serbia remained high throughout the year, the border between them continuing to be patrolled by UN observers (see AR 1993, p. 128). However, the situation eased somewhat in July when Serb units withdrew from positions near Kriva Palanka which they had taken up the previous month.

New elections for both the presidency and the Macedonian Assembly took place on 14 and 30 October, attended by many accusations of unfair practices, as a result of which balloting was repeated in 11 constituencies. President Kiro Gligorov was returned to power in the first round of voting and a new government was formed by Branko Crvenkovski, leading a coalition of centre-left groups called the Alliance for Macedonia (AM) which had fought the elections on a platform of economic reform. The strongly nationalist Internal Macedonian Revolutionary Organization (IMRO) was virtually eliminated as an electoral force, while radical Albanian groups also fared poorly. Although strong enough to rule without partners, the AM renewed its coalition with accommodationist Albanian groups.

SLOVENIA. In January and February talks took place at the level of Prime Ministers in an attempt to resolve the longstanding border dispute between Slovenia and Croatia, concerning four villages in the Istrian region. In the absence of agreement, the National Assembly resolved on 3 October to confirm their Slovene identity, this action being followed a week later by the delivery of a formal Croatian note of protest. The failure to resolve the problem threatened to have consequences for the subsequent demarcation of contested territorial waters by the two countries.

The loose alliance of Liberal Democrats, Democrats, Greens and Socialists, forming the backbone of the governing coalition, was replaced on 12 March by a formal merger creating Liberal Democracy of Slovenia, a centre party with a third of the seats in the Assembly. It faced its first test when Defence Minister Janez Janša was dismissed from his post on 28 March following allegations of his responsibility for misuse of power by the military police. The withdrawal of Mr Jaňsa's Social Democrats precipitated a short-lived crisis within the coalition. The Christian Democrats (CD) continued their support for Premier Drnovšek's leadership until 16 September, when their leader and Foreign Minister, Lojze Peterle, resigned over the issue of the balance of ministerial appointments.

Despite a meeting on 16 June between Mr Drnovsek and his Italian counterpart, Silvio Berlusconi, no progress was made in the discussions over Italy's claims for compensation for ethnic Italians diplaced from Slovenia after 1945. Consequently, Italy continued to block Slovene attempts to secure closer integration with the EU.

INTERNATIONAL MEDIATION. International efforts to bring the disintegration process in former Yugoslavia to a peaceful conclusion were plagued by acute differences between the various interested countries and international organizations over the need for external military intervention, and the form which that might take. The French position was signalled on 3 January in a statement by Defence Minister François Léotard urging US military intervention. At the Brussels meeting of NATO leaders on 10–11 January, the principles governing the use of air strikes in support of UN ground troops, or to ensure the viability of declared 'safe areas' (see AR 1993, p. 125), were agreed. However, a statement the following day by the UK Prime Minister, John Major, and the terms of a motion passed in the Russian Duma on 21 January indicated the strength of reservations about such interventions. On relinquishing his command as head of UN forces in Bosnia on 24 January, General François Briquemont (France) remarked that there was little point in continuing an impossible mission.

Largely in response to a mortar attack on a Sarajevo market place on 5 February, killing 68 people and injuring 167, pressure mounted for effective international action. NATO announced an exclusion zone for heavy weapons around Sarajevo, an ultimatum for compliance being issued for 9 February. In the event, the withdrawal of Serb heavy weapons did not begin until 17 February, after a unilateral Russian diplomatic initiative and the deployment of Russian troops in the exclusion zone. By the end of February the UN forces had begun to take a more 'robust' stance, the new UN commander in Bosnia, Lieutenant-General Sir Michael Rose (UK), authorizing a policy of higher profile military escorts for aid convoys. On 28 February four Serb fighter aircraft were shot down near Banja Luka by NATO aircraft, enforcing for the first time the 'no-fly' zone over Bosnia (see AR 1992, p. 131).

Intervention from the air by NATO forces also played a significant role in stemming an assault by Bosnian Serb forces on the 'safe haven' of Goražde, attempting to secure a major road link. The engagement began in late March, but by 22 April the town had effectively fallen under Serb control. NATO aircraft bombed Serb ground positions on 10 and 11 April to little effect. It was only after a further ultimatum issued by NATO on 22 April that UN special envoy Yasushi Akashi was able to negotiate a ceasefire with Bosnian Serb military leaders. A Serb withdrawal began on 24 April, after the Russian Foreign Minister, Andrei Kozyrev, had indicated that his government would not oppose the use of force by NATO.

In response to the situation in Goražde, on 19 April the Russian President, Boris Yeltsin, issued an appeal for an international summit meeting. This resulted, on 26 April, in the setting up of a Contact Group, consisting of Britain, France, Russia and the USA, with the intention of working towards a full cessation of hostilities in Bosnia-Hercegovina. The same day the UN Security Council voted for the dispatch of an additional 6,500 troops to support its activities in the region. During March the first fruits of the work of the Contact Group emerged in the form of the plan for a Bosnian Federation of Muslims and Croats (see above).

The development of coordinated action in relation to Bosnia was rendered difficult, however, by growing pressure within the USA for the unilateral lifting of the arms embargo. On 11 May the US Senate voted in favour of breeching the embargo (although a related congressional vote on the military budget on 1 July was not carried). The US government also dissented from the formula agreed at a meeting of Foreign Ministers in Geneva on 13 May, when it had been proposed that 51 per cent of Bosnia-Hercegovina should be awarded to the new Muslim–Croat Federation. Reacting to the possibility of unilateral action by the USA, in the belief that this would signal an end to any Serb cooperation with international organizations in Bosnia, the French Foreign Minister, Alain Juppé, indicated that it might be necessary to withdraw the French contingent (currently 6,800 troops) from UN service. A British Foreign Office minister, Douglas Hogg, hinted on 19 May that the withdrawal of British forces might also be considered.

In spite of having signed the agreement creating a new federation, Muslims and Croats were reluctant to support any action which could be interpreted as accepting the permanent division of Bosnia and as *de facto* recognition of the Serbian republic. On the part of the Serbs, international efforts to mediate met with extreme reluctance to concede any land over which they had effective control. For these reasons, the process of international mediation remained extremely difficult and any gains tentative.

On 6 July the Contact Group presented a list of proposals, including a map, which awarded 51 per cent of Bosnian territory to the Muslim–Croat Federation and attempted to avoid earlier deadlocks by placing several key disputed towns under UN or EU protection/administration. A period of intense diplomatic activity ensued, aimed at persuading the various parties to accept the proposals. The Assembly of Bosnia-Hercegovina, convened in special session on 18 July, accepted the plan; but the following day the Bosnian Serb assembly's call for further talks was construed as rejection. On the other hand, the Belgrade government threw in its lot with the Contact Group plan, announcing in August that it would enforce international economic and military sanctions against the Serbian republic in Bosnia. After some hesitation, Belgrade on 15 September agreed to the deployment of international monitors on the Yugoslav–Bosnian border. Consequently, on 24 September the UN Security Council approved a selective and temporary suspension of the sanctions hitherto imposed upon Yugoslavia.

The UN-brokered ceasefire in the Bihać area collapsed on 25 November, resulting in widespread fear of a reversion to all-out war throughout Bosnia-Hercegovina. At the same time, evidence began to accumulate that the Bosnian Serbs were effectively evading some important elements of the UN embargo. In an effort to avert the danger of renewed warfare, former US President Jimmy Carter visited the area the following month at the invitation of the Bosnian Serb leader, Radovan Karadžić, with the result that on 20 December an agreed plan was announced for a general ceasefire. In spite of several local outbreaks of fighting, this came into effect on 23 December and held until the year's end.

The inclusion of Turkish troops among UN forces in Bosnia-Hercegovina after 2 July was widely interpreted as an event of symbolic significance. They were the first Turkish armed forces to serve there since the establishment of the Austro-Hungarian protectorate in 1878 and the first in former Yugoslav territory since 1913.

vii.   ALBANIA

CAPITAL: Tirana   AREA: 29,000 sq km   POPULATION: 3,400,000 ('92)
OFFICIAL LANGUAGE: Albanian   POLITICAL SYSTEM: parliamentary democracy
HEAD OF STATE: President Sali Berisha (since April '92)
RULING PARTIES: coalition of Democratic (DP), Republican (RP) and Social
  Democratic (SDP) parties
PRINCIPAL MINISTERS: Aleksander Meksi (DP/Prime Minister), Dashimir Shehu
  (DP/Deputy Prime Minister, tourism), Dylber Vrioni (Deputy Prime Minister,
  finance), Bashkim Kopliku (DP/Deputy Prime Minister, economic reform),
  Vullnet Ademi (SDP/cabinet general secretary), Alfred Sarreqi (DP/foreign
  affairs), Safet Xhulali (DP/defence), Agron Musaraj (DP/interior), Kudred Cela
  (non-party/justice)
CURRENCY: lek (end-'94 £1=AL157.12, US$1=AL100.43)
GNP PER CAPITA: US$300 ('92 est.)
MAIN EXPORT EARNERS: crude oil, minerals, agricultural products

FOR much of 1994 President Sali Berisha seemed determined to continue the trend towards authoritarianism which had become apparent in 1993. In February the editor of the socialist publication Koha Jone (Our Way) was sentenced under the old penal code for allegedly disclosing defence secrets. The accused was later released and fled abroad. In August Koha Jone suspended publication for a few days following new financial regulations which, said opponents of the government, were contrived to silence criticism because, although newspapers were supposed to meet all their costs, the state was not prevented from subsidizing any publication that it chose to favour.

A further attack upon the government's opponents came in April when charges were finally laid against the former Communist Party leader, Ramiz Alia, and nine of his erstwhile colleagues who had been detained since August 1993. The charges included the misappropriation of state funds and the illegal execution of 22 people in 1951. In July Mr Alia was sentenced to nine years and the others were condemned to lesser terms. In the following month the Supreme Court upheld the 12-year sentence previously passed on Fatos Nano, the former leader of the (ex-communist) Socialist Party of Albania (SPA), who had been arrested in July 1993 (see AR 1993, pp. 133-4)

There were also confrontations with victims of the former communist dictatorship. In May, police in the northern town of Kukes clashed with farmers demanding compensation for the loss of homes inundated during the construction of a hydro-electric scheme in the 1970s. The confrontation escalated when over 150 protesters occupied the town hall, where they remained for over a week; in December compensation had still not been forthcoming and the protesters went on hunger strike. The hunger strike was also the main means of protest used by former political prisoners. There was a nationwide demand from these victims of communist dictatorship for compensation, but the sums suggested were far beyond anything the government could afford. The police acted with considerable vigour against the hunger-strikers, 18 of whom were arrested on 14 August for refusing to comply with a court order to suspend their protest.

Local elections in five areas in June gave the ruling Democratic Party (DP) some encouragement, in that it secured 47 per cent of the vote as against 32.7 per cent for the SPA. The latter, however, insisted that there had been considerable malpractice and continued to demand a general election.

If the DP had been encouraged by the outcome of the local elections, it was to suffer a stunning defeat in the major domestic political issue of 1994. On 3 October President Berisha issued a decree for a referendum to endorse a new constitution. In a vigorous and intensely personal campaign, he argued that a new constitution was necessary to break with the communist past, to ease Albania's path towards closer association with the rest of Europe and to attract inward investment. His opponents, and some of the DP's partners in the ruling coalition, feared that the new constitution would give the President too much power. Held on 6 November, the referendum registered a 54 per cent vote against the new constitution. A month later, in an effort to regain some of his lost prestige, President Berisha carried out a major governmental reshuffle (and Mr Alia's prison sentence was reduced from nine to six years), but the opposition was not mollified and continued to press for a general election.

On the economic front, the year brought some advances. The government reached an agreement with the most important trade union organizations on a new policy for wage and price controls. From January 1995 24 items were to be subjected to regulation, and government and trade union representatives were to meet every six months thereafter to fix wage and pension levels in the light of regulated price movements. There were also successes in the search for foreign loans. In January a Saudi Arabian concern was reported to be willing to invest $100 million in Albania; in September the World Bank promised a loan of $10 million to fund irrigation projects; in November the European Bank for Reconstruction and Development granted $16 million to finance improvements in the electricity grid; and in December Greece at last lifted its veto on a $43 million European Union (EU) credit to ease Albania's trade deficit.

The Greek veto had been imposed because of the serious deterioration in Albano-Greek relations which began in April and which became a serious threat to Balkan stability (see also II.3.v). In April two Albanian soldiers were killed during a raid on an army training camp. As a result of the raid, five ethnic Greek Albanian citizens, all of them members of the Greek minority organization Omonia, were charged with espionage, illegal possession of weapons and fomenting separatism amongst the Greek minority in southern Albania. The trial began in August and ended in September with guilty verdicts and sentences of between six and eight years in prison. The Greek government recalled its ambassador to Tirana, closed its consulate in Gjirokaster, sealed its borders against entry from Albania and, between September and December, expelled in the region of 70,000 illegal Albanian immigrants. The crisis was defused by President Berisha's loss of authority after the referendum, and by pressure on both parties from Germany, which then held the EU presidency. In November the sentences on the 'Tirana Five' were reduced and on 24 December one of them was released.

The crisis in relations with Greece overshadowed Albania's other external problems. The Kosovo issue continued to plague relations with rump Yugoslavia (Serbia and Montenegro), especially after the nomination in May of a Serbian from Kosovo as ambassador to Tirana. Albania remained committed to UN sanctions against the Belgrade regime, although the authorities seemed powerless to stem the flow off goods, including oil, into Montenegro. Relations with Macedonia, despite cooperation on the proposed Balkan highway from Durres via Tirana to Sofia, Skopje and Istanbul, were complicated by the position of the Albanian minority in Macedonia. In February Albania became a signatory to the NATO Partnership for Peace plan (see XII.2; XIX.1).

Albania endured its worst drought for a century in 1994, as well as a cholera outbreak which claimed over 20 lives.

2. WESTERN CIS REPUBLICS—BALTIC STATES

i. RUSSIA—BELORUSSIA—UKRAINE—MOLDOVA—CAUCASIAN REPUBLICS

Russia

CAPITAL: Moscow   AREA: 17,075,000 sq km   POPULATION: 149,000,000 ('92)
OFFICIAL LANGUAGE: Russian   POLITICAL SYSTEM: democratic republic
RULING PARTIES: Russia's Democratic Choice dominates fluid coalition
HEAD OF STATE & GOVERNMENT: President Boris Yeltsin (since June '91)
PRINCIPAL MINISTERS: Viktor Chernomyrdin (Prime Minister), Andrei Kozyrev (foreign affairs), Gen. Pavel Grachev (defence), Gen. Viktor Yerin (interior), Viktor Panskov (finance), Yuri Kalmykov (justice)
CURRENCY: rouble (end-'94 £1=R5,612.60, US$1=R3,587.47)
GNP PER CAPITA: US$2,510 ('92 est.)

Belorussia (Belarus)

CAPITAL: Minsk   AREA: 208,000 sq km   POPULATION: 10,300,000 ('92)
OFFICIAL LANGUAGE: Belorussian   POLITICAL SYSTEM: democratic republic
HEAD OF STATE & GOVERNMENT: President Alyaksandr Lukashenka (since July '94)
PRINCIPAL MINISTERS: Mikhas Chigir (Prime Minister), Syargey Ling (Deputy Prime Minister, economy), Uladzimir Syanko (foreign affairs), Yuri Zakharenka (interior), Anatol Kastenka (defence), Valyantsin Sukala (justice)
CURRENCY: rubel/rouble (see above)
GNP PER CAPITA: US$2,930 ('92 est.)

Ukraine

CAPITAL: Kiev   AREA: 604,000 sq km   POPULATION: 52,100,000 ('92)
OFFICIAL LANGUAGES: Ukrainian   POLITICAL SYSTEM: democratic republic
HEAD OF STATE & GOVERNMENT: President Leonid Kuchma (since July '94)
PRINCIPAL MINISTERS: Vitali Masol (Prime Minister), Viktor Pynzenyk (First Deputy Prime Minister, economic reform), Valerii Shmarov (Deputy Prime Minister, defence), Hennadii Udovenko (foreign affairs), Volodymyr Radchenko (interior), Roman Shpek (economy), Petro Hermanchuk (finance), Vasyl Onopenko (justice)
CURRENCY: karbovanets (end-'94 £1=K169,916.7, US$1=K104,133.0)
GNP PER CAPITA: US$1,820 ('92 est.)

Moldova (Moldavia)

CAPITAL: Chisinau (Kishinev)   AREA: 34,000 sq km   POPULATION: 4,400,000 ('92)
OFFICIAL LANGUAGES: Moldovan   POLITICAL SYSTEM: democratic republic
HEAD OF STATE & GOVERNMENT: President Mircea Snegur
PRINCIPAL MINISTERS: Andrei Sangheli (Prime Minister), Mihai Popov (foreign affairs), Maj.-Gen. Pavel Creanga (defence), Maj.-Gen. Constantin Antoci (interior), Valeriu Chitan (finance), Vasile Sturza (justice)
CURRENCY: rouble (see above)
GNP PER CAPITA: US$1,300 ('92 est.)

Georgia

CAPITAL: Tbilisi   AREA: 70,000 sq km   POPULATION: 5,500,000 ('92)
OFFICIAL LANGUAGES: Georgian & Russian   POLITICAL SYSTEM: democratic republic
RULING PARTIES: Citizens' Union coordinates fluid coalition
HEAD OF STATE & GOVERNMENT: President Eduard Shevardnadze (since Oct '92)
PRINCIPAL MINISTERS: Otar Patsatsia (Prime Minister), Aleksandr Chikvaidze (foreign affairs), Lt.-Gen. Vardiko Nadibaidze (defence), Shota Kviraia (interior), Tevdore Ninidze (justice), Vladimir Papava (economy), David Iakovidze (finance)
CURRENCY: rouble (see above)
GNP PER CAPITA: US$850 ('92 est.)

Armenia
CAPITAL: Yerevan   AREA: 30,000 sq km   POPULATION: 3,700,000 ('92)
OFFICIAL LANGUAGES: Armenian & Russian   POLITICAL SYSTEM: democratic republic
RULING PARTY: Armenian National Movement
HEAD OF STATE & GOVERNMENT: President Levon Ter-Petrosyan (since Aug '90)
PRINCIPAL MINISTERS: Gagik Harutianian (Vice-President), Hrand Bagratian (Prime
   Minister), Vahan Papazian (foreign affairs), Vanik Siradeghian (interior), Vahe
   Stepanian (justice), Serzhik Sarkissian (defence), Levon Barkhodarian (finance),
   Ashot Yeghiazarian (economy)
CURRENCY: rouble (see above)
GNP PER CAPITA: US$780 ('92 est.)

Azerbaijan
CAPITAL: Baku   AREA: 87,000 sq km   POPULATION: 7,400,000 ('92)
OFFICIAL LANGUAGES: Azeri & Russian   POLITICAL SYSTEM: democratic republic
HEAD OF STATE & GOVERNMENT: President Geidar Aliyev (since June '93)
PRINCIPAL MINISTERS: Fuad Kuliyev (Prime Minister), Gasan Gasanov (foreign
   affairs), Maj.-Gen. Mamedrafi Mamedov (defence), Ramil Usubov (interior),
   Samad Sadykov (economy), Fikret Yusifov (finance)
CURRENCY: manat & rouble (see above)
GNP PER CAPITA: US$740 ('92 est.)

ALTHOUGH it was now three years since the end of communist rule and of the USSR itself, the nature of a post-Soviet Russia was more obscure by the end of 1994 than it had been at the outset. The establishment of a powerful presidency under the constitution of December 1993 appeared to offer a guarantee of the continuation of reform; but it had been balanced by the election of a new legislature in which President Yeltsin's communist and nationalist opponents were strongly represented (see AR 1993, pp. 141-2). Influenced by these and other circumstances, the President tended to slow down the pace of reform during a year in which the composition of the Russian government moved in favour of the advocates of gradual change rather than 'shock therapy'. The attempt from December to crush the self-declared independence of the Chechen republic, in which thousands of civilians and poorly-led Russian soldiers were later to lose their lives, led beyond this to a widening gulf between President Yeltsin and the liberal reformers who had previously supported him. There was no sign, by the end of the year, that the economy had begun to reverse the decline dating from last years of Soviet rule. Moreover, although Mr Yeltsin enjoyed a closer relationship with the outside world than his Soviet predecessor, there were signs of greater caution in the economic support that the major Western powers were prepared to give him as the future of Russian reform became increasingly problematic.

The immediate result of the December 1993 elections had been a series of changes in the composition of the Russian government, as the reformists Yegor Gaidar (Deputy Prime Minister) and Boris Fedorov (Finance Minister) withdrew in January and went into opposition. Others, such as Andrei Kozyrev (Foreign Minister) and Anatolii Chubais (responsible for privatization), remained in office; indeed,

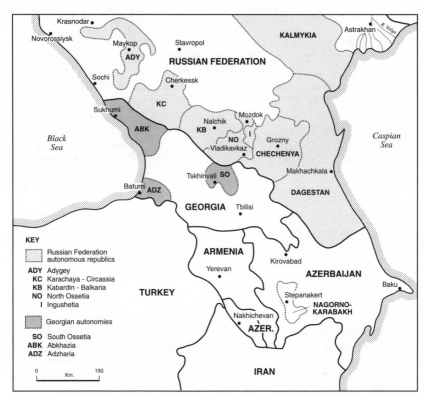

Mr Chubais was promoted to a first deputy premiership in November. As a result, the government increasingly became a *de facto* coalition of representatives of parties that had fought the election with differing, if not incompatible, policies. The authority of Prime Minister Chernomyr-din—who had not openly identified with any of the electoral parties but was understood to favour the gradualist Party of Russian Unity and Concord (PRES)—tended to strengthen during the year, despite occasional rumours of his dismissal. Speaking in January, Mr Cherno-myrdin explained that the 'period of market romanticism had ended' but remained formally committed to a market economy, and to strict monetary and budgetary policies in particular. President Yeltsin, for his part, made it clear in late January that he intended 'firmly to defend reforms and to ensure stability and the continuation of the democratic course'.

The implications of the December elections became clearer in February, when the leaders of the parliamentary resistance to President Yeltsin the previous September and October (see AR 1993, pp. 139-41) were freed under the terms of an amnesty declared by the new State Duma, the lower house of parliament. The most prominent of those released were Aleksandr Rutskoi (until his arrest Mr Yeltsin's Vice-President), Ruslan Khasbulatov (the former parliamentary chairman) and three leaders of the strongly anti-reformist National Salvation Front. The amnesty also brought to an end the proceedings against those who had been involved in the attempted coup in 1991, although one of the accused, General Valentin Varennikov (a former Deputy Interior Minister), refused to be amnestied and was acquitted of treason by the Supreme Court in August.

The conclusion of a Treaty on Civil Accord, on 28 April, appeared to hold out the hope of a wider reconciliation. The document was signed by representatives of 245 social and political organizations and was intended (in the words of Mr Yeltsin) to put a 'final end to civil confrontation'. Its signatories included Mr Gaidar at one end of the political spectrum and Vladimir Zhirinovsky (leader of the ultra-nationalist Liberal Democratic Party) at the other, but not the Communists or the reformist Yavlinsky–Boldryev–Lukin Bloc (Yabloko). They agreed to avoid constitutional changes that were not 'stabilizing' and not to press for early elections, while working to strengthen local self-government and to support the rights of ethnic minorities. Tensions between parliament and government nonetheless continued, leading to the tabling of a vote of no confidence on 27 October that was only narrowly defeated. The concerns of many oppositionists were articulated in an address to the Duma on 28 October by the writer Alexander Solzhenitsyn, who had returned to Russia in May after 20 years of exile: according to his uncompromising analysis, Russia was ruled by an oligarchy concealed by a 'sham democracy' and privatization was a form of 'privateering' that should be dealt with by the courts.

The background to these political events was a continuing economic decline and a deepening social crisis. President Yeltsin, in May, sought to strengthen and extend the process of economic reform by reducing the incidence of several taxes, abolishing quotas and licences for almost all export goods, and exempting recently-established joint ventures from profits tax for three years. In July a presidential decree authorized a second stage of privatization in which enterprises would be auctioned for cash. There were indications, at the same time, that enterprises were being protected from bankruptcy by continuing state credits, while pressure was exerted by the Defence Ministry for more adequate funding of the armed forces. There were conflicting interpretations of economic performance over the year. Official statistics were in any case a less adequate guide than in the past because of widespread evasion of taxes and a broadening non-state sector. They nonetheless suggested a continuing fall in national income, of up to 25 per cent as compared with the early months of 1993. There were some spectacular collapses, including the MMM investment company, whose director, Sergei Mavrodi, was arrested in August (but then elected to the Duma in a by-election and released). The currency itself suffered a dramatic fall on 'black Tuesday', 11 October, when it dropped briefly to an all-time low of 3,926 roubles to the US dollar. The chairman of the Central Bank, Viktor Gerashchenko, resigned shortly afterwards.

Criminality was one of the elements associated with a gradual breakdown of relations between the federal government and the Chechen republic, one of the 89 components of the federation and (in Moscow's view) one of the main sources of public disorder. There had, in fact, been some advance in relations with the other 'autonomies' in the earlier part of the year. In February the Nationalities Minister, Sergei Shakhrai, concluded an agreement with the large and oil-rich republic of Tatarstan allowing it to retain its own constitution and sovereignty 'for a long time'. The agreement gave Tatarstan the right to apply federal legislation on its territory only when it chose to do so, although the federal government retained the right to determine the republic's contribution to the state budget. Another agreement was concluded in August with Bashkortostan, also a Muslim republic (located in the southern Urals) and rich in natural resources. This accord allowed Bashkortostan to raise its own taxes and retain its constitution, while confirming the authority of the federal government to set macroeconomic policy and to regulate defence and foreign affairs.

No such accommodation proved possible with the Chechen republic, where by the end of the year the federal government had launched a fullscale military action to impose its authority. The predominantly Muslim Chechen republic (in the Caucasus—see map on p. 143) had declared its independence from the federation in November 1991 after Major-General Dzhokhar Dudayev had seized power in Grozny (the capital) two months earlier. Relations had steadily worsened, amid some evidence that the central government was seeking to remove President Dudayev from power by exploiting local opposition to his increasingly autocratic rule. An attempt was made on the Chechen leader's life in May, for which the Chechens blamed the Russian security services. President Dudayev himself claimed in June that Russian agents were planning to set off an underground nuclear explosion in order to discredit the breakaway republic. A number of oppositional (i.e. pro-Russian) figures were expelled by the Grozny regime, including Mr Khasbulatov (a Chechen), and there were clashes with local resistance groupings, who appealed to Moscow for support. In July the Russian government denounced the Dudayev administration as 'illegitimate' and threatened to intervene if the lives of Russians were endangered, Russian army units in neighbouring areas being placed on full combat alert. President Dudayev himself declared a state of emergency on 12 October, warning that the republic was 'threatened as never before with the loss of its independence'.

Full-scale military conflict broke out after the Dudayev regime had rejected a demand by President Yeltsin on 29 November that all 'illegal military formations' should lay down their arms within 48 hours. The ultimatum came after an attempt to dislodge President Dudayev from the presidential palace (with covert Russian assistance) had been rebuffed. Russian troops were ordered into the republic on 11 December. Despite predictions of an early victory, they met stiff resistance and suffered heavy losses, particularly among young and apparently poorly-prepared Interior Ministry troops. These forces were reinforced by units of the regular army and an assault began upon Grozny and the presidential palace. At year's end, Chechen forces loyal to President Dudayev were still holding the palace, despite the superior numbers and firepower ranged against them. Casualty figures were minimized by the official Russian media but were reported by independent sources to be heavy on both sides. The Russian authorities acknowledged the deaths of 50 servicemen by the end of the year; the Chechens claimed that the Russian action had caused 800 civilian deaths and over 200,000 refugees. Attempts to negotiate a ceasefire were unavailing, and an order by President Yeltsin on 27 December that civilian targets should be avoided was apparently disregarded by the Russian commanders. For President Dudayev (and many others), the conflict was already reminiscent of the lengthy and damaging Soviet intervention in Afghanistan in 1979–89 and likely to be at least as protracted.

The Chechen war had already had a number of political consequences as the year drew to its violent conclusion. Mr Yeltsin's domestic support fell sharply and he found himself denounced by the liberal reformers who had once been his allies and supporters. Mr Gaidar, for instance, argued that the conflict would prejudice economic reform and lead to a 'police state'. Andrei Sakharov's widow, Yelena Bonner, withdrew from the President's commission on human rights, claiming that the country was 'reverting to totalitarianism'. The Russian human rights commissioner, Sergei Kovalev, appealed from Grozny for an end to a 'crazy massacre', while the Duma voted overwhelmingly on 23 December for a ceasefire and negotiations. The cost of the war, moreover, was increasingly difficult to reconcile with the state budget and had implications for the future of economic reform: estimates were that the cost of military operations and of subsequent reconstruction would exceed £1,000 million, or 4 per cent of annual government revenue. The Chechen war therefore appeared to strengthen the group of predominantly conservative military figures in the Russian Security Council, which was likened by some to the Soviet-era politburo. The action was also welcomed by Mr Zhirinovsky and other extreme nationalists, who took the view that Russian territorial integrity must be preserved at whatever cost. In Chechenya itself, President Dudayev became the focus of a national resistance movement, and there some indications in nearby (particularly Muslim) states that the conflict might widen.

In foreign policy, the year saw a gradual reassertion of Russian national interests and a series of minor incidents (including espionage cases) which suggested that Cold War strains were not entirely a thing of the past. Foreign Minister Kozyrev warned in January that the departure of Russian troops from the 'near abroad' (the former Soviet republics) would create a 'security vacuum' that would inevitably be filled by forces 'directly hostile to Russian interests'. There could be 'no revival of the [Russian] empire', Mr Kozyrev insisted in February; but Russia could not be 'ignored' when major diplomatic actions were being considered and the West should not attempt to restrict Russia's role in international affairs. Russian diplomats, during the year, were particularly concerned to assert an independent role in former Yugoslavia (see III.1.vi) and were generally more sympathetic than the Western powers to their fellow Slavs and Orthodox Christians in Serbia. There was also concern that NATO's Partnership for Peace plan (see XII.2; XIX.1) might be used to incorporate Eastern Europe into the Western sphere of influence. The Russians pressed for special status within the new framework, as well as for special UN status for Russian peace-keeping forces deployed in the former Soviet republics. Although these demands were rejected, Russia followed the other republics by acceding in principle to the Partnership plan in June under an agreement recognizing the country's 'unique and important contribution' to European and international affairs. The possible expansion of NATO into Eastern Europe proved more controversial: Mr Kozyrev asserted in June that there should be 'no haste' in matters of this kind, while President Yeltsin warned in

December that plans to expand NATO membership raised the danger of a 'cold peace' rather than a 'single democratic Europe'.

During a visit to Russia in January, President Clinton of the United States stressed that the US government wanted a 'genuine partnership with a strong and free Russia'. At the same time, the US Secretary of State, Warren Christopher, warned that a revanchist Russian policy would prompt NATO to 'consider the erection of a security barrier'. Russia's relations with the only remaining superpower were not improved by the disclosure in February that a senior CIA official had been arrested on charges of spying for the USSR and then for Russia (see IV.1). The Russians themselves announced the arrest of a senior defence official on charges of spying for British intelligence, and of another accused of spying for Germany. The UK Prime Minister, John Major, was a visitor to Moscow in mid-February and concluded what he described as a 'remarkable and courageous' agreement in which both sides agreed to stand down nuclear missiles hitherto aimed at each other's territory. President Yeltsin visited Spain in April, concluding a treaty of friendship and cooperation, and went to Germany in May for talks with Chancellor Kohl. He visited Germany again in late August to mark the departure of the last Russian troops stationed in Berlin, attracting some comment when he led the local police band in an unscheduled rendition of 'Kalinka'. Following the military withdrawal from Lithuania in 1993, the last Russian troops left Latvia and Estonia in August (see III.2.ii).

In June President Yeltsin was a dinner guest at the Corfu summit of the European Union (EU), with which he signed an agreement on partnership and cooperation. However, there were continuing tensions over the view of some EU member states that the Bosnian arms embargo should be lifted to enable the Bosnian Muslims to resist Serb aggression. This issue also surfaced during Mr Yeltsin's summit meeting with the US President in Washington in September (their fifth in 18 months). The Russian President addressed the United Nations in the course of his visit, calling for a 'disarmament and strategic stability treaty' involving sweeping new cuts in nuclear arms. In circumstances of some controversy, President Yeltsin failed to appear for a planned meeting with the Irish Prime Minister at Shannon airport on 30 September on his return journey. He did, however, meet President Jiang Zemin of China in Moscow in September (see also IX.2.i), as well as, in October, Queen Elizabeth of England, who became the first reigning British monarch to visit Russia since the 1917 revolution.

Russian interaction with the outside world was dominated, as before, by a series of negotiations on Western economic assistance and by a series of Group of Seven (G-7) meetings in which Russia was normally a participant. The World Bank and the IMF, at the start of the year, expressed concern that the Russian government was insufficiently resolute in fighting inflation and in cutting subsidies to industry and agriculture. Finance Ministers and central bank governors of the G-7 countries, meeting in February, agreed to support plans for the improvement of Russia's social security system so as to alleviate the 'social hardships of the transformational process'; at the same time there was a renewed emphasis upon the necessity of fighting inflation and reducing the budgetary deficit if further loans and credits were to be made available. Under a formal agreement in April, the IMF agreed to release US$1,500 million provided there was a reduction in the rate of inflation and appropriate cuts in spending and improvements in tax collection. This was the second tranche of the systemic transformation facility first awarded in June 1993. Russia was for the first time an 'equal partner' in the annual summit of the G-7 nations, held in Naples in July (see XVIII.1), although it had had not yet become a formal G-7 member and was excluded from the summit's economic deliberations. An agreement was reached in October to reschedule a substantial proportion of Russia's commercial debt; the then Deputy Prime Minister, Alexander Shokhin, described it as an 'important vote of confidence from the international financial community'.

Government changed hands in both of the other Slavic ex-Soviet republics during 1994. In BELORUSSIA, the chairman of parliament and de facto head of state, Stanislav Shushkevich, was forced from office when he lost a vote of confidence in January and was succeeded by Mechislau Grib, a lawyer who had previously worked in the USSR Interior Ministry. In March, however, a new constitution was adopted that provided for the introduction of a presidential form of government. The President would be directly elected for a maximum of two five-year terms, would head the armed forces and appoint the cabinet, and would have the power to introduce a state of emergency but not to dissolve parliament. Pending presidential elections, the then Prime Minister, Vyacheslau Kebich, concluded a treaty on economic union with Russia (in April), providing for the removal of trade and currency restrictions and eventually the abolition of a separate Belorussian currency. A programme of privatization was launched in the same month, later than in other post-Soviet republics, involving the issuing of vouchers to the population at large and the sale of state enterprises for such vouchers from July onwards. The presidential elections on 23 June and 10 July were won, sensationally, by Alyaksandr Lukashenka, a former collective farm chairman who had become prominent as an anti-corruption campaigner. He took over 80 per cent of the vote in the second and decisive round, defeating Prime Minister Kebich. As President, Mr Lukashenka appointed a new and more reformist government, and in September presented an 'anti-crisis programme' to deal with the republic's economic difficulties. Under the programme, higher prices were to be balanced by enhanced social security for the least-advantaged.

Relations between UKRAINE and Russia had been complicated by several factors in the past, among them the fate of the ex-Soviet Black Sea fleet (see AR 1993, p. 143). An additional source of tension was provided by the election in January of Yuri Meshkov as the first president of Crimea, with the strong support of its largely Russian-speaking population. Mr Meshkov insisted that there was no immediate prospect of separation from Ukraine, but called a referendum on 27 March on Crimean independence and union with other CIS states. The referendum, which had advisory rather than constitutional force, produced a 70 per cent majority in favour of greater Crimean autonomy, dual citizenship and greater presidential powers. The new Crimean parliament, in turn, adopted legislation in May asserting that its relationship with Ukraine was defined by treaties and agreements (implying an equal relationship) and allowing the local population to hold joint Ukrainian and Russian citizenship. The Ukrainian parliament called for the legislation to be rescinded, whereas President Yeltsin declared in favour of local Crimean sovereignty. President Meshkov, meanwhile, had become engaged in a protracted dispute with the Crimean parliament, which sought to strip him of his powers after a majority of the deputies had disagreed about the formulation of a new Crimean constitution. For its part, the Ukrainian parliament approved a set of constitutional amendments allowing it to rescind, and not simply suspend, Crimean legislation that was in conflict with the republic's constitution.

Political life in Ukraine was shaped during the year by parliamentary elections in March and presidential elections in June and July. The first round of parliamentary elections, on 27 March, produced few clear results but marked a deepening division between the predominantly Russian-speaking east (where left-wing candidates were more successful) and the more traditional west (where nationalists were returned in some strength). The second round, in early April, filled most of the 450 seats in the new parliament; most successful candidates were unaffiliated but among the recognized parties the Communists won the greatest number of seats. In the first round of the presidential elections, on 26 June, President Kravchuk won 38 per cent as against 31 per cent for the former Prime Minister, Leonid Kuchma. In the run-off on 10 July, however, Mr Kuchma was victorious, with 52 per cent as against Mr Kravchuk's 45 per cent. The former manager of a missile factory at Dnepropetrovsk, Mr Kuchma had campaigned for gradual economic reform and closer links with Russia. He placed himself in direct charge of the government on his election, introducing a set of proposals for economic reform in October under IMF guidance involving extensive privatization, agricultural changes, cuts in state subsidies to industry and price increases.

Ukraine had been reluctant to surrender the nuclear weapons that remained on its soil after the dissolution of the USSR, insisting on compensation and Western security guarantees in exchange. An agreement was finally concluded in January between President Kravchuk and his Russian and US counterparts that the missiles would be relinquished; more than 1,600 warheads were involved, representing the world's third largest nuclear arsenal. The weapons were to be dismantled and shipped to Russia, where their uranium would be removed, with various forms of assistance from both Russia and the United States. The Ukrainian parliament had given its preliminary approval to the START I arms reduction treaty in November 1993, but there was strong resistance to the ratification of an agreement that appeared to nationalist deputies to leave the country without adequate defences. In February, nonetheless, START I was finally approved, it being agreed that all nuclear weapons would eventually be surrendered. In December Ukraine went further and signed the Nuclear Non-Proliferation Treaty. Initially hesitant, the republic became an 'associate member' of the CIS economic union in April; it also signed an agreement establishing a payments union and an inter-state economic committee in which Russia would have half of the votes.

There were less dramatic developments in the other, smaller post-Soviet republic to the south of Russia. The longstanding conflict between ARMENIA and AZERBAIJAN continued, with further substantial loss of life although with little change in the balance of forces. The advantage appeared to lie, from the start of the year, with the advancing Azerbaijanis, and a ceasefire negotiated in February was not observed. The Russian Defence Minister announced that 18,000 people had been killed since the conflict began and that over a million had been made homeless. A further ceasefire agreed in July appeared to be more effective. Azerbaijan concluded a ten-year friendship and military cooperation treaty with Turkey in February. Parliamentary elections in MOLDOVA in February resulted in gains for the Agrarian Democratic Party and losses for the pro-Romanian opposition. A referendum in March showed overwhelming support for independence rather than unification with Romania. The Moldovan parliament, at the same time, ratified membership of the CIS and of its economic union. A new constitution was approved in July, defining Moldova as a presidential, parliamentary and neutral republic.

The remaining Caucasian republic, GEORGIA, continued to draw closer to Russia and the other post-Soviet republics during the year, for what appeared to be largely economic and security reasons. In February a summit meeting took place between President Yeltsin and the Georgian head of state, Eduard Shevardnadze, at which 25 agreements were signed, including a treaty of friendship and cooperation. For Mr Shevardnadze the summit was 'one of the major events in 200 years of history between our two peoples'. In a related development in March, the Georgian Supreme

Council approved the republic's membership of the Commonwealth of Independent States. Domestic politics continued to be affected by shooting incidents attributed to paramilitary irregulars and by the ongoing conflict between the Tbilisi government and the separatist republic of Abkhazia, where nationalists were reported to be receiving Russian assistance. The Abkhaz parliament declared independence on 10 February, with the result that fighting resumed in March. However, a ceasefire signed in Moscow in April led on to a further agreement on 14 May providing for military disengagement and the deployment of Russian troops in a peace-keeping capacity. Mr Shevardnadze's own political position appeared to be secured by the rejection of a parliamentary motion of no-confidence on 28 September. Nevertheless, the introduction of food rationing in late 1994 suggested that, in Georgia as in the other post-Soviet republics, the retention of political authority by government would be difficult in the face of deepening economic problems.

ii.   ESTONIA—LATVIA—LITHUANIA

Estonia
CAPITAL: Tallinn   AREA: 45,000 sq km   POPULATION: 1,600,000 ('92)
OFFICIAL LANGUAGE: Estonian   POLITICAL SYSTEM: democratic republic
RULING PARTIES: Fatherland party heads coalition
HEAD OF STATE: President Lennart Meri (since Oct '92)
PRINCIPAL MINISTERS: Andres Tarrand (Prime Minister), Juri Luik (foreign affairs),
   Juri Adams (justice), Kaido Kama (interior), Enn Tupp (defence), Toivo
   Jurgensen (economy)
CURRENCY: kroon (end-'94 £1=K19.36, US$1=K12.37)
GNP PER CAPITA: US$2,760 ('92)

Latvia
CAPITAL: Riga   AREA: 64,000 sq km   POPULATION: 2,600,000 ('92)
OFFICIAL LANGUAGE: Latvian   POLITICAL SYSTEM: democratic republic
RULING PARTIES: Latvian Way heads coalition
HEAD OF STATE: President Guntis Ulmanis (since July '93)
PRINCIPAL MINISTERS: Maris Gailis (Prime Minister), Valdis Birkavs (foreign
   affairs), Vita Terauda (state reform), Andris Piebalgs (finance), Janis Zvanitais
   (economy), Janis Trapans (defence), Janis Adamsons (interior)
CURRENCY: lats (end-'94 £1=L0.86, US$1=L0.55)
GNP PER CAPITA: US$1,930 ('92)

Lithuania
CAPITAL: Vilnius   AREA: 65,000 sq km   POPULATION: 3,800,000 ('92)
OFFICIAL LANGUAGE: Lithuanian   POLITICAL SYSTEM: democratic republic
RULING PARTY: Lithuanian Democratic Labour Party
HEAD OF STATE: President Algirdas Brazauskas (since Nov '92)
PRINCIPAL MINISTERS: Adolfas Slezevicius (Prime Minister), Povilas Gylys (foreign
   affairs), Aleksandras Vasiliauskas (economy), Eduardas Grikelis (finance),
   Romasis Vaiteikunas (interior), Linas Linkevicius (defence)
CURRENCY: litas (end-'94 £1=L6.25, US$1=L3.99)
GNP PER CAPITA: US$1,310 ('92)

THE political systems in the three Baltic republics successfully managed the tribulations as well as the advantages of democracy. One of the casualties strewn along the way was ESTONIA's Prime Minister, Mart Laar. Hailed at a London seminar earlier in the year as a devotee of Thatcherite economic shock therapy, Mr Laar found his own countrymen less enthusiastic. Defections from the governing coalition dominated by his Fatherland party ensued in mid-summer. However, when a vote of no confidence on 28 September ended Mr Laar's interesting premiership, the opposition focused less on policy and more on his 'destructive' and arbitrary leadership style, exploiting his alleged role in the unauthorized sale of Russian roubles after the reintroduction of the kroon as Estonia's official currency in 1993. Parliament subsequently rejected another 'strong man' nominee, central banker Siim Kallas, before endorsing a compromise candidate, Andres Tarrand (a former Environment Minister), as Prime Minister on 27 October. Mr Tarrand also benefited from the opposition's reluctance to force premature elections (due in March 1995). The highly able Foreign Minister, Juri Luik, remained in post to maintain the general direction of Estonia's foreign policy.

In LATVIA high drama was provided in May by the withdrawal of mandates from five members of parliament—including no less a figure than the Foreign Minister, Georgs Andrejevs—on the grounds of their former collaboration with the KGB. Mr Andrejevs explained his own position fully but did the honourable thing and resigned on 4 June. The municipal elections on 29 May also indicated declining support for the ruling coalition headed by Latvian Way. It was eventually split by its junior partner, the Latvian Farmers' Union, because of disagreements over economic policy and agriculture. In July the right-wing National Conservative Party (LNNK) had the chance to form a majority coalition. However, the cabinet presented by LNNK leader Andrejs Krastins on 18 August did not win parliamentary approval, partly because of fears that it would endanger the deal with Russia on troop withdrawal (see below). Instead, Maris Gailis (also of Latvian Way) was accepted on 15 September.

In LITHUANIA the right-wing opposition party, Fatherland Union, mounted a direct challenge to the government's overall economic strategy by forcing a referendum on an opposition proposal that the value of private savings should be restored from the profits of the state's privatization programme. The manoeuvre threatened the entire framework erected by the Lithuanian government for the private sector to create wealth. The outcome confirmed, however, that political common-sense had indeed taken root. Only some 37 per cent of those eligible to vote turned up for the referendum on 27 August and of these only 3 per cent were in favour of the 'wrongful privatization' proposal. Amidst political turbulence, Baltic governments thus preserved an impressive measure of continuity in their policies.

Some of the economic benefits undoubtedly flowing from this achievement were registered by the 1993 'transition report' of the European Bank for Reconstruction and Development (see also XI.5.ii). It placed the Baltic states alongside the Czech and Slovak republics, Hungary and Poland as the ex-communist countries nearest to a market economy. The share of the private sector in these countries was put at around 50 per cent compared with the figure of 5 to 30 per cent in most of the former Soviet republics. Privatization continued to advance in both Estonia and Lithuania, with Latvia lagging behind. As to the legislative framework for the overall transition to a market economy, Estonia forged even further ahead of both Latvia and Lithuania and received most of the foreign direct investment in the three Baltic states. The Deutsche Bank estimated Estonia to be the fastest-growing economy of the three and predicted that its growth rate would outstrip other former Eastern-bloc countries.

A further indicator of Baltic economic progress was the signature in July of trade agreements covering industrial goods between the Baltic republics and the European Union (EU) (see also XI.3). At the time, the German ambassador to Estonia expressed enthusiasm for the speedy conclusion of EU association agreements with the Baltics. In fact, the framework decision to begin the necessary negotiations was not reached by the EU Foreign Ministers until 28 November. Foreign Minister Luik of Estonia promptly reissued his warning about the creation of a 'grey zone' between Russia and Europe if the Baltics were left out of the first EU enlargement in the former Eastern bloc. The Baltic case was marginally helped on 25 November by the decision of the CEFTA states (Czech Republic, Hungary, Poland, Slovakia)—also known as the Visegrad Group—to include the Baltic states in future activities of the grouping.

Inter-Baltic relations continued to develop, notably in that the free trade agreement between the three Baltic states covering industrial goods came into force on 1 April. Under an agreement concluded in June, pan-Baltic political structures were streamlined with a view to enhancing regional cooperation (see XI.5.v). During October the ten countries around the Baltic Sea called on Brussels to formulate an EU programme for the Baltic area, in order to facilitate trans-border and inter-regional cooperation. Finland's adherence to the EU from the start of 1995, in providing the latter with a frontier with former Soviet territory for the first time, undoubtedly increased the pressures for such a programme.

The broader security issues underlying the whole question of enlarging the EU were all too evident in relations between NATO and the Baltic states. The latter speedily signed up for NATO's Partnership for Peace programme (see XII.2; XIX.1) and reaffirmed their commitment to NATO defence standards in their own forces. Cooperation between individual NATO members and the Baltic states on defence matters intensified throughout the year. On 11 September a memorandum of understanding was signed under which Britain and the four Nordic countries would assist the three Baltic states in the formation and training of the much-discussed 600-strong joint peace-keeping battalion of the Baltic states. At the end of October, Latvian, Estonian and Lithuanian troops took part in the Cooperative Spirit 94 exercise in the Netherlands. It was apparent by then that the question was 'when and how', rather than 'if', the Baltic republics would join NATO.

Mr Luik's neat equation about Estonia—'security = normalization + integration'—was true for Latvia and Lithuania too. Normalization referred to relations with Russia. Accompanied by the familiar Russian propaganda about the maltreatment of Russians in the Baltic countries, and prefaced by clumsy brinkmanship from President Yeltsin, the Russian forces at last pulled out of Estonia and Latvia on 31 August. Latvia had to accept a scheme giving social guarantees to Russian military pensioners residing in the country and was obliged to lease the Skrunda radar base to the Russian government for five-and-a-half years. Estonia allowed a substantial number of Russian military pensioners to apply for residence permits and ceded Russia the right to maintain a base at Paldiski until 30 September 1995. A large number of Russian troops who were illegally demobilized on Baltic soil before the evacuation also remained in Estonia and Latvia.

Since Russia refused to acknowledge that its troops had 'occupied' the Baltic countries, 'normalization' was not, however, achieved by their withdrawal. To the very end of 1994, the Russian government insisted—in spite of external findings—that there were human rights violations against Russians in the Baltic states. On 26 June President Yeltsin issued a decree initiating Russia's unilateral demarcation of its border with Estonia, in contravention of the Soviet-Estonian 1920 Tartu peace treaty. During a visit to the disputed Petseri region in November, Mr Yeltsin warned that not 'an inch' of Russian land would be ceded. Russia maintained, in addition, considerable economic pressure, notably by doubling tariffs on goods imported from the Baltic states from 1 July. The Yeltsin administration also tried to use trade talks with Lithuania to improve transit conditions between Russia and its Kaliningrad enclave, which was still home to many thousands of Russian troops. Such pressures served to underline, however, the good sense of the Baltic states in continuing to reorientate their trade towards the rest of Europe.

President Guntis Ulmanis of Latvia used his historic address to the UN General Assembly on 27 September to highlight continuing worries in the Baltic states about Russia, while Mr Luik in turn stressed to the delegates that Baltic security problems were not yet solved. Whilst emphasizing Estonia's willingness to build relations with Russia, the

Estonian Foreign Minister firmly rejected speculation aired earlier by the *Washington Post* to the effect that the Baltics might come to be regarded as a Russian sphere of influence. The Estonian President's colourful February stricture on Russian imperialism—the 'the future of Estonia is also the future of Europe'—assumed greater resonance when President Yeltsin launched an attack on the Chechen republic at the end of 1994 (see also III.2.i). The event prompted further reminders from the Baltic states about parallels with their own recent past. The message was not lost in a year during which the Baltic states inched towards their long-term goal of full European integration.

The extent to which Estonia was already part of the Baltic/Nordic communications network was demonstrated in tragic circumstances on 28 September when the Estonian-owned car ferry *Estonia*, en route from Tallinn to Stockholm, sank in a Baltic Sea storm with great loss of life. It was Europe's worst post-war transport disaster. Of the estimated 1,047 passengers and crew, only 140 survived; of some 900 who perished, 350 were Estonian nationals and most of the others Swedes. Subsequent investigations established that the *Estonia*'s bow door had been broken off by the force of the storm, with the result that sea-water had flooded onto the car deck and quickly capsized the ship. The catastrophe served to intensify international debate about the safety of 'roll-on, roll-off' car ferries. There was also some public recrimination in Sweden about the maritime safety standards applied by the Baltic republics. The grim conclusion at government level was that much more needed to be done to bring about the equalization of standards.

IV THE AMERICAS AND THE CARIBBEAN

1. UNITED STATES OF AMERICA

CAPITAL: Washington, DC   AREA: 9,372,614 sq km   POPULATION: 255,400,000 ('92)
OFFICIAL LANGUAGE: English   POLITICAL SYSTEM: democratic federal republic
HEAD OF STATE & GOVERNMENT: President Bill Clinton, Democrat (since Jan
   '93)
RULING PARTIES: The President is a Democrat but Congress is controlled by the
   Republicans
PRINCIPAL CABINET MEMBERS: Al Gore (Vice-President), Warren Christopher
   (Secretary of State), Robert Rubin (treasury), Bruce Babbitt (interior), Janet
   Reno (Attorney-General) (*for full list see* XIX.6)
INTERNATIONAL ALIGNMENT: NATO, OECD, G-7, OAS, ANZUS, NAFTA
CURRENCY: dollar (end-'94 £1=US$1.56)
GNP PER CAPITA: $23,240 ('92)
MAIN EXPORT EARNERS: machinery & transport equipment, computer technology,
   agricultural products, chemicals, miscellaneous manufactures, financial services,
   tourism

THE second year of the Clinton admininistration was one of continued struggle against charges of financial and personal misconduct (see AR 1993, pp. 149, 152-3, 156) and political opposition. While the 'Whitewatergate' and 'Fornigate' affairs remained unresolved at the year's end, the political map was changed dramatically following the Republican victory in the congressional elections in November. As a result, political pundits held out little hope of President Clinton's achieving his legislative programme or being re-elected in 1996.

More basic issues of presidential security were raised on 12 September when a stolen light aircraft was crashed in the White House grounds immediately in front of President's bedroom. The pilot, named as Frank Corder, was killed in what appeared to be a deliberate suicide rather than an assassination attempt. The Clintons were not actually in residence at the time. Further doubts about security were raised on 29 October when a former US soldier fired on the White House with a semi-automatic weapon in broad daylight. President Clinton was in the building and heard the shots, but no-one was harmed. The gunman was overpowered by bystanders and police officers, and was later charged with damage to government property and illegal possession of a firearm. The President refused to alter his schedule, and at a dinner that night joked that it was 'nice to be home in the safety and security of the White House' after his trip to the Middle East that month. Shots were again fired at the White House in the early hours of 17 December, when a number of bullets hit the south side of the building. No immediate arrests were made. On 20 December Washington police shot and critically wounded a man running towards the White House carrying a large knife.

Other questions of security in the national capital were raised on 23 November when Benny Lee Lawson, a former convict, entered Washington's police headquarters and opened fire with an assault weapon. Two FBI agents and a detective were killed before the assailant, who had earlier been questioned by police conducting a murder inquiry, was himself shot dead. On 21 December a firebomb exploded on a crowded subway train in New York city, causing panic and paralysing the Wall Street area of the city. Police subsequently charged an unemployed computer operator injured in the explosion with the bombing. They believed he was trying to extort money from the transit authority.

In the absence of baseball, because of a strike which began in August over a proposal to limit top players' salaries, the US news was dominated by the scandals surrounding the Clinton administration and by others involving major celebrities. Undoubtedly the most remarkable was the case of the popular former American footballer and present-day film-star, Orenthal James (O.J.) Simpson. Following a hunt and dramatic televised car chase, Mr Simpson was charged with the murder of his ex-wife Nicole and her friend Ronald Goldman on 18 June. When preliminary court proceedings eventually began on 26 September, under the full glare of television cameras, it was dubbed the 'trial of the century', involving as it did American obsessions with race, sex, violence and celebrity. Mr Simpson pleaded not guilty to the double murder charge preferred against him by state prosecutors. It was expected that it would take months merely to select an impartial jury following the intensive news coverage of every detail of the case.

Earlier media interest had focused on the case of the rival ice-skaters Tonya Harding and Nancy Kerrigan. Ms Harding, the US figure-skating champion, was under investigation for involvement in an assault by her ex-husband which had put Ms Kerrigan out of the national championships in January. Both skaters took part in the Winter Olympics in February (see Pt. XVII), Ms Kerrigan winning a silver medal. In a bargain to avoid a prison sentence, Ms Harding subsequently pleaded guilty to conspiring to hinder police investigations and was fined $100,000.

In May the pop super-star Michael Jackson married Lisa Marie Presley (daughter of the late Elvis Presley) in a secret ceremony in Dominica. Questions about Mr Jackson's sexual orientation had been generated by charges of child molestation (see AR 1993, p. 150), but on 21 September the Los Angeles district attorney announced that charges would not be brought because the boy involved no longer wished to proceed. It was reported earlier in the year that Mr Jackson had paid the boy a sizeable settlement in compensation. At the end of November the media reported that Mr Jackson's marriage had ended, although this was not entirely certain as the year ended.

The United States experienced a number of disasters and accidents during the year. The worst occurred on 17 January when 57 people were killed in Los Angeles during an earthquake which measured 6.6 on the Richter scale. Despite massive damage, estimated at $30,000 million, casualties were relatively low because the disaster occurred in the early hours of the morning before the rush-hour had begun. Nonetheless, approximately 25,000 people were left homeless and others had no water or electricity. The governor of California, Pete Wilson, declared southern California a disaster area, while the Clinton administration acted quickly to secure appropriations of emergency funds to provide relief. President Clinton visited Los Angeles on 19 January to inspect the damage. At the beginning of February mudslides closed a number of roads in Malibu and other suburbs of Los Angeles.

Exceptionally cold weather was responsible for more than 90 deaths in January, when a state of emergency was declared in Washington DC, where all offices, non-essential businesses and restaurants were forced to close. More severe snow storms in early February again closed government offices in the federal capital, and forced a shut-down in New York city. In March tornados in Alabama and Georgia resulted in 42 deaths. In July 28 people died in severe flooding in parts of Alabama, Georgia and Florida, the affected areas being promised relief of $60 million by President Clinton. At least six people were killed and many properties were damaged when Hurricane Gordon hit Florida and the Carolinas in late November.

Concerns over air safety were raised following a series of plane disasters. A USAir DC-9 crashed near Charlotte, North Carolina, on 2 July during a thunderstorm, 37 of the 57 people on board being killed. On 9 September a USAir Boeing 737 crashed near Pittsburgh and all 132 on board were killed. All 68 passengers, including seven Britons, died when an American Eagle commuter plane en route from Indianapolis to Chicago crashed in bad weather on 1 November. Another airplane operated by American Eagle crashed near Raleigh-Durham airport in North Carolina on 13 December, killing 15 of the 20 people on board.

On a more positive note, end-of-year figures recorded a fall in violent crime in a number of cities. In New York the number of murders fell by 350, one-fifth lower than the previous year and 650 fewer than in in 1990. Many Americans were saddened, but not surprised, when former President Ronald Reagan, aged 83, announced on 6 November that he was suffering from Alzheimer's disease.

POLITICS AND HOME AFFAIRS. The year began sadly for President Clinton when his mother, Virginia Kelley, died on 6 January aged 70. This personal tragedy did little to deflect criticism from the President, as Senator Robert Dole (Republican) accused him of colluding with the Justice Department to limit the scope of the Whitewater investigation.

President Clinton had earlier asked the Justice Department to appoint a special prosecutor to investigate the allegations relating to the Whitewater affair and the failure of Madison Guaranty Savings and Loan, including the circumstances surrounding the apparent suicide of the White House deputy counsel, Vincent Foster, in July 1993 (see AR 1993, p. 156). On 20 January a senior Republican, Robert Fiske Jr, was appointed to the position.

The final report of the special counsel investigating the Iran-Contra scandal (see AR 1992, pp. 162-3; 1991, pp. 51-2) was published on 18 January. The report suggested that the Iran-Contra operation was not an isolated operation but part of an institutional culture created during the Reagan presidency. Furthermore, the report claimed that President Reagan had known about the affair and had 'knowingly participated or at least acquiesced' in a cover-up. The report also found that former President George Bush had been aware of the plan to sell arms to Iran and use the proceeds to support the Contras in Nicaragua, despite his claims to the contrary; but neither Mr Reagan nor Mr Bush was believed to have wilfully broken the law. Mr Reagan described the investigation as 'excessive and vindictive', while Mr Bush said the report was 'simply wrong'.

The Clinton administration's problems in making senior appointments continued on 18 January when its nominee for Secretary of Defence, Bobby Ray Inman, withdrew. At a press conference, former Admiral Inman said that he was unwilling to face the 'garbage' of scrutiny which accompanied public life, accusing the media of 'modern McCarthyism'. On 25 January President Clinton named the Deputy Defence Secretary, William Perry, as his new nominee for the post. The Senate confirmed the appointment and Mr Perry was sworn in on 3 February.

Also on 25 January, President Clinton gave his first State of the Union address to Congress, broadcast on national television. Appealing alternately to conservatives and liberals, the President called for legislation on health insurance, crime prevention and welfare reform. But he warned Congress that 'if you send me legislation that does not guarantee every American private health insurance that can never be taken away, you will force me to take this pen, veto the legislation, and we'll come right back here and start all over again'. Mr Clinton endorsed the 'three strikes and you're out' provision (a term derived from baseball) making a life sentence mandatory for a third violent or drug-related offence, which was included in the Crime Bill laid before Congress (see below). He also advocated community policing, an expansion in police forces and gun control, as well as federal funds for drug treatment, job training and urban renewal. In a much-quoted passage, President Clinton announced his intention 'to end welfare as we know it' and to limit the time an individual could claim payments. He pledged that the government would provide welfare dependants with 'the support, the job training, the child care you need for up to two years'; after that, he added, 'anyone who can work must—in the private sector wherever possible, in community service if necessary'. The President indicated that he did not intend to propose further cuts in military spending, declaring: 'Nothing is more important to our security than our nation's armed forces.'

Despite positive responses to the State of the Union address, the Clinton admininstration was soon under more pressure over the White-water affair. In March the White House legal counsel, Bernard Nuss-baum, resigned following revelations that he had been monitoring the progress of the Whitewater investigations through meetings with US Treasury officials. Mr Nussbaum was one of ten officials from the White House and Treasury Department subpoenaed on 4 March to appear before a grand jury; he resigned the following day. Mr Clinton said on 3 March that 'as nearly as I can determine, no-one has actually done anything wrong', but that 'it would have been better if the meetings and conversations hadn't occurred'. He ordered White House staff to 'bend over backwards' to help the inquiry go forward. Mr Nussbaum was replaced by Lloyd Cutler, a veteran of the Washington establishment who had held the post under President Jimmy Carter.

On 7 March Mr Clinton's chief of staff, Thomas 'Mack' McLarty, admitted that he had arranged the meetings between Treasury regulators and members of the President's staff which had led to Mr Nussbaum's resignation. The revelations forced Democratic opponents to congressional hearings into Whitewater to back down. The role of the President's wife, Hillary Clinton, through her link with the Rose law firm in Arkansas and her management of the President's financial and business matters also came under increasing scrutiny and criticism from some Republicans. Mr Clinton responded on 7 March by saying of his wife: 'I have never known a person with a stronger sense of right and wrong in my whole life, ever.' The President dismissed comparisons between Whitewater and Watergate, and promised that 'there will not be a cover-up, there will not be an abuse of office in this White House'.

On 10 March, however, 80 Republican congressmen demanded an investigation into whether Mrs Clinton had used insider knowledge as head of the taskforce on health-care reform to trade in health-care stocks. Mrs Clinton broke her silence on 13 March to deny any wrongdoing, but she admitted that 'we made lots of mistakes'. In another statement the following day, she modified earlier claims that she and Mr Clinton had lost $69,000 in the Whitewater deal, saying that she was still trying to ascertain the 'exact figures'. Mrs Clinton's position was not improved by the resignation the same day of Webster Hubbell, an associate attorney-general, who had been a partner with Mrs Clinton in the Rose law firm. He resigned following allegations that he had overcharged the federal government, for whom he had acted in a lawsuit against the accountants of Madison Guaranty. Moreover, the Clintons' denials of wrong-doing did little to stop speculation. In a speech to Congress on 24 March, Congressman Jim Leach asserted that the Whitewater company had illegally transferred money from the Madison Guaranty, and that some of the funds had been used in Clintons' gubernatorial campaign.

Responding on the evening of 25 March, in only his second televised press conference, the President denied all the allegations, but did give a revised figure of $47,000 as the amount that he and his wife had lost in Whitewater. He also announced that he had provided the Whitewater investigation with details of tax returns back to 1977. The effect of these forthright comments was undermined by the disclosure on 25 March that George Stephanopoulos, a senior White House aide, was under investigation for having allegedly attempted to influence Treasury appointments in the Whitewater investigation. On 11 April, moreover, Mrs Clinton revealed that she had failed to report income from investments in 1980, due to an oversight, and would pay $14,615 in back taxes. However, Republican congressmen confirmed on 13 April that the preliminary finding of the special prosecutor, Mr Fiske, was that there was no real evidence that Vincent Foster's death had not been suicide, while other reports refuted Congressman Leach's allegations. The April opinion polls suggested that Mr Clinton had recovered some public support. In part this was due to the more positive news on Whitewater, but also because the President continued to campaign strongly for the health care reforms which had been stuck in congressional committees since being unveiled in 1993 (see AR 1993, pp. 154–5).

Some attention was diverted from President Clinton's troubles by the death of Richard Milhous Nixon on 22 April at the age of 81 (see XX: Obituary). The funeral, at Yorba Linda, California, on 27 April, was declared a national day of mourning and was attended by former Presidents Gerald Ford, Jimmy Carter, Ronald Reagan and George Bush, as well as by Mr Clinton. Another of the great figures from the 1960s was mourned when Jacqueline Onassis, widow of President John F. Kennedy, died of cancer, aged 64, on 19 May (ibid.).

Media interest quickly returned to President Clinton's personal life when, on 6 May, a former Arkansas state employee, Paula Jones, filed charges of sexual harassment, claiming that Mr Clinton had made sexual advances to her in May 1991 while he was governor. A federal judge gave the President until 5 August to respond to the suit in order to allow a determination to be made as to whether presidential immunity applied in the case. Mr Clinton's lawyer filed for immunity on 27 June. On 28 June the Clintons established a legal defence fund to meet the costs of both the Whitewater and the Jones cases, announcing that individual donations would be welcomed. Attention shifted briefly to another senior Democratic politician when on 31 May a grand jury indicted Dan Rostenkowski, former chairman of the House ways and means committee of fraud and corruption. Mr Rostenkowski protested his innocence and said that he would fight to clear his name.

Both Mr and Mrs Clinton testified separately under oath before the the Whitewater special prosecutor on 12 June. On 14 June the Senate voted by 56 votes to 43 in favour of narrowly-focused Whitewater hearings, rather than the wide-ranging ones called for by Republicans. On 30 June President Clinton signed a bill reinstating the Independent Counsel Act, introduced after the Watergate scandal but allowed to lapse in 1992. The act provided for an independent counsel (special prosecutor) to be appointed from outside the executive to investigate allegations against senior government officials. The measure was thought likely (correctly, as it transpired) to affect the position of Mr Fiske adversely and also to expedite the investigation of charges that the Secretary of Agriculture, Mike Espy, had improperly accepted gifts from Tyson Foods, an Arkansas-based company owned by a friend and supporter of President Clinton. In August Attorney-General Janet Reno called for the appointment of a special prosecutor to investigate the claims against Mr Espy. Following investigations of his conduct by the Office of Government Ethics, Mr Espy announced on 3 October that he would resign at the end of the year, although he admitted only to carelessness in his financial affairs. President Clinton subsequently nominated a former congressma, Dan Glickman, who had strong Republican support, to replace Mr Espy.

President Clinton outlined his proposals for welfare reform in a speech on 14 June. The main aim of the programme, which was intended to take effect in 1996, was to force those on welfare for more than two years to sign up for work or training programmes. Increased spending was outlined for education, training and job placement as well as child-care for those on such programmes. The cost was to be met by reducing entitlements and welfare fraud, by tax reforms and by taking money from the corporate superfund tax. In an attempt to improve the administration's performance, President Clinton announced a reshuffle of White House staff on 27 June, replacing the Chief of Staff McLarty with Leon Panetta, formerly Director of the Office of Management and Budget. Senior presidential adviser David Gergen, brought in to improve the admininstration's image in 1993, was moved to foreign affairs in order to improve presentation of foreign policy.

Congressional hearings into the Whitewater affair opened on 26 July with the focus on areas already examined by the special prosecutor. In his first report, Mr Fiske discounted allegations that the death of Vincent Foster had been anything other than suicide. Moreover, although he had found evidence of considerable contact between White House staff and Treasury Department officials, it was insufficient to establish any corrupt intent. The House committee accordingly ruled that the Foster death would not be examined during its investigations. A series of witnesses then appeared before the committee, including the White House legal counsel, Lloyd Cutler, his predecessor, Mr Nussbaum, and ten senior presidential aides and advisers, notably Mr McLarty and Mr Stephanopoulos. When the first hearings closed on 5 August there was considerable criticism of the contacts between White House officials and the Treasury Department, and particularly of Deputy Treasury Secretary Roger Altman, who had given contradictory accounts of the meetings. Mr Altman's position had been undermined by testimony from a senior Treasury Department lawyer, Jean Hanson, and by a diary kept by the Treasury Chief of Staff, Joshua Steiner. Mr Altman resigned on 17 August, as did Ms Hanson a little later. Meanwhile, on 5 August a panel of judges acting under the renewed Independent Counsel Act had dismissed Mr Fiske as the Whitewater special prosecutor and replaced him with Kenneth W. Starr, an office-holder under the two previous Republican administrations. The Clinton administration promised to cooperate with Mr Starr, but hoped that he would not go over 'old territory'.

The Clinton administration faced yet another crisis on 11 August when the Crime Bill failed to pass in the House of Representatives by 225 to 210 votes, after 58 Democrats had joined the Republican opposition. Different forms of new legislation on crime had been approved by the legislature previously, and on 21 April the House had voted by 285 votes to 141 in favour of an omnibus bill. However, the administration's measure was opposed by objectors to gun control and by those unhappy about extending the death penalty. The defeat of a measure so central to the President's social reforms was seen as a major setback and appeared to jeopardize further progress on the health reform proposals. Mr Clinton responded angrily, denouncing Congress for letting down the American people and on 14 August calling upon voters 'to make it clear to members of Congress that, even if they disagree with a particular measure in this Crime Bill, the overall bill is the best, the smartest bill we have ever had in this country'.

At a birthday press conference on 19 August, the President claimed that he liked 'the big fights' and that 'this is an exhilarating time'. Asserting that the Crime Bill was a 'grass-roots, mainstream, non-partisan issue', he urged Republicans and Democrats 'to reach across to each other in good faith' on this measure. The President's campaign evidently had some effect, because on 21 August the House of Representatives approved a watered-down version of the bill. Although it reduced spending on crime prevention measures by $3,000 million compared with the Clinton bill, it still included controls on the sale of 19 types of automatic weapon, extended the death penalty to 60 federal offences (compared with two previously), adopted the 'three strikes and you're out' mandatory life sentence for violent crimes and provided for substantial increases in police forces. After protracted debate, the measure was passed by a margin of one vote in the Senate on 25 August. The President praised those Democrats and Republicans who had supported the measure for putting the country above partisan consideration. Signing the bill on 13 September, Mr Clinton said: 'Never again should Washington put politics and party above law and order.'

The protracted struggle over the Crime Bill left little time for consideration of the President's health-care plan before the congressional recess and mid-term elections. The proposals had been considered by various congressional committees in July, and President Clinton had made it clear he was prepared to consider compromises on the principle of universality and the 'employer mandate' (i.e. the requirement that employers should contribute to costs). However, on 26 September Senate majority leader George Mitchell announced that no further progress could be made. In a written statement, Mr Clinton expressed his regret at this setback, but said he would not give up the 'mission to cover every American and to control health-care costs.'

The mid-term election campaigns began on 5 September and encompassed a number of primaries. In Virginia, Oliver North, the conservatives' hero of the Iran-Contra affair, secured the Republican nomination despite attracting criticism from President Reagan. Washington DC witnessed an amazing political comeback when the former mayor, Marion Barry, gained the nomination as the Democratic candidate on 13 September, virtually assuring him of election in November. Mr Barry had been convicted of cocaine possession in 1990 (see AR 1990, pp. 63–4) but had emerged from prison declaring himself to be a reformed character and appeared to have suffered little political damage among his black constituency. Almost everywhere else, the elections threatened to be a disaster for the Democrats, given the precipitous fall in Mr Clinton's popularity, and some Democratic candidates made a point of distancing themselves from the President when campaigning. Democratic stalwarts Senator Edward Kennedy (Massachusetts) and Governor Mario Cuomo (New York) faced their most serious challenges for years, from Mitt Romney and George Pataki respectively. The incumbent Democratic senator for California, Diane Feinstein, for a time seemed to have little hope against multi-millionaire Michael Huffington (Republican), who made opposition to illegal immigration a central plank of his campaign. However, Mr Huffington lost ground after it became known that he and his high-profile Greek-born, English-educated wife had hired an illegal immigrant as nanny.

The results of the elections, held on 8 November, exceeded most predictions of Democratic losses (see accompanying map). Despite a week of intensive campaigning across the country by President Clinton, the Republican Party gained control of both the Senate and the House

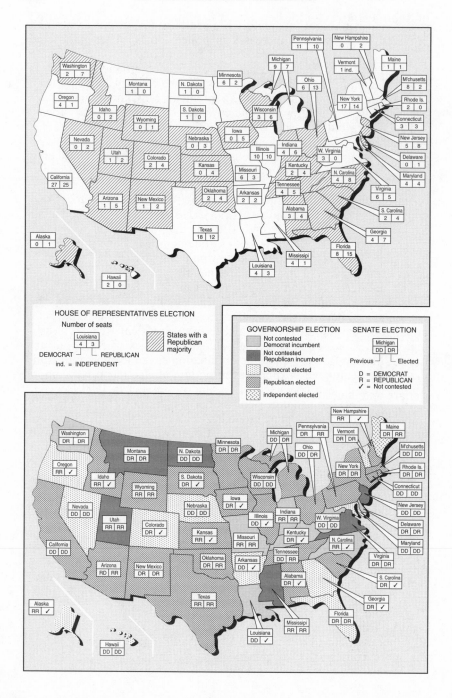

HOUSE OF REPRESENTATIVES ELECTION

Number of seats

Louisiana	
4	3

DEMOCRAT   REPUBLICAN

ind. = INDEPENDENT

States with a Republican majority

GOVERNORSHIP ELECTION   SENATE ELECTION

- Not contested Democrat incumbent
- Not contested Republican incumbent
- Democrat elected
- Republican elected
- independent elected

Michigan	
DD	DR

Previous   Elected

D = DEMOCRAT
R = REPUBLICAN
✓ = Not contested

of Representatives for the first time in 40 years. The electorate delivered a decisive rejection of both President Clinton and the Democrat's programme, in what amounted to a massive electoral shift to the right. With the post-election defection of Senator Richard Shelby of Alabama (previously elected as a Democrat), the Republicans obtained a majority of 53 seats to 47 in the Senate, having gained nine seats in the polling. Not all Democrats were swept away: Senator Kennedy held on to his seat in Massachusetts; Senator Feinstein narrowly defeated Mr Huffington in California; and Mr North failed to defeat the Democratic incumbent, Chuck Robb, in Virginia. But the overall results indicated a powerful conservative tide in US electoral politics.

In the House elections the Republicans gained over 50 seats, to take a total of 230 as against the Democrats' 204. Among the defeated Democrats were the Speaker of the House, George Foley, and Mr Rostenkowski, who was facing trial accused of misuse of government funds (see above). Democratic candidates also lost heavily in the 36 gubernatorial elections, the Republicans gaining 12 states, giving them executive control in 30 out of 50. In New York Mr Cuomo lost his battle with Mr Pataki, despite having the support of the Republican mayor of New York city, Rudolph Giuliano, while in Texas Ann Richards lost to George W. Bush, son of the former President. Among the few Republican defeats was the failure of Jeb Bush to unseat Lawton Chiles (Democrat) in Florida. In California the Republican governor, Pete Wilson, decisively fought off the challenge of Kathleen Brown (Democrat), despite his own apparent unpopularity. A significant factor was Mr Wilson's support for Proposition 187, aimed at limiting welfare and education benefits for illegal immigrants. This proposition was approved by 59 per cent of those voting, but courts in San Francisco and Los Angeles quickly delivered rulings against its being implemented. In the mayoral contests, Mr Barry was duly elected in Washington, DC, discovering on taking office again that the federal capital was on the verge of bankruptcy.

At a press conference after the polls, President Clinton said that the Democrats had been 'held accountable' and accepted his 'share of the responsibility', declaring that he was prepared to work with the Republicans 'to serve all the American people'. At the same time, he warned 'those who would use this election to turn us back' that he would do everything in his power 'to keep anyone from jeopardizing this economic recovery by taking us back to the policies that failed us before'. In a conciliatory telephone call to the President immediately after the results became clear, the new majority leader in the Senate, 71-year-old Robert Dole of Kansas, said: 'I wanted to let you know right up front that we want to work together wherever we can.' Other Republicans claimed a clear mandate for a change of policy. Leading the more conservative element was the aggressive new Speaker of the House, Newt Gingrich of Georgia, who promised to enact the conservatives' ten–point 'contract with America' featuring tax cuts, reduced welfare benefits, increased defence spending and fixed terms for elected officials.

The Whitewater affair surfaced again at the start of December when it was reported that an indictment of the former assistant attorney-general, Mr Hubbell, would be filed before Christmas. Mr Hubell, who had resigned his position in the Justice Department in March (see above), apparently struck a deal with the special prosecutor, Mr Starr, and admitted to mail fraud and tax evasion while working in the Rose law firm in Arkansas. Concurrent reports suggested that Mr Clinton's personal aide, Betsey Wright, and a special assistant, Bruce Lindsey, were also under investigation. More immediately damaging to the Clinton administration was the resignation on 6 December of the much-respected Treasury Secretary, Lloyd Bentsen, whose assertion that his stewardship of economic policy had produced 'the best numbers we have had in 30 years' prompted many to wonder why he had decided to resign. Mr Bentsen's departure was followed by the dismissal of Joyce Elders as Surgeon-General. The first black to hold the post, Ms Elders had publicly suggested that masturbation was 'part of something that perhaps should be taught' in school sex education classes. The President immediately named Robert Rubin, a former co-chairman of the bankers Goldman Sachs, as Mr Bentsen's successor.

On 15 December Mr Clinton attempted to recover lost ground in public opinion, and to steal the Republicans' thunder, when he announced a programme of tax cuts which he described in a television address as 'a middle-class bill of rights'. The President's proposals included tax relief for families earning less than $75,000 a year and with children under 13, protection for pension schemes and allowances for college fees. The lost revenue would be offset by the freezing of non-military spending and by cutbacks in the Departments of Energy, Housing, Transport and Commerce. Implicitly denying that he was copying his opponents, Mr Clinton said that his policy was 'not about left or right' but rather about 'moving forward'. Republicans, and even some Democrats, had earlier attempted to upstage the President by announcing tax-cutting proposals of their own, with the result that Mr Clinton's message received a fairly lukewarm reception.

The President's press secretary, Dee Dee Myers, announced her resignation on 16 December, saying that it was 'time for me to move on'. The chain of resignations continued when the much-criticized head of the Central Intelligence Agency (CIA), James Woolsey, resigned on 28 December. Mr Woolsey had been appointed in 1993 but had taken much of the blame for the Ames spy scandal (see below) and for failing to sack those responsible.

Republicans had their own difficulties at the close of the year. Mr

Gingrich was criticized for accepting a $4.5 million advance from the publishers HarperCollins for a book on his political philosophy and for an edited anthology of political writings. On 30 December Mr Gingrich, the advocate of financial conservatism, announced that he would take only $1 million as an advance and would then earn royalties after publication. Critical comments from Mr Dole, the more moderate Senate majority leader, pointed up divisions within Republican ranks.

THE ECONOMY. On 7 February President Clinton presented Congress with his budget proposals for the 1995 fiscal year (beginning in October 1994). The most significant feature was a reduction in government spending and a projected reduction of the budget deficit to $176,100 million, lower than any since 1989. The one major tax rise—to increase the federal tax on a packet of 20 cigarettes from 24 to 99 cents—was expected to raise $67,000 million over six years to help fund health-care reform. Critics suggested that the budget was based on optimistic projections of economic growth. Nonetheless, the package was approved by the House of Representatives on 11 March by 222 votes to 164 (no Republicans voting in favour) and by the Senate on 25 March by 57 votes to 40. A proposed constitutional amendment to prohibit a federal budget deficit unless specifically approved by Congress failed to get the necessary two-thirds majority in either the Senate or the House in March. The bill had been opposed by the Clinton administration but was supported by leading Republicans.

At the end of June the administration struggled to prevent a currency crisis as the US dollar fell to an all-time low against the Japanese yen. The then Treasury Secretary, Mr Bentsen, denied that the government wanted a weak dollar in order to improve the trade balance, asserting: 'The dollar is not a tool in our trade policy.' This difficulty followed an announcement by the Commerce Department that the US economy was growing at a faster rate than previously anticipated, which in turn fuelled fears of inflation. In August the Federal Reserve added to President Clinton's problems when it raised short-term interest rates for the fifth time in the year. In November it announced a further 0.75 per cent increase (the biggest single rise since 1980), setting the rate at 5.5 per cent in an anti-inflationary move intended to slow growth and prevent the economy from overheating. The Clinton administration had argued for smaller rises, but Mr Bentsen accepted that 'the Federal Reserve is an independent agency with authority to make monetary policy', adding: 'The news on the economy is still good.' Figures showed that production and sales had increased rapidly in October, while unemployment was the lowest for many years, at 5.8 per cent of the registered labour force.

As the year drew to a close, figures were released which showed that the US trade deficit was the highest since 1987. As sales increased in the otherwise buoyant economy, imports exceeded exports by $10,400 million in October. Particularly striking was the ever-increasing trade gap with Japan, which reached a record level of $6,700 million despite the efforts of the Clinton administration to persuade Japan to open its markets to US exports.

SOCIAL AND LEGAL AFFAIRS. Much media attention focused on the trial which began in Manassas, Virginia, on 10 January of Lorena Bobbitt, a manicurist accused of malicious wounding after she had cut off her husband's penis with a kitchen knife in June 1993. She was acquitted by the jury on 22 January after pleading justification on the grounds of Mr Bobbitt's violence towards her. Mr Bobbitt, whose severed part had been sewn back on by surgeons, apparently successfully, was in turn acquitted of a charge of marital rape in November, by which time he had become a media celebrity. More seriously, on 5 February Byron De La Beckworth (73) was convicted in Jackson, Mississippi, for the murder in 1963 of Medgar Evers, a black civil rights activist, and was sentenced to life imprisonment. An avowed 'white supremacist', Mr De La Beckworth had previously been twice acquitted (in 1964) of the crime after all-white juries had failed to agree upon a verdict.

On 26 February the trial of the 11 surviving members of the Branch Davidian religious sect involved in the Waco siege of 1993 (see AR 1993, p. 159) ended when the defendants were acquitted of murder and attempted murder, although five were convicted of manslaughter and others on lesser charges. The verdict indicated that the jury had accepted the defendants' claim to have been acting in self-defence and implied further criticism of the tactics used by the authorities in the siege, in which four federal agents and over 80 sect members died. Nevertheless, eight sect members received prison sentences ranging from five to 40 years on 17 June, while on 8 July one member who had testified against the others was sentenced to three years imprisonment.

A high-ranking officer in the Central Intelligence Agency (CIA), Aldrich Ames, and his wife, Maria del Rosario Casas Ames, were arrested on 21 February on charges of having passed information to the Soviet Union and then Russia over a nine-year period in return for payments totalling more than $2 million. It was stated that the information provided by Mr Ames had betrayed 11 agents working for the CIA, several of whom had been executed. Mr Ames claimed that he had not 'noticeably aided' the Moscow government, but pleaded guilty to charges of espionage and tax evasion on 28 April in return for leniency for his wife. He was sentenced to life imprisonment without parole, while Mrs Ames was later sentenced to 63 months in prison. The case of Mr Ames, who was believed to be the highest-ranking CIA member ever recruited by Moscow, caused great consternation in the United States and generated some strains in US-Russian relations (see below). External ramifications of a different sort were involved in the conviction on 4 March of four Muslim fundamentalists of Middle Eastern origin who had been tried for conspiracy and explosives offences arising from the February 1993 bombing of New York's World Trade Center, which had killed six people (see AR 1993, p. 158). A fifth man, thought to be the ringleader, was still awaiting trial and two others remained at large.

On 7 March Governor Wilson of California signed a new state crime bill into law. It specified that a defendant found guilty of a second violent crime would receive double the usual penalty, plus an additional five years, and a third such felony conviction would lead to a sentence of at least 25 years without parole. This Californian version of the 'three strikes and you're out' concept backed by President Clinton (see above) was intended to punish habitual violent offenders. Other states were preparing similar legislation.

On 6 April Supreme Court Justice Harry A. Blackmun (85), the court's most liberal member, announced his intention to retire at the end of June. The then Senate majority leader, George Mitchell (Democrat, Maine), was widely tipped as a likely replacement, but on 12 April he announced that he did not wish to be considered. On 13 May President Clinton nominated Stephen G. Breyer, chief judge of the court of appeals for the first circuit and chief counsel to the Senate judiciary committee. The Senate confirmed the nomination in July and Judge Breyer was sworn in on 3 August. Before his retirement, Justice Blackmun wrote the majority opinion in a landmark Supreme Court judgment on 19 April in the case of *JEB.* v. *Alabama Ex Rel T.B.*. The Court ruled by six votes to three that sexual discrimination in the selection of juries constituted a violation of the equal protection guaranteed in the 14th amendment of the US constitution, thus extend a 1986 decision that jurors could not be excluded on grounds of race.

A federal jury in Los Angeles on 19 April awarded Rodney King $3,800,000 as compensation for the beating he had received in 1991 from members of the Los Angeles Police Department (see AR 1991, p. 48; 1992, p. 151; 1993, p. 158). The same jury ruled in June that none of the six LAPD officers facing a civil suit from Mr King should be liable for punitive damages.

The Supreme Court ruled on 30 June that a Florida judge had not violated the free-speech rights of anti-abortion protestors when he prohibited them from picketing within 36 feet of an abortion clinic but had done so by limiting the pickets to within 300 feet of the clinic. A new law passed in May had made it a federal crime to block access to abortion clinics. On 9 May a Houston court awarded more than $1 million in damages to a Planned Parenthood clinic which had been blockaded by two leading anti-abortion groups in 1992. One of the worst instances of continuing anti-abortion violence came on 29 July, when a doctor arriving for work was shot dead outside a clinic in Pensacola, Florida, together with his volunteer escort. A leading anti-abortionist and former Presbyterian minister, Paul Hill, was charged with the killings, found guilty in November and sentenced to death. On 30 December a gunman opened fire in two Boston abortion clinics, killing two office workers and wounding several other people. A 22-year-old suspect subsequently arrested by the police appeared to be emotionally disturbed rather than connected with the anti-abortion movement.

On 2 May a Michigan jury acquitted Dr Jack Kevorkian of assisting in the suicide of a terminally-ill patient in August 1993. The decision undermined a Michigan law passed in 1993 banning assisted suicides and matters were further complicated by subsequent rulings of the state's court of appeals. The latter body ruled on 10 May that the 1993 law was unconstitutional but also found that there was no constitutional right to suicide. It therefore ruled that murder charges against Dr Kevorkian, for assisting in the deaths of two women in 1991, could be reinstated.

The notorious serial killer Jeffrey Dahmer (see AR 1993, p. 165) was on 28 November found beaten to death in the prison near Madison, Wisconsin, where he was serving life sentences for 15 murders.

FOREIGN AFFAIRS. At the beginning of the year Mr Clinton took part in the NATO summit in Brussels which launched the Partnership for Peace programme of cooperation with former Warsaw Pact and neutral European states (see XII.2; XIX.1). The President met leaders of the Visegrad Group (the Czech Republic, Hungary, Poland and Slovakia) in Prague on 12 January, before travelling on to Russia for meetings with President Yeltsin (see also III.2.i). While agreement was reached to stop aiming missiles at each other's territory, there were disagreements concerning NATO's plans. During his visit, Mr Clinton made an unprecedented appearance on Russian television before a studio audience and answered questions in an American-style 'town meeting' link-up with other cities. Before returning to the United States, Mr Clinton met President Hafiz al-Asad of Syria in Geneva on 16 January and welcomed the Syrian leader's announcement that he was ready to establish normal relations with Israel in the context of a peace treaty. The two sides decided on the creation of a joint working group to examine bilateral relations.

President Clinton announced the lifting of the 19-year-old US embargo against Vietnam on 3 February, following an earlier vote in favour of the step by the Senate. Mr Clinton said that Vietnam had provided 'significant and tangible' help on the issue of American servicemen still classified as missing in action (the MIAs) during the Vietnam War. However, further progress was required before a restoration of full diplomatic relations could be achieved.

In light of the shock of the Ames case (see above), Secretary of State Warren Christopher summoned the Russian chargé d'affaires on 22 February in order to 'protest in the strongest terms' against the continuation of anti-US Russian espionage activities. Alexander Lysenko, described by the State Department as the chief Russian intelligence officer in the United States, was ordered to leave the country within seven days. When Russia responded on 28 February by expelling the CIA's Moscow station chief, James Morris, the Clinton administration expressed regret but said that it did not plan to take further retaliatory action.

Differences between the United States and Japan over the trade imbalance were discussed during a summit meeting between President Clinton and Prime Minister Morihiro Hosokawa in Washington on 11–12 February, but without substantive result (see IX.2.iv). Mr Clinton said that no agreement was preferable to an empty one, adding: 'Just because we have some disagreements doesn't mean we don't have a good relationship.' Nonetheless, the imposition of US trade sanctions against Japan was openly discussed in subsequent months, during which the US trade deficit with Japan remained colossal.

In a television interview broadcast internationally on 3 May, President Clinton defended his foreign policy. While he denied any wish to see the United States as 'the world's policeman', he said that America could not 'turn our back on the world'. He particularly warned North Korea and Haiti that the US government would take action if their policies did not change. In the case of the former state, prevention of nuclear weapons proliferation was the US aim (see IX.2.vi)—as it was, in different circumstances, in respect of the former Soviet republics. After President Clinton had on 14 March announced the extension of the US moratorium on nuclear testing for a further year to September 1995, agreements were reached two days later with Russia on the inspection of plutonium storage sites and the future closure of reactors in Siberia. The US government also secured an undertaking from Ukraine that it would give up its ex-Soviet nuclear arsenal, Secretary of Defence William Perry promising $100 million in aid to assist with its elimination (see III.2.i; XII.1).

In May President Clinton restored China's most-favoured-nation status, subsequent attempts to suspend the decision being defeated in the House of Representatives on 9 August. On 29 August a new US-China trade agreement signed in Beijing set up joint task forces in key sectors such as telecommunications, aviation, electronics and chemicals, paving the way for new US trade missions to gain access to China's markets. Human rights groups denounced the moves because of the failure to achieve any prior improvement in China's internal security record. Much publicity was given to a New York group which claimed that organs from executed Chinese prisoners were used in transplants without their consent and that some prisoners were kept alive until their organs had been removed.

In June President Clinton joined Allied leaders in Normandy to commemorate the 50th anniversary of the D-Day landings, proclaiming: 'Let us never forget that when they were young these men saved the world.' On 11 July, during a two-day visit to Germany, Mr Clinton acknowledged a special US relationship with Britain but spoke of the 'truly unique relationship' between the United States and Germany, which existed because 'so many of our challenges are just to Germany's east'. Visiting what had been East Berlin on 12 July, the President said: 'America is on your side, now and forever.' His speech attracted criticism, at home and abroad, for appearing to seek to emulate the historic Berlin address of President Kennedy in June 1963.

Following horrific television news coverage of the inter-ethnic slaughter in Rwanda (see VII.1.ii), President Clinton on 22 July announced an emergency airlift of supplies to deal with what he called the 'worst humanitarian crisis in a generation'. After the difficulties experienced by the US forces in Somalia, the administration had hitherto been reluctant to get involved in Rwanda, while Congress had rejected UN appeals aid.

The Clinton administration faced Republican opposition when, on 19 August, the President announced the reversal of the 30-year-old US open door policy for Cuban refugees (see also IV.3.xi). The announcement provoked a further exodus of Cuban 'boat people', large numbers of whom were picked up by the US Coastguard and taken to the US base at Guantánamo (Cuba). Governor Lawton Chiles of Florida declared a state of emergency, while Mr Clinton warned that all future refugees would be detained and returned, asserting that 'the Cuban government will not succeed in dictating US immigration policy'. For the Republicans, Mr Gingrich denounced the move as 'appalling' and accused the administration of a 'total lack of any moral compass in policy toward the Caribbean'. President Clinton also tightened economic pressures on Cuba by banning the sending of remittances from exiles in the United States and placing limits on family visits and medical and food aid to Cuba. The crisis eased after 27 August when Mr Clinton agreed to discussions with a view to allowing 'legal, orderly and safe migration'. An agreement between Cuban and US negotiators on 9 September provided for the controlled provision of US entry visas and the reintroduction of Cuban restrictions on those wishing to leave, although there was no lifting of the US trade embargo against Cuba.

American concerns in the Caribbean increased with the growing crisis over Haiti following the expulsion of the UN-OAS International Civilian Mission in July and the growing refugee crisis (see also IV.3.xii). US forces began to gather offshore and to take part in air and sea operations in preparation for an invasion. On 21 July Mr Clinton asked the United Nations to support an invasion of Haiti, but was faced with opposition to military action in Congress and among the public. In a televised address on 15 September, the President said that the military junta in Haiti was conducting 'a reign of terror', warning its members: 'Leave now or we will force you to leave.' On 17 September a delegation led by former President Jimmy Carter, and including General Colin Powell and Senator Sam Nunn, went to Port-au-Prince to persuade the Haitian military leaders to give up power peacefully. After prolonged negotiations, a last-minute agreement was reached on 18 September, with the result that aircraft carrying US paratroops en route to invade Haiti were recalled and US marines began to land peacefully on 19 September in an operation named 'Uphold Demcracy'. Initially welcomed as a triumph of diplomacy, the Haiti agreement soon attracted criticism, the disquiet increasing when US troops had to stand idly by when local policemen attacked anti-junta demonstrators. After lengthy discussions, the American commander, Lieutenant-General Hugh Shelton, announced that the junta had agreed to restrain the police. On 24 September American forces were involved in a gun battle at a police-station in Cap Haïtien in which ten Haitians were killed. The departure of the junta leaders and the return of President Aristide in October brought greater stability, so that by year's end the Haitian operation was generally regarded as one of the Clinton administration's few external policy successes.

In a statement on 1 September. President Clinton welcomed the IRA ceasefire in Northern Ireland (see I.8; XIX.3), adding that he was 'pleased that the United States has been able to contribute to this process of reconciliation'. Earlier in the year, the US decision to grant an entry visa to the leader of the IRA's political wing, Sinn Féin president Gerry Adams, had caused some strains in relations with London. During his summer vacation at Martha's Vineyard, Massachusetts, the President met the Irish Foreign Minister, Dick Spring, and promised to do 'whatever we can to help'. He also discussed the possibility of a 'peace dividend' in the form of increased US financial contributions to the International Fund for Ireland.

The Clinton administration responded quickly to the news that Iraqi troops had moved close to the Kuwaiti border on 4 October (see V.2.vi; V.3.iii). The US President warned that 'it would be a great mistake' if the Iraqi regime believed that US resolve had weakened. When Iraq failed to pull back its forces immediately, the US government despatched thousands of troops and hundreds of planes to Kuwait in 'Operation Vigilant Warrior'. The subsequent withdrawal of the Iraqi forces was seen as a victory for the Clinton administration.

President Clinton hosted the Washington meeting of King Husain of Jordan and Prime Minister Yitzhak Rabin of Israel on 25 July at which the two leaders signed an agreement formally ending the state of conflict between their countries. In October the US President made a whirlwind visit to the Middle East in support of the peace moves in the region. Following a meeting with President Mubarak of Egypt and PLO leader Yassir Arafat in Cairo, the President travelled on to Jordan to be present at the signing of the peace treaty between Israel and Jordan on 26 October (see V.2.iii; XIX.4). Mr Clinton urged the signatories to follow their words with actions, saying: 'Open your borders, open your hearts.' Speaking before the Jordanian parliament later the same day, he criticized extremists 'who cloak themselves in the rhetoric of religion and nationalism'. On 27 October Mr Clinton became the first US President to visit Syria for over 20 years when he had a brief meeting in Damascus with President Asad. During their joint press conference, Mr Clinton emphasized the importance of Syria reaching a comprehensive peace settlement with Israel. After a brief stopover in Jerusalem, he travelled to Kuwait, where he addressed UN and US forces near the border with Iraq and promised the Kuwaitis that 'the United States and the international community will not allow Baghdad to threaten its neighbours now or in the future'.

One of the first consequences of the Republican victories in the November mid-term elections was the Clinton administration's announcement on 11 November that it would end its support for the UN arms embargo on former Yugoslavia. Reflecting the prevalent US view that the embargo prevented the Bosnian government from being able to defend itself against Serbian aggression, the decision was regretted by the UK and French governments, because they supplied the bulk of UN peace-keeping forces in Bosnia (whereas the United States provided none). On 22 November, as Serbian forces threatened the UN-guaranteed 'safe haven' of Bihać, US Defence Secretary Perry warned that NATO forces would destroy Serbian aircraft if necessary. During the weekend of 26-27 November a US aircraft carrier with 2,000 marines on board sailed into the Adriatic. US political divisions on Bosnian policy intensified on 27 November when Senator Dole accused UN officials in Bosnia of having aided 'the Serb aggressors' and declared NATO policy a failure. A meeting of President Clinton's security advisers later that day resulted in a policy modification to the extent that a White House spokesman indicated agreement with the majority NATO view that the Serbs could not be defeated in Bosnia. Senator Dole, meanwhile, reiterated his criticisms of NATO during a visit to Brussels, where he told officials that the UN forces should withdraw and that the embargo ban should be lifted. Mr Dole refused to moderate his position despite the urgings of Prime Minister Major and other British ministers at a brief meeting in London on 30 November.

That President Clinton was able to win some concessions from the Republicans was apparent when he announced at a news conference on 23 November that Senator Dole had agreed to support ratification of the December 1993 accord of the General Agreement on Tariffs and Trade (GATT). Under the ratification agreement, the administration undertook to review trade dispute decisions of the new World Trade Organization (GATT's projected successsor) and Congress would have the right to opt for US withdrawal if and when three decisions went against US interests. The GATT agreement was passed with over-whelming support in the House of Representatives on 29 November and by a 76–24 majority in the Senate on 1 December. Mr Clinton welcomed the outcome, saying: 'Let's make the GATT vote the first vote of a new era of cooperation.' He signed the agreement on 8 December.

On 9 December President Clinton opened a 'Summit of the Americas' in Miami, Florida, attended by 34 other heads of state or government. He called upon those assembled to seize the 'magic moment' affording a present opportunity to establish free trade and democracy in the western hemisphere. The US President also expressed the hope that the next time such a summit convened 'the leader of a democratic Cuba will take that country's place among us'.

2. CANADA

CAPITAL: Ottawa   AREA: 9,9970,610 sq km   POPULATION: 27,400,000 ('92)
OFFICIAL LANGUAGES: English & French
POLITICAL SYSTEM: federal parliamentary democracy
HEAD OF STATE: Queen Elizabeth II (since Feb '52)
GOVERNOR-GENERAL: Ramon John Hnatyshyn (since Jan '90)
RULING PARTY: Liberal Party (since Oct '93)
HEAD OF GOVERNMENT: Jean Chrétien, Prime Minister (since Oct '93)
PRINCIPAL MINISTERS: Sheila Copps (Deputy Prime Minister, environment), André Ouellet (foreign affairs), Paul Martin (finance), David Collenette (defence), John Manley (industry), Allan Rock (justice)
INTERNATIONAL ALIGNMENT: NATO, OECD, G-7, OAS, NAFTA, Francophonie, Cwth.
CURRENCY: Canadian dollar (end-'94 £1=Can$2.19, US$1=Can$1.40)
GNP PER CAPITA: US$20,710 ('92)
MAIN EXPORT EARNERS: manufactured goods, fabricated & crude materials, agricultural products, tourism

THE possibility of Quebec's secession from the federation dominated the political affairs of Canada in 1994 and promised to come to a head in a referendum on the subject in 1995. The topic gained urgency with the provincial election victory of the separatist Parti Québécois (PQ) in September, some 18 years after it had last come to power in the predominantly French-speaking province.

The PQ had been founded in 1968 by a charismatic journalist, René Lévesque, who became Quebec premier in 1976 but failed, in a referendum four years later, to secure popular endorsement of his proposal for sovereignty combined with economic association with the rest of Canada. Although the PQ continued to govern Quebec until

1985, it did not raise the issue again. M. Lévesque died in 1987 and was eventually succeeded by Jacques Parizeau, an economist and former Quebec finance minister. The PQ was followed in office by the Liberal Party, which combined a belief in the unity of Canada with the aim of winning a special status for Quebec. Its leader, Robert Bourassa, cooperated with Brian Mulroney, head of the national Progressive Conservative Party and Prime Minister of Canada from 1984 to 1993, in an effort to secure this goal. Two major efforts were made to change the constitution of Canada in order to reflect Quebec's aspirations within a reformed federal structure, but they were unsuccessful. The 1990 Meech Lake Accord was turned down by two of the provinces and the 1992 Charlottetown Accord was rejected by the Canadian people in a referendum (see AR 1992, p. 169). The rejections strengthened the movement for separation in Quebec.

M. Bourassa retired as Quebec premier in January 1994, to be replaced by a member of his cabinet, Daniel Johnson (49), who attempted to give a fresh face to a tired government. Calling an election for 12 September, Mr Johnson was fiercely attacked by the PQ for having mismanaged the province's economy. M. Parizeau pointed to Quebec's 10 per cent unemployment rate to emphasize the need for economic growth and job creation. He also raised the dream of independence and pilloried Mr Johnson as the defender of a 'dysfunctional' federalism. In the event, the PQ won 77 seats in the 125-seat assembly (against 33 at dissolution), the Liberals fell from 78 to 47 seats and an additional seat was won by a splinter party. But the two leading parties were almost tied in the popular vote (44.7 per cent for the PQ and 44.3 per cent for the Liberals), so that M. Parizeau could not interpret his victory as a triumph for the cause of separation. Polls revealed that the popular support for Quebec's sovereignty remained fixed at about 40 per cent, almost the same result that had prevailed in the 1980 referendum.

M. Parizeau was sworn in as Quebec's 26th premier on 26 September. Undaunted by the ambivalent electoral verdict, his government prepared for the promised referendum on sovereignty by introducing a draft bill into the legislature on 6 December, asserting Quebec's destiny as 'a sovereign country'. Although the new country would assume all the attributes of independence, it would seek an economic association with the rest of Canada, would continue to use the Canadian dollar as its currency and would allow its citizens to hold Canadian citizenship. Public consultations, organized by 15 regional committees, would begin early in 1995 and would prepare residents for the vote on sovereignty. Voters would be asked to endorse the goal of independence as set forth in the draft legislation. If they did, the act, as passed in the assembly, would come into force a year following the referendum.

Federalist groups branded M. Parizeau's strategy as a dishonest tactic which lacked credibility. In the first place, the bill of 6 December was beyond the power of the legislature of Quebec to enact. Second, the consultative process was so devised as to make sovereignty appear an inevitable result. The process allowed Quebeckers no discussion of continued federalism as an option and deliberately under-represented, in the committee managing the process, areas such as Montreal, where there were sizeable components of English-speaking and ethnic residents. These groups could be expected to vote against independence. Indian and Inuit peoples also denounced the PQ plan, insisting that it did not recognize their desire to remain under the historic protection of the government in Ottawa. If Quebec seceded from Canada, they stated, there could be no quarrel with their right to leave Quebec and remain part of Canada. Prime Minister Jean Chrétien, head of the central government in Ottawa, repudiated M. Parizeau's strategy, while Mr Johnson, speaking for Quebec's federalists, refused to participate in what he termed a 'flawed' consultative process.

Although federalists could take comfort from the fact that separatist sentiment in Quebec had barely increased in 14 years, there were important differences between the situations in 1980 and 1994. The Canadian election of 1993 had brought a separatist party, the Bloc Québécois (BQ), to the federal parliament, where it controlled 54 of Quebec's 75 seats and was thus the largest opposition party in the House of Commons. Its leader, Lucien Bouchard, was a forceful critic of the Chrétien government and a figure of magnetic appeal in Quebec. But M. Bouchard was mysteriously struck down by streptococcus A bacteria, losing his left leg on 1 December as physicians struggled to control the infection. He survived but clearly would be unable to play the leading part that separatists had planned for him in the referendum campaign. As well, in 1994 there was less disposition on the part of the rest of Canada to make major concessions in order to placate Quebec. M. Crétien had ruled out further efforts in the short term to amend the constitution, preferring to meet Quebec's desire for change through *ad hoc* administrative arrangements. Typical of this approach was a plan reached by federal and provincial first ministers on 18 July to dismantle or reduce inter-provincial trade barriers. Found in such fields as food products, government procurement, financial services and labour mobility, the barriers were estimated to cost Canadians about Can$6,500 million annually in increased costs.

The Chrétien government, holding a comfortable majority based on 176 Commons seats out of 295, moved cautiously in its legislative programme in 1994. The government sponsored far-reaching reviews of areas marked out for future action: social assistance, unemployment insurance, health care and foreign and defence policies. It also promised tough measures to deal with the national deficit through assessing the worth of all government spending programmes. The Prime Minister's calm approach to the question of national unity (he insisted that

Quebeckers would reject separation in a popular vote) seemed to reassure Canadians, both inside and outside Quebec, who gave his administration a larger margin of support than it had enjoyed when it took office in November 1993. Although the federalist campaign for the Quebec referendum would be directed by Mr Johnson, there was no doubt that M. Chrétien and other federalist Quebec ministers would play an active part by speaking directly to voters.

Canada climbed steadily out of recession in 1994. Economic growth in the third quarter reached 4.8 per cent on a year-on-year basis, sparked by a record level of exports, mainly to the United States, and marked by the strongest corporate profits in five years. Gross domestic product (GDP) at the end of June, on a seasonally-adjusted basis at market prices, was estimated at Can$739,600 million. Unemployment remained stubbornly high, although by November the jobless rate had fallen to 9.6 per cent of the labour force, the lowest level since the end of 1990. Inflation remained under control, the consumer price index actually falling for several months during the year. In May, for instance, the index fell by 0.2 per cent from the year before as the government reduced taxes on cigarettes in an effort to curtail smuggling from the United States. In November the index stood at minus 0.1 per cent.

The Finance Minister, Paul Martin, presented his first budget on 22 February. It contained no new taxes nor any increases in tax rates. The current unacceptable level of the deficit, running at 5.4 per cent of GDP, preoccupied Mr Martin. He predicted that expenditure restrictions and revenue growth from an expanding economy would reduce the shortfall from Can$45,700 million in the 1993/94 fiscal year to Can$39,700 million in 1994/95. His objective was to achieve a goal set forth by the Liberals in their 1993 election campaign: a deficit amounting to only 3 per cent of GDP by 1996/97. Rising interest rates during the latter months of 1994, increasing the charges on the public debt, threatened to jeopardize this deficit planning for 1994/95. Defence suffered the deepest cuts in Mr Martin's budget, with four large military bases to be closed in the Maritime provinces and Quebec and 16 smaller installations to be eliminated or pared in size. Cuts were also announced for military and civilian personnel, leaving an armed force of 66,700 men and women at the end of a four-year process.

In foreign affairs M. Chrétien adopted a more independent attitude towards the United States than his predecessor had done. In relations with Cuba, for instance, Canada, which had never suspended diplomatic links with the government of Fidel Castro, moved to resume aid which had been cut off in 1978. Canada made it clear that it did not approve of the exclusion of Cuba from the trade conference of the Americas held in Miami in early December (see IV.1). It did not take part in the first phase of the US intervention in Haiti (see IV.3.xii), although later it sent a contingent of the Royal Canadian Mounted Police to help in training Haitians for police duties.

Canada was a major supplier of peace-keeping forces in Croatia and Bosnia, having about 2,000 personnel engaged in monitoring the fighting and helping to distribute food and emergency supplies. M. Chrétien agreed reluctantly with the NATO decision to use air strikes in Bosnia to force the Serbs to withdraw artillery from around Sarajevo and to observe truce agreements (see II.1.vi). As the situation on the ground in Bosnia deteriorated and the Canadian peace-keepers came under increasing danger of attack, the Chrétien government promised to review the efficacy of the Canadian mission early in 1995.

Canadian peace-keepers, mainly communications specialists, were caught in the middle of the savage conflict in Rwanda in the first half of the year (see VII.1.2) before being relieved by a larger UN force during the summer. A Canadian general commanded the first UN Assistance Mission assigned to Rwanda. Altogether in 1994 there were 3,825 Canadian military personnel serving under the UN's command in the Middle East, the Balkans, Africa and Asia.

3. LATIN AMERICA

ARGENTINA—BOLIVIA—BRAZIL—CHILE—COLOMBIA—ECUADOR—
PARAGUAY—PERU—URUGUAY—VENEZUELA—CUBA—
DOMINICAN REPUBLIC AND HAITI—CENTRAL AMERICA
AND PANAMA—MEXICO

i. ARGENTINA

CAPITAL: Buenos Aires   AREA: 2,766,890 sq km   POPULATION: 33,100,000 ('92)
OFFICIAL LANGUAGE: Spanish   POLITICAL SYSTEM: federal presidential democracy
HEAD OF STATE & GOVERNMENT: President Carlos Saúl Menem (since July '89)
RULING PARTY: Justicialist (Peronist) Party (since Dec '89)
PRINCIPAL MINISTERS: Guido di Tella (foreign relations), Óscar Camilión (defence),
    Domingo Cavallo (economy), Carlos Federico Ruckauff (interior), Rodolfo Barra
    (justice)
INTERNATIONAL ALIGNMENT: OAS
CURRENCY: peso (end-'94 £1=AP1.56, US$1=AP1.00)
GNP PER CAPITA: US$6,050 ('92)
MAIN EXPORT EARNERS: wheat, other agricultural produce, manufactures

DIVISIONS surfaced in the opposition Radical Civic Union (UCR) over the decision of former President Raúl Alfonsín Foulkes to support President Carlos Menem's constitutional reform proposals under the so-called Olivos Pact of December 1993. However, when on 10 April elections were held for the Constituent Assembly, which was to meet for a maximum of 90 days, the Peronists (PJ) won 136 seats but failed to gain an overall majority. The UCR won 75 seats with less than 20 per cent of the vote and the dissident Peronist Big Front (FG) won 31 seats and 12.5 per cent. The Convention was formally inaugurated by President Menem on 25 May at Paran, in the province of Entre Rios, and completed its work on 22 August, following which public officials swore allegiance to the new constitution. Two months later a split in the PJ deprived it of an overall majority in the Chamber of Deputies.

Unrest in Jujuy in April relating to the high cost of living echoed earlier disturbances in Santiago del Estero. As the peso became increasingly overvalued, threatening its dollar parity, a presidential decree on 19 November banned all new public-sector expenditure for the remainder of the year. Finance Minister Cavallo blamed the rising cost of the pension system, which had been privatized in May. On 10 June the President had unexpectedly announced his intention to abolish compulsory military service at the end of the current 12-month period. The cost of replacing the 18,700 serving conscripts by volunteers was expected to increase defence spending by 5 per cent. Nevertheless, on 28 September the government had announced that it would not be taking up the last two tranches of its IMF loan.

President Menem, who had caused an uproar on 2 November by publicly defending the role of the armed forces in the 'dirty war' of 1976–83, opened his campaign for re-election in April 1995 on 20 November, with the opinion polls giving him a commanding lead over all other candidates. A week later the UCR, which had earlier nominated Federico Storani as its presidential candidate, replaced him by Horacio Massaccesi, governor of Río Negro. The right-wing Movement for Dignity and Independence (MODIN) nominated its leader, Aldo Rico.

ii. BOLIVIA

CAPITAL: La Paz and Sucre   AREA: 1,099,000 sq km   POPULATION: 7,500,000 ('92)
OFFICIAL LANGUAGES: Spanish, Quechua, Aymará
POLITICAL SYSTEM: presidential democracy
HEAD OF STATE & GOVERNMENT: President Gonzálo Sánchez de Lozada (since Aug '93)
RULING PARTIES: Nationalist Revolutionary Movement (MNR) heads coalition with Túpac Katari Revolutionary Liberation Movement (MRTKL), Civic Solidarity Union (UCS) & Free Bolivia Movement (MBL)
PRINCIPAL MINISTERS: Víctor Hugo Cárdenas (MRTKL/Vice-President), Antonio Araníbar Quiroga (MBL/foreign affairs), Raúl Tovar Pierola (UCS/defence), Fernando Alvaro Cossio (MNR/economic development & finance), René Blattman Bauer (ind./justice)
INTERNATIONAL ALIGNMENT: NAM, OAS
CURRENCY: boliviano (end-'94 £1=Bs7.37, US$1=Bs4.71)
GNP PER CAPITA: US$680 ('92)
MAIN EXPORT EARNERS: natural gas, tin

A 24-hour general strike, called by the Bolivian Workers' Central (COB) for 24 January, had little support. Unrest continued for several weeks but was halted by an agreement with the government on 7 May. Continued tension in the ruling coalition led President Gonzálo Sánchez de Lozada to replace half his cabinet on 26 March, increasing the representation of his Nationalist Revolutionary Movement (MNR) to seven portfolios out of 11. On the same day, former President Jaime Paz Zamora, of the opposition Movement of the Revolutionary Left (MIR), announced his premature retirement from politics, after a report prepared by the Special Force Against the Drugs Trade (FELCN) in conjunction with the US Drugs Enforcement Agency (DEA) had made damaging accusations, strongly denied, that he and members of his family had conspired to conceal evidence of drug-trafficking. The leader of the MIR, Oscar Eid Franco, was arrested on 26 December on similar charges.

On 19 May the government announced a new decree regulating coca production, warning that if it was not accepted by the growers' organization, which had earlier been consulted, compulsory measures would have to be used. However, after widespread demonstrations, the government finally accepted a compromise plan on 22 September which conceded nearly all the disputed points.

Former President Luis García Meza, sentenced *in absentia* in April 1993 to 30 years' imprisonment on various charges of abuse of power (see AR 1993, p. 173), was arrested by Brazilian police in São Paulo on 11 March and held for extradition.

iii. BRAZIL

CAPITAL: Brasília   AREA: 8,512,000 sq km   POPULATION: 153,900,000 ('91)
OFFICIAL LANGUAGE: Portuguese   POLITICAL SYSTEM: federal presidential democracy
HEAD OF STATE & GOVERNMENT: President Itamar Franco (since Dec '92)
PRESIDENT-ELECT: Fernando Henrique Cardoso (to be inaugurated Jan '95)
RULING PARTIES: Brazilian Democratic Movement (PMDB), Liberal Front (PFL),
    Brazilian Social Democratic (PSDB), Progressive (PP) & Workers' (PT) parties
PRINCIPAL MINISTERS: Ciro Gomes (PFL/finance), Beni Veras (ind./planning & budget),
    Celso Luis Nuñez Amorim (ind./foreign affairs), Alexandre de Paula Dupeyrat
    Martins (ind./justice)
INTERNATIONAL ALIGNMENT: OAS
CURRENCY: real (end-'94 £1=R1.33, US$1=R0.85)
GNP PER CAPITA: US$2,770 ('92)
MAIN EXPORT EARNERS: coffee, iron ore, soyabeans, tourism

ON 21 January the congressional committee investigating charges of corruption in the federal budget committee recommended the expulsion of 18 members of the Chamber of Deputies. Debate on constitutional reform resumed, but concluded on 31 May with only six amendments actually approved, including one to reduce the presidential term to four years. On 8 February Congress had agreed to the creation of a Social Emergency Fund (FSE), transferring a wide range of state programmes to federal government control. This was a personal victory for the Finance Minister, Fernando Henrique Cardoso of the Social Democratic Party (PSDB), and marked the first step in a plan to introduce a new dollar-based currency called the real. The real duly became Brazil's official currency on 1 July.

President Itamar Franco (non-party) had difficulty holding together his cabinet in January and was further discredited in the eyes of some the following month when he was filmed during the Rio Carnival dancing with a scantily-dressed part-time prostitute. Sr Cardoso announced his candidature for the presidency on 30 March and was replaced as Finance Minister by Rubens Ricúpero, former ambassador to the United States. Sr Ricúpero was forced to resign on 3 September, however, after he had inadvertently revealed on nationwide television that he had 'massaged' the inflation figures to aid Sr Cardoso's election campaign, and was replaced by Ciro Gomes, governor of Ceará state.

In the first round of the presidential election, held on 4 October, Sr Cardoso won outright, obtaining 53.4 per cent of the votes cast, against 27.0 per cent for his nearest rival, Luís Inácio ('Lula') da Silva of the Workers Party (PT). In Rio de Janeiro, where ballot-rigging had been massive, troops were called in to guard the election officials, and the elections were subsequently annulled. In the second round on 15 November, the PSDB won the governorships of only six of the 27 states, against nine for the Party of the Brazilian Democratic Movement (PMDB), but the PSDB victories included São Paulo, Minas Gerais and Rio de Janeiro (the three most populous states). The PMDB presidential candidate, Orestes Quércia, had been indicted in May on charges of fraud and came a bad fourth in the presidential election (with 4.4 per cent). His party re-emerged as the largest single formation in Congress, with 105 seats in the 517-member Chamber and 23 in the 81-member Senate; but the Cardoso-led coalition (including the PSDB and the Liberal Front Party) won 175 Chamber and 33 Senate seats on a platform of economic and financial stability combined with constitutional reform.

Troops were deployed in Brasília, São Paulo and Belém in May, when the federal police joined other public sector workers in a nationwide strike. Subsequently, on 11 June, President Franco ordered military salaries to be brought into line with those for civil servants. Some 65,000 troops were placed on alert for the elections, after which, in a crackdown on organized drug-trafficking on 18-20 November, teams of soldiers went into the shanty-towns (favelas) of Rio. No significant resistance was encountered. Alleging that the local police were collaborating with the criminals, the army justified their action by describing it as pacification rather than confrontation.

On 12 December the Supreme Court voted 5-to-3 to acquit former President Fernando Collor de Mello of the charge of passive corruption which had led to his resignation, under threat of impeachment, in December 1992 (see AR 1992, pp. 176-7).

iv. CHILE

CAPITAL: Santiago   AREA: 756,000 sq km   POPULATION: 13,600,000 ('92)
OFFICIAL LANGUAGE: Spanish   POLITICAL SYSTEM: presidential democracy
HEAD OF STATE & GOVERNMENT: President Eduardo Frei Ruíz Tagle (since March '94)
RULING PARTY: Christian Democratic Party (PDC) heads Coalition of Parties for Democracy (CPD), which is in coalition with Socialist (PS), Democracy (PPD) & Social Democratic (PSD) parties
PRINCIPAL MINISTERS: Carlos Figueroa Serrano (PDC/interior), José Miguel Insulza (PS/foreign affairs), Alvaro García Hurtado (PPD/economy), Eduardo Aniniat Ureta (PDC/finance), Soledad Alvear (PDC/justice), Edmundo Pérez Yoma (PDC/defence)
INTERNATIONAL ALIGNMENT: OAS, NAM
CURRENCY: peso (end-94 £1=Ch$627.44, US$1=Ch$401.05)
GNP PER CAPITA: US$2,730 ('92)
MAIN EXPORT EARNERS: copper, agricultural products

ON 13 February a joint session of Congress voted for the reduction of the presidential term from eight to the traditional six years, rather than the four agreed the previous year. Eduardo Frei Ruíz Tagle of the Christian Democratic Party (PDC), who had been elected in December 1993 as candidate of the ruling Coalition of Parties for Democracy (see AR 1993, p. 177), was inaugurated as President in the Congress building in Valparaiso on 11 March. It was the first time since 1970 that a peaceful transition of power had occurred between democratically-elected candidates.

The previous day, outgoing President Patricio Aylwin Azócar (PDC) had pardoned three men sentenced for the unsuccessful assassination attempt in 1986 on the then head of state (and still army commander), General Augusto Pinochet (see AR 1986, p. 76). The General, who had the right to hold his army post until 1997, said that the army 'would remain in silence and obey orders'. The continuing constitutional immunity of the armed forces was demonstrated on 17 May when the commander of the Carabineros paramilitary police, General Rodolfo Stange Oelckers, was cleared by a military court of charges of dereliction of duty. The general (who resumed his command) had been accused of serious civil rights abuses and in April had been invited to resign by President Frei. On the other hand, the Supreme Court held on 3 June that the 1978 Amnesty Law did not apply to the two officers of the former secret police who had been convicted in November 1993 of the murder of former Foreign Minister Orlando Letelier in Washington in 1976.

Promising a national crusade against poverty, President Frei appointed Alvaro García of the Party for Democracy (PPD) as Minister for the Economy and Edmundo Pérez Yoma as Minister of Defence. Germán Correa Díaz of the Socialist Party (PS) became Interior Minister but was replaced on 20 September by Carlos Figueroa Serrano, whose Foreign Affairs portfolio was entrusted to José Miguel Insulza (PS).

v.   COLOMBIA

CAPITAL: Bogotá   AREA: 1,141,750 sq km   POPULATION: 33,400,000 ('92)
OFFICIAL LANGUAGE: Spanish   POLITICAL SYSTEM: presidential democracy
HEAD OF STATE & GOVERNMENT: President Ernesto Samper Pizano (since Aug '94)
RULING PARTIES: Liberal Party (PL), Social Conservative Party (PSC) & Alliance for Colombia (AC)
PRINCIPAL MINISTERS: Rodrígo Pardo García-Peña (PL/foreign affairs), Horacio Sepra Uribe (PL/interior), Guillermo Perry Rubio (PL/finance), Fernando Botero Zea (PL/defence), Néstor Humberto Martínez Neira (PL/justice)
INTERNATIONAL ALIGNMENT: NAM, OAS
CURRENCY: peso (end-'94 £1=Col$1,301.04, US$1=Col$831.60)
GNP PER CAPITA: US$1,330 ('92)
MAIN EXPORT EARNERS: coffee, oil & oil derivatives

THE 1994 event in Colombia that hit the world's headlines was the murder in Medellín on 2 July of the country's leading footballer, Andrés Escobar, whose 'own goal' against the United States had effectively put the national side out of the World Cup finals in the USA (see Pt. XVII). Violence continued throughout the year. An attempt by the Army of National Liberation (ELN) on 17 January to assassinate the then Finance Minister, Rudolf Hommes Rodríguez, was specifically linked to the government's free market policies. Nevertheless, in congressional and local elections on 13 March the ruling Liberal Party (PL) retained its majority and left-wing parties lost ground. On 20 March the US State Department complained of the unhelpful attitude towards drug-trafficking of the Colombian Attorney-General, Gustavo de Grieff. There was wider international criticism of a decision by the Constitutional Court on 6 May, by five votes to four, that laws against the personal possession of drugs were unconstitutional because they violated 'rights of privacy and free development of the personality'. Aerial spraying of coca fields was halted in December following complaints from farmers.

In the first round of the presidential elections, postponed from 8 to 29 May to encourage greater participation, Ernesto Samper Pizano (PL) headed Andrés Pastrana Arango of the Social Conservative Party (PSC) by a small margin. In the second round on 19 June, Sr Samper (a 43-year-old economist who had previously served as Development Minister) was elected with 50.37 per cent of the vote. His political opponents were believed to have been behind reports (strongly denied) that his campaign had been financed by the Cali drugs cartel.

The main task of President Samper's government, which was sworn in on 7 August, was to deal with the challenge of the revitalized Simón Bolívar National Guerrilla Coordinating Board (CNGSB), which had stepped up attacks in the last weeks of the outgoing presidency. In September and October indications came from both the ELN and the Colombian Revolutionary Armed Forces (FARC) that they were prepared to enter into dialogue with the government; by then, however, a new guerrilla group called the Popular Front of National Liberation (FPLN) had emerged. On 3 November guerrillas ambushed a police caravan, killing 11 officers and one student in a school bus that was caught in the crossfire. A further 21 people died in a clash between FARC guerrillas and security forces near San Pedro (in Antioquia department) on 21 November. By then the President had announced, on 17 November, that his government was prepared to enter into peace talks without preconditions, this initiative being greeted positively by the ELN's Francisco Galán. On 22 November General Ramón Emilio Gil Bermúdez, who had served as commander of the armed forces since 1992 and who was known to have resisted the idea of dialogue, was replaced by General Hernando Camilo Zúñiga Chaparro. On 9 December the government signed a social pact with representatives of business and labour.

An earthquake on 6 June, measuring 6.0 on the Richter Scale, killed at least 269 people in the village of Toez in south-western Colombia and devastated communities in the Páez river valley.

vi. ECUADOR

CAPITAL: Quito   AREA: 270,500 sq km   POPULATION: 11,000,000 ('92)
OFFICIAL LANGUAGE: Spanish   POLITICAL SYSTEM: presidential democracy
HEAD OF STATE & GOVERNMENT: President Sixto Durán Ballén (since Aug '92)
RULING PARTIES: Republican Unity Party (PUR) and Ecuadorian Conservative Party
  (PCE) hold presidency and vice-presidency respectively, Social Christian Party
  (PSC) dominates Congress
PRINCIPAL MINISTERS: Alberto Dahik Garzoni (Vice-President), Galo Leoro Franco
  (foreign affairs), Abraham Romero (government & justice), Gen. José Gallardo
  Román (defence), Modesto Correa San Andres (finance), José Vicente
  Maldonado (industry), Gustavo Galindo (energy & mines)
INTERNATIONAL ALIGNMENT: NAM, OAS
CURRENCY: sucre (end-'94 £1=S/.3,554.40, US$1=S/.2,271.91)
GNP PER CAPITA: US$1,070 ('92)
MAIN EXPORT EARNERS: oil & oil derivatives, coffee, bananas

THE government of President Sixto Durán Ballén began the year facing strong criticism of its free market policies from the United Workers' Front (FUT). Having failed to persuade Congress to agree to increase value-added tax to compensate for declining oil revenue, the government decided instead to raise petrol prices by 71 per cent. This provoked serious riots in major cities from 27 January, until the Court of Constitutional Guarantees ruled on 11 February that the increase was unconstitutional. On 1 March President Durán Ballén announced that a plebiscite on constitutional reform would be held at the congressional elections on 1 May, but the opposition-controlled Supreme Electoral Tribunal (TSE) ruled that such a consultation would be illegal.

In the elections themselves, the two government parties and pro-government independents lost their majority in Congress, retaining control of only 11 of the 77 seats, which were divided between 12 parties and two independents. The right-wing opposition gained a commanding position, the Social Christian Party (PSC) led by Jaime Nebot Saadi advancing to 26 seats in total (emerging as a national party in the process) and the Roldosista Party of Ecuador (PRE) to 11 seats. An attempt by the new right-wing majority to reverse 30 years of slow land reform by means of a Land Development Law passed on 13 June led to massive protests from the National Confederation of the Indigenous Population of Ecuador (CONAIE), before the Court of Constitutional Guarantees ruled the law unconstitutional on 23 June. An amended law guaranteed the rights of those who directly worked land, whether as individuals or associations.

On 3 May Ecuador reached an agreement with commercial banks (under the US Brady Plan) to restructure $4,500 million of its capital debt and $3,100 million of interest, the IMF on 11 May approving a standby credit of SDR 130 million to assist the arrangement. In September, however, Diego Paredes Peña was forced to resign as Foreign Minister by a congressional vote of censure on his handling of external relations. In October, moreover, the Minister of Energy and Mines, Francisco Acosta Coloma, was also forced out, after being criticized for licensing the US Texaco oil company to operate in Ecuadorian Amazonia.

vii. PARAGUAY

CAPITAL: Asunción   AREA: 406,752 sq km   POPULATION: 4,500,000 ('92)
OFFICIAL LANGUAGE: Spanish   POLITICAL SYSTEM: republic
HEAD OF STATE & GOVERNMENT: President Juan Carlos Wasmosy (since Aug '93)
RULING PARTY: Colorado Party
PRINCIPAL MINISTERS: Angel Roberto Feisart (Vice-President), Luís María Ramírez
    Boettner (foreign affairs), Carlos Podestá (interior), Crispiano Sandoval (finance),
    Hugo Estigarribia Elizeche (defence), Juan Manuel Morales (justice & labour),
    Ubaldo Scavone (industry & trade)
INTERNATIONAL ALIGNMENT: OAS
CURRENCY: guarani (end-'94 £1=G2,994.10, US$1=G1,913.77)
GNP PER CAPITA: US$1,380 ('92)
MAIN EXPORT EARNERS: cotton, soyabeans, meat

THE country's two major labour federations, the Workers' Unitary Central (CUT) and the National Workers' Confederation (CNT), staged a 24-hour general strike on 2 May, demanding pay increases and a halt both to privatization and to economic integration with Argentina, Brazil and Uruguay within the Southern Cone Common Market (Mercosur). The government of President Carlos Wasmosy, which for months had faced rural unrest, deployed tanks around Asunción, at least 20 demonstrators being killed in clashes with security forces, including peasant leader Sebastin Larrosa. On 24 September the President carried out a reshuffle of the armed forces command, strengthening the position of the army commander-in-chief, General Lino Oviedo, whose associate, General Roosevelt Benítez, was appointed head of the joint chiefs of staff.

viii. PERU

CAPITAL: Lima AREA: 1,285,000 sq km POPULATION: 22,400,000 ('92)
OFFICIAL LANGUAGES: Spanish, Quechua & Aymará
POLITICAL SYSTEM: presidential democracy
HEAD OF STATE & GOVERNMENT: President Alberto Keinya Fujimori (since July '90)
RULING PARTY: New Majority-Change 90 heads government coalition
PRINCIPAL MINISTERS: Efrain Goldenberg Schreiber (Prime Minister, foreign affairs), Jorge Camet Dickman (economy & finance), Gen. E.P. Víctor Malca Villanueva (defence), Fernando Vega Santagadea (justice), Gen. Juan Briones Davila (interior)
INTERNATIONAL ALIGNMENT: NAM, OAS
CURRENCY: new sol (end-'94 £1=NS3.41, US$1=NS2.18)
GNP PER CAPITA: US$950 ('92)
MAIN EXPORT EARNERS: copper, petroleum products

A major split was reported in the Sendero Luminoso guerrilla movement, whose imprisoned leader, Abimael Guzmán ('Presidente Gonzalo'), was said by the goverment to have called on his followers to surrender (see AR 1993, p. 180), whereas militants led by Oscar Ramírez Durand ('Feliciano') favoured continued armed struggle. A total of 6,000 former guerrillas had surrendered under the 'law of repentance' before it expired on 31 October, casualties in the internal conflict having fallen to some 300 in the previous 12 months.

The main beneficiary was the President, Alberto Keinya Fujimori, who continued to rule by decree while running for re-election in April 1995. In a serious assault on judicial autonomy, in February the President arranged for the cases against nine members of the armed forces accused of the abduction and murder in July 1992 of nine students and a professor from the University of La Cantuta to be transferred from a civil to a military court, which sentenced two majors to 20 years' imprisonment and the rest to between one and 15 years. Although the President had the support of the Democratic Constituent

Congress (CCD)—which had no jurisdiction in the matter—the Prime Minister, Alfonso Bustamente y Bustamente, resigned and was replaced on 17 February by the Foreign Minister, Efrain Goldenberg Schreiber. On 28 July the President claimed that terrorism had been defeated. Nevertheless, on 13 November the government extended the existing state of emergency in Lima and Callao for a further 90 days, citing continuing terrorist activity as its justification. Renewed guerrilla actions in December cost at least 26 lives.

The campaign for the 1995 elections was enlivened by a public breach in August between President Fujimori and his 44-year-old wife, Susana Higuchi. The President, having changed the constitution to permit his re-election, had issued a decree banning his wife from running for public office, at which she had protested. Finding that the door to her apartments in the presidential palace had been welded shut to prevent her leaving, she was released only after she had shouted out of the window to reporters and members of the public that her husband was a 'heartless, ruthless, corrupt dictator' who allowed violations of human rights to occur daily. Shortly afterwards she announced her intention to contest the presidency herself, but the National Election Board (JNE) ruled in October that her '21st Century Harmony Party' had failed to obtain the necessary 100,000 signatures. Undeterred, she subsequently formed an electoral alliance with the Police–Military Front (FREPOL), consisting of retired military and police personnel, which was recognized by the JNE on 28 November. In December she announced that she had commenced both divorce and annulment proceedings against her estranged husband.

The President continued to enjoy strong support on account of his apparent success on the economic front. After a period of contraction between 1987 and 1991, the economy grew by over 10 per cent in 1994, while inflation fell to around 20 per cent and foreign investment, stimulated by a far-reaching programme of privatization, rose steeply. Meanwhile, Sr Fujimori's leading rivals for the presidency—former UN Secretary-General Javier Pérez de Cuéllar (74) and Alejandro Toledo (47), a native Quechua-speaking banker—trailed in the opinion polls. Only six of the 15 organizations standing in the forthcoming elections were prepared to sign an agreement to conduct a clean and non-violent campaign. President Fujimori's New Majority–Change 90 was not one of them.

ix. URUGUAY

CAPITAL: Montevideo AREA: 176,200 sq km POPULATION: 3,100,000 ('92)
OFFICIAL LANGUAGE: Spanish POLITICAL SYSTEM: presidential democracy
HEAD OF STATE & GOVERNMENT: President Luis Alberto Lacalle Herrera (since '90)
PRESIDENT-ELECT: Julio María Sanguinetti (to be inaugurated March '95)
RULING PARTY: National (Blanco) Party heads coalition
PRINCIPAL MINISTERS: Gonzalo Aguirre Ramirez (Vice-President), Sergio Abreu
  Bonilla (foreign relations), Angel M. Gianola (interior), Ignacio de Posadas
  (economy & finance), Daniel Hugo Martins (defence), Miguel Angel Galán
  (industry & energy)
INTERNATIONAL ALIGNMENT: OAS
CURRENCY: new peso (end-'94 £1=NUr$8.82, US$1=NUr5.64)
GNP PER CAPITA: US$3,340 ('92)
MAIN EXPORT EARNERS: wool, meat

IN presidential elections on 27 November, victory in a three-way contest
went to the leading candidate of four running under the banner of
the opposition Colorado Party, 58-year-old former President Julio
Sanguinetti. His party obtained 617,470 votes to 595,936 for the
ruling National Party (Blancos), which in turn was only narrowly
ahead of the left-wing Progressive Encounter, the former Broad Front
(Frente Amplio), with 585,109. In a record turnout of 89.4 per cent,
the result was the closest in the country's history. Sr Sanguinetti
fought and won the campaign on the need to provide employment
and to develop manufacturing industry, while his main rival, Juan
Andrés Ramírez, who was endorsed by President Luis Lacalle Herrera,
defended the administration's record of fiscal rectitude, low inflation and
privatization. In simultaneous congressional elections, the Colorados
won 11 of the 30 Senate seats, the Blancos ten and Progressive Encounter
nine, while the 99 seats in the Chamber of Deputies were distributed in
similar proportions.

x. VENEZUELA

CAPITAL: Caracas AREA: 912,000 sq km POPULATION: 20,200,000 ('91)
OFFICIAL LANGUAGE: Spanish POLITICAL SYSTEM: presidential democracy
HEAD OF STATE & GOVERNMENT: President Rafael Caldera Rodríguez (since Feb '94)
RULING PARTIES: 17–party National Convergence coalition
PRINCIPAL MINISTERS: Miguel Angel Burelli Rivas (foreign affairs), Ramón Escovar
  Salom (interior), Julio Sosa Rodríguez (finance), Gen. Orozco Graterol
  (defence), Erwin José Arrieta (energy & mines), Rubens Creixems (justice)
INTERNATIONAL ALIGNMENT: OAS, NAM
CURRENCY: bolivar (end-'94 £1=Bs265.76, US$1=Bs169.87)
GNP PER CAPITA: US$2,910 ('92)
MAIN EXPORT EARNERS: oil, aluminium

UNREST continued at the introduction of value-added tax in September
1993 by the government of acting President José Ramón Velásquez

(see AR 1993, p. 182), with the result that President-elect Rafael Caldera Rodríguez supported a decision on 10 January to fix prices of basic foodstuffs and medicines. Before his inauguration on 2 February, Dr Caldera unexpectedly 'invited' the Defence Minister, Vice-Admiral Rádames Muñoz León, and the military commanders to resign. Proclaiming 1994 a year of stabilization and promising a sustained anti-inflationary campaign, the new President appointed the banker and businessman Julio Sosa Rodríguez as Finance Minister and prominent diplomat Miguel Angel Burelli Rivas as Foreign Minister. In a gesture of goodwill towards the armed forces, on 13 February he ordered the release of 23 officers and other ranks who had been imprisoned for participation in attempted coups in 1992 (see AR 1992, pp. 183-4); most of the rest, including their leader, Lieutenant-Colonel Hugo Chávez Frías, were amnestied on 26 March. On 18 May the Supreme Court issued a warrant for the arrest of former President Carlos Andrés Pérez; hearings on the corruption charges against him eventually began at the end of November.

The new government faced challenges on two fronts. A strike by thousands of public sector workers resulted in water shortages in Caracas, while violent crime continued to rise (more than 3,400 people being killed in the first nine months of the year). On 12 May the government announced that all major cities would be 'militarized' and on 7 November the National Guard were deployed to patrol urban areas in support of the police. Meanwhile, cross-border attacks by Colombian guerrillas resulted in the deployment of additional forces in the frontier zone and the signature on 22 November of an agreement with Colombia providing for joint operations.

The currency continued to be in a state of crisis. The collapse of the country's second-largest commercial bank, Banco Latino, led to the issue of warrants for the arrest of 83 executives. Despite the resignation on 26 April of the central bank president, Ruth de Krivoy, her successor, Antonio Casas González, was unable to halt the fall of the bolívar. Additional taxes were announced on 25 May in an effort to reduce the fiscal deficit and on 27 June the government adopted emergency powers to try to stem the collapse in economic confidence, including the suspension of six civic and economic guarantees contained in the constitution. This action provoked a confrontation with Congress, which on 21 July voted to restore five of them, obliging the government, after several days of confusion, to shelve the emergency powers strategy. Eventually, on 12 September, a two-year economic stabilization plan was announced. By the end of 1994 the government had taken over some 70 per cent of the banking system, but still faced acute financial and social difficulties.

xi. CUBA

CAPITAL: Havana AREA: 115,000 sq km POPULATION: 10,800,000 ('92)
OFFICIAL LANGUAGE: Spanish POLITICAL SYSTEM: republic, one-party communist
    state
HEAD OF STATE & GOVERNMENT: President Fidel Castro Ruz (since Jan '59)
RULING PARTY: Cuban Communist Party (PCC)
PRINCIPAL MINISTERS: Gen. Raúl Castro Ruz (1st Vice-President, defence), Roberto
    Robaina González (foreign relations), Gen Abelardo Colomé Ibarra (interior),
    José Luis Rodríguez García (finance & prices), Antonio Rodriques Maurell
    (Deputy Premier, planning), Alfredo Jordan Morales (agriculture)
INTERNATIONAL ALIGNMENT: NAM
CURRENCY: peso (end-'94 £1=Cub$1.56, US$1=Cub$0.99)
GNP PER CAPITA: n.a.
MAIN EXPORT EARNERS: sugar & sugar products

WHILE strenuous efforts continued to be made to safeguard health and
social services, the Cuban economy continued its decline. Speaking in
Santiago de Cuba to mark the 35th anniversary of the revolution,
President Fidel Castro Ruz described 1993 as 'our toughest year'. Power
cuts of eight to 12 hours a day had become commonplace because of
lack of fuel. Under a deal signed in March, Russia agreed to deliver
2.5 million tonnes of oil in exchange for a million tonnes of sugar. The
sugar harvest—undertaken with only 22 per cent of normal resources,
according to Vice-President Carlos Lage—was again a failure: at 4
million tonnes it was 10 per cent less than the poor harvest of 1992/93.

On 12 May a special session of the National Assembly of People's
Power (ANPP) enacted a package of measures to halt the depreciation of
the currency, curb profiteering and reduce the budget deficit. However,
Cuba remained critically short of foreign exchange, with the result that
on 1 November Russia announced that it was suspending shipments,
even though it had earlier declared that it would honour the commitment
of the former Soviet Union to provide the necessary credits for the
completion of the nuclear power plant at Cienfuegos.

When Vice-President Raúl Castro made the keynote address at
celebrations on 26 July to mark the 41st anniversary of the Moncada
uprising, he blamed the US embargo for an incident on 13 July in
which 32 would-be refugees had drowned when their escape vessel
had sunk. Many people continued to perish in the attempt to reach
the United States across the shark-infested Florida Straits. In Havana,
violent clashes had again occurred on 11 February round the offices of
the US special interests section of the Swiss embassy, following a rumour
that US visas were to be issued. In an effort to improve relations with
the outside world, the government had convened a special conference
on immigration in Havana on 22–24 April, although the most hostile
exile organizations were not invited.

A serious crisis developed when on 11 August President Castro
indicated that Cuba would no longer try to stop refugees leaving
the island, precipitating a greatly increased outflow. The Clinton

administration responded on 19 August by suspending the granting of automatic refugee status, banning further entry to the United States and establishing holding camps for would-be refugees at the US base at Guantánamo Bay (Cuba) and in Panama (see IV.1). The immediate crisis eased on 9 September, however, when Cuba and the United States agreed on measures to stem the flow of refugees; it was reported that the US side had pledged that measures on Cuba's part to liberalize trade would be reciprocated. At the end of September a new law was announced opening up all sectors of the Cuban economy to foreign participation and on 20 December, after the ANPP had approved the 1995 budget, official Cuban sources disclosed that a new convertible peso was to be introduced.

The first independent opinion survey to be conducted in Cuba since before Dr Castro came to power in 1959 took place in November. Designed by the *Miami Herald* newspaper and CID–Gallup, it showed that 58 per cent of the sample believed that the revolution's successes outweighed its failures and that 48 per cent described themselves as revolutionaries. The US embargo was cited as the main cause of the country's problems.

xii.   HAITI AND THE DOMINICAN REPUBLIC

Haiti

CAPITAL: Port-au-Prince   AREA: 27,750 sq km   POPULATION: 6,700,000 ('92)
OFFICIAL LANGUAGE: French   POLITICAL SYSTEM: military/presidential
HEAD OF STATE & GOVERNMENT: President Jean-Bertrand Aristide (elected Dec '90,
   deposed Sept '91, restored to power Oct '94)
CURRENCY: gourde (end-'94 £1=G29.85, US$1=G19.08)
GNP PER CAPITA: US$370 ('90)
MAIN EXPORT EARNERS: light manufactures, coffee, tourism

Dominican Republic

CAPITAL: Santo Domingo   AREA: 48,400 sq km   POPULATION: 7,300,000 ('92)
OFFICIAL LANGUAGE: Spanish   POLITICAL SYSTEM: presidential democracy
HEAD OF STATE & GOVERNMENT: President Joaquín Balaguer Ricardo (since Aug '86)
CURRENCY: peso (end-'94 £1=RD$20.69, US$1=RD$13.22)
GNP PER CAPITA: US$1,050 ('92)
MAIN EXPORT EARNERS: sugar, metals, tourism

DESPITE his blindness and his 87 years, President Joaquín Balaguer of the DOMINICAN REPUBLIC told delegates of the ruling Social Christian Reformist Party (PRSC) on 6 January that he intended to run for a seventh term of office. He received an overwhelming vote of confidence, but in the first round of the elections, held on 16 May, obtained only 42.5 per cent of the votes recorded against 41.4 per cent for José Francisco Peña Gómez of the centre-left Dominican Revolutionary Party (PRD). The campaign was marked by vicious racist attacks on Sr Peña Gómez (a black) by the official media and evidence of 'massive fraud', according to observers from the Organization of American States (OAS).

Faced with widespread protest strikes and demonstrations, Sr Balaguer at first rejected requests by both the PRD and the US State Department that fresh elections be held. Fortunately, as a result of mediation by the Catholic Church and the OAS, the three major parties agreed on 10 August to ban consecutive presidential terms, to replace the government-dominated Central Electoral Board (JCE) and to hold fresh elections on 16 November 1995. Meanwhile, President Balaguer was sworn in for a reduced term on 16 August and appointed former Vice-President Carlos Morales Troncoso as his new Foreign Minister.

In HAITI, despite some US and local misgivings, Fr Jean-Bertrand Aristide was restored to the presidency in October following an un-opposed landing on 19 September by 2,000 US marines. Elected in December 1990, Fr Aristide had been in exile in the United States since the military coup of September 1991 (see AR 1991, p. 79). The US intervention had been authorized by the UN Security Council on 31 July (see IV.1; XI.1). That it was unopposed was largely due to a compromise agreement secured in Port-au-Prince on 18 September by former US President Jimmy Carter in talks with junta leader General Raoul Cédras and his nominee for President, Emile Jonassaint, who had been elected by Haitian deputies on 11 May but had not been recognized by the US government.

Government in Haiti had been paralysed at the beginning of the year when Congress was inquorate and acting Prime Minister Robert Malval was unable to assemble his cabinet, while the UN embargo hit hard at the poorest sectors of society. Fr Aristide had rejected all previous attempts to reach a solution involving an amnesty for the military leaders, while the Duvalierist Revolutionary Front for the Advancement and Progress of Haiti (FRAPH) had mobilized to defeat the embargo and prevent Fr Aristide's restoration. After the US intervention, attacks on pro-Aristide demonstrators by the Haitian military continued largely unhindered by the occupying forces until the return of the President to Haiti aboard a US aircraft on 15 October. The junta leaders, whom the President had amnestied on 10 October, quietly left the island prior to his arrival.

On 17 October President Aristide wrote to the president of the Haitian episcopal conference accepting the latter's request that he relinquish the priesthood (the Vatican having been the only sovereign state to recognize the military regime). The new Prime Minister nominated on 25 October was Smarck Michel, a wealthy businessman who had served as Minister of Commerce in 1990–91. The new cabinet, sworn in on 8 November, retained six members of the transitional government appointed by the outgoing M. Malval. Virtually its first task was to deal with the consequences of Hurricane Gordon, which hit the island on

13–14 November, leaving over 800 dead and more than 10,000 homeless. On 20 December a provisional electoral council was formed to oversee forthcoming legislative elections.

xiii. CENTRAL AMERICA AND PANAMA

Guatemala
CAPITAL: Guatemala City   AREA: 109,000 sq km   POPULATION: 9,700,000 ('92)
OFFICIAL LANGUAGE: Spanish   POLITICAL SYSTEM: presidential democracy
HEAD OF STATE & GOVERNMENT: President Ramiro de León Carpio (since June '93)
CURRENCY: quetzal (end-'94 £1=Q8.77, US$1=Q5.61)
GNP PER CAPITA: US$980 ('92)
MAIN EXPORT EARNERS: coffee, sugar, cotton, petroleum, cardamom, bananas

El Salvador
CAPITAL: San Salvador   AREA: 21,400 sq km   POPULATION: 5,400,000 ('92)
OFFICIAL LANGUAGE: Spanish   POLITICAL SYSTEM: presidential democracy
HEAD OF STATE & GOVERNMENT: President Armando Calderón Sol (since June '94)
RULING PARTY: National Republican Alliance (Arena)
CURRENCY: colón (end-'94 £1=C13.71, US$1=C8.76)
GNP PER CAPITA: US$1,170 ('92)
MAIN EXPORT EARNERS: coffee, cotton, sugar

Honduras
CAPITAL: Tegucigalpa   AREA: 112,000 sq km   POPULATION: 5,400,000 ('92)
OFFICIAL LANGUAGE: Spanish   POLITICAL SYSTEM: presidential democracy
HEAD OF STATE & GOVERNMENT: President Carlos Roberto Reina Idiaquez (since Jan '94)
RULING PARTY: Liberal Party of Honduras (PLH)
CURRENCY: lempira (end-'94 £1=L14.56, US$1=L9.30)
GNP PER CAPITA: US$580 ('92)
MAIN EXPORT EARNERS: bananas, coffee, tourism

Nicaragua
CAPITAL: Managua   AREA: 120,000 sq km   POPULATION: 3,900,000 ('92)
OFFICIAL LANGUAGE: Spanish   POLITICAL SYSTEM: presidential democracy
HEAD OF STATE & GOVERNMENT: President Violeta Chamorro (since April '90)
RULING PARTY: National Opposition Union (UNO)
CURRENCY: córdoba (end-'94 £1=C$11.05, US$1=C$7.06)
GNP PER CAPITA: US$340 ('92)
MAIN EXPORT EARNERS: coffee, cotton, sugar, bananas

Costa Rica
CAPITAL: San José   AREA: 51,000 sq km   POPULATION: 3,200,000 ('92)
OFFICIAL LANGUAGE: Spanish   POLITICAL SYSTEM: presidential democracy
HEAD OF STATE & GOVERNMENT: President José María Figueres (since May '94)
RULING PARTY: National Liberation Party (PLN)
CURRENCY: colón (end-'94 £1=C256.87, US$1=C164.19)
GNP PER CAPITA: US$1,960 ('92)
MAIN EXPORT EARNERS: coffee, bananas, tourism

Panama
CAPITAL: Panama City   AREA: 77,000 sq km   POPULATION: 2,500,000 ('92)
OFFICIAL LANGUAGE: Spanish   POLITICAL SYSTEM: presidential
HEAD OF STATE & GOVERNMENT: President Ernesto Pérez Balladares (since Sept '94)
RULING PARTY: Democratic Revolutionary Party (PRD) heads coalition
CURRENCY: balboa (end-'94 £1=B1.56, US£1=B1.00)
GNP PER CAPITA: US$2,420 ('92)
MAIN EXPORT EARNERS: bananas, prawns, sugar, canal dues

In GUATEMALA, talks between the government and the opposition Guatemalan National Revolutionary Unity (URNG), suspended in May 1993 (see AR 1993, p. 187), were resumed on 6 January. An agreement reached in March and finally signed on 17 June provided for a reciprocal end to the violence that had afflicted the country for the past 34 years. A 'commission for historical clarification' (CEH) would examine responsibility for atrocities during that period, in which more than 100,000 had died and 50,000 had disappeared. According to the Attorney-General's office, there had been more than 13,000 civil rights violations in 1993 and the number appeared to be on the increase, although it was hoped that a new penal code effective from 1 July would improve the situation. The government–URNG agreement was to be supervised by a UN Mission for Guatemala (MINUGUA), members of which began to arrive in the country on 21 November (see also XI.1).

Meanwhile, President Ramiro de León Carpio had reshuffled his cabinet on 19 January, appointing Marithza Rúiz de Vielman as Foreign Minister in place of Arturo Farjado Maldonado, and Ana Ordoñez de Molina as Finance Minister vice Richard Aitkenhead Castillo. In a referendum held on 30 January, despite a low turnout (17.5 per cent), the President obtained 67.9 per cent of the votes cast for his anti-corruption package of constitutional reforms. As a result, the current Congress was dissolved and fresh elections ordered. Ten days after the assassination of the president of the Constitutional Court on 1 April, President de León placed the army in charge of internal security.

At the legislative elections held on 14 August the Guatemalan Republican Front (FRG), led by General (retd.) Efraín Ríos Montt, won 32 of the 80 seats and was able to propose him as president of Congress despite his grim record on civil rights (see AR 1983, p. 86). But the National Advancement Party (PAN) had taken 24 seats, the Christian Democrats (PDC) 13, the National Centre Union (UCN) eight and the National Liberation Movement (MLN) two, so that these opposition parties were able to block General Ríos Montt's election when the eight members of the National Centre Union (UCN) abstained.

The 1992 peace agreement continued to hold in EL SALVADOR, although its implementation was not yet complete and the UN Security Council twice voted to extend the mandate of the UN Observer Group in El Salvador (ONUSAL). In the first round of elections held on 20 March (and marked by numerous irregularities, according to ONUSAL), the hardline presidential candidate of the ruling Nationalist Republican Alliance (Arena), Armando Calderón Sol, just failed to gain the necessary overall majority. In the second round on 24 April, he heavily defeated Rubén Zamora, joint candidate of Democratic Convergence and the Farabundo Martí National Liberation Front (CD–FMLN), by 818,264 votes (68.2 per cent) to 378,980 (31.6 per cent). In simultaneous legislative elections, Arena maintained its plurality. Although the FMLN polled strongly in its first parliamentary contest, by the end of 1994 two of its more radical components had withdrawn.

Sworn in on 1 June, President Calderón Sol appointed Oscar Alfredo Santamaria as Foreign Minister and Luis Enrique Cordova as Minister for the Economy. Following the election, despite continuing violence involving the army and the discredited National Police (PN), the UN sponsored talks on an agreed programme of social and political reform. On 26 November the Archbishop of San Salvador, Mgr Arturo Rivera y Damas, who had mediated the agreement between the government and the FMLN guerrillas, died at the age of 71.

Carlos Roberto Reina was sworn in as President of HONDURAS on 27 January, vowing to make substantial increases in social expenditure. He appointed Ernesto Paz Aguilar as Foreign Minister and Delmer Urbizo Panting as Minister of Economy and Commerce. Military service, which Congress had voted in May to abolish, was reinstated on 1 August following an ultimatum to the President from the Commander-in-Chief of the Armed Forces. Soon afterwards statements were published from two guerrilla groups, one of which, the Morazanista Patriotic Front (FPM), had previously claimed responsibility for a bomb attack on 4 July at Comayagua. Both uttered threats against all involved in the passage of the new government's structural adjustment plan, which, however, was adopted on 14 October.

The position of President Violeta Chamorro of NICARAGUA was strengthened by dissension in the ranks of the opposition Sandinista National Liberation Front (FSLN). At a special congress of the former ruling party held on 20–22 May, the orthodox wing re-elected its standard bearer, former President Daniel Ortega Saavedra, as FSLN secretary-general and voted former Vice-President Sergio Ramírez Mercado off the national directorate. Sr Ramírez then lost his alternate's seat in Congress when Sr Ortega reclaimed it in September. But the FSLN congressmen did not choose Sr Ortega as their leader, their preference being instead for the moderate Dora María Tellez. On 7 June some 30 former Sandinistas occupied Managua Cathedral and on 28 July a radical FSLN splinter-group, the Front for Popular Struggle (FLP), occupied León Cathedral in protest against unemployment and poverty. Similar actions were carried out by former Contras. In October Fr Ernesto Cardenal, the former Minister of Culture, formally resigned from the FSLN and Carlos Fernando Chamorro (son of the President) was dismissed as editor of the party newspaper, *Barricada*. Attempts by the US Congress to block aid to the government were, however, unsuccessful. On 23 August Congress endorsed a new military code designed to enhance civilian primacy, while on 24 November it approved, by 72 votes to nil with six abstentions, a series of constitutional amendments designed to reduce the powers of the presidency. The first Central American summit devoted to ecological issues was held in

Managua on 13–14 October (see XIV.3). In December the President finally named the new chief of the army to replace General Humberto Ortega in February 1995, her choice falling on another left-wing Sandinista, Major-General Joaquín Cuadra Lacayo.

Victory in the presidential elections held on 6 February in COSTA RICA went to the candidate of the opposition National Liberation Party (PLN), José María Figueres, the 39-year-old son of former President José Figueres Ferrer. He obtained 739,181 votes to 710,403 votes for the candidate of the ruling Social Christian Unity Party (PUSC), Miguel Angel Rodríguez, while the PLN won 28 of the 57 seats in the Legislative Assembly, against 25 for the PUSC and four for independents.

Presidential elections held on 8 May in PANAMA were considered by international observers to have been free and fair. Victory went to a 48-year-old US-educated millionaire businessman, Ernesto Pérez Balladares, of the Democratic Revolutionary Party (PRD) of former President Omar Torrijos Herrera. His main challenger was Mireya Moscoso de Gruber, widow of former President Anulfo Arias Madrid and president of the Democratic Alliance (AD), of which the Arnulfista Party (PA) of President Guillermo Endara Gallimany was a member. Sr Pérez Balladares obtained 33.3 per cent of the votes cast to 29.1 per cent for Sra Moscoso, while Rubén Blades of the centre-left Movimiento Papa Egoró, a popular salsa singer who had campaigned against official corruption, came third with 17.7 per cent. On 6 June President Endara used his residual powers to pardon a number of prominent political figures, including former President Eric Arturo Delvalle. Sr Pérez Balladares was sworn in on 1 September, appointing Olmedo Miranda (PRD) as Treasury Minister and an independent, Gabriel Lewis Galindo, as Foreign Minister. He promised peace and reconciliation, an amnesty for a further 222 people, including associates of General Manuel Noriega, and a 'state of emergency' against crime and corruption.

xiv.   MEXICO

CAPITAL: Mexico City   AREA: 1,958,000 sq km   POPULATION: 85,000,000 ('92)
OFFICIAL LANGUAGE: Spanish   POLITICAL SYSTEM: federal presidential democracy
HEAD OF STATE & GOVERNMENT: President Ernesto Zedillo Ponce de Léon (since Dec '94)
RULING PARTY: Party of the Institutionalized Revolution (since 1929)
PRINCIPAL MINISTERS: José Angel Gurría Treviño (external relations), Esteban Moctezuma Barragán (interior), Gen. Enrique Cervantes Aguirre (defence), Guillermo Ortíz Martínez (finance), Ignacio Pichardo Pagaza (energy), Antonio Lozano (Attorney-General)
INTERNATIONAL ALIGNMENT: OAS, NAFTA, OECD
CURRENCY: peso (end-'94 £1=Mex$7.71, US$1=Mex$4.93)
GNP PER CAPITA: US$3,470 ('92)
MAIN EXPORT EARNERS: oil, motor machinery, coffee, tourism

ON New Year's Day the previously unknown Zapatista National Liberation Front (EZLN) seized control of three towns in the southern state of Chiapas (Ocosingo, Altamirano and Las Margaritas) and also attacked the historic tourist city of San Cristóbal de las Casas, where they ransacked and set fire to the palace of justice before retreating into the mountains. The former state governor, General (retd.) Absalón Castellanos Domínguez, was seized at his cattle ranch, bundled into a truck with two of his cows and taken as a hostage. On his release on 16 February, he stated that he agreed that the social injustice cited by the EZLN as the root cause of the revolt really existed.

The government of President Carlos Salinas de Gortari, celebrating entry on 1 January into the North American Free Trade Area (NAFTA), was much embarrassed. Within a week, the guerrillas had extended their control to the towns of San Miguel and Guadalupe Tepayac, the country was on nationwide alert, a fifth of Mexico's army had been deployed to the region and more than 145 people had been killed, some by summary executions and other atrocities. On 10 January the President reshuffled his cabinet, dismissing his Interior Secretary, José Patrocinio González Garrido, a former governor of Chiapas. Two days later he accepted the urgent advice of the Bishop of San Cristóbal by calling a truce and appointing Manuel Camacho Solís, the Secretary of External Relations (who had been passed over for the presidential nomination in 1993), to negotiate with the insurgents.

The presidential campaign, which had officially opened on 7 January, was abruptly interrupted when the candidate of the ruling Party of the Institutionalized Revolution (PRI), Luis Donaldo Colosio Murrieta (see AR 1993, p. 191), was fatally shot at a campaign rally at Tijuana on 23 March. The presumed assassin arrested at the scene of the crime, Mario Aburto Martínez (23), was on 31 October sentenced to 42 years' imprisonment for premeditated murder. The official report that he had acted alone was, however, greeted with derision when it appeared on 12 July, with the result that three days later the President reopened the inquiry. Meanwhile, Sr Salinas moved quickly to nominate a new candidate acceptable to the PRI hierarchy. The obvious choice, Sr Camacho, immediately ruled himself out of contention, so the President's choice fell on Ernesto Zedillo Ponce de León, an economist who had studied at Yale University and had served as Minister of Budget and Planning in 1988-92 and as Secretary of Education in 1992-93.

With the powerful support of the government party, Sr Zedillo campaigned hard during the summer on a pledge to continue the policies of Sr Salinas. In the presidential contest on 21 August, he obtained 48.77 per cent of the votes cast (according to tabulations used in the press) and a convincing majority over the candidate of the right-wing National Action Party (PAN), Diego Fernando de Cevallos, who gained 25.94 per cent. The PRI preferred to calculate the percentages after excluding the invalid votes (2.8 per cent in a turnout of 77.7 per cent), so that Sr Zedillo could claim to have won more than 50 per cent. Either way, it was clear that the PRI had recorded its lowest share of a poll since it came to power in 1929. Cuauhtémoc Cárdenas Solórzano of the reformist Party of the Democratic Revolution (PRD), standing as candidate of the National Democratic Alliance (ADN), came a poor third, with 16.6 per cent, and five other candidates all won less than 1 per cent. Sr Cárdenas, who on 7 February had declared his 'peacable' support for the EZLN, had not been well received by them in May. A lacklustre performance in Mexico's first presidential TV debate, on 12 May, had not helped his cause; nor had the fact that nearly 300 PRD activists had been murdered since Sr Salinas took office in 1988.

In simultaneous congressional elections, the PRI retained control of the 500-member Chamber of Deputies, winning 300 seats (compared with 320 in 1991) against 119 for the PAN, 71 for the PRD and ten for the Labour Party (PT). In the Senate, which was enlarged from 64 to 128 members, the PRI's post-election seat tally was 95, against 25 for the PAN and eight for the PRD. On 28 September the PRI secretary-general, José Francisco Ruiz Massieu, was assassinated while getting into his car in Mexico City, the motive of the presumed killer (who was arrested) remaining unclear at year's end. Sr Ruiz Massieu was replaced by Maria de los Angeles Moreno, leader of the reformist faction of the PRI in Congress. President-elect Zedillo was sworn in on 1 December, appointing Jaime Serra Puche to the key post of Secretary of Finance.

Meanwhile, the situation in Chiapas had deteriorated into near anarchy. The PRI candidate for governor, Eduardo Robledo Rincón, had been declared officially elected in the August balloting, with 50.46 per cent of the vote compared with 39.40 per cent for his PRD opponent, Amado Avendaño Figueroa, who had been seriously injured on 26 July when a truck without number plates rammed his car. In September 20,000 Tojolobal Indians, organized by the independent Union of Agricultural Workers (CIOAC), had declared themselves autonomous. Shortly afterwards, on 10 October, the EZLN leader, 'Subcommandante Marcos', broke off contact with the government negotiator. Violence then escalated, as peasants armed themselves against the attacks of paramilitary forces organized by ranchers, one group of angry peasants kidnapping the interim governor, Javier López Moreno, and holding him hostage for several hours.

On the eve of his inauguration as governor of Chiapas on 8 December, Sr Robledo offered to resign if the EZLN laid down their arms—an offer which came to nothing. On 19 December EZLN guerrillas, who controlled about one-fifth of the state, demonstrated their ability to slip through army cordons, erecting roadblocks which proclaimed 'liberated zones' and occupying the town of Simojovel.

The government had advance warning of this move and on 21 December took advantage of it to devalue the new peso from 3.34 to 4.00 against the US dollar, deftly placing the blame on the Chiapas guerrillas. Within 24 hours, however, while fresh troops and tanks moved into place around the guerrilla bases, the devaluation had revealed the fundamental weakness of the Mexican economy, notably its dependence on short-term loans. As capital flooded out of the country, the government lost control of the financial situation and allowed the peso to float, with the result that it immediately lost a further 20 per cent of its value and continued to drift downwards, precipitating a major crisis of investors' confidence. The dismissal of Sr Serra Puche as Finance Secretary on 29 December (after less than a month in office) and the announcement of an emergency economic plan by President Zedillo seemed unlikely to restore the financial credibility of the new administration. Meanwhile, a truce between the government and the EZLN had been announced on 28 December.

4.   THE CARIBBEAN

JAMAICA—GUYANA—TRINIDAD & TOBAGO—BARBADOS—BELIZE—
GRENADA—THE BAHAMAS—WINDWARD AND LEEWARD ISLANDS—
SURINAME—NETHERLANDS ANTILLES AND ARUBA

i.   JAMAICA

CAPITAL: Kingston   AREA: 11,000 sq km   POPULATION: 2,400,000 ('92)
OFFICIAL LANGUAGE: English   POLITICAL SYSTEM: parliamentary democracy
HEAD OF STATE: Queen Elizabeth II   GOVERNOR-GENERAL: Howard Cooke
RULING PARTY: People's National Party (PNP)
HEAD OF GOVERNMENT: Percival J. Patterson, Prime Minister (since March '92)
PRINCIPAL MINISTERS: Seymour Mullings (Deputy Prime Minister, agriculture), Paul Robertson (foreign affairs & trade), Omar Davies (finance), K.D. Knight (national security & justice), David Coore (Attorney-General)
INTERNATIONAL ALIGNMENT: NAM, ACP, OAS, Caricom, Cwth.
CURRENCY: Jamaican dollar (end-'94 £1=J$49.95, US$1=J$31.93)
GNP PER CAPITA: US$1,340 ('92)
MAIN EXPORT EARNERS: bauxite/alumina, bananas, sugar, tourism

CRIME and the economy were the major themes confronting the social democratic People's National Party government during 1994. Prime Minister P.J. Patterson called for a 'moral reawakening' to combat drug-related and political violence. As in 1993, however, the year saw over 650 homicides, damaging the prospects of the tourist trade, the island's major growth sector. The controversial Suppression of Crimes Act (1974), which established the so-called 'gun courts' and gave extensive powers to the police, was repealed in March after the National Security Minister, Keith Knight, conceded that the legislation, lately applied in only three localities, had become counter-productive. However, a new Constabulary Act restored some of the exceptional powers.

The question of capital punishment came to the fore in December when the judicial committee of the Privy Council rejected an appeal by Albert Huntley, whose 1983 murder conviction had been reclassified as a capital offence in 1992. This refuelled the debate over the role of the Privy Council, sitting in London, as the supreme judicial authority for some Commonwealth states. The ruling disappointed international campaigners against the death penalty, who had welcomed a 1993 ruling which required the commutation of scores of sentences. No executions had been carried out since 1988, but the Huntley case left over 100 prisoners on death row, with the government publicly committed to recommencing executions.

Inflation, which was 25 per cent in 1993, rose to 27 per cent during 1994. This was despite measures taken to stabilize the Jamaican dollar, which had fallen sharply in the latter part of 1993. In February the government liberalized foreign exchange rules and curtailed the black market; hotels and merchant banks were licensed to join the official market, although 20 per cent of their purchases had to be sold on to the Bank of Jamaica. Other expansionary measures in the February package included a bond issue and interest rate reductions, and later the government sold off 70 per cent of the national airline. The overall effect was to slow, but not halt, the depreciation of the currency.

Although the conservative Jamaica Labour Party under Edward Seaga had secured the establishment of a parliamentary select committee to consider electoral reforms, its effectiveness in opposition was limited by its having only five seats in the 60-member House of Representatives and only eight of 21 in the Senate. It also remained marginalized in local government, controlling only one of the 13 councils. Local elections which had been postponed from mid-1993 were again put off until 1995.

ii. GUYANA

CAPITAL: Georgetown   AREA: 215,000 sq km   POPULATION: 806,000 ('92)
OFFICIAL LANGUAGE: English   POLITICAL SYSTEM: cooperative presidential
     democracy
HEAD OF STATE & GOVERNMENT: President Cheddi Jagan (since Oct '92)
RULING PARTY: People's Progressive Party–Civic (PPP-C)
PRINCIPAL MINISTERS: Sam Hinds (Vice-President & Prime Minister), Clement
     Rohee (foreign affairs), Asgar Ali (finance), Feroze Mohamed (home affairs),
     Bernard de Santos (justice)
INTERNATIONAL ALIGNMENT: NAM, ACP, OAS, Caricom, Cwth.
CURRENCY: Guyana dollar (end-'94 £1=G$222.02, US$1=G$141.91)
GNP PER CAPITA: US$330 ('92)
MAIN EXPORT EARNERS: bauxite, sugar, rice

THE first local elections in 24 years took place on 8 August, resulting in a victory for the centre-left People's Progressive Party–Civic (PPP-C) of President Cheddi Jagan. Of the 71 neighbourhood and municipal councils contested, the PPP-C won 49, but failed to capture Georgetown. The capital, once a stronghold of the right-wing opposition People's National Congress (PNC), gave 12 of its 30 council seats to a new formation, Good and Green for Georgetown (GGG). An offshoot of the Forum for Democracy created in 1993 by former PNC Prime Minister Hamilton Green, the GGG grouping pushed the PNC into second place with 10 seats, leaving eight to the PPP-C. The PNC retained control of the second city, Linden.

The leftist Working People's Alliance boycotted the polls because of a disagreement over the structures of local government and also in protest at the alleged resurgence of ethnic politics. The PPP was traditionally identified with the Asian-descended population, while the PNC and the GGG vied for the African-descended voters. Later in the year the sensitivity of community relations was demonstrated when the government proposed to downgrade the Mashramani or Republic Day holiday (23 February) in favour of Independence Day (26 May). Protests from the African community, which particularly valued Mashramani, forced the government to back down.

A parliamentary select committee was established to review the constitution. A less formal inter-party committee on the issue agreed that a comprehensive reform would be completed prior to the next general elections, due in 1997.

The economy continued to grow and inflation fell to around 16 per cent, still some way off the 4 per cent targeted by the IMF for 1994–96. An enhanced structural adjustment facility agreed with the IMF in mid-year left little room for manoeuvre on public spending. A ceiling imposed on wage rises led to some labour unrest. Government stakes in the banking, engineering, commerce and transport sectors were privatized during the year, further sales of holdings in bauxite mining being scheduled for 1995.

iii. TRINIDAD & TOBAGO

CAPITAL: Port of Spain   AREA: 5,128 sq km   POPULATION: 1,300,000 ('92)
OFFICIAL LANGUAGE: English   POLITICAL SYSTEM: parliamentary republic
HEAD OF STATE: President Noor Mohammed Hassanali (since March '87)
RULING PARTY: People's National Movement (PNM)
HEAD OF GOVERNMENT: Patrick Manning, Prime Minister (since Dec '91)
PRINCIPAL MINISTERS: Ralph Maraj (foreign affairs), Wendell Mottley (finance & tourism), Keith Sobion (Attorney-General), Kenneth Valley (trade & industry), Barry Barnes (energy)
INTERNATIONAL ALIGNMENT: NAM, ACP, OAS, Caricom, Cwth.
CURRENCY: Trinidad & Tobago dollar (end-'94 £1=TT$8.87, US$1=TT$5.67)
GNP PER CAPITA: US$3,940 ('92)
MAIN EXPORT EARNERS: oil, chemicals, tourism

PRIME Minister Patrick Manning's People's National Movement survived the year without facing major challenges to its dominant position on Trinidad. Opposition parties remained split: the National Alliance for Reconstruction (NAR), the major political force on Tobago, failed to agree a joint slate with the United National Congress for a by-election in August, prompting the resignation of NAR leader Selby Wilson.

Privatization of utilities and industrial holdings helped offset a continuing decline in oil revenues. Despite union opposition, Mr Manning's government pressed ahead with structural adjustment policies aimed at slimming down the state sector and fostering growth areas, principally tourism. The country was, however, unsuccessful in its application for membership of the NAFTA trading bloc (of the USA, Canada and Mexico).

Law and order issues were once again prominent. Troops were brought onto the streets in January to support police patrols. Human rights campaigners were shocked when convicted murderer Glen Ashby was hanged at Port of Spain prison on 14 July, before his appeal could be heard by the Privy Council in London. The Council's stay of execution arrived by fax minutes after the hanging, five days before Ashby would have qualified for commutation through having spent five years on death row. The haste with which Ashby was dispatched reflected government anxiety to assuage public alarm about violent crime. Amnesty International deplored the hanging, which was said to breach assurances given by Attorney-General Keith Sobion. The UN Human Rights Committee also rebuked the government for its apparent violation of the due process guarantees in the International Covenant on Civil and Political Rights, and undertook to pursue Ashby's case posthumously. Two others among the 25 prisoners on Trinidad's death row secured a stay of execution in July, and subsequent commutations.

Any international embarrassment which the government felt arising from the Ashby case was alleviated not only by the domestic popularity of its hard line but also by a subsequent Privy Council case which went in its favour. The Council was asked to reconsider the legality of the pardon granted to 114 participants in the Jamaat al-Muslimeen rebellion in 1990. Those concerned had been freed in 1992 after the Privy Council had upheld a High Court ruling on procedural grounds; the amnesty was ratified in 1993 by the High Court (see AR 1993, p. 194), but in October the Privy Council allowed a fresh appeal and set aside the amnesty, returning the matter to Trinidadian jurisdiction.

Under current government plans, Tobago's status as a constitutional and economic 'poor relation' to the larger island was to be tackled by enhanced autonomy and investment in infrastructure. Substantial progress in this direction was expected before the next elections to the Trinidad & Tobago House of Representatives and to the Tobago Assembly, due in December 1996.

iv. BARBADOS

CAPITAL: Bridgetown   AREA: 430 sq km   POPULATION: 259,000 ('92)
OFFICIAL LANGUAGE: English   POLITICAL SYSTEM: parliamentary democracy
HEAD OF STATE: Queen Elizabeth II   GOVERNOR-GENERAL: Dame Nita Barrow
RULING PARTY: Barbados Labour Party (BLP)
HEAD OF GOVERNMENT: Owen Arthur, Prime Minister (since Sept '94)
PRINCIPAL MINISTERS: Billie Miller (Deputy Prime Minister, foreign affairs & trade),
    David Simmons (Attorney-General, home affairs), Reginald Farley (industry)
INTERNATIONAL ALIGNMENT: NAM, ACP, OAS, Cwth.
CURRENCY: Barbados dollar (end-'94 £1=BDS$3.14, US$1=BDS$2.01)
GNP PER CAPITA: US$6,540 ('92)
MAIN EXPORT EARNERS: sugar, tourism, light manufactures, chemicals

DISPUTES in February and March over patronage prompted the resignations of three members of the increasingly unpopular government
of ailing Prime Minister Erskine Sandiford. Dissatisfaction with Mr
Sandiford's austerity programme led to his losing a House of Assembly
confidence motion on 7 June, when some representatives of his Democratic Labour Party (DLP) voted with the opposition and others resigned
from the party. Although the margin of defeat did not require him to
do so, the Prime Minister subsequently announced the dissolution of
parliament for a general election on 6 September, the first to be held
ahead of schedule since independence in 1966. Mr Sandiford was in
July replaced as DLP leader by his erstwhile Finance Minister, David
Thompson, but remained Prime Minister.

The election ended eight years of DLP rule, the party retaining just
eight of its 18 seats. The social democratic Barbados Labour Party
(BLP), led since mid-1993 by Owen Arthur, increased from ten seats
to 19, with 48.3 per cent of the vote to 38.4 per cent for the DLP.
Some 12.7 per cent voted for the National Democratic Party, product
of a 1989 schism in the DLP, but this party secured only one seat.

Mr Arthur took office as Prime Minister on 7 September and
appointed nine other cabinet ministers, assuming himself ministerial
responsibility for defence and security, finance and economic affairs, and
information. All three women in the parliamentary BLP were appointed
to the cabinet, including Billie Miller as Deputy Prime Minister and
Minister of Foreign Affairs, Foreign Trade and International Business.

Unemployment remained over 25 per cent throughout the year. Mr
Sandiford had declared in January that growth in tourism would be the
main engine of economic recovery, and on taking office Mr Arthur
confirmed the commitment to export-led growth, while denying that
he planned a devaluation of the Barbados dollar to speed it along. The
Barbados dollar maintained its fixed rate of BDS$2 to US$1 throughout
the year.

v. BELIZE

CAPITAL: Belmopan AREA: 23,000 sq km POPULATION: 199,000 ('92)
OFFICIAL LANGUAGE: English POLITICAL SYSTEM: parliamentary democracy
HEAD OF STATE: Queen Elizabeth II
GOVERNOR-GENERAL: Sir Colville Young
RULING PARTY: United Democratic Party (UDP)
HEAD OF GOVERNMENT: Manuel Esquivel, Prime Minister (since June '93)
PRINCIPAL MINISTERS: Dean Barrow (Deputy Prime Minister, foreign affairs), Eduardo
   Dito Juan (natural resources), Elito Urbina (home affairs), Salvador Fernández
   (trade & industry)
INTERNATIONAL ALIGNMENT: NAM, ACP, Caricom, Cwth.
CURRENCY: Belize dollar (end-'94 £1=BZ$3.13, US$1=BZ$1.99)
GNP PER CAPITA: US$2,220 ('92)
MAIN EXPORT EARNERS: sugar, citrus products, fish, tourism

As in every year since independence in 1981, the main issue in 1994 was Belize's relations with the neighbouring republic of Guatemala. The United Democratic Party (UDP) of Prime Minister Manuel Esquivel had a more cautious approach in this matter than the People's United Party (PUP) government which it had narrowly defeated in the previous year's elections (see AR 1993, pp. 196–7). The UDP line was endorsed in local government elections in March, in which the ruling party captured a majority of town boards from the PUP.

The 1,000–strong British garrison completed its evacuation of Belize in October. The United Kingdom retained a jungle warfare training centre and was to give support to the country's 650-strong Defence Force. The withdrawal indicated British confidence, not wholly shared by the UDP government, in the future good conduct of Guatemala, notwithstanding political instability and occasional nationalistic sabre-rattling in that country in the run-up to the August congressional election (see IV.3.xiii). Guatemala had formally renounced its longstanding territorial claim on Belize as recently as 1991, in an accord also involving maritime rights (see AR 1991, p. 89); the Esquivel government proposed to renegotiate the deal to recover some of the maritime concessions and further entrench guarantees of respect for Belizean sovereignty.

Guatemalan reassertions of territorial and maritime claims in 1994 were denounced in June at the Foreign Ministers' meeting of the Caribbean Community (CARICOM) hosted by Belize, whose status received support from a visit by Queen Elizabeth, its head of state, in February. It was further bolstered by neighbouring states in June when Belize was admitted as an observer at the 25th summit of Central American heads of state in Costa Rica (see XI.6.vi). Belize also took part in the regional environmental summit held in Nicaragua in October (see XIV.3).

vi. GRENADA

CAPITAL: St George's AREA: 344 sq km POPULATION: 91,000 ('92)
OFFICIAL LANGUAGE: English POLITICAL SYSTEM: parliamentary democracy
HEAD OF STATE: Queen Elizabeth II GOVERNOR-GENERAL: Sir Reginald O. Palmer
RULING PARTY: National Democratic Congress (NDC)
HEAD OF GOVERNMENT: Nicholas Brathwaite, Prime Minister (since March '90)
PRINCIPAL MINISTERS: George Brizan (agriculture, trade & industry), Francis Alexis
  (Attorney-General)
INTERNATIONAL ALIGNMENT: NAM, ACP, OAS, Caricom, Cwth.
CURRENCY: East Caribbean dollar (end-'94 £1=EC$4.22, US$1=EC$2.69)
GNP PER CAPITA: US$2,310 ('92)
MAIN EXPORT EARNERS: agricultural products, nutmeg, tourism

NICHOLAS Brathwaite, Prime Minister since 1990 and leader since 1989 of the centrist National Democratic Congress (NDC), resigned his party post on 27 August following widespread criticism of his government's austerity programme. At an NDC convention on 4 September he was succeeded as party leader by the Agriculture Minister, George Brizan, but pending elections in 1995 he remained Prime Minister, with a number of other portfolios, including external relations, home affairs and finance.

Opposition forces remained divided. The New National Party led by Keith Mitchell was split among internal factions, while the old Grenada United Labour Party led by eccentric former Premier Sir Eric Gairy appeared unlikely to recapture its past hegemony. Other active parties included the National Party and two formations launched in 1993, the Initiative for Better Representation and the United Republican Party.

Legislation was introduced to levy income tax, which had been abolished in 1986 but readopted in principle in 1993. The tax was to be implemented effectively from 1995 on income over EC$10,000, in bands from 10 to 30 per cent. This reflected the difficulty experienced since 1986 in maintaining government services on the basis of revenue from indirect taxation; capital expenditure had become almost entirely dependent on overseas aid, including in 1994 a US$8.5 million soft loan from Kuwait towards infrastructure improvements. The broader economic picture showed an increasing reliance on tourism, which almost equalled the 40 per cent contribution to GDP of the declining agricultural export sector.

Phyllis Coard, sentenced to life imprisonment for conspiracy in the 1983 overthrow of the New Jewel Movement government, completed her tenth year in prison despite continuing pressure from international human rights organizations.

vii. THE BAHAMAS

CAPITAL: Nassau   AREA: 14,000 sq km   POPULATION: 262,000 ('92)
OFFICIAL LANGUAGE: English   POLITICAL SYSTEM: parliamentary democracy
HEAD OF STATE: Queen Elizabeth II   GOVERNOR-GENERAL: Sir Clifford Darling
RULING PARTY: Free National Movement (FNM)
HEAD OF GOVERNMENT: Hubert Ingraham, Prime Minister (since Aug '92)
PRINCIPAL MINISTERS: Janet Gwennett Bostwick (foreign affairs, justice &
    immigration), Maurice Elijah Moore (labour), Brent Symonette (tourism)
INTERNATIONAL ALIGNMENT: NAM, ACP, OAS, Cwth.
CURRENCY: Bahamas dollar (end-'94 £1=B$1.56, US$1=B$1.00)
GNP PER CAPITA: US$12,070 ('92)
MAIN EXPORT EARNERS: tourism, petroleum products

THE consequences of the crisis in Haiti (see IV.1; IV.3.xii) provided a serious distraction from the campaign of the Free National Movement (FNM) government to uncover and prosecute the corruption institutionalized by the Progressive Liberal Party (PLP) regime which it had succeeded in 1992. The commission of inquiry set up in early 1993 (see AR 1993, pp. 198-9), but adjourned in August after a legal challenge, resumed its hearings in 1994. These were continuing in December, although no criminal charges had yet ensued.

Efforts were made throughout the year to relocate many of the estimated 40,000 Haitian refugees who arrived in the aftermath of the September 1991 military coup. Despite summary repatriations, many thousands remained in the Bahamas at the year's end, representing a serious strain on resources and—in view of illegal onward migration—on relations with the United States. The tourism industry, accounting for over 60 per cent of GDP, remained stagnant. Measures taken to bolster public finances and to service the foreign debt included tax increases and plans to privatize the Bahamasair national airline, although the sell-off was delayed by corruption investigations. Other privatizations were planned for telecommunications, water services and power.

On 9 November the Deputy Prime Minister, Orville 'Tiny' Turnquest, resigned from the cabinet and from parliament pending his appointment as Governor-General, his posts of Foreign Minister and Attorney-General going to the Justice Minister, Janet Bostwick. Mr Turnquest had in February demanded an apology for the suggestion by a US federal prosecutor that he had accepted money from the Medellín drugs cartel.

viii. WINDWARD AND LEEWARD ISLANDS

St Kitts & Nevis
CAPITAL: Basseterre AREA: 260 sq km POPULATION: 42,000 ('92)
OFFICIAL LANGUAGE: English POLITICAL SYSTEM: parliamentary democracy
HEAD OF STATE: Queen Elizabeth II
GOVERNOR-GENERAL: Sir Clement Athelston Arrindell
RULING PARTY: People's Action Movement (PAM)
HEAD OF GOVERNMENT: Kennedy A. Simmonds, Prime Minister (since Feb '80)
CURRENCY: East Caribbean dollar (end-'94 £1=EC$4.22, US$1=EC$2.69)
GNP PER CAPITA: US$3,990 ('92)
MAIN EXPORT EARNERS: sugar, agricultural produce, tourism

Antigua & Barbuda
CAPITAL: St John's AREA: 440 sq km POPULATION: 66,000 ('92)
OFFICIAL LANGUAGE: English POLITICAL SYSTEM: parliamentary democracy
HEAD OF STATE: Queen Elizabeth II
GOVERNOR-GENERAL: James B. Carlisle
RULING PARTY: Antigua Labour Party (ALP)
HEAD OF GOVERNMENT: Lester Bird, Prime Minister (since March '94)
CURRENCY: East Caribbean dollar (see above)
GNP PER CAPITA: US$5,980 ('92)
MAIN EXPORT EARNERS: tourism, miscellaneous manufactures

Dominica
CAPITAL: Roseau AREA: 750 sq km POPULATION: 72,000 ('92)
OFFICIAL LANGUAGE: English POLITICAL SYSTEM: parliamentary republic
HEAD OF STATE: President Crispin Sorhaindo (since Oct '93)
RULING PARTY: Dominica Freedom Party (DFP)
HEAD OF GOVERNMENT: Dame Eugenia Charles, Prime Minister (since July '80)
CURRENCY: East Caribbean dollar (see above)
GNP PER CAPITA: US$2,520 ('92)
MAIN EXPORT EARNERS: bananas, tourism

St Lucia
CAPITAL: Castries AREA: 616 sq km POPULATION: 155,000 ('92)
OFFICIAL LANGUAGE: English POLITICAL SYSTEM: parliamentary democracy
HEAD OF STATE: Queen Elizabeth II
GOVERNOR-GENERAL: Sir Stanislaus A. James
RULING PARTY: United Workers' Party (UWP)
HEAD OF GOVERNMENT: John Compton, Prime Minister (since '64)
CURRENCY: East Caribbean dollar (see above)
GNP PER CAPITA: US$2,920 ('92)
MAIN EXPORT EARNERS: agricultural products, tourism

St Vincent & the Grenadines
CAPITAL: Kingstown AREA: 390 sq km POPULATION: 109,000 ('92)
OFFICIAL LANGUAGE: English POLITICAL SYSTEM: parliamentary democracy
HEAD OF STATE: Queen Elizabeth II GOVERNOR-GENERAL: David Jack
RULING PARTY: New Democratic Party (NDP)
HEAD OF GOVERNMENT: James F. Mitchell, Prime Minister (since '72)
CURRENCY: East Caribbean dollar (see above)
GNP PER CAPITA: US$1,990 ('92)
MAIN EXPORT EARNERS: bananas, tourism, agricultural produce

THE crisis which followed the November 1993 election in ST KITTS
& NEVIS (see AR 1993, p. 200) continued into 1994, following the
decision of Governor-General Sir Clement Arrindell to invite Kennedy
Simmonds of the outgoing People's Action Movement to form a

coalition government with the Nevis Reformation Party, although the two parties commanded only five seats in the 11–member National Assembly. Supporters of the main opposition St Kitts-Nevis Labour Party (SKLP) participated in street protests, party leader Denzil Douglas demanding fresh elections as the only way to resolve the impasse. A state of emergency declared in December 1993 extended for several days into the new year; church mediation secured an end to the rioting, but there were two large demonstrations in January. The SKLP boycotted parliament until, in October, it secured an agreement that fresh elections would be held no later than mid-November 1995.

Deputy Prime Minister Earl Sydney Morris resigned in sensational circumstances in November after two of his sons were charged with drug-related offences and a third was murdered. A police superintendent murdered while working on the case had investigated the disappearance in June of a Kittitian diplomat also allegedly involved in drugs. Mr Morris was succeeded by Agriculture Minister Hugh Heyliger, who also assumed the Youth portfolio. Tourism continued to grow in a competitive climate, encouraged by tax breaks in the February budget. A proposal to privatize the state-owned St Kitts Sugar Manufacturing Company met opposition from the SKLP and the trade unions.

In ANTIGUA & BARBUDA, general elections on 8 March, observed by the OAS, were generally agreed to have been fairer than previous polls. They renewed for five years the mandate of the Antigua Labour Party (ALP) led by Lester Bird, who thereupon succeeded his father, Vere Bird Sr, as Prime Minister. The ALP's majority was, however, trimmed from 15 to 11 of the 17 seats in the House of Representatives. The opposition was strengthened by a merger of other anti-government forces with the United Progressive Party (UPP) led by Baldwin Spencer. The revitalized UPP took five seats, while the remaining seat was filled by the Barbuda People's Movement.

DOMINICA's ruling Dominica Freedom Party (DFP) ended the year preparing for a general election against a confident opposition. The United Workers' Party and the Dominica Labour Party were hoping to overturn the narrow majority secured in 1990 by the conservative DFP led by Brian Alleyne, who had in 1993 succeeded Dame Eugenia Charles, although she remained Prime Minister. In April public transport workers were involved in serious disturbances, prompting the declaration of a state of emergency in the capital, Roseau, which was lifted only after the government backed down on a proposed licence fee increase. The ravaging of the banana industry by the tropical storm Debbie in September further increased the country's trade deficit.

Also severely hit by Debbie was ST LUCIA, where Prime Minister John Compton had already announced a 48 per cent fall in banana revenues during 1993, necessitating an austerity budget presented in April. After September, when the storm destroyed at least 40 per cent of the 1994 crop, the picture was even more grim. Some 10,000 small growers in Dominica and St Lucia were reckoned to have lost the year's harvest. In October Mr Compton helped to secure permission for the Windwards to buy in so-called 'dollar bananas' to meet European Union export commitments, but he predicted a 30 per cent loss of GDP in 1995.

Elections in ST VINCENT & THE GRENADINES on 24 February restored a parliamentary opposition to Prime Minister James 'Son' Mitchell's National Democratic Party (NDP) government. The NDP was returned for a third term, albeit with 12 seats in the House of Assembly compared with its 1989 clean sweep of all 15. The opposition St Vincent Labour Party (SVLP) and Movement for National Unity (MNU) fought the election in alliance under SVLP leader Vincent Beache, securing three seats. The alliance subsequently launched three legal challenges to the election results, none of which were resolved by the year's end.

The poll (brought forward from May) followed divisions in the ruling NDP and the resignation in January of a minister, Burton Williams, who failed to secure re-election. There was some disorder in the latter part of the campaign, one person being killed and 65 injured on the eve of voting. On 16 October the SVLP and MNU consolidated their advance by merging to form the Unity Labour Party, headed by Mr Beache and with former MNU leader Ralph Gonsalves as his deputy.

The banana industry, normally accounting for 60 per cent of the country's exports, fared badly in 1994 despite the limited impact of tropical storm Debbie, which caused enormous losses elsewhere in the archipelago (see above). Market conditions having resulted in export earnings falling by one-third in 1993, the 1994 budget included measures to aid the restructuring of the banana industry. The NDP government restated its commitment to closer economic cooperation and the political unification of the Windward Islands.

ix. SURINAME

CAPITAL: Paramaribo   AREA: 163,000 sq km   POPULATION: 404,000 ('92)
OFFICIAL LANGUAGE: Dutch   POLITICAL SYSTEM: republic, under military tutelage
HEAD OF STATE: President Ronald Venetiaan (since Sept '91)
RULING PARTIES: New Front (for Democracy and Development), consisting of the
    Suriname National (NPS), Progressive Reform (VHP) and Unity and Harmony
    (KTPI) parties, plus the Suriname Labour Party (SPA)
PRINCIPAL MINISTERS: Jules Ajodhia (Vice-President, head of government),
    Subhaas Chandra Mungra (VHP/foreign affairs), Siegfried Gilds (SPA/defence),
    Rufus Nooitmeer (NPS/regional development), Ruben Setroredjo (home affairs),
    Soeshil Girjasing (justice & police)
INTERNATIONAL ALIGNMENT: NAM, ACP, OAS
CURRENCY: Suriname guilder (end-'94 £1=Sf516.74, US$1=Sf330.29)
GNP PER CAPITA: US$4,280 ('92)
MAIN EXPORT EARNERS: bauxite/alumina, aluminium, rice

FACED with increasing internal unrest, the ruling New Front (NF) coalition gave up the struggle to maintain an IMF-backed structural adjustment programme. The economy was in disarray; drastic taxes introduced in 1993 to restrict oil consumption helped to keep the inflation rate over 75 per cent for the third successive year, and by December it was unofficially reported to be running at 240 per cent. As in 1993, there was a lengthy debate over exchange rate policy; at the insistence of the IMF, the independent central bank in July replaced the four-tier system with a unified rate. When the bank floated the guilder in October, it depreciated from 180 to over 300 to the US dollar within days, as compared with the official end-1993 rate of 1.78.

The collapse of the currency led to the reimposition of an official rate in December, along with price controls and food subsidies. President Ronald Venetiaan attributed what amounted to the abandonment of the three-year market reforms to the non-arrival of promised Dutch aid, whereas the Netherlands said that any aid was conditional on a favourable IMF report.

Although the opposition, including the National Democratic Party of former military ruler Desi Bouterse, continued to press for the bringing forward of elections (not due constitutionally until 1996), its National Assembly members voted with the NF in May in favour of Suriname joining CARICOM on the same basis as the Bahamas—that is, as a full member of the political community but outside the common market. The application was deferred at CARICOM's July meeting, but Suriname could expect to enjoy closer ties with its neighbours as a member of the new Association of Caribbean States (see XI.6.vi).

Popular protests in October against the collapse of the currency were described by Vice-President Jules Ajodhia as 'an excellent idea'. In November and December, student and trade union protests against government economic policy led to a number of arrests and to the temporary closure of schools. A strike by customs officers in November had caused the closure of borders; there were also labour disputes in the health service, the utilities and the private sector, many centring on the fact that wage inflation was bringing workers into higher tax bands. Most protests were unarmed, although in March a previously-unknown Suriname Liberation Front briefly held 26 workers hostage at a hydroelectric project in an attempt to force President Venetiaan's resignation.

x.   NETHERLANDS ANTILLES AND ARUBA

Netherlands Antilles
CAPITAL: Willemstad (Curaçao)   AREA: 800 sq km   POPULATION: 194,000 ('92)
OFFICIAL LANGUAGES: Dutch, Papiamento, English
POLITICAL SYSTEM: parliamentary democracy under Dutch crown
GOVERNOR: Jaime M. Saleh
RULING PARTIES: National People's Party (PNP) heads coalition
HEAD OF GOVERNMENT: Miguel Pourier, Prime Minister (since March Dec '94)
CURRENCY: Neth. Antilles guilder (end-'94 £1=NAf2.80, US$1=NAf1.79)
GNP PER CAPITA: US$5,300 ('88)
MAIN EXPORT EARNERS: oil, tourism

Aruba
CAPITAL: Oranjestad   AREA: 193 sq km   POPULATION: 67,000 ('92)
OFFICIAL LANGUAGE: Dutch
POLITICAL SYSTEM: parliamentary democracy under Dutch crown
GOVERNOR: Olindo Koolman
RULING PARTIES: People's Electoral Movement (MEP) heads coalition
HEAD OF GOVERNMENT: Nelson Oduber, Prime Minister (since Feb '89)
CURRENCY: Aruba guilder (end-'92 £1=Af2.80, US$1=Af1.79)
GNP PER CAPITA: US$12,000 ('88)
MAIN EXPORT EARNERS: oil, tourism

POLITICAL disarray was the motif of 1994 in the NETHERLANDS ANTILLES, after the surprise outcome of the referendum on the largest island, Curaçao, rejecting *status aparte* (see AR 1993, p. 202). The interim non-party Prime Minister of Curaçao, Alejandro 'Jandi' Paula, held office until elections on 25 February ousted the coalition based on the National People's Party (NVP). The newly-formed Antillean Reconstruction Party (PAR) emerged as the largest party, its leader, Miguel Pourier, heading the coalition which took office on 31 March.

The Dutch government was keen to see action against corruption, the narcotics trade and money-laundering, and to secure political stability. Scandals over kickbacks on infrastructure projects caused considerable public resentment and led to a higher degree of Dutch oversight of the local administration.

A referendum on 14 October resulted in resounding majorities on St Maarten and the smaller islands of St Eustasius and Saba in favour of their existing constitutional position within the Netherlands Antilles. However, 32 per cent on St Maarten voted for autonomy within the Kingdom of the Netherlands. Support for full independence was negligible, as it had been on Curaçao.

In ARUBA, the coalition led by the centre-left People's Electoral Movement (MEP) was accused by the opposition Aruban People's Party (AVP) of having ties with organized crime. Although the charges were strenuously denied by Prime Minister Nelson Oduber, they contributed to conflict with the MEP's coalition partners, the Aruban Patriotic Party (PPA) and National Democratic Action (ADN), with the result that Mr Oduber announced his government's resignation on 17 April. He led an interim MEP administration while trying to negotiate a pact with the AVP, rather than hold fresh elections only one year into the parliamentary term, but this proved impossible.

When polling took place on 29 July, the AVP won ten seats to the MEP's nine, leaving the Aruban Liberal Organization (ALO) with two seats and the balance of power. The APP and ADN lost their representation. On 30 August agreement was reached on the formation of an AVP-ALO government, headed by AVP leader Henny Eman.

V MIDDLE EAST AND NORTH AFRICA

1. ISRAEL

CAPITAL: Jerusalem AREA: 22,000 sq km POPULATION: 5,200,000 ('92)
OFFICIAL LANGUAGE: Hebrew POLITICAL SYSTEM: parliamentary democracy
HEAD OF STATE: President Ezer Weizman (since March '93)
RULING PARTIES: Israel Labour Party (ILP) heads coalition with Meretz & Yi'ud
parties
HEAD OF GOVERNMENT: Yitzhak Rabin (ILP), Prime Minister (since July '92)
PRINCIPAL MINISTERS: Shimon Peres (ILP/foreign affairs), Michael Harish (ILP/trade &
industry), Avraham Shohat (ILP/finance), David Libai (ILP/justice), Shimon Shitrit
(ILP/economy)
CURRENCY: new shekel (end-'94 £1=NIS4.72, US$1=NIS3.02)
GNP PER CAPITA: US$13,220 ('92)
MAIN EXPORT EARNERS: diamonds, machinery, agricultural produce, tourism

THE peace process with the Arab world was the dominant feature
of Israel's year in 1994. The signing of the Declaration of Principles
between Israel and the Palestine Liberation Organization (PLO) in
Washington in September 1993 (see AR 1993, pp. 204–6, 210, 557-63)
provided the impetus that the flagging process needed desperately.

The high point of the year was the signing, on 26 October in Wadi
Araba, of a full peace treaty between Israel and Jordan (see V.2.iii;
XIX.4). This was matched by the steady erosion of the barriers to
direct contacts between Israel and the broader Arab and Muslim world.
The year also revealed the long road that Israel and the Palestinians
still had to travel before a true and lasting peace was achieved. The
expectations generated by the high drama on the White House lawn were
not met by the realities and achievements on the ground. Negotiations
between Israel and the Palestinians were fraught with difficulties and
uncertainties. Terror and violence by Israeli militant settlers and Islamic
fundamentalists aimed at killing both civilians and the fragile peace
process cast a dark shadow. Exploratory contacts between Israel and
Syria, for all the efforts of the Americans, seemed to be going nowhere
fast. On the domestic front, the Israeli government was engaged in
continual efforts over the year to broaden the base of its coalition and
to shore up the fading public support for its policies.

Of all the tracks of the Arab-Israeli peace process, the obstacles to
the normalization of relations between Israel and Jordan were the least
difficult to surmount. Ever since (and even before) the establishment
of the state of Israel, Jordanian and Israeli leaders had been engaged
in an almost continual secret dialogue. After King Husain relinquished
any claim over the future of the West Bank in 1988, the substantive
issues between the two sides concerned a small area of approximately
380 square kilometres in the Arava desert and the allocation of water

resources of the Yarmuk and Jordan rivers. Timing, rather than substance, was the principle issue at stake for Jordan's ruler. It was the developments between Israel and the Palestinians that spurred him to grasp the nettle and move boldly ahead.

The groundwork for the Israeli-Jordanian peace treaty had been laid in the preceding years following the Madrid peace conference in 1991. On 14 September 1993, one day after Yitzhak Rabin (the Israeli Prime Minister) and Yassir Arafat (the PLO leader) had shaken hands on the Declaration of Principles, Israel and Jordan put their signatures on a common agenda for future negotiations. For the first part of 1994, Israeli-Jordanian talks took place in the shadow of the negotiations between Israel and the PLO over the implementation of their accord. However, after the signing of the Gaza-Jericho Agreement in Cairo on 4 May (see V.2.i; XIX.2), the speed of events between Israel and Jordan was breathtaking. On 18 July Israeli and Jordanian negotiators conducted an unprecedented non-secret meeting in the region, held in a desert tent straddling both sides of the border. Two days later the Israeli Foreign Minister, Shimon Peres, and the Jordanian Prime Minister, Abdul Salam Majali, met publicly on the Jordanian side of the Dead Sea. Within a week the public reconciliation between the two sides was completed with the signing in Washington, by Mr Rabin and King Husain, of a joint peace declaration bringing a formal end to their state of belligerency.

A series of high-level meetings in August and September paved the way for the signing of a full peace treaty, in the full glare of the world's media, at the end of October. The treaty, signed with warmth and open smiles, received widespread support across the Israeli public and political spectrum and was overwhelmingly endorsed by the Knesset (the Israeli legislature) by a majority of 105 to three, with six abstentions. On 10 November King Husain made his first public visit to Israel, crossing the Jordan river to meet Mr Rabin on the shores of the Sea of Galilee. One month later the two sides sealed their new spirit of friendship with the exchange of ambassadors and the opening of embassies in Tel Aviv and Amman.

Mr Rabin, Mr Peres and Mr Arafat were jointly awarded the 1994 Nobel Peace Prize for their efforts in trying to resolve the Israeli-Palestinian conflict. However, translating principles into realities on the ground proved to be a far harder task. After months of delay and arduous negotiations, bordering at times on the acrimonious, Israel and the PLO on 4 May signed the Cairo agreement, setting out provisions for the implementation of Palestinian self-rule in the Gaza Strip and Jericho and the withdrawal of Israeli forces from those areas, to be replaced by a 9,000-strong Palestinian police force. The agreement contained detailed arrangements covering legal, civil, security and economic activities. An appointed 24-member Palestine National Authority (PNA) was created to manage Palestinian affairs in Gaza-Jericho in place of the Israeli military administration. Elections in the Gaza Strip and the whole of the West Bank, which under the terms of the Declaration of Principles were due to take place on 13 July, were postponed under the new agreement, the revised target date being October. At the end of June Israeli and Palestinian official embarked on a series of meetings aimed at extending Palestinian self-rule beyond Gaza and Jericho. These talks resulted in the signing on 29 August of an 'agreement on the preparatory transfer of powers and responsibilities' whereby Palestinian authority in the remainder of the Israeli-occupied West Bank would be extended to cover five spheres of activity: tourism, health, social welfare, direct taxation and education.

These diplomatic achievements took place amidst an atmosphere of growing violence between Israelis and Arabs. Extremists from both sides of the Israeli-Palestinian divide sought to derail the peace process by resorting to terrorism against innocent civilians. On 25 February, a Jewish extremist from the Israeli settlement of Kiryat Arba, Dr Baruch Goldstein, opened fire on worshippers praying in the Ibrahimi Mosque at the Tomb of the Patriachs in Hebron, killing 29 Palestinians and wounding over 60 others. Attacks by Islamic militants against Jewish targets in the occupied territories and within Israel itself resulted in the deaths of nearly 100 Israeli civilians in 1994. In April the Hamas fundamentalist movement launched three attacks against civilians in the Israeli towns of Ashdod, Afula and Hadera. The award of the Nobel Peace Prize was overshadowed by a suicide bomb attack by a Hamas extremist on a crowded bus travelling in the heart of Tel Aviv on 19 October, leaving 22 dead and injuring 47 others. Such terrorism steadily undermined support amongst the Israeli public for the negotiations with the Palestinians—a trend exacerbated by Mr Arafat's luke-warm condemnation of the attacks and by his seeming unwillingness or inability to control Hamas. The growing level of violence persuaded the government that it could not safely redeploy Israeli troops from the major population centres in the West Bank in preparation for Palestinian elections, as called for in the Declaration of Principles. The delay led to yet another postponement in the holding of such elections.

The progress of Israel's exploratory contacts with Syria was beset by frustrations. The year ended as it had begun with a public meeting between US President Bill Clinton and President Asad of Syria (see also V.2.iv), the first in Geneva in January and the second in Damascus at the end of October as part of Mr Clinton's tour of the Middle East. In the intervening months, US Secretary of State Warren Christopher strove to bring the two sides closer together, several times shuttling energetically between Jerusalem and Damascus. By the end of the year, however, an Israeli-Syrian reconciliation was seemingly no nearer than it had been at the start.

The breakthrough with the Palestinians and the mutual recognition between Israel and the PLO was the catalyst for the development of relations between Israel and the broader Arab world. The principal channel for the new contacts was the multilateral track of the peace process, dealing with functional issues such as water, the environment and regional economic development. This enabled Gulf states such as Bahrain, Qatar, Oman and the North African governments of Tunisia and Morocco to host meetings with the full and open participation of Israel—a prospect which would have been unimaginable only a few years previously. A series of open bilateral meetings between Israeli ministers and their Arab counterparts included an official visit by Mr Rabin to Oman on 26 December, while there were decisions to open reciprocal 'interest sections' by Israel on the one hand and Morocco and Tunisia on the other. Another important spin-off arising from the multilateral talks was the gradual erosion of the Arab economic embargo against Israel, as indicated by the formal decision by the Gulf Cooperation Council states in September to end their secondary and tertiary boycott of Israel (see also V.3.iii).

A number of other diplomatic 'firsts' were recorded in 1994. Mr Rabin became the first Israeli Prime Minister to pay an official visit to Japan, while an unprecedented visit by President Ezer Weizman to Turkey in January was reciprocated by one to Israel by Turkish Prime Minister Tansu Çiller in November. President Weizman also represented Israel at the inauguration of Nelson Mandela as the new President of South Africa in May. Diplomatic relations were exchanged with the Vatican (see also II.2.viii), while the remaining African states which had not yet restored the diplomatic ties with Israel severed during the Yom Kippur War of 1973 did so in the course of the year.

On the domestic front, Mr Rabin spent the year trying to widen the parliamentary base of his coalition government. In his eagerness to entice the (ultra-orthodox Sephardi) Shas party back into the government fold, the Prime Minister offered them a wide range of legislative powers in religious and civil affairs, much to the consternation of the left-wing Meretz coalition partner and even of some members of his own Labour Party. Civil rights movements, horrified by the prospect of freedoms being curtailed, turned to the courts and petitioned the Supreme Court in an effort to block the prospective coalition deal. In the event, Mr Rabin's assiduous courting of Shas was to no avail. However, in December he did succeed in securing the backing of the two Knesset deputies of the Yi'ud faction, which had split earlier in the year from Rafael Eitan's rightist Tsomet party. This still left the government three votes short of a clear majority of 61 and reliant on the tacit support of the Arab Democratic Party and the communist-dominated Hadash (Democratic Front for Peace and Equality).

The domestic shock of the year was the humiliating defeat suffered by the Labour Party in the elections to the powerful Histadrut trade union federation in May. For the first time since its formation in 1920, Labour lost control of the organization. The elections were won by the 'Ram' list headed by the former Minister of Health, Haim Ramon, who had resigned in February when his radical reforms of the health service had been derailed by the manoeuvres of traditionalist trade unionists. Mr Ramon, who had been expelled from the Labour Party after declaring his intention to run a separate list, was able to attract an unlikely coalition of other Labour renegades, the left-wing Meretz and the ultra-orthodox Shas for his reformist platform.

The government's political problems were compounded by the sluggish performance of the economy in 1994 and a return to double-digit inflation. Its credibility was particularly damaged by the highly unpopular imposition of capital gains tax on the stock market, a measure adopted despite repeated previous assurances that no such step would be taken.

2. ARAB WORLD AND PALESTINIANS—EGYPT—JORDAN—SYRIA— LEBANON—IRAQ

i. THE ARAB WORLD AND THE PALESTINIANS

THE affairs of the Palestinian Arabs and their Israeli neighbours—less than seven million people all told—attracted more Western attention than those of over 100 million Arabs elsewhere; but all, including the Palestinians, were powerfully affected by the growing influence of uncompromising Islam, the so-called fundamentalism. Egypt was the most populous and important Arab state; but even there, despite its substantial Christian minority and traditional tolerance between races and creeds, Islamic zealots disputed government control of some areas and damaged one of Egypt's essential industries, tourism. Algeria seemed to be sinking into anarchy and deprivation under Islamist attack. In states under secular, firm and often despotic control, such as Iraq, Syria and Libya, Islamic influence was less politically powerful.

There was an accompanying decline of pan-Arab sentiment. In Egypt it had lost its force decades earlier. The Iraqi dictator had always put his own survival above any other consideration. Jordan's ruler decided to cultivate his own garden and followed the late President Sadat in making peace with Israel. Pan-Arabism had never been strong in Lebanon, the Gulf or the Maghreb, except in republican Libya, whose leader was too wayward to be a persistent crusader. Even the Syrian dictator seemed likely to put Syrian above pan-Arab considerations if he could thereby recover the Golan.

The ascendancy of Islamic fundamentalism over pan-Arabism was evident in the halting progress of the Israeli-Palestinian peace process in 1994. The previous year had given grounds for hope that Palestinian self-government, if not statehood, might be attainable (see AR 1993, pp. 204-6, 209-12, 557-63). Palestinian leaders no longer hoped for an Arab state conterminous with pre-1948 Palestine; the chauvinist Likud government in Jerusalem had been replaced by one no longer dreaming of *Eretz Israel* from the Mediterranean to the Jordan. The Russians had neither power nor will to intervene. The USA might still, even under the new Democratic President, resist Zionist pressure and adopt a pragmatic policy in the Middle East.

These hopes proved vain. In Israel the Labour-led government was unready to defy the Jewish activist settlers. Hints from Foreign Minister Shimon Peres that they might be removed were not followed up. Israel did not accept UN Security Council resolution 904 calling on it to disarm the settlers. For their part, the Palestinians were deeply divided. The Fatah leadership remained dominated by the erratic but plausible charisma of Yassir Arafat, an autocrat without administrative experience or talent, whose association with Saddam Husain of Iraq had alienated Westerners and some Arabs. Many respectable Palestinians, often intellectuals, some of whom Mr Arafat had excluded from his inner councils, refused or hesitated to participate in the new structures. Really on the outside were the Islamic fundamentalists (themselves divided between the mainstream Hamas and the smaller but more extreme Jihad Islami), who were embittered by the harshness of Israel's security services, averse to gradualism dictated by weakness and prone to violence.

Such an attitude by the fundamentalists strengthened the resolve and the power of Jewish extremists, whose reprisals in their turn provoked more Arab violence. On both sides one outrage followed, and provoked, another outrage (see also V.1). The 25 February slaughter by an American Jewish settler of Palestinian worshippers in a Hebron mosque was the ghastliest; the assassin himself was overpowered and beaten to death. Several Palestinian suicide bombers blew themselves up with their victims. There was also fighting between Arabs: on 18 November the newly-installed Palestinian police opened fire when attacked by Islamists, 12 people being killed. Many Arabs were murdered on suspicion of collaboration.

The peace process faced great incompatibilities, the biggest being on the Israeli side, namely, an inability to accept the eventual withdrawal of Jewish settlements from the West Bank and the Gaza Strip (where Palestinian desperation was deepest) or from the Golan Heights, whose recovery by Syria would probably induce President Asad to make peace. It also remained clear that no Israeli government, Likud or Labour, could swallow the re-division of Jerusalem. Nevertheless, Mr Arafat repeatedly demanded it, first in a draft constitution in May and most publicly at a conference in Casablanca (Morocco) in October.

Although Mr Rabin undertook to block Arab self-government in east Jerusalem, the Israelis were—officially at least—prepared to accept the stalling formulation contained in the 1993 Israel–PLO Declaration of Principles. Article V of this document left decisions on Jerusalem and the settlements to the third year of the interim period.

Following a partial accord in Cairo on 9 February, Mr Rabin and the PLO leader met again in the Egyptian capital on 4 May and completed an agreement on Palestinian self-rule in the Jericho area and the Gaza Strip (see XIX.2). It assigned legislative and executive powers in the two areas to a Palestinian authority and established a 9,000-strong Palestinian police force, while Israel was to remain responsible for the security of Jewish settlements and for the external security of the self-rule areas. Associated confidence-building measures included an Israeli pledge to release some 5,000 Palestinian detainees. In accordance with the agreement, PLO policemen entered the Gaza Strip on 10 May, while on 13 May Israeli forces withdrew from Jericho, ending a 27-year occupation. After some delay, Mr Arafat made a triumphal return to Gaza on 1 July, declaring it to be 'the first free Palestinian land'. On 5 July he flew on to the West Bank and in Jericho installed what the PLO called the Palestinian National Authority (PNA)—the Israelis preferred simply 'Palestinian authority'—with himself as chairman. The newly-appointed PNA, effectively a Palestinian cabinet, had been transported from the previous PLO seat in Tunis and on 26 June had held its inaugural session in Gaza, where it subsequently established itself.

The Israel-PLO agreement was strongly opposed by Hamas and by other militant Palestinian groups and was regarded with suspicion by some moderate Palestinian leaders. Arab-Jewish bloodshed and intra-Palestinian score-settling and division continued. Each major multiple killing delayed the implementation of the agreement, notably the holding of Palestinian elections, which were deferred from July to October but had still not been held by year's end.

On 29 April Israeli and PLO representatives, meeting in Paris, had also signed an accord to cover economic relations for the five-year interim period. Under a transitional agreement concluded in August, administrative functions in the remainder of the Israeli-occupied West Bank were to be gradually passed to the PNA, beginning with education and ending four months later with taxation and health.

This apparent progress only intensified one of the the PNA's major difficulties—lack of money. The Israelis had spent money, however sparingly, running the occupied territories; the PNA had practically none to spend. Already-small tax receipts were further reduced by frequent Israeli border closures, on security grounds, which stopped tens of thousands of Palestinians from going daily to work in Israel. In January the Palestinian Economic Council for Development and Reconstruction (PECDAR), operating from Tunis, had under-estimated the prospective

annual deficit at $158 million, of which donors were expected to provide
$120 million. Of the subsequent reported offers of financial help from
Europe and elsewhere, nearly all were for development, which raised the
question of where day-to-day expenses were to come from meanwhile.
In May Warren Christopher, the US Secretary of State, urged donors
to earmark 25 per cent of their aid for administrative expenses. In
October, however, the PNA member responsible for planning said
that, of a pledged $700 million in donations, only $100 million had
arrived. President Mubarak of Egypt pointed out that continued delays
in providing money would provoke yet more violent opposition to the
peace process. At the end of November prospective donors met in
Brussels and agreed to meet a budget shortfall of $125 million, the
UK government undertaking to provide $4.5 million to help to pay the
Palestinian police.

With no end in sight to the cycle of killings, 1994 closed with a group
of Jewish colonists clearing the ground for a new settlement in the West
Bank. The same Israeli government which in 1992 had appeared to be
determined to halt new Jewish settlement (see AR 1992, pp. 207–8)
this time merely suggested that the colonists should choose some less
provocative site. Against this background, the conferring of the 1994
Nobel Peace Prize jointly on Mr Arafat, Mr Rabin and Mr Peres did
not meet with universal approval.

ii.   EGYPT

CAPITAL: Cairo   AREA: 1,000,000 sq km   POPULATION: 54,700,000 ('92)
OFFICIAL LANGUAGE: Arabic   POLITICAL SYSTEM: presidential democracy
HEAD OF STATE & GOVERNMENT: President Mohammed Husni Mubarak (since '81)
RULING PARTY: National Democratic Party (NDP)
PRINCIPAL MINISTERS: Atif Sidqi (Prime Minister), Kamal Ahmed Ganzouri (Deputy
   Premier, planning), Yusuf Amin Wali (Deputy Premier, agriculture), Fld
   Marsh. Mohammed Hussein Tantawi (defence), Amr Mohammed Moussa (foreign
   affairs), Gen. Hussein Mohammed al-Alfi (interior), Mohammed Ahmed al-Razaz
   (finance), Farouk Seif al-Nasr (justice)
INTERNATIONAL ALIGNMENT: NAM, Arab League, OAPEC, ACC, OAU, ICO, Francophonie
CURRENCY: Egyptian pound (end-'94 £1=LE5.33, US$1=LE3.41)
GNP PER CAPITA: US$640 ('92)
MAIN EXPORT EARNERS: oil & gas, cotton, tourism, agricultural produce

As in 1993, the fundamentalists aimed to weaken Egypt's ties with the
West, damage the economy and thus increase poverty and discontent.
The Palestinian question (see V.2.i) helped them by heightening anti-
Western and anti-government sentiment. In foreign affairs, President
Husni Mubarak played an important but uncomfortable role as mediator
between Western and Arab governments.

Fundamentalists attacked the police and the latter riposted firmly.
An anti-terrorist general was shot in Cairo on 9 April and his deputy

in Asyut 11 days later. Militant leaders arrested or shot included two from the most active group, the Jama'at al-Islamiya (Islamic League). The novelist and 1988 Nobel Prize winner, Naguib Mahfouz, survived an assault on 14 October. The emergency laws in force since 1981 were renewed for another three years. Violence was also directed against foreign tourists and investors, whom the Jama'at expressly warned to stay away. A cruise ship on the Nile was attacked. Between January and November around 80 people died, including policemen, militants and tourists. By 31 March tourist numbers were down by 29 per cent on 1992. Since then 55 people had been condemned to death for terrorism and 39 executed, including five for the attempted murder of a government minister and two for plotting to murder the President. In September Amnesty International criticized Egypt's human rights record, alleging 'grossly unfair' military trials and 16 suspected deaths under torture.

Fundamentalism was strong among lawyers; one who had defended fundamentalists was arrested and died in gaol, provoking a demonstration by 6,000 lawyers and a hunger strike. There was, however, some reaction against fundamentalism, the press in particular denouncing attempts to return Egypt to the Middle Ages. A repentant fundamentalist secured a large audience for his confessions; and an anti-fundamentalist film was a popular success in Cairo. The government's hosting of the UN World Population Conference (unpopular with fundamentalists) brought 20,000 delegates—and 4,000 journalists—to Cairo in mid-September (see XI.1). Though criticized by Muslim extremists and the Vatican, it passed off peacefully.

In early January a property millionaire was arrested and opposition newspapers alleged that an ex-minister had tried to bribe the press to suppress the story. The courts also revealed other stories of corruption, especially in the grant of building licenses (see AR 1992, p. 211). These were ventilated by an opposition leader, whom the Prime Minister and others sued for defamation. The case was dropped in August.

On 2 November a thunderstorm ignited an army fuel depot in southern Egypt and more than 450 people died in fires caused by blazing fuel. Another 63 drowned in flash floods at the same time.

In foreign affairs, much of President Mubarak's time went on the Middle East peace process. He was constantly involved as middle-man and increasingly voiced his concern about the deteriorating economy of the Israeli-occupied territories. The US and Israeli governments continued to expect his support in dealings with the PLO and with the unyielding Syrian President. Mr Mubarak was uncomfortably placed between Egypt's financial obligations to the US government and the opposite pull of anti-Israeli feeling. The February massacre of Arab worshippers in Hebron (see V.1) raised public feeling higher than anything since the riots of 1977 (see AR 1977, p. 182). The opposition demanded the expulsion of the Israeli ambassador; 10,000 Azhar students chanted anti-Israel and anti-Jewish slogans. The Foreign Minister opposed punitive action but held Israel responsible for the security of Palestinians under occupation.

In November the American press claimed that US aid to Egypt was in question because the Cairo government had disregarded US wishes by maintaining relations with Libya. These reports, although denied in Washington, were partly confirmed when President Mubarak urged a Western reappraisal of Qadafi regime. While relations with Sudan remained bad (see V.4.i), Egypt was reported to be seeking to increase its influence in the Maghreb: in November the Egyptian Foreign Minister was in Algiers applying to join the Arab Maghreb Union.

Commenting on Egypt's economic situation, the US embassy saw only inconclusive signs of recovery and growth. Radical action on stock Western lines was constantly urged by the US goverment, the IMF and the World Bank—privatization, tariff reduction, balanced budgets, reduced subsidies, realistic exchange rates and so on. The Egyptians declined to do all these things as quickly as was demanded. They began offering public enterprises for sale, lowering tariffs at the top, freeing transfers across the exchanges and moving towards exchange rate reform. But they maintained that the need for domestic political support limited their power to close loss-making enterprises. Although in late January Egypt had received pledges of another $2,000 million in aid, a further reduction of its debts was delayed and the IMF urged another devaluation. The President replied firmly: 'There will be no devaluation and no rise in the price of dollars.' Unemployment, highest among the under-20s, was around 17.5 per cent. On the other hand, Egypt won a UN prize for reducing the annual growth rate of its population, while the IMF was satisfied to find that the government deficit was down to 8 per cent of GDP and inflation to 7.3 per cent.

iii. JORDAN

CAPITAL: Amman AREA: 97,000 sq km POPULATION: 3,900,000 ('92)
OFFICIAL LANGUAGE: Arabic POLITICAL SYSTEM: monarchy
HEAD OF STATE & GOVERNMENT: King Husain ibn Talal (since Aug '52)
PRINCIPAL MINISTERS: Abdul Salam Majali (Prime Minister, defence & foreign affairs), Sammi Gammouh (finance), Salameh Hammad (interior), Hisham l-Tal (justice), Rima Khalaf (trade & industry)
INTERNATIONAL ALIGNMENT: NAM, Arab League, ACC, ICO
CURRENCY: dinar (end-'94 £1=JD1.10, US$1=JD0.70)
GNP PER CAPITA: US$1,120 ('92)
MAIN EXPORT EARNERS: phosphates, chemicals, cement

KING Husain had long been in touch with the Israeli government and had resented the concealment from him by Yassir Arafat of the negotiation of the Israel-PLO Declaration of Principles signed in September 1993 (see AR 1993, pp. 210, 557-63). By autumn 1994 he had himself concluded a separate peace with Israel (see V.1; XIX.4). This unlocked the door to greater Western financial assistance and provided a buffer to interference from across the Jordan. Popular reactions to peace with Israel were not uncontrollable and the King's own energies appeared to be standing the strain.

On 7 January the PLO sent a mission of reconciliation to Amman and signed a non-political economic agreement. A visit by the King to Washington on 21 January did not suggest any new line. On 10 February Mr Arafat came to Amman to explain the interim agreement he had just reached with Israel (see V.2.i). The Hebron massacre later that month interrupted Jordan's talks with Israel and brought Jordan and the PLO closer together. Meanwhile, Jordan and the United States came into conflict over the latter's naval interference with Iraq's trade through Aqaba, resulting in much-reduced shipping and port receipts. After King Husain had threatened to boycott peace talks, the Americans eventually agreed to lift the blockade and to have the trade monitored by other means.

Still distancing Jordan from the PLO's negotiations, the Deputy Prime Minister described the Israel-PLO agreement of 4 May as 'an independent Palestinian matter'. On 19 May the King met the Israeli Prime Minister, Yitzhak Rabin, in London and then went to Damascus for talks with President Asad. A turning-point came on 7 June in the shape of new administrative and procedural agreements with Israel, after which Jordan negotiated without the PLO. The new situation was underlined by an extensive ministerial reshuffle on 8 June, although the Jordanian cabinet was still headed by Abdul Salam Majali, a known supporter of rapprochement with Israel. In Washington, on 20–22 June, the King discussed how to cover Jordan's debts.

After practical issues had been covered on 18–19 June, King Husain and Mr Rabin (in the presence of President Clinton) signed a declaration in Washington on 25 July ending 46 years of Jordanian-Israeli belligerency. Jerusalem was not covered by the declaration, which did, however, recognize Jordan's 'present special role' in the city. (A Jordanian minister later promised the Palestinians that no agreement on Jerusalem would be concluded with Israel without consulting them.) On 26 July both the King and Mr Rabin addressed the US Congress. There followed financial arrangements to reduce Jordan's $6,700 million foreign debt: the USA would waive nearly one-third of $950 million owing (an agreement to do so in three stages being signed in late September), while the British government undertook to convert $92 million of Jordanian debt into a grant.

The Israel-Jordan treaty itself was signed by Mr Rabin and King Husain on 26 October on the border between the two countries.

Both parties accepted the frontiers defined under the British Palestine mandate (i.e. excluding the West Bank from Jordanian sovereignty), while Jordan agreed to grant 25-year leases to existing Israeli settlers on its territory and was to receive some Israeli land in exchange. Military alliances with third parties were banned and reciprocal diplomatic representation was to be established (the two missions being opened in December). The Straits of Tiran and the Gulf of Aqaba would be open to all nations; and Jordan's special position in Jerusalem was acknowledged. The latter provision was particularly offensive to the Palestinians, in which context Crown Prince Hasan of Jordan (always the voice of reason) promised at an Islamic economic conference in Morocco in November that Jordan would surrender care of the Holy Places to the Palestinians after completion of their negotiations with Israel. However, this later promise did not carry the sanctity of the treaty.

The Israel-Jordan treaty was ill-received by the Palestinians in the occupied territories, both PLO and Hamas, and was also attacked by Islamists and left-wingers in the Jordanian parliament. In reply, the King described it as a historic achievement and spoke harshly of its opponents. The treaty was ratified by 55 votes to 24 on 6 November. There was some ministerial opposition: the Deputy Prime Minister resigned on 5 December, while two former Prime Ministers protested and one of them had to leave the Senate. In the broader Arab world, there was no repeat of the vigorous opposition generated by the 1979 Egypt-Israel peace treaty, although Jordan's sympathy for Iraq during the Gulf War was still resented by Saudi Arabia. King Fahd avoided seeing King Husain when he went on pilgrimage in March, but agreed without enthusiasm to restore diplomatic relations between the two countries.

The year's momentous events heightened internal tensions. In mid-January death sentences were passed on five men accused of plotting to murder the King in 1993. Ten days later fundamentalists launched a series of attacks on cinemas, nine suspected perpetrators being arrested. In late December a further 11 Islamist militants were sentenced to death for similar attacks and for plotting the overthrow of the government. Such executions had already caused concern to Amnesty International and the government was also criticized at home and abroad for regularly prosecuting the press. By April 20 such cases had been reported.

The government could not count on the unconvincingly large parliamentary majorities enjoyed by some neighbouring regimes. In January the budget was approved by 55 votes to 21, i.e. opposed by nearly 30 per cent of the deputies. The lower house minority against ratifying the treaty with Israel was similarly over 30 per cent, accurately reflecting popular sentiment according to local opnion polls.

The year began with the usual financial difficulties. Not all the aid promised for 1993 had arrived; a third of export earnings had gone in loan repayments; and foreign debts were the equivalent of 130 per cent of annual GNP. Against this background, government departments were required to cut their expenditures by 10 per cent. In May an aid donors' meeting in Paris agreed to provide $200 million for 1994, while the IMF produced another $180 million, conditional on the imposition of a flat 14 per cent sales tax (which was opposed by parliament). In June the Paris Club of creditors agreed to reschedule $1,215 million of Jordan's debt over 20 years and to grant a ten-year grace period. The state's finances were then transformed, because of the peace treaty with Israel, by the large debt write-offs described above.

Bahjat Talhouni, who had served several terms as Prime Minister between 1960 and 1970 and more recently had sat in the Senate, died on 30 January aged 82 (see XX: Obituary). King Husain's mother, Queen Zain, died on 26 April.

iv. SYRIA

CAPITAL: Damascus   AREA: 185,000 sq km   POPULATION: 13,000,000 ('92)
OFFICIAL LANGUAGE: Arabic   POLITICAL SYSTEM: presidential
HEAD OF STATE & GOVERNMENT: President Hafiz al-Asad (since March '71)
RULING PARTY: Baath Arab Socialist Party
VICE-PRESIDENTS: Abdul Halim Khaddam, Zuheir Masharqa & Col. Rifa'at al-Asad
PRINCIPAL MINISTERS: Mahmud Zuabi (Prime Minister), Gen. Mustafa Tlas
    (Deputy Premier, defence), Salim Yassin (Deputy Premier, economic affairs),
    Faruq al-Shara (foreign affairs), Husain Hassun (justice), Mohammed Harbah
    (interior)
INTERNATIONAL ALIGNMENT: NAM, Arab League, OAPEC, ICO
CURRENCY: Syrian pound (end-'94 £1=LS35.54, US$1=LS22.72)
GNP PER CAPITA: US$1,160 ('91)
MAIN EXPORT EARNERS: oil, cotton, textiles

THERE was again little change in Syria's internal or foreign politics. Talk of relaxations in government control was not followed by much significant action. The ageing President, Hafiz al-Asad, had never abandoned Syria's right to recover the entire Golan Heights from Israel in one go and was not to be coaxed by Americans or Israelis into settling for less. In 1994 he appeared less committed than before to pursuing pan-Arab goals outside Syria's own vital interests, although the latter clearly continued to include Lebanon (see V.2.v).

The US and Israeli governments behaved as if persistence and patience would eventually bring President Asad round. President Clinton twice, in January and October, went to meet him, first in Geneva and then in Damascus, becoming the first US President to visit Syria for 20 years. His Secretary of State, Warren Christopher, visited Damascus several times in the course of the year. These encounters, and other meetings in Cairo under President Mubarak's auspices, produced no authentic or public statements which could be interpreted as weakening Syria's stand. In

October the Foreign Minister, appearing on Israeli TV, repeated Syria's demand for a full Israeli withdrawal from the Golan.

For its part, the Israeli government was under pressure from Israeli settlers on the Golan. Prime Minister Yitzhak Rabin did at one moment suggest that to retain the whole area would mean another war with Syria; but in October Foreign Minister Shimon Peres said that no return of the Golan would be possible before 1999, while in November Mr Rabin said that Syria's price for peace—return of the Golan—was too high. Syria's reaction to Jordan's peace treaty with Israel (see V.2.iii) was not encouraging for a Golan agreement. In October, in Cairo, President Asad described as 'blasphemous' the provision in it whereby Jordan allowed Israeli settlers to stay on as Jordan's tenants. Relations between the Syrian and Israeli peoples were more human, however. When President Asad lost his son Basil (see below), a mission of condolence by Israeli Arabs, led by a Knesset deputy, visited Damascus. In February the Syrian government offered exit visas to all the remaining Syrian Jews (numbering about 1,200), although most chose to stay.

Syria continued to play an important role in Lebanon, where Prime Minister Rafiq Hariri had the confidence of the Damascus government (see V.2.v). But the Syrians could still not safely leave Lebanon to itself, and several crises in Beirut were resolved by hurried top-level visits to Damascus. Shia villagers in southern Lebanon continued to wage a guerrilla war against the Israelis and their local collaborators in the Israeli-controlled 'security zone'; but they were supported and inspired more by Tehran than by Damascus, which would do nothing to help until it had recovered the Golan.

Russia actively encouraged President Asad to negotiate with Israel and wanted to recover at least part of some $10,000 million owed by Syria to the former Soviet government. At Russian-Syrian talks held in Damascus in the spring, Moscow reportedly agreed to supply more arms and to waive 80 per cent of Syria's debt, it being anticipated that the rest would come from the Gulf states, on whom Syria had established a claim by fighting for Kuwait in the 1991 Gulf War. Meanwhile, there were still about 2,000 Russian experts, some military, in Syria. Debts to others, especially Germany and France, were around $700 million. A delegation from the Paris Club of creditors visited Damascus in December to discuss them. German-Syrian trade was currently in Syria's favour owing to German imports of Syrian oil.

The economy was still dominated by the state; there were no private banks. The collapse of some unofficial finance houses led to a new law to control their operations. But in September, when addressing parliament, President Asad advocated more flexibility in the management of public sector companies. This was followed by a decree enabling them to deal commercially and increasing their independence. In November the Prime Minister, inaugurating the new parliament, announced reforms in banking and some unification of exchange rates. Other changes were reported in December; the private sector could now import directly goods previously bannned or handled only by government agencies.

General elections were held on 24 August, the Baath and its allies winning 167 seats and independents the remaining 83. Some 7,000 candidates presented themselves and a turnout of over 50 per cent was reported. Ten of those elected for Damascus were wealthy businessmen, a class reportedly beginning to enter politics. In the course of the year, Amnesty International reported that, although thousands of political prisoners had been released and international observers admitted to political trials, violations of human rights had not ceased; some prisoners, Amnesty believed, had been secretly executed.

On 21 January President Asad's eldest son Basil, who had been tipped as his eventual successor, was killed in a road accident. The next son, Bashir, was told to take over his brother's role, especially in the fight against corruption.

v.   LEBANON

CAPITAL: Beirut   AREA: 10,000 sq km   POPULATION: 3,781,000 ('92)
OFFICIAL LANGUAGE: Arabic   POLITICAL SYSTEM: presidential, based on power-sharing
HEAD OF STATE & GOVERNMENT: President Elias Hrawi (since Nov '89)
RULING PARTIES: government of national unity
PRINCIPAL MINISTERS: Rafiq Hariri (Prime Minister, finance), Michel al-Murr (Deputy
    Premier, interior), Muhsin Dallul (defence), Faris Buwayz (foreign affairs),
    Bahij Tabbarah (justice), Hagob Yarman Dermerdjian (economy & trade)
INTERNATIONAL ALIGNMENT: NAM, Arab League, ICO, Francophonie
CURRENCY: Lebanese pound (end-'94 £1=LL2,576.73, US$1=LL1,647.00)
MAIN EXPORT EARNERS: agricultural products, precious metals & jewels

THERE was little change of pattern in Lebanese affairs in 1994. In foreign relations Syrian influence was paramount, having installed the Prime Minister, Rafiq Hariri, in October 1992. Though a dynamic figure, Mr Hariri needed Syrian support and hesitated less than before to invoke it. His successes, as both millionaire businessman and statesman, sometimes aroused jealousy and opposition. He clearly thought that, since no Lebanese could solve the problems posed by the continued Israeli control of southern Lebanon, they were better ignored. Instead, he concentrated on planning and financing the reconstruction of Beirut.

Nevertheless, the Israeli-run security zone (SZ) retained its media prominence. The Shia-manned, Iranian-inspired Hizbullah regularly attacked Israeli forces or their Christian Lebanese protégés. These forces took sometimes disproportionate reprisals, perhaps mainly to satisfy Israeli public opinion; they had little effect on Hizbullah. As fighting raged in February-March, the USA and Israel warned the Lebanese government to curb Hizbullah—a task possible only with

Syrian assistance, which Syria would not give. Mr Hariri replied that Israel could secure peace only by evacuating Lebanese territory. In May the Israelis abducted a Shia leader for interrogation over the disappearance of an Israeli airman in 1986 (see AR 1986, p. 192), causing Lebanon to protest to the UN Security Council. A week or so later Israel responded to Hizbullah attacks by carrying out a raid in which 50 people were killed.

Not all violence involved Hizbullah. In January the Jordanian chargé d'affaires in Beirut was murdered, reportedly by members of the rejectionist Abu Nidal group; a number of suspects were later arrested in Amman. On 12 April an Iraqi dissident was also murdered, supposedly by Iraqi agents; Lebanon severed relations with Iraq and expelled or arrested members of its embassy. A battle in a refugee camp near Tyre in November between pro- and anti-Arafat Palestinians left seven dead.

The murder of ten Lebanese in a Maronite church on 27 February was attributed variously to the (Christian) Forces Libanaises (FL), to Israeli agents and to the Syrians. Many FL members, including their deputy commander, were arrested. On 23 March the FL were officially banned and a month later Samir Geagea, the FL leader, was also arrested, together with some FL militiamen, and charged with the church massacre and the 1990 assassination of Dany Chamoun (see AR 1990, p. 213). Mr Geagea was brought to trial in November. Reporting on the church massacre had been immediately banned by the government, which began to impose various controls on the media—reportedly against the advice of the Prime Minister. These controls were designed, it was said, to silence opposition by the Maronites.

All this tended to obscure the problem of thousands of Palestinian refugees in Lebanon, mostly in camps near Sidon or Beirut. They had never been very welcome in Lebanon, having at one time involved themselves in the civil war and become a target for the Israelis. Now that the war was over, the authorities wanted the makeshift Palestinian slums cleared away. The Foreign Minister therefore proposed in the spring that they should be redistributed outside Lebanon—in Gaza or Jericho or wherever else they could find a home; in no case would they be allowed Lebanese citizenship. When Walid Jumblatt (Minister of State for Refugee Affairs) proposed in August that 3,000 of them should be re-housed in Sidon, the cabinet renewed its opposition to permanent Palestinian settlement. In an analogous 'Lebanon for the Lebanese' trend, the government refused work permits for Syrians and Egyptians who had flocked in to the country.

After disagreements with colleagues, Mr Hariri twice left office in a huff (in May and December), but was soon coaxed back by the Syrians during emergency visits to Damascus. Mr Hariri's May resignation signalled his distaste for the Lebanese tradition of subordinating efficient administration to confessional balance. He wanted the best people, no matter what their religion, and refused to leave the nomination of Maronites to their co-religionists. Ironically, his aim of appointing more technocrats and fewer sectarians meant that, although he was himself a Muslim, there would be more Christians in government.

Both of Mr Hariri's resignations produced a sharp fall in the Lebanese currency. His experience in, and encouragement of, business suited the financial community, which also welcomed his brainchild, the Solidere company and its project to rebuild central Beirut (see AR 1993, p. 220). This enterprise had already, early in 1994, enticed $650 million of Lebanese money back from abroad; by September Solidere shares had risen by 70 per cent. There was also a revival of tourism in 1994. However, government economic policy was not universally approved. A parliamentary committee rejected an attempt to have the budget passed simultaneously with a development plan thought to be too ambitious. Nor was Solidere immune from criticism. Mr Hariri would, it was said, profit from its potentially huge operations and its acquisition of building land at preferential prices, while being able to place his cronies in jobs.

In general, there was perhaps too much new construction, in that many existing buildings remained empty. New capital, though increasing, tended to accumulate in high-interest bank deposits and short-term securities. The fruits of economic growth were slow in trickling down. Wages had fallen in real terms and the trade unions demanded rises of up to 88 per cent, which the Prime Minister said could not be afforded at present. In April the unions postponed an anti-government demonstration on pay, but the issue loomed again as the year came to an end.

vi. IRAQ

CAPITAL: Baghdad   AREA: 438,000 sq km   POPULATION: 19,165,000 ('92)
OFFICIAL LANGUAGE: Arabic   POLITICAL SYSTEM: presidential
HEAD OF STATE & GOVERNMENT: President Saddam Husain (since July '79), also
    Prime Minister & Chairman of Revolutionary Command Council
VICE-PRESIDENT: Taha Mohieddin Maarouf
RULING PARTY: Baath Arab Socialist Party
PRINCIPAL MINISTERS: Tariq Aziz (Deputy Premier), Watban Ibrahim al-Hasan
    (interior), Muhammed Said Kazim al-Sahhaf (foreign affairs), Lt-Gen. Husain
    Kamil al-Majid (industry & military industrialization), Safa Hadi Jawad (oil),
    Ali Hasan al-Majid (defence), Shabib Lazim al-Maliki (justice)
INTERNATIONAL ALIGNMENT: NAM, Arab League, OPEC, OAPEC, ACC, ICO
CURRENCY: dinar (end-'94 official rate £1=ID0.87, US$1=ID0.56)
MAIN EXPORT EARNERS: oil & gas

THE year saw no improvement in Iraq's international standing, deteriorating economy and brutal dictatorship. By simulating another imminent attack on Kuwait (see also V.3.iii), President Saddam Husain gave

London and Washington a valid argument for maintaining sanctions. Their opposition continued even after the Iraqi leader had, upon the failure of his manoeuvre, belatedly recognized Kuwait's independence, although other states wanted the sanctions relaxed. Kurdistan remained lost to Baghdad, little though that profited its divided and factious inhabitants. Not much could be done to protect Iraq's southern marshmen from the Baghdad regime, which continued to destroy their environment. Nor was life easy for non-Kurdish, non-Shia Iraqis.

Sanctions had already removed, seemingly, Iraq's ability to wage war on its neighbours but were renewed every 60 days, despite French, Russian and Chinese reluctance. France and Russia hoped, once sanctions were ended, to recover some of the money that Iraq owed them. The US and British governments, however, seemed unlikely to relent while President Saddam remained in power. In March President Clinton said that the United States would maintain sanctions as long as oppression continued in northern and southern Iraq. This was a restatement of earlier positions: in December 1993 the US representative at the UN had declared that Iraq must first end repression in the north and south and convince the Security Council 'that it is now a responsible member of the international community'.

In any case, Iraq had not yet unambiguously recognized Kuwait's independence and frontiers. In October the Iraqis lent force to this objection by massing their troops on the Kuwaiti frontier. The United States, Britain and France sent warships to the Gulf and on 15 October the UN Security Council ordered Baghdad to withdraw all the troops recently moved up (see XI.1). By then US reconnaissance was reporting an Iraqi withdrawal, although spokesmen in Washington said that they had not withdrawn far enough and opposed ending sanctions even if Iraq did recognize Kuwait. A Russian mediation attempt was rebuffed by the Western powers, but on 8 November Iraqi Deputy Premier Tariq Aziz was in Moscow, reportedly trying to bargain recognition of Kuwait for Russian help in getting the sanctions lifted. The Russian Foreign Minister, Andrei Kozyrev, returned with him to Baghdad and on 10 November was present when the National Assembly ratified the decree finally recognizing Kuwait's sovereignty and frontiers.

Iraq asserted that sanctions should now be lifted, but the US and British governments insisted on their maintenance until Iraq had complied with other UN resolutions. The Security Council, while deciding yet again to renew sanctions, welcomed Iraq's new attitude. On 26 November Iraq acknowledged the UN's right to monitor its long-term weapons programme. On 10 December Mr Aziz visited Moscow again, no doubt to remind Russia of the need to reward Iraq for good behaviour; Mr Kozyrev conceded that there had been 'some intransigence' at the UN. A still small voice, that of President Saddam's half-brother and brother-in-law, Barzan Takriti, was meanwhile heard—

from the safety of Geneva—observing that Iraq's 1990 invasion of Kuwait and its October 1994 troop movements had been a mistake. President Saddam continued to refuse, on grounds of sovereignty, the UN's offer to allow Iraq to export some oil to fund the relief of hardship. Such a sale, the UN pointed out, might also help to reopen the Kirkuk-Dörtyol pipeline, which was still holding 30 million barrels of (stationary) oil. In August negotiations to clear the pipeline seemed near completion, but nothing had transpired by year's end.

In Kurdistan, despite apparent previous reconciliations, Kurds of the Barzani (KDP) and Talabani (PUK) factions were more divided than ever. A pro-Iranian group, the Islamic Movement of Iraqi Kurdistan (IMIK), had also appeared, indicating the Iranian government's greater interest in the Kurds. Clashes between the PUK and IMIK caused an estimated 200 deaths between December 1993 and the signature of a peace agreement between the two groups on 17 February. Fighting between the Kurdish factions resumed in May and continued for most of the year despite periodic peace talks in Paris and elsewhere. Many hundreds were reported killed and Amnesty International accused both sides of torture and executions of civilians. On 24 November another PUK/KPD peace agreement promised fresh elections in 1995 after the holding of a census; meanwhile, a power-sharing system would include representatives of non-Kurdish commumnities. On 25 November the Kurdistan assembly accepted the resignation of the Kurdish government.

Also in Kurdistan, US warplanes on 14 April shot down (by mistake) two UN helicopters carrying 22 UN personnel and two Kurds. Later in the year lack of funds threatened to halt UN relief operations. The Foreign Ministers of Iran, Turkey and Syria met in February and in August to discuss Kurdistan, emphasizing their support for Iraq's territorial integrity. Nevertheless, Turkish forces crossed the frontier in their war with Turkish Kurds and set up a frontier security zone (see also II.3.vii).

The Baghdad government increased its control in the south, especially by draining the marshes (see AR 1992, p. 222; 1993, p. 223). In the spring suspected rebel positions were reportedly bombed and local inhabitants expelled, contributing to an estimated 50 per cent reduction in the marsh population. The World Wild Life Fund, using satellite photographs, reported that 43 per cent of the marshes had been drained since 1985.

There were the usual stories of unsuccessful revolts against the regime. A crowd reportedly stormed the Baath party headquarters in the southern city of Amara and cut off the ears of party officials. In Baghdad three bombs were exploded, one killing four people. A former chief of intelligence defected in Kurdistan, reporting that President Saddam had lost the support of the security forces. But there was little to suggest any solid threat to the regime. In various ministerial changes, the Iraqi leader increased his powers and in May made himself Prime Minister. No-one else seemed to count much, except Vice-President Taha Yasin Ramadan and Deputy Premier Aziz. In late November the latter's supervision of foreign affairs reportedly passed to President Saddam himself after Iraq's further poor showing at the UN.

The dinar collapsed in 1994, the market rate falling from 170 to the US dollar to around 650 by October. Foreign exchange shortage forced the closure of 15 of Iraq's missions abroad. Many people, especially children, were suffering malnutrition and its attendant diseases. In September the government severely reduced rations, prices doubled and the UN food programme said it would need 100,000 tonnes of emergency supplies. Scarcity bred illegal methods to combat and to exploit it, through theft and profiteering, and the government punished such activities harshly. In February 30 currency dealers were reported to have been executed. In June the Revolutionary Command Council ordered the amputation of hands for convicted thieves; some criminals were to be permanently branded. Alcohol was banned in public places; bars and discotheques were closed.

3.   SAUDI ARABIA—YEMEN—ARAB STATES OF THE GULF

i.   SAUDI ARABIA

CAPITAL: Riyadh   AREA: c.2,000,000 sq km   POPULATION: 13,300,000 ('92 est.)
OFFICIAL LANGUAGE: Arabic   POLITICAL SYSTEM: monarchy
HEAD OF STATE & GOVERNMENT: King Fahd ibn Abdul Aziz (since June '82), also
   Prime Minister
PRINCIPAL MINISTERS: Crown Prince Abdallah (First Deputy Premier), Prince Sultan
   (Second Deputy Premier, defence), Prince Nayef (interior), Prince Saud al-Faisal
   (foreign affairs), Muhammad Ali Aba al-Khail (finance & national economy),
   Hisham Nazer (petroleum & energy), Abdullah ibn Muhammad ibn Ibrahim al-
   Shaikh (justice)
INTERNATIONAL ALIGNMENT: NAM, Arab League, OPEC, OAPEC, GCC, ICO
CURRENCY: riyal (end-'94 £1=SRls5.87, US$1=SRls3.75)
GNP PER CAPITA: US$7,510 ('92)
MAIN EXPORT EARNERS: oil & gas

MANY of the problems which had troubled Saudi Arabia in 1993 persisted in 1994; indeed, some were intensified. The year began with an announcement that government expenditure was to be cut by nearly 20 per cent, with the aim of achieving a balanced budget in 1995. Few observers believed that this was a realistic target, and so it proved. The economy remained relatively sluggish, as oil income showed little growth; and the overall budget deficit was estimated still to be around 10 per cent of gross domestic product at the end of the year. Government spokesmen denied the more 'alarmist' predictions made by some foreign economic commentators. But it was clear that the cost of the 1990–91 war against Iraq, coupled with a measure of financial mismanagement, had in effect removed the 'safety net' of very large overseas reserves. Barring a substantial and sustained rise in oil prices, future economic growth was therefore likely be much slower than the rate to which many Saudis had become accustomed.

As in 1993, the government sought to delay some of its payments to both domestic and foreign suppliers, and this prompted several complaints. In November details were published of the new five-year development plan which was to come into effect at the end of the year. It stated that the government now hoped to achieve a balanced budget by the year 2000. In order to do so, an ambitious scheme for the privatization of several large state-owned industries was announced. In addition, the government said that it would be seeking to deepen and broaden its revenue base, and to 'rationalize' a range of very costly state subsidies. Those for wheat farming had already been reduced, and in late December the price of petrol was increased sharply, as was the cost of electricity supplied to major consumers. During the year there were reports of power black-outs in several cities, and it became clear that some urban electricity and water supply systems were coming under increasing strain as demand continued to increase.

On the political front, too, there were some sources of disquiet. The Consultative Council established by the King in 1993 (see AR 1993, p. 224) began its deliberations, but no details of them were made public. In March censorship was extended, as the government banned the use, importation and manufacturing of television satellite dishes. In April a prominent businessman believed to be living in Sudan, Usama Binladin, was stripped of his Saudi nationality. He was reported to be a close friend and supporter of the Sudanese religious leader, Hassan al-Turabi, who had been very critical of the Saudi government. In June the former first secretary at the Saudi embassy to the United Nations, Muhammad al-Khilewi, sought political asylum in the USA. He claimed to have a large number of documents allegedly showing that his government had provided financial support for terrorist groups in the Middle East, that it had helped to fund Iraq's nuclear arms programme, that it had tried to exercise electronic surveillance over various Jewish political organizations in the USA, and that it was guilty of numerous violations of human rights at home. For good measure, Mr Khilewi accused other members of the Saudi diplomatic service of fraud and corruption. These charges were given much international publicity by faxes distributed by the London-based Committee for the Defence of Legitimate Rights, a Saudi opposition group, one of whose leaders, Muhammad al-Massaari, requested political asylum in Britain. This was refused in November, and his appeal against the decision was still pending at the end of the year. In late September over 150 Saudis were arrested on the grounds that they were 'inciting religious dissension' within the country, but most had been released by the end of October.

On 4 October King Fahd announced the creation of a new Higher Council for Islamic Affairs under the chairmanship of the Second Deputy Prime Minister and Minister of Defence, Prince Sultan. Its members included several other prominent royal princes, and it became clear that its task was to act as a form of administrative 'ombudsman' for economic, educational, foreign policy and social issues, as well as for more specifically religious matters. The new body was widely seen as another attempt by the government to limit the growing influence of some of the more militant religious leaders and preachers.

The annual pilgrimage in May saw a number of political protests by Iranian Muslims. In the course of the religious ceremonies, over 250 people were killed in a stampede outside Mecca on 23 May. The government declined to take part in the UN World Population Conference held in Cairo in September (see XI.1). With the exception of Qatar, Saudi Arabia's relations with the other members of the Gulf Cooperation Council remained relatively cordial (see V.3.iii); but those with neighbouring Yemen deteriorated disastrously during the year (see below).

ii. YEMEN

CAPITAL: Sanaa AREA: 540,000 sq km POPULATION: 13,000,000 ('92)
OFFICIAL LANGUAGE: Arabic POLITICAL SYSTEM: presidential democracy
RULING PARTIES: General People's Congress (GPC) heads coalition with Yemeni
    Alliance for Reform (Al-Islah)
HEAD OF STATE & GOVERNMENT: President (Gen.) Ali Abdullah Saleh (since '90)
PRINCIPAL MINISTERS: Brig.-Gen. Abd Rabbuh Mansur Hadi (Vice-President),
    Abdul Aziz Abdul-Ghani (GPC/Prime Minister), Abdul-Wahab Ali al-Ounsi
    (Al-Islah/Deputy Premier, foreign affairs), Mohammad Said al-Attar (GPC/Deputy
    Premier, industry), Abdul Qadir Abd al-Rahman Ba Jammal (GPC/Deputy
    Premier, planning & development), Rabbi al-Mutawakkil (GPC/interior), Abdul
    Wahhab Lufti al-Dailami (Al-Islah/justice), Brig.-Gen. Abdul-Malik al-Sayani
    (GPC/defence), Mohammad Ahmad al-Junaid (ind./finance)
INTERNATIONAL ALIGNMENT: NAM, Arab League, ACC, ICO
CURRENCY: rial & dinar (end-'94 £1=YRls88.30 or YD0.69, US$1=YRls55.44 or YD0.44)
GNP PER CAPITA: US$520 ('91)
MAIN EXPORT EARNERS: oil, agricultural products

FOR Yemen, 1994 was a tragic year. Hopes of strengthening the country's new-found unity were dashed as growing political tensions erupted into an all-out civil war. At the same time, relations with Saudi Arabia became more acrimonious and hostile than they had been for many years. While the general election of 1993 had been welcomed with great public enthusiasm (see AR 1993, pp. 225–6), personal relations between President Ali Abdullah Saleh (former leader of North Yemen) and Vice-President Ali Salim al-Bid (former leader of South Yemen), remained mutually hostile and suspicious. The year opened with the latter continuing to refuse to leave his political home-base in Aden to assume his official position in Sanaa. Various external powers endeavoured to break the political deadlock by seeking a new power-sharing agreement between the country's three largest political parties—President Saleh's General People's Congress (GPC), Vice-President al-Bid's Yemen Socialist Party (YSP) and the Islamically-inspired Yemeni Alliance for Reform (Al-Islah) led by Sheikh Abdullah bin Hussein al-Ahmar.

On 18 January representatives of these three parties initialled a 'document of pledge and agreement', but neither the President nor the Vice-President would at first accept it. The government of Jordan then intervened and the two Yemeni leaders both signed the document in Amman on 20 February. The agreement covered various military and security matters, and promised a review, and then the possible revision, of the constitution largely to meet earlier demands made by the YSP. The agreement was soon to become a dead letter, however, as clashes broke out between former South Yemeni soldiers stationed in former North Yemen, and vice versa. At first the most serious fighting occurred at Zinjibar, north-east of Aden, but the number of clashes quickly grew. In late March a committee was established to try to negotiate the separation of the former northern and southern army units. In addition to senior officers from both those forces, it also included representatives from Jordan and Oman, as well as the French and US military attachés in Sanaa. The actions of that committee secured a lull in the fighting, but this proved to be brief. By mid-April both Oman and Jordan had, in effect, abandoned their attempts at mediation, and efforts made by Egyptian officials also proved unsuccessful. By the end of April fighting was widespread, and several former South Yemeni units in the north were reported to have suffered heavy casualties. The Vice-President then ordered the former southern airforce to attack targets in the north, including the presidential palace in Sanaa. In response, the former northern airforce bombed Aden, and both cities also suffered long-range missile attacks.

On 21 May Vice-President al-Bid, who had by now moved his headquarters to the Hadrahmaut because of the attacks on Aden, announced the creation of a new state in the south, the Democratic Republic of Yemen (DRY). Many Yemenis believed that he had done this at the behest of the Saudi Arabian government, which had been angered by the Yemeni government's stance at the UN over Iraq's invasion of Kuwait in 1990. With the collapse of the Soviet Union, moreover, Riyadh no longer saw any danger of marxism spreading northwards from Aden. The Saudi government certainly appeared to favour the rapid diplomatic recognition of the new regime in the south, and there were many reports of military and economic assistance being supplied to it by Riyadh. The military forces of former North Yemen proved, however, to be the stronger. Despite various UN Security Council and Arab League resolutions calling for a ceasefire, the war continued with attacks on several oilfields and other important economic installations. This prompted the evacuation of foreign technical personnel, and led to a decline in petroleum production. Russian diplomatic efforts, together with those of other countries, produced a series of ineffective ceasefire agreements in June and early July. By the end of July it was clear that the former North Yemeni forces had achieved a 'victory'.

In early September the YSP elected a new leadership after many of its prominent officials (including Vice-President al-Bid) had fled into exile, from where some of them vowed 'to continue the struggle against the dictatorship of President Saleh'. On 28 September the House of Representatives in Sanaa adopted a series of constitutional reforms which greatly strengthened the political role of the President, to which post General Saleh was formally re-elected on 1 October for a five-year term. On 6 October he appointed a new Council of Ministers, in which the key posts were retained by members of the GPC, although the number of representatives from Al-Islah rose from six to nine. Some independent ministers were also appointed, but there were no cabinet posts for any members of the new YSP.

The aftermath of the war was therefore a legacy of bitterness, suspicion and deep distrust both within Yemen and also between that country and Saudi Arabia. The Yemeni economy, which was already very weak, suffered considerable physical damage, and hopes of attracting vital foreign investment virtually disappeared. The politics of violence, and of tribal rivalries, had once again exacted a heavy price in Yemen.

iii.   ARAB STATES OF THE GULF

United Arab Emirates

CONSTITUENTS: Abu Dhabi, Dubai, Sharjah, Ras al-Khaimah, Fujairah, Umm al-Qaiwin, Ajman

FEDERAL CAPITAL: Abu Dhabi   AREA: 77,000 sq km   POPULATION: 1,700,000 ('92)

OFFICIAL LANGUAGE: Arabic   POLITICAL SYSTEM: federation of monarchies

HEAD OF STATE & GOVERNMENT: Shaikh Zayad bin Sultan al Nahayyan (Ruler of Abu Dhabi), President of UAE (since '71)

CURRENCY: dirham (end-'94 £1=Dh5.75, US$1=Dh3.67)

GNP PER CAPITA: US$22,020 ('92)

MAIN EXPORT EARNERS: oil & gas

Kuwait

CAPITAL: Kuwait AREA: 18,000 sq km POPULATION: 1,410,000 ('92)
OFFICIAL LANGUAGE: Arabic POLITICAL SYSTEM: monarchy
HEAD OF STATE & GOVERNMENT: Shaikh Jabir al-Ahmad al-Jabir as-Sabah (since '77)
CURRENCY: dinar (end-'94 £1=KD0.47, US$1=KD0.30)
GNP PER CAPITA: US$16,150 ('89)
MAIN EXPORT EARNERS: oil & gas

Oman

CAPITAL: Muscat AREA: 300,000 sq km POPULATION: 1,600,000 ('92)
OFFICIAL LANGUAGE: Arabic POLITICAL SYSTEM: monarchy
HEAD OF STATE & GOVERNMENT: Shaikh Qaboos bin Said (since '70)
CURRENCY: rial (end-'94 £1=OR0.60, US$1=OR0.38)
GNP PER CAPITA: US$6,480 ('92)
MAIN EXPORT EARNERS: oil & gas

Qatar

CAPITAL: Doha AREA: 11,400 sq km POPULATION: 508,000 ('92)
OFFICIAL LANGUAGE: Arabic POLITICAL SYSTEM: monarchy
HEAD OF STATE & GOVERNMENT: Shaikh Khalifah bin Hamad al-Thani (since '72)
CURRENCY: riyal (end-'94 £1=QR5.69, US$1=QR3.64)
GNP PER CAPITA: US$16,750 ('92)
MAIN EXPORT EARNERS: oil & gas

Bahrain

CAPITAL: Manama AREA: 685 sq km POPULATION: 530,000 ('92)
OFFICIAL LANGUAGE: Arabic POLITICAL SYSTEM: monarchy
HEAD OF STATE & GOVERNMENT: Shaikh Isa bin Sulman al-Khalifah (since '61)
CURRENCY: dinar (end-'94 £1=BD0.59, US$1=BD0.38)
GNP PER CAPITA: US$7,130 ('91)
MAIN EXPORT EARNERS: oil & gas, aluminium

THE general atmosphere within the Gulf throughout 1994 was one of consolidation. Nonetheless, the Iraqi threat was brought suddenly to life when, in mid-October, American intelligence sources revealed that up to 80,000 Iraqi troops, many of them from the Republican Guards, were massing close to Iraq's border with Kuwait (see also V.2.vi). The UN Security Council condemned the Iraqi move and demanded that Iraq forego all future troop movements in the southern region of the country (see also XI.1). The United States backed up the UN demand by moving up to 40,000 troops into the region, together with more than 600 aircraft and a large naval task force. The Gulf Cooperation Council (GCC) condemned the Iraqi move and Kuwait mobilized 20,000 troops. A British task force also moved into the Gulf and the French sent one frigate.

Iraqi compliance with UN demands allowed American and British forces in Kuwait to be removed, the remaining 7,800 US troops being withdrawn just before Christmas. Iraq was also persuaded by Russian mediation to recognize its new UN-designated border with Kuwait on 12 November, although this did little to convince the Security Council to remove the sanctions regime against Baghdad. Kuwaiti and

Iraqi negotiators met in Geneva in September to discuss the issue of 600 Kuwaitis still missing after the 1990 invasion and subsequent war. Kuwait also filed official reparations claims worth $80,000 million with the UN reparation claims commission in October, alongside earlier claims for the same amount filed in May and representing individual and company claims against Iraq.

One feature of the year was the growth in popular resentment against Gulf governments. In Kuwait this was contained by the increasing participation of the National Assembly in political life. The Assembly did, however, question the foreign investment policy of the government and its $12,000 million defence procurement policy, originally laid down in 1992. There were also heated debates on proposals to eliminate the budget deficit either through taxation or through the removal of subsidies. The powerful role of the Islamists in the Assembly, where they held a significant minority of the seats, was underlined in December when the deputies approved a law separating the sexes in a new university.

The Kuwaiti government's readiness to respond to Assembly opinion was underlined when Ali Khalifah al-Sabah—the former Oil Minister— was arrested with three others and accused of defrauding the state by embezzlement from funds of the Kuwait Oil Transport Company. Five persons—four Iraqis and one Kuwaiti—were sentenced to death in June for the attempted assassination of former US President George Bush the previous year (see also IV.1). Seven other persons were sentenced to long prison terms. An assembly proposal to make the *sharia* the sole source of law was rejected by the government in July. The Kuwaiti cabinet was reshuffled in April, when Oil Minister Ali Ahmad al-Baghli, usually considered an Islamist sympathizer, was replaced by Abdelmohsin Midij al-Midij, who was close to the liberal wing in the Assembly.

The Omani government also underwent a minor reshuffle at the start of the year. In mid-year, it was announced that the January 1992 Consultative Council was to be enlarged from 59 to 80 members and that women would be able to stand for election in Muscat itself. The tensions within Omani society were underlined in August when a foreign-supported Islamist network was uncovered and 200 persons were arrested. Bahrain also experienced widespread popular unrest in its Shia community in December, when several days of riots culminated in up to nine deaths and 1,600 arrests, according to the Islamic Front for the Liberation of Bahrain. Government sources blamed the disturbances on demonstrators who stoned a charity marathon after it was condemned by a Shia divine, Sheikh Ali Salman; he was said to have returned two years earlier after spending a long period studying at Qom in Iran. They also suggested that the ensuing riots had been planned by 'outside' organizations.

Opposition sources, however, claimed that the Bahrain crisis had started in mid-November after an appeal by four former parliamentarians who had organized a 3,000-signature petition for the restoration of the 1973 Assembly (disbanded in 1975). Widescale arrests followed, to prevent the petition being presented to the Emir on 16 December, Bahrain's national day. The charity marathon incident, which occurred on the same day, coincided with a demonstration in Manama outside the Ministry of Labour over unemployment, which had been condemned by Sheikh Ali Salman. At end-1994 there were 15,000 people unemployed, mainly members of the majority Shia community, who faced fierce job competition from the 60,000-strong foreign migrant community. Police intervention ushered in five days of rioting in which at least one policeman was lynched.

The rioting in Manama in December coincided with the annual GCC heads of state meeting and was thus a great embarrassment to the Bahraini government. The summit confirmed the decisions of an earlier GCC Finance Ministers' conference in Riyadh in mid-September which sought to unify monetary and economic policies as a first step towards creating a free trade area in the Gulf. In April the GCC military committee was inaugurated in Dubai as part of the process of integrating Gulf defence forces. A common security strategy pact was signed by all GCC states except Kuwait and Qatar at the end of November. The GCC also condemned Iranian attitudes towards the Abu Musa dispute and supported a UAE decision, in December, to refer the matter to the International Court of Justice (ICJ) at The Hague. Earlier, Qatar had decided to refer its maritime boundary dispute with Bahrain to the ICJ (see also XI.1.i).

In late September the GCC agreed to follow Kuwait's lead and remove the secondary and tertiary boycotts against Israel, as a contribution to the advancing peace process in the Middle East (see V.1; V.2.i). Individual Gulf states also moved towards closer relations with Israel during the year. In February Qatar proposed a $1,000 million gas pipeline to supply Israel and the new Palestinian entity for a 25-year period—although the construction of such a line would have to await a formal peace agreement. Oman hosted a conference on regional water issues in April, as part of the multilateral peace process, in which an Israeli delegation took part. The Israeli Prime Minister, Yitzak Rabin, visited Oman at the end of the year.

Qatar threatened to open diplomatic relations with Iran during the year, much to the disgust of its partners in the GCC. Russia tried to reassert its role in the Gulf during a visit by the Russian Foreign Minister, Andrei Kozyrev, in November. A trade accord was signed between Russia and Kuwait, and Russia agreed to supply $750 million worth of armoured personnel carriers, apparently in part-settlement of its $1,100 million debt to Kuwait. The UAE was able to achieve a final settlement to the BCCI scandal (see AR 1991, pp. 24–5, 229; 1992, p. 231), at the price of dropping its own claims against the failed bank. In the domestic arena, the UAE decided to base criminal law on the *sharia* in February and the UAE Oil Minister, Yusuf bin Umayr bin Yusuf, unexpectedly resigned for personal reasons in the same month.

In economic terms, 1994 opened with a growing anxiety in the Gulf about the persistent weakness of world oil prices and continuing sluggishness in demand. It was only after March, when 'hedge-fund' investment in oil forced prices upwards, that this anxiety began to dissipate. Nonetheless, Gulf states continued to consider that revenue levels should be governed by export volumes, rather than price levels. Indeed, OPEC as a whole saw production rise by 5 per cent in 1993 and Kuwait's production levels were the highest for 14 years.

Kuwaiti production remained consistently at around 2 million barrels per day (b/d) through the year, plans being announced in January to expand production capacity from the current level of 2.5 million b/d to 3 million b/d by 2010. Qatar announced at the start of the year that its production capacity was to be raised over the next three years by 50 per cent towards 600,000 b/d. In Oman, on the other hand, specific measures were taken to try to persuade OPEC and non-OPEC oil producers to bolster prices. The Oil Minister, Said bin Ahmed al-Shanfari, unsuccessfully sought in February to persuade oil producers to rein in production by 5 per cent in order to improve world price levels. At the same time, Oman's own production capacity rose to 800,000 b/d, a 3 per cent increase over the preceding year.

In the UAE, where production levels consistently exceeded the state's OPEC quota, Dubai announced plans at the start of the year to revive its flagging oil production—which had fallen from 415,000 b/d in 1991 to an estimated 260,000 b/d in 1994—to 345,000 b/d within a year. In April Abu Dhabi announced similar plans to increase capacity from 2.4 million b/d to 2.6 million b/d by the end of 1995. Production capacity had increased to 2.5 million b/d by the end of the year, while production levels remained above 2 million b/d, with Abu Dhabi producing 1.85 million b/d and Dubai 315,000 b/d. Plans were also mooted in June to link the gas-gathering systems in Oman, the UAE and Qatar together in order to improve gas reinjection schemes.

Gas production was also important in the Gulf energy picture during 1994. Qatar continued development of the North Field, at an estimated eventual cost of up to $8,000 million, and engaged in negotiations with Iran over the associated South Pars Field. The major gas liquefaction project, involving Qatargas, Total, Marubeni, Mitsui and Mobil, obtained finance worth $2,000 million from Japan. However, the Eurogas project, in which the Italian company Snam had a 30 per cent stake, was shelved after a disagreement between Qatar and Italy over gas prices. Oman revalued its reserves in March and claimed proved reserves of 20,000,000 million cubic feet of gas and 4,700 million barrels of oil. The Sultanate also pushed ahead with the $9,000 million Bimmah liquified natural gas project, on which site preparation started in October. The proposed Oman-India gas pipeline project was, however, postponed in mid-year.

The budgetary situation throughout the Gulf during 1994 underlined the twin problems of financial stress caused by the Gulf War and of chronically depressed oil prices. Kuwait managed to reduce its budget deficit to $5,000 million from a previously estimated level of $9,000 million, before foreign investment revenues were included. Although much of this was covered by expected foreign investment income of $6,000 million—so that in the 1993/94 financial year the actual budget deficit was only $705 million—the government was still left with a financing gap of $1,500 million, partly because oil revenues fell to $21,000 million from a predicted level of $26,000 million in the 1993/94 financial year.

The reduction in the Kuwaiti deficit was the effect of cuts made in response to demands from the National Assembly for a 20 per cent across-the-board expenditure reduction; as a result, the Assembly passed the new budget in September. Kuwait still faced problems, however, in that $2,800 million of the $17,000 million cost of the Souk al-Manakh stock crisis was still unpaid, while the United States demanded payment of the cost of transferring troops to defend Kuwait in October. The latter demand seemed likely to lead to a further 25 per cent cut in development spending or a 10 per cent tax increase.

Oman also tried to cut its budget expenditure during the year, although defence expenditure continued at a level of 30 per cent of total proposed expenditure and oil revenues were predicated on a rise in oil prices. By September estimates of Oman's current-account deficit had tripled to $904 million—some 8 per cent of GDP—and the government had to seek external financing to resolve it. A $300 million syndicated loan raised in June indicated that there would be little difficulty in achieving this. Oman nevertheless faced serious economic problems, as a World Bank report made clear in November. It suffered from chronic budget deficits (averaging $870 million annually, equivalent to 23 per cent of government revenues), adverse export trends and declining investment. In these respects, it was similar to the other Gulf states but, unlike them, it had little capital reserves to tide it over. The World Bank pointed out that Oman was, in effect, drawing on its capital by depending on oil and gas revenues to fund current expenditure and it recommended a far more energetic push towards privatization as a means of countering these trends. In response, Oman announced the most ambitious privatization plans of any state in the Gulf, and began to reconsider some of its foreign investment proposals, such as the planned oil investments in Kazakhstan.

Despite its domestic political troubles, Bahrain built on its economic successes of 1993, when it achieved a trade surplus of $200 million and a reduced current-account deficit of $450 million, together with a reduction in foreign debt to $2,580 million. Both Alba and Bapco announced ambitious expansion plans, and the new South Hidd container port was on schedule for completion in 1999. The offshore banking sector contracted once again, to a value of $60,200 million in September compared with $60,930 million in September 1993.

Qatar faced a more stringent year as budget spending was cut by 19.5 per cent in July and additional finance was sought for development projects associated with the North Field. The UAE also faced a difficult year, with the economy stagnating because of reduced oil revenues, although the non-oil economy grew by 6 per cent in 1993. The Jebel Ali free port expanded by another 140 companies during 1993 to a total of 603 companies, the most active sector of which (187 companies) was engaged in manufacturing (which was growing by 4 per cent per year). In June the UAE proposed increased GCC economic integration through customs tariff unification at 4 per cent throughout member states. In September Kuwait joined Bahrain and the UAE as members of the GATT, and it was expected that Oman and Qatar would not be far behind.

4. SUDAN—LIBYA—TUNISIA—ALGERIA–MOROCCO—WESTERN SAHARA

i. SUDAN

CAPITAL: Khartoum   AREA: 2,500,000 sq km   POPULATION: 26,500,000 ('92)
OFFICIAL LANGUAGE: Arabic   POLITICAL SYSTEM: military regime
HEAD OF STATE & GOVERNMENT: President (Gen.) Omar Hasan Ahmed al-Bashir
  (since Oct '93), previously Chairman of Revolutionary Command Council
PRINCIPAL MINISTERS: Gen. Zubir Mohammed Saleh (Vice-President), El-Tayyib
  Ibrahim Mohammed Khair (interior), Hussein Suliman Abu Saleh (foreign
  affairs), Abdallah Hasan Ahmed (finance), Maj.-Gen. Hasan Abdel Rahman Ali
  (defence), Abdul Aziz Shiddu (justice)
INTERNATIONAL ALIGNMENT: NAM, Arab League, OAU, ACP, ICO
CURRENCY: dinar (end '94 £1=D48.62, US$1=D31.08)
GNP PER CAPITA: US$480 ('88)
MAIN EXPORT EARNERS: cotton, agricultural products

THE Sudanese-UK diplomatic strains generated by the Archbishop of Canterbury's unofficial visit to Christian southern Sudan at the turn of the year (see AR 1993, p. 233) contrasted sharply with the increasing warmth of Sudan's relations with France in 1994. High-ranking Sudanese government officials and security chiefs visited France, while French companies were involved in oil exploration in Sudan, the building of Juba international airport and the restarting of the Jonglei Canal project. The high point came in August when Sudan announced the capture in Khartoum of Illich Ramírez Sánchez, known as 'Carlos the Jackal', who was turned over to the French authorities (see also II.2.ii). This event was interpreted as an attempt, albeit largely unsuccessful, to change Sudan's image as a country officially supporting terrorism. Sudan's continuing support of extremist Islamic groups led to an arms embargo being applied on Sudan by the Foreign Ministers of the European Union (EU).

Uganda complained about Sudan's support for the northern-based dissident group called the Lord's Resistance Army; in response, Sudan accused Uganda of allowing weapons to reach the insurgent Sudan People's Liberation Army (SPLA). Sudan denied that it was involved in an attack on Eritrea in which 20 invaders from Sudan led by an Eritrean commander were killed. Moreover, Eritrea, Ethiopia and Malawi accused Sudan of supporting Muslim groups in their countries. Sudan asked the Eritrean government to begin repatriating Eritrean refugees living in Sudanese territory. The Sudanese ambassador to Somalia was kidnapped in April but later released, the government denying that a ransom had been paid for his release. Sudan's relations with Egypt were further strained due to the government's confiscation of 16 Egyptian rest-houses and other properties. The Egyptian government rejected Sudanese accusations that it had been involved in a coup attempt allegedly mounted by the Umma Party (UP) in June. Sadiq al-Mahdi, the UP leader, was arrested but released later after denying involvement in any coup attempt. Faced with such regional hostility (as well as broader international condemnation), the Sudanese regime initiated talks on integration with Libya, its only sympathetic neighbour.

In February an armed attack on a mosque in Omdurman belonging to Ansar al-Sunna, a small religious group, resulted in many deaths. The government stated that the vehicle and weapons used in the operation had been stolen from a police station, whereas opposition groups alleged that the attack had been organized by the government. One of the attackers was later hanged in public. An estimated 50,000 people displaced by the civil war in the south were expelled from Khartoum. The US government and the EU presidency protested against the expulsions and the associated violent attacks on those involved. The government rejected a UN report which accused Sudan of human rights' abuses against rebel forces in the south.

In accordance with the policy of implementing strict Islamic codes, the government decreed that all female students must cover all parts of their bodies except the face and hands. Further, students were required to report for military training to the Popular Defence Force (PDF), an organization under the control of the Muslim fundamentalists, or risk losing their places at academic institutions.

The Umma and Democratic Unionist parties, the main opposition groups, rejected approaches by the pro-government National Islamic Front (NIF) for a reconciliation. In April the government approved legislation providing for general elections on a constitutional referendum, although no firm date was set. The interim President, General al-Bashir, appointed 54 new members to the country's unelected transitional Assembly. In pursuance of its policy of administrative decentralization, the government created a further 17 new states in February, bringing the total to 26. To appease the southern Sudanese, George Kongor Arop, a Christian, was appointed second Vice-President in February, while Agnes Lokudu became governor of the southern Bahr-Jabal state, the first woman to be so appointed. Aldo Ajo Deng, the deputy speaker in the transitional Assembly, decided to remain in exile, accusing the present regime of trying to impose Islam on the south. A minor ministerial reshuffle in July saw the appointment of a hardliner, Al-Tayib Ibrahim Muhammed, as Interior Minister.

Despite efforts to reconcile the rival factions of the SPLA, fighting continued between them. From early 1994 government forces launched a major offensive against SPLA strongholds in the south, capturing a number of towns and villages. As increasing numbers of refugees crossed the borders into Zaïre and Uganda, they were subjected to air attacks and bombing by the government. The SPLA accused Zaïre and the Central African Republic of allowing Sudanese troops to attack the SPLA from within their territory. A number of meetings in Nairobi between government representatives and the SPLA failed to resolve the conflict in the south. The SPLA wanted a united Sudan and not an Islamic Sudan—a demand which was unlikely to be accepted by the existing regime. Some southern Sudanese expressed a separatist view, as evidenced when the SPLA-United faction, under the leadership of Riak Macher, changed its name to the Movement for the Independence of Southern Sudan.

In view of the escalation of civil conflict, the French oil company Total decided to withdraw from its exploration in southern Sudan. On the other hand, the government agreed in principle that Arakis Energy of Canada should construct an oil pipeline from Heglig and Unity fields to Port Sudan. In September the IMF suspended its earlier proceedings for the expulsion of Sudan, which obtained more time to fulfil promises to reform its financial policy and to begin refunding its $1,700 million debt. The United Nations appealed for $279 million in food and energy aid for Sudan, to compensate for poor agricultural production in the north. In view of its international isolation, in 1994 Sudan received only $28 million from the OPEC Development Fund and the Jeddah-based Islamic Development Bank for agricultural and irrigation rehabilitation projects. The government continued to devalue its currency and the central bank announced the end of currency exchange control, leaving banks free to determine currency parities. This contributed to soaring inflation, which put daily basic commodities beyond the means of many people.

ii. LIBYA

CAPITAL: Tripoli   AREA: 1,760,000 sq km   POPULATION: 4,867,000 ('92)
OFFICIAL LANGUAGE: Arabic   POLITICAL SYSTEM: socialist 'state of the masses'
HEAD OF STATE: Col. Muammar Qadafi, 'Leader of the Revolution' (since '69)
GOVERNMENT LEADERS: Abd al-Majid al-Qaud (sec. of Gen. People's Committee), Mohammed Bait al-Mal (planning & finance), Omar Mustafa al-Muntassir (foreign affairs & international cooperation), Abdullah Salem al-Badri (energy), Fathi Bin Shatwan (industry)
INTERNATIONAL ALIGNMENT: NAM, OPEC, OAPEC, AMU, OAU, ICO
CURRENCY: dinar (end-'94 £1=LD0.56, US$1=LD0.36)
GNP PER CAPITA: US$5,310 ('89)
MAIN EXPORT EARNERS: oil & gas

WHEN the General People's Congress met in January, the Lockerbie affair was high on the agenda but the statement issued at the end of the session contained no hint that a compromise was possible and instead accused the USA of using sanctions to continue its policy of oppressing Libya. In a speech in Misurata in February, Colonel Qadafi declared that the Lockerbie affair was closed, but two weeks later proposed that the two accused men be tried by an Islamic court in the USA, Britain or any other country so long as the court officials were all Muslims. The proposal was rejected by the British Foreign Office. After the secretary of the Arab League held talks in Tripoli at the end of February, the official Libyan press agency JANA accused the League of giving in to US pressure over UN sanctions and declared that Libya wished to play no further part in the organization. In February President Clinton renewed US sanctions against Libya, originally imposed in 1986, and reaffirmed his determination to see the two Libyans accused of the Lockerbie bombing extradited to face trial. He described Libya as an exceptional threat to US national security and interests.

In April the UN Security Council voted to maintain sanctions against Libya. The US government continued to press for an oil embargo but most of its European allies were unwilling to support any further tightening of sanctions. In June Libya proposed that the two Libyan suspects should be tried by a Scottish jury at the International Court of Justice at The Hague. The proposal won support in the Security Council from China and the Non-Aligned countries, while the Organization of African Unity called on the UN to reconsider sanctions against Libya. Nevertheless, when sanctions came up for review in August, the Security Council voted to keep existing measures in place for a further 120 days. The Libyan proposals were clearly aimed at winning international sympathy and support rather than at resolving the problem. An intransigent Colonel Qadafi, who maintained links with radical Palestinian groups, appeared determined not to give the two men up and convinced that the real motive behind sanctions was to remove him from power.

During the early part of the year, a series of press reports once again cast doubts on Libya's involvement in the bombing of the Pan Am airliner in 1988 and suggested that Syria, Iran and the Popular Front for the Liberation of Palestine might have been implicated. Attention focused on a report that the Swiss electronics firm which manufactured the detonators used to trigger the bomb planted on the flight had supplied these devices to the Stasi (the former East German security service) as well as to Libya. One of the key elements in the prosecution's case against Libya had been the fact that Libya alone had purchased detonators from the Swiss firm. However, when a member of the Abu Nidal group, on trial for murder in Beirut, claimed responsibility for the bombing, the credibility of his confession was questioned and it was rumoured that he had been forced to make the statement under pressure from his organization. Sanctions against Libya were again renewed without change by the Security Council on 30 November after the regular 120-day review.

One of the consequences of the imposition of sanctions was the return of the feared Committees of the Revolutionary Movement to the forefront of Libyan politics. The secretaries of these committees had become political commissars supervising government departments, the people's congresses, the judiciary, the security forces and the army. The main objective of the movement's domestic section was to suppress internal dissent while its international section became more powerful than the Foreign Ministry. The movement expressed its vehement opposition to any concessions in the Lockerbie affair. Mohammed Said, head of the movement's day-to-day operations, was reported to have replaced Abdul-Salem Jalloud as Colonel Qadafi's second-in-command. Major Jalloud had not been seen in public since October 1993.

In what was interpreted as a move to strengthen the regime's repressive armory in hunting down opponents, Colonel Qadafi announced in September the creation of Socialist People's Commands in every commune. Each command appeared to be responsible for denouncing opponents of the regime in its own district or all its members faced collective punishment. There were persistant rumours that the main threat to the regime could come from tribal rivalries and reports that tensions had arisen between the Qadafia, the Libyan leader's own tribe, and the Maghara and Warfella. There were examples of the regime demanding the public denunication of alleged traitors by fellow tribesmen. The first official confirmation of the attempted coup in October 1993 (see AR 1993, p. 236) came in March when a

Libyan television broadcast alleged 'confessions' by three army officers and a student, all members of the Warfella tribe. In April Colonel Qadafi accused elements in the armed forces of harbouring 'fascist aspirations'.

In February the International Court of Justice ruled against Libya's claim to the Aouzou Strip in northern Chad (see XV.1.i). Libya and Chad had agreed in 1989 to accept the Court's ruling over the disputed territory. Following an agreement signed in April at Sirte, Libya completed its withdrawal by the end of May.

iii. TUNISIA

CAPITAL: Tunis   AREA: 164,000 sq km   POPULATION: 8,400,000 ('92)
OFFICIAL LANGUAGE: Arabic   POLITICAL SYSTEM: presidential
HEAD OF STATE & GOVERNMENT: Gen. Zayn al-Abdin Ben Ali (since Nov '87)
RULING PARTY: Constitutional Democratic Rally (RCD)
PRINCIPAL MINISTERS: Hamid Qarwi (Prime Minister), Habib Ben Yahia (foreign affairs), Abdullah Khalal (interior), Sadok Chaabane (justice), Abdelaziz Ben Dhia (defence), Nouri Zorgati (finance), Sadok Rabah (economy)
INTERNATIONAL ALIGNMENT: NAM, Arab League, OAPEC, AMU, OAU, ICO
CURRENCY: dinar (end-'94 £1=D1.54, US$1=D0.99)
GNP PER CAPITA: US$1,720 ('92)
MAIN EXPORT EARNERS: tourism, oil & gas, phosphates, olive oil

THE presidential and legislative elections on 20 March brought few surprises. President Ben Ali was re-elected for a second term, winning a reassuring 99.91 per cent of the vote according to official sources, which also reported that 94.89 per cent of eligible voters had participated in the election. He was the only candidate. Abderrahmane el-Hani, a lawyer and leader of a political party not recognized by the government, and Moncef Marzouki, the former president of the Ligue Tunisienne des Droits de l'Homme (LTDH) and an obstinate critic of the regime's human rights record, had both been arrested after announcing their intention to stand for the presidency. In the parliamentary elections the ruling Rassemblement Constitutionnel Démocratique (RCD) swept to victory, winning 97.73 per cent of the vote and taking all 144 seats allocated under the majority list system.

The RCD demonstrated that its capacity to mobilize its forces had grown even stronger since its reorganization. Its carefully orchestrated electoral campaign, centred on the key words 'safety', 'prosperity' and 'consensus', just as much as the regime's achievements in economic development and women's rights, swayed the voters in favour of continuity. The tragic situation in neighbouring Algeria (see V.4.iv) no doubt served as a powerful counter-model. The divided and increasingly marginal opposition secured only 2.27 per cent of the vote and thus failed to obtain more than the 'quota' of 19 seats reserved for parties which did not secure a majority in the constituencies. The Mouvement des Démocrates Socialistes (MDS) was allocated ten of the guaranteed seats, the Harakat Ettajdid (Renewal Movement) four, the Union Démocratique Unioniste (UDU) three and the Parti de l'Unité Populaire (PUP) two.

The opposition parties enticed into the National Assembly by the offer of a handful of seats had no power and did not threaten the dominant position of the ruling party and the President. Given the RCD's overwhelming victory in the elections, its claims to have crushed 'Islamic fundamentalist' groups inside Tunisia and reports of divisions within the exiled leadership of the outlawed Nahda (Renaissance) party, there was considerable speculation about why the regime was so unwilling to tolerate any criticism and why its authoritarian grip on the country appeared to be hardening. A growing gap was apparent between the regime's talk of democracy and a personalized government which stifled all opposition in the name of stability.

Observers pointed in particular to the apparently vindictive arrests of Mr el-Hani and Mr Marzouki, to the harsh sentence imposed in April on Hamma Hammami (secretary of the banned Parti Ouvrier Communiste Tunisien), to press censorship and to the continued repression of Islamist sympathizers. There were those who argued that the government was afraid to relax its strict contols in case this resulted in a resurgence of the Islamist threat. Others accused the government of merely using the threat from militant Islam as an excuse to crush all opposition movements. Some more cynical observers felt that the regime was able to act in an increasingly arrogant manner because it could count on the support of key foreign investors and the majority of Tunisians who, it was argued, were willing to accept restrictions on political freedoms and human rights in return for stability and economic prosperity.

Criticism of the regime continued both at home and abroad. Despite the election of a more moderate council and the resignation of Mr Marzouki, in April the LTDH renewed its calls for greater freedom of opinion, expression and organization. In May the League expressed its support for a petition signed by over a hundred Tunisian women, mainly professionals, which deplored 'grave violations' of human rights in Tunisia, 'pressures imposed on the press' and restrictions on freedom of expression. In November the UN Commission of Human Rights expressed its disquiet at the harsh treatment of detainees, including the use of torture, at the banning of several foreign newspapers and at the restrictions imposed on the activities of political parties. In mid-July Mr Marzouki was freed 'provisionally' and some believed that his trial might be postponed indefinitely. Legal action against the women petitioners was also called off, moves which were interpreted as an attempt to improve Tunisia's poor record on human rights.

The PLO offices in Tunis were closed in June as Yassir Arafat and the Palestinian leadership prepared to move to Gaza (see V.2.i). The official farewell ceremonies for Mr Arafat on 11 July were attended by President Ben Ali and were worthy of a head of state, but few Tunisians regretted the PLO's departure. The first party of Israeli tourists to visit Tunisia since its independence arrived in June and direct telephone links were established with Israel in July. In October the Tunisian and Israeli Foreign Ministers met in New York and agreed in principle to open interest sections in the Belgian embassies in Tel Aviv and Tunis. At a meeting at the State Department, Habib Ben Yahia (Tunisia's Foreign Minister) stated that this was only the first step to full diplomatic relations.

In April President Ben Ali handed over the presidency of the Arab Maghreb Union (AMU) to General Zéroual of Algeria. Little progress had been made in translating AMU rhetoric into reality or in developing a unified Maghreb. Relations with Morocco were strained during the year after Tunisia expelled several hundred Moroccans and the Moroccan government protested that some of its nationals had been maltreated. The Organization of African Unity held its 30th annual meeting in Tunis in June, at which President Ben Ali assumed the OAU presidency (see XI.6.i). South Africa took part for the first time. In May Tunisia had announced that diplomatic relations with South Africa would be established.

iv.   ALGERIA

CAPITAL: Algiers   AREA: 2,382,000 sq km   POPULATION: 26,300,000 ('92)
OFFICIAL LANGUAGE: Arabic   POLITICAL SYSTEM: quasi-military regime
HEAD OF STATE & GOVERNMENT: President (Brig.-Gen.) Liamine Zéroual (since Jan '94)
PRINCIPAL MINISTERS: Mokdad Sifi (Prime Minister), Mohammed Salah Dembri (foreign affairs), Abderrahmane Meziane Cherif (interior), Ahmed Benbitour (finance), Mohammed Teguia (justice), Amar Mekhloufi (industry & energy)
INTERNATIONAL ALIGNMENT: NAM, Arab League, OPEC, OAPEC, AMU, OAU, ICO
CURRENCY: dinar (end-'94 £1=DA67.35, US$1=DA43.05)
GNP PER CAPITA: US$1,840 ('92)
MAIN EXPORT EARNERS: oil & gas

ALGERIA's 'descent into madness', to use the words of one Algerian journalist, continued during a year marked by escalating violence as efforts to initiate dialogue between the military-backed regime and the Islamist opposition failed. The national dialogue conference in late January was boycotted by almost all the main political parties and proved to be a fiasco. Having failed in their efforts to appoint Abdelaziz Bouteflika (Foreign Minister in 1963–79) as the new head of state, members of the Higher Council of State named the Defence Minister, General Lamine Zéroual, as President and he was sworn in on 31 January. The eight-member Higher Security Committee, mainly composed of senior army officers, was believed to have played a major part in General Zéroual's selection.

One of the most respected members of the senior officer corps, General Zéroual was regarded as sharing the views of 'les conciliateurs' within the ruling elite. Unlike many officers who had held commanding positions in the Algerian military hierarchy since 1988, he had never served in the French army but had joined the Armée de Libération Nationale at the age of 16 and had fought in the guerrilla struggle inside Algeria during the war of independence. On his appointment as head of state, General Zéroual retained the defence portfolio and the cabinet under Redha Malek remained unchanged for the time being. In his first public statement, the new President called for 'serious dialogue' to find a way out of the country's crisis and made cautious overtures to those members of the banned Front Islamique du Salut (FIS) who were prepared to renounce violence.

On 11 April Redha Malek (one of 'les éradicateurs', who had dismissed any rehabilitation of the banned FIS) resigned and President Zéroual appointed Mokdad Sifi, hitherto Equipment Minister, as the new Prime Minister. Mr Malek had resigned the day after the government had finally agreed a new accord with the IMF opening the way for a debt-rescheduling agreement—a controversial move that was bound to provoke new tensions within an already faction-torn ruling establishment. The majority of Mr Sifi's new government team were technocrats or senior civil servants. Changes included the departure of Salim Saadi (an éradicateur and close associate of Mr Malek) from the Interior Ministry; the transfer of Mourad Benachenhou to head the new Ministry for Industrial Restructuring; and the return of Sassi Lamouri to the highly sensitive post of Religious Affairs Minister.

In May, President Zéroual inaugurated the National Transition Council, an interim legislature of 200 appointed members, which was supposed to provide a forum for debate until the holding of new parliamentary elections. Of the main political parties, only the 'moderate' Islamist party, Hamas, agreed to participate in the new body, which was the target of ridicule in the media. Indeed, the regime consistently failed to involve a majority of the leading legalized political parties in its efforts to promote dialogue. It was only in August that the President managed to get five leading legalized parties to join dialogue talks aimed at drawing up an acceptable peace formula. Even then there was disagreement among the parties over whether or not to include the banned FIS.

In a surprise move in early September, President Zéroual ordered the release from prison of the two most senior FIS leaders, Abbasi Madani and Ali Belhadj, and their transfer to house arrest. The decision prompted the resignation of the government's spokesperson,

Leila Aslaoui (a feminist and *éradicateuse*), but failed to break the deadlock between the regime and the FIS. At the end of October, the President announced that neither Mr Madani nor Mr Belhadj was willing to renounce violence or to participate in talks. Before his release, Mr Madani had stated that he was willing to consider calling a halt to the FIS military campaign if certain conditions were met. General Zéroual was unable to concede on a number of these demands, namely the rescinding of the ruling outlawing the FIS, the release of all imprisoned FIS members and the admission of the FIS armed wing into the dialogue talks. The President's ability to compromise was limited because of the objections of leading *éradicateurs* in the military, while the FIS political leadership was under pressure from radical militant groups opposed to any dialogue with the regime.

From mid-year there were persistent reports of splits, mergers and conflicts within the Islamist opposition. Particular uncertainty surrounded the relationship between the political and military wings of the FIS and between the FIS and its rival, the more radical Groupe Islamique Armé (GIA), whose forces dominated the military struggle against the regime. After the release of Mr Madani and Mr Belhadj, the GIA reiterated its rejection of any ceasefire, reconciliation or dialogue and threatened to kill Islamist leaders who participated in talks with the 'renegade' regime. However, in July Anouar Haddam, the FIS spokesman in Washington, issued a statement claiming that an agreement had been reached in May to merge the armed forces of the FIS with those of the GIA. A communique from Rabah Kebir, the main FIS spokesman in exile, immediately denied that any such merger had taken place, while Mr Haddam later denied joining the GIA and stated that he was still a member of the FIS. There was further confusion in August when the GIA announced that it was creating its own government-in-exile and named Mr Haddam as its foreign minister. In September it was reported that Mohammed Said, a senior FIS official who had defected to the GIA, had been appointed GIA leader, although other reports stated that Mr Said would remain in the FIS. The identity of the GIA leadership remained the subject of rumour and contradictory reports. Numerous defections of FIS activists to the GIA were reported.

At the end of October President Zéroual announced that he would hold presidential elections before the end of his mandate in 1996, an initiative rejected by several leading legalized opposition parties and condemned by the exiled FIS leadership. In the same speech, the President accused the FIS leadership of consolidating extremism instead of acting to halt the violence, and announced the promotion of the hardline Chief of Staff, Major-General Mohammed Lamari, to the rank of lieutenant-general.

During the first year of the Zéroual presidency, for all the talk of dialogue, the suicidal slide into civil war continued, and some of the barbarous acts reported recalled the worst days of the struggle for independence. The regime admitted in September that 10,000 people had died in the conflict since early 1992; Amnesty International put the death toll at 20,000, half of them ordinary citizens, who were bearing the brunt of the violence. These figures could well have underestimated the scale of the death toll, as daily killings went unreported by a heavily-censored media. Tens of thousands of Algerians had been driven into exile, many from the country's educated elite. An Amnesty International report released in October painted a grim picture of a country where civilians were living in a state of fear—threatened and killed by Islamist militants for not obeying their orders and by the security forces in retaliation for Islamist raids. In Kabylia, a region traditionally alienated from the regime but strongly opposed to the Islamist militants, Berber villagers began organizing armed patrols.

There was a continued exodus of foreign nationals, at least 60 of whom had been been killed by end-1994, including two engineers shot dead at an oil drilling site in the first reported Islamist attack on the hydrocarbon sector. After four GIA guerrillas who had hijacked an Air France airbus were killed by French counter-terrorist police at Marseilles airport on 26 December (see II.1.ii), four Catholic priests were murdered in Algeria in retaliation. The guerrillas had planned to blow up the plane over Paris.

v. MOROCCO

CAPITAL: Rabat   AREA: 460,000 sq km   POPULATION: 26,200,000 ('92)
OFFICIAL LANGUAGE: Arabic   POLITICAL SYSTEM: monarchy
HEAD OF STATE & GOVERNMENT: King Hassan II (since '61)
PRINCIPAL MINISTERS: Abdellatif Filali (Prime Minister, foreign affairs), Driss Basri
    (interior, information), Mohammed Idrissi Alami Machichi (justice), Mourad
    Charif (finance & investment), Abdellatif Guerraoui (energy & mines)
INTERNATIONAL ALIGNMENT: NAM, Arab League, AMU, ICO
CURRENCY: dirham (end-'94 £1=DH13.94, US$1=DH8.91)
GNP PER CAPITA: US$1,030 ('92)
MAIN EXPORT EARNERS: phosphates, agricultural products, tourism

IN February radical Islamist and leftist students clashed again at Fez University and courses were suspended indefinitely after security forces moved in. Political tensions mounted again at the end of the month when the Lamrani government banned a 24-hour general strike planned for 25 February called by the Confédération Démocratique du Travail (CDT) to protest about falling living standards and low wages. Some 11 CDT activists were arrested in Casablanca during the week before the proposed strike. The banning order was condemned by most opposition parties and by the three national trade unions. The government invited the opposition to take part in the reopening of the 'social dialogue' scheduled to begin on 15 March.

At the end of April a number of parliamentary by-elections were held following a judicial decision on complaints of irregularities during the 1993 parliamentary elections (see AR 1993, pp. 241–2). Of the 14 seats at issue, which were contested by 88 candidates, the Union Socialiste des Forces Populaires (USFP) won two and the Istiqlal three, while the Rassemblement Nationale des Indépendants (RNI), which had won five of the seats in June 1993, retained only two. Nevertheless, the opposition parties again complained of irregularities during the voting. In May, after persistent pressure from the unions, the government finally made concessions on pay, increasing minimum agricultural and industrial wages by 10 per cent from 1 July.

On 25 May King Hassan replaced Mr Lamrani as Prime Minister with Abdellatif Filali, hitherto Foreign Minister and another member of the king's inner circle (his son Fouad, chairman of Omnium Nord-Africain, was married to the King's eldest daughter). The change was thought to be due in part to Mr Lamrani's opposition to accelerating and widening the privatization programme. Within a few days of taking office, Mr Filali stated that he had started to consult with all political parties in the House of Representatives about the political, economic and social situation; however, after a week of such consultations, he made no changes to the cabinet list presented to the King on 7 June. The new Prime Minister retained the foreign affairs and cooperation portfolio. Radical reforms were predicted with the aim of promoting economic growth and development, Mr Filali confirming that his government saw privatization as a vital element in boosting domestic investment and as encouraging foreign investment and expertise. It was announced that the sale of 'strategic assets' such as power, water and transport could no longer be ruled out. In July Mohammed Saghou was dismissed as Finance Minister for too lax a budget policy; he was replaced by Mourad Charif, hitherto Foreign Trade Minister. King Hassan continued his efforts to draw the parliamentary opposition parties into a coalition government, in October offering them the post of Prime Minister as an inducement.

In June Mr Filali announced that the national television service would begin broadcasting news bulletins in the three main Berber 'dialects'. In August the King declared that Berber 'dialects' were an integral part of Morocco's authenticity and history and would soon be taught in state schools, at least at elementary level. This appeared to mark a major change in policy towards the Berber-speaking minority, making up almost a third of the population. Berber cultural associations had flourished in recent years, attracting many young activists. In May, after a peaceful demonstration by the Tilelli Association at Errachidia demanding official recognition of Tamazight (the Berber language), seven supporters had been arrested and charged with threatening state security.

Nevertheless, the regime remained nervous of any challenge to its authority and determined to crack down on organized labour, students and other dissenting groups. In August, after gunmen shot two Spanish tourists in Marrakesh, the Interior Ministry launched a massive security operation amidst fears that the vitally important tourist industry was being targeted. Within days, two French nationals of North African origin were arrested and charged with the murders, while in the following two months several hundred suspects, most of them Algerian-French or Moroccan-French, were arrested and accused of terrorist activities. The net spread to France, where police arrested associates of the two men charged with the Marrakesh murders and asserted that they were part of an Islamist terrorist cell. Claiming that two of the suspects still being sought were in the pay of the Algerian secret service, the Moroccan government on 26 August imposed visa requirements for Algerian nationals and others of Algerian origin, including French nationals. The Algerian government denied that it was sponsoring terrorism and on 27 August sealed its border with Morocco. By October, however, tension with Algeria had eased somewhat: in a gesture of goodwill, Algeria appointed a permanent ambassador to Rabat.

After talks with King Hassan on 3 June, the Israeli Foreign Minister, Shimon Peres, told the press that the two countries had agreed to renew or establish telecommunications links and at a later date to establish 'representations of some kind'. At the beginning of September Morocco and Israel agreed to open 'liaison offices' in Rabat and Tel Aviv, marking a further step towards full Moroccan recognition of Israel. The move was criticized by the opposition parties, which urged caution until a comprehensive Middle East peace settlement had been achieved. Morocco became the first Arab state to announce that it would open a 'liaison bureau' with the new Palestinian authority in Gaza (see V.2.i).

vi.   WESTERN SAHARA

CAPITAL: Al Aaiún   AREA: 252,000 sq km   POPULATION: 164,000 ('82)
STATUS: regarded as under its sovereignty by Morocco, whereas independent Sahrawi
   Arab Democratic Republic (SADR) was declared by Polisario Front in 1976

DESPITE the passing of another year, the Western Sahara dispute remained unresolved. In January Charles Pasqua, the French Interior Minister, paid a private visit to Al Aaiún, the first time that a senior French minister had visited the disputed territory. In March the UN Secretary-General, Dr Boutros Boutros-Ghali, told the Security Council that the UN had three options: to go ahead with the planned referendum by the end of 1994 even if one or both sides in the dispute disagreed; to cancel plans for the referendum and withdraw most of the UN peace-keeping force; or to continue with talks between Morocco and the Polisario Front in order to draw up acceptable voter lists. Polisario rejected the first two options and demanded that the third option, which it claimed favoured Morocco, should be 'revised and reformulated'. The Security Council decided to go ahead with plans to hold the referendum and announced that the UN mission to identify voters would be completed by 30 June. The Secretary-General was asked to continue his efforts to reach agreement between the two sides on the difficult issue of voter participation.

At the end of April Erik Jensen, the UN diplomat in charge of the registration process, stated that Polisario had accepted a UN voter registration plan proposed under Security Council resolution 907 and that a UN voter identification commission would start registering voters in June. However, despite a joint statement on 31 May from Mr Jensen and Driss Basri (the Moroccan Interior Minister) confirming a June start, registration of voters did not in fact begin until 28 August. Morocco adopted familiar blocking techniques and at first refused to allow the presence of observers from the Organization of African Unity (OAU) at the identification of voters, which proved to be a slow process. In November (when the voter registration was supposed to have been completed), the UN announced that plans to hold the referendum in February 1995 would have to be delayed by several months because of problems of identifying potential voters.

During a visit to the region at the end of November, Dr Boutros-Ghali warned Morocco and Polisario of serious consequences if progress was not achieved in preparations for the referendum. In mid-December the UN Secretary-General stated that the referendum could be held in October 1995 but told the Security Council that a major reinforcement of UN personnel was essential if identification and registration of the large number of applications already received were to be completed in time. Progress towards a peaceful solution of the long-running dispute was not helped by the deterioration in relations between Morocco and Algeria (see V.4.v). The new Algerian President, General Zéroual, appeared to adopt a less flexible position on Western Sahara and angered Morocco by referring to it as 'an illegally occupied country' at a meeting of the OAU in August.

VI EQUATORIAL AFRICA

1. ETHIOPIA—ERITREA—SOMALIA—DJIBOUTI—KENYA—TANZANIA—UGANDA

i. ETHIOPIA

CAPITAL: Addis Ababa   AREA: 1,128,000 sq km   POPULATION: 54,800,000 ('92)
OFFICIAL LANGUAGE: Amharic   POLITICAL SYSTEM: presidential
RULING PARTY: Ethiopian People's Revolutionary Democratic Front (EPRDF)
HEAD OF STATE: President Meles Zenawi (since July '91)
PRINCIPAL MINISTERS: Tamirat Laynie (Prime Minister), Alemayehu Dhaba (finance),
    Tekedel Forsido (agriculture), Mehitema Solomon (justice), Seyoum Mesfin
    (foreign affairs), Kuma Demeksa (interior), Siye Abraha (defence)
INTERNATIONAL ALIGNMENT: NAM, OAU, ACP
CURRENCY: birr (end-'943 £1=Br8.47, US$1=Br5.42)
GNP PER CAPITA: US$110 ('92)
MAIN EXPORT EARNERS: coffee, agricultural produce

CONSTITUENT Assembly elections were held on 5 June, except in the Somali-inhabited Ogaden region, where they were postponed. Despite attempts at mediation by the US Carter Center, the major opposition parties—including the All-Amhara People's Organization (AAPO), the Oromo Liberation Front (OLF) and the Ogaden National Liberation Front (ONLF)—all boycotted the elections, leaving the field open for the numerous ethnically-based parties affiliated with the Ethiopian People's Revolutionary Democratic Front (EPRDF), which won 478 of the declared seats. Five seats went to opposition parties and 25 to independents, ten of them in Addis Ababa. Although the conduct of the elections was generally peaceful and well-organized, the verdict of independent observers as to whether the results fairly represented the wishes of the Ethiopian people was expressed in very guarded terms.

A draft constitution for the 'Federal Democratic Republic of Ethiopia' was approved by the Constituent Assembly on 8 December. In keeping with the doctrine of ethnic federalism espoused by the ruling EPRDF, this stated that 'sovereignty resides in the nations, nationalities and peoples of Ethiopia', rather than in the people as a whole, and granted each nation, nationality or people rights of self-determination up to and including secession. State ownership of all land was retained. Unusually for Africa, the system of government was parliamentary rather than presidential, executive power being vested in a Prime Minister and Council of Ministers responsible to an elected Council of Peoples' Representatives and the presidency being purely titular.

Human rights organizations, including Amnesty International, expressed increasing concern over conditions in the country. From January onwards leading members of ONLF were arrested and several were killed or died in military custody. In Addis Ababa a number of journalists disappeared or were detained, while several hundred demonstrators were arrested outside the High Court on 20 September while protesting against the imprisonment of the AAPO leader, Professor Asrat Woldeyes. In the Oromo-inhabited area of western Ethiopia a large number of people were arrested on 6 September, while attending the funeral of an elderly businessman who had been killed by government forces. These incidents, including reports of torture, reinforced growing uncertainty within the country and abroad over the sincerity of the government's commitment to open and democratic governnment. There were, however, no reports of serious armed opposition to the regime.

Exiled former leader Mengistu Haile-Maryam angered his Zimbabwean hosts in February by issuing a statement in opposition to the current government, despite undertakings not to participate in politics. A formal request for his extradition was delivered to the Zimbabwean government, but not acted on. Trials of 66 officials of the former regime (including 21 *in absentia*), accused of major human rights abuses, formally opened on 13 December but were adjourned until March 1995.

Following poor rains and pest infestations in 1993, there were food shortages in much of the country. Although widespread famine was averted, the government Relief and Rehabilitation Commission (RRC) reported 10,000 famine-related deaths in south-western Ethiopia in mid-1994, while over seven million people were dependent on relief food. The main July-September rains were good in most of the country, but a food shortfall of 750,000 tonnes was predicted for 1995. Other areas of the economy appeared to be improving, in response to the encouragement of a free market, and the World Bank announced a major commitment in support of the reform programme in 1994/95.

ii.   ERITREA

CAPITAL: Asmara   AREA: 94,000 sq km   POPULATION: 3,500,000 ('93 est.)
OFFICIAL LANGUAGES: Arabic & Tigrinya   POLITICAL SYSTEM: presidential
RULING PARTY: People's Front for Democracy and Justice (PFDJ)
HEAD OF STATE & GOVERNMENT: President Issaias Afewerki (since May '93)
PRINCIPAL MINISTERS: Petros Solomon (foreign affairs), Ali Said Abdella (internal affairs), Mesfin Hagos (defence), Fozia Hashim (justice), Haile Weldetensae (finance & development)
CURRENCY: birr (end-'94 £1=Br8.47, US$1=Br5.42)

THE third congress of the Eritrean People's Liberation Front (EPLF) was held in February at Nakfa, symbolic centre of the long struggle which culminated in independence in May 1993 (see AR 1993, pp. 245–6). As part of the normalization of the political process, the EPLF converted itself from a national liberation front into a political party, called the People's Front for Democracy and Justice (PFDJ), and committed itself to an eventual multi-party system. For the present, however, opposition parties remained banned, pending the introduction of a new constitution, which was expected to take three years. The PFDJ executive committee was extensively restructured to include only three members of the former EPLF executive, in addition to the President, Issaias Afewerki. These changes generally displaced former marxist hardliners and guerrilla fighters in favour of pragmatists and administrators.

Reintegration of former fighters remained a problem, and an attempted demonstration by disabled veterans in July was suppressed. The popular former EPLF commander, Mesfin Hagos, was appointed Defence Minister in November. About half a million Eritrean refugees remained in Sudan, but agreement was reached with the UNHCR in September for the voluntary repatriation of 25,000 of them. President Issaias, in his 1994 New Year message, reported the attempted infiltration of Eritrea by a Muslim fundamentalist group associated with the ruling National Islamic Front in Sudan; all 20 members were reportedly killed. Relations between Eritrea and Sudan subsequently deteriorated, and Eritrea formally broke diplomatic relations in December (see also V.4.i). Relations with the Ethiopian government remained very close. At the Organization of African Unity (OAU) summit in Tunis in June, President Issaias criticized the OAU for its minimal impact on Africa's problems (see XI.6.i). He called for its reorganization on a regional basis, with a restructured secretariat and full summits only every two or three years rather than annually.

Eritrea joined the IMF and World Bank, receiving praise from Bank officials for its realistic approach to development issues. The Bank provided credits of $50 million for economic recovery, education and port development. Foreign aid and loans received in 1994 included $53 million from the European Union. Following very poor rains and pest infestation in 1993, the harvest amounted to only 20 per cent of requirements, so that most of the population remained dependent on relief food. Despite good 1994 rains in most of the country, the estimated harvest still amounted to less than half of requirements.

iii. SOMALIA

CAPITAL: Mogadishu   AREA: 638,000 sq km   POPULATION: 8,300,000 ('92)
OFFICIAL LANGUAGES: Somali & Arabic   POLITICAL SYSTEM: none
HEAD OF STATE: none
INTERNATIONAL ALIGNMENT: NAM, OAU, ACP, Arab League, ICO
CURRENCY: shilling (end-'94 £1=SoSh4,096.37, US$1=SoSh2,618.33)
GNP PER CAPITA: US$120 ('90)

WITH the progressive withdrawal of UN forces and the failure of the Somali factions to agree on any effective political settlement, Somalia relapsed into the conditions of anarchy which had prevailed before the arrival of US and later UN forces from December 1992 (see AR 1993, p. 247). The approval by the UN Security Council on 4 February of a revised mandate for the UNOSOM II peace-keeping operation signalled a shift from an attempt to enforce a political settlement towards reconciliation. However, a 'peace agreement' signed in Nairobi on 24 March between the two main adversaries, Mohammed Farah Aydid's Somali National Alliance (SNA) and a grouping of factions led by his rival, Ali Mahdi Mohammed, rapidly broke down. Other attempted settlements also collapsed. All but a token force of US troops left Somalia on 24 March, together with the Canadian, South Korean and all the European contingents, leaving UNOSOM in the hands of Asian and African forces, amongst which the largest contingents were from Pakistan, India, Indonesia and Egypt.

Fierce fighting frequently broke out between different factions, notably in the southern port of Kismayu in February and in Mogadishu in June, October and December. Peace-keeping soldiers and aid workers were kidnapped from time to time but usually released. By the end of the year, however, more than 100 peace-keepers had been killed since December 1992. Many of the aid agencies still operating in Somalia withdrew their personnel as it became progressively more difficult to assure their safety, culminating in the withdrawal of the UN World Food Programme in October. Although the 1994 harvest was good and ample stocks of food aid had been shipped to the country, much of it was looted and adequate distribution became impossible. A cholera epidemic broke out in March.

The UN mandate was extended by the Security Council, first to 31 October and then to March 1995. However, Indian forces (one of the most effective contingents) withdrew by the end of the year, and several of the remaining contingents were themselves implicated in the sale or looting of UN equipment. Some US$4 million in cash was stolen from the UN compound in April. President Clinton offered US military assistance to help cover the final UN withdrawal in 1995.

In the northern region, which had declared itself independent as the Republic of Somaliland in 1991 (see AR 1991, p. 251), the ruling Somali National Movement (SNM) split between President Mohammed Ibrahim Egal and his predecessor, Abdelrahman Abdel Ali, who allied himself with the SNA and called for the reincorporation of Somaliland into Somalia. In August President Egal expelled UN forces from Somaliland, whose independence the UN had refused to recognize. Fighting between the two groups broke out in the northern capital of Hargeisa in November, about 50,000 refugees fleeing to Ethiopia, but forces loyal to President Egal remained in control.

iv. DJIBOUTI

CAPITAL: Djibouti AREA: 23,000 sq km POPULATION: 546,000 ('92)
OFFICIAL LANGUAGES: Arabic & French POLITICAL SYSTEM: presidential
RULING PARTY: Popular Rally for Progress (RPP)
HEAD OF STATE: President Hassan Gouled Aptidon (since '77)
PRINCIPAL MINISTERS: Barkat Gourad Hamadou (Prime Minister), Ahmad Bulaleh
    Barreh (defence), Ahmed Aden Youssouf (finance), Muhammad Ali Muhammad
    (economy & trade), Abdou Bolok Abdou (foreign affairs), Idris Harbi Farah
    (interior), Moumin Bahdon Farah (justice)
INTERNATIONAL ALIGNMENT: NAM, OAU, ACP, Arab League, ICO, Francophonie
CURRENCY: Djibouti franc (end-'94 £1=DF277.87, US$1=DF177.61)
GNP PER CAPITA: US$480 ('81)
MAIN EXPORT EARNERS: agricultural products

FOLLOWING defeats inflicted by government forces in 1993, the Afar-based opposition Front for the Restoration of Unity and Democracy (FRUD) split in March, former leader Ahmed Dini Ahmed being ejected by a new 13-member executive council led by Ahmed Ougoureh Kible. Under French auspices, the new FRUD leadership entered into peace talks with President Hassan Gouled Aptidon's government, a peace agreement being announced on 12 June. The security situation was nonetheless precarious, and many Afar refugees remained in Ethiopia and Eritrea.

v. KENYA

CAPITAL: Nairobi AREA: 580,000 sq km POPULATION: 25,700,000 ('92)
OFFICIAL LANGUAGE: Kiswahili & English POLITICAL SYSTEM: presidential
HEAD OF STATE & GOVERNMENT: President Daniel Arap Moi (since '78)
RULING PARTY: Kenya African National Union (KANU)
PRINCIPAL MINISTERS: George Saitoti (Vice-President, planning & development),
    Stephen Kalonzo Musyoka (foreign affairs), Francis Lotodo (home affairs),
    Musalia Mudavadi (finance), Amos Wako (Attorney-General)
INTERNATIONAL ALIGNMENT: NAM, OAU, ACP, Cwth.
CURRENCY: shilling (end-'94 £1=Ksh70.16, US$1=Ksh44.85)
GNP PER CAPITA: US$310 ('92)
MAIN EXPORT EARNERS: coffee, tea, petroleum products, tourism

TO the satisfaction of international donors, Finance Minister Musalia Mudavadi continued to demonstrate his commitment to economic reform. Thus he removed the restrictions on local borrowing by foreign-controlled companies in February and effectively revoked the Exchange Control Act in May. His austere budget for 1994/95 announced recurrent and development expenditure of approximately Ksh 183,000 million (then about US$3,660 million), of which some 76 per cent was recurrent. Detailed budget provisions included a reduction in the top rate of value-added tax from 40 to 30 per cent, the imposition of a temporary drought levy on high income earners (over four million people currently faced starvation) and the introduction of excise duty on petroleum products to meet the cost of improving the national infrastructure. In June Kamlesh Pattni, a leading Kenyan businessman, and four former Central Bank of Kenya officials were arrested and charged with financial fraud.

In October the government announced the deregulation of the oil industry: future pricing was to be determined by market forces. The anxiety of petrol companies to obtain foreign exchange to replenish their fuel stocks reversed the trend in the currency markets, which had seen the value of the Kenya shilling rise and demand for the US dollar plummet. The government proposed to cut subsidies to the parastatals—still an avenue for political patronage—and regarded the private sector as the main engine of economic growth. However, President Daniel Arap Moi said that structural adjustment programmes would not be followed blindly and in October outlined plans to reduce the impact of these programmes on vulnerable groups in society. Other corrective action included increases in the general and agricultural minimum wage of 20 and 15 per cent respectively, announced in May. The government also planned to create 600,000 jobs and to cut unemployment (some 20 per cent of the workforce being without jobs). It also proposed to reduce the over-manned, inefficient and allegedly corrupt civil service by retrenching 16,000 employees a year over the next three years.

In January the government proscribed *Kenya: Return to Reason*, a book highly critical of the President by Kenneth Matiba, then leader of the opposition FORD-Asili (but subsequently suspended by his party executive), while the police confiscated the 14 January issue of *The People*, a weekly newspaper which Mr Matiba published. In the same month the veteran (Luo) politician Oginga Odinga, leader of FORD-Kenya and a former national Vice-President, died at the age of 82 (see XX: Obituary). In July Africa Watch (a US-based human rights organization) stated that government harassment of political opponents had increased since the December 1992 elections. However, its report did not deter international donors from continuing to supply aid, which was increasingly channelled through non-government organizations and relief agencies rather than through the government.

A weak and divided opposition failed to present a united front at by-elections in June, enabling the ruling Kenya African National Union (KANU) to win three seats in a primarily Luhya area of Western province. Heading a government widely seen as autocratic and oppressive, President Moi tightened his grip on power in the face of widespread popular discontent. The press was under attack; opposition MPs were arrested; university lecturers and government hospital doctors took strike action over pay; and the police broke up meetings organized by the opposition. The *New African* believed that the independence of the judiciary was also threatened.

Members of the government were alleged to be fanning ethnic violence, particularly directed against the Kikuyu, who were suspected of trying to stage a political comeback. Kikuyu smallholders in the Rift Valley area adjoining the Masai Mara park were among the chief sufferers. The President retaliated by accusing the media, and the *Daily Nation* especially, of exciting ethnic animosity and criticized church leaders for making inflammatory statements from the pulpit.

In March Dr Richard Leakey resigned as director of the Kenya Wildlife Service (KWS), having been falsely accused of mismanagement, racism and corruption by two cabinet ministers and other political enemies, who were jealous of his achievement in building the KWS into a large and financially-powerful organization. He was replaced by Dr David Western, another white Kenyan conservationist. Kenya Airways, under a new management structure, made a profit for the first time in its 17-year history; the long-term objective was to privatize the airline. The brewing industry was hard hit by the importation of cheaper South African beer, while agriculturists had to face increased South African competition in cereals. Crime was out of control in Nairobi, the capital, where over a million people lived in slum conditions. AIDS continued to spread at an alarming rate. The results of the 1989 census were finally released; opposition leaders alleged that the figures showing the distribution of population had been 'doctored'.

vi. TANZANIA

CAPITAL: Dar es Salaam/Dodoma AREA: 945,000 sq km POPULATION: 25,900,000 ('92)
OFFICIAL LANGUAGES: Kiswahili & English POLITICAL SYSTEM: presidential
HEAD OF STATE & GOVERNMENT: President Ali Hassan Mwinyi (since '85)
RULING PARTY: Chama cha Mapinduzi (CCM)
VICE-PRESIDENTS: Cleopa D. Msuya (Prime Minister), Salmin Amour (President of Zanzibar)
PRINCIPAL MINISTERS: Ernest Nyanda (home affairs), Jakaya M. Kikwette (finance), Joseph Clemence Rwegasira (foreign affairs), Kighoma Ali Malima (industry & trade), Samuel Sitta (justice & constitutional affairs)
INTERNATIONAL ALIGNMENT: NAM, OAU, ACP, Cwth.
CURRENCY: shilling (end-'94 £1=Tsh819.29, US$1=Tsh523.67)
GNP PER CAPITA: US$110 ('92)
MAIN EXPORT EARNERS: coffee, cotton, tropical foodstuffs

THE government continued with an economic reform programme backed and monitored by the IMF and the World Bank, the largest single contributor. The main focus of the 1994/95 budget was to improve revenue collection and reduce spending. Total planned expenditure was TSh 514,284 million (then about US$1,029 million), of which 70.5 per cent was allocated to recurrent and 29.5 per cent to development expenditure. Critics were worried about over-reliance on donor funding and the overall impact of the structural adjustment programme (SAP), which hit hardest those in marginal groups and resulted in massive redundancies, labour unrest and student riots. As from 1 July, the government increased the salaries of its employees and of parastatal personnel by 100 per cent, at the same time raising the minimum wage to TSh 10,000 per month.

Minerals were expected to replace agriculture as the dominant sector of the economy and an increase in the current annual economic growth rate of 4.1 per cent was anticipated. A total of 22 state-owned industries were being privatized, while another 117 were earmarked for divestiture; joint ventures with foreign companies were encouraged. An Investment Promotion Centre identified potential investors and advised on investment opportunities; it approved over 90 projects in the tourism sector.

Some donor countries, including the United Kingdom, threatened to withdraw aid unless steps were taken to stamp out tax evasion—the result of a weak and inefficient tax system—and corruption. Dr Julius Nyerere undermined the authority of Ali Hassan Mwinyi, his successor as President, by speaking out publicly against high-level corruption, a slack administration and the uncritical adoption of IMF and World Bank directives, which meant, he said, that Chama cha Mapundizi (CCM), the ruling party, was preaching socialism while practising capitalism. He also pointed to dissent within CCM, which, however, had easily defeated a divided opposition in by-elections early in the year. In November President Mwinyi appointed an official inquiry to investigate charges against individuals accused of defrauding the government. However, the government went only a little way in 1994 to meet the concern of aid donors at the lack of press freedom. In December, faced with mounting donor pressure, the President appointed Jakaya Mrisho Kikwette as Minister of Finance in place of Professor Kighoma Malima (alleged to be a tax evader) and replaced John Malecela, the strongly reformist Prime Minister, with Cleopa Msuya (hitherto Industry and Trade Minister), who also became First Vice-President and was thought to have presidential aspirations.

Early in the year prolonged drought led to acute shortages of food in the five northern regions; some 1.5 million people were at risk. The government withdrew from the Pan-Africanist Congress of South Africa the right to use Tanzania as a guerrilla base. Faced with mounting South African competition, port charges were cut and the Tanzania-Zambia Railway Authority (Tazara) floated its cargo freight rates, allowing customers to bargain for preferential terms. In November Tanzania and the other ten member-states of the Southern African Development Community (SADC) agreed in Arusha to form a (non-permanent) regional rapid deployment force to deal with regional conflicts and attempted coups (see also XI.6.i).

Tabled in June, the Zanzibar budget forecast total expenditure of over TSh 43,000 million (about US$86 million), approximately half to be spent on economic development. Government revenue was to be strengthened and tax collection improved. Relations with the mainland were uneasy. President Salmin Amour's government wanted the right to an independent foreign policy and complained that Zanzibar was not given its fair share of donor-funded national development projects. The government was accused of harassing its opponents, banning their meetings and using the tightly-controlled state radio and television to discredit them. Followers of the Zanzibari wing of the opposition Civic United Front (CUF) were dubbed on television 'the donkeys from Dubai', but were thought capable of defeating the increasingly unpopular CCM in the multi-party elections scheduled for October 1995.

Dr Nyerere had no confidence in President Amour's leadership in Zanzibar and fought hard to preserve the union from detractors on both sides. In July, however, five major parties on the mainland staged a demonstration calling for a separate Assembly and government for Tanganyika. Concern grew on the mainland that Zanzibar's reliance on Islamic countries for sympathy and support was leading to an influx of Muslim fundamentalists to the islands. Under a constitutional amendment adopted in December, to come into effect after the next elections, the President of Zanzibar would no longer automatically be a Vice-President in the union government.

vii. UGANDA

CAPITAL: Kampala AREA: 240,000 sq km POPULATION: 17,500,000 ('91)
OFFICIAL LANGUAGE: English POLITICAL SYSTEM: presidential
HEAD OF STATE & GOVERNMENT: President Yoweri Museveni (since Jan '86)
RULING PARTY: National Resistance Movement (NRM) heads broad-based coalition
PRINCIPAL MINISTERS: Speciosa Wandira Kazibwe (Vice-President, gender & community development), Kintu Musoke (Prime Minister), Eriya Kategaya (First Deputy Premier), Paul Ssemogerere (Second Deputy Premier, public service), Ruhakana Rugunda (foreign affairs), Joshua Mayanja–Nkangi (finance & planning), Crispus Kiyonga (internal affairs), Joseph Ekemu (justice)
INTERNATIONAL ALIGNMENT: NAM, OAU, ACP, Cwth.
CURRENCY: shilling (end-'94 £1=Ush1,435.29, US$1=Ush917.41)
GNP PER CAPITA: US$170 ('92)
MAIN EXPORT EARNERS: coffee, cotton

RESTRUCTURING of the economy went ahead with strong support from the World Bank and other donors. Emphasis was placed on further privatization, improved incentives for the public sector and financial reform. In the latter context, US organizations took over the management of the badly-run Uganda Commercial Bank and other commercial banks and helped with the restructuring of the Bank of Uganda. The 1994 budget set total expenditure at USh 857,000 million (then about US$857 million), of which some 53 per cent was recurrent and the remainder development expenditure; the bulk of the latter was to be externally funded. GDP was expected to grow at 5.5 per cent as against 4 per cent the previous year.

Under the budget terms, public wages and salaries were raised by 40 per cent, the sales tax on essential foodstuffs was increased to 10–12 per cent and withholding tax by 2 per cent; value-added tax was to be introduced in July 1996. It was also planned that Uganda's dependence on coffee would be reduced, in which context cocoa was proving to be a popular alternative in the west of the country. Privatization of the Cocoa Marketing Board and the Lint Marketing Board was scheduled. Reform achievements included a market-determined exchange rate and a liberal foreign exchange system. However, the financial system remained weak and foreign debt was a heavy burden. The size of both the army and the civil service was to be further reduced.

Elections for a Constituent Assembly to debate the new draft constitution were held on 28 March. More than 1,500 candidates contested the 214 elective seats as individuals, though the parties compaigned openly beforehand. The elections attracted a large turnout and were generally free and fair. President Yoweri Museveni's supporters scored resounding victories in Buganda and the west and won some seats in the east, though most seats in the east and north were captured by members of opposition parties. The elected members were joined by 10 presidential nominees and 56 others appointed by special interest groups, including trade unions, women's and youth organisations, and two each from the four main opposition parties.

In November 36 Assembly members walked out in protest when a committee chairman stated that the constitution should prolong the rule of the National Liberation Movement for a further five years and retain the nine-year ban against political campaigning. In the same month the President carried out a major cabinet reshuffle, appointing a woman minister, Speciosa Wandira Kazibwe, as Vice-President and naming Kintu Musoke as Prime Minister; Paul Ssemogerere, leader of the Democratic Party, was moved from foreign affairs to public service. A new law curtailed the substantial press freedom which had hitherto existed under President Museveni, who accused journalists of indulging in personal invective to the neglect of the wider public interest.

Despite the government's comprehensive and vigorous AIDS campaign, some 1.5 million people were believed to be infected with the HIV virus, with adverse effects on food output. The deadline for Asians expelled by Idi Amin in 1972 to reclaim property left behind was extended to 30 April 1995. President Museveni denied in May that he was supplying arms to the Rwandan Patriotic Front (which had helped him in the Ugandan civil war) and called for limited foreign intervention in Rwanda to stop genocide (see VII.1.ii). Solon Iguri Gafabusa I was crowned the 27th *Mukama* (King) of Bunyoro. The train service between Uganda and Kenya was resumed during the year, while Uganda Airways, in order to boost tourism, launched a flight package linking Kampala and Mombasa.

2.   GHANA—NIGERIA—SIERRA LEONE—THE GAMBIA—LIBERIA

i.   GHANA

CAPITAL: Accra   AREA: 240,000 sq km   POPULATION: 15,800,000 ('92)
OFFICIAL LANGUAGE: English   POLITICAL SYSTEM: presidential
HEAD OF STATE & GOVERNMENT: President Jerry Rawlings (since Nov '92), previously
    Chairman of Provisional National Defence Council (since '81)
PRINCIPAL MINISTERS: Kow Nkensen Arkaah (Vice-President), Kwesi Botchwey
    (finance & economic planning), Obed Y. Asamoah (foreign affairs & justice),
    Mahamad Iddrisu (defence), Col. (retd) E. M. Osei-Owusu (interior)
INTERNATIONAL ALIGNMENT: NAM, OAU, ACP, Cwth.
CURRENCY: cedi (end-'94 £1=C1,621.35, US$1=C1,036.34)
GNP PER CAPITA: US$450 ('92)
MAIN EXPORT EARNERS: cocoa, gold, minerals

Stirred by the December 1992 elections (see AR 1992, p. 257), the political pot had settled down in the succeeding year (see AR 1993, pp. 255-6), with the result that in 1994 Ghana began to turn away from politics and towards economics. At national level, President Rawlings's government was more tolerant, while the opposition New Patriotic Party under Professor Adu Boahen was more conciliatory. At local level, however, there were ugly scenes in the Northern region during February and March when age-old animosities flared into tribal conflict between the Nanumba and Konkomba. More than 6,000 people were reportedly killed in and around the Nanumba town of Bimbilla and the regional capital, Tamale; thousands more were made homeless in the fighting, which erupted on 3 February over land disputes. The army was sent in and shot a number of Konkomba young men in its attempt to restore order.

The economy grew during the year—even in the north, where existing gold reserves at Bole were re-mined under licence by Takoradi Gold of Australia. The ore was at a shallow depth of 50 metres and offered good returns under open-cut methods of extraction. With assistance from the European Investment Bank and other sources, manganese production increased at Nsuta-Wassaw in the Western region, despite declining world demand. Moreover, De Beers of South Africa signed an agreement with the government to boost the country's output of diamonds, undertaking to pay $1 million for a feasibility study to extend the life of the existing mine at Akwatia on the River Birim. Diamond output was expected to double to over 400,000 carats in 1994/95.

The outstanding event of the year in the economic sphere was the public offer in March–April of shares in the Ashanti Goldfields Corporation (AGC) on the Accra stock market. Shares worth between $18 million and $25 million were bought by local institutions and private investors, including the five free shares given to each of some 10,000 AGC employees. The distribution was worth a total of $168 million, amounting to 37 per cent of the value of the Accra stock market and some 10 per cent of total bank liquidity—a huge addition to Ghana's finances which the government was quick to exploit by settling part of its debts by means of a bond issue. The majority of the share issue was traded in London, but the local flotation reflected the new-found strength of the local stock exchange. The issue was part of the restructuring programme being undertaken with the help of large inflows of aid from the IMF, in which context officials were seeking to transfer some 35 state enterprises to the private sector.

Overall, the economy grew by 5 per cent during the year and inflation was contained to 25–30 per cent, as compared with a rate of 140 per cent a decade earlier. A number of overseas companies based in Ghana showed substantial profits, including Unilever, Standard Chartered, Mobil and Guinness. But there were also problems, some of which were the perverse result of success. For example, demand for electricity was expected to double by the end of the century and was already outrunning supply. Growing domestic and industrial power consumption could not be met from the Akosombo Dam, where low rainfall and poor flow levels on the River Volta meant that much of the country was experiencing one-day-a-week cuts in supply. In September exports from the Volta River Authority were halted, while power was cut to the US-owned American Aluminium company. The obvious remedy was to import electricity from neighbouring countries, but this would force consumer prices to rise and was therefore politically difficult for President Rawlings. The year ended without any solution to the problem being found.

On 28 October the High Court in London ruled on a libel case brought by Kojo Tsikata (a former adviser to President Rawlings) against *The Independent* newspaper. The case related to the murder in June 1982 of three judges and an army officer (see AR 1982, p. 230) and the execution in August 1983 of Joachim Amartey Kwei of the then ruling Provisional National Defence Council (see AR 1983, p. 220). Judgment was given in favour of *The Independent*.

In the sphere of external policy, Ghana acted as convenor in regional efforts to implement the Cotonou peace accord reached by the ECOWAS governments in mid-1993 on the internal conflict in Liberia (see VI.2.v). Relations with Togo were normalized, after many years of friction, by the appointment on 16 November of a Ghanaian ambassador to Lomé.

ii.   NIGERIA

CAPITAL: Lagos   AREA: 924,000 sq km   POPULATION: 88,500,000 ('92 est.)
OFFICIAL LANGUAGE: English   POLITICAL SYSTEM: transitional
HEAD OF STATE & GOVERNMENT: General Sani Abacha, Chairman of Provisional
   Ruling Council and Federal Executive Council (since Nov '93)
PRINCIPAL MINISTERS: Lt-Gen. D.O. Diya (Vice-Chairman of Federal Executive
   Council), Babagana Kingibe (foreign affairs), Anthony Asuquo Ani (finance),
   Don Etiebet (petroleum), Michael Agbamuche (justice), Alex Ibru (internal
   affairs)
INTERNATIONAL ALIGNMENT: NAM, OAU, OPEC, ICO, ACP, Cwth.
CURRENCY: naira (end-'94 £1=N34.42, US$1=N22.00)
GNP PER CAPITA: US$320 ('92)
MAIN EXPORT EARNERS: oil & gas

IT was another unhappy year for Nigeria, with the economy continuing in the doldrums and the country in a state of constant political crisis. On 10 January General Sani Abacha, who had taken power in November 1993 (see AR 1993, pp. 258–9), personally presented the 1994 budget and abandoned the market reforms dating from 1986—a move that caused alarm among foreign economists and aid donors. Interest rates were cut and foreign exchange controls reimposed (the exchange rate being fixed at N 22 to the US dollar), which led to fears of shortages in the shops and further inflation, then running at between 50 and 60 per cent. Free repatriation of export earnings was also curtailed. As a result of these measures, any agreement with the IMF was effectively ruled out.

Nigeria urgently needed to reschedule its international debts, which stood at $31,000 million and were costing $6,000 million a year to service (almost as much as the expected total revenue from oil sales in 1994). Oil output was running at 1.8 million b/d. The then Finance Minister, Kalu Idika Kalu (who had previously supported devaluation and accomodation with the IMF), argued that the budget measures were inevitable if Nigeria was to stimulate its industrial output, currently only 35 per cent of capacity. Some 75 per cent of foreign exchange sold by the government was going to the industrial sector.

On 16 January General Abacha inaugurated a 19-member National Constitutional Conference Commission, headed by retired judge Idu Kawu, with a brief to supervise the elected body which was to determine the country's political future. The first details of the government's transitional programme were released on 22 April and elections for National Constitutional Conference (NCC) delegates were set for 28 May. A draft constitution was to be presented to the Provisional Ruling

Council (PRC) on 28 November and to be made public at the end of December. The next phase of the transition would begin in January 1995.

The elections for the NCC in May were widely boycotted by the pro-democracy groups. The Yoruba heartland saw almost total boycotts, no-one voted in Lagos during the first three hours of polling and there was much apathy everywhere. The call for the boycott was organized by the new National Democratic Coalition (Nadeco), an alliance of politicians, former army officers and civil rights groups. Nadeco was particularly active during May, causing the police to issue a reminder that all non-government political activity was illegal. Nevertheless, coinciding with a national broadcast by General Abacha on 12 June, Nadeco called for a week of protests. In his national broadcast, General Abacha pledged to restore democracy but warned his opponents that they faced the full force of the law if they acted illegally.

In response to the Nadeco call, demonstrations took place throughout June. On 19 June some 2,000 students at the Federal University of Technology (Akure) called for an immediate end to military rule and the installation as President of Moshood Kashimawo Olawale (M.K.O.) Abiola of the Social Democratic Party (SDP), who had been heading the poll in the aborted June 1993 elections (see AR 1993, pp. 257-8). There were also protests at the University of Port Harcourt, while on 24 June 1,000 market women and hundreds of trade unionists marched in protest through Lagos and were tear-gassed by the police. Mr Abiola was arrested on 23 June, having been hunted by the authorities following an address to a 3,000-strong crowd in Lagos on 11 June, when he had declared himself to be President, army chief and head of the country's legal government. On 25 June a federal court ordered the authorities to produce Mr Abiola after he had challenged his arrest. In July the government charged him with treason and twice refused to produce him, leading the presiding High Court judge to describe the government action as a 'blatant and unconstitutional challenge to judicial authority'. In the latter part of the year the opening of Mr Abiola's trial was repeatedly postponed, in part because of his poor health. In October the federal High Court declared his continued detention to be illegal.

Having been opened by General Abacha on 27 June, the NCC proposed in November that the presidency should alternate between a northerner and a southerner and adopted the principle that any party gaining 10 per cent of the seats in the legislature should be guaranteed representation in the cabinet. It proposed multi- rather than two-party politics for Nigeria and named 2 January 1997 as the date for a return to democratic government after a two-year transition period. However, at the very end of the year the NCC changed its collective mind and recommended 1 January 1996 as the date for a return to civilian rule, calling upon the PRC to work out a timetable accordingly.

The deteriorating state of the economy was highlighted in April when Nigeria (one of the world's leading oil producers) was obliged to import 100,000 tonnes of petrol after a week of chronic fuel shortages due to production troubles at its refineries. On 4 July members of the National Union of Petroleum and Natural Gas Workers (Nupeng) began a sympathy strike in support of Mr Abiola and a return to democracy. As chaos mounted, the union leaders were arrested on 6 July and the army took over fuel distribution. Clashes between strikers and the military on 18 July led to 20 deaths; further violence followed in Abuja and Lagos at the end of the month. The Nigerian Labour Congress (NLC) called for an indefinite strike on 3 August but then suspended its decision to allow negotiations to take place with the government. General Abacha described the continuing oil strike as 'economic sabotage' and dismissed the union executives. On 12 August a court reinstated the union leaders, but on 19 August 25 union activists were arrested. Having brought the sector to a standstill for two months, the oil strike was finally called off by Nupeng on 4 September 'in the interests of the suffering masses of Nigeria, the economy and the oil industry'.

Meanwhile, an increasingly isolated General Abacha had in August dismissed the chiefs of staff of the army and navy (Major-General Mohammed Chris Ali and Rear-Admiral Allison Madueke) and had then dismissed the directors of all but one of the state-owned companies and agencies. On 6 September, moreover, the government issued a series of decrees which effectively gave it absolute power, enabling it in the first instance to ban three newspapers and two magazines for six months. The Nobel literature laureate, Wole Soyinka, had his Nigerian passport and a UN travel pass confiscated, but later arrived in Paris (on a French visa apparently obtained in Benin) and denounced the 'despotic and corrupt military regime'. The chairman of the Campaign for Democracy, Bello Ransome Kuti, was arrested and briefly imprisoned.

At the end of September General Abacha increased the PRC from 11 to 25 members. Criticism of his regime continued through October and on 17 October, without explanation, the Finance Minister, Kalu Idika Kalu, was dismissed, a development which led to a 12 per cent fall in the value of the naira. In a stock-taking speech after a year in power, General Abacha claimed in November that the army had seized power 'to halt the drift towards anarchy', adding as regards the economic situation: 'If we return to food production and agriculture and resume our abundant interests in mining, our earnings from these sectors will surpass that from oil . . .' But his words could not disguise the fact that the year had been one of almost non-stop economic chaos and political unrest.

iii. SIERRA LEONE

CAPITAL: Freetown AREA: 72,000 sq km POPULATION: 4,400,000 ('92)
OFFICIAL LANGUAGE: English POLITICAL SYSTEM: military dictatorship
HEAD OF STATE & GOVERNMENT: Capt. Valentine E. M. Strasser, Chairman of
   Supreme Council of State (since May '92)
PRINCIPAL MINISTERS: Lt Julius Maada Bio (Chairman of Council of State
   Secretaries), Abbas Bundu (foreign affairs), John Karimu (finance), Victor
   Brandon (development & planning), Franklyn Kargbo (justice)
INTERNATIONAL ALIGNMENT: NAM, OAU, ICO, Cwth.
CURRENCY: leone (end-'94 £1=Le930.28, US$1=Le594.62)
GNP PER CAPITA: US$160 ('92)
MAIN EXPORT EARNERS: diamonds, coffee, cocoa

PROMISES of an early end to the two-year insurrection in the districts adjoining war-torn Liberia (see VI.2.v) failed to materialize, despite claims of government military successes, additional military assistance from Ghana and renewed offers of a ceasefire and negotiations with the insurgent Revolutionary United Front (RUF). Instead, RUF forces extended their operations to areas previously unaffected, killing or taking hostage a number of Europeans, including two British VSO volunteers in November. Two new opposition groups also announced themselves, the National Front for the Restoration of Democracy and the Sierra Leone Initiative for Peace.

More serious were reported rifts in the security forces between senior and junior officers in the army and between the Supreme Council of State (SCS) in Freetown, led by Captain Valentine Strasser, and soldiers at the front. Fourteen senior officers, including Brigadier Jusu Gortor, were dismissed and disaffected soldiers turned increasingly to banditry in the war zone. Twelve soldiers were executed in November for murder and armed robbery.

The military setbacks also cast doubts on the SCS's ability to advance its programme of a staged return to elected government by 1996 and the rehabilitation of the war-ravaged economy. Given the extent of the fighting, it proved impossible to carry out voter registration in March, or to hold a national referendum on the revised draft constitution in May and district council elections in November. Dialogue with the RUF was frustrated by uncertainties about its political demands and leadership. Economic recovery, despite some encouraging successes, also depended on an end to hostilities. The June budget claimed reductions in both inflation and government debt, but later it was officially admitted that the war was consuming 75 per cent of government resources.

iv.   THE GAMBIA

CAPITAL: Banjul   AREA: 11,300 sq km   POPULATION: 989,000 ('92)
OFFICIAL LANGUAGE: English   POLITICAL SYSTEM: military regime
HEAD OF STATE & GOVERNMENT: Lt Yahya Jammeh, Chairman of Armed Forces
    Provisional Ruling Council (since July '94)
PRINCIPAL MINISTERS: Lt Edward Singateh (Vice-Chairman of AFPRC, defence),
    Capt. Lamin Bajo (interior), Bala Garba-Jahumpa (finance), Bolong Sonko
    (external affairs), Fafa Idrissa M'bai (justice)
INTERNATIONAL ALIGNMENT: NAM, OAU, ACP, ICO, Cwth.
CURRENCY: dalasi (end-'94 £1=D15.13, US$1=D9.67)
GNP PER CAPITA: US$370 ('92)
MAIN EXPORT EARNERS: groundnuts & groundnut products

THREE decades of elected government and multi-party politics came
to an end on 22 July with the overthrow of President Sir Dawda
Jawara and his People's Progressive Party (PPP) government in a
bloodless coup organized by a group of junior army officers. The Armed
Forces Provisional Ruling Council (AFPRC), under the chairmanship
of Lieutenant Yahya Jammeh, claimed widespread corruption and
electoral malpractices on the part of the government as the reasons
for the coup; but it was likely that there were also tensions and
grievances within the 800-strong Gambian army. The army's action
was generally welcomed by the public, as was its decision to investigate
the assets of ex-ministers and senior officials. In contrast, the coup met
with strong condemnation from the international donor community.
President Jawara escaped to exile in London, where he set himself up
in opposition to the new regime.

The five-man military junta sought to broaden its support by co-
opting 11 civilian ministers, including four women and two former PPP
ministers. The anti-corruption drive was extended to include action
against street crime, drugs and prostitution—all measures which met
with the approval of the public. However, support for the AFPRC began
to slip in October when it announced that it would remain in power
for a further four years. At the same time, major international donors
terminated or reduced aid. The most damaging action resulted from the
UK Foreign Office's advice to British tourists not to visit The Gambia.
The ensuing sharp drop in tourists severely hit hotel bookings.

Counter-measures by the AFPRC, such as the restoration of diplomatic relations with Libya and the courting of neighbouring countries,
could not prevent a serious decline in trade and revenue. Mounting
domestic criticism, including an abortive army counter-coup on 11
November (in which there were a number of deaths) and the effects
of economic sanctions, persuaded the AFPRC to set up a 22–strong
National Consultative Committee in December to determine the public
response to its transition programme.

v.   LIBERIA

CAPITAL: Monrovia   AREA: 97,750 sq km   POPULATION: 2,371,000 ('92)
OFFICIAL LANGUAGE: English   POLITICAL SYSTEM: confused
HEAD OF STATE & GOVERNMENT: David Kpormakor, Chairman of Council of State
   (since March '94)
PRINCIPAL MINISTERS: Dorothy Musuleng-Cooper (foreign affairs), Wilson Tarpeh
   (finance), Laveli Supwood (justice), Sandee Ware (defence), Samuel Saye Doike
   (internal affairs)
INTERNATIONAL ALIGNMENT: NAM, OAU, ACP
CURRENCY: Liberian dollar (end-'94 £1=L$1.56, US$1=L$1.00)
GNP PER CAPITA: US$450 ('87)
MAIN EXPORT EARNERS: iron ore, rubber, coffee

IT was another year of dashed expectations with the civil war dragging on into its fifth year. Hopes of a new peace settlement brokered by ECOWAS, the UN and the Ghanaian government failed to materialize as the warring factions squabbled over political office, dishonoured agreements and renewed hostilities against each other. For much of the year the war seemed to go badly for Charles Taylor's Liberian National Patriotic Front (LNPF), the faction most responsible for the break-down of earlier peace initiatives. Internal fighting between rival elements, a split between Mr Taylor and Tom Woewiyu and other LNPF ministerial nominees to the new Liberian national transitional government and increased attacks by United Liberation Movement of Liberia (Ulimo) and two new opposition groups, the Lofa Defence Force (LDF) and the Liberia Peace Committee (LPC), forced Mr Taylor to abandon his capital, Gbarnga, and to retreat across the border into Côte d'Ivoire in October. However, fighting within Ulimo between the Mandingo faction of Alhaji Kormah and a Krahn faction led by General Roosevelt Johnson, enabled the LNPF leader to recover much lost territory and partially reoccupy his abandoned capital in December.

As ever, the major stumbling-block to an agreed settlement was the unwillingness or inability of the various rival groups to stick to agreements. The Interim Government of National Unity (IGNU), headed by Dr Amos Sawyer, was replaced by a Liberian National Transitional Government (LNTG) in March, but it was May before disagreements about the distribution of posts among the warring factions were resolved. The new government's brief to bring about the disarming of the rival groups and return Liberia to elected civilian rule by September proved impossible to fulfil. By October only some 3,500 of an estimated 60,000 fighters had been disarmed and fighting continued among the principal contestants.

International pressure from ECOWAS and the UN Security Council brought the combatants together at a peace conference in August and to further meetings at Akosombo in Ghana in September and November, leading to a new ceasefire agreement on 28 December. Few expected the agreement to last. The economic situation remained as unpromising as ever. The LNTG, with no resources of its own, remained confined to the capital, Monrovia, and dependent on external support. Much of the population, subjected to renewed atrocities from all sides, chose to live outside the country.

3. SENEGAL—GUINEA—MALI—MAURITANIA—CÔTE D'IVOIRE— BURKINA FASO—NIGER—TOGO AND BENIN—CAMEROON—CHAD —GABON AND CENTRAL AFRICAN REPUBLIC—CONGO— EQUATORIAL GUINEA

i. SENEGAL

CAPITAL: Dakar   AREA: 196,000 sq km   POPULATION: 7,800,000 ('92)
OFFICIAL LANGUAGE: French   POLITICAL SYSTEM: presidential democracy
HEAD OF STATE & GOVERNMENT: President Abdou Diouf (since '81)
RULING PARTY: Socialist Party (PS) heads coalition
PRINCIPAL MINISTERS: Habib Thiam (Prime Minister), Papa Ousmane Sakho
   (economy, finance & planning), Madieng Khary Dieng (armed forces),
   Jacques Baudin (justice), Moustapha Niasse (foreign affairs), Djibo Laity Ka
   (interior), Robert Sagna (agriculture)
INTERNATIONAL ALIGNMENT: NAM, ACP, ICO, Francophonie
CURRENCY: CFA franc (end-'94 £1=CFAF834.94, US$1=CFAF533.68)
GNP PER CAPITA: US$780 ('92)
MAIN EXPORT EARNERS: agricultural products & fish, chemicals

THERE were fears at the beginning of the year that the 50 per cent devaluation of the CFA franc (the currency of the Communauté Financière Africaine) announced on 11 January would have a particularly dramatic effect on Senegal. This was partly because of the high volatility of Senegal's politically-conscious urban population, but also because it had few exportable resources, other than groundnuts, fish and phosphates, and had high import dependence, especially for food.

The year's political turbulence began with violent demonstrations in Dakar in February, in which six policemen were killed. The violence came when an opposition demonstration was commandeered by Islamic fundamentalists, but the main protest was against worsening inflation (notwithstanding government efforts to control basic commodity prices). In this tense situation, the international community moved in to help the government control the situation. The devaluation meant that the value of economic aid increased (as did the value of debt, which once again had to be partially waived). Senegal had always been one of Africa's most highly-aided countries, and immediate efforts were made to step up flows, spearheaded by the International Monetary Fund (IMF) and the World Bank. These institutions had been among the most vociferous campaigners for a devaluation of the over-valued CFA franc, and were now anxious to bestow the funds that they had been provisionally witholding.

The IMF awarded a standby credit of $30 million in March, following the adoption of a structural adjustment programme immediately after the devaluation in January. In August this was followed up with a full structural adjustment facility of $192 million. The World Bank pledged $60 million, although this had not been disbursed by the end of the year. Other donors, especially France, matched these commitments, welcoming an increase in tourism and exports, as well as a return of private capital. Senegal's basic problems remained unsolved, however.

The February demonstration marked the high-point of political tensions in 1994, as they were followed by the arrest of the two most active opposition leaders, Maître Abdoulaye Wade of the Parti Démocratique Sénégalais (PDS) and Landing Savané of the And-Jef movement. Mᵉ Wade and M. Savané had both been excluded from the coalition set up after the 1993 presidential elections, and Mᵉ Wade had also been under suspicion for allegedly being implicated in the assassination of the vice-president of the Electoral Commission in May 1993 (see AR 1993, p. 263). That charge was dropped, however, and in August Mᵉ Wade and M. Savané (already out on bail) were acquitted of implication in violent affray. In September relatively lenient prison sentences of between six months and two years were passed on 80 people convicted of taking part in the riots although the prosecutor had called for death sentences. They were members of an Islamic organization called the Moustarchidine wal Moustarchidate (Men and Women Who Seek the Truth), which had been banned after the riot. Its leader, Moustapha Sy, had already been sentenced to a year's imprisonment for incitement.

There were further signs of political détente later in the year, when a new grouping called Bokk Sopi Senegal (Unite to Change Senegal)—composed of the PDS, And-Jef and the party of the veteran former Prime Minister, Mamadou Dia—called for a national consensus, to serve as the basis of a 'social pact'. Although this move was criticized by some trade union organizations, Mᵉ Wade met with President Abdou Diouf at the end of the year, his imminent entry into the government being widely predicted.

ii. GUINEA

CAPITAL: Conakry AREA: 246,000 sq km POPULATION: 6,100,000 ('92)
OFFICIAL LANGUAGE: French POLITICAL SYSTEM: military regime
HEAD OF STATE & GOVERNMENT: Brig.-Gen. Lansana Conté, Chairman of Transitional
    Committee for National Recovery (since '84)
PRINCIPAL MINISTERS: Kozo Zomanigui (foreign affairs), Maj. Abdourahmane Diallo
    (defence), El-Hadj Camara (finance), Salifou Sylla (justice) Alseny René Gomez
    (interior)
INTERNATIONAL ALIGNMENT: NAM, OAU, ACP, ICO, Francophonie
CURRENCY: Guinean franc (end-'94 £1=GF1,566.80, US$1=GF1,001.47)
GNP PER CAPITA: US$510 ('92)
MAIN EXPORT EARNERS: bauxite, oilseeds

A sullen mood was prevalent in the wake of the December 1993 presidential elections (see AR 1993, p. 264) which had been won by the incumbent, General Lansana Conté, who had been one of the main instigators of the military coup of 1984 and had ruled the country ever since. Having been under pressure to democratize, he had ensured his victory by means which had been heavily criticized by the opposition. The annulment of the election in two opposition strongholds did little to appease the critics.

In the post-election atmosphere, the country seemed near to paralysis. Some observers saw it coming increasingly under the control of a new strong man, Interior Minister René Alseny Gomez. Reports of a failed coup attempt in June were denied, but several army officers were briefly detained without explanation. It took seven months for the newly-elected President to produce a new government, which contained few surprises, except that seven new ministries were created. The ascendancy of M. Gomez was confirmed. In September political meetings were banned following a clash between police and members of the opposition Rassemblement du Peuple Guinéen (RPG) led by Alpha Condé. Tensions increased as forces started to mobilize for the first multi-party parliamentary elections, due in the first part of 1995. The opposition was highly critical of the government's decision not to allow some two million expatriate Guineans to vote. M. Gomez said that such voting had caused 'particular problems' during the presidential elections.

iii. MALI

CAPITAL: Bamako   AREA: 1,240,000 sq km   POPULATION: 9,000,000 ('92)
OFFICIAL LANGUAGE: French   POLITICAL SYSTEM: presidential
HEAD OF STATE & GOVERNMENT: President Alpha Oumar Konaré (since April '92)
RULING PARTY: Alliance for Democracy in Mali (ADEMA)
PRINCIPAL MINISTERS: Ibrahim Boubakar Keita (Prime Minister), Djounkouma Traore
   (defence & mines), Djounkouma Traoré (foreign affairs), Soumeyla Cissé
   (finance & trade), Cheikna Détteba Kamissoko (justice)
INTERNATIONAL ALIGNMENT: NAM, OAU, ACP, ICO, Francophonie
CURRENCY: CFA franc (end-'94 £1=CFAF834.94, US$1=CFAF533.68)
GNP PER CAPITA: US$310 ('92)
MAIN EXPORT EARNERS: cotton, agricultural products

LIKE some of the other poorer countries in the franc zone, Mali was badly affected by the 50 per cent devaluation of the CFA franc on 11 January, although it did receive the financial boost of more external aid and improved export earnings, especially from cotton and newly developed gold mines. But the impact of the devaluation on prices caused a new wave of urban discontent, as well as anti-French feeling. France was accused of engineering the devaluation and of backing the strong-arm methods of President Alpha Oumar Konaré against student demonstrators in February. This episode led to the resignation of the Prime Minister, Sekou Sow, who was replaced by Aboubakar Keita, and to the departure of several parties from the ruling coalition. The result was increased political tensions for much of the rest of the year.

Political problems were compounded by the continuing spectre of renewed civil war involving dissident Touaregs in northern Mali. The peace accord signed at Tamanrasset in 1992 (see AR 1992, p. 266) seemed increasingly frayed at the edges, and the situation worsened when eight people, including an imam, were killed in an attack on Gao in October, Mali became increasingly critical of a 'pro-Touareg lobby' in Europe, and there were also suspicions that Libya and Sudan were fomenting trouble surreptitiously in the Touareg area (see also VI.3.vii).

iv. MAURITANIA

CAPITAL: Nouakchott   AREA: 1,000,000 sq km   POPULATION: 2,100,000 ('92)
OFFICIAL LANGUAGES: French & Arabic   POLITICAL SYSTEM: quasi-military
RULING PARTY: Democratic and Social Republican Party (PRDS)
HEAD OF STATE & GOVERNMENT: President (Col.) Moaouia Ould Sidi Mohammed
   Taya (since Jan '92), previously Chairman of Military Council of National
   Salvation (since '84)
PRINCIPAL MINISTERS: Sidi Mohammed Ould Babaker (Prime Minister), Mohammed
   Salem Ould Lekhal (foreign affairs), Mohammed Lemine Salem Ould Dah
   (interior), Sow Adema Samba (justice), Lemrabet Sidi Mahmoud Ould Cheikh
   Ahmed (finance), Taki Ould Sidi (planning), Col. Ahmed Ould Minnih (defence)
INTERNATIONAL ALIGNMENT: NAM, Arab League, ICO, OAU, ACP, AMU, Francophonie
CURRENCY: ouguiya (end-'94 £1=OM190.75, US$1=OM121.92)
GNP PER CAPITA: US$530 ('92)
MAIN EXPORT EARNERS: iron ore, fish

THE year began with heightened political activity around municipal elections held on 28 January and 4 February—the first test of the multi-party system since the presidential and parliamentary elections of 1992 (see AR 1992, p. 267). The ruling Republican Democratic and Social Party (PRDS) won 172 of the 208 districts, while the opposition Union of Democratic Forces (UDF) won 17 districts and the remaining 19 went to independents. Although there was over 70 per cent participation, the ruling party experienced a reduction in its support compared with the 1992 poll. These elections were followed in April by those to one-third of the seats in the Senate, in which the PRDS won 16 of the 17 seats available for contesting, thus maintaining its large majority in the upper house. The woes of the opposition increased in June when two parties, El Hor (the party of the Haratines, the black former slaves) and the Movement of Independent Democrats left the UDF, claiming that its leader, Ahmed Ould Abdallah, was too authoritarian.

Later in the year there were more frictions with Mali and increasing government worry over the activities of Islamic fundamentalists, allegedly supported by Sudan and the Algerian opposition. Relations with Senegal to the south continued to improve, a new agreement on security being signed at the end of the year. There was renewed concern at a deteriorating financial and economic situation, which the opposition, despite its divisions, was beginning to exploit.

v.   CÔTE D'IVOIRE

CAPITAL: Abidjan   AREA: 322,000 sq km   POPULATION: 12,900,000 ('92)
OFFICIAL LANGUAGE: French   POLITICAL SYSTEM: presidential
HEAD OF STATE & GOVERNMENT: President Henri Konan Bédié (since Dec '93)
RULING PARTY: Democratic Party of Côte d'Ivoire (PDCI)
PRINCIPAL MINISTERS: Daniel Kablan Duncan (Prime Minister, economy & finance),
   Amara Essy (foreign affairs), Léon Konan Koffi (defence), Emile Constant
   Bombet (interior), Faustin Kouamé (justice)
INTERNATIONAL ALIGNMENT: NAM, OAU, ACP, Francophonie
CURRENCY: CFA franc (end-'94 £1=CFAF834.94, US$1=CFAF533.68)
GNP PER CAPITA: US$670 ('92)
MAIN EXPORT EARNERS: cocoa, coffee, timber

THE beginning of the year was dominated by the preparations for the funeral of Félix Houphouët-Boigny, founder of the nation and President of the Republic for 33 years, who had died on 7 December (see AR 1993, pp. 266, 593–4). The funeral was held on 7 February, in the great basilica that he had built in his home town of Yamoussoukro, and had been preceded by a number of traditional events, as well as a lying-in-state in Abidjan. The funeral was attended by a number of African leaders, but was mainly notable for the mass descent on Côte d'Ivoire of the French political élite. Not only were President Mitterrand and Prime Minister Balladur present, but also former President Giscard d'Estaing and former Prime Ministers Chirac, Messmer, Barre, Mauroy, Rocard and Cresson, as well as several former Foreign and Cooperation Ministers and the octogenarian Jacques Foccart, General de Gaulle's *éminence grise* on African affairs. The late President's remains were buried in a private mausoleum, following traditional ceremonies.

With the funeral over, the new President, Henri Konan Bédié, moved to consolidate his position. In April he took over the leadership of the ruling Parti Démocratique de la Côte d'Ivoire (PDCI), although some of his opponents in the party split off in June to form the Rally of Democratic Republicans (RDR), led by Djeny Kobbina. Former Prime Minister Alassane Ouattara, who had contested the presidential succession with M. Konan Bédié, left the country for a senior post at the IMF. There was speculation that he might return to contest the 1995 presidential elections.

In the meantime, luck seemed to be on the new President's side. Not only did the CFA franc devaluation in January operate in Côte d'Ivoire's favour by boosting earnings from its varied cash crop exports, but also the high world prices of cocoa and coffee helped to replenish the country's depleted treasury.

vi. BURKINA FASO

CAPITAL: Ouagadougou   AREA: 275,000 sq km   POPULATION: 9,300,000 ('91)
OFFICIAL LANGUAGE: French   POLITICAL SYSTEM: transitional
HEAD OF STATE & GOVERNMENT: President (Capt.) Blaise Compaoré (since Dec '91),
    previously Chairman of Popular Front (since '87)
RULING PARTY: Organization for Popular Democracy–Labour Movement
PRINCIPAL MINISTERS: Youssouf Ouedraogo (Prime Minister), Thomas Sanon
    (external relations), Roch Christian Kaboré (finance & planning), Timothée Somé
    (justice),Yarga Larba (defence)
INTERNATIONAL ALIGNMENT: NAM, OAU, ACP, ICO, Francophonie
CURRENCY: CFA franc (end-'93 £1=CFAF436.79, US$1=CFAF295.23)
GNP PER CAPITA: US$290 ('91)
MAIN EXPORT EARNERS: cotton, agricultural produce

A quiet year politically featured the making of preparations for further multi-party electoral contests in 1995 and 1996. The divided opposition was trying to regroup itself, but reacted surprisingly mildly to the hardships of the CFA franc devaluation in January. At the end of the year, observers said that among the franc zone countries Burkina Faso had coped better than some others with the devaluation, both in controlling inflation and in keeping to structural adjustment, and had benefited from increased aid as a result of the devaluation. Meanwhile, President Blaise Compaoré tried to shed his 'cowboy' image by involving himself in regional mediation. He brokered an accord between Niger and its Touareg rebels signed in Ouagadougou on 23 October (see VI.3.vii). He was also, ironically, cast as a mediator in Liberia, despite being one of the players in that country's civil war (see VI.2.v).

vii. NIGER

CAPITAL: Niamey   AREA: 1,267,000 sq km   POPULATION: 8,200,000 ('92)
OFFICIAL LANGUAGE: French   POLITICAL SYSTEM: transitional
HEAD OF STATE & GOVERNMENT: President Mahamane Ousmane (since April '93)
RULING PARTY: Alliance of the Forces of Change coalition
PRINCIPAL MINISTERS: Souley Abdoulaye (Prime Minister), Abdourahamane Hama
    (foreign affairs), Abdou Labo (defence), Amadou Tahirou (justice), Mohammed
    Moudi (finance & planning)
INTERNATIONAL ALIGNMENT: NAM, OAU, ACP, ICO, Francophonie
CURRENCY: CFA franc (end-'94 £1=CFAF834.94, US$1=CFAF533.68)
GNP PER CAPITA: US$280 ('92)
MAIN EXPORT EARNERS: uranium, metal ores

A difficult year in the Niger Republic proved a testing time for the new multi-party democracy of President Mahamane Ousmane, who had been elected in 1993 (see AR 1993, p. 268). On the one hand, the deepening economic and social crisis obtained no immediate relief from the CFA franc devaluation of 10 January, partly because of the continued depression of the world uranium market; on the other, the rebellion of Touaregs in the north, where several armed movements were grouped in the Coordination of the Armed Resistance (CRA), became a greater threat. One of the Touaregs' main grievances was that the 1991 national conference, which led to the democratic transition, had not taken account of their grievances. Armed attacks in the Agadès area in the north increased in intensity, until contacts made with assistance from Algeria and France in September led to peace talks in Ouagadougou (the Burkina Faso capital) and the signing of a provisional ceasefire agreement on 23 October (see also VI.3.vi).

The ceasefire agreement secured the approval of the National Assembly, which was more than could be said of successive governments of appointed by the the President. Prime Minister Mahamadou Issoufou resigned in late September after his Niger Party for Democracy and Socialism (PNDS) had left the ruling Alliance of the Forces of Change (AFC) amid claims of presidential encroachment on the government's authority. Another factor was unhappiness within the PNDS as regards the structural adjustment policies which the government had been attempting to impose. A new government under Souley Abdoulaye of the President's Democratic and Social Convention promptly lost a vote of confidence on 16 October. President Mahamane was accordingly forced to dissolve parliament and call parliamentary elections for early in 1995.

viii.　TOGO AND BENIN

Togo
CAPITAL: Lomé　AREA: 57,000 sq km　POPULATION: 3,900,000 ('92)
OFFICIAL LANGUAGES: French, Kabiye & Ewe　POLITICAL SYSTEM: transitional
HEAD OF STATE: President Gnassingbe Eyadema (since '67)
HEAD OF GOVERNMENT: Edem Kodjo, Prime Minister (since April '94)
CURRENCY: CFA franc (end-'94 £1=CFAF834.94, US$1=CFAF533.68)
GNP PER CAPITA: US$390 ('92)
MAIN EXPORT EARNERS: phosphates, cocoa

Benin
CAPITAL: Porto Novo　AREA: 113,000 sq km　POPULATION: 5,000,000 ('92)
OFFICIAL LANGUAGE: French　POLITICAL SYSTEM: presidential
HEAD OF STATE & GOVERNMENT: President Nicéphore Soglo (since April '91)
CURRENCY: CFA franc (end-'94 £1=CFAF834.94, US$1=CFAF533.68)
GNP PER CAPITA: US$410 ('92)
MAIN EXPORT EARNERS: cotton, palm products

THE beginning of the year saw another outbreak of mayhem in TOGO that may have been an incursion, or an attempted coup, and the end of the year brought rumours of another coup attempt. Nevertheless, 1994 was generally a quiet year, largely devoted to President Gnassingbe Eyadema's attempts to master his domestic political situation. After a clearly-rigged presidential election in 1993 (see AR 1993, p. 269), multi-party parliamentary elections were held on 6 and 20 February under relatively objective conditions, although the presence of international observers did not prevent some abuses. Although the opposition parties collectively won the election, the President subsequently managed to detach Edem Kodjo's small Union for Justice and Democracy (UTD) from the opposition alliance. After several weeks of political attrition, M. Kodjo became Prime Minister in April, with support of the ruling Togolese People's Rally (RPT). He survived in power until the end of the year, despite predictions to the contrary. The end of the year also saw a thaw in relations with Ghana, although there were still large numbers of Togolese refugees in both Ghana and Benin.

Democratic politics in BENIN continued to be turbulent, as President Nicéphore Soglo continued to survive without a proper majority in the National Assembly. Tensions increased in the run-up to parliamentary elections due early in 1995. President Soglo himself, having tried to remain above party politics, eventually became leader of the Benin Renaissance Party (PRB), founded by his wife Rosine in 1992. The country continued to enjoy its new-found reputation as a democratic success story, but did not find that this status brought any more aid. Some special relief came to both Togo and Benin in the wake of CFA franc devaluation in January, although the resultant inflation generated agitation from Benin's trade unions and students, whose reputation for turbulence was maintained.

ix.   CAMEROON

CAPITAL: Yaoundé   AREA: 475,000 sq km   POPULATION: 12,200,000 ('92)
OFFICIAL LANGUAGES: French & English   POLITICAL SYSTEM: transitional
HEAD OF STATE & GOVERNMENT: President Paul Biya (since '82)
RULING PARTY: Cameroon People's Democratic Movement (RDPC)
PRINCIPAL MINISTERS: Simon Achidi Achu (Prime Minister), Edouard Akame
    Mfoumou (defence), Justin Naioro (economy & finance), Ferdinand Leopold
    Oyono (foreign affairs), Douala Montomé (justice)
INTERNATIONAL ALIGNMENT: NAM, OAU, ACP, ICO, Francophonie
CURRENCY: CFA franc (end-'93 £1=CFAF834.94, US$1=CFAF533.68)
GNP PER CAPITA: US$820 ('92)
MAIN EXPORT EARNERS: oil, cocoa, coffee, aluminium

THE year proved to be a confused and disappointing one for Cameroon, both economically and politically. Of the countries of the CFA franc zone, it had seemed to be one of those in a good position to take advantage of the devaluation in January. For a number of reasons, this did not prove to be the case, notably because oil revenues, which could have been expected to double in CFA terms, had in fact been mortgaged for several years in advance. The oil, in any case, was slowly running out, and the political disruptions of the early 1990s had had a prejudicial effect of agricultural production for exports: in periods of uncertainty, the peasants preferred to go for food crops. Although Cameroon had quietly achieved greater respectability with the World Bank and the IMF (which made new funds available in 1994), the government's reluctance to embark on economic reform continued to annoy the Washington institutions. In particular, the civil service remained highly overblown but politically difficult to cut down.

Politically, although the opposition was going through a period of division and demoralization, President Paul Biya and the ruling Cameroon People's Democratic Movement lacked the confidence to embark on either a much-touted constitutional debate or to hold much-postponed municipal elections. Palpably dependent on his own Beti-Bulu ethnic base, the President resorted essentially to distractions, notably a border conflict over the Bakassi peninsula with Nigeria, which threatened to become a shooting war in March-April (see also VI.2.ii). Although Nigeria accused France of offering military support to Cameroon, all the evidence was that French backing was only lukewarm and that France, because of its substantial interests in both countries, was pushing for a peaceful solution. The decision by Cameroon to refer the matter to the International Court of Justice at The Hague was thought to have resulted from pressure from France and the European Union as a whole (see also XV.1.i).

x.   CHAD

CAPITAL: Ndjaména   AREA: 1,284,000 sq km   POPULATION: 6,000,000 ('92)
OFFICIAL LANGUAGES: French & Arabic   POLITICAL SYSTEM: presidential
HEAD OF STATE & GOVERNMENT: President (Col.) Idriss Déby (since Dec '90)
PRINCIPAL MINISTERS: Delwa Kassiré Koumakoye (Prime Minister), Ahmat
    Abderahmane Haggar (foreign affairs), Abderahmane Miskine Izzo (interior &
    security), Patake Albert Pahimi (finance), Maj. Loum Hinassou Laina (justice)
INTERNATIONAL ALIGNMENT: NAM, OAU, ACP, ICO, Francophonie
CURRENCY: CFA franc (end-'94 £1=CFAF834.94, US$1=CFAF533.68)
GNP PER CAPITA: US$220 ('92)
MAIN EXPORT EARNERS: cotton, agricultural products

IT was another difficult year for the fragile rule of President Idriss Déby, even if less dramatic than previous years. Because of endless incursions, and a wave of strikes and insecurity, the democratic transition originally foreseen for April 1994 was postponed for a year. A draft constitution was prepared by July (although the opposition parties complained about lack of adequate consultation), but had still not been submitted to the planned referendum by the end of the year. President Déby, by a process of attrition, displayed increasing confidence that he could face an electoral test. One sign of this was the way he organized the removal of a possible presidential rival, Lol Mahamat Choua, from the speakership of the interim parliament in October.

The major political problem continued to be the disaffection of the far south, where the exactions of President Déby's Republican Guard became deeply unpopular. With assistance from the Central African Republic, a peace with Lieutenant Moise Kette, one of the southern rebel leaders, was brokered in Bangui in August. Under the agreement, 150 former army officers were reintegrated. However, armed resistance under hardliner Laokein Barde was continuing at the end of the year, in support of a demand for a 'federal' solution that was totally unacceptable to the northerners.

Although fears of penetration by Islamic fundamentalists continued to be expressed in the south, President Déby achieved the balancing-act of maintaining good relations with France, Libya and Sudan simultaneously. Evidence of this came when Libya accepted the judgment in favour of Chad made by the International Court of Justice on the Aouzou Strip (see also XV.1.i). In light of the ruling, Libyan troops were withdrawn at the end of May.

xi.   GABON AND CENTRAL AFRICAN REPUBLIC

Gabon

CAPITAL: Libreville   AREA: 268,000 sq km   POPULATION: 1,200,000 ('92)
OFFICIAL LANGUAGE: French   POLITICAL SYSTEM: presidential
HEAD OF STATE & GOVERNMENT: President Omar Bongo (since '67)
RULING PARTY: Gabonese Democratic Party (PDG)
PRIME MINISTER: Paulin Obame-Nguema (since Oct '94)
CURRENCY: CFA franc (end-'94 £1=CFAF834.94, US$1=CFAF533.68)
GNP PER CAPITA: US$4,450 ('92)
MAIN EXPORT EARNERS: oil & gas, manganese

Central African Republic

CAPITAL: Bangui   AREA: 623,000 sq km   POPULATION: 3,200,000 ('92)
OFFICIAL LANGUAGE: French   POLITICAL SYSTEM: transitional
HEAD OF STATE & GOVERNMENT: President Ange-Felix Patassé (since Sept '92)
RULING PARTY: Central African People's Liberation Party (MPLC) heads coalition
PRIME MINISTER: Jean-Luc Mandaba (since Oct '93)
CURRENCY: CFA franc (end-'94 £1=CFAF834.94, US$1=CFAF533.68)
GNP PER CAPITA: US$410 ('92)
MAIN EXPORT EARNERS: coffee, diamonds, timber

THE year in GABON started with a backlash of troubles arising from the contested re-election of President Omar Bongo in December 1993 (see

AR 1993, p. 272). A state of alert imposed then, involving government and opposition, was not lifted until April. Talks were opened in Paris with the aim of breaking the 'political and economic deadlock' in the country. The talks finally matured in September, when a far-reaching agreement was concluded by some 50 delegates variously representing the 'presidential tendency' and the opposition. It led to the installation in October of a new coalition government under Paulin Obame-Nguema to replace that of Casimir Oye Mba (which had been appointed in March). One of the main opposition parties, the National Rally of Woodcutters (RNB), declined to support the new government.

In the CENTRAL AFRICAN REPUBLIC, the emphasis was more on economic recovery as the newly-elected President, Ange-Felix Patassé, tried to consolidate his position. The local effects of the CFA franc devaluation in January were said to be mixed. Although improvements in export earnings from commodities such as cotton were registered, urban hardship from the unavoidable inflation caused continuing discontents. At the end of the year a constitutional referendum was held on, among other things, extending the presidential term from four to six years and introducing regional decentralization. The proposals were approved by over 80 per cent of those voting (whose number was low), amid opposition criticism of the haste of the consultation and claims that opponents of the proposals had been denied access to the media.

xii. CONGO

CAPITAL: Brazzaville AREA: 342,000 sq km POPULATION: 2,400,000 ('92)
OFFICIAL LANGUAGE: French POLITICAL SYSTEM: transitional
HEAD OF STATE & GOVERNMENT: President Pascal Lissouba (since Aug '92)
RULING PARTY: Pan-African Union for Social Democracy (UPADS)
PRINCIPAL MINISTERS: Gen. Jacques Joachim Yhombi-Opango (Prime Minister),
    Benjamin Bounkoulou (foreign affairs), Moungounga N'Guila Nkomba (economy
    & finance)
INTERNATIONAL ALIGNMENT: NAM, OAU, ACP, Francophonie
CURRENCY: CFA franc (end-'94 £1=CFAF834.94, US$1=CFAF533.68)
GNP PER CAPITA: US$1,030 ('92)
MAIN EXPORT EARNERS: oil & gas, timber

MUCH of the year was spent in coping with the submerged political crisis, which manifested itself in armed faction fighting pursuant to the disputed parliamentary elections of June and October 1993 (see AR 1993, pp. 273–4). The year began with open fighting between rival militias, which included the presidential tendency backing President Pascal Lissouba and the 'ninjas' of the Bakongo leader in Brazzaville, Bernard Kolelas. With the estimated death toll running into hundreds, on 31 January a ceasefire was signed by deputies from President Lissouba's Pan-African League for Social Democracy and from the

Congolese Movement for Democracy and Integral Development led by M. Kolelas. Violence nevertheless continued sporadically, and was said by some to have been inflamed by militia of a 'third force' supporting former President Sassou Nguesso. As rumours of an army coup surfaced regularly, the President reinforced his security with Israeli specialists.

In August, however, there was a formal reconciliation between parliamentary leaders of the two main factions, followed by the election of M. Kolelas as mayor of Brazzaville. One consequence of this development was the setting-up of an alliance of northern political parties in the Assembly, grouping 15 deputies, including those of M. Sassou Nguesso's Congolese Labour Party. In October President Lissouba and M. Kolelas appeared together at a rally. Although the violence continued sporadically, there was talk at the end of the year of a coalition government of the two main groupings, excluding the northern parties. Observers noted the damage which the instability had done to the Congolese economy, which meant that advantage had not been taken of the CFA franc devaluation of January.

xiii. EQUATORIAL GUINEA

CAPITAL: Malabo   AREA: 28,000 sq km   POPULATION: 437,000 ('92)
OFFICIAL LANGUAGE: Spanish   POLITICAL SYSTEM: transitional
HEAD OF STATE & GOVERNMENT: President (Brig.-Gen.) Teodoro Obiang Nguema
    Mbasogo (since Aug '79)
RULING PARTY: Democratic Party of Equatorial Guinea (PDGE)
PRINCIPAL MINISTERS: Siale Bileka Silvestre (Prime Minister), Anatolio Ndong Mba
    (Deputy Prime Minister, economy & finance), Miguel Oyanyo Ndong Mifumu
    (foreign affairs), Júlio Ndong Ela Mangue (interior)
INTERNATIONAL ALIGNMENT: NAM, OAU, ACP, Francophonie
CURRENCY: CFA franc (end-'94 £1=CFAF834.94, US$1=CFAF533.68)
GNP PER CAPITA: US$330 ('92)
MAIN EXPORT EARNERS: cocoa, timber, coffee

THE grim and dreary cycle of events in this sad little dictatorship continued to repeat itself, after the half-hearted attempts, under pressure from despairing Western donors, to introduce a multi-party democracy in 1993 (see AR 1993, p. 274). Municipal elections due to be held in November were delayed, after the government had frozen its relations with the opposition in August, following 'vile and insulting behaviour' by the opposition leader, Severo Motta Nsa, during a visit to Spain. This followed a deterioration in relations with Spain at the beginning of the year in which aid was suspended and the Spanish ambassador temporarily recalled following the expulsion of the Spanish consul in the mainland town of Bata. In February Amnesty International produced a report that contained criticisms of the government's human rights record.

In October the Speaker and Deputy Speaker of the National Assembly resigned in protest against the poor management of the country by the government. Both had been members of the ruling Democratic Party of President Teodoro Obiang Nguema Mbasogo, the resignations coming shortly after a wave of arrests of opposition personalities in Malabo and on the mainland.

VII CENTRAL AND SOUTHERN AFRICA

1. ZAÏRE—BURUNDI AND RWANDA—GUINEA-BISSAU AND CAPE VERDE—SÃO TOMÉ & PRÍNCIPE—MOZAMBIQUE—ANGOLA

i. ZAÏRE

CAPITAL: Kinshasa   AREA: 2,345,000 sq km   POPULATION: 39,800,000 ('92)
OFFICIAL LANGUAGE: French   POLITICAL SYSTEM: presidential
HEAD OF STATE & GOVERNMENT: President (Marshal) Mobutu Sese Seko (since '65)
RULING PARTY: Popular Movement for Renewal (MPR)
PRINCIPAL MINISTERS: Léon Kengo Wa Dondo (Prime Minister), Gustave Malumba M'Bangula (Deputy Premier, interior), Adml. Mavua Mudima (Deputy Premier, defence), Kamanda Wa Kamanda (Deputy Premier, justice), Lunda Bululu (foreign affairs), Pay-Pay Wa Kasige (finance), Bahati Lukuebo (budget), Katanga Mukmadiya Mutumba (economy), Mutombo Bakafwa N'Senda (mines)
INTERNATIONAL ALIGNMENT: NAM, OAU, ACP, Francophonie
CURRENCY: zaïre (end-'94 £1=Z4,975.00, US$1=Z3,179.93)
GNP PER CAPITA: US$220 ('90)
MAIN EXPORT EARNERS: copper, other minerals, oil

'ZAïRE', wrote John Darnton in the *New York Times*, 'is coming to represent a new spectre in Africa—the stateless country. Where once there was the "big-man rule" of President Mobutu Sese Seko, there is now what some Zaïreans are calling "no-man rule".'

The President's two assets remained his control of the best-equipped sections of the security forces and his access to presses to print bank notes; against him was ranged most of the people, with no arms and no money. 'We cannot overthrow him', explained one opposition politician, 'but he cannot overthrow us.' 'There is no such thing as society here', wrote *The Independent*'s Africa correspondent, Richard Dowden, after visiting a number of urban areas. 'There are the rich, a be-suited clan of about 100 families, and there are 40 million poor people. The lucky ones are "clients", protected by a "patron" in a hierarchy of wealth. The rest live in the Iron Age.'

The country's infrastructure was in a state of near-total collapse. Of the extensive road network at the time of independence 85 per cent was reckoned to have reverted to bush. Hospitals, clinics and schools had been forced to close for lack of funds. Malnutrition was widespread, AIDS rife and bubonic plague reported in eastern Zaïre. 'When the water system breaks down', Dowden reported, 'the poor get cholera, the rich can buy Perrier.' Yet 'the death of government has not', Dowden concluded, 'created a catastrophe': Kinshasa 'bubbles with commerce and street life. People are too busy staying alive or making money to think about politics.' And some vestiges of the state survived in the form of ritual: in Kisangani Dowden found that the traffic came to a halt at 7.30 every morning for the ceremony of raising the national flag.

At the start of the year Zaïre was in the unusual situation of having two Prime Ministers, two governments, two parliaments and one President (see AR 1993, pp. 276–7). For the President's opponents, grouped together in the Sacred Union, Etienne Tshisekedi was the legitimate Prime Minister and the High Council of the Republic (HCR) the only legal parliament. The President's supporters had formed themselves into a group calling itself the Political Forces of the Conclave (FPC) with members of the President's party, the Popular Movement for Renewal (MPR), in prominent positions, Faustin Birindwa as Prime Minister and the National Assembly as their parliament.

In January the President announced that the two legislatures were to be merged to form the HCR–Parliament of Transition. In April this new body endorsed the Transitional Constitutional Act to regulate the transition to democracy. The terms of the act appeared to strengthen the position of the Prime Minister in relation to the President, awarding the government control of the armed forces and the central bank.

In June the new legislature held elections for the post of Prime Minister, from which Kengo Wa Dondo emerged as a clear winner with 72 per cent of the votes. This result was a serious setback for M. Tshisekedi, whose supporters regarded him as the only legitimate candidate. Once again the President had revealed his ability to divide his opponents: M. Kengo's election was made possible only by splitting the ranks of the Sacred Union. The new Prime Minister, who had served in that capacity on two occasions in the 1980s but had later joined the opposition, was seen as a man of the centre with a reputation for efficiency. The only way the radicals could express their disapproval was to call on their supporters to stay at home and transform the capital into 'a dead city'. But this tactic, effectively employed on a number of occasions in the past three years, no longer worked: 'confronted with the *fait accompli* of M. Kengo's election, ordinary Zaïreans', wrote one observer, 'have displayed an extraordinary collapse of morale'.

M. Kengo's programme was well designed to attract support both at home and abroad: freeing the central bank from the President's control, ending the irresponsible printing of money, curbing corruption in the public sector, embarking on a policy of privatization and imposing discipline on the security forces. From the start, the Prime Minister could count on the backing of the French government; gradually the country's other two backers, the United States and Belgium, began to reconsider their policy of withholding all aid so long as President Mobutu remained in power. The crisis over Rwanda (see VII.1.ii) in fact played into the President's hands. By granting international agencies easy access to the Rwandan refugee camps in eastern Zaïre and by not obstructing the brief French military intervention, the President effectively ingratiated himself with some sections of the international community. His attendance at a summit meeting hosted by President Mandela in Pretoria in July was a further indication of his diplomatic rehabilitation.

Realists continued to express their doubts about the ability of the new government effectively to tackle the country's problems. In July the Prime Minister dismissed the governor of the central bank (although it was not until November that the governor, a nominee of the President, actually quit his office). Almost all Zaïre's neighbours were in a state of turmoil: refugees, some bearing arms, moved in from Angola, southern Sudan, Burundi and in their hundreds of thousands from Rwanda. In Shaba the local administration had declared its autonomy and changed the province's name back to Katanga. But while neighbouring countries had fallen apart as a result of armed conflict and civil war, Zaïre's implosion was the result of horrendously bad government, for which the President was directly responsible. However, with no widely acceptable alternative leader in sight, the year ended once again with President Mobutu still in power, confounding all the confident predictions of his imminent downfall.

ii.   BURUNDI AND RWANDA

Burundi

CAPITAL: Bujumbura   AREA: 28,000 sq km   POPULATION: 5,800,000 ('92)
OFFICIAL LANGUAGE: French & Kirundi   POLITICAL SYSTEM: presidential
HEAD OF STATE & GOVERNMENT: President Sylvestre Ntibantunganya (since April '94)
RULING PARTIES: Front for Democracy in Burundi (Frodebu) and Union for National
    Progress (Uprona) head coalition
CURRENCY: Burundi franc (end-'94 £1=FBu387.99, US$1=FBu247.99)
GNP PER CAPITA: US$210 ('92)
MAIN EXPORT EARNERS: coffee, tea

Rwanda

CAPITAL: Kigali   AREA: 26,300 sq km   POPULATION: 7,300,000 ('92)
OFFICIAL LANGUAGES: French & Kinyarwanda   POLITICAL SYSTEM: presidential
HEAD OF STATE & GOVERNMENT: President Pasteur Bizimungu (since July '94)
RULING PARTIES: Rwandan Patriotic Front (FPR) heads coalition
CURRENCY: Rwanda franc (end-'94 £1=RF216.50, US$1=RF138.38)
GNP PER CAPITA: US$250 ('92)
MAIN EXPORT EARNERS: coffee, tea, tin

ON 6 April the executive jet carrying President Juvénal Habyarimana of RWANDA and President Cyprien Ntaryamira of Burundi from peace talks in Tanzania was shot down as it was coming in to land at Kigali airport. No impartial investigation of the crash could be conducted, but it was widely believed that the perpetrators, who had access to ground-to-air missiles, were extremist members of the Presidential Guard strongly opposed to peace with the Tutsi-dominated Rwandan Patriotic Front

(FPR). Within hours of the crash, first the Rwandan capital, then other parts of the country became the scene of a pogrom directed not only against local Tutsi but also against any Hutu associated with parties in opposition to the President's party, the National Republican Movement for Democracy and Development (MNRD). The pogrom rapidly developed a genocidal intensity, leading to appalling scenes of violence comparable to the atrocities committed in the 1970s by the Khmers Rouges in Cambodia.

Although the international community was taken by surprise, local observers had noticed many ominous developments in the preceding months. The FPR's invasion of Rwanda, launched in 1990, served powerfully to exacerbate ancestral Tutsi-Hutu hostility. The peace treaty signed at Arusha in August 1993 (see AR 1993, p. 279) had promised an end to the conflict through the formation of a transitional government in which all parties, including the FPR, would be represented. At the same time, a United Nations force (UNAMIR in its English acronym, MINUAR in French) had been sent to help prepare the ground for a general election in 1995. However, as early as September 1993 the agreement had run into difficulties when the various parties failed to agree on the nomination of their representatives to the transitional government. Meanwhile, Hutu militants were working out contingency measures. The Rwandan army began providing weapons and training for the members of two party political militias, one drawn from the MRND and known as Interahamwe (Those Who Attack Together), the other, Impuzamugambi (Those With a Single Purpose), drawn from the MRND's extremist ally, the Coalition for the Defence of the Republic (CDR). Training for these militias intensified in early 1994. At the same time, a private radio station—reportedly owned by members of the President's inner circle—began a campaign of hate-filled propaganda directed against the Tutsi generally and also against Hutu opponents of the President's party. This radio campaign grew steadily more virulent after 6 April.

Among the first victims of the violence was the Prime Minister, Agathe Uwilingiyimana, and ten Belgian UN soldiers sent to protect her. Other ministers also died, together with prominent Hutu human rights activists. The immediate response of the international community was to evacuate all foreign nationals. On 21 April the UN Security Council voted to reduce the size of UNAMIR/MINUAR from 2,500 to 270—a decision which was reversed on 17 May. It was then agreed that the UN force should be increased to 5,000 (see XI.2), although it proved impossible to provide so many UN troops immediately.

Meanwhile, the country had become the scene of two distinct conflicts: the FPR resumed its offensive, while Hutu extremists went on the rampage in most areas, some of the worst massacres taking place in churches to which Tutsi had fled for sanctuary. By June the death toll was put at between 200,000 and 500,000, while many more people had left their homes to seek refuge in Tanzania or Zaïre.

On 19 July, having occupied Kigali and most other major towns, the FPR announced victory in the civil war and went on to form a government based on the terms of the 1993 Arusha agreement, but excluding—at least for the time being—members of the MNRD and allied parties. The international community could have little impact on the internal situation in Rwanda: a French military force which entered western Rwanda in June was withdrawn by September. Aid agencies concentrated on the huge refugee camps in Tanzania and Zaïre. Here the situation was exacerbated by Hutu militants forcibly dissuading refugees from returning home, spreading stories of alleged Tutsi atrocities. On 8 November the UN Security Council established an International Criminal Tribunal for Rwanda to prosecute those responsible for genocide. By the end of the year the new government in Kigali had clearly embarked on a policy of reconciliation, one of its most practical measures being the establishment of military re-education centres for 'harmonization training' to prepare soldiers from the defeated army for enrolment in a new 'patriotic army'.

BURUNDI was overshadowed not only by the catastrophe in Rwanda but also by the consequences of the failed coup of October 1993. According to the findings of an international commission, most members of the security forces had been actively or passively involved in that attempt, which had led to the death of the country's first democratically elected President, Melchior Ndadaye (see AR 1993, p. 278). Violence was always close to the surface: in March soldiers shot 400 people dead in the capital, Bujumbura during protests against a number of dismissals ordered by the government. But the sudden death of the new President, Cyprien Ntaryamira, elected by the National Assembly as M. Ndadaye's successor in January, in the air crash on 6 April (see above) did not lead to any political breakdown. The Speaker of the National Assembly, Sylvestre Ntibantunganya, was formally appointed acting President and was later elected to the presidency in September. After protracted negotiations, all the main parties agreed to a Convention of Government stipulating the terms for power-sharing, with the opposition parties being granted about 45 per cent of ministerial and ambassadorial posts and provincial governorships. To Hutu militants this compromise was a betrayal of their cause but they were confronted by security forces 95 per cent Tutsi in composition and by a local magistracy only 13 of whose 231 office-holders were Hutu. Inevitably, therefore, Burundi's Hutu extremists began making contact with the armed Hutu irreconcilables from Rwanda who were thronging the refugee camps just beyond Burundi's borders. For both countries the presence of so many embittered and often heavily-armed men presented a deeply ominous threat for the future.

iii.   GUINEA-BISSAU AND CAPE VERDE

Guinea-Bissau
CAPITAL: Bissau   AREA: 36,000 sq km   POPULATION: 1,000,000 ('92)
OFFICIAL LANGUAGE: Portuguese   POLITICAL SYSTEM: presidential
HEAD OF STATE: President (Brig.-Gen.) João Vieira (since '80)
HEAD OF GOVERNMENT: Manuel Saturnino da Costa (since Oct '94)
RULING PARTY: African Party for the Independence of Guinea and Cape Verde
   (PAIGC)
CURRENCY: peso (end-'94 £1=PG21,215.10, US$1=PG13,560.30)
GNP PER CAPITA: US$220 ('92)
MAIN EXPORT EARNERS: groundnuts, agricultural products

Cape Verde
CAPITAL: Praia   AREA: 4,000 sq km   POPULATION: 389,000 ('92)
OFFICIAL LANGUAGE: Portuguese   POLITICAL SYSTEM: emerging democracy
HEAD OF STATE: President Antonio Mascarenhas Monteiro (since March '91)
RULING PARTY: Movement for Democracy (MPD)
HEAD OF GOVERNMENT: Carlos Veiga, Prime Minister (since Jan '91)
CURRENCY: Cape Verde escudo (end-'94 £1=CVEsc129.72, US$1=CVEsc82.92)
GNP PER CAPITA: US$850 ('92)
MAIN EXPORT EARNERS: cashew nuts, fish

ON 3 July GUINEA-BISSAU held its first multi-party legislative and presidential elections with an electorate numbering 400,000. Of the 100 parliamentary seats, a clear majority of 64 went to the party that had ruled the country since independence, the African Party for the Independence of Guinea and Cape Verde (PAIGC). Of the opposition parties, Guinea-Bissau Resistance/Bafata Movement (RGB/MB) won 16, the Party for Social Renovation (PRS) 12 and the Union for Change (UM) six, the remainder going to smaller parties. In the first round of the presidential election the PAIGC's candidate, General João Vieira, the country's President since his military coup in 1980, won 46 per cent of the votes, 21.9 per cent going to his leading opponent, Kumba Iala of the PRS. In the second round the PRS candidate (who came from the Balanta, the largest of the country's 30 ethnic groups) secured the backing of all the other opposition parties and won 48 per cent to General Vieira's 52 per cent. Restiveness in the Balanta-dominated army was seen as a likely cause of future tensions.

In CAPE VERDE, signs of division in the ruling Movement for Democracy (MPD) emerged in March when several leading members of the party resigned and spoke of forming a new party.

iv.   SÃO TOMÉ & PRÍNCIPE

CAPITAL: São Tomé   AREA: 965 sq km   POPULATION: 121,000 ('92)
OFFICIAL LANGUAGE: Portuguese   POLITICAL SYSTEM: emerging democracy
HEAD OF STATE & GOVERNMENT: President Miguel Trovoada (since March '91)
RULING PARTY: Movement for the Liberation of São Tomé and Príncipe–Social
   Democratic Party (MLSTP-PSD)
PRINCIPAL MINISTERS: Carlos Graça (Prime Minister), Guilherme Posser da Costa
   (foreign affairs), Joaquim Rafael Branco (economic affairs), Carlos Quaresma
   Batisa de Souza (planning & finance), Alberto Paulino (interior)
INTERNATIONAL ALIGNMENT: NAM, OAU, ACP
CURRENCY: dobra (end-'94 £1=Db1,485.14, US$1=Db949.28)
GNP PER CAPITA: US$360 ('92)
MAIN EXPORT EARNERS: cocoa, copra

A political crisis not unlike that of 1992 (see AR 1992, p. 281) arose in July when President Miguel Trovoada clashed with the government over the budget, appointed a new Prime Minister, dissolved the National Assembly and called elections for October. These proved a disaster for the Democratic Convergence Party (PCD), whose representation in the 55-member Assembly was reduced from 33 to 14. The Movement for the Liberation of São Tomé and Príncipe (MLSTP), which had ruled the islands as a one-party state from 1974 to 1991 and was now sub-titled 'Social Democratic Party', increased its representation from 21 to 27 seats and formed the new government. The remaining 14 seats went to Independent Democratic Action (ADI).

v.   MOZAMBIQUE

CAPITAL: Maputo   AREA: 800,000 sq km   POPULATION: 16,500,000 ('92)
OFFICIAL LANGUAGE: Portuguese   POLITICAL SYSTEM: presidential
HEAD OF STATE & GOVERNMENT: President Joaquim Chissano (since '86)
RULING PARTY: Front for the Liberation of Mozambique (Frelimo)
PRINCIPAL MINISTERS: Pascoal Mocumbi (Prime Minister), Eneias da Conceiçao
   Comiche (economic & social affairs), Leonardo Simão (foreign affairs), Aguiar
   Real Mazula (defence), José Abudo (justice), Manuel Mucananda (home affairs),
   Tomas Salomao (planning & finance)
INTERNATIONAL ALIGNMENT: NAM, OAU, ACP
CURRENCY: metical (end-'94 £1=Mt10,099.40, US$1=Mt6,455.35)
GNP PER CAPITA: US$60 ('92)
MAIN EXPORT EARNERS: sea food, cashew nuts

IN accordance with the terms of the peace treaty of 1992 (see AR 1992, pp. 281–3), although a year later than originally planned, Mozambique held its first multi-party elections in October. Polling stations were open from 27 to 29 October, the final results being released on 19 November. Over the elections hung the shadow of Angola's dreadful experience (see VII.1.vi) with its many painful parallels with the situation in Mozambique: a protracted and appallingly destructive civil war in part fomented by outsiders and ending in stalemate; a long and difficult period of negotiations for peace, with outsiders acting as intermediaries;

the calling-in of UN personnel to monitor the process of demobilization of the rival armies and the holding of elections; and elections generally thought to have been free and fair but producing a result which the loser refused to accept and which led to a return to armed conflict even more violent than anything that had gone before. That events in Mozambique eventually worked out differently was due to three main factors.

Learning from the débâcle in Angola, the UN Security Council saw to it that the United Nations Operation in Mozambique (ONUMOZ) had a staff at least seven times the size of the UN presence in Angola in 1992, with 6,000 soldiers and 1,100 police drawn from many different countries (see also XI.1). Much credit was clearly due to the energy and political shrewdness of the UN special representative, Aldo Ajello, an Italian journalist and politician, who paid special attention to the vital importance of ensuring the participation of the National Resistance Movement (MNR or RENAMO). For this reason, a special UN trust fund with an initial capital of $12 million was established to provide the means for the NMR to organize itself into a political party. The fund also boosted the morale of the MNR leader, Afonso Dhlakama, by providing him with a lavish sea-side villa in Maputo, a bullet-proof Mercedes and the means for international travel.

The process of demobilization was carried through far more thoroughly in Mozambique than it had been in Angola. By the end of July it was reckoned that almost all the 80,000 troops of the ruling Frelimo and the 20,000 MNR guerrillas had passed through demobilization centres. Far less successful was the effort to build up a new national army, the Mozambique Armed Defence Force (FADM). So reluctant were most ex-combatants to commit themselves to a formal military career that only a third of the required 30,000 came forward, these containing an inevitable disproportion of officers and senior NCOs.

The third factor which served to strengthen the peace process in Mozambique was the greater vulnerability of the MNR leader to external pressure as compared with the UNITA leader, Jonas Savimbi. This was clearly shown on the very eve of the October elections, when Mr Dhlakama suddenly announced that the MNR would boycott the voting process, alleging unfairness to his party in the arrangements. Immediately the MNR leader found himself under pressure from UN and diplomatic representatives in Maputo, from members of the Catholic Church and of the British company Lonrho (who had played key roles in the original peace negotiations) and most important of all from President Mugabe of Zimbabwe and the representatives of the South African President, Nelson Mandela. Lacking backers for his ill-conceived ploy, Mr Dhlakama called off the boycott.

As it turned out—to the surprise of those who thought of the MNR only as a peculiarly brutal guerrilla movement guilty of numerous well-attested atrocities—the MNR did remarkably well in the elections. Of the 4.9 million votes cast in the presidential election, Mr Dhlakama won 33 per cent against 53 per cent for the incumbent Frelimo candidate, Joaquim Chissano, the remaining votes being divided among ten other candidates. In the elections for the 250 seats in the National Assembly, Frelimo won 129 with 44.3 per cent of the votes cast, the MNR 112 (37.8 per cent) and the Democratic Union (the only other party to pass the qualifying threshold of 5 per cent) nine (5.1 per cent). Eleven smaller parties failed to secure representation. Thus re-established as President, Mr Chissano rejected suggestions that he should follow the South African example and form a coalition government of national reconciliation, while Mr Dhlakama said he would accept the role of leader of the opposition.

vi.   ANGOLA

CAPITAL: Luanda   AREA: 1,247,000 sq km   POPULATION: 9,700,000 ('92)
OFFICIAL LANGUAGE: Portuguese   POLITICAL SYSTEM: transitional
HEAD OF STATE & GOVERNMENT: President José Eduardo dos Santos (since '79)
RULING PARTY: Popular Movement for the Liberation of Angola-Workers' Party
   (MPLA-PT) heads nominal coalition
PRINCIPAL MINISTERS: Marcelino Moco (Prime Minister), Col.-Gen. Pedro Maria
   Tonha 'Pedale' (defence), Andre Pitra 'Petroff' (interior), Venancio da Silva
   Moura (external relations), Paulo Tchipilika (justice), José Pedro De Morais
   (planning), Augusto da Silva Tomas (finance)
INTERNATIONAL ALIGNMENT: NAM, OAU, ACP
CURRENCY: kwanza (end-'94 £1=Kw793,011.90, US$1=Kw506,879.00)
GNP PER CAPITA: US$610 ('89)
MAIN EXPORT EARNERS: oil, coffee, diamonds

ON 20 November representatives of the MPLA and Unita signed a peace agreement, known as the Lusaka Protocol, at a ceremony in the Zambian capital attended by a number of African heads of state and other dignitaries. Significantly, although President dos Santos of Angola (MPLA) was present, the Unita leader, Jonas Savimbi, did not attend, claiming that it was too dangerous for him to travel to Zambia. The agreement was the product of months of hard bargaining that had started in Lusaka in November 1993 under the auspices of the UN special representative, Alioune Blondin Beye of Mali. Five days earlier the two sides agreed to a ceasefire to be monitored by the United Nations Angola Verification Mission (UNAVEM II). It was hoped that UNAVEM II would eventually involve the deployment of up to 7,000 UN personnel, whose task would include overseeing the demobilization of the armed forces of the two sides and their merging in a new national army and police force. The peace agreement laid down provisions for 'the adequate participation of Unita members at all levels and in the various institutions of political, administrative and economic activity'. It specified precisely the senior posts to be held by Unita, including four at full ministerial and seven at deputy ministerial level, as well as three provincial governorships and seven deputy governorships.

Both sides had come under international pressure to reach an agreement. A new factor in the situation was the influence of the new South African government under President Mandela, who invited the Presidents of Angola, Mozambique and Zaïre to a summit meeting in Pretoria in July. President Mobutu of Zaïre, the only head of state to provide consistent support for Unita, had not met President dos Santos since the abortive Gbadolite agreement of June 1989 (see AR 1989, pp. 279–80). It was clearly in the interest of all the other governments in southern Africa to see an end to the war in Angola, but the amount of leverage at their disposal was limited. Far more important in bringing the two sides together were developments taking place on the battlefield; even as the negotiators were meeting in Lusaka, heavy fighting continued in many parts of Angola.

At the start of the year Unita had control of an estimated 70 per cent of the country and seemed to be in an immensely powerful position. However, since early 1993 the MPLA government had been busy acquiring new equipment for the Angolan Armed Forces (FAA), total military expenditure between January 1993 and July 1994 being put at $3,500 million (compared with a total of $4,700 million spent on arms in the five years from 1987 to 1991). Russia, maintaining a tradition established by the Soviet Union, was by far the largest source of supply, but substantial purchases were also made in Brazil, North Korea, Portugal, Spain and a number of other countries. The government also began to recruit foreign 'military consultants' for training, security and combat duties, the majority being engaged through a private firm in Pretoria. Another morale-boosting factor was the personality of the Army Chief of Staff, General João de Matos, to whom was ascribed much of the credit for 'the new coherence in the government's military strategy'.

In the first half of the year the major areas of conflict were Cuito and Malanje, where government garrisons were under strong Unita pressure, and Huambo, which had been captured by Unita in March 1993 and made the movement's capital but was regularly bombed by government planes. In July the situation began to change following breakthrough by the garrison in Cuito and a successful government offensive in the diamond-producing north-east, an area of vital economic importance to Unita. In late October came significant government advances in northern Angola, where Unita forces were driven from the important oil town of Soyo and two provincial capitals, Uige and M'Banza Congo. On 10 November government forces recaptured Huambo, which was a particularly significant reverse for Dr Savimbi.

As always, it was the civilian population that suffered most, especially when, because of the fighting, one side or the other denied international relief agencies access to areas where the local population was dependent on outside aid to ward off starvation. A report brought out by Human Rights Watch Africa in November provided detailed evidence of 'the violations of the rules of war' by both sides. These included the aerial bombardment or shelling of civilian populations, the indiscriminate laying of anti-personnel mines, the recruitment of child soldiers, dis-appearances, summary executions and torture.

The civilian population suffered, too, from the massive imbalance in government expenditure: one estimate for 1993 put the government's defence budget at $475 million compared with $18 million set aside for health and $12 million for education. The massive expense of the arms purchases in 1993–94 could be met only by mortgaging the country's revenues for years to come. The task of returning to peace was made all the more difficult for thousands of Angolan peasants by the indiscriminate sowing of mines, especially by Unita, in many agricultural areas.

Within days of the signing of the peace agreement there were reports of breaches of the ceasefire. There was also evidence of divided counsels on both sides, setting hawks against doves and militarists against civilians. Some Unita commanders, reflecting their leader's frequent rhetoric about a 'long march' and the need to contemplate 30 years of war, argued the case for returning to guerrilla tactics in the bush. General de Matos, the architect of the MPLA's recent military successes, dreamt of dealing more hammer blows to finish off the rebels as a fighting force. Some civilian leaders stressed the need for national reconciliation and Dr Savimbi expressed willingness to abide by the peace agreement. But it was noted in Luanda that there was a sharp contrast between public response to the peace agreement of 1991 and that of 1994: the first had been greeted with jubilation and an upsurge of optimism; the second evoked only a mood of sombre scepticism. Desperately war-weary in a war-shattered land, most people found their lives reduced to a grim struggle for survival.

2. ZAMBIA—MALAWI—ZIMBABWE—NAMIBIA—BOTSWANA—SWAZILAND

i. ZAMBIA

CAPITAL: Lusaka   AREA: 750,000 sq km   POPULATION: 8,300,000 ('92)
OFFICIAL LANGUAGE: English   POLITICAL SYSTEM: presidential
HEAD OF STATE & GOVERNMENT: President Frederick Chiluba (since Nov '91)
RULING PARTY: Movement for Multi-Party Democracy (MMD)
PRINCIPAL MINISTERS: Brig.-Gen. Godfrey Miyanda (Vice-President), Benjamin Y. Mwila (defence), Remmy Mushota (foreign affairs), Ronald Penza (finance), Chitalu Sampa (home affairs), Amusa Mwanamwamba (legal affairs)
INTERNATIONAL ALIGNMENT: NAM, OAU, ACP, Cwth.
CURRENCY: kwacha (end-'94 £1=K1,086.63, US$1=K694.55)
GNP PER CAPITA: US$420 ('90)
MAIN EXPORT EARNERS: copper, zinc, cobalt

THE London *Financial Times*, in a special survey published on 24 October, commented: 'Zambia marks the 30th anniversary of independence today in a sombre mood. . . . Mismanagement . . . and misfortune, including regional wars, have taken their toll. Life expectancy is falling, infant mortality is rising, and per capita income is lower today than it was 30 years ago.' According to one recent estimate, 85 per cent of Zambians were living below the poverty datum line. Yet the situation was not entirely bleak. Indeed, the *Financial Times* could describe the economic situation as 'brighter than at any time since the early 1970s'.

The annual inflation rate, having reached 400 per cent in the last years of the Kaunda regime, had fallen to 30 per cent. As a result of the removal of protective tariffs and of foreign exchange controls, consumers could benefit from the inflow of cheaper commodities, especially from Zimbabwe and South Africa, while Zambian producers were forced to adapt to competition. Government revenues were rising, to the satisfaction of aid donors and IMF officials, and a start had been made on privatizing the dominant parastatals although only ten out of some 150 had so far changed hands. In particular, President Chiluba's government had not yet embarked on what was seen as its toughest and most necessary act—the privatization of Zambia Consolidated Copper Mines (ZCCM). The mines were in desperate need of new capital and modern technology, both available only from foreign investors. But privatization would mean many redundancies—probably more than 10,000 of the 50,000-strong workforce, whose members formed the country's labour aristocracy. Moreover, most miners, being Bemba, were of the same ethnic group as the President, and among his most loyal supporters.

Zambians appreciated the greater media freedom than had ever been possible under ex-President Kaunda's form of autocracy, but the lack of progress in improving social services generated an uncomfortable feeling that 'the medicine of the structural adjustment plan might prove too strong for the patient'. The government's standing was seriously affected by the resignation or dismissal of cabinet ministers who had been among the founders of the ruling Movement for Multi-Party Democracy (MMD). Most of the 13 ministers who left office in 1992–94 came from the country's southern provinces, a fact which inevitably gave weight to the charge that the government was dominated by northerners, especially Bemba.

A confusing situation was compounded by allegations of high-level involvement in drug-dealing—for long a profitable activity in a country which had become an important conduit for the channelling of narcotics to the lucrative South African markets. According to the wits of Lusaka, MMD now stood for 'Mass Movement of Drug-dealers'. In this more critical atmosphere, Kenneth Kaunda, so decisively defeated in 1991, began putting himself forward as a potential national saviour. Also prominent was Baldwin Nkumbula (leader of the National Party, whose father Harry had been the most prominent nationalist politician of the early 1950s), who struck a populist note by urging that the mines must always be kept in state hands.

ii. MALAWI

CAPITAL: Lilongwe   AREA: 118,500 sq km   POPULATION: 9,100,000 ('92)
OFFICIAL LANGUAGE: English   POLITICAL SYSTEM: presidential, one-party state
HEAD OF STATE & GOVERNMENT: President Bakili Muluzi (since May '94)
RULING PARTIES: United Democratic Front (UDF) heads coalition with Malawi
    National Democratic Party (MNDP), United Front for Multi-Party Democracy
    (UFMD) & Alliance for Democracy (Aford)
PRINCIPAL MINISTERS: Justin Malewezi (UDF/First Vice-President), Chakufwa
    Chihana (Aford/Second Vice-President), Aleke Banda (UDF/finance, planning &
    development), Edward Bwanali (UDF/external affairs), Peter Fachi (UDF/justice),
    Cassim Chilumpha (UDF/defence), Wenham Nakanga (UDF/home affairs)
INTERNATIONAL ALIGNMENT: NAM, OAU, ACP, Cwth.
CURRENCY: kwacha (end-'94 £1=MK24.08, US$1=MK15.39)
GNP PER CAPITA: US$210 ('92)
MAIN EXPORT EARNERS: tobacco, tea, sugar

'WE have emerged from ruthless oppression disguised as discipline. We have now freed ourselves from the yoke of injustice, corruption and poverty.' Thus, to wildly cheering crowds, did Bakili Muluzi, newly-elected President of Malawi, announce the start of a new era in the country's history at his inauguration in the Kamuzu stadium, Blantyre, on 21 May. It was not just a political event: in what had been one of the most tightly-controlled societies in Africa, there was clearly a deep cultural significance in this moment of liberation for the people of Malawi.

Malawi's first multi-party elections since independence, held on 17 May, were contested by three major parties. The incumbent President, Dr Hastings Kamuzu Banda, in spite of his age (he was officially 88 but probably in his mid-90s) and his recent ill-health, insisted on being the presidential candidate of the Malawi Congress Party (MCP), most of whose supporters lived in the central provinces. Of the two main opposition parties, the Alliance for Democracy (Aford) was as solidly based in the north, while the United Democratic Front (UDF) had equally strong support in the more populous south and also in some of the country's urban centres. The UDF chose as its candidate a wealthy Muslim businessman, Bakili Muluzi, who had been a member of the MCP until 1983 and had held the post of general secretary in the 1970s. Aford's candidate, Chakufwa Chihana, had come to prominence in 1992 when he had made a dramatic call for 'a conference of democratic forces' (see AR 1992, p. 287). In the presidential elections, Mr Muluzi won 47.3 per cent of the vote, Dr Banda 33.6 per cent and Mr Chihana 18.6 per cent. The final results for the 177 seats in the National Assembly (after some re-runs) gave the UDF 86, the MCP 56 and Aford 35. Coalition talks between the UDF and Aford broke down on 1 June, and for a time Aford formed an uneasy partnership with the MCP in opposition. On September 24, however, Mr Chihana joined the government as Second Vice-President and five of his party colleagues were also given ministerial posts.

iii.   ZIMBABWE

CAPITAL: Harare   AREA: 390,000 sq km   POPULATION: 10,400,000 ('92)
OFFICIAL LANGUAGE: English   POLITICAL SYSTEM: presidential
HEAD OF STATE & GOVERNMENT: President Robert Mugabe (since Dec '87),
   previously Prime Minister (since April '80)
RULING PARTY: Zimbabwe African National Union-Patriotic Front (ZANU-PF)
PRINCIPAL MINISTERS: Simon Muzenda (Vice-President), Joshua Nkomo (Vice-
   President), Didymus Mutasa (senior minister, national affairs), Bernard Chidzero
   (senior minister, finance, planning & development), Nathan Shamuyarira
   (foreign affairs), Emmerson Munangagwa (justice), Moven Mahachi (defence),
   Dumiso Dabengwa (home affairs)
INTERNATIONAL ALIGNMENT: NAM, OAU, ACP, Cwth.
CURRENCY: Zimbabwe dollar (end-'94 £1=Z$13.08, US$1=Z$8.36)
GNP PER CAPITA: US$570 ('92)
MAIN EXPORT EARNERS: tobacco, gold, tin, tourism

AFTER two years of drought and recession, 1994 brought a modest upturn in Zimbabwe's economy. GDP rose by 4.5 per cent, bolstered by improved performances across the productive sectors: mining output was up by 5 per cent, manufacturing industry grew 6 per cent and agricultural earnings benefited from improved world prices. Tourism boomed in particular, earning close on Z$1,000 million, a 36 per cent increase on the previous year. In Harare the transformation of the capital's skyline by new high-rise office and shopping complexes—including the architecturally-striking headquarters of both the ruling ZANU-PF party and the Central Reserve Bank—seemed to mirror the economic recovery.

   In the fourth year of the government's five-year Economic Structural Adjustment Programme (ESAP), real benefits were at last evident. In January the Zimbabwean dollar was devalued by 17 per cent and a range of market reforms and trade liberalization measures were introduced to encourage external investment. Further substantial loans (see AR 1993, p. 288), this time from the International Monetary Fund (IMF) and totalling Z$1,100 million, effectively underwrote the country's balance-of-payments deficit and made possible a relaxation in exchange control regulations. Despite the resulting stimulus to business and manufacturing industry, President Mugabe remained strongly critical of the influence of international donors, referring in August to the 'financial imperialism' of the World Bank and the IMF.

   The benefits of the ESAP came at a price, however. Real per capita expenditure on health and education continued to decline, while restrictions on public sector pay awards led to unprecedented labour unrest, including wildcat strikes by such pivotal professional groups as junior doctors, public prosecutors, bank staff and postal workers. Unemployment rose above one million, or 24 per cent of the total workforce. Economic recovery was further compromised by continuing high inflation, which fluctuated between 20 and 25 per cent over the year. The improved financial climate masked the fact that ordinary Zimbabweans faced an increase of more than 100 per cent in the cost of drugs and medical care over 12 months, rises of 27 per cent in the price of food, and an increase of over 30 per cent in the cost of transport. Direct taxation also rose, reaching 45 per cent of personal income.

The government came under repeated criticism for its high-spending, high-borrowing fiscal policy. The budget tabled on 28 July provided for an increase in state spending of Z$20,700 million, a full 15 per cent of GDP, pushing interest rates to levels which inhibited private business investment. Also in July, the government launched a national social security scheme which aimed, in the long term, to provide welfare and pension benefits across the nation. Government-owned utility companies and parastatals continued to devour huge public subsidies while delivering manifestly lacklustre results. The Zimbabwe Electricity Supply Authority (ZESA) recorded substantial losses for the year, while the state steel company (ZISCO), despite having received Z$1,400 million in government funds since 1980, was forced to deny rumours of imminent bankruptcy. The government announced plans for the privatization of parastatals 'as a matter of urgency'.

Despite widespread unpopularity, the government approached the end of its third five-year term with little fear that President Mugabe's ZANU-PF would lose the general election due in spring 1995. It had no effective opposition, and indeed little tolerance of it. The Forum Party, an amalgam of dissident factions (see AR 1993, p. 289), suffered from internal division and indifferent leadership, while the new ZimRights movement, set up to monitor human rights violations, was denounced by the government in June as a 'dangerous organization' and as a 'front for the opposition'. ZANU-PF showed no sign, moreover, that it believed itself vulnerable to the pro-democracy forces that had overthrown the founding nationalist governments of neighbouring Zambia and Malawi. After 14 years of continuous rule, the party had become virtually synonymous with government. It continued to use the outdated formal vocabulary of its marxist-leninist heritage, and moves to drop the honorific title of 'comrade' were quashed. Opponents noted that despite the rhetoric of socialist democracy, the party vetoed any ballot for the posts of president and vice-president at its annual conference in September.

The most momentous event of Zimbabwe's year occurred outside its borders. The April election and advent of majority government in South Africa (see VII.3) reconfigured the geopolitics of the region and placed

Zimbabwe more centrally within the Southern African Development Community (SADC). Welcoming the political transformation of Zimbabwe's neighbour and leading trading partner, President Mugabe made a state visit to South Africa in August. Formal diplomatic relations were established for the first time and the renewal of trade agreements was discussed in the context of existing bilateral exchanges worth a comfortable Z$2,000 million annually. In reality, however, Zimbabwe risked being upstaged by its powerful and sophisticated neighbour, whose return to the international economy introduced a glamorous competitor for international investment.

The perennial issue of land ownership continued to polarize opinion in Zimbabwe (see AR 1992, pp. 290–1; 1993, p. 289). The gradual implementation of the Land Acquisition Bill of 1992 involved the appropriation of some five million hectares from 4,000 mainly white commercial farmers. In April, however, the Catholic Commission for Justice and Peace revealed that 98 farms acquired for resettlement had in fact been leased to government officials and senior civil servants. President Mugabe, apparently innocent of the scandal, responded by compelling the Minister of Lands, Agriculture and Water Development, Kumbirai Kangai, to cancel the leases; but his government remained committed to the land redistribution policy. With agriculture employing 70 per cent of the country's workforce and contributing 22 per cent of GDP, critics of the policy emphasized the fundamental importance of planned farm management and warned of the danger of creating 'a wilderness of seriously overused land'.

The economic progress of a year described as 'very peaceful and stable' by President Mugabe was overshadowed in December by the threat of renewed drought. A two-month delay to the start of the rainy season, together with a plague of army worm in the newly-planted fields, persuaded the Grain Marketing Board to stockpile a million tonnes of maize as insurance against a recurrence of the nightmare conditions that Zimbabwe had faced in 1992.

iv.   NAMIBIA

CAPITAL: Windhoek   AREA: 824,000 sq km   POPULATION: 1,500,000 ('92)
OFFICIAL LANGUAGES: Afrikaans & English   POLITICAL SYSTEM: presidential
   democracy
HEAD OF STATE: President Sam Nujoma (since March '90)
RULING PARTY: South West Africa People's Organization (SWAPO)
PRINCIPAL MINISTERS: Hage Geingob (Prime Minister), Theo-Ben Gurirab
   (foreign affairs), Peter Mueshihange (defence), Hifikepunje Pohamba (home
   affairs), Ngarikutuke Tjiriange (justice), Gerhard Hanekom (finance),
   Andimba Toivo ja Toivo (mines & energy)
INTERNATIONAL ALIGNMENT: NAM, OAU, SADC, Cwth.
CURRENCY: South African rand (end-'94 £1=R5.55, US$1=R3.54)
GNP PER CAPITA: US$1,610 ('92)
MAIN EXPORT EARNERS: minerals

ON 28 February the Walvis Bay enclave and Atlantic port as well as the 12 associated Penguin Islands were transferred from South Africa to Namibia, in accordance with an agreement reached in August 1993 (see AR 1993, pp. 290-1). After months of negotiations involving the South African and Namibian governments as well as representatives of the South African multi-party constitutional talks, the formalities and procedures of the Transfer of Walvis Bay Act had been announced in December 1993. Under the terms of this bill, Walvis Bay's military base was to be taken over by Namibia, South Africans resident in Walvis Bay at the date of the transfer could retain their citizenship, and former South Africans who chose to return to South Africa would be permitted to reapply for citizenship. Following the transfer, in March Namibian President Sam Nujoma opened a free trade zone in the port. Noting that the newly-integrated territory was a strategic gate to the emerging markets of southern and western Africa as well as those of Latin America, Mr Nujoma pointed out Walvis Bay's 'enormous potential to become a major port of container trans-shipment along the Atlantic coast'. Construction of new port facilities began in April and would complement the proposed trans-Kalahari and Caprivi highway schemes linking Namibia with South Africa's commercial hub around Johannesburg and with Botswana, Zambia and Zimbabwe.

The first post-independence elections were held on 7–8 December. Eight political parties met the deadline for registration: the ruling South West Africa People's Organization (SWAPO), the main opposition Democratic Turnhalle Alliance (DTA), the Democratic Coalition of Namibia (DCN), the Monitor Action Group, the United Democratic Front (UDF), the Federal Convention of Namibia, the South West Africa National Union (SWANU) and the Workers' Revolutionary Party. Only two presidential candidates were nominated—President Nujoma for SWAPO and the DTA leader, Mishake Muyongo. In a 76 per cent turnout, SWAPO won 72.7 per cent of the vote and 53 of the 72 Assembly seats (compared with 57 per cent and 41 seats in the pre-independence 1989 election), while the DTA secured 15 seats with 20.4 per cent (against 21 seats and 28 per cent in 1989). Of the other parties, the UDF won two seats and the Monitor Action Group and the DCN one each. Mr Nujoma polled 76.3 per cent in the presidential election.

Its two-thirds Assembly majority gave SWAPO the power to alter the constitution, probably to allow Mr Nujoma to run for a third term and possibly, in the view of some analysts, to turn Namibia into a single-party state. The President had given an undertaking that he would test any such alterations in a nationwide referendum. The election results were contested by the DTA, which accused SWAPO of using state funds to finance its campaign. The Alliance's poor showing reflected its failure to offer alternative ideas and policies during the previous four years, rather than SWAPO's stupendous success in government.

Namibian independence had not emancipated the poor from poverty. After three years of real GDP growth—0.8 per cent in 1990 and 5.6 per cent in both 1991 and 1992—1993 saw a contraction of 3.3 per cent. This was mainly the result of low commodity prices, particularly for diamonds and uranium, although a 3 per cent annual rate of population increase did not help. The unemployment level was estimated at between 35 and 40 per cent during 1994. A five-year national development plan to be implemented in 1995 provided for the revitalization of existing basic sectors, particularly fishing and mining, and an expansion of manufacturing and tourism. The Chevron oil exploration programme off Namibia's southern coast and the creation in November of the NAMDEB diamond partnership between De Beers and the government appeared to bode well for the future.

v.   BOTSWANA

CAPITAL: Gaborone   AREA: 580,000 sq km   POPULATION: 1,400,000 ('92)
OFFICIAL LANGUAGE: English   POLITICAL SYSTEM: presidential democracy
HEAD OF STATE & GOVERNMENT: President Sir Quett Ketumile Masire (since '80)
RULING PARTY: Botswana Democratic Party (BDP)
PRINCIPAL MINISTERS: Festus Mogae (Vice-President, finance, development &
    planning), Ponatshego Kedikilwe (presidential affairs), Lt.-Gen. Mompati Merafhe
    (external affairs), B.K. Temane (home & labour affairs)
INTERNATIONAL ALIGNMENT: NAM, OAU, SADC, ACP, Cwth.
CURRENCY: pula (end-'94 £1=P4.27, US$1=P2.73)
GNP PER CAPITA: US$2,790 ('92)
MAIN EXPORT EARNERS: diamonds, copper-nickel, beef

AFTER landslide victories in all previous general elections since independence from Britain in 1966, Sir Quett Ketumile Masire's ruling Botswana Democratic Party (BDP) won the 15 October poll with a much-reduced majority and 53.1 per cent of the popular vote. Holding all but three seats in the previous 34-member Assembly, the BDP won 26 seats in the expanded 40-seat lower house. The opposition Botswana National Front (BNF) under Kenneth Koma took 13 seats, while one seat remained to be decided later in a by-election. Four of the BNF victories were for key seats in the capital, Gaborone, and the party achieved an impressive 37.7 per cent of the vote.

The swing to the BNF had been widely predicted as a result of rising unemployment, slow economic growth and government corruption scandals. In February it was reported that 14 ministers and MPs owed the National Development Bank the equivalent of about US$1 million in unpaid interest on loans—among them President Masire, who owed nearly $100,000. This and other such revelations prompted the government to establish a Directorate of Corruption and Economic Crime under the direction of a retired British police officer, Graham Stockwell.

Botswana had a history of impressive post-independence economic growth, mainly through the development of diamond and copper-nickel resources, and its accumulated foreign exchange resources of around $4,300 million had enabled it to become the first sub-Saharan African country to lend money to the IMF. However, falling diamond prices (though production remained at record levels), coupled with a sizeable public sector (accounting for about 50 per cent of GDP), resulted in unemployment rising to 21 per cent by August 1994 (up from 14 per cent in 1991) and a slow-down in economic growth to 1.8 per cent in 1993, compared with 4 per cent in 1992.

vi.   LESOTHO

CAPITAL: Maseru   AREA: 30,000 sq km   POPULATION: 1,900,000 ('92)
OFFICIAL LANGUAGES: English & Sesotho
POLITICAL SYSTEM: monarchy
HEAD OF STATE: King Letsie III (since Nov '90)
RULING PARTY: Basotho Congress Party (BCP)
HEAD OF GOVERNMENT: Ntsu Mokhehle, Prime Minister (since April '93)
PRINCIPAL MINISTERS: Moeketsi Senaona (finance & planning), Shakhane Molhlehe (trade, industry & tourism), Lesao Lehohla (home affairs), Kelebone Maope (justice)
INTERNATIONAL ALIGNMENT: NAM, OAU, SADC, ACP, Cwth.
CURRENCY: loti/maloti (end-'94 £1=M5.55, US$1=M3.54)
GNP PER CAPITA: US$590 ('92)
MAIN EXPORT EARNERS: diamonds, wool

HOSTILITIES broke out in January between two factions of the 2,000-strong Royal Lesotho Defence Force (RLDF) over a 100 per cent pay increase demand. This grievance was, however, used as a smokescreen for broader political goals, illustrating the difficulties many in the RLDF had in readjusting to normal life after six years of military rule had been ended by the elections in March 1993 (see AR 1993, pp. 292-3). In this, their dissatisfaction was stirred up by the opposition Basotho National Party (BNP) under Evaristus Sekhonyana, which had suffered a landslide election defeat at the hands of Ntsu Mokhehle's Basotho Congress Party (BCP).

Although the two RLDF sides—the rebel Makoanyane and the loyalist 'Headquarters' factions—ceased fighting early in February, the underlying issues remained unresolved. On 14 April rogue RLDF elements shot dead the Deputy Prime Minister, Selometsi Baholo, and kidnapped four other ministers, although the latter were later released unharmed. Mr Baholo had earlier represented Lesotho at crisis talks convened in Gaborone in January by President Masire of Botswana with the aim of ending the bloodbath. This meeting had also been attended by President Mugabe of Zimbabwe, the then South African

President, Mr F.W. de Klerk, and the South African ANC president, Nelson Mandela.

On 17 August King Letsie III effectively seized power in a royal coup, dismissing Prime Minister Mokhehle and his cabinet. Human rights lawyer Hae Phoofolo was sworn in as chairman of a Provisional Council to rule for 12 months and Mr Sekhonyana was appointed as Minister of Foreign Affairs. It appeared that a request by Mr Mokhehle that southern African leaders should send a peace-keeping force to Lesotho to quell the army uprising lay behind the King's action. The coup provoked an immediate general strike, which ended only when southern African leaders (Presidents Mandela, Mugabe and Masire) opened talks with King Letsie in Pretoria on 23 August in an attempt to defuse the crisis. This was followed in September by the signing of an agreement between Mr Mokhehle and the King restoring the ousted Prime Minister and democratic rule. In November, following a further southern African summit in Pretoria, it was announced that King Letsie's father, King Moshoeshoe II, who had been deposed four years earlier, was to be restored to the throne.

The ongoing instability in Lesotho served to revive suggestions that the kingdom—landlocked and entirely surrounded by South African territory—should become the tenth South African province. Although this concept was provided for originally under the Union of South Africa Act of 1909, apartheid rule in South Africa had made it a non-starter. With the advent of multi-racial democracy, however, incorporation of Lesotho received support from South Africa's National Union of Mineworkers (whose 30,000 Basotho members included its president, James Motlatsi) as well as from some opposition parties in Lesotho, notably the BNP. In May Mr Mokhehle dismissed such ideas, claiming that no particular purpose would be served by a change in Lesotho's status. He did not, however, rule out joint discussions on the boundary issue with South Africa's Orange Free State province.

The motivation of those favouring incorporation appeared to stem from fears of reduced employment prospects for Basotho mineworkers in South Africa. With unemployment in Lesotho having risen from 23 per cent in 1986 to 40 per cent in 1991, the consequences of a reduction in the number of migrant Basotho mineworkers from the current figure of 120,000 were seen as potentially catastrophic. Almost half of Lesotho's GNP was derived from this source, as against 8 per cent from the agricultural sector (employing over 70 per cent of the domestic workforce). On the positive side, phase 1A of the Lesotho Highlands Water Project remained on track for completion in 1996. In addition to yielding substantial royalties for the government and boosting electricity supply, the completed project was expected to create employment and to benefit tourism and communications infrastructure.

vii. SWAZILAND

CAPITAL: Mbabane   AREA: 17,350 sq km   POPULATION: 858,000 ('92)
OFFICIAL LANGUAGES: English & Siswati   POLITICAL SYSTEM: monarchy
HEAD OF STATE & GOVERNMENT: King Mswati III (since '86)
PRINCIPAL MINISTERS: Prince Jameson Mbilini Dlamini (Prime Minister), Shishayi
    Nxumalo (Deputy Prime Minister), Isaac Shabangu (finance), Solomon Dlamini
    (foreign affairs), Prince Sobandla (home affairs), Chief Maweni Simelane (justice)
INTERNATIONAL ALIGNMENT: NAM, OAU, SADC, ACP, Cwth.
CURRENCY: lilangeni/emalangeni (end-'94 £1=E5.55, US$1=E3.54)
GNP PER CAPITA: US$1,090 ('92)
MAIN EXPORT EARNERS: sugar, agricultural products

ALTHOUGH political parties had been banned in Swaziland since 1973, the October 1993 elections to a 65-member lower house (see AR 1993, p. 294) were seen as a stage in the reform of the monarchical *tinkhundla* (traditional) political system and were ultimately expected to result in the adoption of a bill of rights and a freely-elected legislature. Meanwhile, in the absence of a strong parliamentary opposition to the government, this role was taken on in 1994 by Swaziland's trade unions.

From June to August the country was hit by a series of strikes called by unions demanding pay increases and the abandonment of government plans to curb public spending. Provoked by a 47 per cent rise in the monthly transport allowances for cabinet ministers and senior civil servants, the strikes marked the emergence of the unions as a quasi-political opposition to the rule of King Mswati III. Prominent in the movement was the president of the Swaziland National Association of Teachers (SNAT), Meshack Masuku, who publicly questioned the nature of ministerial selection (only six of the 17 ministers being elected MPs). In September the Confederation for Full Democracy in Swaziland (a group of banned Swazi political parties) warned that civil war could ensue if the government did not hold free elections. In November activities at the University of Swaziland were suspended because of political unrest.

In late June the Deputy Prime Minister, Shishayi Nxumalo, announced a nine-point plan to stimulate the economy. These measures included a review of investment and tax incentives, infrastructure, the work permit system and small-business support mechanisms; the creation of an investment centre; deregulation of the economy; the creation of a countrywide marketing strategy; and the renegotiation of border-post hours and visa requirements. Soon afterwards King Mswati inaugurated an economic *vusela* (review) as the next stage in mapping out a long-term economic development strategy.

Swaziland, Mozambique and South Africa signed a cooperation agreement in August aimed at curbing cross-border smuggling, principally of arms and drugs. It was also hoped that the democratic elections in both South Africa and Mozambique would lead to the normalization of transport and trade flows in the region.

3. SOUTH AFRICA

CAPITAL: Pretoria   AREA: 1,220,000 sq km   POPULATION: 39,800,000 ('92)
OFFICIAL LANGUAGES: Afrikaans, English & nine African languages
POLITICAL SYSTEM: transitional multi-racial democracy
HEAD OF STATE & GOVERNMENT: President Nelson Mandela (since May '94)
RULING PARTIES: African National Congress (ANC), National Party (NP) & Inkatha
 Freedom Party (IFP) form government of national unity
PRINCIPAL MINISTERS: Thabo Mbeki (ANC/First Deputy President), F.W. de Klerk
 (NP/Second Deputy President), Alfred Nzo (ANC/foreign affairs), Joe Modise
 (ANC/defence), Dullah Omar (ANC/justice), Chris Liebenberg (ind./finance),
 Roelof ('Pik') Botha (NP/mineral & energy affairs), Chief Mangosuthu Buthelezi
 (IFP/home affairs)
INTERNATIONAL ALIGNMENT: NAM, OAU, SADC, Cwth.
CURRENCY: rand (end-'94 £1=R5.55, US$1=R3.54)
GNP PER CAPITA: US$2,670 ('92)
MAIN EXPORT EARNERS: precious & base metals, minerals

IT was probably the most memorable year in South African history—the year in which 350 years of white domination were finally brought to a close. The reforms begun in 1990 by President F.W. de Klerk of the National Party (NP), including the unbanning of the African National Congress (ANC) and other anti-apartheid parties and the release of political leaders such as Nelson Mandela, had come to final fruition on 22 December 1993 with the enactment in parliament of a constitutional bill providing for full democracy and the election of a government of national unity for a transitional term of five years (see AR 1993, pp. 294-300, 565-71). Four months later, on 26–29 April, voters went to the polls in South Africa's first non-racial democratic elections, which resulted in a massive victory for the ANC and the inauguration of Mr Mandela as President on 10 May.

    The terms of the constitution agreed in late 1993 provided for a Transitional Executive Council, an Independent Electoral Commission (IEC) and an Independent Media Commission to ensure free and fair elections. The bicameral legislative arm was to consist of a National Assembly of 400 members elected by proportional representation (200 from national party lists and 200 from provincial party lists) and a 90-member Senate composed of ten members elected by each of the nine provincial legislature. These two bodies would form a Constituent Assembly, which would decide on the final constitution to take effect after the next elections in 1999.

    Under the transitional constitution, South Africa was divided into nine provinces, namely Western Cape, Northern Cape, Eastern Cape, KwaZulu-Natal, Orange Free State, Pretoria-Witwatersrand-Vereeniging (PWV), North-West, Eastern Transvaal and Northern Transvaal. All the so-called 'bantustans'—the six self-governing and four 'independent' black homelands (Transkei, Bophuthatswana, Venda and Ciskei)—were abolished. Pressure from the right-wing parties for a federal constitution resulted in the provinces being accorded wide-ranging powers, to be exercised by provincial legislatures of between 30 and 100 members. However, national questions such as the environment, economic policy and internal security were reserved for the central government, which also had responsibility for external relations, defence and monetary policy.

The period leading up to the elections was characterized by outbreaks of extreme political violence. The spectre of civil war loomed large between those committed to the interim constitution and a broad opposition grouping designated the Freedom Alliance (FA) and led by General (retd.) Constand Viljoen. The FA consisted of disparate Zulu forces under the leadership of Chief Mangosuthu Buthelezi, leader of the Zulu-based Inkatha Freedom Party (IFP), various black homeland leaders and conservative Afrikaner groups allied within the Afrikaner Volksfront (AVF), including Eugene Terreblanche's paramilitary Afrikaner Resistance Movement (AWB). The violence reached endemic proportions in the early months of 1994, as running battles were waged between IFP-aligned Zulus and more radical ANC activists in the townships of the East Rand and in areas of Natal.

The violence scaled new heights in March when some 5,000 AWB and other Afrikaner forces invaded the north-western homeland of Bophuthatswana in an attempt to prop up the ailing government of Chief Lucas Mangope (an FA member) in the face of ANC-led protests against his decision to boycott the elections. Speedy deployment of South African government troops ensured the failure of the invasion, which witnessed the gunning-down of two wounded AWB prisoners by a Bophuthatswana policeman in full view of the international media. The débâcle served to intensify divisions between the AWB and General Viljoen, who broke ranks with the AVF and formed the Freedom Front (FF), which promptly registered for the elections. This split was a major setback for the broader FA, from which it never recovered in 1994.

The extent of violence was brought home to ordinary South Africans on 28 March when an IFP march past the ANC headquarters in the centre of Johannesburg, to demonstrate support for King Goodwill Zwelithini of the Zulus, degenerated into wholesale slaughter. In a gun-battle involving police, marchers and sharpshooters firing from buildings, over 30 marchers were killed and nearly 300 injured. The Law and Order Minister, Hernus Kriel, responded by immediately declaring 11 magisterial districts around Johannesburg to be areas of unrest. In April, moreover, a state of emergency was declared in KwaZulu-Natal in a bid to halt the spiral of violence. All this made the inclusion of the IFP in the electoral process seem most unlikely as polling day approached.

However, to the amazement and relief of most South Africans, all the major actors agreed in the end to participate in the April elections. Although the Conservative Party under Ferdi Hartzenberg maintained

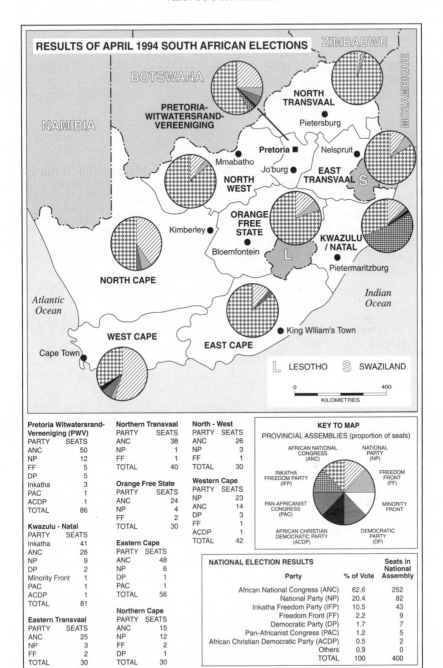

RESULTS OF APRIL 1994 SOUTH AFRICAN ELECTIONS

Pretoria Witwatersrand-Vereeniging (PWV)

PARTY	SEATS
ANC	50
NP	12
FF	5
DP	5
Inkatha	3
PAC	1
ACDP	1
TOTAL	86

Kwazulu - Natal

PARTY	SEATS
Inkatha	41
ANC	26
NP	9
DP	2
Minority Front	1
PAC	1
ACDP	1
TOTAL	81

Eastern Transvaal

PARTY	SEATS
ANC	25
NP	3
FF	2
TOTAL	30

Northern Transvaal

PARTY	SEATS
ANC	38
NP	1
FF	1
TOTAL	40

Orange Free State

PARTY	SEATS
ANC	24
NP	4
FF	2
TOTAL	30

Eastern Cape

PARTY	SEATS
ANC	48
NP	6
DP	1
PAC	1
TOTAL	56

Northern Cape

PARTY	SEATS
ANC	15
NP	12
FF	2
DP	1
TOTAL	30

North - West

PARTY	SEATS
ANC	26
NP	3
FF	1
TOTAL	30

Western Cape

PARTY	SEATS
NP	23
ANC	14
DP	3
FF	1
ACDP	1
TOTAL	42

NATIONAL ELECTION RESULTS

Party	% of Vote	Seats in National Assembly
African National Congress (ANC)	62.6	252
National Party (NP)	20.4	82
Inkatha Freedom Party (IFP)	10.5	43
Freedom Front (FF)	2.2	9
Democratic Party (DP)	1.7	7
Pan-Africanist Congress (PAC)	1.2	5
African Christian Democratic Party (ACDP)	0.5	2
Others	0.9	0
TOTAL	100	400

its boycott, many right-wing Afrikaners were brought into the process through the creation of General Viljoen's FF. Moreover, after an unsuccessful international attempt led by Dr Henry Kissinger and Lord Carrington to mediate between the government, Mr Mandela and Chief Buthelezi, a last-ditch effort facilitated by Kenyan academic Washington Okhumu and the South African Consultative Business Movement secured the IFP's agreement to participate only a week before polling. This meant that the 40 million ballot papers (which had been printed in the United Kingdom) had to be reprinted, further complicating already complex arrangements.

Afrikaner diehards launched a bombing campaign just before the elections, killing 21 people in separate attacks, including one on Johannesburg's Jan Smuts airport and another on the ANC regional office in the city. Nevertheless, the polling process was characterized by enormous goodwill, with over 19.7 million people turning out to vote, some queuing for up to ten hours to cast their ballots. Under the spotlight of the international media and several thousand Commonwealth and international election observers, the main voting exercise on 27 April (following balloting by the elderly, infirm and pregnant on 26 April) was extended for two further days in light of chaotic delays at polling stations. Counting also proved to be slow, the final results not being announced by the IEC chairman, Justice Johan Kriegler, until 6 May.

The ANC received an overwhelming majority, winning 62.6 per cent of the votes cast and 252 seats in the 400-member National Assembly, although short of the two-thirds majority needed to rewrite the constitution forthwith. The NP gained 82 seats with a 20.4 per cent slice of the overall vote, just sufficient to to ensure the appointment of Mr de Klerk as one of the two Deputy Presidents, the other being the ANC's Thabo Mbeki. The IFP won 10.5 per cent and 43 Assembly seats, while General Viljoen's FF came in next with nine seats (2.2 per cent), followed by the moderate Democratic Party with seven (1.7 per cent), the Pan-Africanist Congress with five (1.2 per cent) and the African Christian Democratic Party with two (0.5 per cent). None of a collection of smaller parties—which included the Soccer Party, the Federal Party, the Women's Rights Peace Party, the African Muslim Party, the African Moderates Congress Party, the Luso-South African Party, the Minority Front Party, the Workers' List Party, the African Democratic Movement and the Keep it Straight and Simple Party (KISS)—managed to secure representation. In the simultaneous elections for the nine provincial legislatures, the ANC obtained majorities in seven, the exceptions being KwaZulu-Natal, where the IFP was declared the winner, and Western Cape, which was won by the NP.

On 10 May Nelson Mandela was inaugurated as President of South Africa. International guests from 180 national delegations included

Prince Philip representing Queen Elizabeth (the head of the Common-wealth), US Vice-President Al Gore and first lady Hillary Clinton, Prime Minister Benazir Bhutto of Pakistan, PLO leader Yassir Arafat and President Fidel Castro of Cuba. During the gala event, held at the Union Buildings in Pretoria and attended by 60,000 people, President Mandela addressed the nation, urging South Africans to forge a 'rainbow nation at peace with itself'. Declaring that hope had been implanted in the breasts of millions of people, he continued: 'We enter into a covenant that we shall build the society in which all South Africans, both black and white, will be able to walk tall, without any fear in their hearts, assured of their inalienable right to human dignity.' At a later VIP luncheon, the new President said that the new government would rely on persuasion and not on the brute force of the past to rebuild the nation.

In the post-election government of national unity, the ANC took 18 of the 27 ministerial posts, including the portfolios of defence, foreign affairs, justice, labour, land affairs, public enterprises, public works, and trade and industry, and nine of the 13 deputy minister posts. The NP was represented by six ministers (responsible for finance, agriculture, constitutional development and provincial affairs, environmental affairs and tourism, mineral and energy affairs, and welfare and population development) and by three deputy ministers. As the third participating party, the IFP was allocated three ministerial portfolios (including home affairs) and one deputy minister. The new government included representatives of all of South Africa's main racial groups.

Following the successful conclusion of the elections, South Africa was quickly accepted back into the international community, taking its seat in the UN General Assembly in June (see XI.1), rejoining the Commonwealth in July (see XI.2) and gaining admission to the OAU in May and the Southern African Development Community in August (see XI.6.i). All remaining sanctions, including the UN arms embargo, were lifted in May. President Mandela's first official visit abroad was to Mozambique in July, though he maintained an active schedule throughout the year, including trips to Tunis to address the June OAU summit and to the United States in October. In July President Mitterrand of France became the first head of state to visit South Africa since the election, this being interpreted by some as an attempt by Paris to gain Pretoria's support for the French intervention in Rwanda (see II.1.ii; VII.1.ii). In September the UK Prime Minister, John Major, addressed parliament in Cape Town, some 34 years after the last British Prime Minister to visit South Africa, Harold Macmillan, had delivered his famous 'wind of change' speech in the same house (see AR 1960, pp. 2, 86-7).

While the new South Africa, and the President in particular, main-tained a high profile abroad, inside the country there were growing rumblings of discontent, elements of which were foreshadowed by a warning from the Congress of South African Trade Unions (COSATU) that its alliance with the ANC had been purely for electoral purposes. The month of July saw an escalation in labour disputes in various industries across the country, including a six-week strike by 25,000 motor assembly workers and other disputes involving a major retail chain, the mining sector and court interpreters. Threatened strikes in the public service, including the police force, failed to materialize in 1994, but the issues involved carried over into the new year. The new Public Service Ministry faced seemingly impossible tasks: not only to create a new service from the 15 administrations inherited from the previous government but also to implement affirmative action policies on behalf of non-whites while reducing the size of the bureaucracy—all this without dismissing any of the 1.2 million incumbent public employees. Alongside demands for salary parity from existing employees, over 1.3 million applications were received for the 11,000 affirmative action posts on offer.

The redressing of imbalances in government departments was illustrated by the appointment of 16 new ambassadors in December. Yet this process was fraught with controversy. Of the 16 new posts, 11 went to ANC members, three to career diplomats in the Department of Foreign Affairs (DFA), one to the former leader of the Democratic Party (Dr Zach de Beer) and one to a notable of the former homeland of KaNgwane. Soon after the appointments were announced, however, two of the three DFA appointees were reallocated. More controversially, the ambassadorial appointment of the former leader of the ANC in Western Cape, Dr Allan Boesak, was suspended pending further inquiries into allegations of financial misappropriation in his Foundation for Peace and Justice.

The reconstruction and integration of the security forces, which had been expected to be complicated by emotional issues and unrealizable aspirations, proceeded relatively smoothly until former members of the ANC's military wing, Umkhonto we Sizwe (Spear of the Nation), staged a stike in October at the Wallmannsthal training camp north of Pretoria. The mutinous elements objected to their alleged shabby treatment in the new South African National Defence Force (SANDF), being formed as an amalgamation of the old South African Defence Force with ANC and PAC former guerrillas; but they were given short shrift by President Mandela. Those refusing to return to barracks were given the choice of returning within seven days or being cashiered. Over 2,000 were subsequently discharged. The annual defence budget rose from R 10,700 million to R 12,000 million to accommodate integration costs. The former ANC chief of staff, Siphiwe Nyanda, was appointed as acting Chief of Staff of the new SANDF in July.

Political stability was seen by the new government to be unavoidably linked to social and economic improvement for non-whites, in which context the ANC's reconstruction and development programme (RDP) became the country's economic blueprint. The RDP proposed to make amends for the years of apartheid by building one million houses, electrifying 2.5 million dwellings, providing free and compulsory education for all children, creating 2.5 million jobs and redistributing 30 per cent of all arable land in the next five years. In his State of the Nation address at the opening of parliament on 24 May, President Mandela committed his government to financial restraint and cooperation with the private sector. As the first stage of the RDP, he announced the provision of free medical care for young children and a primary school feeding scheme, these being the key areas in the initial allocation of R 2.500 million to the programme. In September the ANC Minister without Portfolio, Jay Naidoo, unveiled further RDP projects that would cost R 3,000 million, while in December the government allocated a total of R 6,000 million to the RDP for the period 1995–96.

Despite assurances of economic support from the United States, Britain, France, Japan and Canada, continuing political and criminal violence mitigated against the promised flow of foreign investment to South Africa. Although fewer policemen were killed in 1994 than 1993 (228 as opposed to 271), labour militancy and uncertainty about government investment and financial policies (especially the two-tier rand system) were powerful negative factors. The susceptibility of the South African financial markets to international opinion was illustrated by the damaging effect of the resignation announcement of Derek Keys (NP) as Finance Minister in July, only two weeks after he had presented the new budget. President Mandela moved quickly to limit further damage to the value of the rand by replacing him with former Nedbank chief, Chris Liebenberg, with effect from October.

Although President Mandela opened South Africa's first international defence show on 22 November, thereby demonstrating government support for the armaments industry, ministers were torn between the economic benefits of expanding arms sales and the morality of doing so. This issue was heightened by sittings in November and December of the Cameron commission of inquiry into the controversial export of South African weapons to Yemen earlier in the year and by the resultant publication of details of arms exports during the apartheid years.

The year ended with an agreement in principle by the cabinet that South Africa should assist in UN peace-keeping operations in Angola (see VII.1.vi). At the same time, there were growing fears about the negative economic and political effects of illegal immigration into the country from neighbouring states. While the government attempted to maintain a friendly and open image with its neighbours, conversely it became increasingly likely to employ harsh methods of control against illegal trade and immigrants.

Signals of growing discontent among ANC supporters at the slow pace of government action on black upliftment were evident from the outcome of the party's national conference held in Bloemfontein in December. Militant members swept the board in elections for the ANC national executive committee, the first five places being taken by General Bantu Holomisa, Pallo Jordan (Minister of Posts, Telecommunications and Broadcasting), Peter Mokaba (an Assembly member), Mac Maharaj (Transport Minister) and Winnie Mandela (Deputy Minister of Arts, Culture, Science and Technology), the estranged wife of the President.

While 1994 was a year of historic change and hope for the future, it was clear at its close that the post-election honeymoon was over. In retrospect, perhaps, South Africans of various shades had expected both too little and too much. Violent revolution did not occur, as many had feared, but neither did the massive inflow of foreign investment previously anticipated as South Africa's reward for finding a political solution to its internal conflict.

VIII SOUTH ASIA AND INDIAN OCEAN

1. IRAN—AFGHANISTAN—CENTRAL ASIAN REPUBLICS

i. IRAN

CAPITAL: Tehran AREA: 1,650,000 sq km POPULATION: 59,600,000 ('92)
NATIONAL LANGUAGE: Farsi (Persian) POLITICAL SYSTEM: Islamic republic
SPIRITUAL LEADER: Ayatollah Seyed Ali Khamenei (since June '89)
HEAD OF STATE & GOVERNMENT: President (Hojatolislam) Hashemi Ali Akbar
  Rafsanjani (since July '89)
OTHER MEMBERS OF PRESIDENCY: Seyed Mohammed Mir-Mohammedi (Deputy
  President), Hassan Ebrahim Habibi (First Vice-President), Seyed Mohajerani
  (Vice-President, legal and parliamentary affairs), Massoud Roghani Zanjani
  (Vice-President, planning and budget), Reza Amrollahi (Vice-President, atomic
  energy), Massoud Razavi (Vice-President, state employment), Mehdi Manafi
  (Vice-President, environment), Seyed Mostafa Hashemi-Taba (Vice-President,
  physical education), Hossain Moussavi (domestic & foreign policy adviser),
  Seyed Mansur Razawi (administrative affairs adviser), Seyed Hoseyn Marashi
  (head of presidential office)
PRINCIPAL MINISTERS: Ali Akbar Velayati (foreign affairs), Mohammed Forouzandeh
  (defence), Morteza Mohammed Khan (economic affairs & finance), Gholamreza
  Agazadeh (oil), Ali Mohammed Besharati (interior & security), Hojatolislam
  Ismail Shostari (justice)
INTERNATIONAL ALIGNMENT: NAM, OPEC, ICO, ECO
CURRENCY: rial (end-'94 £1=Rls2,705.50, US$1=Rls1,729.31)
GNP PER CAPITA: US$2,200 ('92)
MAIN EXPORT EARNERS: oil & gas, carpets

INTERNAL political divisions between the factions constituting the
Islamic regime were exacerbated in 1994. The position of President
Ali Akbar Rafsanjani came under direct threat. On 1 February five
shots were fired at the President during a ceremony at the mausoleum
of Ayatollah Khomeini. He was uninjured but the incident served to
underline the growing frustrations among the population at the regime's
failure to advance political development. Stalemate existed between
the President, who wished for speedier economic change within the
country, and hardliners who perceived the political and religious costs of
modernization to be a threat to the stability of the revolutionary republic.
Hashemi Rafsanjani also suffered from the enforced resignation of his
brother as head of the state broadcasting authority in February.

To add to the government's difficulties, there was a major terrorist
incident at the shrine of the Imam Riza in Meshhed on 10 June,
when at least 24 people died and 70 persons were injured. Although
attributed to the opposition Mujahideen Khalq (MKO), the explosion
was probably the work of Iranian Sunni groups seeking revenge for the
regime's destruction of their religious properties. August brought rioting
in the western city of Qazvin, which was denied status as a full province
with an independent budget in a Majlis vote early in the month. Feeling

over the provincial issue and latent dissatisfaction with the regime for other political and economic causes rapidly spilled over into a fullscale emergency. Hashemi Rafsanjani attempted to secure his own future as President by proposing an amendment to the constitution which would enable him to stand for a third term in the presidential elections in 1997.

In December the regime faced a serious crisis as a result of the death of Grand Ayatollah Araki, who was the premier cleric in the Shia world. Ayatollah Ali Khamenei, the official spiritual guide (*rahbar*) in Iran, was put forward as a successor, largely in order to secure religious supremacy for the regime. However, Iranian and other Shia schools were not in favour of this arrangement—opposition which left the Iranian government looking unconvincing as a form of 'government of God' in the Khomeini mould, while Ayatollah Khamenei appeared to be publicly discountenanced. This was the second occasion within a year that the weakness of the regime's Islamic credentials had been exposed (see AR 1993, p. 302).

Iranian isolation from the world community persisted in 1994. The US State Department officials again denounced Iran as an outlaw country on grounds of its support for international terrorism, its poor record on human rights and its opposition to the Middle East peace process through its links with Hizbullah and Hamas. Diplomatic conflicts with Britain arose over allegations that the Iranian authorities had given succour to the IRA, a round of tit-for-tat expulsions of diplomats following in May. In mid-year John Major (UK Prime Minister) accused Iran of being a terrorist state, although UK-Iranian strains over the Salman Rushdie issue faded somewhat. Iran's relations with the rest of the European Union were also difficult. France made concessions to Iran in January when two Iranians wanted in Switzerland on murder charges were repatriated to Tehran. France also sought to play down the political importance of the trial in September of three Iranians accused of being implicated in the murder of former Prime Minister Shapour Bakhtiar in 1991.

In the Middle East region Iranian policies of rapprochement with the Arab states made little progress. In March Iran disputed with Saudi Arabia a reduced quota of annual *hadj* pilgrims allocated to Iran; Saudi Arabia was also criticized by the Iranian leadership for its intervention in the Yemeni civil war. Iran's conflict with the United Arab Emirates over the ownership of the Persian Gulf islands of Abu Musa and the two Tunbs remained unresolved, the UAE Interior Minister calling in August for Iran to accept international arbitration on the dispute. Relations with Turkey were damaged in January when Turkish aircraft bombed Kurdish-populated Iranian villages in the north-west border area, as a result of which Iran submitted a claim for $1 million in damages. Allegations in the Turkish press that Iran was actively involved in training Turkish Islamic terrorists and that the Iranian embassy in Ankara was involved in supporting terrorist operations in Turkey were denied in Iran.

Iran took an ambivalent stance with respect to Iraq. Masoud Barzani, leader of the Kurdistan Democratic Party (KDP), visited Tehran in October to thank Iranians for their support for the Kurds' struggle against the Baghdad regime. In November Iranian troops intruded into Iraqi territory in pursuit of MKO guerrillas and the Iranian air force bombed MKO bases in Iraq, provoking strong Iraqi protests. On the other hand, Ali Akbar Velayati (Iranian Foreign Minister) called in September for the United Nations to lift its embargo against Iraq. A bright note for foreign policy was the attendance of an Iranian delegation led by Hojatolislam Mohammed Taskhiri at the World Population Conference held in Cairo in September (see XI.1). Iranian delegates were well received and their contributions to the debate widely acclaimed. Elsewhere in the Middle East area, Iranian opposition to the Arab–Israeli peace process engendered a great deal of antipathy in Arab government circles, including the PLO. Speaking at the UN General Assembly in September, Ali Akbar Velayati condemned the peace process as contrary to natural justice and doomed to failure.

Iran's internal political weakness and its meagre successes in foreign policy were as nothing, however, in comparison with its domestic economic difficulties. In September oil exports were running at an average of 2.6 million barrels per day (b/d), from an output of 3.6 million b/d, barely matching the average for 1993. The oil price rose in the mid-year period, to give some increment in oil income, but overall the forecast for oil revenues in 1994 was less than $12,000 million. The seriousness of the position was recognized by the Majlis in January when the 1993/94 (Iranian year) budget forecast for oil revenues was $10,500 million within total expenditures of the equivalent of $39,000 million, of which $18,500 million represented the general state budget. Even even this austerity budget appeared to be at risk of carrying a large deficit, since the government's access to new credits was restricted by its deteriorating credit-worthiness. Iranian foreign debt stood at $32,000 million and the country faced a worsening balance-of-payments problem, symptomized by late payment on letters of credit for imports and the rescheduling of sovereign debt. German banks and trading companies alone rescheduled DM 5,300 million of debt during the year.

The Iranian rial continue to lose value. Its official rate against the US dollar in November was at 1,749, but it was trading at 2,750 on the free market. An attempt on 1 October to stop illegal trading in foreign exchange appeared to fail entirely. The government relinquished many of its subsidies on essential products in the face of the financial crisis, but in November proposed subsidizing and controlling the prices of a residual 23 items, including wheat, flour and bread. Inflation persisted at over 50 per cent during the year, inflamed by rising import prices and the shortage of housing in urban areas. There was exasperation among the mass of the population at the deteriorating economic situation and continuing falls in personal incomes. As a signpost to an improving future, the Majlis in November promised to implement the second five-year plan (1995–2000), involving expenditure of $80,000 million at the free market exchange rate. Some two million new jobs were to be created and the base of the economy diversified away from oil. Meanwhile, in part making good the shortcomings of the public sector, private enterprise, aided by some piecemeal privatization, expanded in 1994, with both small-scale industry and farming generally experiencing a growth in output.

ii.   AFGHANISTAN

CAPITAL: Kabul   AREA: 650,000 sq km   POPULATION: 21,500,000 ('92 est.)
OFFICIAL LANGUAGES: Pushtu, Dari (Persian)   POLITICAL SYSTEM: presidential
HEAD OF STATE & GOVERNMENT: President Burhanuddin Rabbani (since June '92)
PRINCIPAL MINISTERS: Arsalan Rahmani (acting Prime Minister), Ahmed Shah
    Ahmedzay (Second Deputy Premier), Najibullah Lafraie (foreign affairs),
    Ahmad Rashid Irshadi (finance), Gen. Mohammed Younis Qanouni (defence,
    acting), Monshi Abdolmajid (interior, acting)
INTERNATIONAL ALIGNMENT: NAM, ICO
CURRENCY: afghani (end-'94 £1=Af5,414.45, US$1=Af3,460.82)
GNP PER CAPITA: US$168 ('82)
MAIN EXPORT EARNERS: agricultural products

CIVIL war continued to convulse Afghanistan. Throughout 1994 competing mujahideen factions continued to litter Kabul with dead bodies and piles of rubble. Several years after the abject Soviet troop withdrawal from Afghanistan in February 1989, there was no noticeable peace dividend for a land which remained a single country only theoretically.

In the continuing battle for Kabul, the opportunist warlord Abdul Rashid Dostam, of Uzbek origin, withdrew his support from President Burhanuddin Rabbani (in office since June 1992) and deployed his forces in support of the President's bitterest opponent, Prime Minister Gulbuddin Hekmatyar. Despite several peace efforts by Afghan and international bodies, the fighting showed no signs of coming to an end. Over 12,000 were killed, tens of thousands were wounded and hundreds of thousands abandoned the capital, which was almost razed to the ground by rocket and artillery fire. There was no functioning economy across most of the country and starvation was rife. Kabul's infrastructure was destroyed, there being no water, telephone or electricity for much of the year. Following the well-nigh complete withdrawal of UN and national diplomatic personnel, only a few international aid agencies remained to make occasional distributions of food and first aid.

Military alliances between warlords, once formed substantially on the basis of ethnic or religious affiliation, now seemed to spring almost entirely from opportunism and a desire to obtain more power. In addition, the country's territory was increasingly used as a base for Tajik guerrillas attempting to spread Islamic militancy in the ex-Soviet Central Asian republics, especially in Uzbekistan.

Afghanistan's more westerly northern neighbour, Turmenistan, was emerging as the principal regional focus for new links to the south, including a proposed railway through western Afghanistan to Pakistan. Some regarded this idea as impractical, in that Afghanistan had no railways and was still plagued by civil war. But Pakistani officials claimed that in discussions on the proposal they had received promises of support from the Afghan tribal chiefs in control of the relevant areas and pointed out that western Afghanistan had been relatively peaceful in recent years. The existing road connecting Pakistan with Turkmenistan through Afghanistan, via Kandakar and Herat, was in bad condition. Pakistan sent a convoy of goods along the road to arrive for Prime Minister Benazir Bhutto's visit to Turkmenistan in early November. This and earlier such exercises helped Pakistani experts to estimate that $300 million needed to be spent on the road.

The continuing civil war in Afghanistan in 1994 not only prevented the country from rejoining the international community and from making a start on economic reconstruction; it also contributed considerably to the destabilization of the Central Asian region as a whole. Afghan guerrilla veterans were, moreover, reported to be active in the ranks of armed Islamic extremist forces in Algeria, Lebanon and former Yugoslavia.

In the last quarter of 1994 a hitherto unknown fighting force called the Taleban emerged in Afghanistan, based in the Pakistan border area. Consisting mainly of former students and fiercely opposed to the Kabul regime, it quickly demonstrated a combination of military prowess and uncompromising Islamic fundamentalism.

iii.   KAZAKHSTAN—TURKMENISTAN—UZBEKISTAN—KYRGYZSTAN—TAJIKISTAN

Kazakhstan

CAPITAL: Almaty   AREA: 2,717,300 sq km   POPULATION: 17,000,000 ('92)
OFFICIAL LANGUAGE: Kazakh   POLITICAL SYSTEM: republic
RULING PARTY: Congress of People's Unity of Kazakhstan (CPUK)
HEAD OF STATE & GOVERNMENT: President Nursultan Nazarbayev
PRINCIPAL MINISTERS: Akezhan Kazhageldin (Prime Minister), Kasymzhomart Takayev (foreign affairs), Col.-Gen. Sagadat Nurmabagambetov (defence), Bulat Bayekenov (interior), Nagashibay Shaykenov (justice), Aleksandr Pavlov (finance), Nurlan Balgynbayev (oil & gas)
CURRENCY: tenge/rouble   GNP PER CAPITA: US$1,680 ('92)

Turkmenistan

CAPITAL: Ashgabat   AREA: 448,100 sq km   POPULATION: 3,900,000 ('92)
OFFICIAL LANGUAGE: Turkmen   POLITICAL SYSTEM: republic
RULING PARTY: Democratic Party of Turkmenistan (DPT)
HEAD OF STATE & GOVERNMENT: President (Gen.) Saparmurad Niyazov
PRINCIPAL MINISTERS: Khan Akhmedov (Prime Minister), Boris Shikhmyradov
    (Deputy Premier, foreign affairs), Hakim Ishanov (Deputy Premier, oil & gas),
    Lt-Gen. Danatar Kopekov (defence), Kurban Mukhamed Kasimov (interior),
    Tagandurdy Halliev (justice), Mukhamed Abalakhov (economics & finance)
CURRENCY: manat   GNP PER CAPITA: US$1,230 ('92)

Uzbekistan

CAPITAL: Tashkent   AREA: 447,400 sq km   POPULATION: 21,500,000 ('92)
OFFICIAL LANGUAGE: Uzbek   POLITICAL SYSTEM: republic
RULING PARTY: People's Democratic Party (PDP)
HEAD OF STATE & GOVERNMENT: President Islam Karimov
PRINCIPAL MINISTERS: Abdulhashim Mutalov (Prime Minister), Bakhtiar Hamidov
    (Deputy Premier, finance), Abdulaziz Komilov (foreign affairs), Maj.-
    Gen. Rustan Ahmadov (defence), Vyacheslav Kamalov (interior), M. Abdusalamov
    (justice)
CURRENCY: sum   GNP PER CAPITA: US$850 ('92)

Kyrgyzstan

CAPITAL: Bishkek   AREA: 198,500 sq km   POPULATION: 4,500,000 ('92)
OFFICIAL LANGUAGE: Kyrgyz   POLITICAL SYSTEM: republic
RULING PARTY: Democratic Movement of Kyrgyzstan (DMK)
HEAD OF STATE & GOVERNMENT: President Askar Akayev
PRINCIPAL MINISTERS: Apas Jumagulov (Prime Minister), Roza Otunbayeva (foreign
    affairs), Kamchibek Shakirov (finance), Col. Madalbek Moldashev (internal
    affairs), Mukar Cholponbayev (justice), Murzakan Subanov (defence)
CURRENCY: som   GNP PER CAPITA: US$820 ('92)

Tajikistan

CAPITAL: Dushanbe   AREA: 143,100 sq km   POPULATION: 5,600,000 ('92)
OFFICIAL LANGUAGE: Tajik   POLITICAL SYSTEM: republic
RULING PARTY: People's Party of Tajikistan(PPT)
HEAD OF STATE & GOVERNMENT: President Imamali Rakhmanov
PRINCIPAL MINISTERS: Jamshed Karimov (Prime Minister), Talbak Nazarov (foreign
    affairs), Maj.-Gen. Aleksandr Shlyapnikov (defence), Yakub Salimov (interior),
    Anvarsho Muzaffurov (finance), Shavkat Ishmoilov (justice)
CURRENCY: rouble   GNP PER CAPITA: US$490 ('92)

IN all five ex-Soviet Central Asian republics attempts were made in 1994
to give the electorate the opportunity to express its opinion through
the ballot box. In practice, however, these efforts were, in most cases,
marred by serious procedural shortcomings.

On 15 January the Turkmen public was invited to take part in
a nationwide referendum on the question of whether or not the
President, Saparmurad Niyazov, should be granted a five-year extension
to his term of office; the result was a 99.5 per cent vote in favour,
uncomfortably reminiscent of the unanimous votes of the Soviet period.
The referendum held in Kyrgyzstan on 30 January, asking whether or not
the citizens of the Republic wanted President Akayev to remain in office
until the end of his legally-stipulated term, elicited a similarly monolithic
96 per cent 'yes' vote; subsequent analysis of the results suggested that
there had been a high level of vote-rigging in the provinces.

The Kazakhstan parliamentary elections, held on 7 March, also came in for much criticism. The CSCE observers noted that up to a third of the votes had been cast by proxy and should therefore have been disallowed. Other irregularities included harassment of candidates of whom the government did not approve in the run-up to the elections and blocking of media access to polling stations. Of the 177 seats in the new parliament, only 23 were won by deputies who seemed likely to constitute an opposition faction. The ethnic balance was biased in favour of the titular group: Kazakhs won approximately 66 per cent of the seats (although representing only 44 per cent of the total population) and Russians around 28 per cent (although forming 36 per cent of the population); the remainder of the seats were won by minority groups (Ukrainians, Germans and Jews).

The presidential elections in Tajikistan, held on 6 November, were even more problematic. The only candidates were the incumbent head of state, Imamali Rakhmanov, and the former Prime Minister, Abdumalik Abdullozhonov. International agencies refused to send observers on the grounds that it would have been well-nigh impossible to ensure a fair election when so much of the country was controlled by gun law. Support for the two candidates was divided along traditional clan/regional lines, the power base of Mr Rakhmanov being in the south and that of Mr Abdullozhonov in the north. The former won by a relatively narrow (in Central Asian terms) 25 per cent margin; nevertheless, the rival faction immediately claimed that there had been gross violations of the electoral law and blatant falsification of the results.

The Turkmen parliamentary elections, held on 11 December, were a much calmer affair—an occasion for feasting and merry-making rather than for expressing dissident opinions. Only one seat out of 50 was contested by more than one candidate, so the victory of the ex-communist Democratic Party of Turkmenistan was a foregone conclusion. The only republic to break the mould of predictable voting in accordance with government preferences was Uzbekistan. In the parliamentary elections held on 25 December, although two-thirds of the candidates were drawn from the President's People's Democratic Party (the erstwhile Communist Party), preliminary end-of-year estimates suggested that the electorate had voted overwhelmingly in favour of independents from the provinces.

The economic decline of the five republics remained acute, but in the course of the year there were signs of a tentative stabilization in some areas. In July the Uzbek government phased in the sum as the national currency unit, replacing the transitional sum-coupons which had been in circulation since late 1993. At the same time, determined efforts were made by Uzbekistan to implement the monetarist policies recommended by the IMF. These included firm limits to the amount of cash in circulation, the capping of wages, the lowering of tax rates combined with a widening of the tax base, and a drive to establish convertibility through the relatively free sale of dollars. Commercial and foreign banks were granted a six-month tax holiday (until 1 January 1995). The first stage of the privatization programme (housing and small enterprises) was accomplished smoothly and according to schedule, although the second stage, that of larger enterprises, encountered some difficulties, mostly the result of an inadequate infrastructure.

In Turkmenistan, tight controls on economic policy were also maintained. A privatization programme was introduced in January, whereby the trade and services sectors were scheduled to be given over to private ownership by the end of the year. On the whole, progress was satisfactory. President Niyazov recognized that privatization of industry would mean large-scale unemployment, but introduced measures to minimize the social burden. In Kyrgyzstan, the national currency (the som) introduced in May 1993 maintained its value against the dollar better than the other Central Asian currencies, but this was in large part due to exceptionally lenient IMF and World Bank credits, which provided a seemingly limitless supply of dollars at currency auctions. Nevertheless, President Akayev had hoped for more aid and was displeased by the stringent terms laid down by donor governments; some of the latter accused the Kyrgyz government of abusing the funds that had already been provided. A more encouraging development was the signature by the Kyrgyz government, after months of dispute and hesitation, of a general agreement with the Canadian mining firm Cameco for development of the Kumtor gold field. Progress in other areas, however, was slower. The privatization programme was plagued by corruption and organizational chaos; by July accusations were rife that only some 6 per cent of the 5,000 enterprises that were supposed to have been privatized had actually passed into private ownership. By September Kyrgyzstan's national income was down by 28.6 per cent, industrial output by 26 per cent and agricultural output by 22 per cent compared with the first nine months of 1993.

In Kazakhstan, the situation was little better. The mid-year economic statistics revealed that GDP was down by 27 per cent compared with the same period in 1993; that industrial output had fallen by 29 per cent and investment by 60 per cent; and that some 600 enterprises had suspended production and another 100 had closed down completely. Unofficial estimates put unemployment at between 400,000 and 600,000; unemployment benefits, however, had been calculated on the basis of a mere 92,200 jobless people. A three-stage economic recovery programme, launched in July, committed the government, in the July-December phase, to using 'its own resources and minimal external loans' to finance budget and balance-of-payments deficits. Some Kazakh commentators characterized the country's problems as systemic and political rather than economic; there was strong criticism of the government's over-enthusiastic adherence to IMF-dictated policies which, it was felt, were unsuited to conditions in Kazakhstan.

Tajikistan's economy, not surprisingly, continued its downward trajectory. Prime Minister Samadov travelled to Russia, the USA and several West European countries in May seeking financial assistance in the order of $100 million to aid in the reconstruction of the country's ravaged industrial and agricultural sectors. However, possible donors felt that the Tajik government had not succeeded in formulating a realistic fiscal programme and were therefore unwilling to commit funds.

Turkmenistan and Kazakhstan made determined efforts in 1994 to solve the crucial problem of export pipelines for their respective gas and oil resources. The project for a Turkmenistan-Europe gas pipeline, to run via Iran and Turkey, was significantly advanced by the Turkish government's agreement, signed at the end of October, to buy 15,000 million cubic metres of natural gas per annum from Turkmenistan, starting in 1997. It was agreed that the first segment of the pipeline, scheduled to reach the Iranian-Turkish border by June 1997, was to be part-financed by the Iranians and Turks. The Kazakhs continued to encounter political difficulties over the route of the proposed oil pipeline from the Tengiz field. The preferred option remained that the pipeline would cross Russian territory to the Black Sea terminal at Novorossiisk. However, the Russians demanded that Chevron, the foreign partner in the joint venture to develop the Kazakh oilfield, should pay a high portion of the construction costs of the pipeline, in return for a mere 25 per cent stake in its ownership. Chevron was unwilling to make this concession; by the end of the year the matter had still not been resolved. The Russians applied similar pressure to British Gas and Agip (France), Kazakhstan's intended foreign partners in the exploitation of the Karachaganak oil and gas field, demanding that 15 per cent of their proposed stakes be ceded to Russia. Negotiations were still in progress at the end of the year; it seemed likely that British Gas and Agip would join forces with the Caspian Sea Consortium in their ongoing efforts to conclude an agreement for the Tengiz oil pipeline.

Uzbekistan also suffered problems related to energy exports, in the form of non-payment for supplies of gas already provided to other members of the Commonwealth of Independent States (CIS). By November the Kazakh debt alone was in excess of $100 million. The Uzbeks accepted a Kazakh offer of grain and oil products in part payment, but rejected other Kazakh proposals. The problem was still unresolved at the end of the year. The Turkmens, who likewise suffered from non-payment of debts by CIS users, did, however, agree in December to an arrangement whereby their major debtor, Ukraine, would immediately repay $350 million (out of credits provided by the IMF) and supply Turkmenistan with consumer goods worth $200 million.

The outstanding balance of $713 million was rescheduled, for repayment over a longer period.

The civil war in Tajikistan continued, punctuated by talks at various levels and venues between the government and the opposition. The most recent round, held in October in Islamabad, coincided with the beginning of the ceasefire that had previously been agreed at talks in Tehran. It was very nearly derailed by the murder of the Vice-Premier of the Dushanbe government, Munavarsho Nazriyev, on the very day that the talks opened. Nevertheless, the opposition representatives, headed by Kazi Turadzhonzade (former head of the Muslim establishment in Tajikistan), showed greater pliancy than previously. An extension to the ceasefire was agreed, but no lasting solution to the situation was reached. In particular, there was no agreement on the formation of a neutral coalition government, although there were some indications that opposition leaders might be allowed to participate in the parliamentary elections scheduled to be held in 1995. In December the Interior and Security Ministries, in a first step towards restoring law and order, had some success in their campaign to confiscate arms from all non-government paramilitary formations.

The integration of the Central Asian region, proposed in 1993, remained largely confined to attempts to form a customs and economic union between Uzbekistan, Kazakhstan and Kyrgyzstan; it was further underpinned by a pact, signed in February, on military cooperation. Links with the CIS, especially Russia, remained strong, despite numerous disagreements over supplies and payment. The Kazakh government finally agreed to the withdrawal to Russia of the strategic nuclear weapons stationed on its territory, in return for international guarantees as to its national security and financial compensation (the amount as yet unspecified) for the weapons-grade uranium in the nuclear warheads (see also XII.2). Negotiations were also conducted with the Russian Ministry of Defence to establish a basis for the exploitation of the Semipalatinsk nuclear test site, located in Kazakhstan, as part of a joint Kazakh-Russian defence programme. A similar approach was under consideration for the operation of the Baikonur space centre in central Kazakhstan.

2. INDIA—PAKISTAN—BANGLADESH—SRI LANKA—NEPAL—BHUTAN

i. INDIA

CAPITAL: New Delhi   AREA: 3,287,000 sq km   POPULATION: 883,600,000 ('92)
OFFICIAL LANGUAGES: Hindi & English   POLITICAL SYSTEM: parliamentary democracy
HEAD OF STATE: President Shankar Dayal Sharma (since July '92)
RULING PARTIES: Congress (I) forms minority government
HEAD OF GOVERNMENT: P.V. Narasimha Rao, Prime Minister (since June '91)
PRINCIPAL MINISTERS: Dinesh Singh (external affairs), Manmohan Singh (finance),
    S.B. Chavan (home affairs), Bajram Jakhar (agriculture), Pranab Mukherjee
    (commerce)
INTERNATIONAL ALIGNMENT: NAM, SAARC, Cwth.
CURRENCY: rupee (end-'94 £1=Rs49.08, US$1=Rs31.37)
GNP PER CAPITA: US$310 ('92)
MAIN EXPORT EARNERS: precious stones, textiles, tea, tourism

THE sheer size and complexity of India's political system and economy meant that there were apparently contradictory signs of both success and failure during the year, depending on the focus of the observer. In the sphere of foreign policy it was a relatively quiet and constructive year, apart from acerbic exchanges with Pakistan over Kashmir, featuring accusations and counter-accusations of interference in each other's domestic affairs (see also VIII.2.ii). The Indian Prime Minister, P.V. Narasimha Rao, paid official visits to Germany in February, to the United Kingdom in March, to the United States in May and to Russia in June, all of them promotional, business-oriented tours in some respects. During 1994 India sought to stake out or to safeguard its place in the emerging new world order, especially in relation to the dynamic economies of the Asia–Pacific region.

Perhaps the clearest sign of India's turn away from economic autarky was its decision to sign the draft treaty for the creation of a World Trade Organization as the successor to GATT, whose lengthy Uruguay Round negotiations India had helped to conclude in December 1993 (see AR 1993, pp. 408, 534, 574-86) by making major concessions on Western intellectual property rights. At the 1994 UN General Assembly session, India in October signalled its claim to a permanent Security Council seat, maintaining that India should be included in any expansion of the Council to make it more representative. As if to back its claims, India had already sent or pledged forces to several recent UN peace-keeping operations, including those in Cambodia, Somalia, Rwanda and Haiti. India also showed marked interest, considering that it was a non-member, in the activities of ASEAN and APEC (see XI.6.iii). In September China's Defence Minister paid a five-day visit to India, the highest-level military visitor from China to do so since the Sino-Indian War of 1962.

On the nuclear proliferation issue, Mr Rao stated categorically on 11 June that India would not 'give up the choice of producing a bomb'.

The Prime Minister made this comment whilst rejecting a demand by the right-wing opposition Bharatiya Janata Party (BJP) that India should produce a nuclear weapon forthwith. The US government continued to press India to sign the Non-Proliferation Treaty (NPT), but India continued to refuse, saying that the treaty discriminated against countries that did not already have nuclear arms.

In by-elections across India on 26 May, the ruling Congress (I) party retained five seats, giving it 269 of the 531 occupied seats in the lower house. Although the BJP retained a seat in Meerut, Uttar Pradesh, on its platform of Hindu nationalism. the result was seen as an endorsement of Mr Rao's government. However, four state elections held in early December resulted in Congress (I) suffering one of the worst drubbings in its history. Subsequent bitter internal wrangling centred on the Prime Minister's leadership qualities and on the wide-ranging programme of pro-market economic reforms he had encouraged since taking office in 1991. In the state elections, Congress (I) was reduced to a rump in two key southern states which it had previously governed, Andhra Pradesh and Karnataka, as well as in the small Himalayan state of Sikkim. In the coastal state of Goa, also among the smallest of the Indian Union's 25 states, Congress (I) lost its majority in the state assembly but hung on to power by forming a coalition.

The scale of the rout for Congress (I) seemed to dismay Prime Minister Rao, who had campaigned vigorously in all four states, telling voters that the outcome would be a test of the popularity of his government and its economic policies. Within a few days of these dire election results, the Health, Food and Rural Development Ministers (respectively B. Shankaranand, Kalpnath Rai and Rameshwar Thakur) tendered their resignations from the government in the context of efforts by Congress (I) to clean up an image tainted by corruption allegations. The resignations brought to four the number of cabinet ministers who had resigned after being named in connection with either a sugar import scandal or a $1,200 million stock market scandal. Harsh exchanges ensued at party meetings held to review the state results. Senior Congress (I) leaders were quoted in several Indian newspapers as saying that Mr Rao might have to be ousted if the next round of state elections in February 1995 turned out as badly for the party. Their mood reflected fears within the ruling party that it was heading for defeat at the national elections due no later than May 1996.

Mr Rao received a further blow on 24 December, when his Human Resources (i.e. education) Minister, Arjun Singh, resigned from the cabinet and delivered a scathing denunciation of the Prime Minister's style of leadership and failure to curb corruption. Significantly, Mr Singh did not resign from parliament or the Congress (I) working committee (the party's day-to-day ruling body), clearly signalling that he would be offering himself as an alternative leader at some future date. In a seven-page letter of resignation, Mr Singh called for a full investigation into who had benefited from a recent $850 million securities scandal—this being clearly aimed at one of Mr Rao's sons, whose name was associated with a company allegedly involved in the shady dealings. He also called for an apology to Muslims for the government's failure to protect the Babri mosque in Ayodhya, which had been torn down two years earlier by Hindu fanatics (see AR 1992, pp. 311, 445-6). Mr Singh was reported to be close to the late Rajiv Gandhi's influential widow, Sonia Gandhi, and certainly seemed to be trying to give that impression. A week of mourning for India's former President, Giani Zail Singh, who died on 25 December (see XX: Obituary), gave the Prime Minister a welcome, if temporary, respite from internal party recriminations and manoeuvrings.

After several years of continuous depreciation, the Indian rupee remained steady against major currencies for most of 1994. This was only achieved, however, because of the active intervention of the Reserve Bank of India (RBI). India's export houses and industrial groups monitored the RBI's moves carefully and began to lobby for a big devaluation of the rupee in order to protect exports. By the end of the year commentators were predicting that the government would advance the timing of a free float of the rupee (i.e. a devaluation).

India's booming stock markets had been given a sharp jolt in December 1993 when the Securities and Exchange Board of India banned the *badla* system, which allowed speculators to take positions without backing securities. Trading volumes dropped dramatically in January, while brokers lobbied frantically to get *badla* restored. The market remained subdued until March-April, though foreign institutions cashed in on the unusually low prices by buying stock through off-market transactions. Towards the end of April trading began to pick up and in June the sensitive index of the Bombay Stock Exchange (BSE) crossed the 4,000 mark.

Seven foreign brokers registered themselves for operations in India in 1994, while the freedom to raise funds abroad provided a domestic stock market stimulus. Even so, foreign and domestic investments in India's industrial projects declined in real terms, according to a survey conducted by the Centre for Monitoring the Indian Economy (an independent Bombay-based research agency). The survey, covering more than 3,000 industrial projects with a total envisaged investment of Rs 7,764 million, showed a sharp increase in investment intentions but 'very poor growth' in project implementation. 'While the investments envisaged in projects at the proposal stage had grown by nearly 46 per cent, those in projects actually being implemented grew by a meagre 4.4 per cent', the survey noted. Total investments had increased by 24 per cent over the previous year, but most of this was accounted for by new projects which had been announced but had yet to be implemented.

Science and technology enjoyed increasingly high status in India, which boasted of having the second-largest English-speaking scientific and technical manpower resources in the world (after the USA). In the three years since the start of India's economic liberalization, IBM, Motorola, Hewlett-Packard, Texas Instruments and Digital Equipment had all established operations there, to take advantage of India's cheap but sophisticated labour force. Higher education in science and technology had expanded enormously in recent decades, certainly well beyond the economy's capacity to absorb the output of graduates and PhDs. As a result, India had become one of the world's main exporters of technical skills—and according to some estimates was repaying, through the export of skilled human capital, more than it was receiving in foreign aid.

Recent rapid growth in Indian computer software exports was being achieved despite the fact that in many ways India was an unlikely candidate to be a major force in such a sophisticated industry. It had one of the lowest concentrations of computers in the world: seven for every 10,000 people, against an estimated world average of 250, 1,070 in Singapore and a US figure of 2,500. Even in basic telecommunications facilities, India still had one of the world's poorest telephone networks. Its export growth in computer software and skills therefore seemed to fly in the face of conventional wisdom about development, to the effect that a strong domestic market was essential in order to be able to compete internationally.

In mid-September India experienced an outbreak of pneumonic plague, beginning in the city of Surat (in the state of Gujarat) and soon spreading to other western states, creating panic as it did so. By the end of September at least 47 people were officially reported to have died, although unofficial figures put the death toll at more than 100 and the number of people affected at between 1,500 and 2,500. The outbreak resulted in much national and international criticism of the union government and its health policies and also of the governments of the states affected. In fact, the health authorities moved swiftly and largely successfully to control the epidemic.

Ten years after a blanket of lethal gas from a Union Carbide pesticide plant had wrought havoc in the central Indian city of Bhopal (see AR 1984, p. 276), questions of responsibility and of compensation still remained unresolved. While the compensation fund set aside by the company had reached the $500 million mark, only a tiny percentage of the money had so far reached the victims. Even the cause of the gas leak remained a source of sharp disagreement. The Indian government, non-governmental groups and the Indian media asserted that Union Carbide's negligence and poor management were to blame. Union

Carbide continued to maintain that the disaster was caused by an act of sabotage by an unidentified disgruntled plant worker. The resolution of such issues, related to what was probably the world's worst-ever industrial catastrophe to date in terms of lives lost, remained beset by confusion, allegations of corruption and legal challenges by individuals and groups.

India's population of some 900 million in 1994 was growing so fast—by about 18 million a year—that at present comparative rates of growth it was set to overtake China (currently with about 1,200 million people) as the world's most populous country some time after 2020. Population increase created numerous problems. A majority of Delhi's ten million inhabitants already lived in overcrowded tenements with insufficient water and electricity. With 6,319 people per square kilometre, the capital had the highest population density (and one the highest pollution levels) of any Indian city. Only 40 per cent of the 145 million Indian couples in the reproductive age group were believed to practise contraception, the momentum of the post-independence family planning programme having been lost during the state of emergency declared by Indira Gandhi in 1975.

It became clear at the end of 1994 that India intended to maintain a strength of 120,000 Gurkha troops within its army. In contrast, the British army (which had 45 Gurkha battalions during World War II) was committed to reducing its Gurkha strength by half, to 2,500 men, by 1996.

Three very different prominent Indians died during the year: Hajj Mastan Mirza (in July), India's best-known gangster and don of Bombay's multi-billion crime syndicate in the 1960s and 1970s, aged 72; Swaran Singh (in October), former Foreign Minister of India, aged 87; and Giani Zail Singh (in December), President of India 1982–87, aged 78 (see XX: Obituary).

ii. PAKISTAN

CAPITAL: Islamabad   AREA: 804,000 sq km   POPULATION: 119,300,000 ('92)
OFFICIAL LANGUAGE: Urdu   POLITICAL SYSTEM: parliamentary democracy
HEAD OF STATE: President Farooq Leghari (since Nov '93)
RULING PARTY: Pakistan People's Party (PPP)
HEAD OF GOVERNMENT: Benazir Bhutto, Prime Minister (since Oct '93)
PRINCIPAL MINISTERS: Ahmed Asif Ali (foreign affairs), Naseerullah Babar (home affairs), Aftab Shaban Mirani (defence), N.D. Khan (law & justice)
INTERNATIONAL ALIGNMENT: NAM, ICO, SAARC, Cwth., ECO
CURRENCY: rupee (end-'94 £1=PRs48.14, US$1=PRs30.77)
GNP PER CAPITA: US$420 ('92)
MAIN EXPORT EARNERS: cotton, textiles, rice

BENAZIR Bhutto's government remained in office for the whole of the year, but this success was against a backdrop of constant confrontation with the opposition. Violent conflict in Karachi and other parts of the country seemed beyond the control of the government.

Ms Bhutto and the Pakistan People's Party (PPP) had come to power in November 1993 following the electoral defeat of Nawaz Sharif's Pakistan Muslim League (PML) and its allies (see AR 1993, pp. 317-8). She had also been able to secure the election as President of PPP member Farooq Leghari. After some weeks of manoeuvring, Ms Bhutto engineered the downfall in April of the PML-dominated government in North-West Frontier Province (NWFP) and the installation of a PPP ministry. This required the use of the President's discretionary power. In the Punjab, by contrast, she was unable to establish her supremacy and had to share power in an awkward partnership with Manzoor Wattoo, the leader of a dissident faction of the Muslim League. In Sindh the PPP retained power throughout the year, although under difficult circumstances. The provincial government in Baluchistan remained under the control of a local coalition.

Mr Sharif made it clear even before the NWFP episode that he did not recognize the legitimacy of Ms Bhutto's government, and used every device at his disposal to make life difficult for her. National Assembly sessions throughout the year were turned into shouting-matches between government and opposition. In September Mr Sharif stepped up the tempo by launching a concerted campaign of street demonstrations and other forms of direct action. He also tried, but failed, to enlist the support of Altaf Hussain, the leader of the Muhajir Qaumi Movement (MQM) (see below). It seemed to many observers that the former Prime Minister was trying to create a situation in which the army would feel obliged to intervene and call fresh elections, perhaps after a suitable pause. The army, however, studiously refused to become directly involved.

Having herself used similar tactics in 1993 against Mr Sharif's government, Mr Bhutto responded aggressively to his challenge. Close colleagues of the PML leader were arrested for participating in street action, and a former head of the Intelligence Bureau who was close to Mr Sharif was arrested. On 13 November Mr Sharif's elderly father, Mian Muhammad Sharif, was arrested in connection with alleged offences to do with his business affairs. This was widely considered to be a form of pressure on his son, although Mr Sharif senior was released after a short while.

There was a major bank scandal during the year. The founder of the Mehran Bank (Pakistan's leading private bank, established in the wake of economic reform) was alleged to have embezzled Rs 2,100 million, it being claimed that politicians and army leaders had received regular payoffs. Attempts were also made to implicate the President himself in the scandal.

The PPP itself came more clearly under the direct leadership of Ms Bhutto, whose husband, Asif Zardari, came to play a significant role in policy-making. There seemed little room for dissent and disagreement within the party, and many of its erstwhile liberal supporters from the urban middle class withdrew from active participation. In December the Law Minister, Iqbal Haider, was forced to resign following differences over how to treat the opposition. At the beginning of the year there had been a major confrontation with Ms Bhutto's estranged brother Murtaza, at that point still in gaol on terrorism charges, who had failed to make much headway in the elections but who still enjoyed some local support in the family's home area. Several people were killed on 5 January in clashes near the tomb of the late Zulfikar Ali Bhutto. Murtaza Bhutto was released from gaol in June but failed to elicit much support elsewhere in the country.

Violence flared up in a number of areas, but by far the most serious was the situation in Karachi, the capital of the province of Sindh and the country's largest city. Here the army had been in control of law and order since mid-1992, and had been conducting a campaign to wrest control of the city from the MQM, an ethnic movement whose main aim was to maintain the strength of the Urdu-speaking former refugees who had come to the city immediately after independence in 1947. In September the MQM took the logical step of demanding that the city be made into a separate province within Pakistan; but this was fiercely opposed by the Sindhi-speaking population of the area.

The army had succeeded in forcing Altaf Hussain, the MQM leader, into exile in London, but had not been able to take full control of the situation. During 1994, especially in the second half, the level of violence increased steadily, with as many as 250 being killed in the month of November alone. The death toll for the whole year was put at around 900. At least three separate types of conflict were identified. Members of the MQM targeted the security forces, especially after the June sentencing of Mr Hussain *in absentia* to a gaol term of 27 years. There was a great deal of internecine fighting between the members of the MQM loyal to Mr Hussain and a faction opposed to him. There were also sectarian clashes between Sunni and Shia groups. At the end of the year the army was withdrawn from the streets.

In early November there was an uprising in Malakand district (a tribal area of NWFP) which in form seemed to belong to the colonial period but in fact reflected the continuing tensions created as the Pakistan state sought to take control of traditionally autonomous regions. Led by the Tehrik Nifaz-i-Shariat Muhammadi, local tribesmen demanded the enforcement of Islamic law instead of the normal Pakistani laws that were to be implemented following a Supreme Court ruling in February. In fact, the Islamic law demanded by the protesters was very similar to the earlier rules in force in the area. In the course of the protest, thousands of armed men took over towns in the area and held government officials hostage. Large numbers of paramilitaries were needed to control the situation, the death toll being at least 40.

The Prime Minister made a number of foreign visits, partly, so her opponents alleged, as a distraction from difficulties at home. Perhaps the most successful was to the UN World Population Conference in Cairo in September, where her status as a progressive woman leader in a large Muslim country gave her a special position.

Relations with India remained as dificult as ever, largely because of the impasse over Kashmir, whose anti-Indian militants continued to receive active and vocal support from Pakistan. At the beginning of the year, proposals by India for confidence-building measures were rejected by Pakistan as inadequate and a distraction from the central issues. During the year diplomats from the two countries found themselves used as pawns in the struggle, and several were physically attacked. In March the Pakistan consulate in Bombay was closed, as was the Indian consulate in Karachi at the end of December. Pakistan suffered a major diplomatic setback in March when it was forced to withdraw a resolution on Kashmir at a meeting in Geneva of the UN Human Rights Commission. Hoped-for support from China and Iran was not forthcoming and it was clear that the resolution would be defeated if it were not withdrawn. A similar move later in the year to raise the Kashmir question at the UN General Assembly also ended in failure. In December the Prime Minister attended the Casablanca summit of the Islamic Conference Organization and was able to get a sympathetic resolution passed on the Kashmir question. Nevertheless, Pakistan felt itself to be losing the arms and technology race with India, as the latter made further successful missile tests and in June began to bring its indigenously-developed Prithvi missile into operation.

The year saw concerted efforts by the United States to try to bring the governments of South Asia into line on the nuclear issue. Visits by high-ranking US officials, including one in April by Deputy Secretary of State Strobe Talbott, were intended to bring India and Pakistan into multilateral discussions on security issues. At the same time, efforts were made to persuade Pakistan to impose a unilateral cap on its nuclear programmes in return for the delivery of the F-16 warplanes that had originally been ordered in the late 1980s. Pakistan was not prepared to accept such a deal, however. The situation was not improved by a statement in August by Mr Sharif (the former Prime Minister) that Pakistan did in fact possess a nuclear weapon.

Pakistan continued to be affected by the civil war in Afghanistan (see VIII.1.ii). In January it closed its borders to refugees from the fighting, while in the following month there was a failed attempt in Islamabad to take children hostage against demands for money and food for Afghanistan. While Pakistani agencies had longstanding links with the

Hekmatyar side in the civil war, there were signs during 1994 that the government was trying to disengage.

The economy made only modest progress (inflation being higher than anticipated), although the foreign exchange situation improved sharply and the fiscal deficit was reduced. GDP growth in 1993/94 was put at 3.9 per cent. The 1993/94 cotton crop was down to 7.6 million bales, 40 per cent less than the record harvest of 1991/92, and excessive rain and viral diseases later in the year damaged the prospects for the 1994/95 harvest. Inconsistent government policies exacerbated the impact on the economy, and a number of spinning mills remained closed. There were also shortfalls in sugar production which had an impact on consumer prices. Against this background, there was strong resistance to efforts in the budget on 9 June to raise revenue through a new general sales tax and by giving increased powers to income tax officers. A business strike at the end of June forced the government to suspend or withdraw these measures.

In September the US Energy Secretary visited Pakistan together with a number of leading US businessmen. Considerable interest was expressed in the possibility of investment in the energy sector, where the government was offering generous terms. Foreign investors bought the bulk of the shares in Pakistan Telecommunication Company when 12 per cent were privatized during the year, although there was criticism of the amateurish way the placement was handled. It was clear during the year that the government intended to maintain its commitment to privatization and foreign investment, this approach being rewarded by a large IMF credit facility in February and aid pledges of $2,500 million for 1994/95.

iii.   BANGLADESH

CAPITAL: Dhaka   AREA: 144,000 sq km   POPULATION: 114,400,000 ('92)
OFFICIAL LANGUAGE: Bengali   POLITICAL SYSTEM: parliamentary democracy
HEAD OF STATE: President Abdur Rahman Biswas (since Oct '91)
RULING PARTIES: Bangladesh National Party (BNP)
HEAD OF GOVERNMENT: Begum Khaleda Zia, Prime Minister (since March '91)
PRINCIPAL MINISTERS: Mirza Gholam Hafiz (law & justice), A.S.M. Mustafizur Rahman (foreign affairs), Saifur Rahman (finance), Abdul Matin Choudhry (home affairs), Maj.-Gen. (retd.) Majedul Haq (agriculture, irrigation & flood control)
INTERNATIONAL ALIGNMENT: NAM, ICO, SAARC, Cwth.
CURRENCY: taka (end-'94 £1=Tk62.27, US$1=Tk39.80)
GNP PER CAPITA: US$220 ('92)
MAIN EXPORT EARNERS: jute, fish

THIS was a year of acute political unrest, turmoil and deadlock, especially in the capital city of Dhaka. Opposition groups vainly tried to unseat the incumbent Bangladesh National Party (BNP) government of Begum Khaleda Zia and to install a caretaker administration pending the holding of fresh general elections. In effect, however, a political stalemate dominated the national scene throughout the year.

Following a BNP by-election victory in March, the main opposition parties alleged that it been achieved by bribery and corruption. Thenceforth, the Awami League (AL) mostly boycotted parliament to press its demand that general elections should be held much earlier than 1996 (the latest date constitutionally permissible). The BNP government refused, claiming that there was no constitutional provision for the installation of an interim caretaker government, as demanded by the opposition. In attempts to outflank the AL, the BNP tried, with rather mixed success, to improve its relations with the other opposition parties, the two main ones being the Jatiya Party of ex-President Ershad and the Islamist Jamaat-i-Islami.

The opposition followed up its parliamentary boycott with a series of nationwide agitations. A number of general strikes and 'sieges' featuring rail and road blockades were organized, bringing in their wake strong criticism from the business community. On 18 April eight small but influential opposition parties formed a new group, the Left Democratic Front, as part of opposition pressure for early elections. The Front included the National Socialist Party, the Workers' Party and the Communist Party of Bangladesh, the last reputedly having strong support among industrial workers.

The Commonwealth Secretary-General, Chief Emeka Anyaoku, while on an official visit to Dhaka in September, offered to try to set up a dialogue between the government and the opposition with a view to resolving the impasse. After both sides had agreed to the proposal, the former Governor-General of Australia, Sir Ninian Stephen, became Chief Anyaoku's mediator. After several weeks in Dhaka, however, Sir Ninian had to admit failure. As he left Bangladesh he was accused by the AL leader, Sheikh Hasina, of partisanship on the government's side.

Under an agreement of 18 January between India, Bangladesh and Chakma tribal leaders, a first batch of 282 Chakmas who had been languishing in refugee camps in India's north-eastern Tripura state crossed into Bangladesh. Subsequently, further batches of refugees (estimated to number about 56,000 in all, including a sprinkling of other tribal groups in Tripura) returned cautiously to Bangladeshi soil. Since the Chakma insurgency began in 1973, more than 3,500 people had been killed. The rebels wanted autonomy for the Hill tracts (of some 14,200 square kilometres) and the expulsion from them of some 300,000 Bengali-speaking settlers. In order to achieve their accord, both Dhaka and the insurgents modified their earlier positions, the guerrillas agreeing to an extended truce and to enter into further peace talks.

In late May a senior official of the UN High Commissioner for Refugees (UNHCR) announced that the repatriation of some 200,000

Rohingya refugees who had fled to Bangladesh from Burma would be completed by the end of 1995. Werner Blatter, director of the UNHCR's regional bureau for Asia and Oceania, said that repatriation would resume in late June or early July after the reconstruction of cyclone-damaged camps.

On 29 July some 100,000 demonstrators converged on Dhaka in a protest rally organized by 13 Islamist religious organizations to demand the enactment of a law against blasphemy and the punishment of author Taslima Nasreen. It was claimed that she had defamed the Koran in a recent interview, thus compounding the alleged blasphemies committed in her novel *Lajja*, published in 1993 (see AR 1993, p. 320). Ms Nasreen at first sought legal protection from the courts in Bangladesh, perhaps in the hope that she could remain in her own country, albeit in a safe house. Soon, however, she opted for the security of the West and took up residence in Sweden.

On the economic front, businessmen, entrepreneurs and government ministers sought to further free-market policies (see AR 1993, p. 320) and to attract new international investment. It was clear, however, that the country's ability to attract investment was vitiated by the prevailing political atmosphere of strikes and opposition protest actions, with the result that some businessmen demanded legislation to ban strikes. There were some signs that the economy was registering improvements: growth reached 5 per cent in the year to June, the budget deficit was much reduced, savings increased and the current-account deficit was estimated to be only 2 per cent of GDP by the end of the year. Nevertheless, the domestic political crisis over the legitimacy of the government threatened to undermine the positive economic trends.

The Prime Minister paid official visits to Japan and Malaysia in March and October respectively, in each case heading large business delegations seeking to improve bilateral trade relations as well as to attract investment. As current chairperson of the South Asian Association for Regional Cooperation (see XI.6.iii), Begum Khaleda visited Bhutan in October and planned to visit all the other members before the next SAARC summit, which was postponed several times but was eventually rescheduled to be held in 1995 in New Delhi.

iv.   NEPAL

CAPITAL: Kathmandu   AREA: 147,000 sq km   POPULATION: 19,900,000 ('92)
OFFICIAL LANGUAGE: Nepali   POLITICAL SYSTEM: parliamentary democracy
HEAD OF STATE: King Birendra Bir Bikram Shah Deva (since '72)
RULING PARTY: United Communist Party of Nepal (UCPN)
HEAD OF GOVERNMENT: Man Mohan Adhikari, Prime Minister (since Nov
   '94)
PRINCIPAL MINISTERS: Madhav Kumar Nepal (Deputy Prime Minister, defence, foreign
   affairs), Bharat Mohan Adhikari (finance), Subhash Chandra Nembang (law,
   justice & parliamentary affairs)
INTERNATIONAL ALIGNMENT: NAM, SAARC
CURRENCY: rupee (end-'94 £1=NRS77.24, US$1=NRS49.37)
GNP PER CAPITA: US$170 ('92)
MAIN EXPORT EARNERS: agricultural products, tourism

THE main event for Nepal in 1994 was the general election, held in November, barely four years after attempts had first been made to institute parliamentary democracy and to clip the powers of King Birendra (see AR 1990, pp. 324-5). It was also a year in which the Nepalese people came face to face with the uncertainties of competitive political pluralism. Allegations of corruption and mismanagement against the government led by the Nepali Congress (NC) had been mounting over the preceding four years, causing repeated street agitation by the opposition. Two by-elections in February, caused by the death of sitting MPs, glaringly exposed the factionalism in the NC. Subsequently, for weeks on end, the machinery of government was virtually at a standstill. In the wake of the by-elections, political passions were also running high amongst the rival parties.

Furthermore, India became involved in controversy with Nepal when armed Indian police, allegedly in hot pursuit of Pakistani terrorist agents, entered Kathmandu in April and carried out unauthorized searches of a residential building, but found no terrorists. This led to Nepalese from all walks of life holding public protest meetings in the capital, and the affair simmered on for several months to become one of the contentious issues in the November polls.

Prime Minister Koirala resigned on 10 July after losing a vote of no confidence owing to NC defections. The King immediately dissolved parliament and called an early general election, requesting Mr Koirala to head a caretaker government until then. Eventually held on 15 November, the election was the second in Nepal's still brief recent history of representative democracy, the first having taken place in 1991 (see AR 1991, p. 319). Violence during the campaigning and polling was relatively low. The voter turnout, at about 58 per cent, was lower than the 65.2 per cent recorded in 1991, which led some commentators to claim that there was growing disillusionment with the main political parties.

The final results were indecisive, giving rise to a fortnight of post-election political uncertainty. Led by 74-year-old Man Mohan Adhikari, the United Communist Party of Nepal (UCPN) headed the returns with 88 seats in the 205-member Pratinidhi Sabha (House of Representatives), 15 short of an overall majority. In second place was the NC with 83 seats (compared with 110 in 1991), while the monarchist Rashtriya Prajatantra Party (RPP) took 20, the Nepal Mazdoor Kisan Party four, the Nepal Sadhbhavana Party three and independents seven. With the NC deciding to go into opposition, the Communists failed to enlist the support of the anti-Koirala NC faction and found the pro-palace RPP unwilling to join any coalition, King Birendra therefore invited the UCPN leader to form a minority government, as allowed for in the newly-drafted constitution.

At the swearing-in ceremony held on 30 November at the Narayanhiti Royal Palace in Kathmandu, a nine-member cabinet assumed office with Mr Adhikari as Prime Minister. The UCPN general secretary, Madhav Nepal, became Deputy Prime Minister in charge of the critical portfolios of foreign affairs and defence. Mr Adhikari swore to be loyal and faithful to the monarch and the Hindu kingdom and himself took on the palace affairs portfolio—ironical twists of fortune, since earlier in his life he had spent 17 years in prison for his involvement in attempts to overthrow the monarchy.

In a nationwide broadcast immediately afterwards, the new Prime Minister promised to encourage business interests whilst also helping the landless; at the same time, he criticized his predecessor for having harmed Nepal by his 'attempts to sell off the Nepalese public sector units to Indian capitalists'. Mr Adhikari said that he would soon initiate a dialogue with the Indian government across the entire range of bilateral relations and would review Nepal's treaty with India, adding that updating it was vital 'in a changed international context'. According to the UCPN leader, India and China were equal friends of Nepal's.

The vexed issue of Bhutanese refugees in Nepal (see VIII.2.v) seemed no closer to a solution in 1994. A senior UN representative held talks with government officials in Kathmandu and visited the camps, while ministerial talks aimed at resolving problems were said to be making progress in mid-year. However, a fifth round of talks scheduled for the autumn were postponed by Nepal because of its election.

King Birendra paid a six-day visit to France in September, followed by unofficial visits to Russia, Italy and the United Arab Emirates. Crown Prince Dipendra made official visits to Thailand in June, India in September and China in November. Diplomatic relations were established with South Africa, Guyana and Slovakia, bringing the number of countries having diplomatic relations with Nepal to 108.

v. BHUTAN

CAPITAL: Thimphu   AREA: 46,500 sq km   POPULATION: 1,500,000 ('92)
OFFICIAL LANGUAGES: Dzongkha, Lhotsan, English   POLITICAL SYSTEM: monarchy
HEAD OF STATE & GOVERNMENT: Dragon King Jigme Singye Wangchuk (since
   '72)
PRINCIPAL MINISTERS: Lyonpo Dawa Tsering (foreign affairs), Lyonpo Dago Tshering
   (home affairs), Lyonpo Dorji Tshering (finance), Lyonpo Om Pradhan (trade &
   industry), Lyonpo Chenkyab Dorji (planning)
INTERNATIONAL ALIGNMENT: NAM, SAARC
CURRENCY: ngultrum (end-'94 £1=N49.08, US$1=N31.37)
GNP PER CAPITA: US$180 ('92)
MAIN EXPORT EARNERS: tourism, cement, timber

THE refugee crisis with Nepal (see AR 1993, pp. 322–3) continued
to loom large among the problems of this land-locked, mountainous
state, with its series of north-south valleys cutting thin swathes in
the Himalayas between India and China/Tibet. Ministerial talks, with
some postponements and reschedulings, continued throughout the year
between Bhutan and Nepal on classifying the refugees from Bhutan
(variously estimated at between 85,000 and just over 100,000), who
were huddled in camps in eastern Nepal.

A joint verification team of ten members, five from each side, was
agreed to in principle to define the status of Bhutanese refugees. Four
categories were distinguished: (i) bona fide Bhutanese nationals who
had been forced to leave Bhutan; (ii) Bhutanese who had emigrated
from Bhutan to Nepal and had thus forfeited Bhutanese nationality
according to the laws of Bhutan; (iii) non-Bhutanese refugees; and
(iv) Bhutanese who had committed criminal acts. During 1994 the
number of southern Bhutanese residents leaving for camps in Nepal was
greatly reduced, while the numbers of supervised returnees increased.
Nevertheless, by the end of the year it was clear that the problem was
unlikely to be fully resolved in the immediate future.

Economic issues pressed keenly on the populace throughout 1994,
with somewhat contradictory consequences. In March Bhutan's financial
institutions adopted more cautious guidelines for lending, largely in
order to deal with growing numbers of unrecoverable loans and over-
valuations of assets. In mid-July King Jigme instructed the financial
institutions and business community to act urgently to resolve the loan
repayments problem, reportedly involving bad debts currently totalling
the equivalent of some US$9 million. Grant and aid assistance from
the Indian government, especially in power generation, remained the
basis of Bhutan's economic planning. India's overall commitment to
Bhutan's seventh plan (1992–97) was N 5,000 million for mutually-
agreed programmes, plus N 2,500 million in development subsidies.

In March Bhutan joined the Geneva-based World Intellectual Property Organization, being in the process of preparing its first copyright
law.

vi. SRI LANKA

CAPITAL: Colombo AREA: 64,500 sq km POPULATION: 17,400,000 ('92)
OFFICIAL LANGUAGES: Sinhala, Tamil, English
POLITICAL SYSTEM: presidential democracy
RULING PARTIES: Sri Lanka Freedom Party (SLFP) heads People's Alliance coalition
HEAD OF STATE & GOVERNMENT: President Chandrika Bandaranaike Kumaratunga
 (since Nov '94)
PRINCIPAL MINISTERS: Sirimavo Bandaranaike (Prime Minister), Lakshman
 Kadirgamar (foreign affairs), Ratnasiri Wickremanayake (home affairs), Kingsley
 Wickremaratne (trade), D.M. Jayaratna (agriculture)
INTERNATIONAL ALIGNMENT: NAM, SAARC, Cwth.
CURRENCY: rupee (end-'94 £1=SLRs77.70, US$1=SLRs49.66)
GNP PER CAPITA: US$588 ('93)
MAIN EXPORT EARNERS: textiles, tea, rubber, tourism

IN an eventful year, Sri Lanka voted for a change of President and of government, and the new administration launched a process intended to lead to a resolution of the country's long-running ethnic conflict. Chandrika Bandaranaike Kumaratunga, the candidate of the left-wing People's Alliance headed by the Sri Lanka Freedom Party (SLFP), decisively won the presidential poll held on 9 November. She had earlier led the Alliance to a narrower victory in the parliamentary elections on 16 August, winning 105 seats in the 225-member legislature, with the then ruling United National Party (UNP) taking 94 seats. The peaceful transfer of governmental power after 17 years of UNP rule—the fifth change since independence in 1948—confirmed the strength of the country's democratic tradition.

The new President, aged 49, had the distinction of being the daughter of two former Prime Ministers, namely Solomon and Sirimavo Bandaranaike. While her success drew attention to the dynastic element in South Asian politics, Mrs Kumaratunga gave ample evidence of leadership qualities in her own right. Having lost her father to an assassin's bullet in 1959 while she was a teenager, she saw her husband, Vijaya Kumaratunga, a popular film actor turned radical politician, murdered in 1988 by gunmen believed to have been sent by the Sinhalese chauvinist Jatika Vimukti Peramuma (JVP). After seeking safety abroad with her two young children for a while, she had a swift political rise on returning home to rejoin the SLFP founded by her father. She quickly achieved dominance in the party at the expense, to some extent, of her mother, who had earlier expected to be the Alliance presidential candidate but had to be content with the less powerful post of Prime Minister. She also triumphed over her younger brother, Anura, who had defected to the then ruling UNP in 1993 in exchange for a cabinet post (see AR 1993, p. 325). Maternal efforts to end this sibling rivalry were unsuccessful.

The three-month period between the two elections was one of enforced 'cohabitation' between President Dingiri Banda Wijetunge of the UNP and Prime Minister Kumaratunga of the Alliance. Mr Wijetunge had been chosen by parliament to serve out the six-year term of President Premadasa after the latter's assassination in May 1993; under the somewhat bizarre constitution devised by former President Jayewardene, he not only became head of government and commander-in-chief but was also entitled to hold the portfolios of his choice. In the event, President Wijetunge insisted on being Defence Minister but avoided obstructing Mrs Kumaratunga and her Alliance ministers. Originally intending to contest the 1994 presidential election, he bowed out after the UNP lost the parliamentary election in August.

Ranil Wickremasinghe, then UNP Prime Minister, expected to be made the party's presidential candidate, but he was narrowly beaten in a party contest by Gamini Dissanayake. The latter, together with Lalith Athulathmudali, had formed the Democratic United National Front (DUNF) after leading an unsuccessful bid to impeach President Premadasa in 1992; but Mr Athulathmudali had been assassinated a week before President Premadasa, following which Mr Dissanayake had abandoned the DUNF to rejoin the UNP. In the 1994 presidential election, Mr Dissanayake was conducting a vigorous campaign when he too was killed, with 55 others, in a bomb attack at a political rally in Colombo on 23 October that recalled the 1991 slaying of India's Rajiv Gandhi (see AR 1991, pp. 310, 322). Suspicion centred on the Liberation Tigers of Tamil Eelam (LTTE), the militant Tamil movement waging a secessionist war in the north-east, which was believed to have used a suicide bomber in each case. Mr Dissanayake had incurred the LTTE's wrath by supporting the deployment of the Indian Peace-keeping Force in Sri Lanka to do battle with the Tigers in the late 1980s. Following Mr Dissanayake's assassination, the UNP sought to capitalize on the sympathy factor by naming his politically-inexperienced widow, Srima, to take his place in the presidential contest.

Mrs Kumaratunga made peace talks with the LTTE a key part of her election platform, along with ending corruption and jettisoning the executive presidency in favour of a return to a parliamentary form of government. On becoming Prime Minister, she relaxed the economic embargo on Tiger-controlled areas and sent officials to open preliminary talks with the LTTE. However, Mr Dissanayake's killing caused further talks to be postponed. In campaigning to secure his widow's election, the UNP tried to discredit Mrs Kumaratunga for wishing to continue talks with the LTTE, which the party blamed for the assassination of its candidate. Mrs Kumaratunga refused to backtrack on her peace overtures and was vindicated by the massive support she received in the presidential poll. The results showed that she had been elected as Sri Lanka's first woman head of state with 62.3 per cent of the popular vote, against 35 per cent for Mrs Dissanayake.

Two rounds of talks with the LTTE before the end of the year were preliminary, ground-preparing exchanges, not involving political heavyweights on either side or key issues relating to devolution of power to Tamil areas. Fears were voiced—perhaps shared by at least some in the military—that the LTTE was eager to have a ceasefire because it wished to rebuild its strength, as it had done during prolonged talks with the Premadasa government in 1989.

Popular support among Tamils for the peace process was manifested in the welcome given to Colombo's negotiating team in the northern city of Jaffna. There was also some evidence of rising disenchantment among Tamils with the LTTE leadership. In January Tamil protests, in Sri Lanka and abroad, prevented the execution by the LTTE of its former deputy leader, Gopalaswamy Mahendrarajah (also known as Mahattaya), who had been accused of passing information to Indian intelligence.

The Alliance government pledged to continue its predecessor's free-market economic policies, including privatization of state-run enterprises, but to give such policies a human face. While investors looked for confirmation of such pro-market professions, Sri Lanka's trade unions, previously kept on a tight rein by the UNP government, seemed ready to flex their muscles in the new climate. A wave of labour unrest marked the turn of the year. Increases in government spending—first by the UNP government to win votes and then by the new administration to help its low-income supporters—threatened to widen the budget deficit to 9 per cent of GDP in 1994 (from 6.5 per cent in 1993). Mrs Kumaratunga promised fiscal prudence, in the knowledge that the IMF and World Bank would press for it. Observers agreed that her task would become easier if the talks with the Tamils yielded a peace dividend. GDP growth was estimated to have fallen below the impressive 6.9 per cent achieved in 1993, but foreign reserves improved, as exports of manufactures and tourism continued to expand.

3. INDIAN OCEAN STATES

i. MAURITIUS

CAPITAL: Port Louis   AREA: 2,040 sq km   POPULATION: 1,100,000 ('92)
OFFICIAL LANGUAGE: English   POLITICAL SYSTEM: parliamentary democracy
HEAD OF STATE: President Cassam Uteem (since June '92)
RULING PARTIES: coalition of Mauritian Socialist Movement (MSM), Mauritian Militant Movement (MMM) and Organization of the Rodrigues People (OPR)
HEAD OF GOVERNMENT: Sir Anerood Jugnauth (MSM), Prime Minister (since '82)
PRINCIPAL MINISTERS: Prem Nababsing (MMM/Deputy Prime Minister, planning & development), Ramduthsing Jaddoo (MSM/external affairs), Ramakrishna Sithanen (MSM/finance)
INTERNATIONAL ALIGNMENT: NAM, OAU, ACP, Cwth., Francophonie
CURRENCY: rupee (end-'94 £1=MRs28.24, US$1=MRs18.05)
GNP PER CAPITA: US$2,700 ('92)
MAIN EXPORT EARNERS: sugar, textiles, manufactured goods, tourism

THE country's economic boom continued apace in 1994. Based on extensive liberalization and diversification into light industry and tourism and enjoying cross-party support, the boom had brought about a doubling of income per head since 1980.

At a meeting of the 22-member Preferential Trade Area (PTA) in Grand Bay on 17–23 October (see also XI.6.i), the Prime Minister, Sir Anerood Jugnauth, urged other African countries to adopt and adapt the Mauritius model to secure sustained growth. It was pointed out that Mauritius, in contrast with much of continental Africa, had made great headway in the past decade in the area of social and economic development and had acquired wide experience in implementing structural adjustment strategies and establishing new areas of production, such as export processing zones.

The 1994/95 budget contained plans to privatize Air Mauritius and other state-owned companies and to develop an offshore financial sector, a free port and other services. It also promised further measures to improve market efficiency and to stimulate savings and investment. The economy was expected to record 5 per cent growth in 1994. With unemployment down to 1.5 per cent of the labour force, inflation was relatively high at 9.5 per cent in mid-year, not least owing to the tight labour market and rising wages. Interest rates were raised in the second half of the year to curb inflationary pressures. Cyclone Hollanda struck Mauritius on 10–11 February, killing two people, making around 1,900 homeless and causing damage estimated at US$135 million. Around a fifth of the sugar crop, a key foreign-exchange earner, was lost.

The Prime Minister carried out a cabinet reshuffle on 27 August. The main change was that Ramduthsing Jaddoo, hitherto Minister of Manpower Resources, became Minister of External Affairs. He replaced Ahmud Swaley Kasenally, who became Minister of Energy, Water Resources and Postal Services. On 29 November Paul Bérenger, leader of the opposition Mauritian Militant Movement (MMM), and Jean-Claude Raoul de l'Estrac, the Industry Minister and leader of the Mauritian Militant Renewal (RMM), both resigned their parliamentary seats, after daring each other to do so in a dispute over allegations of fraud in the 1991 election. The RMM had been formed in 1993 by an MMM faction which had preferred to remain in the government notwithstanding the dismissal of M. Bérenger as Foreign Minister (see AR 1993, p. 326).

Police on 24 July arrested the head of the civil service, Sir Bhinod Bacha, on suspicion of murder, arson, conspiracy and obstructing police inquiries into a fire at his mansion in early June which had killed his wife and nine-year-old son. A lady-friend of Sir Bhinod's was arrested on similar charges. The affair was the most sensational for years in Mauritius and dominated the popular press for weeks, raising concern over trial by the media.

Another case which preoccupied public opinion throughout the year was that of the novel *The Rape of Sita* by Lindsey Collen, a white South African resident in Mauritius. Dealing with the fate of Sita, the much-revered consort of the god-king Rama of Hindu mythology, the book had been denounced in the press on its publication in December 1993. Quickly withdrawn by the author and publishers, it had then been formally banned by the government on the grounds that it might be blasphemous. Some religious Hindus accused Ms Collen of 'raping Hinduism', but many women commended her for highlighting the plight of females in Hindu society.

In October the media reported that one of the world's rarest falcons had eaten one of the world's rarest pigeons in Mauritius. The incident happened on the Île aux Aigrettes. The falcon was a Mauritius kestrel, whose numbers in the wild had fallen to four before a breeding programme had raised them to 250. It apparently ate one of the chicks of the first Mauritius pink pigeons reintroduced into the wild after another successful breeding programme had saved that species from extinction.

ii.   SEYCHELLES, COMOROS AND MALDIVES

Seychelles
CAPITAL: Victoria   AREA: 454 sq km   POPULATION: 69,000 ('92)
OFFICIAL LANGUAGES: Seychellois, English, French   POLITICAL SYSTEM: presidential
RULING PARTY: Seychelles People's Progressive Front (SPPF)
HEAD OF STATE & GOVERNMENT: President France-Albert René (since '77)
PRINCIPAL MINISTERS: James Michel (defence, finance & communications),
   Danielle de St Jorre (foreign affairs, planning)
CURRENCY: rupee (end-'94 £1=SR7.77, US$1=SR4.97)
GNP PER CAPITA: US$5,460 ('92)
MAIN EXPORT EARNERS: tourism, copra, fish

Comoros
CAPITAL: Moroni   AREA: 1,860 sq km   POPULATION: 510,000 ('92)
OFFICIAL LANGUAGES: Arabic & French   POLITICAL SYSTEM: presidential
RULING PARTY: Rally for Democracy and Renewal (RDR)
HEAD OF STATE & GOVERNMENT: President Said Mohammed Djohar (since '89)
PRINCIPAL MINISTERS: Halifa Houmadi (Prime Minister), Said Mohammed Sagaf
   (foreign affairs), Amadi Abdoulbastu (finance & budget), Mohammed
   Abdouwahabi (interior)
CURRENCY: franc (end-'94 £1=FC628.63, US$=FC401.81)
GNP PER CAPITA: US$510 ('92)
MAIN EXPORT EARNERS: vanilla, agricultural products, tourism

Maldives
CAPITAL: Malé   AREA: 300 sq km   POPULATION: 229,000 ('92)
OFFICIAL LANGUAGE: Divehi   POLITICAL SYSTEM: presidential
HEAD OF STATE & GOVERNMENT: President Maumoun Abdul Gayoom (since
   '78)
PRINCIPAL MINISTERS: Fathuhulla Jameel (foreign affairs), Abdulla Jameel (home
   affairs), Mohammed Rashid Ibrahim (justice)
CURRENCY: ruffiya (end-'94 £1=R18.40, US$1=R11.76)
GNP PER CAPITA: US$500 ('92)
MAIN EXPORT EARNERS: tourism, fish, coconuts

AFTER the reintroduction of multi-party politics in SEYCHELLES in 1993 (see AR 1993, p. 328), the René government embarked on a programme of economic liberalization and diversification. This involved selling off state-owned companies, attracting foreign investment, establishing an offshore financial sector, reducing reliance on tourism (currently generating nearly three-quarters of foreign earnings) and continuing to develop fishing, agriculture and food processing. On 22 November the government announced the establishment of an international business authority, of government and private-sector representatives, to promote the country as a trading centre. The aim was to capitalize on the islands' location between Asia and Africa by setting up institutions for offshore banking, free port trade, ship registration and an export zone.

In April the Roman Catholic bishop of Seychelles, Felix Paul, was quoted in a magazine as saying that he had watched pornographic films and had tried growing marijuana. He resigned on 31 May after the Vatican had called on him to do so. He subsequently claimed that the real reason the Vatican had wanted him to resign was the frank comments he had made on a range of controversial issues during evidence to a constitutional commission in 1992 and 1993.

Despite the confusion surrounding the parliamentary elections in COMOROS at the end of 1993 (see AR 1993, p. 329), when the ruling Rally for Democracy and Renewal (RDR) had been returned to power with an absolute majority in highly dubious circumstances, President Said Mohammed Djohar appointed the RDR secretary-general, Mohammed Abdou, as the new Prime Minister. The new government included several close supporters of the President's son-in-law, Mohammed Nchangama, who was widely believed to be the power behind the throne and was thought to have waiting his chance to become President himself. The opposition parties condemned the elections as an abandonment of any pretence at multi-party democracy and formed a Forum for National Recovery (FRN) to coordinate their activities.

As well as campaigning against the abuse of democracy, the FRN also criticized the effects of a 25 per cent devaluation of the Comoro franc in January. This action followed the 50 per cent devaluation of the CFA franc of the African franc zone (see VI.3; XI.6.i), whose parity Comoros had hitherto followed. A series of subsequent public sector strikes and protests culminated in a violent riot in June on the island of Mohéli which left several people dead and injured.

In October Mr Abdou was suddenly dismissed by the President and replaced by Halifa Houmadi, an RDR leader drawn from the parastatal sector. His new government included a group of non-political technocrats, purportedly to bring about an improvement in the islands' rickety economy. Its appointment served to intensify disaffection within the ruling party.

Public life in the MALDIVES in 1994 was dominated by growing calls for political reform, in particular for the legalization of political parties and a separation of powers, most of which continued to rest with President Maumoun Abdul Gayoom. Another major source of public disaffection with the government was widespread corruption.

The general election on 2 December was widely seen as a referendum on President Gayoom's leadership. The 40 elective seats in the Majlis (parliament) were contested by 229 independent candidates (a further eight deputies being appointed by the President). Reformist candidates were allowed to stand, but political parties, public meetings and campaign speeches remained banned. Although five candidates were detained during the campaign and one was convicted of corruption, the authorities intervened far less than in previous elections and foreign observers deemed the vote to have been fair. Among the reformists elected to the new parliament were two former ministers, Abdullah Kamaluddeen and Ahmed Mujutaba.

President Gayoom had recognized the popular mood in favour of change in his fourth-term inauguration speech in November 1993 (see AR 1993, pp. 329-30). But in an interview during the election campaign he claimed there were no restrictions on freedom of expression and criticized parliamentarians for not holding ministers to account. He also said that he was not opposed to a multi-party system in principle but believed it could destabilize the country.

The Maldives hit the international headlines in late 1994 in connection with a major spying scandal in neighbouring India. On 20 October Mariam Rasheeda, a 31-year-old former junior officer in the Maldivian army, was arrested in Bangalore, India, in a routine police operation after she had let her visa expire. Under questioning, she confessed to using sexual favours and bribes to acquire classified information from Indian space and defence scientists and to selling it to unnamed customers. Another Maldivian woman, Fauzia Hussain, was thereupon arrested on suspicion of being her controller, while two leading scientists from the Indian Space Research Organization (ISRO) and two Indian businessmen were also arrested. It was unclear who had been the recipient of the information, which concerned details of key systems in India's advanced missile and space programme, but media speculation centred on Pakistan.

In a twist to the affair related directly to the Maldives, Indian police announced on 9 December that a diary kept by Ms Rasheeda described a plot to kill President Gayoom. She told the police that she was a member of the (Maldivian) National Security Force and had been sent to India to investigate the plot, which she claimed had been hatched by an exiled opposition leader. The Maldives government refused to comment on the allegations and denied that Ms Rasheeda was an intelligence officer.

iii. MADAGASCAR

CAPITAL: Antananarivo   AREA: 587,000 sq km   POPULATION: 12,400,000 ('92)
OFFICIAL LANGUAGES: Malagasy & French   POLITICAL SYSTEM: presidential
RULING PARTIES: Comité des Forces Vives forms loose coalition
HEAD OF STATE & GOVERNMENT: President Albert Zafy (since Feb '93)
PRINCIPAL MINISTERS: Françisque Ravony (Prime Minister, finance), Emmanuel
   Rakotovahiny (agriculture & rural development), Jacques Sylla (foreign
   affairs), Tovonanahary Rabetsitonta (economy), Ralahy Nelson Rabenirainy
   (justice), Charles Clément Séverin (interior), Gen. Charles Rabenja (armed
   forces)
INTERNATIONAL ALIGNMENT: NAM, OAU, ACP, Francophonie
CURRENCY: Malagasy franc (end-'94 £1=FMG5,691.14, US$1=FMG3,637.67)
GNP PER CAPITA: US$230 ('92)
MAIN EXPORT EARNERS: coffee, vanilla, cloves

AFTER the political excitement of 1992 and 1993, and the slow-motion
removal of the military regime of President Ratsiraka (see AR 1993,
pp. 330–1), Madagascar gradually settled into the different rhythms
(and headaches) of multi-party democracy. This exercise became, in
1994, inextricably intertwined with the demands of economic reform,
as pressed for by the international community, especially by the IMF
and the World Bank. At the beginning of the year, Cyclone Geralda was
the worst to hit Madagascar since 1927, causing extensive destruction in
the north and east of the island and leaving 500,000 homeless. Particular
damage was done to agriculture, especially to the rice harvest, with the
result that Madagascar received substantial international emergency
aid.

A programme of economic reform was adopted by the new civilian
government, involving a floating exchange rate for the Malagasy franc,
the creation of private banks and a stock exchange, and the privatization
of state enterprises. But there was opposition from different quarters
in parliament, and relations with the Washington financial institutions
remained ambiguous. In June a group of opposition deputies said to be
sympathetic to ex-President Ratsiraka tabled a motion of censure against
President Albert Zafy and Assembly Speaker Richard Andriamanjato
for negotiating 'parallel' government loans without IMF blessing. It was
reported that the Prime Minister, Françisque Ravony, had returned from
Washington without an agreement for a new loan facility. Although the
censure motion was rejected, political turbulence continued to the end
of the year, as the Prime Minister could not count on the support of
the Forces Vives Rasalama (FVR), which had the largest number of
members of the Assembly.

In July President Zafy alleged that an attempted coup had been
foiled, and for good measure criticized members of the Assembly for
'absenteeism and drunkenness'. In August, after months of political
haggling, M. Ravony produced a definitive government list, which had
the support of an Assembly majority. The defeat of the censure motion
had helped to break the logjam, and also led to the confirmation in office

of the Finance Minister, Yvon Raserijoana, the architect of the reform programme. He was confirmed despite the Assembly's disapproval of his ongoing conflict with the central bank governor, whose departure was sought by the IMF. At the end of the year, however, the Assembly showed its continuing independence by rejecting a government budget proposal to impose a tax on petroleum products, thus diminishing the budget's credibility. Moreover, when the central bank governor was dismissed by M. Raserijoana, the latter was quickly forced to resign by pressure from angry parliamentarians.

IX SOUTH-EAST AND EAST ASIA

1. MYANMAR (BURMA)—THAILAND—MALAYSIA—BRUNEI— SINGAPORE—INDONESIA—PHILIPPINES—VIETNAM— CAMBODIA—LAOS

i. MYANMAR (BURMA)

CAPITAL: Yangon (Rangoon)   AREA: 676,500 sq km   POPULATION: 43,700,000 ('92)
OFFICIAL LANGUAGE: Burmese   POLITICAL SYSTEM: military regime
HEAD OF STATE & GOVERNMENT: Gen. Than Shwe, Chairman of State Law and
  Order Restoration Council and Prime Minister (since April '92)
PRINCIPAL MINISTERS: Vice-Adml. Maung Maung Khin (Deputy Premier), Lt-Gen.
  Tin Tun (Deputy Premier), U Ohn Gyaw (foreign affairs), Lt-Gen. Mya Thinn
  (home affairs), Brig.-Gen. Win Tin (finance), Brig.-Gen. David Abel (planning &
  economic development)
CURRENCY: kyat (end-'94 £1=K9.19, US$1=K5.87)
GNP PER CAPITA: US$200 ('86)
MAIN EXPORT EARNERS: teak, rice, minerals

IN 1994 political events continued to dominate in Burma. Aware that economic prosperity depended ultimately on a resolution of the country's political conflicts, the ruling State Law and Order Restoration Council (SLORC) extended negotiations with insurgent groups and began talks with imprisoned leader of the National League for Democracy (NLD), Daw Aung San Suu Kyi.

The SLORC strategy of brokering separate peace deals with the insurgents (see AR 1993, p. 332) continued to succeed in 1994. The SLORC concluded a peace treaty with the powerful Kachin Independence Army on 24 February, while negotiations were also conducted with Karen and Mon insurgents along the Thai-Burmese border during the year. In contrast, the SLORC stepped up its military campaign against the drug warlord Khun Sa and his Mong Tai Army (MTA). Burmese military advances, including the capture of Mong Kyawt, dealt a serious blow to Khun Sa as they cut off the drug baron's main source of opium in northern Burma. At year's end, fresh Burmese military attacks raised the possibility that Khun Sa might be soon forced out of the drug trade.

The opening of direct talks between Ms Suu Kyi and the SLORC was signalled when the imprisoned NLD leader was able to have a meeting with visiting US congressman William Richardson on 14 February. The dialogue began in September when Ms Suu Kyi had a meeting with the SLORC Chairman, General Than Shwe, and the military intelligence leader, Lieutenant-General Khin Nyunt. A further meeting was held on 29 October, and subsequently the NLD leader was permitted to meet with imprisoned colleagues Tin Oo (NLD chairman) and Kyi Maung

(NLD secretary). Although Ms Suu Kyi was still under house arrest in late December, it appeared likely that a resolution to the political stalemate between the SLORC and the NLD would occur in 1995.

These meetings occurred against a backdrop of continued international pressure on the SLORC. The Americans debated resolutions condemning the Burmese regime in Congress, and a visit to Rangoon on 31 October by the US Deputy Assistant Secretary of State for East Asian and Pacific Affairs, Thomas Hubbard, was a chance for the Americans to reiterate their position.

In contrast, Asian countries persisted with a policy of 'constructive engagement'. The year was marked by visits to Rangoon by the Singapore Prime Minister, Goh Chok Tong, and by the Indonesian Foreign Minister, Ali Alatas. In July Thailand invited Burma to the opening and closing ceremonies of the ASEAN summit in Bangkok (see XI.6.ii). In December Japan announced the resumption of official development assistance to Burma from April 1995 for humanitarian purposes. These measures reflected in part growing regional concern over Burma's close links with China (see AR 1993, p. 333). In 1994 relations between Burma and China continued to strengthen, trade between Burma and neighbouring Yunnan being estimated at nearly US$1,000 million. Military cooperation also continued: a mid-December visit to China by the SLORC's Lieutenant-General Tin Oo resulted in an arms deal worth a reported $400 million.

The SLORC continued to pursue a policy of gradual economic opening to the outside world in 1994. In conjunction with multinational firms, the government began to develop two offshore natural gas fields in the Andaman Sea; it also invited bids from international companies for gold and copper prospecting in north and central Burma. At year's end, the government was even consulting with Japan's Daiwa Securities about the establishment of a capital market in the country. Yet the persistence of grave human rights abuses perpetuated by the Burmese army continued to cast a shadow over the regime's economic plans.

Speculation continued in 1994 as to the likely political effects of the future demise of the 83-year-old Ne Win. The prospect of an outbreak of political infighting in the SLORC upon his death appeared more likely than ever as tensions grew between the army and the intelligence services. As in previous years, uncertainty persisted over the direction that Burmese politics would take in a post-Ne Win era.

ii.   THAILAND

CAPITAL: Bangkok   AREA: 513,000 sq km   POPULATION: 58,000,000 ('92)
OFFICIAL LANGUAGE: Thai   POLITICAL SYSTEM: constitutional monarchy
HEAD OF STATE: King Bhumibol Adulyadej (Rama IX) (since June '46)
RULING PARTIES: Democrat Party heads coalition
HEAD OF GOVERNMENT: Chuan Leekpai, Prime Minister (since Sept '92)
PRINCIPAL MINISTERS: Banyat Banthatthan, Gen. Arthit Kamlang-ek, Maj.-Gen.
   Chamlong Srimuang, Suphachai Panitchaphak (Deputy Premiers), Gen. Wichit
   Sukmak (defence), Thaksin Shinawatra (foreign affairs), Tharin Nimmanhemin
   (finance), Maj.-Gen. Sanan Kachornprasart (interior), Sawai Pattano (justice)
INTERNATIONAL ALIGNMENT: ASEAN, NAM
CURRENCY: baht (end-'94 £1=B39.28, US$1=B25.11)
GNP PER CAPITA: US$1,840 ('92)
MAIN EXPORT EARNERS: textiles, rice, tapioca, rubber, gems, fish products, tourism

TWO long-running scandals marred Thailand's international reputation in 1994. In May it was revealed that an opposition MP, Thanong Siripreechapong, had been indicted in the USA on serious drug-trafficking charges. He resigned as a member of the Chart Thai Party but denied the allegations. At the end of May a second MP, Mongkol Chongsuthamanee of the Chart Pattana Party, was similarly revealed to have had his US visa revoked. A series of stories circulated that as many as 17 serving and former MPs were also on a US drugs blacklist. At a closed-door session of the House of Representatives on 28 July, the then Foreign Minister, Prasong Sonsiri, accused the deputy leader of the opposition Chart Thai Party, Vatana Asavahame, of involvement in drug-trafficking. Earlier it had been revealed that Mr Vatana had also had his US visa application denied.

The second débâcle concerned the Saudi gems affair dating from 1989, when a Thai worker had stolen gems valued at US$20 million from a Saudi prince's residence in Riyadh. When the Thai police returned the recovered gems in 1990 they proved to be largely counterfeit. In early 1994 a Thai gem dealer was rumoured to have evidence of Thai police involvement in the scam. In July his wife and son were found battered to death and on 12 September a police officer investigating the case was charged with involvement in the murders. He in turn implicated Thailand's police chief, General Pratin Santiprabhob, who resigned his position, although charges against him and another senior police officer were quickly dropped for lack of evidence. At year's end eight people stood indicted for the abduction and murder of the dealer's wife and son.

The year saw Thailand's relations with Cambodia sour over allegations of Thai military support for the Khmers Rouges (KR) (see IX.1.ix). A comment to the same effect by the Australian Foreign Minister, Gareth Evans, provoked a sharp retort from the Thai government. In November Prime Minister Chuan refused a US government request to station military supply ships in the Gulf of Thailand, citing possible misunderstandings with Thailand's neighbours. In contrast, the opening of the first bridge across the lower reaches of the Mekong river, at a ceremony on 8 April attended by King Bhumibol, cemented relations with Laos (see IX.1.x).

A cabinet reshuffle on 26 October brought 11 representatives of the Palang Dharma (PD) party and three more MPs of the New Aspirations Party (NAP) into the government, including Major-General Chamlong Srimuang, the newly re-elected PD leader, as a Deputy Prime Minister. Most contentious was the appointment of non-elected media and telecoms tycoon Thaksin Shinawatra as Minister of Foreign Affairs, replacing Prasong Sonsiri. Major-General Chamlong was reputed to have pressed for the appointment, which was criticized as representing a return to 'money politics'.

As the year ended, the Chuan government ran into further turmoil on 8 December when the NAP, led by the Interior Minister, General Chavalit Yongchaiyut, left the ruling coalition to join the opposition in fighting proposed constitutional amendments. Faced with presiding over a minority government, the Prime Minister asked the Chart Pattana Party to join the coalition, an arrangement which most commentators viewed as distinctly uncomfortable given the party's links with the military junta that had seized power in the 1991 coup (see AR 1991, pp. 331-2). Following the changes, the ruling coalition controlled 201 seats in the 360-seat parliament. An extensive cabinet reshuffle followed soon after, in which Sanan Kachornprasart, a Democrat MP, was appointed Interior Minister. The roots of the crisis lay in the defeat of the government over constitutional reforms aimed at barring unelected local officials from serving on local councils.

In November the Thai parliament approved a new copyright law. In response, the US government stated that Thailand would be removed from the 'priority watch list' of countries which it considered guilty of intellectual property theft.

iii.   MALAYSIA

CAPITAL: Kuala Lumpur   AREA: 132,000 sq km   POPULATION: 18,600,000 ('92)
OFFICIAL LANGUAGE: Bahasa Malaysia   POLITICAL SYSTEM: federal democracy
HEAD OF STATE: Ja'afar ibni Abdul Rahman, Sultan of Selangor (since April '94)
RULING PARTY: National Front coalition
HEAD OF GOVERNMENT: Dr Mahathir Mohamad, Prime Minister (since '81)
PRINCIPAL MINISTERS: Anwar Ibrahim (Deputy Premier, finance), Abdullah Ahmad
   Badawi (foreign affairs), Najib Tun Razak (defence), Hamid Albar (justice),
   Rafidah Aziz (trade & industry)
INTERNATIONAL ALIGNMENT: NAM, ASEAN, ICO, Cwth.
CURRENCY: ringitt (end-'94 £1=M$3.99, US$1=M$2.55)
GNP PER CAPITA: US$2,790 ('92)
MAIN EXPORT EARNERS: oil, palm oil, timber, rubber, tin

FROM August onwards the government took measures to crush the Al-Arqam Islamic revivalist movement (named after a companion of the Prophet), which had been founded in 1968 by a religious teacher called Ashaari Muhammad. The movement was declared illegal by the National Fatwa Council because of its deviant religious teachings, after the Prime Minister, Dr Mahathir Mohamad, had described it as a threat to national security. Ashaari Muhammad was detained in Malaysia on 2 September on being deported from Thailand, where he had been in exile. He was released from detention on 28 October following an appearance on state television during which he recanted his teachings. The next day he announced that Al-Arqam was 'a thing of the past'.

In September Rahim Thamby Chik, chief minister of Malacca and president of the youth wing of the United Malays National Organization (UMNO), took leave of both offices pending the outcome of investigations into allegations that he had engaged in sexual relations with an under-age girl. After he had formally resigned the following month, the Attorney-General announced that criminal proceedings would not be brought against him, although charges of abuse of power and corruption were instituted in November. This scandal was given additional political significance by Dr Mahathir, who interpreted its disclosure as part of a challenge to his leadership. At UMNO's annual assembly in November, the Prime Minister invoked the analogy of Brutus from Shakespeare's *Julius Caesar* in warning off contenders for his office.

Sabah's chief minister, Joseph Pairin Kitingan, was found guilty of corruption on 17 January and fined, although the amount set by the court was below the threshold for automatic disbarment from holding public office. A week previously, he had dissolved the state legislature, for which new elections were held on 18–19 February. The ruling United Sabah Party was returned to office with a reduced majority of 25 out of 48 seats. Mr Pairin was sworn in for a further term as chief minister on 21 February, but he resigned on 17 March following the virtual disintegration of his party through defections to the state wing of the federal ruling National Front coalition. The latter formed a new government the next day, headed by Sakaran Dandai, previously federal Minister of Lands and Cooperative Development.

On 25 February the Malaysian government went well beyond its 'buy British last' policy of 1981 (see AR 1981, p. 287) by banning UK companies from competing for new government contracts. The decision was announced by Deputy Premier Anwar Ibrahim in retaliation for allegations in the London *Sunday Times* of financial impropriety by Dr Mahathir and other ministers and government officials. The allegations arose from investigative reporting into the terms of a British loan to finance the construction of the Pergau Dam (including a 600-megawatt hydroelectric power station) in Malaysia's east coast state of Kelantan, with particular reference to any entanglement between such aid and Malaysian orders for British-made armaments. Ironically, Malaysia's ban was announced within hours of its air force taking delivery of the first batch of 28 British Aerospace Hawk jet-trainers procured under a memorandum of understanding of September 1988.

Efforts by both sides to repair Anglo-Malaysian relations eventually resulted in the lifting of the ban on 7 September, after the editor of the *Sunday Times* had moved to a new post with an American television station. On 10 November the High Court in London ruled that the British government had acted unlawfully by authorizing a concessionary loan from its foreign aid budget to finance the Pergau Dam. However, any renewed threat to Anglo-Malaysian relations passed when Douglas Hurd, the Foreign Secretary, made it clear that the UK government would meet its contractual obligations. In a deal involving counter-trade in palm oil and other products, Malaysia agreed on 7 June to purchase 18 Russian MiG fighter aircraft, this marking Russia's first sale of military equipment to a non-communist country in South-East Asia since the break-up of the Soviet Union.

Dr Mahathir received Singapore's Prime Minister, Goh Chok Tong, on the island of Langkawi on 7 September, when it was agreed that the jurisdiction dispute over the Singapore Strait island of Pedra Branca (called Pulau Batu Puteh in Malaysia) would be referred to a third party such as the International Court of Justice. Talks between Dr Mahathir and President Suharto of Indonesia in Jakarta a week later failed to make progress on a similar dispute over the islands of Sipadan and Ligitan off the coast of eastern Borneo, Malaysia's proposal for third party arbitration being rejected.

In February the Malaysian censorship board banned the internationally-acclaimed US film *Schindler's List* on the grounds that its story (about Nazi Germany's extermination of Jews during World War II) 'reflects the privileges and the virtues of a certain race only' (see also XVI.1.v). The ban was overturned by the government in March on condition that scenes of nudity and violence were cut, but the film was not shown in Malaysia because its distributors, United International, refused to permit any cuts to be made. In July the Malaysian government reaffirmed its refusal to establish diplomatic or trade relations with Israel, following the revelation that King Ja'afar's brother, Tunku Abdullah, had visited the Jewish state. Tunku Abdullah's passport was impounded for one day as a political gesture, but in October the government announced that Malaysians would be permitted to visit Jerusalem for work or religious purposes.

Dr Mahathir attended the summit meeting of the Asia-Pacific Economic Cooperation (APEC) forum in Indonesia in November (see XI.6.iii), publicly subscribing to the common resolve on the desirability of freer regional trade and investment. Immediately afterwards he issued reservations about his government's position on the pace and scope of trade liberalization which were seen as reflecting his general reservations about the role of APEC.

iv. BRUNEI

CAPITAL: Bandar Seri Bagawan   AREA: 5,765 sq km   POPULATION: 273,000 ('92)
OFFICIAL LANGUAGES: Malay & English   POLITICAL SYSTEM: monarchy
HEAD OF STATE & GOVERNMENT: Sultan Sir Hassanal Bolkiah (since '67)
PRINCIPAL MINISTERS: Prince Mohammed Bolkiah (foreign affairs), Prince Jefri
     Bolkiah (finance), Pehin Dato Haji Isa (internal affairs), Pengiran Bahrin (law)
INTERNATIONAL ALIGNMENT: NAM, ICO, ASEAN, Cwth.
CURRENCY: Brunei dollar (end-'94 £1=B$2.81, US$1=B$1.46)
GNP PER CAPITA: US$15,390 ('87)
MAIN EXPORT EARNERS: oil & gas

THE Foreign Ministers of Brunei and Malaysia and their officials held an inaugural joint commission meeting (JCM) in the Malaysian resort of Langkawi in April. An agreement was reached on adopting a bilateral approach to resolving Brunei's longstanding claim to Limbang, which had been a part of adjoining Sarawak (now a Malaysian state) for over a century. The two governments also agreed to set up a joint committee on disputed land and maritime boundaries. In October President Ali Akbar Rafsanjani of Iran visited Brunei for official talks with Sultan Hassanal Bolkiah.

At a meeting in London in mid-December the Sultan of Brunei and the UK Prime Minister, John Major, signed a memorandum of cooperation on defence sales, in the context of a renewal of the agreement providing for the stationing of a battalion of the British Gurkha Rifles in Brunei.

v. SINGAPORE

CAPITAL: Singapore   AREA: 620 sq km   POPULATION: 2,800,000 ('92)
OFFICIAL LANGUAGES: Malay, Chinese, Tamil, English
POLITICAL SYSTEM: parliamentary
HEAD OF STATE: President Ong Teng Cheong (since Aug '93)
RULING PARTY: People's Action Party (PAP)
HEAD OF GOVERNMENT: Goh Chok Tong, Prime Minister (since Nov '90)
PRINCIPAL MINISTERS: Lee Kuan Yew (senior minister), Lee Hsien Loong (Deputy
     Prime Minister), Wong Kan Seng (home affairs), Richard Hu Tsu Tau (finance),
     Shanmugam Jayakumar (foreign affairs & law), Lee Boon Yang (defence &
     labour), Yeo Cheow Tong (trade & industry)
INTERNATIONAL ALIGNMENT: NAM, ASEAN, Cwth.
CURRENCY: Singapore dollar (end-'94 £1=S$2.28, US$1=S$1.46)
GNP PER CAPITA: US$15,730 ('92)
MAIN EXPORT EARNERS: machinery & equipment, petroleum products, financial
     services, tourism

THE caning in May of an 18-year-old US citizen, Michael Fay, after he had been convicted of acts of vandalism generated heated but mixed international responses. President Clinton appealed to President Ong Teng Cheong for the sentence of six strokes with a rattan cane to be commuted, but Singapore's cabinet advised only that it be reduced to four strokes as a way of accommodating the appeal from the head of a friendly state without compromising the principle that persons convicted of vandalism should be caned. The government of Singapore was strongly confirmed in its position by extensive popular support for the punishment in the United States. An early US response to the caning was to oppose Singapore's offer to hold the first ministerial meeting of the new post-GATT World Trade Organization.

Less media attention was generated in June when 17-year-old Shiu Chi Ho from Hong Kong, who was charged with vandalism at the same time as Michael Fay, received six strokes of the cane after his initial sentence of 12 strokes had been halved. In September Johannes van Damme, a Dutch citizen, became the first Westerner to be hanged under Singapore's anti-drugs legislation after being found guilty in 1993 of trafficking in heroin.

The limits to press freedom in Singapore were demonstrated in March when two journalists (one of them the editor of *Business Times*, Patrick Daniel) and three economists were fined after being found guilty of violating the Official Secrets Act. They had been charged in 1993 with illegally disclosing the government's estimate of economic growth for the second quarter of 1992 a few days before its official release (see AR 1993, p. 338). Despite fulsome public apologies from the defendants, legal action for damages over articles appearing in the *International Herald Tribune* was taken by Senior Minister Lee Kuan Yew and Deputy Prime Minister Lee Hsien Loong in September, and by Lee Kuan Yew alone in December, while the government filed contempt of court charges in November in respect of one article.

On 21 November the Registrar of Societies approved the formation of the Singapore People's Party, which had been set up by a breakaway faction of the Singapore Democratic Party following an abortive attempt to expel its founder and parliamentary leader, Chiam See Tong (see AR 1993, pp. 338–9).

Prime Minister Goh Chok Tong visited Myanmar in March, becoming only the second head of government (after that of Laos) to acknowledge personally the authority of the military junta which had engaged in savage repression of unarmed demonstrators in 1988 (see also IX.1.i). Lee Kuan Yew paid his first visit to Israel in mid-May and then went on to visit Jordan. At a conference in Singapore later in the month, Mr Lee warned China that it would alienate the countries of South-East Asia if it interfered in their internal affairs or pursued a policy of expansionism in the South China Sea. In October, however, the former Singapore Prime Minister accepted the office of honorary chairman at the founding conference of the International Confucian Association held in Beijing.

vi. INDONESIA

CAPITAL: Jakarta   AREA: 1,905,000 sq km   POPULATION: 184,300,000 ('92)
OFFICIAL LANGUAGE: Bahasa Indonesia   POLITICAL SYSTEM: presidential, army-
   backed
HEAD OF STATE & GOVERNMENT: President (Gen. rtd.) Suharto (since '68)
RULING PARTY: Joint Secretariat of Functional Groups (Golkar)
PRINCIPAL MINISTERS: Gen. Try Sutrisno (Vice-President), Susilo Sudarman
   (political affairs & security), Saleh Afiff (economy), Ali Alatas (foreign affairs),
   Yogi S. Memet (home affairs), Gen. Edi Sudrajat (defence & security),
   Mar'ie Muhammad (finance), Utoyo Usman (justice)
INTERNATIONAL ALIGNMENT: NAM, ASEAN, ICO, OPEC
CURRENCY: rupiah (end-'94 £1=Rp3,438.77, US$1=Rp2,198.00)
GNP PER CAPITA: US$670 ('92)
MAIN EXPORT EARNERS: oil & gas

THE economic growth characteristic of modern Indonesian development persisted in 1994, while the political scene continued to be dominated by the government's repressive East Timor and civil rights policies.

In January an austere budget of the equivalent of US$33,100 million was passed which sought to balance declining oil and gas receipts, and concerns about foreign debt of over $90,000 million, with development plans in the energy, transport and education sectors. The year also witnessed further initiatives to attract foreign investment (see AR 1993, p. 341). On 2 June a major deregulation package was approved whose key provision was the ending of a requirement that foreign firms surrender majority control of their operations to Indonesian firms after 15 years. This step was followed in October by new legislation to reform the country's tax system. The government also embarked on its first international privatization with the $1,000 million flotation of the Indosat telephone company in the largest equity issue ever made in the developing world. Yet the main economic event of the year was the massive influx of foreign investment—in excess of $23,000 million in 1994, more than double the previous record set in 1992.

The underlying strength of the economy was reflected in annual growth of 6.5 per cent in 1994, equal to that of 1993. A rise in oil prices from $16 to $20 a barrel for Sumatran crude contributed to the favourable economic situation, as did a rise in non-oil and gas exports during the year. Impressed with Indonesia's economic record, international donors pledged $5,200 million in official development assistance for 1994/95, up 1.7 per cent from the previous year. Still, revelations about bad debts held by state banks—and notably the Golden Key scandal, involving the misappropriation of $420 million in loans from the Indonesian Development Bank—were a reminder that political 'cronyism' continued to exist in certain economic sectors.

On the political front, 1994 was a mixed year for the government. President Suharto's international reputation was enhanced as a result of his chairmanship of the Asia-Pacific Economic Cooperation (APEC)

summit which met in Indonesia in November and backed trade liberalization in the region (see XI.6.iii). Yet Indonesia's continued violation
of human rights in East Timor and elsewhere in the country remained
a source of political trouble. Notwithstanding efforts in 1993 to project
a more favourable image over East Timor (see AR 1993, p. 340), the
government continued to be the focus of international criticism over
this issue. Unrest in this province continued throughout the year, and
an invasion of the US embassy in Jakarta by 29 East Timorese students
dominated international media coverage during the APEC summit. East
Timor was also the subject of discussions between President Suharto and
President Bill Clinton at the summit. Yet in late 1994 there appeared
little prospect of an early resolution to this conflict.

The arrest of union leaders also increased doubts about the government's 'openness' (*keperbukaan*) policy. Labour unrest in the country
flared into the open in April when a union demonstration against
local firms in Medan turned into a major anti-Chinese riot. The
government responded by crushing the independent union movement.
By year's end, many union leaders were under detention, including
Muchtar Pakpahan, head of the Indonesian Worker's Welfare Union
(the country's largest independent union). In another move that caused
domestic and international dismay, the Suharto regime closed three news
magazines popular with Indonesia's middle-class for their attempts to
highlight policy differences within the government over the purchase of
39 former East German naval vessels (see AR 1993, p. 341).

Plans in late 1994 to clamp down on Indonesia's non-governmental
organizations raised the prospect of continued political disquiet in the
country in 1995. In the process, political troubles once again threatened
to distract attention in the coming year from Indonesia's impressive
economic achievements.

vii. PHILIPPINES

CAPITAL: Manila   AREA: 300,000 sq km   POPULATION: 64,300,000 ('92)
OFFICIAL LANGUAGE: Filipino   POLITICAL SYSTEM: presidential democracy
HEAD OF STATE & GOVERNMENT: President Fidel Ramos (since May '92)
RULING PARTIES: Lakas ng Edsa/National Union of Christian Democrats heads
    coalition
PRINCIPAL MINISTERS: Joseph Estrada (Vice-President), Roberto Romulo (foreign
    affairs), Gen. Renato de Villa (defence), Franklin Drilon (justice), Ernesto Leung
    (finance), Rafael Alunan (interior)
INTERNATIONAL ALIGNMENT: NAM, ASEAN
CURRENCY: peso (end-'94 £1=P38.17, US$1=P24.40)
GNP PER CAPITA: US$770 ('92)
MAIN EXPORT EARNERS: electrical goods, textiles, agricultural products, minerals

THERE were signs in 1994 that an economic recovery was occurring
in the Philippines. However, political controversy dogged President

Ramos, and a politically damaging U-turn over an oil levy threatened to undermine his ability to produce further economic reforms.

Trouble for the President began early in the year as a levy on oil sales threatened to result in retail price increases of up to 28 per cent. An anti-oil levy coalition, the Kilusang Pollback, organized highly effective popular protests, while the Communist Party of the Philippines set off bombs at the offices of oil companies. Faced with a nationwide strike, President Ramos backed down and cancelled the oil levy on 23 February. He then began a search for funds to make up for the estimated P 10,100 million ($367 million) shortfall caused by this decision so as to avert the withdrawal of an International Monetary Fund (IMF) credit facility to the country. Plans to collect additional revenue through a crackdown on tax evasion in the banking sector and the establishment of a national lottery drew opposition. The eventual decision to extend value-added tax (VAT) to the service sector, and to impose an increased tax on stockmarket transactions, prompted a new round of protests. However, the solution was sufficient for the IMF to approve a long-delayed $684 million credit facility on 24 June. This opened the way for a systematic rescheduling of the national debt as well as the infusion of fresh aid money. In July the World Bank pledged $5,600 million in assistance for 1994–95.

These moves reflected cautious but growing international confidence in the Philippines economy. A big boost in 1994 was the alleviation of the electricity power cuts that had hampered business in the Manila area so much in the previous year. As production increased, so too did exports, which rose 19.5 per cent in the first nine months of the year alone. More importantly, foreign investment increased dramatically with approvals to September running at the equivalent of $14,000 million, or five times the 1993 rate. With inflation holding at around 7.5 per cent and annual economic growth estimated to be in excess of 3 per cent, the peso began to gain value towards year's end. Passage of a new banking law permitting increased foreign participation, as well as approval of the December 1993 GATT agreement (see AR 1993, pp. 408, 534, 574-86), provided further reassurance to the international community.

Nevertheless, various disputes in 1994 were a reminder of the factionalism still plaguing the country's politics. In a replay of the oil levy controversy, the extended VAT legislation prompted popular and political opposition. It also resulted in growing tensions between President Ramos and the opposition-dominated Senate, and led to the defection of 20 congressmen, including House of Representatives majority leader Ronaldo Zamora, from the Ramos faction. The President responded on 26 August by announcing that his party, the Lakas–National Union of Christian Democrats (Lakas-NUCD), and the erstwhile opposition Laban ng Demokratikong Pilipino (LDP) would form a grand coalition to implement a common legislative programme.

More importantly, the new coalition was to field a common slate of candidates in the 1995 congressional and local elections. Although it was already showing signs of deep divisions by year's end, the coalition nevertheless represented the most powerful political force in the country as attention turned to the election campaign.

viii. VIETNAM

CAPITAL: Hanoi   AREA: 330,000 sq km   POPULATION: 69,300,000 ('92)
OFFICIAL LANGUAGE: Vietnamese   POLITICAL SYSTEM: socialist republic
RULING PARTY: Communist Party of Vietnam (CPV)
HEAD OF STATE: President (Gen.) Le Duc Anh (since Sept '92)
PARTY LEADER: Do Muoi, CPV general secretary (since June '91)
PRINCIPAL MINISTERS: Gen. Vo Van Kiet (Prime Minister), Nguyen Manh Cam
    (foreign affairs), Lt-Gen. Bui Thien Ngo (interior), Gen. Doan Khue (defence),
    Ho Te (finance), Nguyen Dinh Loc (justice)
INTERNATIONAL ALIGNMENT: NAM
CURRENCY: dong (end-'94 £1=D17,323.6, US$1=D11,072.9)
MAIN EXPORT EARNERS: crude oil, rise, textiles, seafood

AFTER months of speculation, the US economic embargo of Vietnam was lifted on 3 February, following the adoption by the Senate in late January of a non-binding resolution urging the lifting of sanctions and a series of missions to Vietnam by US politicians and military personnel (see also IV.1). The embargo had been imposed on North Vietnam in 1964 and had been in force on unified Vietnam since the end of the war in 1975. However, President Bill Clinton stressed that the full restoration of diplomatic relations would have to await further progress on the issue of the MIAs (US servicemen listed as 'missing in action'). In a further step towards normalization, Hanoi and Washington on 21 May agreed to establish liaison offices in their respective capitals.

The Prime Ministers of Singapore and Thailand, respectively Goh Chok Tong and Chuan Leekpai, both visited Hanoi in March and lent their support to Vietnam's plans to join the Association of South-East Asian Nations (ASEAN). It was unofficially disclosed at the end of November that Vietnam would become ASEAN's seventh member in mid-1995. During October tension between Vietnam and China over the disputed Spratly Islands intensified, the Chinese deploring Vietnam's prospecting for oil in disputed territory, while Vietnam accused China of systematic territorial violations. However, during a landmark visit to Vietnam in November by President Jiang Zemin of China, Hanoi and Beijing agreed to set up an expert group to negotiate the settlement of the Spratly Islands dispute and to resolve border disagreements without recourse to force, or the threat of force.

The ruling Communist Party of Vietnam (CPV) held its first-ever mid-term national conference in January. Details were sketchy, but the delegates confirmed their commitment to the process of renovation (*doi moi*). Fears of growing corruption arising out of the reform process were reinforced in February when a former Energy Minister, Vu Ngoc Hai, was sentenced to three years' imprisonment for corruption. He was the highest-ranking government official to be tried to date.

At a World Bank-sponsored meeting of aid donors in Paris in mid-November, US$2,000 million in aid was pledged for 1995 and the government's economic reform policies were highly praised. GDP growth for 1994 was forecast at a healthy 8.5–9.0 per cent, but inflation rose to 14.4 per cent for the 12 months to November. The discovery of a new oilfield off southern Vietnam was announced by a subsidiary of Mitsubishi Oil of Japan in June. In mid-September British Petroleum revealed that the large natural gas field discovered in 1993 (see AR 1993, p. 345) had estimated recoverable reserves of 350 million barrels of oil equivalent.

A visit by Prime Minister Vo Van Kiet to Russia in mid-June led to the signing of a treaty of friendship and two agreements of cooperation. The former instrument effectively downgraded the previous Soviet-Vietnamese friendship and cooperation treaty, removing any provision for military support in the event of an attack on either party.

A meeting of the International Conference on Indo-Chinese Refugees in Geneva on 14 February endorsed a plan to repatriate some 52,000 'boat people' held in camps in South-East Asia by the end of 1995.

ix. CAMBODIA

CAPITAL: Phnom Penh   AREA: 181,000 sq km   POPULATION: 9,050,000 ('92)
OFFICIAL LANGUAGE: Khmer   POLITICAL SYSTEM: monarchy
HEAD OF STATE: King Norodom Sihanouk (elected Sept '93)
RULING PARTIES: United National Front for an Independent, Neutral, Peaceful and Cooperative Cambodia (FUNCINPEC) and Cambodian People's Party (CPP) head coalition
PRINCIPAL MINISTERS: Norodom Ranariddh (First Prime Minister), Hun Sen (Second Prime Minister), Sar Kheng (Vice-Prime Minister, interior), Ing Kiet (Vice-Prime Minister, public works), Keat Chhon (economy & finance), Ing Huot (foreign affairs), Tea Banh (defence), Tie Chamrat (defence), Gen. Peng Pat (defence), Gen. El Vansarat (defence), Chem Snguon (justice)
CURRENCY: riel (end-'94 £1=R4,054.16, US$1=R2,591.35)
GNP PER CAPITA: US$200 ('91)

IN early July the government foiled a coup attempt led by Norodom Chakkrapong (a former Vice-Prime Minister), General Sin Song (former Interior Minister) and Sin Sen (State Secretary for the Interior). Sin Song and Chakkrapong, both former members of the Cambodian People's Party (CPP), had been expelled from the government after alleged involvement in another attempted coup in June 1993. Sin Song and Sin

Sen were arrested while Chakkrapong fled the country. The government also arrested 14 Thai citizens at Phnom Penh airport, allegedly weapons experts flown in to assist in the coup; five were quickly released but the rest were charged and sentenced to suspended gaol terms. While the Thai government vigorously denied any role in the coup attempt, allegations later emerged that Vice-Prime Minister Sar Kheng and 42 others had been involved. Commentators saw the plot as indicating a split in the CPP. On 4 September Sin Song escaped from prison and on 28 October a Cambodian court sentenced him, *in absentia*, to a 20-year gaol sentence. In early November Sin Song was arrested in Bangkok, whereupon the Cambodian government requested his return to Phnom Penh.

Fighting between troops of the Cambodian government and Khmers Rouges (KR) guerrillas intensified in January when government forces advanced in strength towards the northern KR headquarters at Anlong Veng, which they took at the beginning of February. KR commander Ta Mok moved his forces eastwards into Preah Vihear province before counter-attacking. By the beginning of March Anlong Veng was back in KR hands. The Cambodian government claimed an even more significant victory on 19 March—the capture of the KR headquarters at Pailin, under KR control since late 1989. But by 19 April Pailin too had been recaptured by the KR. In early May the KR came close to overwhelming the key city of Battambang.

At the end of May the KR and the Cambodian government attended a conference on 'peace and national reconciliation' in Pyongyang (North Korea), organized by King Norodom Sihanouk. Further talks were held in mid-June in Phnom Penh. However, the KR demanded power-sharing before any ceasefire, with the result that the talks reached deadlock. In response, the government closed KR offices in Phnom Penh and expelled all KR officials. On 7 July the National Assembly controversially outlawed the KR, while offering an amnesty to rank-and-file guerrillas who surrendered within six months. Two days later the KR announced the formation of an alternative 'provisional government of national union and national salvation'. However, towards the end of the year defections from the KR increased as rebels took advantage of the government's amnesty offer.

A cabinet reshuffle was approved by the National Assembly on 20 October. The most notable change was the replacement of the Economy and Finance Minister, Sam Rangsi, by Keat Chhon. Sam Rangsi was highly regarded and had taken a tough anti-corruption stance; the government's claim that his removal was to retain ministerial unity was discounted by most commentators. On 24 October the Minister for Foreign Affairs and International Cooperation, Prince Norodom Sereivut, resigned in solidarity with Rangsi, stating that 'we must show. . . there are some honest people'.

The Thai Prime Minister, Chuan Leekpai, visited Phnom Penh in January, the first such visit for many years. However, the trip coincided with fresh, and embarrassing, allegations—vigorously denied—of Thai military support for the KR. With the fall of Pailin, the war of words between the Cambodian and Thai governments intensified. Both Cambodian Prime Ministers, Norodom Ranariddh and Hun Sen, accused the Thais of assisting the KR and even of helping Pol Pot to escape from Pailin.

In April two Britons and an Australian were kidnapped by the KR, which eventually (in mid-November) admitted to their killing, branding them 'spies and colonials'. On 26 July three tourists (French, British and Australian) travelling on a train in Kompot province were also kidnapped by the KR. The government announced the discovery of their bodies on 1 November and there was a spate of mutual recrimination over the failure to secure their release. The KR admitted to their 'execution' in mid-November, claiming they were spies. In October Chhouk Rin, the commander of the KR forces involved in their seizure, defected to the government and received an amnesty—to the outrage of the Australian, British and French governments. The episode raised the possibility that military aid might be cut. The failure to prosecute Chhouk Rin was allegedly because a trial would reveal that government forces were also involved in the train attack. In November the Cambodian authorities recovered the bodies of 17 Thai loggers murdered by the KR in Preah Vihear province.

The second meeting of the International Committee on the Reconstruction of Cambodia held in Tokyo on 10–11 March pledged US$486 million in aid for 1994 and applauded the government's market reforms. On 6 May the IMF agreed an enhanced structural adjustment facility amounting to $120 million to finance the reform programme for 1994–96. At the beginning of August the National Assembly passed a new, and overdue, investment law providing foreign investors with tax exemption on profits for eight years and various other incentives.

A controversial immigration law, which some saw as permitting the expulsion of ethnic Vietnamese residents of Cambodia, was passed by the National Assembly on 26 August. On 4 November the cabinet approved a draft press law, to the dismay of press associations and human rights groups, which saw it as potentially undermining press freedom. Severe flooding affected the southern and western provinces in August; damage was costed at $200 million.

x. LAOS

CAPITAL: Vientiane AREA: 237,000 sq km POPULATION: 4,400,000 ('92)
OFFICIAL LANGUAGE: Laotian POLITICAL SYSTEM: people's republic
RULING PARTY: Lao People's Revolutionary Party (LPRP)
HEAD OF STATE: President Nouhak Phoumsavan (since Nov '92)
HEAD OF GOVERNMENT: Gen. Khamtay Siphandon, LPRP chairman (since Nov '92)
  and Prime Minister (since Aug '91)
PRINCIPAL MINISTERS: Gen. Phoune Sipaseuth (vice-premier, supervising foreign
  affairs), Khamphoui Keoboualapha (Vice-Prime Minister, planning & co-
  operation), Brig.-Gen. Choummali Saygnasone (defence), Asang Laoli
  (interior), Khamouan Bouppha (justice), Somsavat Lengsavat (foreign affairs),
  Khamsai Souphanouvong (finance)
INTERNATIONAL ALIGNMENT: NAM
CURRENCY: new kip (end-'94 £1=KN1,127.28, US$1=KN720.54)
GNP PER CAPITA: US$250 ('92)
MAIN EXPORT EARNERS: textiles, electricity, coffee, minerals, timber

ON 8 April the first bridge across the lower reaches of the Mekong
river was officially opened in a ceremony attended by King Bhumibol
of Thailand, President Nouhak Phoumsavan of Laos and the Prime
Ministers of Laos, Thailand and Australia (General Khamtay Siphandon,
Chuan Leekpai and Paul Keating respectively). The so-called Friendship
(or Mitaphaab) Bridge, which had been financed by Australia, provided
a link between the north-eastern Thai town of Nong Khai and the Lao
capital of Vientiane. It was expected to ease transport constraints in
Laos, the only land-locked country in South-East Asia.

The National Assembly passed new investment and labour laws in
March, to be enforced within 60 days. As an incentive to foreign
investors, the investment law lowered some import taxes and the tax on
net profit, streamlined the approval process and rescinded the 15-year
foreign investment period limit hitherto in force. The labour law was
intended to provide better protection for both workers and employers.

2. CHINA—TAIWAN—HONG KONG—JAPAN—
SOUTH KOREA—NORTH KOREA—MONGOLIA

i. PEOPLE'S REPUBLIC OF CHINA

CAPITAL: Beijing AREA: 9,600,000 sq km POPULATION: 1,198,500,000 ('94)
OFFICIAL LANGUAGE: Chinese POLITICAL SYSTEM: people's republic
HEAD OF STATE: President Jiang Zemin (since March '93)
RULING PARTY: Chinese Communist Party (CCP)
PARTY LEADER: Jiang Zemin, CCP general secretary (since June '89)
CCP POLITBURO STANDING COMMITTEE: Jiang Zemin, Li Peng, Qiao Shi, Li Ruihuan,
  Zhu Rongji, Liu Huaqing, Hu Jintao
CCP CENTRAL COMMITTEE SECRETARIAT: Hu Jintao, Ding Guangen, Wei Jianxing,
  Wen Jiabao, Ren Jianxin
CENTRAL MILITARY COMMISSION: Jiang Zemin, chairman (since Nov '89)
PRINCIPAL MINISTERS: Li Peng (Premier), Zhu Rongji (Vice-Premier, governor of
  central bank), Zou Jiahua (Vice-Premier), Qian Qichen (Vice-Premier, foreign
  affairs), Li Lanqing (Vice-Premier), Liu Zhongli (finance), Wu Yi (foreign trade
  & economic cooperation), Chi Haotian (defence), Jia Chunwang (state security),
  Tao Siju (public security), Xiao Yang (justice)
INTERNATIONAL ALIGNMENT: independent, orientated towards Third World
CURRENCY: renminbi (RMB) denominated in yuan (end-'94 £1=Y8.58, US$1=Y5.80)
GNP PER CAPITA: US$373 ('92) at market exchange rate, US$1,910 ('92) at purchasing
  power parity
MAIN EXPORT EARNERS: textiles, mechanical & electrical goods, mineral products,
  light manufactures, agricultural products

ECONOMIC construction remained at the centre of China's domestic
agenda during 1994, although there was increasing concern about the
weak ideological and organizational base of the Chinese Communist
Party (CCP), in part prompted by a deterioration in public order. At
home, a buoyant economic performance masked some of the problems
associated with rapid growth, such as upward pressure on prices and the
emergence of supply bottlenecks of key goods and services. Meanwhile,
the momentum of foreign trade expansion was maintained and realized
overseas investment showed a significant increase. Measures to improve
social stability were less successful—not least in parts of the countryside,
where the situation was said to be out of control. Paralysis of grassroots
party organizations was one contributory factor. Another was the
existence of enormous numbers of surplus rural labourers, many of
whom migrated to major cities, but failed to find productive
employment and turned in increasing numbers to crime.

A series of high-level diplomatic tours highlighted the importance
attached by the government to improving its foreign relations and
enhancing China's global position. Active participation in the sixth Asia-
Pacific Economic Cooperation (APEC) summit meeting in November
(see XI.6.iii) also underlined the significance of China's regional role.
Within the Asia-Pacific region, reciprocal visits to Beijing and Seoul
by government leaders underlined the strength of the axis being forged
between China and South Korea (see also IX.2.v). The potential benefits
to both sides of closer economic ties between China and Japan were

reflected in increased trade and investment flows, although the legacy of history overshadowed their non-economic relations (see IX.2.iv). Major obstacles also surrounded continuing talks between non-governmental representatives from Taiwan and the People's Republic (see IX.2.ii), while the opposing views of the Chinese and Hong Kong governments on Governor Patten's constitutional proposals remained irreconcilable (see IX.2.iii). High-level talks in Washington and Beijing generated more hopeful developments in Sino-American relations and President Clinton's decision to delink the award of China's most-favoured-nation (MFN) status was a significant watershed (see IV.1). The presence of the French Premier in China and that of Premier Li Peng in Germany were perhaps the most conspicuous signs of a mutual desire for closer ties between China and Western Europe.

Official statistics for 1993 and 1994 offered clear evidence of a booming economy. In 1993 the annual rate of GDP growth was 13.4 per cent, making China the world's fastest-growing major economy. During the same period, agriculture and industry grew by 4 and 20.2 per cent respectively, while fixed investment surged by 58.6 per cent. In 1994 GDP growth of 11.8 per cent was recorded, while industrial and fixed investment growth slowed to 18 and 27.8 per cent respectively. The 1994 figures indicated some apparent success in meeting earlier demands for slower growth in order to cool down what had widely come to be regarded as serious economic overheating. The reality was otherwise. The rate of domestic inflation remained stubbornly high and the supply of many key commodities and services was well below the demands of current growth. Against the background of a mere 2.2 per cent growth in coal production in 1993 and the re-emergence, after several decades, of China as a net oil importer, the energy constraint was especially serious.

Rapid but unbalanced growth characterized China's trade performance in 1993, with imports rising by 29 per cent, compared with only 8 per cent for exports. The outcome was a trade deficit of US$12,200 million—the first such deficit since 1989 and the largest since 1985. In 1994, however, major export recovery reversed the previous trends, and by the end of the year a surplus of $5,300 million had been achieved. Meanwhile, utilized foreign investment rose by an astonishing 91.5 per cent in 1993, as China absorbed $25,800 million of foreign direct investment (FDI). The upward momentum was maintained, albeit at a slower rate, during 1994, although contracted investment fell sharply. There was evidence of a greater involvement in China's economy by multinationals, not least through their participation in high-tech, large-scale infrastructural projects.

As in previous years, Li Peng's government work report, delivered to the second session of the Eighth National People's Congress (NPC) on 10 March, focused on China's economic situation. He confirmed that the main thrust of current reform efforts was to create a 'socialist market economy' and to implement associated changes in tax, financial and investment systems. Further decentralization of enterprise decision-making powers and price rationalization remained high priorities. Premier Li also revealed that the door to traders and foreign investors would be opened even wider and he called for closer scientific and technological cooperation with overseas partners.

But the Premier did not ignore the less favourable aspects of China's economic situation and his report was in some ways a familiar litany of problems still confronting the government. Most serious were the excessive scale of fixed investment and high level of inflation, the persistence of structural economic irrationalities and the inefficiency of state-owned enterprises. Such difficulties were compounded by the poor state of public order and the weakness of government administration. Addressing himself to ways of correcting the structural imbalances and easing the pressures of excessive growth, Premier Li warned against the 'blind' pursuit of growth and urged localities to formulate output targets commensurate with their individual circumstances. He called for more rational functional and regional patterns of investment in order to direct funds to key sectors, such as energy, raw and semi-finished materials, transport and telecommunications. He also proposed to introduce tighter controls on construction activities, including halting the establishment of development zones

The single issue which dominated economic debate in 1994 was inflation. Despite the introduction of remedial measures in mid-1993 (see AR 1993, p. 350), prices continued to rise. By the end of the year the annual rate of urban inflation had reached 25.9 per cent (second only to the previous post-1949 peak level of 1988). In the first half of 1994 the overall retail price index increased by a further 20 per cent. Cities were worst hit and there were warnings that inflation had reached the 'limit of urban residents' tolerance'. But, ominously, there were hints that price increases were also causing considerable rural discontent. The persistence of inflationary pressure was attributed to continued rises in fixed investment and consumer spending, fuelled by excessive expansion of the money supply. The government's inability to control price rises was reflected in upward revisions of the annual rate of inflation—from 16 per cent in August (already well above the 10 per cent target) to 21 per cent by the end of the year. Against this background, it was clear that China would remain committed to a tight fiscal policy throughout 1995.

The dangers of neglecting the needs of agriculture and reaffirmation of its fundamental role in China's development were recurring themes. Widely differing agricultural and industrial growth rates (see above) indicated fundamental structural imbalance in the economy. But there was abundant evidence of problems in the farm sector itself: falling (even negative) investment, the weakness of its scientific base, the widespread closure of local rural technology centres and the slow growth of peasant income (especially for grain farmers). An article in the *People's Daily* (8 December) most dramatically highlighted official concern in the face of lagging farm growth. It warned that the 'desperate' agricultural situation threatened future economic growth and improvements in living standards and urged that, in the interests of economic and political stability, prioritization of agriculture should be made 'the party's basic ideological guiding principle for economic work'.

Economic conditions in the state enterprise sector were a source of concern throughout 1994. State-owned enterprises (SOEs) still contributed about half of industrial output, but accounted for less than 7 per cent of national industrial growth. In part, this reflected the rapid expansion of rural and foreign-funded industrial enterprises. But it was also the result of depressed efficiency, highlighted in falling profits, rising losses, increasing indebtedness and inadequate investment. As a major source of profits and taxes remitted to the government, the increasing incidence of loss-making SOEs—by mid-1994, more than 45 per cent of them were in deficit—posed a serious threat to the effective implementation of public sector policy. In the face of a rapidly deteriorating situation, there was strong support for mergers or auctions of loss-making units. Official encouragement extended to the use of foreign capital and establishment of joint ventures in order to renovate, up-grade and modernize SOEs—though not to the adoption of wholesale privatization. Above all, the greater use of bankruptcy for ailing SOEs was advocated. Awareness of earlier unsuccessful attempts to implement bankruptcies underlined the need to devise ways of creating an effective social security framework, settling enterprise debts and finding new jobs for displaced workers. To this end, a new Bankruptcy Law was to be promulgated during 1995.

With law and order increasingly undermined, officials called for intensified efforts to curb criminal activities (including road and rail banditry, prostitution, drug-trafficking, the abduction and sale of women and children, and gang-based murder, robbery and theft). Conditions in the countryside were acute, it being apparent that violent crime was rising faster in some rural areas than in the cities. The situation was exacerbated by the failure to allocate sufficient funds and manpower to enforce the law and maintain social order. Rural police stations were often manned by just two or three officers and in some places there were none at all. A major contributory factor was the existence of a huge army of surplus rural labourers, officially estimated at 130 million. Whether they remained in the countryside or joined the major cities' 'floating population' (2.81 million migrants arrived in Shanghai in 1993 and at one point up to 70,000 were entering Beijing every day), many of those who failed to find jobs turned to crime. Nor was this likely to be a short-term problem. It was estimated that by the year 2000 some 68 million urban residents would be seeking employment, in addition to more than 200 million jobless peasants.

Deteriorating social order was mirrored in poor party discipline and the susceptibility of government officials and cadres to corruption and criminal activities. The seriousness of the situation was reflected in Jiang Zemin's warning that such problems threatened the very stability of both party and state. According to the President, the solution lay in renewed emphasis on ideological and political work (including proper provision for the selection and promotion of cadres of proven integrity and ability) in order to strengthen leadership at all levels. Above all, asserted President Jiang, the supreme authority of the central leadership should be maintained.

The proceedings of the fourth plenum of the 14th CCP central committee (25–28 September) underlined the urgency of such issues. In contrast to the economic focus of previous plenary sessions, the primary concern of the 1994 meeting was party building. The guidelines to which it gave expression emphasized the tasks of improving work style and eliminating corruption in party ranks in order to strengthen the authority of the CCP throughout the country. To these ends, it commended the virtues of hard work and organizational rationalization. In particular, the guidelines demanded intensified political and ideological education in order to reassert the central role of democratic centralism as the 'fundamental organizational and leadership system of the party', described as essential to the successful creation of a socialist market economy. Implicit in such advocacy was the belief that the effective establishment of a socialist market economy was inseparable from the maintenance of the supreme authority of the central leadership. It was a theme which was to dominate major policy statements during the last quarter of the year.

Problems of low morale affected not only party ranks but also members of the armed forces. Changing economic and social conditions had weakened military discipline just when heightened vigilance and unquestioning obedience were required. Hence the need for renewed efforts to enhance the role of the military in facilitating reform and development. Just how important the economic role of the military had already become was shown in the fact that 77.4 per cent of Chinese defence industry's total production now comprised civilian goods, compared with a mere 8.1 per cent in 1978. Meanwhile, official reports pointed to the need to enhance the professional competence of the People's Liberation Army (PLA) through improved training and the purchase of advanced military technology. In response to the lessons of the Gulf War, combined service training was enhanced. In addition, the State Council made available $5,000 million to facilitate the purchase of Russian military hardware (including Su-35s, Su-30

MKs, Il78 mid-air refuelling aircraft, Il76-MF air transports and T-80 tank technology).

China conducted two underground nuclear tests in 1994 (in June and October). In their defence, official sources rehearsed the familiar argument that China possessed nuclear weapons solely for defence purposes. They insisted that the Chinese government remained committed to the destruction of all such weapons and the realization of a comprehensive nuclear test ban.

The death occurred on 11 December of Yao Yilin (aged 77). He had held vice-ministerial posts during the 1950s but was dismissed from office during the Cultural Revolution. Following his rehabilitation in 1973, he resumed high office, his career culminating in appointments as Head of the State Planning Commission and Vice-Premier of the State Council. Meanwhile, a link with China's imperial past was severed when Aisin Giorro Pu Jie, the brother of the last emperor of the Qing Dynasty, died on 27 February at the age of 87.

EXTERNAL RELATIONS. Li Peng's government work report summarized recent achievements in China's foreign relations, pointing to a further improvement, during 1993, in relations with Russia, Germany, France and countries of the Asia-Pacific. He spoke of favourable prospects for expanded trade and economic cooperation with Western Europe. As for Sino-American relations, they were best pursued in a global context and from a long-term perspective.

An authoritative statement of China's assessment of the international situation was contained in Qian Qichen's address to the 49th session of the UN General Assembly on 28 September. The Foreign Minister argued that fundamental changes had occurred in recent years, characterized by a shift towards 'multi-polarity' and a greater role for economic factors in foreign relations. He conceded a general tendency towards détente, but warned that 'hegemonism and power politics' had not been entirely eliminated. New destabilizing factors had emerged, which underlined the increasing complexity and volatility of international conditions. A key issue was how to resolve regional disputes, in which context Foreign Minister Qian reaffirmed China's commitment to the UN Charter and other norms governing foreign relations—not least, impartiality and the avoidance of interference in a country's internal affairs.

Jiang Zemin, Li Peng, Qian Qichen and other government leaders undertook diplomatic tours in 1994, which took them to the USA, Europe, Japan, Russia, the Middle East, South-East Asia and South America. In terms of their immediate implications, however, the most significant developments were those which took place within the Asia-Pacific region. Especially so were reciprocal visits which President Kim Young Sam of South Korea and Premier Li Peng made to each other's capitals (October-November). The visits underlined the growing importance of closer trade and foreign investment flows, with merchandise trade having reached $11,400 million in 1993, already making China South Korea's third-largest trading partner (and Korea, China's sixth-largest). On both occasions the situation in North Korea was a topic for discussion (see IX.2.vi), the two sides agreeing on the desirability of working together in order to help improve stability there and on the Korean peninsula as a whole.

High-level meetings between Chinese and Japanese government leaders also highlighted the importance to both countries of forging closer bilateral relations. In 1993 Japan overtook Hong Kong to become China's top trading partner and in the first half of 1994 merchandise trade increased by a further 24.7 per cent. Meanwhile, despite warnings that continued Chinese nuclear testing (see above) could jeopardize Japanese overseas development assistance to China, an agreement was reached whereby the Japanese government undertook to extend loans worth 580,000 million yen in 1996–98. The funds, though less than requested by China, were to be used mainly for the implementation of environmental projects.

History again cast a shadow over the more positive aspects of Sino-Japanese relations. During his visit to China in March, the Japanese Prime Minister, Morihiro Hosakawa, spoke with regret of the 'intolerable suffering' which Japan's 'invasion and colonial rule' had brought to so many Asian countries. But his interpretation of what constituted a correct attitude towards history was not shared by some of his colleagues, who subsequently continued to deny Japanese responsibility for deliberately unleashing a 'war of aggression' against China. In one instance, a Japanese minister even denied the authenticity of the 'Nanjing massacre' in 1937. Such statements were the source of dismay and anger among Chinese officials.

In his work report, Li Peng reaffirmed China's commitment to the principle of 'one country, two systems' as the basis for reunification with Taiwan, Hong Kong and Macao. He added that China was determined to effect smooth transfers of government in Hong Kong (1997) and Macao (1999) in accordance with the provisions of the relevant Basic Laws of the two regions. Outside the economic sphere, the process of rapprochement between the mainland and Taiwan was halting, although the momentum of talks between non-governmental representatives of the two countries was maintained (see IX.2.ii). Nevertheless, cross-Straits economic ties continued to strengthen in 1994, Taiwan having become China's second-largest source of foreign investment.

Two incidents were the source of considerable mutual embarrassment to China and Taiwan during the year. The first occurred in March, when 24 Taiwanese tourists on a pleasure cruise on Lake Qiandao (Zhejiang province) were killed, following an outbreak of fire which sank the boat. Investigations by the mainland authorities eventually pointed to the involvement of three criminals, who were arrested and tried for robbery, arson and murder, and subsequently executed. The incident temporarily soured relations and interrupted the cross-Straits dialogue, although talks were later resumed. The second episode took place in November, when Taiwanese troops fired shells which accidentally hit a suburban area of Xiamen (Amoy), causing injuries to four people. The Taiwanese authorities expressed regret for what had happened.

Some improvement in relations between China and the United States was detectable during 1994. A series of meetings between senior officials reflected both sides' keen desire to increase trade and to broaden economic cooperation, as well as to promote closer ties in other areas. Warren Christopher (US Secretary of State), who travelled to Beijing in March, spoke of a 'businesslike and productive' atmosphere surrounding his talks with Qian Qichen on MFN and human rights issues and indicated that differences between the two sides were narrowing. In August the US Secretary of Commerce (Ron Brown) visited China, where he discussed a wide range of economic and other questions. Prior to his return to Washington, Mr Brown stated that the visit had exceeded his expectations and revealed that consultations on human rights would be resumed in the near future. Finally, in October, the arrival in Beijing of William Perry (US Secretary of Defence) for talks with his counterpart, Chi Haotian, marked the resumption of high-level military exchanges between China and the United States. Such contacts had been halted since the 1989 political upheavals in the Chinese capital.

President Clinton's announcement that he intended to detach the annual MFN review process from China's human rights record marked another watershed in Sino-American relations. The decision, which was widely seen as a means of facilitating closer American involvement in trade and economic cooperation with the mainland, was welcomed in China, although the reception was qualified by demands for the simultaneous removal of existing sanctions. Attendance by Mr Clinton and Jiang Zemin at the sixth APEC ministerial meeting in Indonesia allowed a second presidential summit to take place there on 14 November. Both leaders spoke with satisfaction of the progress towards closer ties, achieved since their previous (November 1993) meeting in Seattle (see AR 1993, p. 356). President Clinton reaffirmed his decision to de-link the MFN review process, while President Jiang reiterated his government's willingness to enter into discussions on human rights on the basis of 'equality and mutual respect'.

That major obstacles nevertheless continued to impede realization of the full potential of the Sino-American relationship was made clear by the fate of bilateral negotiations on China's re-entry into the General Agreement on Tariffs and Trade (GATT). China had long insisted on its right, as a developing country, to regain full membership of GATT, and was also seeking to be a founding member of the successor World

Trade Organization (WTO). However, China's unilateral imposition of a deadline—1 January 1995—for readmission to GATT served to increase the difficulties surrounding its membership application. In confirming the deadline, China's Trade Minister, Wu Yi, warned that unless China's membership was renewed by the end of December, the government would cancel all the undertakings it had made during the previous eight years of discussions. The initial response of the US government was that it could not negotiate under the shadow of what it regarded as an ultimatum. Talks did, however, take place in Geneva, but insufficient progress was achieved to break the impasse. Only after the discussions had failed in an atmosphere of acrimony was there any sign of a softening of China's attitude, when Vice-Premier Li Lanqing indicated that his government would support a proposal that its accession to the new WTO be delayed until July 1995, on condition that China was by then assured of readmission to GATT before its final demise.

The renewed momentum of the development of closer relations between China and Western Europe was maintained during 1994, the most notable aspect of this process being the further strengthening of ties between China and its two most important European economic partners, France and Germany. Following the difficulties which had affected Sino-French relations as a result of the sale by France of 60 Mirage jets to Taiwan (see AR 1993, p. 355), the arrival in Beijing of Premier Edouard Balladur in April provided concrete evidence that those relations had returned to their former level. Meanwhile, in July, Li Peng's visit to Germany provided an opportunity for an exchange of views with senior government leaders, including Chancellor Kohl and Klaus Kinkel (German Foreign Minister), over a wide range of economic, political and human rights issues.

With Great Britain alone in Western Europe, Chinese relations remained at a low ebb for much of the year, dominated still by disagreements over Hong Kong. A report on Sino-British relations by the foreign affairs select committee of the UK House of Commons was criticized by China for allegedly failing to recognize that Governor Patten's constitutional proposals for Hong Kong had violated the Sino-British Joint Declaration, the Basic Law and other relevant agreements and understandings. Li Peng was only one of several senior officials who blamed Britain for causing the irrevocable breakdown of bilateral talks on the arrangements for 1994–95 elections in the British colony. In September, however, more conciliatory statements by Qian Qichen and Douglas Hurd in the course of a meeting at the UN in New York offered the prospect of some degree of rapprochement.

Visits by Viktor Chernomyrdin (the Russian Prime Minister) and Andrei Kozyrev (Foreign Minister) to China, and by Jiang Zemin to Russia, reflected both countries' desire to establish closer relations, especially in the economic sphere. Statistics for 1993 showing that bilateral trade had risen by 30 per cent seemed to confirm that closer economic ties were indeed being forged. However, less encouraging were statistics for the first half of 1994, showing that such trade had fallen back by 37 per cent. The principal reason was said to be a sharp contraction in the level of barter trade.

Participation in the sixth APEC summit in Indonesia in November by senior Chinese government officials (including Jiang Zemin, Qian Qichen and Wu Yi) signalled China's determination to assume a full role in the organization's development. The Chinese Foreign Minister expressed his government's support of APEC's goal of trade and investment liberalization throughout the Asia-Pacific region. He urged that associated policies should be based on the different economic levels of APEC members and called for major efforts to narrow intra-regional differentials in order to promote the joint development and common prosperity of all of them.

ii. TAIWAN

CAPITAL: Taipei   AREA: 35,981 sq km   POPULATION: 20,944,000 ('93)
OFFICIAL LANGUAGE: Chinese   POLITICAL SYSTEM: presidential
HEAD OF STATE & GOVERNMENT: President Lee Teng-hui (since Jan '88)
RULING PARTY: Kuomintang (KMT)
PRINCIPAL MINISTERS: Lien Chan (Prime Minister), Hsu Li-teh (Vice-Premier),
    Frederick Chien Fu (foreign affairs), Wu Po-hsiung (interior), P.K. Chan
    (economic affairs), Lin Chen-kuo (finance), Sun Chen (defence), Ma Ying-jeou
    (justice)
CURRENCY: New Taiwan dollar (end-'94 £1=NT$41.13, US$1=NT$26.29)
GDP PER CAPITA: US$10,677 ('93)
MAIN EXPORT EARNERS: manufactured goods, electronics, machinery

CONSTRAINED by the competing and often successful claims of the government of the People's Republic to be the sole representative of China, the authorities in Taipei nevertheless continued their efforts to raise Taiwan's profile overseas. In this connection, the tour of three South-East Asian countries which President Lee undertook in February, on the pretext of a private 'holiday', was a significant event. All three countries—the Philippines, Thailand and Indonesia—enjoyed formal diplomatic relations with mainland China, so that the President's presence in each was a matter of some diplomatic delicacy. Indeed, China made clear its strong opposition to such 'vacation diplomacy' and accused the Taiwanese authorities of seeking to use such trips to create 'two Chinas' through attempts to establish unofficial, but substantive, relations overseas.

There were other signs of a continuing diplomatic offensive by Taiwan. One was the unannounced visit to Mexico by the Taiwanese Premier (Lien Chan) in June. Another was the establishment of formal diplomatic relations with the equatorial African state of Burkina Faso in February, accompanied by Taiwanese promises of economic and technical assistance. Beijing condemned the action as 'money diplomacy' and severed its own diplomatic relations with Burkina. An official invitation by Sheikh Ahmad al-Fahad, president of the Olympic Council of Asia (OCA), for President Lee to attend the Asian Games in Japan in October appeared to be another victory for Taiwan's diplomatic offensive. But subsequent threats by mainland China to boycott the Games, combined with diplomatic pressure, resulted in an OCA statement to the effect that 'no political figure will be invited to or accommodated at the 12th Asian Games'. In this way, the invitation was effectively withdrawn, leaving President Lee with no alternative but to protest and to abandon his hoped-for visit. Meanwhile, however, Japan agreed that Vice-Premier Hsu Li-teh, as the person responsible for Taiwan's bid to host the Asian Games in 2002, would be allowed to travel to Japan.

The US State Department revealed in September that American policy towards its links with Taiwan would be adjusted in the interests of facilitating more effective bilateral relations. Specific changes included allowing high-level meetings to be held in government offices and re-naming Taiwan's de facto embassy in the USA (previously, the Coordination Council for North American Affairs) as the Taipei Economic and Cultural Representative Office. Washington's denial that the moves constituted a shift from its one-China policy failed to convince the authorities in Beijing, who warned that the action would lead to serious consequences. Ironically, Taiwanese sources also expressed regret that more radical changes had not been introduced.

Having lost its UN seat to the PRC in 1971, Taiwan undertook another major propaganda effort in 1994 in support of its bid to regain membership. But for the second year in succession its attempt to have the matter placed before the UN General Assembly was unsuccessful. The Taiwanese Foreign Minister, Frederick Chien, insisted that efforts to regain a seat on the UN would continue.

Further talks between non-governmental representatives of Taiwan's Straits Exchange Foundation (SEF) and the mainland Association for Relations Across the Taiwan Straits (ARATS) took place during 1994. Initial positive results were interrupted by a cooling of relations in the wake of the Lake Qiandao incident (see IX.2.i). But renewed progress was reflected in the arrival in Taipei on 3 August of the ARATS vice-chairman, Tang Shubei, for discussions with his Taiwanese counterpart, Chiao Jen-ho. Despite an inauspicious start—Tang Shubei's arrival was marked by a demonstration in favour of Taiwan's independence—the four-day meeting marked the highest-level cross-straits contact since 1949 and facilitated an exchange of views and apparent agreement on a wide range of issues. Such progress notwithstanding, the sixth round of SEF–ARATS talks in November failed to fulfil expectations, as the Taiwanese side opposed demands by ARATS representatives that earlier agreements on the repatriation of hijackers and illegal immigrants should be made retroactive.

On 2 June eight Taiwanese generals were impeached by the Control Yuan, following charges that they had wasted taxpayers' money through their involvement in an arms scandal. It was the most serious such case ever to have been undertaken by the Control Yuan. The eight men included a national policy adviser (General Kuo Ju-lin) and national security adviser (General Chen Hsing-ling) to President Lee.

Although the ruling Kuomintang (KMT) maintained its position as the biggest party in local elections in December, it also suffered the most serious setbacks amongst the competing parties. With 49 per cent of the vote overall, KMT candidates won 91 out of 175 seats contested in the Taiwan provincial assembly and in the Taipei and Kaohsiung city councils. By comparison, the Democratic Progressive Party (DPP) and the Chinese New Party (CNP) secured 32 and 6 per cent of votes respectively. Reports indicated, however, that at the municipal level the KMT's showing was disappointing: not only did it lose the Taipei mayoral election, but also DPP and CNP candidates gained at its expense in many city council seats.

Taiwan's economic growth in 1993 was just under 6 per cent, taking average per capita GNP to US$10,677. Inflation was held below 3 per cent and the unemployment rate was a mere 1.24 per cent. There was a slackening of foreign trade growth, exports and imports rising by 4.2 and 7 per cent respectively. Cross-straits economic relations, however, expanded significantly: mainland sources indicated that indirect trade increased by 23.7 per cent, while contracted investment reached $6,700 million (making Taiwan mainland China's second-largest source of overseas capital, after Hong Kong). Forecasts pointed to significant renewed growth in merchandise trade in 1994, although GNP growth seemed likely to remain at about the same level as in the previous year.

iii. HONG KONG

CAPITAL: Victoria   AREA: 1,073 sq km   POPULATION: 6,019,000 ('93)
STATUS: UK dependency due to revert to Chinese sovereignty on 1 July 1997
GOVERNOR: Chris Patten (since July '92)
CURRENCY: Hong Kong dollar (end-'94 £1=HK£12.10, US$1=HK$7.74)
GDP PER CAPITA: US$18,500 ('93)
MAIN EXPORTS: manufactured goods, textiles, financial services

DEVELOPMENTS in 1994 were again overshadowed by deteriorating Sino-British relations, associated with Governor Chris Patten's constitutional reform proposals. There were, however, signs of rapprochement in some areas. The inability of the Chinese and Hong Kong governments to reach a political compromise was most dramatically signalled in China's abandonment of the 'through train' concept and its intention to dismantle any political structure created out of the 1994–95 elections, as soon as it assumed power in Hong Kong in 1997. Representatives of the Preliminary Working Committee (PWC) for the PRC Preparatory Committee for the Hong Kong Special Administrative Region (HKSAR) meanwhile successfully proposed that an Interim Legislative Council should be set up in order to oversee the retrocession of the Colony's sovereignty.

The first part of Mr Patten's political reform package was passed by Legislative Council (Legco) on 24 February. The next day the controversial second-phase legislation was gazetted, prior to being submitted to Legco the following month. China's response was to reaffirm the irrevocable breakdown of Sino-British negotiations. A spokesman warned that, if the legislation were implemented, the 'component parts of the British political body administering Hong Kong'— Legco, the district boards and the municipal councils—would be terminated on 1 July 1997. They would be replaced by a new three-tiered framework, on which members of existing bodies, elected in 1994–95, might still be allowed to serve, provided that they fulfilled the requirements of the Basic Law and other criteria.

Intense lobbying by supporters and opponents took place prior to voting on the second-phase legislation and a last-minute amendment, seeking to dilute the proposals, failed only by a single vote (with two abstentions). In the event, the legislation was passed by Legco on 30 June, albeit by a narrow margin (32 votes to 24). The first part of the reform package had already resulted in lowering the voting age from 21 to 18. Approval of the second stage set the scene for a further extension of the franchise and an increase in the number of Legco seats open to direct election. It also led to the enactment of retaliatory Chinese legislation in order to provide a formal framework in which the intention to dismantle the new Hong Kong political structure could be implemented.

On 5 October Governor Patten delivered his third annual policy address, entitled 'Hong Kong: A Thousand Days and Beyond'. In addition to addressing economic and social issues, the report reaffirmed the Hong Kong government's commitment to cooperation with Beijing during the transition to Chinese sovereignty and put forward conciliatory proposals in an effort to improve political relations between the two sides. In particular, it sought to strengthen informal relations between the administration and PWC members, gave an undertaking to support the first HKSAR chief executive and promised cooperation with the Chinese authorities on defence responsibilities. Such concessions were, however, less than persuasive in Beijing. Official Chinese reaction was to dismiss the report as 'empty words' and to accuse Mr Patten of stalling in order to extend British authority over Hong Kong beyond 1997.

Against this background, representatives attending the 11th session of the PWC's political affairs group in Beijing on 7 October approved a motion to establish an Interim Legislative Council for Hong Kong. The new body was to be in place by early 1996 and would, like its colonial parent, consist of 60 members, no more than 20 per cent of whom would be of non-Chinese nationality or drawn from those who enjoyed a right of abode overseas. The body would have a temporary status—no more than 12 months—and its main remit would be to institute necessary revisions to existing local laws in the aftermath of the retrocession of sovereignty.

The very fact that two meetings of the Sino-British Joint Liaison Group took place in 1994 was regarded by some as an encouraging sign. Although progress was slow, the two sides did reach agreement on the use of existing defence sites in the colony. Another tangible achievement was the realization, after 30 months of negotiations, of an agreement on the financing of Hong Kong's new airport at Chek Lap Kok. Under its provisions, the Hong Kong government undertook to allocate HK$60,300 million to the project and to cap the level of project-related government borrowing at HK$23,000 million. The new airport was due to be in operation by 1997. It would initially have an annual capacity of 35 million passengers and a million tonnes of freight, though these figures would subsequently rise to 87 million and 9 million tonnes respectively.

In September just over 33 per cent of registered voters took part in Hong Kong's first fully democratic elections. Of the 346 vacant seats on the 18 district boards, 167 were won by independents, mostly without any clear political affiliations. The pro-democracy Democratic Party, established through a merger of two former liberal political organizations (the United Democrats of Hong Kong and Meeting Point), did best among the party lists, emerging with 75 seats. The four parties owing varying allegiance to China secured a total of 68 seats, the Democratic Alliance for the Betterment of Hong Kong winning 37 of these.

Despite political uncertainties, Hong Kong's economy remained buoyant. Thanks to a reduction in inflation (from 9.4 to 8.5 per cent, year on year) and real GDP growth of 5.5 per cent (the largest annual increase since 1988), average per capita GDP reached US$18,500 in 1993, three times the level of 1970. Underlying the 13 per cent growth of exports in 1993 was the symbiotic economic relationship which now existed between Hong Kong and China (especially Guangdong). China accounted for 35 per cent of the colony's external trade during 1993, while Hong Kong contributed some two-thirds of all foreign investment in China. In his speech on the 1994/95 budget on 2 March, the Financial Secretary, Hamish Macleod, drew special attention to the important role of the service sector (service exports having grown by 8 per cent)—in particular of financial services, which now accounted for about 10 per cent of GDP. Mr Macleod added that, with inflation held at 8.5 per cent and total trade expanding by 17 per cent annually, GDP growth in real terms was once again likely to reach 5.5 per cent in 1994, increasing per capita GDP to around US$20,600.

iv.   JAPAN

CAPITAL: Tokyo   AREA: 378,000 sq km   POPULATION: 124,500,000 ('92)
OFFICIAL LANGUAGE: Japanese   POLITICAL SYSTEM: parliamentary democracy
HEAD OF STATE: Emperor Tsugu no Miya Akihito (since Jan '89)
RULING PARTIES: Social Democratic Party of Japan (SDPJ), Liberal-Democratic Party
     (LDP) & New Party Harbinger (Sakigake)
HEAD OF GOVERNMENT: Tomiichi Murayama (SDPJ), Prime Minister (since June '94)
PRINCIPAL MINISTERS: Yohei Kono (LDP/Deputy Prime Minister, foreign affairs),
     Isao Maeda (LDP/justice), Masayoshi Takemura (s/finance), Ryutaro Hashimoto
     (LDP/international trade & industry), Hiromu Nonaka (LDP/home affairs),
     Tokuichiro Tamazawa (LDP/defence agency)
INTERNATIONAL ALIGNMENT: OECD, G-7, security pact with USA
CURRENCY: yen (end-'94 £1=Y156.09, US$1=Y99.77)
GNP PER CAPITA: US$28,190 ('92)
MAIN EXPORT EARNERS: transport & electronic equipment, other manufactured goods,
     financial services

THE year was one of bewildering political realignments after four decades of remarkable stability under Liberal-Democratic Party (LDP) cabinets until the July 1993 elections (see AR 1993, pp. 363-4). It opened with Morihiro Hosokawa of the Japan New Party (JNP) still heading the multi-party centre-left coalition formed in August 1993. But it was clear that this grouping was united only by a desire for power and a general interest in political reform and was divided both by personalities and by specific policy preferences. Mr Hosokawa had given himself a deadline of the end of January to secure the passage of his constitutional reform legislation in the upper house of the Diet; but there were acute disagreements among the coalition partners, largely over the wisdom of converting to single-seat constituencies for electoral purposes. Mr Hosokawa was forced to water down his proposals by consultation with the LDP opposition, on which basis they were passed by the end of the session.

Before going to Washington on 11 February, Mr Hosokawa announced the introduction of a consumption tax to compensate for cuts in income tax which he was then proposing (but was later forced to withdraw because of intense opposition). President Clinton tabled a large number of trade demands, including the application of numerical targets for Japanese imports into the United States. Mr Hosokawa broke with tradition by declining to accept any such demands and the summit broke up without resolution of the issue. It was known by then that the Prime Minister was anxious to resign because his domestic policies and methods had been criticized within the government coalition and in the country at large. When the newspapers raised the subject of financial irregularities in which he had been involved some years earlier, he used the occasion to tender his resignation on 8 April.

After three weeks of difficult negotiations, Tsutomu Hata of the Japan Renewal Party (Shinseito), hitherto Finance Minister, was elected Prime Minister on 25 April. He retained most members of the previous Hosokawa cabinet. But his major coalition partner, the Social Democratic Party of Japan (SDPJ), was excluded from a new parliamentary grouping called Kaishin (Innovation) organized by Mr Hata's supporters at the instigation of Ichiro Ozawa, the highly influential co-leader of Shinseito (and former LDP secretary-general). The SDPJ ministers therefore resigned from the governing coalition, which consequently lost its majority. Although the SDPJ made a compact that it would not seek to bring down the government until the long-overdue 1994 budget was passed, the inevitable defeat of Mr Hata on a vote of no confidence came on 25 June, obliging him to give up the reins of office.

The outcome of several days of backroom negotiations came as a shock to most Japanese. It was announced that the SDPJ, long regarded as an ideological party of the left, had teamed up with the LDP, Japan's main party of the right and the SDPJ's long-term rival. Headed by the SDPJ chairman, Tomiichi Murayama (70), the new coalition also included the small New Party Harbinger (Sakigake). The senior cabinet places were divided up among the three parties, the LDP taking seven, the SDPJ four and Sakigake two. The key posts of Deputy Prime Minister and Foreign Minister were given to the LDP leader, Yohei Kono, while other major portfolios also went to the LDP.

In order to grasp the political power which the party had not enjoyed since 1947, the SDPJ leadership was ready to distance itself from most of the party's traditional socialist policies. It now accepted the legitimacy of Japan's Self-Defence Forces, use of the national flag and anthem, the continuation of the US-Japanese alliance and the need for economic deregulation. The LDP entered into this strange combination because its supporters had been demoralized by being out of office since the 1993 elections. Nevertheless, the marriage of convenience was by its nature unstable; and commentators found it difficult to forecast how long it would last.

The political situation had stabilized in time for Mr Murayama and Mr Kono to attend the Naples G-7 summit in July, where they gave undertakings to other world leaders to pursue economic reform policies in Japan in order to stimulate the global economy. Mr Murayama also used the occasion to have direct talks with President Clinton of the USA, especially on the delicate issue of North Korea and its nuclear potential (see IX.2.v). Bilateral talks also resumed in July aimed at closing the huge US-Japan trade gap by opening Japanese markets to American goods and services. The robust US tactics involved the threat that, unless concessions were made by the end of September, the 'Super 301' Trade Law would be applied. This was averted by an agreement of 1 October covering eight sectors, including insurance, flat glass, telecommunications and medical equipment. Japan had not given way over market shares or the import of car parts; nevertheless, the trade deals which were advantageous to the Americans were deeply resented by Japanese producers. In bilateral terms, the issue of the Japanese trade surplus was not resolved by any means, but the temperature of further negotiation was cooled. The implications of the partial US-Japan settlement for Europe were taken up during the visit to Japan by a European Union delegation in November.

After two years of severe contraction, the recession had come officially to an end in October 1993. The country's growing industrial productivity and the surge in the Tokyo stock market during 1994 appeared to confirm that recovery was in progress, although the pace was necessarily slow. There was much scope for structural reform and deregulation, the need for which had been endorsed by most of Japan's top business federations. This prompted the government in September to follow up its predecessor's attempts of February by introducing a package of measures to stimulate the economy. In order to accommodate the SDLP's long-standing opposition to indirect taxation, income tax cuts introduced in November were stated to be only temporary.

An extraordinary session of the Diet began on 1 October. It had to carry through the final stages of the previous coalition's programme of electoral reform, which had been debated over several years as a way of defeating 'money politics'. The bill was passed on 21 November. Its effect was to replace Japan's familiar multi-member constituencies with 300 single-seat constituencies in a lower house of 500 seats (reduced from 511), the other 200 to be elected by proportional representation in 11 electoral districts. It also provided for an annual subsidy for registered political parties and severe penalties for politicians who exceeded legal limits in the donations they received.

Japan continued to be preoccupied with its relations with the rest of Asia. The main outward expression of this preoccupation in 1994 came in October with the holding of the Asian Games in Hiroshima, which were a success despite the threat of a boycott from Beijing (see also IX.2.ii). On the diplomatic front, Mr Murayama held important talks on Asian issues during a visit in August to South-East Asia, taking in the Philippines, Vietnam, Malaysia and Singapore. Japan also took an important part at ASEAN meetings (although it was not a member) and at the APEC summit in Indonesia in November (see XI.6.iii), associating itself with Asia-Pacific issues without distancing itself from the interests of the United States. In September Japan modestly put forward its case for a seat on an enlarged UN Security Council, largely based on the country's economic success but also claiming that Japan had a leadership role among Asian countries.

At the same time, however, there were severe criticisms from Asian countries over Japan's understanding of its role in the Asia-Pacific region in the 1930s and 1940s. Two cabinet ministers, Shigeto Nagano and Shin Sakurai, were forced to resign because of public statements by them which played down the misdemeanours of the Japanese military during the war. Japan was faced in particular by the claims of 'comfort women' from Korea and South-East Asian countries who had been abused by Japanese soldiers. While refusing demands for individual compensation, the Tokyo government announced a package of 'atonement measures' amounting to the equivalent of $1,000 million. On the occasion of the anniversary of the end of World War II in August, Mr Murayama also expressed Japan's apologies for the war along the lines of similar statements made by his predecessors.

The autumn was taken up with a restructuring of political parties in anticipation of the electoral reforms coming into force. Due mainly to the efforts of Mr Ozawa, the various reformist groups which had emerged since 1991, and had formed the core of the Hosokawa and Hata ministries, joined together in September under the name of Kaikaku (Renovation). Three months later, at a launching in Yokohama on 10 December, the alliance became a unified formation under the title of Shinshinto or New Frontier Party (NFP). One by one, the nine constituent parties held meetings and went into voluntary liquidation, although some factions broke away because of their distrust of the NFP. In a leadership election, the office of NFP president went decisively to Toshiki Kaifu, who had been LDP Prime Minister in 1989–91 and had earned popularity as an apostle of reform. Despite his many opponents in political circles, Mr Ozawa was given the influential post of NFP secretary-general. In specific policy terms, the new party was not notably at variance with the governing coalition. On the other hand, it was strongly committed to the elimination the old political system, with its factions and intra-party strife and the corruption which seemed to be its inevitable by-product.

The new political framework, which seemed to favour large parties, came into force on 25 December. At the end of the year the Murayama government had an overall majority of 35 seats in the lower house of the Diet but faced much dissent within its constituent parts. Splits within the SDPJ were emerging and the meltdown of political loyalties was still continuing. The NFP represented a formidable opposition force, even though it did not include the Japan Communist Party (JCP) and a number of small splinter groups. Its bitter hostility to a weak coalition government presaged a test of strength in a general election. Until the will of the electorate was tested, however, it seemed unlikely that there had been a definitive realignment of Japanese political forces.

Emperor Akihito visited various countries during the year, in particular paying state visits to the USA in June and to France and Spain in the autumn. He was accompanied on these visits by the Empress, who had recovered from a throat condition which had made speech difficult. Several serious natural disasters in 1994 caused a number of fatalities, notably an earthquake and tidal waves in islands off Hokkaido in October and another earthquake beneath the ocean north-east of Tokyo in December. There were also many lesser earthquakes on the main island of Honshu, leading some seismologists to predict that a major catastrophe was imminent.

It was announced in October that the Japanese novelist Kenzaburo Oe had won the 1994 Nobel Prize for Literature (see XVI.3).

v.   SOUTH KOREA

CAPITAL: Seoul   AREA: 99,143 sq km   POPULATION: 44,056,000 ('93)
OFFICIAL LANGUAGE: Korean   POLITICAL SYSTEM: presidential democracy
HEAD OF STATE & GOVERNMENT: President Kim Young Sam (since Feb '93)
RULING PARTY: Democratic Liberal Party (DLP)
PRINCIPAL MINISTERS: Lee Hong Koo (Prime Minister), Hong Jae Hyong (Deputy
   Prime Minister, finance and economy), Kim Deok (Deputy Prime Minister,
   unification), Gong Ro Myung (foreign affairs), Kim Yong Tae (home affairs),
   Lee Yanh Ho (defence), Ahn Woo Mahn (justice)
CURRENCY: won (end-'94 £1=SKW1,223.61, US$1=SKW788.50)
GNP PER CAPITA: US$8,411 ('94 est.)
MAIN EXPORT EARNERS: automobiles, electronics, steel, ship-building, clothing &
   textiles, footware

THE economy of the Republic of Korea (South Korea) continued to grow robustly during 1994, giving the government the impetus to seek admission to the OECD in 1996. In order to achieve entry, however, the government was told in May that it must increase technological innovation and achieve greater administrative deregulation as well as more efficient use of its labour force. These demands compelled the government to restructure itself. In early December President Kim Young Sam announced the merger of the powerful Economic Planning Board with the Ministry of Finance to form the Finance and Economic Board, which would coordinate all financial activities and economic planning. In line with these moves the Ministries of Construction and Transport were also merged into a super–ministry.

A sign of the changing nature of the South Korean economy was the increasing dependence of small businesses on cheap, foreign labourers in order to maintain economic competitiveness. In March the government announced that it intended to expel all of the estimated 100,000 foreign workers, who were to be replaced by 20,000 legally-registered workers. In early June the Federation of Small Businesses requested that the permitted number should be increased to 30,000. By the end-June deadline for the expulsions, there were still 54,275 illegal workers in the country. Nevertheless, large numbers of legalized workers were brought in from countries such as Nepal and the Philippines.

President Kim kept a firm hand on the reins of government, twice carrying out major cabinet reshuffles. On 18 April Lee Hoi Chang resigned as Prime Minister and was replaced on 21 April by Lee Young Duk, hitherto Minister for Unification. He in turn was replaced on 17 December by Lee Hong Koo, Lee Young Duk's successor at the Unification Ministry and architect of South Korea's so-called *nordpolitik*. These and other changes were seen as a clear indication of President Kim's desire to reshape the functioning and structure of the South Korean government in the light of eventual Korean unification.

The issue which dominated world media coverage of the Korean peninsula in 1994 was the question of North Korea's nuclear weapons potential and its reluctance to submit to inspection by the International Atomic Energy Agency (IAEA). An agreement concluded in New York on 25 February, by which North Korea undertook to admit IAEA inspectors, appeared to defuse the confrontation. Moreover, South Korea hoped that its announcement on 3 March of the suspension of joint military exercises with the USA and its offer of economic investment in North Korea would ease tensions. By mid-March, however, the February agreement seemed to have broken down completely and North Korea was threatening war if its sovereignty was infringed (although South Korea played down the significance of such threats). On 14–24 May the then South Korean Foreign Minister, Han Sung Joo, made an extended tour of friendly states in order to arrive at a common policy towards North Korea. Former US President Jimmy Carter arrived in Seoul on 13 June to act as a mediator, but the South Korean government was initially afraid that President Kim Il Sung of North Korea would use the visit to avoid UN sanctions without changing his stance. Upon Mr Carter's return to Seoul from Pyongyang, however, the South Koreans on 21 June accepted Kim Il Sung's proposal to meet Kim Young Sam 'anywhere, anytime, without conditions'.

Further progress was made on 28 June when Lee Hong Koo (then South Korean Minister for Unification) and Kim Young Sun (of the North Korean Assembly's unification policy committee) signed an agreement providing for a meeting between the two Korean Presidents in Pyongyang on 25–27 July. However, Kim Il Sung died on 8 July (see IX.2.vi; XX: Obituary), after which assertions that the 28 June agreement remained valid were not translated into an actual top-level meeting between the two sides. On 15 August President Kim Young Sam announced a three-phase plan for unification (which he said 'may be sudden and unexpected') and offered North Korea investment capital and technical assistance to building light-water nuclear reactors. Thereafter, the issue of North Korean intentions remained a paramount concern for the South Korean government, which welcomed the new US-North Korean agreement signed in Geneva on 21 October. This stipulated that North Korea would obtain US diplomatic recognition and assistance on its peaceful nuclear projects, in return for abandoning its alleged nuclear weapons programme and submitting to international inspection (see also XII.3). The following month South Korea announced various initiatives to improve relations with the North, but little progress was made by year's end owing to the uncertainty of the succession in North Korea.

State visits in 1994 continued to show South Korea's wide range of diplomatic and economic contacts, including visits from President Iliescu of Romania, Premier Li Peng of China, President Frei of Chile, President Walesa of Poland and Prime Minister Yitzhak Rabin of Israel. Overseas trips by President Kim Young Sam included state visits to Japan, China, Russia, the Philippines, Indonesia and Australia. While in Moscow on 1–4 June, he secured a commitment that Russia would stop selling or supplying military equipment to North Korea and was told by President Yeltsin that the Soviet-North Korean defence treaty was a dead letter. The Russians also handed over sensitive archival material on the origins of the Korean War which demonstrated the high degree of cooperation by Stalin and Mao Zedong in North Korea's plans to conquer the South. While in Indonesia in November, President Kim attended the Asia–Pacific Economic Cooperation (APEC) summit in Bogor (see XI.6.iii).

The effect of South Korea's economic strength on regional geopolitical relations was indicated by the opening of additional air links with the People's Republic of China. In February both Korean carriers (Korean Air and Asiana) began direct flights to Beijing; by 22 December direct flights by airlines of both nations were in operation between Seoul and several other Chinese destinations. Also noteworthy was the increasing numbers of Russians travelling by ship from Vladivostok to the South Korean port city of Pusan to purchase goods for re-sale in Russia.

vi.   NORTH KOREA

CAPITAL: Pyongyang   AREA: 123,370 sq km   POPULATION: 22,646,000 ('93)
OFFICIAL LANGUAGE: Korean   POLITICAL SYSTEM: people's republic
RULING PARTY: Korean Workers' Party (KWP)
HEAD OF STATE & PARTY LEADER: (vacant)
PRINCIPAL MINISTERS: Kang Song San (Prime Minister), Kim Yong Nam (foreign affairs), Marshal Oh Jin U (defence), Lt-Gen. Paek Hak Nom (public security), Hong Sok Hyong (state planning), Yun Ki Chong (finance)
CURRENCY: won (end-'94 £1=NKW3.36, US$1=NKW2.15)
GNP PER CAPITA: US$943 ('93)
MAIN EXPORT EARNERS: minerals, metallurgical products, cement, agricultural products, textiles & clothing

THERE was a paucity of official information on North Korea in 1994, because in August 1993 the authorities had ceased sending newspapers and other information materials abroad. Particularly acute was the dearth of news from North Korea on the resolution of the nuclear weapons inspection issue and on the succession to Kim Il Sung. Most of what was reported about these major questions therefore came from Western or South Korean sources. It seemed, however, that the North Korean regime was using the issue of its nuclear capability partly to gain external concessions but mainly to shore up its domestic position by demonstrating its strength against the outside world. This scenario helped to explain North Korea's erratic diplomacy with the United States and South Korea (see IX.2.v), the real issue for the regime being, not its nuclear weapons capability, but the continuing disintegration of the state itself.

Over the past four years North Korea's economy had contracted nearly 20 per cent. By mid-June 1994 there were numerous indications of growing food and energy shortages, leading to serious disenchantment with the regime. A small but steady trickle of people managed to reach South Korea, among the most dramatic cases being the escape of some 200 North Korean loggers from semi-slave labour camps in Russian Siberia. In March the South Korean government agreed to take 100 of these loggers, the first group of whom arrived in Seoul on 18 May.

Strong disenchantment amongst key members of the elite sector was indicated by some defections, notably of the son-in-law of the North Korean Premier. Such disaffection perhaps explained the government's announcement early in 1994 that North Korean archaeologists had discovered the bones of the mythical founder of the Korean state, Tan'gun. The authorities proceeded to erect an enormous pyramidal tumulus over the alleged grave site, which became a key pilgrimage site in line with the regime's depiction of itself as the authentic inheritor of Korean history and tradition.

A major crisis for the regime was the death of Kim Il Sung on 8 July at the age of 82 (see XX: Obituary). For a brief period, the world was treated to the theatrical spectacle of North Koreans en masse paying hysterical homage to the memory of the deceased 'Great Leader'. An elaborate funeral was held on 19 July. Subsequently, there were a series of confusing reports about who was running the country, it being unclear whether the late dictator's son, Kim Jong Il, had fully achieved the succession intended by his father. At year's end a new cabinet had still not been formally announced nor had there been a formal statement of the succession of Kim Jong Il. One view in South Korea was that the younger Kim was seriously ill, suffering from heart problems and diabetes.

At the same time, there were also clear indications that some members of the leadership favoured an opening to the outside world and were actively seeking capital assistance. It was revealed in South

Korea that the chairman of the giant conglomerate Daewoo visited Pyongyang twice in 1994 (in June and July). This was followed on 30 August–5 September by a visit by a delegation from the US Chamber of Commerce, including representatives of Motorola, General Motors, Ford, IBM and Hewlett–Packard.

vii. MONGOLIA

CAPITAL: Ulan Bator   AREA: 1,565,000 sq km   POPULATION: 2,250,000 ('94)
PRINCIPAL LANGUAGE: Halh (Khalkha) Mongolian
POLITICAL SYSTEM: republic ruled by reformed communist party
HEAD OF STATE: President Punsalmaagiyn Ochirbat (since Sept '90)
RULING PARTY: Mongolian People's Revolutionary Party (MPRP)
PARTY LEADER: Büdragchaagiyn Dash-Yondon, MPRP secretary-general
PRINCIPAL MINISTERS: Puntsagiyn Jasray (Prime Minister), Choyjilsürengiyn Pürevdorj
    (Deputy Prime Minister), Lhamsürengiyn Enebish (Deputy Prime Minister),
    Tserenpiliyn Gombosüren (foreign relations), Lt-Gen. Shagalyn Jadambaa
    (defence), Tsevegmidiyn Tsogt (trade & industry)
INTERNATIONAL ALIGNMENT: NAM
CURRENCY: tögrög (end-'94 £1=T641.71, US$1=T410.17)
GNP PER CAPITA: US$100 ('93)
MAIN EXPORT EARNERS: copper ore, livestock, agricultural products

SKIRMISHING between the ruling Mongolian People's Revolutionary Party (the reformed communist party) and the opposition National Democratic and Social Democratic parties continued to threaten Mongolia's political stability in 1994. Opposition dissatisfaction stemmed from the MPRP's monopoly of government resulting from the representational imbalance in the Great Hural (national assembly). Resorting to extra-parliamentary action, the opposition launched demonstrations and hunger strikes in April focusing on allegations of official corruption. The government rejected calls for its resignation and introduced new restrictions on demonstrations. However, the three parties eventually achieved a 'political consensus' under which new laws would be drafted to impose a code of moral behaviour on officials and ease the government monopoly of the official media. A commission was set up to examine the electoral law. The government later intensified the campaign against corruption with autumn crackdowns on bankers and illegal immigrants.

The dispute over language policy came to a head in July when the MPRP majority in the Great Hural forced through a resolution postponing until 2001 implementation of the legislature's decision in 1990 to reintroduce the classical Mongolian language and script for official publications in 1994. President Ochirbat vetoed the resolution, but the Hural rejected his veto. The resolution also confirmed the continued use of the Cyrillic (Russian) script adopted for Mongolian some 50 years previously.

The Great Hural approved the formation of three new provinces, named Darhan-Uul, Orhon and Govsümber, around the previously independent towns of Darhan and Erdenet and the former Soviet army base of Choyr respectively. Ex-Prime Minister Dashiyn Byambasüren gave up his seat in the Great Hural and left the MPRP to found the Mongolian Democratic Renewal Party, being elected its chairman.

Opinion polls indicated the continuing popularity of Prime Minister Puntsagiyn Jasray, but he came under attack at the Great Hural's autumn session over the growing crisis of poverty. A total of 137,826 Mongolian families had been categorized as 'poor' (meaning living below the monthly subsistence level of US$7–8) and 32,245 families as 'very poor' (having per capita income of less than 40 per cent of the subsistence level). To reduce the proportion of 'poor' people from 25 to 10 per cent by the year 2000, the government launched an $84 million relief programme supported by the Asian Development Bank (ADB), the World Bank, UNICEF and Denmark.

Inflation declined to 145 per cent in the year to January and to 69 per cent in the year to June 1994, when it was on course to meet the IMF's targets of 51.5 per cent for 1994 and 12 per cent for 1995. However, the uneven development of private enterprise and foreign trade was threatening the IMF's GDP growth predictions of 2.4 per cent for 1994 and 3 per cent for 1995. The 1994 cereals harvest of 424,800 tonnes was below expectations, but livestock surviving from birth in 1994 exceeded 8.5 million, maintaining the herds at just over 26 million head.

Road, rail and air transport were seriously affected by shortages of imported petrol and diesel. The Mongolian Gazryn Tos and US Nescor Energy companies' joint-venture drilling operation in East Gobi province struck oil at 920 metres at Tsagaan Els in December, raising hopes that Mongolia might be able to meet some of its demand for petroleum products from its own resources from 1995–96 onwards. A Chinese standard-gauge (1,435-millimetre) railway spur and electric power transmission line were completed from Erenhot in Inner Mongolia—the terminus of the Mongolian Railway's Russian broad-gauge (1,520-millimetre) track—across the border to Zamyn-Üüd, where a new international goods yard was under construction with a soft loan from Japan.

The ADB issued tenders for the construction of hundreds of miles of hard-top roads from Darhan to Erdenet and from Ulan Bator east to Baganuur and south to Choyr and Saynshand. The British firm Wimpey and a German partner were carrying out improvements to the runway and terminal building at Ulan Bator (Buyant-Uhaa) airport under a US$32 million scheme backed by the ADB. The Mongolian airline MIAT returned its single Tu-154 to Aeroflot and acquired a second Boeing 727 to open a weekly service to the Kazakh capital, Almaty. An airport departure tax of US$8 (US$12 for VIPs) was introduced.

International donors' pledges for 1994 as of November amounted to US$82.8 million in aid and US$172.8 million in loans. More than ECU 10 million was on offer for administrative reform schemes in Mongolia, up for tender following the European Union's decision to include Mongolia in TACIS (the EU's programme of 'technical assistance to CIS' countries).

Following release of Mongolia's foreign policy 'concept' by the Great Hural, Tserenpiliyn Gombosüren (the Foreign Relations Minister) said that the top-priority objective was to ensure the country's security and national interests by diplomatic means. He explained that this meant maintaining a policy of equal relations with Russia and China while developing relations with the West, Asian states. the United Nations and the IMF, other CIS members and East European countries, and developing countries.

'We respect the Mongolian people's choice of their own course of development', declared the Chinese Premier, Li Peng, during an official visit to Mongolia in April. According to Premier Li, China's policy towards Mongolia, based on its five principles of peaceful coexistence, combined respect for Mongolia's independence, sovereignty and territorial integrity with the development of trade and economic cooperation on the basis of equality, support for Mongolia's policy of freedom from nuclear weapons and foreign troops and willingness to see Mongolia develop relations with other countries. A Mongolian–Chinese Treaty of Friendly Relations and Cooperation signed by Premier Li and Prime Minister Jasray emphasized non-interference in each other's internal affairs and regular consultation.

Addressing the UN General Assembly in October, Mr Gombosüren said that Mongolia was ready to join the international nuclear test monitoring network and supported the indefinite prolongation of the Nuclear Non-Proliferation Treaty. Mongolia protested against Chinese nuclear tests in June and October (see IX.2.i). President Ochirbat paid state visits to India, Thailand, Laos and Vietnam in February, signing new treaties and agreements in each country.

X AUSTRALASIA AND SOUTH PACIFIC

i. AUSTRALIA

CAPITAL: Canberra AREA: 7,687,000 sq km POPULATION: 18,000,000 ('94)
OFFICIAL LANGUAGE: English POLITICAL SYSTEM: federal parliamentary democracy
HEAD OF STATE: Queen Elizabeth GOVERNOR-GENERAL: Bill Hayden
RULING PARTY: Australian Labor Party (ALP)
HEAD OF GOVERNMENT: Paul Keating, Prime Minister (since Dec '91)
PRINCIPAL MINISTERS: Brian Howe (Deputy Prime Minister, housing & regional
    development), Ralph Willis (treasury), Kim Beazley (finance), Gareth Evans
    (foreign affairs), Peter Cook (industry, science & technology), Robert Ray
    (defence), Michael Lavarch (Attorney-General)
INTERNATIONAL ALIGNMENT: ANZUS, OECD, Cwth.
CURRENCY: Australian dollar (end-'94 £1=A$2.02, US$1=A$1.29)
GNP PER CAPITA: US$17,260 ('92)
MAIN EXPORT EARNERS: minerals, meat & agricultural products, basic manufactures

THE major political issue dominating the Australian media was the
future of the Liberal Party, which celebrated its 50th anniversary at
Albury (where it was founded) in late October. The Australian Labor
Party (ALP) remained in office nationally and strengthened its position
towards the end of the year. There were no state elections in 1994 and
the Northern Territory remained under Country Liberal Party control
at the election of 4 June. An important group of national by-elections
indicated changing fortunes for the major parties and gave some
encouragement for minor candidates. The economy showed continuing
signs of improvement but by December this was being damped down
again by rising interest rates designed to limit inflationary pressure.
Drought conditions prevailed over large areas, causing considerable
hardship for primary producers. Unemployment levels remained high,
though falling below 10 per cent in the second half of the year. The
Australian dollar rose steadily throughout the year but share prices
remained fairly stagnant. A new timetable produced a May budget
predicting a deficit of A$11,720 million.

The failure of the conservative coalition to win the 1993 election (see
AR 1993, pp. 374-5) caused continuing crises within the Liberal Party
and between it and its ally, the National Party (NP). These reflected
personal tensions, rivalry between New South Wales and Victoria,
ideological divisions between 'wets' and 'dries' and the impact of several
moral issues such as homosexuality, racial vilification and Aboriginal
land rights. In Queensland, where the NP remained stronger than
the Liberals, there were tensions over seat allocation and a proposed
merger. The 'Fightback' policies on which the 1993 election was fought
were steadily repudiated, starting in January with a strong criticism from
the party president, Tony Staley. Senator Bronwyn Bishop emerged
temporarily as a press and opinion-poll favourite (see AR 1993, p. 376).

But her poor showing in the Sydney (Mackellar) by-election which put her into the House of Representatives on 26 March removed her from leadership contention. In the same month the ALP temporarily headed the opposition in opinion polls for the first time for a year, this reversal casting doubt on the future of the Liberal leader, John Hewson.

By mid-April the 'economic rationalist' Fightback programme was being declared 'dead' by the media and its architect, Dr Hewson, began to stake out a liberal position on moral issues in contrast to his emerging rival, former leader John Howard. In early March Dr Hewson had shocked his conservative colleagues by endorsing the annual Gay and Lesbian Mardi Gras, which took place within his constituency. He followed this by criticizing Mr Howard's previous attitudes on Asian immigration and taxation policy. But support slipped away from Mr Hewson, who was damaged when deputy Liberal leader Peter Reith retired to the back benches in May and whose fate was sealed later the same month by the desertion of former party leaders Malcolm Fraser and Andrew Peacock and of Mr Staley. In a 43–36 vote by the Liberal parliamentary caucus on 23 May, he was replaced as leader by Alexander Downer of South Australia, whose deputy, Peter Costello, was from Victoria. Mr Downer was regarded as a traditional conservative and Mr Costello as an 'economic rationalist', although their support was not ideologically consistent. Their election ended the New South Wales grip on the Liberal leadership represented by Dr Hewson and his predecessor, John Howard.

The change of leadership gave only a temporary respite to divisions within the Liberal Party. By the end of the year Mr Downer's position had become as insecure as Dr Hewson's had been previously, his opinion-poll support having dropped sharply from August onwards. He was able to steer rule changes through the anniversary Liberal conference at Albury on 29 October, giving more power to the party centre to determine the selection of candidates. But by then he had already removed Dr Hewson from his front-bench team (on 26 August) and had made some serious public errors, especially on Aboriginal policy. He also antagonized the NP with his proposal for an alternative to the government's racial vilification legislation, any form of which was opposed by the NP (and generally by the media), whereas there was strong pressure in favour of the ALP proposal from the ethnic and Jewish lobbies. Mr Downer had a public dispute with these lobbies and then with the Aboriginal and Torres Strait Islander Commission, both in November. The NP was further annoyed by Mr Downer's failure to oppose the Human Rights (Sexual Conduct) Bill, by which the government sought to override Tasmanian laws making homosexual practices between adults illegal (the only such laws remaining in Australia). Several conservative Liberals and Nationals opposed the bill, Mr Downer's line on which provoked the resignation of the NP Senate leader, Ron Bosworth, on 9 December. By the end of the parliamentary year Mr Downer had reached a low point in the opinion polls. Some party colleagues were actively working against him and Mr Howard was emerging as a serious contender to retrieve the Liberal leadership.

In contrast to the opposition parties, the ALP remained remarkably calm. Its national conference in September endorsed a proposal that within ten years 35 per cent of its candidates in winnable seats would be women. Official support was given to the celebration of the centenary of women's suffrage in South Australia. The conference also resolved to lease airports to private operators and to sell the government share in the national shipping line. It failed to change current policy limiting uranium mining to three mines, despite support for a change from the ALP Prime Minister, Paul Keating. The party unanimously reaffirmed its support for a republic by 2000, but there was no debate or elaboration. Party rules were changed to expand the size of the conference but to reduce the size of the national executive. Both measures moved the party further away from its original federal structure based on state branches.

The ALP had some difficulties with 'ethnic branch stacking'—the practice of signing up members from ethnic minority groups in order to influence the selection of candidates. Rule changes in Victoria largely blocked this practice, which drew attention to the discrepancy between the ethnic character of constituencies and their representatives in parts of Sydney and Melbourne. More starkly, the murder of a state ALP politician, John Newman, at his home in Cabramatta (Sydney) in September was attributed to his opposition to Asian drug gangs operating in his area, which contained one of the largest Vietnamese and Chinese concentrations in Australia. However, no arrest had been made by the end of the year and no evidence was produced of links between the murder and organized crime. In an unconnected event, which also went unprosecuted, the National Crime Authority offices in Adelaide were severely damaged by a bomb explosion in March in which one police officer was killed. Concern about organized crime encouraged the national government to seek agreement with the states on a uniform crime code.

In the absence of national or state elections, some major by-elections indicated political trends and influenced careers, if somewhat uncertainly. The contests were caused by the resignations of several important politicians: John Kerin (Werriwa), Neil Blewett (Bonython) and John Dawkins (Fremantle) of the ALP; and Andrew Peacock (Kooyong), Jim Carlton (Mackellar) and Michael Mackellar (Warringah) of the Liberal Party. As all but Fremantle were safe seats, the other major party did not put up a candidate in most cases, with the result that there was a higher than normal vote for independents, most prominently for anti-immigration candidates in Warringah, Mackellar and Bonython and for a Green in Kooyong. More importantly, new talent was introduced, including Carmen Lawrence (former premier of Western Australia) for the ALP and Bronwyn Bishop, Tony Abbott (director of Australians for a Constitutional Monarchy) and Petro Georgiou for the Liberals. Mr Georgiou, previously director of the party in Victoria, was the first Greek-born candidate to be elected to the national parliament. All were front bench material and Carmen Lawrence was immediately made Minister for Health.

The continuing reckoning for the commercial speculations of the previous decade brought more businessmen back into court (see AR 1990, p. 373; 1992, p. 372; 1993, p. 377). Alan Bond appeared in bankruptcy proceedings throughout the year, while John Elliott (formerly of Elders IXL) was committed for trial on 9 December after a long and public struggle with the National Crime Authority. Laurie Connell of Perth was sentenced to five years for conspiracy on 12 May, but the continuing attempts to extradite Christopher Skase from Spain finally failed on appeal in December, when a Spanish court ruled that he was unfit to travel. The former premier of Western Australia, Brian Burke, was sentenced to two years for fraud on 15 July and his former deputy premier, David Parker, to 12 months for theft on 17 September.

Prime Minister Keating opened the Australian-funded bridge between Thailand and Laos in April. A forum of South Pacific leaders was held in Brisbane in August. Australia took a major role at the Asia-Pacific Economic Cooperation forum at Bogor (Indonesia) in November, in pursuit of its aim to liberalize trade in the region (see XI.6.iii). Otherwise, foreign policy controversy mainly surrounded issues peripheral to Australian interests but of concern to groups within Australia, such as conditions in Indonesian-controlled East Timor (see IX.1.vi) or the uprising in the Papua New Guinean island of Bougainville (see X.1.ii). In response to mass demonstrations by Greek Australians, the government ruled that immigrants from the 'Former Yugoslav Republic of Macedonia' would be officially described as 'Slav Macedonians', a solution which made nobody very happy. Liberal leaders such as Mr Downer and the Victorian premier, Jeff Kennett, publicly supported the Greek case that the new republic had no historical right to call itself Macedonia. The ALP was in a difficult position, in that it received considerable support from both Greeks and Slavs, especially in Melbourne, where most of the agitation took place.

In late December the arrival of several boatloads of Chinese from Beihai in southern China caused some concern. These people had previously been relocated from Vietnam and were seeking to migrate to Australia without official approval. In accordance with current policy, they were detained pending examination for refugee status, putting considerable pressure on existing detention facilities at Port Hedland. Over 1,000 such 'boat people' arrived in 1994, more than for many years, causing the opposition parties to call for negotiations with China to prevent unauthorized departures.

The opening of a third runway at Sydney airport, to reduce congestion, caused great concern among those in the new flight paths over densely inhabited areas of central Sydney. Local councils organized a peaceful occupation of the airport in December and there was a political impact on the ALP as holder of most of the affected constituencies. The Civil Aviation Authority, responsible for air safety, was the subject of much critical inquiry during the year, following a number of small plane crashes and disaffection within its ranks. In early December the national government annoyed many of its supporters by endorsing the renewal of wood-chipping licences in forests, and some pundits endorsed the claim of the conservation movement that this isssue could lose the ALP the next election.

Australia did exceptionally well at the Commonwealth Games in Canada, winning a record 182 medals (see Pt. XVII). Among those who died during the year were the writer Mary Durack, the social researcher Professor Ronald Henderson, the public service reformer Dr Peter Wilenski and the actor Frank Thring.

ii.   PAPUA NEW GUINEA

CAPITAL: Port Moresby   AREA: 463,000 sq km   POPULATION: 4,100,000 ('92)
OFFICIAL LANGUAGES: Pidgin, Motu, English
POLITICAL SYSTEM: parliamentary democracy
HEAD OF STATE: Queen Elizabeth   GOVERNOR-GENERAL: Wiwa Korowi
RULING PARTIES: People's Progress Party (PPP) heads coalition
HEAD OF GOVERNMENT: Sir Julius Chan, Prime Minister (since Aug '94)
PRINCIPAL MINISTERS: Chris Haiveta (Deputy Prime Minister, finance & planning),
   Mathias Ijape (defence), Arnold Marsipal (justice), Nakikus Konga (home affairs)
INTERNATIONAL ALIGNMENT: NAM, ACP, Cwth.
CURRENCY: kina (end-'94 £1=K1.84, US$1=K1.18)
GNP PER CAPITA: US$950 ('92)
MAIN EXPORT EARNERS: copper, coffee, palm oil, cocoa

THE year was one of diverse crises for Papua New Guinea. Governmental instability, the continuing secessionist conflict in Bougainville and a major natural disaster contributed to a continuing climate of national disequilibrium.

At the end of August the Supreme Court found that Prime Minister Paias Wingti of the People's Democratic Movement (PDM) had behaved illegally in 'ambushing' parliament into a technically unnecessary reappointment vote the previous September. He was judged to have misused the constitutional reform of 1991 setting an 18-month period of immunity for 'new' governments from no-confidence votes (see AR 1991 p. 373). A new parliamentary vote for the premiership was ordered, from which Mr Wingti withdrew after the Deputy Prime Minister and People's Progress Party (PPP) leader, Sir Julius Chan, formed an alliance with the opposition Pangu Pati. Sir Julius was elected Prime Minister by a large majority on 30 August. Part-Chinese and with strong business and family links with the islands region, he had been the country's second post-independence Prime Minister in 1980–82 and was widely regarded as one of Papua New Guinea's most able politicians.

On taking office, Sir Julius attempted to use the momentum of governmental change and his 'islander' identity to break the deadlock over the five-year-old secession crisis on the island of Bougainville (see AR 1993, p. 379). Although slowly reoccupying rebel-held areas, government forces had been incapable of extinguishing the revolt by the Bougainville Revolutionary Army (BRA). Long-standing accusations of human rights abuses against the government culminated, in March, in a call by the UN Human Rights Commission for an international investigation. The request was flatly rejected by Mr Wingti, then Prime Minister. Initially the moves of the new Chan government appeared to be successful. In early September it signed a ceasefire agreement with BRA military leader Sam Kauona in Honiara (the Solomon Islands' capital) and a regional peace-keeping force was established drawing contingents from Fiji, Tonga and Vanuatu. However, substantive settlement talks which were arranged for Arawa (in Bougainville itself) on 10 October did not take place. The BRA failed to appear, citing (as on previous occasions) fears for the safety of its delegation and claiming lack of good faith on the part of the government. The peace-keeping force was withdrawn and Sir Julius expressed his interest in pursuing talks with non-BRA Bougainvilleans with a view to isolating the rebels. In the meantime, the low-intensity but dirty war continued.

On 19 September long-feared volcanic eruptions in East New Britain effectively destroyed the provincial capital of Rabaul, choking it with a layer of ash several metres deep and turning the harbour into solid pumice stone. Well-practiced evacuation plans, in place since a previous series of eruptions in the late 1930s, kept casualties to a remarkably low level. Inevitably, however, there were considerable economic consequences following the extinction of a major commercial and trading centre. Papua New Guinea's nascent tourist industry also suffered from the destruction of one of the loveliest towns in the South Pacific region.

Certain adjustments in the tone, if not the substance, of foreign policy were predicted with the change of Prime Minister. Mr Wingti's Melanesian nationalism, in evidence on economic and resource issues at the annual South Pacific Forum held in Brisbane in mid-year (see

XI.6.iv), was replaced by the PPP leader's more emollient, 'business-minded' approach to regional relationships, particularly that with Australia.

2. NEW ZEALAND—SOUTH PACIFIC

i. NEW ZEALAND

CAPITAL: Wellington   AREA: 270,000 sq km   POPULATION: 3,400,000 ('92)
OFFICIAL LANGUAGE: English   POLITICAL SYSTEM: parliamentary democracy
HEAD OF STATE: Queen Elizabeth   GOVERNOR-GENERAL: Dame Cath Tizard
RULING PARTY: National Party (NP)
HEAD OF GOVERNMENT: Jim Bolger, Prime Minister (since Oct '90)
PRINCIPAL MINISTERS: Don McKinnon (Deputy Prime Minister, external relations),
   Bill Birch (finance), Paul East (Attorney-General), Warren Cooper (defence),
   Doug Graham (justice), John Falloon (agriculture)
INTERNATIONAL ALIGNMENT: ANZUS (suspended), OECD, Cwth.
CURRENCY: New Zealand dollar (end-'94 £1=NZ$2.44, US$1=NZ$1.56)
GNP PER CAPITA: US$12,300 ('92)
MAIN EXPORT EARNERS: meat & meat products, wool, dairy products, manufactures,
   tourism

CONVINCING economic growth was recorded in 1994, amidst conditions of social flux and political uncertainty. On an annual basis, the economy (GDP) grew by 4 per cent, the best result for over a decade. By December, government accounts recorded a surplus of NZ$2,300 million, which was double a mid-year budget forecast. Notwithstanding a 4 per cent appreciation of the currency, export returns for dairy, wool and timber products increased, while tourism boomed as the country's leading earner of foreign exchange. Retail, manufacturing and service activities showed strong growth and unemployment fell to 8 per cent of the total workforce.

While the increase in consumer prices remained below 2 per cent, pressures from heightened building activity and record imports saw the Reserve Bank tighten money supply with 90-day bill rates at 9 per cent. This led the trading banks to raise home mortgages to around 11 per cent. The government increased social spending on beneficiaries and faced further charges associated with the costs of its restructured health system, while overseas debt payment remained a priority. Helped by a stronger local currency, net public debt decreased by 5 per cent to NZ$35,000 million. Given the unusual circumstances of running a surplus, the government faced vociferous demands for accelerated spending from educational and social services, whose spokesmen insisted that they faced a backlog of previous under-funding. Public contest over the 'social deficit' also included the issue of housing, where church groups identified a 22 per cent increase in serious need since 1992.

In a widely-leaked announcement in December, the government outlined its proposals for a final settlement of some 400 outstanding Maori land claims currently before the Waitangi Tribunal. To be allocated over the next decade and amounting to approximately NZ$1,000 million, the proposed settlement was strongly promoted by the government as an offer deserving of national support. Although these terms were rejected by some leading Maori, in December the government reached a major settlement, for NZ$170 million, with the northern Tainui tribe, including a formal apology by the Crown for land confiscation in 1863 and the return of 14,000 hectares.

Notwithstanding its flimsy parliamentary majority, the National Party (NP) government of Jim Bolger consolidated its standing as economic circumstances improved. Exploiting the continuing animosity between his Alliance and Labour opponents, the Prime Minister increased his popularity through effective political management and consultation. In March he helped to instigate a public debate on the country's constitutional future by revealing his colours as a genuine republican. It became clear that he was unenthused by the imperial honours system and by the continuing use of the Privy Council in London as the highest court of appeal, and keen that New Zealand should identify more with the Asia-Pacific region.

A particular policy headache which the Bolger government continued to face was health service restructuring. Here it misdiagnosed the ability of the Crown Health Enterprise (CHE) system—which it had established—to cope within the commercial culture within which it was now meant to operate (see AR 1992, pp. 376–7). The original intention of having a reformed health system removed from fiscal risk went badly awry in 1994. In March there was a NZ$405 million three-year injection of additional funding, this being followed by a NZ$880 million debt write-off. In October a further three-year NZ$534 million boost for CHE funding was announced, designed to reduce ever-lengthening hospital waiting lists. Further uncertainty occurred when the government banned tobacco sponsorship of some major sporting events and shortly afterwards abolished the Public Health Commission, an independent body it had established to promote health awareness.

The resignation from parliament of former Finance Minister Ruth Richardson in July caused a by-election in the South Island constituency of Selwyn on 13 August, when the NP narrowly retained the seat against the Alliance, with Labour coming a poor third. The government thus retained an effective two-seat majority in the House of Representatives (the Speaker being drawn from Labour ranks). Politically, there was considerable positioning by parliamentarians preparing themselves for the inception of 'mixed member proportional' (MMP) representation at the next general election (see AR 1993, p. 381). In September Ross Meurant, parliamentary under-secretary for agriculture, defected from the NP to form a new Right of Centre (ROC) party. By allowing Mr Meurant to remain in his administration, in effect now a coalition, Mr Bolger managed to retain a parliamentary majority. Soon afterwards, Peter Dunne (Labour) defected to form the Future New Zealand Party, while at least two other NP backbenchers indicated that they would be leaving the party early in 1995, either to form new parties or to link up with existing organizations.

The prospective introduction of MMP was also complicated when Maori petitioners took the government to court, claiming that it had failed to publicize adequately the options open to Maori voters in a referendum held early in 1994. This was designed to determine the number of seats allocated for Maori representation in direct proportion to those opting to join or remain on the Maori electoral roll. The referendum result indicated that five such seats should be provided, one more than allocated under the outgoing system of representation. The petitioners claimed that, with better government funding and publicity, more voters would have opted to go on the Maori electoral roll. In a ruling that critics believed saw the bench dabbling unduly in politics, Justice McGechan found narrowly for the government but uttered words hinting that the petitioners had a case. They then appealed against the ruling, the outcome remaining undecided at year's end.

In November the Alliance leader (and former Labour president), Jim Anderton, stunned supporters with his resignation from the party leadership. Highly regarded and popular, Mr Anderton was replaced by the less experienced Sandra Lee, who became the first Maori woman to lead a political party in New Zealand. The other minor formation with parliamentary representation, the New Zealand First Party, experienced a decline in its standing, as did leader Winston Peters, although his persistent allegations of tax fraud by firms operating in and out of New Zealand and the Cook Islands resulted in a formal inquiry. Under parliamentary privilege, Mr Peters castigated top officials in the Inland Revenue and the Serious Fraud Office for their handling of the issue and also released a voluminous compendium of documentation detailing his allegations. In a controversial move, the Solicitor-General advised that the inquiry should be conducted by formal judicial procedure rather than be subject to the politics of a select committee of parliament. In retaliation, a senior Labour frontbencher, Michael Cullen, attacked the integrity of the judge chosen to head the inquiry. The gist of Mr Peters' allegations, subsequently verified by numerous news media exposures, was that some New Zealand-registered companies had committed tax frauds in collusion with the Cook Islands government. The allegations and the ongoing inquiry strained relations between Canberra and the Cook Islands.

A serious interruption occurred in New Zealand's normally close relations with Australia when the Keating government in Canberra unexpectedly made a late withdrawal from the scheduled commencement of a bilateral aviation agreement. Initially proposed by Mr Keating, the accord would have allowed airlines from both countries to compete in each other's markets under a common aviation policy. At the core of the dispute lay Australia's concern that Air New Zealand could take international business from Australian carriers, to the possible detriment of a much-delayed privatization of Qantas scheduled for April 1995. The off-handed manner of the Australian withdrawal on the eve of the Asia-Pacific Economic Cooperation (APEC) summit in Indonesia (at which Australia endorsed liberalized trade in services) clearly strained trans-Tasman political relations.

A steady improvement in relations with the United States occurred as Washington restored high-level diplomatic and political contacts in February. This did not entail a revival of the ANZUS pact or a revocation of New Zealand's continuing ban on nuclear-powered or nuclear-armed vessels. At the United Nations, New Zealand completed its two-year term on the Security Council, having ignored opposing pressure from some permanent members by insisting that a UN presence should be deployed in strife-torn Rwanda (see VII.1.ii; XI.1). In Bosnia, New Zealand contributed a 250-strong company for UN peace-keeping duties, this step being taken despite some official misgivings. It also succeeded in formulating an international convention designed to protect the safety and security of UN personnel in peace-keeping and humanitarian operations. Another feature was New Zealand's key role in drawing up the procedure for war crimes tribunals dealing with Bosnia and Rwanda. In the UN General Assembly, New Zealand was alone among Western countries in supporting a resolution endorsing a proposal by the World Health Organization that the International Court of Justice should deliver an advisory opinion on the legality of the use of nuclear weapons (see XV.1.i).

In its international economic relations, New Zealand announced further tariff cuts on manufactured goods, encouraged local businesses to take advantage of the opportunities available under the GATT trade liberalization agreement and supported similar proposals announced at the November APEC summit. In the South Pacific, New Zealand settled a long-standing claim concerning phosphate exploitation on Nauru by agreeing to pay NZ$15 million in compensation. It also reduced rules of origin requirements for imports under the South Pacific regional trade and cooperation agreement.

ii. SOUTH PACIFIC

Fiji
CAPITAL: Suva   AREA: 18,375 sq km   POPULATION: 750,000 ('92)
OFFICIAL LANGUAGES: Fijian & Hindi   POLITICAL SYSTEM: republic
HEAD OF STATE: President Ratu Sir Kamisese Mara
HEAD OF GOVERNMENT: Maj.-Gen. Sitiveni Rabuka, Prime Minister (since May '92)
CURRENCY: Fiji dollar (end-'94 £1=F$2.20, US$1=F$1.41)
GNP PER CAPITA: US$2,010 ('92)
MAIN EXPORT EARNERS: sugar, agricultural products, tourism

Solomon Islands
CAPITAL: Honiara   AREA: 28,000 sq km   POPULATION: 335,000 ('92)
OFFICIAL LANGUAGE: English   POLITICAL SYSTEM: parliamentary democracy
HEAD OF STATE: Queen Elizabeth   GOVERNOR-GENERAL: Moses Puibangara Pitakaka
HEAD OF GOVERNMENT: Solomon Mamaloni, Prime Minister (since Oct '93)
CURRENCY: Solomon Islands dollar (end-'94 £1=SI$5.15, US$1=SI$3.29)
GNP PER CAPITA: US$710 ('92)
MAIN EXPORT EARNERS: timber, copra, fish, tourism

Vanuatu
CAPITAL: Port Vila   AREA: 12,000 sq km   POPULATION: 151,000 ('91)
OFFICIAL LANGUAGES: English, French & Bislama   POLITICAL SYSTEM: parliamentary
HEAD OF STATE: President Fred Timakata (since Jan '89)
HEAD OF GOVERNMENT: Maxime Carlot Korman, Prime Minister (since Dec '91)
CURRENCY: vatu (end-93 £1=VT180.20, US$1=VT121.80)
GNP PER CAPITA: US$1,150 ('91)
MAIN EXPORT EARNERS: copra, agricultural products, tourism

Cook Islands
CAPITAL: Avarua   AREA: 4,200 sq km   POPULATION: 20,000 ('90)
STATUS: New Zealand associated territory
HEAD OF GOVERNMENT: Geoffrey A. Henry, Prime Minister

Western Samoa
CAPITAL: Apia   AREA: 2,830 sq km   POPULATION: 161,000 ('91)
OFFICIAL LANGUAGES: Samoan & English   POLITICAL SYSTEM: monarchy
HEAD OF STATE: Susuga Malietoa Tanumafili II (since '62)
HEAD OF GOVERNMENT: Tofilau Eti Alesana, Prime Minister (since '88)
CURRENCY: tala (end-'93 £1=WS$3.86, US$1=WS$2.61)
GNP PER CAPITA: US$960 ('91)
MAIN EXPORT EARNERS: cocoa, copra, agricultural products, tourism

Kiribati
CAPITAL: Tarawa   AREA: 1,000 sq km   POPULATION: 75,000 ('92)
OFFICIAL LANGUAGE: English   POLITICAL SYSTEM: presidential
HEAD OF STATE & GOVERNMENT: President Teburoro Tito (since Sept '94)
CURRENCY: Australian dollar   GNP PER CAPITA: US$700 ('92)
MAIN EXPORT EARNERS: copra, phosphates, tourism

Tonga
CAPITAL: Nuku'alofa   AREA: 750 sq km   POPULATION: 100,000 ('91)
OFFICIAL LANGUAGES: Tongan & English   POLITICAL SYSTEM: monarchy
HEAD OF STATE: King Taufa'ahua Tupou IV (since '65)
HEAD OF GOVERNMENT: Baron Vaea, Prime Minister (since Aug '91)
CURRENCY: pa'anga (end-'93 £1=T$2.18, US$1=T$1.47)
GNP PER CAPITA: US$1,280 ('91)
MAIN EXPORT EARNERS: agricultural products, tourism

French Polynesia
CAPITAL: Papeete   AREA: 4,200 sq km   POPULATION: 202,000 ('91)
STATUS: French overseas territory
HEAD OF GOVERNMENT: Gaston Flosse, president of territorial government

New Caledonia
CAPITAL: Nouméa   AREA: 19,000 sq km   POPULATION: 165,000 ('90)
STATUS: French overseas territory
HEAD OF GOVERNMENT: Simon Loueckhole, president of territorial congress

Wallis and Futuna Islands
CAPITAL: Mata-Utu   AREA: 274 sq km   POPULATION: 12,500 ('91)
STATUS: French overseas territory
HEAD OF GOVERNMENT: Soane Mani Uhila, president of territorial assembly

Belau
CAPITAL: Koror   AREA: 460 sq km   POPULATION: 15,000 ('90)
OFFICIAL LANGUAGE: English
POLITICAL SYSTEM: independent republic in free association with USA
HEAD OF STATE & GOVERNMENT: President Kuniwo Nakamura (since Nov '92)
CUURENCY: US dollar

Marshall Islands
CAPITAL: Dalap-Uliga-Darrit   AREA: 200 sq km   POPULATION: 50,000 ('92)
OFFICIAL LANGUAGES: English & Marshallese
POLITICAL SYSTEM: independent republic in free association with USA
HEAD OF STATE & GOVERNMENT: President Amata Kabua (since May '79)
CURRENCY: US dollar
MAIN EXPORT EARNERS: copra, tourism

Guam
CAPITAL: Agana   AREA: 542 sq km   POPULATION: 139,000 ('92)
STATUS: unincorporated territory of USA
GOVERNOR: Joseph F. Ada (Republican)

IN FIJI former coup leader Sitiveni Rabuka was returned to office following a February general election. His Fijian Political Party won 31 seats in the 70-member legislature to again form a coalition with the small General Voters' Party and two independents. Major-General Rabuka's main Fijian rival, Joseph Kamikamica, lost his seat, while in the contest for seats reserved for Indians the National Federation Party increased its representation from 14 to 20, primarily at the expense of the Fijian Labour Party. After first reducing the size of his cabinet, the Prime Minister then expanded it in August, making Filip Bole Minister of Foreign Affairs.

The SOLOMON ISLANDS faced a constitutional crisis in October when Francis Billy Hilly's government collapsed following the resignation of five ministers. Although he had support from only 17 of the 47 members of the legislature, Mr Hilly refused to resign until parliament reconvened. He also refused to accept Governor-General Pitakaka's move to dismiss him, referring the question to the High Court, which found that the Governor-General could not dismiss the Prime Minister short of parliament convening and passing a vote of no confidence. Eventually, however, Mr Hilly resigned and elections were held, resulting in Solomon Mamaloni returning to office backed by 25 members of parliament.

VANUATU experienced continuing unrest in the public service, where strikes and major layoffs occurred. Maxime Carlot Korman's government survived a vote of no confidence, while inter-party squabbling delayed the election of Jean Marie Leye as the country's first francophone President. In May a group expelled from former Prime Minister Walter Lini's National United Party formed the People's Democratic Party. The latter entered into coalition with the Korman-led government, providing it with a narrow working majority in the 46-member legislature.

In the COOK ISLANDS, March elections saw Sir Geoffrey Henry's Cook Islands Party returned to office with an increased majority of 20 of the 25 seats in parliament. Allegations from New Zealand politician Winston Peters that the Henry government was heavily implicated in dubious tax practices (see X.2.i) did little to harm the Cook Islands Party's electoral performance. During the election campaign the government sought to defuse a financial scandal over an abortive hotel project by blaming the previous government for signing the controversial deal.

In WESTERN SAMOA, a July report by the chief auditor implicated seven cabinet ministers and senior officials in financial malfeasance. The same report indicated that the country's airline was in a chronic state of insolvency and proving a serious drain on an already fragile economy.

A parliamentary election in KIRIBATI in July ended 15 years of rule by the National Progressive Party of Teatao Teannaki, whose government had collapsed in May amid allegations of corruption. Power passed to the Maneaban Te Mauri party, which secured the election of Teburoro Tito as President in September.

The pro-democracy movement in TONGA launched the kingdom's first political party, the People's Party. A local businessman, Huliki Watab, was elected as its chairman. The government announced moves to privatize public bodies, while the central bank was given added monetary instruments.

In FRENCH POLYNESIA, the vice-president of the territorial assembly, Milou Ebb, launched a new political party entitled Te Avei'a Mau, its key objective being greater autonomy from France. The territorial assembly's operations were impeded for a month as representatives heeded only the calls of their respective leaderships to attend. The suspension of nuclear testing by France continued to afflict the territory's economy (see also II.1.ii), engendering unresolved disputes over appropriate taxation.

In NEW CALEDONIA, the churches decided to support the movement for independence from France, a new nickel mine commenced operations and new sales taxes were introduced to compensate for a decline in nickel earnings. Police from New Caledonia were flown into the French overseas territory of WALLIS AND FUTUNA, where striking workers fire-bombed government facilities and demanded improved essential services and non-religious schools.

In Micronesia, the remaining legal complications in BELAU's constitutional status (see AR 1993, p. 387) were finally resolved, enabling the Republic to proceed to independence in October and UN membership shortly thereafter, although under its compact of free association with the United States the latter remained responsible for its foreign policy and defence.

In the MARSHALL ISLANDS, President Kabua announced a feasibility study for the use of one of the country's radioactivity-contaminated islands as a dump for the long-term storage of nuclear wastes. Economic considerations were seen as paramount, it being claimed that the venture could earn US$50 million a year for 20 years. Documents declassified in the United States revealed that in the 1950s people from nuclear test sites, such as Bikini, were deliberately settled in areas of high radioactivity to facilitate study of the long-term effects of radiation ingestion.

In November elections Democrats gained control of the governorship and legislature of the US territory of GUAM.

XI INTERNATIONAL ORGANIZATIONS

1. UNITED NATIONS AND ITS AGENCIES

THE refusal of member states to provide forces to halt the genocide in Rwanda reflected the air of caution which characterized 1994 as the United Nations approached its 50th anniversary. Still reeling from the criticisms of its operation in Somalia, the UN nevertheless made progress in a number of conflict arenas. Preparations for the UN's 50th anniversary gathered pace during the year under the direction of Gillian Sorensen, an under-secretary-general.

In a focus on development issues in his third annual report to the General Assembly in September, the UN Secretary-General, Dr Boutros Boutros-Ghali, sought 'to correct the common misperception of the United Nations as an organization dedicated primarily to peace-keeping'. He added: 'Economic and social questions have long occupied the major part of UN efforts. Such work has become all the more important today precisely as conflicts are increasingly recognized to have economic and social origins.' In the same vein he appealed for 'post-conflict nation-building' to 'incorporate more dynamic approaches aimed not at returning to the pre-conflict status quo but at addressing the underlying causes of the manifestations of the crisis'.

49th GENERAL ASSEMBLY. The General Assembly began its 49th session on 20 September by electing Amara Essy (Côte d'Ivoire) as its president. Argentina, the Czech Republic, Nigeria, Oman and Rwanda began two-year terms on the UN Security Council on 1 January 1994. Only one veto was used by a Security Council member in 1994: the Russian Federation vetoed a draft resolution on Bosnia and Hercegovina on 2 December.

The Republic of Palau (Belau) became the 185th member of the United Nations on 15 December (see below and X.2.ii).

FINANCE & ADMINISTRATION. Pressure from the United States for a UN 'Inspector-General' led to the unanimous approval of General Assembly resolution 48/218 B on 29 July creating the Office of Internal Oversight Services. The function of the Office, headed by Karl Theodor Paschke (an under-secretary-general), was to provide a single, independent oversight authority to examine all activities carried out at UN headquarters and in the field. Despite improvement over 1993, the UN continued to face chronic funding arrears from member states during 1994, especially for peace-keeping (see accompanying table). On

29 November the General Assembly established an ad hoc intergovern-mental working group to study the principle of 'capacity to pay' as the fundamental criterion in determining the scale of assessments for contributions to the UN's regular budget.

SECURITY COUNCIL REFORM. Momentum increased during 1994 for modifications to the membership of the UN Security Council. The General Assembly's 'open-ended working group on the question of equitable representation on and increase in the membership of the Security Council' held 22 meetings from 19 January to 2 September. Issues raised by member states included the expansion of Council membership, transparency in the Council's working methods, issues of efficiency and effectiveness, and possible modifications to the veto power of the permanent members. The official report of the group to the General Assembly's 48th session in September was brief, stating that

SUMS OWED TO THE UN BY THE 15 MAJOR CONTRIBUTORS AS AT
31 DECEMBER 1994

State	% of UN regular budget that states must pay	Owed to regular budget[a] US$	Owed to peace-keeping budget[a] US$	Total outstanding to UN[a] US$
USA	25.00	274,851,724	220,871,331	495,723,055
Japan	12.45	0	50,252,507	50,252,507
Germany	8.93	0	24,654,228	24,654,228
Russia	6.71	459,918	506,986,794	507,446,712
France	6.00	0	83,210,972	83,210,972
UK	5.02	0	7,908,035	7,908,035
Italy	4.29	0	5,352,335	5,352,335
Canada	3.11	0	0	0
Spain	1.98	0	19,150,898	19,150,898
Ukraine	1.87	41,405,490	136,890,525	178,296,015
Brazil	1.59	16,174,854	8,333,061	24,507,915
Australia	1.51	0	0	0
Netherlands	1.50	0	1,870,669	1,870,669
Sweden	1.11	0	0	0
Belgium	1.06	0	4,278,527	4,278,527
Sub-total	82.13	305,891,986	1,069,759,882	1,375,651,868
All other UN Member States	17.87	174,199,069	216,658,244	390,857,313
TOTAL OUTSTANDING		480,091,055	1,286,418,126	1,766,509,181

[a]These figures include arrears from previous years

no conclusions had been reached, save that there was 'a convergence of views that the membership of the Council should be enlarged'. The 49th Assembly asked the working group to continue its discussions and to submit a further report. Behind the scenes, support grew for permanent seats for Japan and Germany, and for increased representation (in a form to be negotiated) for states from Africa, Asia and Latin America.

In a separate development, concern was expressed by a number of 'non-aligned' states over the decline in the number of formal open meetings of the Council, whose work was increasingly undertaken in private with no public record kept. As a consequence, a working group of the Council on procedure and documentation made a number of proposals for increasing the transparency of the Council's deliberations. The Council agreed on 16 December to meet more often in open session. A small step towards greater consultation by the Security Council with member states contributing personnel to UN peace-keeping operations was also taken. The Council would now meet 'as a matter of course' before deciding to extend, terminate or consider 'significant changes' in a particular peace-keeping operation. This followed the rejection of initial efforts by New Zealand and Argentina to bring about monthly consultations with troop-contributing countries.

INTERNATIONAL LAW. During the course of the 48th General Assembly, the International Court of Justice (ICJ) had a record number of 13 cases before it (see XV.1.i). At its 46th session (1994), the International Law Commission (the body entrusted with primary responsibility for the codification and development of international law) adopted a draft statute for a permanent international criminal court. The jurisdiction of the court would encompass serious crimes of international concern, including genocide, aggression, war crimes, crimes against humanity, terrorism and illicit drug-trafficking.

The General Assembly's sixth committee (legal) voted on 25 November to approve a draft resolution by which the General Assembly would consider the deletion of the term 'enemy state' from the UN Charter.

PEACE-KEEPING OPERATIONS. The Secretary-General issued a report on 14 March entitled 'Improving the Capacity of the United Nations for Peace-keeping' and containing concrete proposals regarding stand-by arrangements, civilian policy, training, the principle of UN command, the strengthening of the secretariat and the recruitment of civilian personnel. Dr Boutros-Ghali also made proposals on the budgetary and financial aspects of peace-keeping. By September 1994 22 member states had made written offers totalling over 31,000 troops available on a stand-by basis for peace-keeping operations. However, when the secretariat asked for troops to protect refugee camps as violence escalated in

Rwanda, not a single state was at first willing to provide any personnel (see below).

On 1 August the first-ever meeting took place between the UN Secretary-General and the heads of regional organizations in an attempt to enhance UN-regional cooperation. Topics considered included the training of peace-keeping personnel from regional organizations, coordination of command and control for joint peace-keeping operations and coordination of the implementation and verification of sanctions under Chapter VII of the UN Charter.

LIBYA AND CHAD. On 3 February the ICJ delivered its judgment on the Aouzou Strip territorial dispute between Libya and Chad (see V.4.ii; VI.3.x; XV.1.i). Both countries agreed to abide by the decision, and in resolution 915 of 4 May the Security Council established the UN Aouzou Strip Observer Group (UNASOG) to observe the implementation of the agreement. The chief military observer of UNASOG announced that the withdrawal of the Libyan administration and forces from the Aouzou Strip area had been completed by 30 May, in fulfilment of the ICJ ruling; consequently, the Security Council terminated the mandate of UNASOG on 13 June.

Evidence emerged at the end of 1994 from US intelligence agencies which threw doubt on the alleged responsibility of Libya for the bombing of Pan Am flight 103 over the Scottish town of Lockerbie in 1988. Fundamental questions were therefore raised about the *raison d'être* of the continued UN sanctions imposed against the Libyan state.

ANGOLA. The Angolan government and the opposition National Union for the Total Independence of Angola (Unita) approved a new mandate for the UN Angola Verification Mission (UNAVEM II) at peace talks in Lusaka on 5 September (see VII.1.vi). In response, the Security Council decided not to strengthen the existing oil and arms embargo against Unita. On 21 November the Security Council welcomed the signing of the Lusaka Protocol by the government and Unita; on 8 December it agreed to restore the strength of UNAVEM II to its previous level of 476 observers.

MOZAMBIQUE. The UN Operation in Mozambique (ONUMOZ) completed the demobilization of more than 70,000 government and RNM (RENAMO) troops on 31 August (see VII.1.v.). On 21 November the Security Council adopted resolution 960 endorsing the results of the elections held on 27–29 October, after special representative Aldo Ajello had declared that the electoral process was free and fair.

RWANDA. At the start of the year the situation in Rwanda was relatively calm as the country began preparations for national elections.

On 6 January the UN Security Council reaffirmed its approval of the deployment of the UN Assistance Mission for Rwanda (UNAMIR), including the early deployment of a second infantry battalion to the demilitarized zone. However, delays in the establishment of a transitional government led to heightened tensions and on 5 April the Security Council passed resolution 909 expressing its concern at the deterioration in security in Rwanda. The next day a plane crash at Kigali airport in which the Presidents of Rwanda and Burundi were killed sparked off wholesale slaughter in Rwanda, including the murder of ten Belgian UN soldiers, which in turn led to the collapse of the ceasefire between the Rwandan Patriotic Front (FPR) and the then government (see VII.1.ii). On 20 April the Secretary-General reported to the Security Council that further massacres could be averted only by an immediate and massive reinforcement of UNAMIR and a change in its mandate to allow UN troops to coerce opposing forces into a ceasefire. He reflected that this would require several thousand additional troops and could require that UNAMIR be given enforcement powers under Chapter VII of the UN Charter. However, in part because of memories of the political disaster of the UN Operation in Somalia (see below), the major contributing countries decided to withdraw their contingents. The Council, in its resolution 912 (1994) of 21 April, then had little choice but to reduce UNAMIR to a minimal level.

In consequence, UNAMIR could do little to stop an orgy of killing which cost the lives of up to 500,000 Rwandese. Despite the passage of another Security Council resolution on 17 May calling for UNAMIR to be strengthened to 5,500 troops, only Ethiopia, Ghana and Senegal were immediately willing to send contingents. On 25 May Dr Boutros-Ghali revealed that he had 'begged' various heads of state to send troops, adding that the international community's response to Rwanda had been a 'scandal'. In the absence of an effective UN operation, the Council on 22 June authorized member states to use 'all necessary means' to assist in humanitarian relief (resolution 929 of 22 June). This legitimized the temporary deployment of a French-led non-UN force in late June (see also II.1.ii) and the establishment of a protection zone in south-west Rwanda. Having stabilized the internal situation, the French withdrew in late August and were gradually replaced by UNAMIR forces, to which other African states had by now pledged contingents.

Throughout the summer the UNHCR and other agencies struggled to cope with an outflow of an estimated two million Rwandan refugees to Zaïre and Tanzania. On 8 November Dr Boutros-Ghali called on the Security Council to dispatch up to 12,000 UN troops to control the violence that had erupted in the UN-supervised camps. On the same day the Council established the International Criminal Tribunal for Rwanda, with a mandate to prosecute those responsible for genocide 'and other serious violations of international humanitarian law' committed in Rwanda between 1 January and 31 December 1994.

SOMALIA. The year saw a winding-down of UN involvement in Somalia (see also VI.1.iii). After the failure of the US-led attempt to arrest General Aydid, all detainees of the latter's Somali National Alliance (SNA) were released in January. The Council decided on 4 February (resolution 897) to authorize the gradual reduction of the UNOSOM II force level down to 22,000; to abandon coercive means, relying instead on the cooperation of the Somali parties; and to protect the important ports, airports and essential infrastructure in Somalia. In the wake of resolution 897, the UN acting special representative, Lansana Kouyaté, successfully normalized relations between UNOSOM II and the SNA, while a meeting of 19 Somali clan leaders signed a nine-point peace agreement at Kismayo on 24 June. Nevertheless, the security situation deteriorated significantly over the summer. Reporting to the Security Council in the autumn, the Secretary-General concluded that any success by UNOSOM in the security field had been achieved by diplomatic rather than military means, so that the force could be reduced in size. The Security Council passed resolution 954 on 4 November, stating that UNOSOM would not be continued after March 1995 because of the political impasse in the country.

SOUTH AFRICA. On 14 January the Security Council expanded the mandate of the UN Observer Mission in South Africa (UNOMSA) to include observation of the April multi-racial elections (see VII.3). The electoral mission, consisting of 2,120 observers, was the largest ever mounted by the United Nations. Following the inauguration of the Mandela government of national unity, the Security Council voted on 25 May to end the arms embargo against South Africa dating from 1963. A South African delegation resumed participation in the General Assembly on 23 June. At that session, the Assembly terminated the mandate of its special committee against apartheid and removed the question of apartheid from its agenda.

WESTERN SAHARA. The UN Mission for the Referendum in Western Sahara (MINURSO) was beset by continuing delays in fulfilling its task in 1994, caused largely by Morocco (see V.4.vi). MINURSO's identification commission had intended to start the process of voter identification and registration on 28 August, but adequate staff were still not in place at the end of the year. On 15 November the Security Council expressed its concern over the slow speed of the voter identification operation.

NORTH KOREA. Despite agreeing to IAEA inspection of its seven declared nuclear facilities in February, the government of North Korea blocked access to IAEA inspectors the following month (see IX.2.v; IX.2.vi). On 23 March the IAEA declared North Korea to be in non-compliance with its safeguards agreement. After North Korea had ignored Security Council calls for inspections on 31 March and 30 May, the IAEA announced on 3 June that verification of whether nuclear material had been diverted for weapons-grade plutonium production could not be undertaken because of deliberate discharge operations by North Korea at one of its nuclear reactors. North Korea formally withdrew from the IAEA in June, and the US government responded first with threats of sanctions and then by entering into bilateral negotiations in Geneva. On 21 October the two sides signed a new agreement by which, in return for certain US concessions, North Korea again agreed to submit to IAEA inspection. On 28 November an IAEA team confirmed that North Korea was complying with the required nuclear 'freeze'.

GUATEMALA. Members of the UN Mission for Guatemala (MINU-GUA) started arriving in the country on 21 November to supervise the implementation of human rights accords between the government and the opposition Guatemalan National Revolutionary Unity (see IV.3.xiii).

HAITI. There was considerable success during 1994 in achieving the UN's goal of restoring democracy to Haiti (see IV.3.xii). On 6 May the Security Council adopted resolution 917, imposing expanded sanctions on the Haitian military regime and stating that they would not be lifted until the regime had facilitated the creation of the proper environment for the deployment of the UN Mission in Haiti (UNMIH). Amid rising tension, on 31 July the Council adopted resolution 940, by which it authorized member states to form a multinational force and to use all necessary means to facilitate the departure of the military leadership and the return of President Aristide. US troops landed unopposed on 19 September, followed by 60 UN observers. The UN special envoy for Haiti, Dante Caputo, resigned the same day, criticizing what he called 'the US decision to act unilaterally'. Nevertheless, the Security Council lifted sanctions against Haiti on 29 September, this being followed by the restoration of President Aristide in October.

CYPRUS. During 1994 the UN special representative, Joe Clark, focused on securing the agreement of both Cypriot communities to implementing the confidence-building measures tabled by Dr Boutros-Ghali in July 1993. Detailed proposals were presented to the parties on 21 March but soon met resistance, first from the Turkish Cypriot side and then from both sides. On 27 July 1994 the Secretary-General advised the Council that his mission of good offices should be suspended unless evidence of a commitment to a negotiated settlement became evident. On 29 July the Council adopted resolution 939 advocating renewed negotiations, but no substantive progress was made at subsequent informal meetings between the leaders of the two communities in October and November.

FORMER YUGOSLAVIA. Two new UN officials took up post in January: Yasushi Akashi (Japan) arrived in Zagreb (Croatia) to take over as the Secretary-General's special representative for former Yugoslavia, while Lieutenant-General Sir Michael Rose (UK) became commander of the UN Protection Force (UNPROFOR) in Bosnia (see also III.1.vi). On 8 July the Security Council appointed Richard J. Goldstone (South Africa) as prosecutor of the international tribunal responsible for the prosecution of persons responsible for serious violations of international humanitarian law in the territory of the former Yugoslavia (see AR 1993, p. 396).

In Croatia, despite a ceasefire agreement on 29 March, UNPROFOR had difficulties in implementing other parts of its mandate, namely the demilitarization of the UN-protected areas (UNPAs), the return of refugees and displaced persons to their homes, the restoration of Croatian authority in the UNPAs and the 'pink zones', and the establishment of border controls. On 30 September, however, the Croatian government reversed its opposition to a renewal of UNPROFOR's mandate and on 2 December signed an economic agreement with the Croatian Serbs covering the opening of routes, rail lines and other communications as well as the restoration of utilities.

In the aftermath of the February shelling of a crowded Sarajevo market, an effective ceasefire in the city was negotiated by UNPROFOR, with NATO's assistance. On 1 March a ceasefire agreement was signed in Washington between the government of Bosnia and the Bosnian Croat party, preparing the way for the signature on 18 March of a federation agreement between the Muslim and Croat communities in Bosnia. Over the summer, however, the situation in Bosnia generallly, and in Sarajevo in particular, began to deteriorate. The negative features included a resumption of widespread sniping, the intermittent closure of Sarajevo airport, blockades of humanitarian aid convoys, restrictions on UNPROFOR's freedom of movement and repeated violations of the 20-kilometre heavy-weapons exclusion zone around the Bosnian capital.

As fighting continued into the autumn, on 29 October the UN and NATO agreed new, more robust rules for ordering air strikes, as a result of which operations by NATO warplanes against Serbian positions grew in magnitude. In November the US government announced that it would no longer enforce the arms embargo against former Yugoslavia, in light of its belief that the ban was unfair to the Bosnian Muslims. On the aid front, the UN launched an inter-agency appeal for $242 million to provide humanitarian aid to former Yugoslavia over the first six months of 1995.

One major criticism of the UNPROFOR operation was that it was failing to meet the expectations of non-Serb Bosnians that it would ensure the safety of the UNPAs. In a report dated 1 December, Dr Boutros-Ghali recommended that the Security Council should redefine the regime of safe areas in order to protect civilian populations and ensure the delivery of humanitarian assistance. He argued that the safe areas in former Yugsoalvia must be clearly delineated and completely demilitarized.

IRAQ/KUWAIT. During the year significant progress was made on the verification and monitoring of Iraqi weapons of mass destruction by the UN Special Commission (UNSCOM) and the IAEA. UNSCOM completed the destruction of Iraq's chemical weapons stocks and closed down the facility which had produced them. The site was turned over to the Iraqis in June. The last shipment of irradiated fuel from the Tuwaitha nuclear reactor was taken away in February, thus completing the removal of nuclear fuel from Iraq.

The international community grew concerned at the deployment of 80,000 Iraqi troops on the Kuwaiti border at the start of October, this action drawing an immediate response from the Security Council and US-led military deployments in the Gulf (see also IV.1; V.2.vi; V.3.iii). The speedy withdrawal of Iraqi forces defused the crisis, in light of which the Council on 15 October adopted resolution 949 imposing fresh restrictions on the Iraq's deployment of troops within its national borders. In November Iraq stepped up its diplomatic campaign for the lifting of UN sanctions. On 16 November the Security Council welcomed Iraq's formal acceptance of Kuwait's sovereignty, territorial integrity, political independence and international boundaries, but took no steps to modify the sanctions regime.

Evidence of gross human rights violations in Iraq continued to be prominent in 1994. In a report to the General Assembly's third committee on 25 November, the special rapporteur of the UN Human Rights Commission on Iraq heavily criticized Iraq as 'a barbaric regime'. Pointing to recent government decrees announcing amputation of ears and feet and forehead branding as punishments for petty thievery, the rapporteur called for the UN to deploy human rights monitors in Iraq.

ISRAEL/PALESTINE. The Security Council reacted to the February massacre by a Jewish settler of Muslim worshippers in the West Bank town of Hebron (see V.1; V.2.i) by adopting resolution 904 calling for the implementation of measures to guarantee the safety and protection of Palestinian civilians throughout the occupied territories, including the establishment of a temporary international or foreign presence. In accordance with resolution 904, a contingent of observers known as the Temporary International Presence in Hebron was deployed in Hebron from May to August. The UN Secretary-General and other UN bodies welcomed the conclusion in May of the Israeli-PLO agreement on the implementation of Palestinian self-rule in the Gaza Strip and Jericho area as well as the Israel-Jordan peace treaty signed in October (see XIX.1; XIX.4).

OTHER INTERNATIONAL DISPUTES. In January Dr Boutros-Ghali dispatched a mission to Portugal, Indonesia, East Timor and Australia regarding the question of East Timor (see IX.1.vi). A round of UN-brokered talks took place between the Foreign Ministers of Indonesia and Portugal in Geneva on 6 May.

On 14 February Mahmoud Mestiri was appointed to head a UN special mission to Afghanistan after serious hostilities had broken out the previous month (see VIII.1.ii). Mr Mestiri undertook a series of consultations between the parties, but fighting continued in Kabul and other parts of the country throughout the year.

Following reports that the security situation in Burundi was rapidly deteriorating (see VII.1.ii), the Security Council sent a UN fact-finding mission to that country on 11 August. It also passed a number of resolutions on the conflict in Yemen (see V.3.ii) and sent a special envoy; however, the resolutions were ignored as the Sanaa government imposed a military 'solution'.

ENVIRONMENT AND DEVELOPMENT. A report by the UN Secretary-General called *An Agenda for Development*, published on 25 May, failed to generate significant momentum within the UN and other bodies on addressing the problems of development cooperation. The report had gone through many drafts, finally emerging as a document focusing on 'principles' of development rather than on specific recommendations. Dr Boutros-Ghali explained that 'rather than proposing specific solutions, the report seeks to provide a comprehensive framework for thinking about the pursuit of development as a means of building foundations for enduring human progress'. In private, however, a number of developing countries expressed disappointment at the report's lack of concrete proposals. The outcome was that a follow-up report containing specific recommendations for the implementation of *An Agenda for Development* was issued by the Secretary-General on 11 November.

At its second session (16–27 May), the Commission on Sustainable Development discussed progress on the implementation of Agenda 21, adopted by the 1992 UN Conference on Environment and Development in Rio de Janeiro (see AR 1992, pp. 546-52). The Commission gave special consideration to the cross-sectoral components of Agenda 21, the critical elements of sustainability and the financial resources and mechanisms required for the implementation of the programme.

The 1982 UN Convention on the Law of the Sea entered into force on 16 November, a year after its ratification by the theshold number of 60 signatory states.

AIDS. A sharp annual rise of 60 per cent in the number of cases of AIDS worldwide was reported by the World Health Organization (WHO) on 1 July (see also XIV.1). In his opening address to an 'AIDS summit' in Paris on 1 December, the UN Secretary-General said that he was declaring a 'planetary emergency'. He pointed to the shortcomings in the international community's response to AIDS, particularly the lack of linkage between global and national efforts, and said that remedial action was being hampered by commercial competition to find cures.

HUMAN RIGHTS. On 14 February the General Assembly approved the appointment of José Ayala Lasso (Ecuador) as the first-ever UN High Commissioner for Human Rights. At its 50th session held in Geneva from 31 January to 11 March, the Commission appointed a special rapporteur on 'the elimination of violence against women'.

POPULATION AND DEVELOPMENT CONFERENCE. The International Conference on Population and Development was held in Cairo on 5–13 September under the auspices of the UN Fund for Population Activities. It was the first UN conference convened explicitly to address population concerns as they related to sustained economic growth, sustainable development, poverty alleviation, gender equality and reproductive health. The proceedings aroused fierce controversy, resulting in a boycott by some Arab states and a concerted campaign by the Vatican and certain Catholic and Muslim countries to remove parts of the proposed programme of action on the grounds that it implicitly legitimized abortion and promoted extramarital sex.

TRUSTEESHIP COUNCIL. The UN Trusteeship Council was formally suspended on 25 May under General Assembly resolution 2200 (LXI). This action was taken because Belau, the last UN trust territory, had at last resolved the obstacles to its compact of free association with the United States and to UN membership as a sovereign state (see X.2.ii).

WOMEN. The UN Commission on the Status of Women, acting as a preparatory body for the Fourth World Conference on Women, to be held in Beijing in September 1995, continued work on the draft final document for the conference. Talks on the merging of the

International Research and Training Institute for the Advancement of Women (INSTRAW) and the UN Development Fund for Women (UNIFEM) were postponed until the 50th session of the General Assembly (1995–96).

2. THE COMMONWEALTH

SOUTH Africa returned to membership of the Commonwealth on 1 June, within a month of the government of national unity taking office under President Nelson Mandela (see VII.3). It was 33 years and one day after South Africa had withdrawn because of the unacceptability of its apartheid policies. Acquisition of a 51st member was a boost for the Commonwealth and was seen as recognition of the decades of support it had given to the anti-apartheid struggle. It also finally removed a source of recurring tension between Britain and the rest of the Commonwealth.

The Commonwealth won regard in South Africa in that country's final transition to full democracy because of its attempts at conflict resolution, help in legal and constitutional advice, technical assistance, and training of black professionals and officers for the diplomatic service. Also influential was the quality of the work of the 119-strong Commonwealth Observer Group to South Africa (COGSA), sent for the elections and headed by Michael Manley, former Prime Minister of Jamaica. The Group's report concluded that inadequacies and irregularities in the election process were not widespread, and that 'in the final analysis the elections represented a free and clear expression of the will of the South Africa people'. On a Commonwealth initiative, 50 agencies attended an international donors' conference on 'human resource development' co-sponsored by the United Nations in Cape Town (26–28 October) to work out a funding and coordination mechanism for South Africa's reconstruction and development programme.

The year saw a mixture of success and setback in the drive to improve the quality of democracy in Commonwealth member countries, as launched by the 1971 Harare Declaration. While South Africa was in the throes of rebirth, early in 1994 Commonwealth diplomats visited Lesotho several times to mediate in the complex situation arising from disputes between the recently-elected government of Dr Ntsu Mokhehle, the army and the monarchy (see VII.2,vi). With firm support from Mr Mandela and Presidents Mugabe of Zimbabwe and Masire of Botswana, the Commonwealth Secretary-General, Chief Emeka Anyaoku, helped to devise a package that restored stability.

In May successful elections brought multi-party rule to Malawi and the end of the 30-year autocracy of Dr Hastings Kamuzu Banda (see

VII.2.ii). A smooth election, which brought to power Bakili Muluzi, was observed by an 11-member Commonwealth Observer Group, led by the former Deputy Prime Minister of Malaysia, Dato Musa Hitam. The Group reported that the Malawi voters had 'been able to exercise their will in an open and transparent manner.'

Eight Commonwealth observers, led by Mrs Justice A.S. Msosa of Malawi, were in Namibia for the presidential and National Assembly elections in December (see VII.2.iv). They concluded that, five years after independence, the elections had shown that 'the culture of democracy had gathered strength and maturity'. The picture was not so rosy for the Commonwealth in West Africa, where a coup in The Gambia ousted its longest-serving leader, Sir Dawda Jawara (see VI.2.iv), while in Nigeria the military government increased repression and made no progress towards civilian rule (see VI.2.ii). In Sierra Leone growing civil war threatened to disrupt the timetable for civilian rule (see (VI.2.iii). As a Nigerian, Chief Anyaoku was particularly exercised by the fact that the Commonwealth's three present military regimes were all in West Africa. On two visits to Nigeria, he tried to persuade General Sani Abacha to restore democracy and to release political prisoners. There was some response in Lagos, but he had no success with the new rulers of The Gambia, who ignored his approaches.

There were worries elsewhere in the Commonwealth. Bitter disputes in Bangladesh between Prime Minister Begum Khaleda Zia and opposition leader Sheikh Hasina, causing much civil unrest (see VIII.2.iii), led to an invitation to the Secretary-General to mediate. He proposed a basis for reconciliation and sent a former governor-general of Australia, Sir Ninian Stephen, to Dhaka as his personal envoy. After a month, however, Sir Ninian withdrew, concluding that 'my continued presence will serve no useful purpose.'

The 15th Commonwealth Games, held in Victoria (Canada) in August (see Pt. XVII), were notable for the return of South Africa, so long the subject of Commonwealth boycotts and sporting acrimony, and for the full integration of disabled athletes for the first time in international games. Alongside the Games, Victoria staged a spectacular Commonwealth Arts Festival, further establishing the event in the Commonwealth calendar.

Britain signalled a slightly warmer political attitude to the Commonwealth when it reversed its decision to stop funding the London-based Commonwealth Institute from 1996. It announced financing on a reduced scale until at least 1999—a decision which meant that the Institute still had to raise considerable private-sector donations.

Commonwealth Finance Ministers, meeting in Malta on 26–28 September, backed a British proposal to relieve Third World debt payments by means of selling up to 10 per cent of IMF gold reserves. Commonwealth Education Ministers met in Islamabad on 27 November–1 December. To promote greater intra-Commonwealth student mobility, seven countries pledged fellowships for the first time under the Commonwealth scholarship and fellowship programme. The target set was that 2,000 students annually should benefit from the programme by the year 2000. Britain, Canada and British Columbia made new funding pledges (and 26 other countries offered help) for the Commonwealth of Learning, the distance education organization based in Vancouver.

The non-governmental Commonwealth continued to grow. A Commonwealth Local Government Forum and a Commonwealth Network of Business Organizations were set up in March. The Forum aimed to share the practice of good governance by promoting local democracy and decentralized, participatory government. The Network planned to develop better business ties between 1,000 organizations. The Commonwealth Health Foundation, launched in October, aimed to fund health care projects, exchange health workers and set up a health system and resources information centre.

A new Commonwealth deputy secretary-general (political) was appointed to take over in 1995, namely Krishnan Srinivasan, the retiring Indian foreign secretary (head of the external affairs civil service), who was to replace Sir Anthony Siaguru of Papua New Guinea. Also new at the secretariat was journalist Michael Fathers of New Zealand, who took over from Patsy Robertson of Jamaica as director of the information and public affairs division.

3. EUROPEAN UNION

EUROPEAN Union (EU) affairs were dominated by constitutional issues for most of the year, as the Delors era drew to a close. Negotiations were concluded for the accession of four candidate countries (three actually joined); elections were held for the European Parliament; and a new European Commission president was nominated, together with his team. Firm commitments were given to the countries of Central and Eastern Europe that they were on the path to EU membership.

No sooner had the Maastricht Treaty on European Union taken effect, in November 1993 (see AR 1993, pp. 402–3), than the battle lines began to be drawn over the future shape of the Union. For the British, enlargement was seen as a welcome way of sapping the drive to European integration. For many other member states it dictated a further deepening of the Community and more effective decision-making procedures.

ENLARGEMENT. Despite early doubts, the tight timetable for completing the accession negotiations with Austria, Finland, Norway and Sweden was met. The outgoing European Parliament was able to vote on enlargement at its final session in Strasbourg on 4 May. The Parliament had to muster 259 votes in favour out of a possible 517; in the event, more than 370 members voted to accept the terms of accession.

The treaty setting up a half-way house to full membership, the European Economic Area (EEA), took effect on 1 January, extending the Community's single-market legislation to Austria, Finland, Iceland, Norway and Sweden (the other two EFTA members, Switzerland and Liechtenstein, remaining outside). But many contentious issues remained for the full accession talks. There were difficulties over regional policy, farming and budget contributions, as well as particular national issues such as Norwegian whaling, alcohol monopolies and the right of Community citizens to own second homes in the candidate countries. Spain and Portugal held out for improved fishing rights in Norwegian waters.

Voting in the enlarged Community was the subject of a damaging dispute which set the UK government against the rest. The British thought initially that the Italians and Spanish were with them, but their support ebbed away as other issues were resolved. In question was the number of weighted votes which could block legislation in the Council of Ministers. The British argued that this should remain unchanged at 23, even though the arithmetic of enlargement meant that the total votes would be increased when the new member countries joined. The crisis held up the conclusion of the accession talks and was only resolved at an emergency meeting in Greece on 26–27 March. It was agreed that, if members of the Council representing a total of 23–26 votes indicated their intention to oppose the adoption of a decision by qualified majority, the Council would 'do all in its power to reach . . . a satisfactory solution that could be adopted by at least 68 votes'. It was agreed that the formula would be re-examined at the 1996 Inter-Governmental Conference (IGC).

After the European Parliament had voted in favour of enlargement, the four candidate countries embarked on their referendum campaigns. The Austrians were the first to go to the polls (on 12 June) and returned a two-thirds majority in favour of membership (see II.2.vi). On 16 October the Finns voted by 57–43 per cent to join the Union (see II.2.v) and on 13 November Sweden opted to join with 52 per cent of the voters in favour (see II.2.iv). Norway's government delayed its referendum until 28 November in the hope that positive results in the other countries might produce a 'yes', but again in vain: the poll result was a 52 per cent majority against membership, narrower than in 1972 but still decisive (see II.2.iii). Some quick readjustment was therefore necessary to prepare for a Union of 15 countries rather than 16. In the enlarged European Parliament a simple majority would require 314 votes out of 626, while a qualified majority in the Council would need 62 votes out of 87.

EUROPEAN PARLIAMENT. Turnout for the June European elections was 56.5 per cent overall, two points down on the 1989 poll. A low figure had been expected in the UK, where just over 36 per cent of the electorate voted (see I.2). It was a bigger surprise that in the Netherlands the figure was below 36 per cent, indicating a deep shift in Dutch public opinion against the EU (see II.1.v). Also below the 36 per cent mark was Portugal. A swing to the right in Germany (see II.1.i), Italy (see II.1.iii) and the Netherlands was offset by the Labour Party's decisive victory in the UK, 62 Labour members being returned out of a total British contingent of 87. With the notable exception of Germany, voters in most member countries rejected their governing parties. In the new Parliament, the Socialists formed the largest group, with 198 seats out of 567, followed by the Christian Democrats with 157, the Liberals with 43 and the Communists with 28. More than 90 members, principally from France and Italy, had no established European groups to join. The right-wing Forza Italia plus allies had 29 members by the end of the year, enough to form its own political group, whereas the French National Front and other ultra-right contingents remained unattached.

The Parliament quickly had its first taste of the new role conferred on it by the Maastricht Treaty. The co-decision method, which gave MEPs stronger veto powers and joint decision-making through a conciliation procedure, was applied in several policy areas in the latter half of 1994. The Parliament also fought to extend its say in technical matters where the European Commission exercised delegated powers. However, when Chancellor Kohl travelled to Strasbourg in December to report on the Essen summit, only about 20 per cent of the members were in the chamber. Responding to criticism of the German presidency of the EU, the Chancellor commented: 'If this is the image you want to present, you should not be surprised by election results.'

COMMISSION PRESIDENCY. The president of the European Commission, Jacques Delors of France, had dominated Community business since being appointed in 1985 and was generally reckoned to have brought a new sense of purpose and strategic vision to European affairs. Most member states sought a change in style in choosing his successor, in keeping with a less powerful Commission and a more managerial function, but the politicking which surrounded the choice led to bitter conflicts. The Dutch Prime Minister, Ruud Lubbers, was the early favourite, but he had upset the German government with his grudging view of German unification. It was then put about that the French and Germans favoured the appointment of Jean-Luc Dehaene, the Belgian Prime Minister. However, the way in which the selection process was apparently being sewn up by a Franco-German alliance provoked intense resentment in the UK House of Commons. Already beset by internal difficulties in the Conservative Party, Prime Minister Major decided to block the choice.

The issue dominated the Corfu summit on 24–25 June. The British refused to budge, despite support for Mr Dehaene from 11 of the 12 member countries. The incoming German presidency was therefore forced to convene a special European Council in Brussels on 15 July, when Jacques Santer, who had been Luxembourg's Prime Minister since 1984, was chosen to succeed M. Delors. Almost immediately M. Santer had to present himself to the European Parliament, which had decided to debate and vote on his appointment. He said in his speech that in his view federalism was the opposite of centralism, adding: 'The more Europe is decentralized, the stronger it is.' Resentment of British tactics, in particular the implication (not founded on any clear evidence) that M. Santer would be more receptive to a British view of Europe than Mr Dehaene, led to a close vote. Members voted by 260 to 238 to approve the nomination of the Luxembourg Prime Minister.

The formal appointment of M. Santer and his team of 20 commissioners from 15 member countries was conditional on European Parliament approval of the whole college. The nominees included five women, among them the former French Prime Minister, Edith Cresson. Eight members were reappointed from the previous Commission, including Sir Leon Brittan (UK) and Hans van den Broek (Netherlands), both of whom were keen to have the high-profile portfolio of Eastern and Central Europe. The prize went to the Dutchman, thanks to strong German support, but only after a fierce contest. Sir Leon had earlier bid for the Commission presidency, so that losing the portfolio he wanted was a bitter disappointment, even though he retained responsibility for the remainder of the EU's external relations.

MULTI-SPEED EUROPE. The impending enlargement of the EU in January 1995, and the prospect that the countries of Central and Eastern Europe might join by the turn of the century, fuelled a debate about the nature of European integration, foreshadowing the 1996 IGC on the Maastricht Treaty. There were three camps: the British government, which wanted to end talk of European integration and to concentrate on making the internal market work better and on foreign policy cooperation; the French and German view that the political base of the Union should be strengthened and extended to economic and monetary union, although without strengthening the power of Brussels; and the traditional proponents of European integration, pushing for stronger central institutions.

Before the German presidency began on 1 July, Chancellor Kohl said that he was determined 'to free ourselves from the notion that everything that has a European dimension automatically falls under the jurisdiction of Brussels'; this, he said, would be a German priority. The debate hotted up in the autumn, when the idea of a 'variable geometry' Europe gathered pace. Herr Kohl endorsed a paper produced by his own Christian Democratic Union, which advocated a multi-speed Europe in which the Benelux countries, France and Germany would be in a central group, leaving the inadequate and the reluctant, including Italy, the UK, the EFTA entrants and the East Europeans, to move on at their own pace.

The French approach was somewhat different, reflecting a wish to develop the external relations and security components of the Union, where Britain would have a key role to play. Prime Minister Balladur talked in an interview with *Le Figaro* of a 'diversification' of the EU structure to cope with enlargement, envisaging three overlapping circles: the European Union with a single market and a common foreign and security policy; a smaller group building an organization on the monetary and military level; and a wider circle encompassing the new member countries to the east.

One theme common to most continental views of the European Union's future was that no one country should be able to block progress which the others might wish to make.

EASTERN EUROPE AND RUSSIA. The process of drawing the Central and East European countries (CEECs) more closely into the EU's economic and political orbit continued. Early in the year so-called Europe Agreements were formally signed with Poland and Hungary, setting out a framework for political dialogue, economic relations and assistance programmes. These accords had already been operating in essentials for a couple of years, and interim agreements were also in place with the Czech Republic, Slovakia, Romania and Bulgaria. A partnership and cooperation agreement was also signed with Ukraine. On 1 April Hungary submitted a formal request for membership of the European Union (see III.1.iii); Poland followed suit one week later (see III.1.i).

The European Commission established a 1994 funding programme of 150 million ecu to promote cross-border cooperation with countries sharing a common border with the EU and funds were set aside for a 'Democracy Programme' for 11 CEECs. A similar programme was launched for the former Soviet republics. Sir Leon Brittan, then still responsible for relations with the CEECs, said that the Community had contributed 4,300 million ecu to these countries in the first five years of the PHARE assistance programme, a further 7,000 million ecu being proposed for 1995–99. [At end-1994 1 ecu = £0.7871 or US$1.2300.]

President Yeltsin was invited to the June summit in Corfu, where a partnership and cooperation agreement was signed between the EU and Russia. This offered the prospect of free trade in the next century if Russian reforms were sufficiently advanced. Direct investment by EU companies in Russia would be freely allowed, as well as the repatriation of investments and profits, and European firms there would be treated at least as well as Russian or other foreign firms. Moscow also agreed to remove restrictions on European banks. The agreement did not envisage the immediate removal of tariffs, a process which would be tied in with Russian membership of GATT. A safeguard clause was included to deal with dumping.

The Corfu summit also looked forward to 'enlargement of the Union to the east and to the south'—a theme which acquired momentum as the year progressed and was a high priority for the German presidency. At the Essen summit in December it was confirmed that those Central European countries which had signed Europe Agreements would be eligible to join the EU by the end of the century, although no accession negotiations could begin until the 1996 IGC had taken place and the proper functioning of EU institutions could be assured. The Commission had prepared a pre-accession strategy discussing what the CEECs would need to do to prepare their economies, banking and legal systems for membership. This general approach was endorsed at the December Essen summit, which asked the Commission to prepare a White Paper by June 1995. An annual report was to be prepared on implementation of the strategy in the period leading to EU membership.

THE MEDITERRANEAN. The heavy emphasis on Central Europe provoked member countries like Spain and France to demand similar treatment for the Mediterranean countries, a policy made more critical by the Algerian crisis and the damage which it could inflict on France in terms of political instability, terrorism and immigration (see II.1.ii; V.4.iv). It was therefore agreed at Essen that the EU should develop its relations with Mediterranean countries, holding a special conference under Spanish presidency in the second half of 1995 and possibly making available a budget line of 5,500 million ecu. It was confirmed that accession would be open to Malta and Cyprus in the same way as for the EU's eastern neighbours.

URUGUAY ROUND. The concluding conference of the GATT Uruguay Round was held in April in Marrakesh (Morocco), where 120 countries signed the deal which had been negotiated in the previous December (see AR 1993, pp. 406-8, 534, 574-86). Efforts then had to be made to ratify the agreement by the end of the year. At one stage the European deadline seemed at risk, owing to a dispute between the Commission and the Council of Ministers as to which was competent to deal with certain aspects of the agreement, especially in the longer-term context of the successor World Trade Organization. Formally asked to give its ruling, the European Court of Justice finished its deliberations in

November, giving time for the procedure to be completed by the end of the year. The Court laid down strict limits as to which aspects of the GATT agreement were the exclusive competence of the Commission. It said that international trade in goods, including coal and steel products, was the full responsibility of the Community/Union, as was the cross-border supply of services, whereas the movement of persons to set up business in another country, intellectual property rights and trade services had to be shared between the Community and member states (see also XV.1.ii).

TRADE. The Community's trade relations with the United States and Japan entered a period of relative calm with the conclusion of the Uruguay Round. A bilateral agreement on public procurement was reached with the USA in the margins of the Marrakesh meeting, governing central government purchases, non-federal purchasing by American cities and electricity generation. The trade deficit with Japan narrowed during the year, but there was concern that deals between the USA and Japan could divert cheap imports to European markets.

FOREIGN POLICY AND DEFENCE. Despite the newly-introduced Maastricht Treaty, with its special emphasis on foreign policy, the United Nations took over full responsibility for humanitarian and peace-keeping activities in ex-Yugoslavia during the year (see III.1.vi). The profile of the Western European Union (WEU), which was intended by Maastricht to become the 'defence identity' of the Union, diminished during the year. At the NATO summit on 10–11 January an effort was made to define the respective roles of the European Union and the Alliance, but the EU as such was not represented at the meeting; nor was President Clinton's Partnership for Peace initiative discussed within the EU (see XII.1; XIX.1). 'Separable but not separate' was the phrase used to describe the relationship between the WEU and NATO. The communique from the summit confirmed the 'enduring validity and indispensability of our Alliance [which] reflects a European security and defence identity gradually emerging as the expression of a mature Europe'. NATO leaders—including Presidents Mitterrand and Clinton—said that they had agreed to adapt the Alliance's political and military structures to reflect the full spectrum of its roles and the development of the emerging European identity. The French President said that there had been a significant change of tone between the EU and the USA, adding that Europe's defence identity no longer caused problems in principle.

The communique was full of direct quotes from the Maastricht Treaty. The summit welcomed its entry into force and the launching of the European Union, which would 'strengthen the European pillar of the Alliance while reinforcing the trans-Atlantic link and will enable European allies to take greater responsibility for their common security and defence'. It emergd from the summit that the collective assets of the Alliance could be made available for WEU operations undertaken by the European allies in pursuit of their common foreign and security policy, an approach which fitted in with the USA's policy of reducing its military commitments in Europe. President Clinton said in a speech to young Europeans at Brussels town hall that Europe remained central to the interests of the United States, but added that 'our bonds with Europe will be different than they were in the past'.

There were signs of movement on the diplomatic front. The French Minister for Europe, Alain Lamassoure, spoke of his concern about the lack of structures to implement the EU's common foreign and security policy. He did not wish to see such responsibilities handed over to the European Commission or to the Council of Ministers—implying that some new secretariat could be set up, perhaps further removed from the existing institutions than the Maastricht Treaty envisaged. The British were also showing signs of new thinking: Defence Secretary Malcolm Rifkind invited his German and French counterparts to talks in London to discuss the implications of the NATO summit.

On the diplomatic front, the Council of Ministers continued to make policy through press statements, commenting on different stages of the war in Bosnia-Hercegovina, welcoming developments in South Africa and deploring the horrors of Rwanda. A particular difficulty was the Greek blockade of Macedonia because of the Balkan republic's alleged threat to the Greek province of the same name. The Commission took Greece to the European Court on grounds that the embargo was impeding operation of the single market, but was refused an interim order (see II.3.v; XV.1.ii).

INTERNAL MARKET. The legislative scene became quieter after the surge in European law of the previous ten years. The outgoing Commission was unable to agree on controversial proposals, such as those for the long-term future of the VAT system in trade between member states, and there were signs that the Council presidency was taking increasing responsibility for new initiatives and for brokering deals among ministers—tasks which had in the past been the prerogative of the Commission.

There was substantial movement on telecommunications, where the pace of technical progress in a rapidly-changing global market threatened to leave the Community behind. There was agreement to liberalize voice telephony by 1998 in most member countries, and steps were taken to open up cable and satellite communications systems to competition. The Bangemann Group, comprising leaders in the telecoms industry, reported to the Corfu summit on the need for Europe to become part of the 'information society', where the new technologies would transform the lives of its citizens (see also XIV.2).

ECONOMIC AND MONETARY UNION. Early in December the EU Finance Ministers agreed that the 15 per cent fluctuation bands introduced into the exchange rate mechanism after the currency crisis of the previous year (see AR 1993, pp. 403–4) should be continued, endorsing an opinion drawn up by the newly-established European Monetary Institute (EMI). The EMI, which was foreseen as the precursor of a European central bank in the Maastricht Treaty, was established in Frankfurt (Germany) at the beginning of the year. It noted in its opinion that the wider bands had prevented large exchange-rate depreciations and excessive exchange-rate intervention, which would have had inflationary consequences. It called for the existing arrangements to be maintained.

The possibility of moving to economic and monetary union by 1999, as foreseen in the Maastricht timetable, was widely discounted in commercial and banking circles—including German central bankers—but the Finance Ministers continued to work in the hope that the improving economic situation would make it a realistic prospect. The fact remained that only Ireland and Luxembourg fulfilled the criteria on budget deficits and public debt laid down by Maastricht. The banks themselves warned that they would need at least five years to plan for a single currency.

European economies were showing signs of rapid recovery from recession by the end of the year, achieving overall growth of about 2 per cent, which was expected to rise to 3 per cent in 1995. This did not translate into dramatic improvements in labour markets, though. The Commission reported an unemployment rate of more than 11 per cent for the Union as a whole. It said that the burden of social charges which had to be paid by employers was increasingly felt, amounting to an average of 45 per cent on top of wages. President Delors told the European Parliament that there should be no question of cutting down on direct wages, but that additional charges should be reduced. He persisted with the idea that environmental taxation could be used to replace employment taxes and charges.

SOCIAL AFFAIRS. Although there was growing concern about the cost of new labour legislation, the Council continued to work on the programme of measures which had been set out in the mid-eighties. Implacable British opposition to the establishment of works councils on a mandatory basis meant that this legislation was re-submitted under the Maastricht protocol and was adopted by 11 member countries. Britain also objected to proposals which would give part-time workers similar rights to those employed full time. This legislation was also expected to be agreed under the protocol during 1995. Meanwhile, European Court judgments formed an important element in Community social affairs, especially in the field of equality of treatment in pension provision between men and women (see XV.1.ii).

4. OECD—NON–ALIGNED AND DEVELOPING COUNTRIES

i.   ORGANIZATION FOR ECONOMIC COOPERATION AND DEVELOPMENT (OECD)

THE December 1994 edition of the OECD's main report, the semi-annual *Economic Outlook*, was notable for an upward revision in the forecast for overall economic growth in 1995, to 3 per cent in real terms (with inflation at 2.3 per cent). Real growth was expected to continue at almost this level (2.9 per cent) through 1996, as Japan and European member countries moved ahead but the USA, hitherto heading the growth surge, slipped back to 2.0 per cent growth (and 3.2 per cent inflation). The overall OECD figures given for 1994 were 2.8 per cent real growth and 2.1 per cent inflation. December's optimistic growth forecast was accompanied, however, by a call for member countries to use this 'golden opportunity' to address longer-term structural problems, particularly with regard to labour market reform.

The annual *Employment Outlook*, published on 19 July, had warned that record levels of unemployment in 1994 (35 million in the OECD as a whole, or 8.5 per cent of the workforce) would fall only slightly, to 34.5 million, in the second half of 1995. The picture for European member countries would actually deteriorate, from 11.7 to 11.8 per cent unemployment.

An OECD paper, prepared for the G-7 special summit on employment issues held in Detroit (USA) in March, had come under attack from US economists in particular for failing to make appropriate macroeconomic policy recommendations (such as the relaxation of the tight monetary stance maintained by the German Bundesbank) to reduce unemployment. The OECD secretary-general, Jean-Claude Paye, had then presented the more detailed analysis of the *OECD Jobs Study*, commissioned in 1992, to the organization's annual meeting in Paris on 7–8 June. Its recommendations notably included increasing working-time flexibility and reducing minimum wage legislation and employment security measures, with the objective of removing rigidities in employment practices. The report acknowledged the need for a 'safety net', but nevertheless urged member countries to consider cuts in unemployment benefit as part of an overhaul of policies to tackle the global jobs crisis.

The OECD was seriously divided through much of the year over its choice of secretary-general. The French incumbent, M. Paye, was seeking a third term from 1 October with support concentrated among European member countries, while the USA backed the rival candidacy of Donald Johnston of Canada, believing that he would 're-energize' the organization and provide 'political-level leadership'. The former UK Chancellor of the Exchequer, Lord (formerly Nigel) Lawson, and Lorenz Schomerus of Germany, were peripheral candidates. Deadlock persisted long enough to make necessary the appointment of an interim secretary-general (Staffan Sohlman of Sweden) for October and November. Finally, on 29 November, it was agreed that M. Paye should hold the post until 31 May 1996 and that Mr Johnston should then take office for a full five-year term.

One criticism of M. Paye concerned budgetary controls, highlighted when the UK announced in mid-December its intention to cease contributions from 1996 to the semi-autonomous OECD Development Centre. The OECD's workload stretched increasingly into areas of social policy, as in its employment study (see above) or the hosting of a conference on 6–7 July on ways of paying for the care of the rising proportion of elderly people in the populations of member countries. Also completed in 1994 were (i) a voluntary code of conduct to combat the use of bribery in international business transactions (on 29 April) and (ii) an agreement on eliminating subsidies to shipbuilding (on 17 July). The latter was finally signed in Paris on 21 December (to take effect from January 1996) after concessions had been made to overcome French resistance.

The OECD's Development Assistance Committee (DAC) published its annual (1993) report on official development assistance (ODA) on 24 March, followed on 23 June by its report on financial flows during 1993 to developing countries and countries in transition. According to the latter, member countries' ODA was down sharply in 1993, by 7.8 per cent in real terms to an aggregate of $54,800 million (only 0.29 per cent of GDP). Total financial flows to developing countries, however, were up from $153,000 million to $160,000 million, a record high. The high level of private flows, in bonds, equities and direct investment (mainly from the United States), more than outweighed a decline in bank lending.

Mexico joined the OECD on 18 May as its 25th member. Plans were approved in June to open negotiations for South Korea to join by end-1996, while the next enlargement was generally expected to involve the inclusion of the four so-called 'partners in transition' countries—Poland, Hungary, the Czech Republic and Slovakia—all of which applied for OECD membership in early 1994. A Declaration on Cooperation was signed with Russia on 8 June, aimed at strengthening the transition process and the development of economic institutions. The first high-level informal meeting in the OECD's dialogue with 'dynamic non-member economies' took place in Tokyo on 19 October.

ii.   NON-ALIGNED MOVEMENT AND DEVELOPING COUNTRIES

THE '11th' ministerial conference—actually the eighth in the triennial series—of Foreign Ministers of the Non-Aligned Movement (NAM) was held in Cairo from 31 May to 3 June. Its first action was to admit the new South African government to membership, bringing the total to 112 countries. Eritrea, Somalia and seven small island countries did not send representatives to the Egyptian capital (and the Yugoslavs were excluded), so 102 members were present in Cairo. Azerbaijan was admitted to observer status and Italy to guest status. The application from Macedonia, outstanding since 1992, and Russia's request in February 1994 for guest status, both controversial, were deferred for further consideration.

The greatest triumph in the history of the NAM was realised in May when South Africa completed the transition to majority rule (see VII.3). Since its formation in 1961, the elimination of apartheid had been one of the Movement's prime goals. During the South African elections, a team of Indonesian officials formed an NAM observer mission, working with the UN and Commonwealth missions (see XI.2). At Cairo the NAM Foreign Ministers were able welcome the end of sanctions on South Africa, wind up its Committee on South Africa and pay tribute to President Mandela. There was also a sense of optimism over the Israeli-Palestinian agreement on self-rule in Gaza and the Jericho area (see V.1; V.2.i; XIX.2). Hope was qualified by worries about achieving a complete Israeli withdrawal, the problem of settlements and horror at the February massacre in Hebron. The Iranians objected to the consensus on this question, because they regarded dealings with Israel and the offer of security guarantees to Israel as being 'a turning-point in the Movement's stand'.

So-called regional conflicts involving NAM members, notably those in Bosnia–Hercegovina, Rwanda, Somalia, Sierra Leone and Afghanistan, were seen as a threat to the Movement as a whole. All the responses showed an unresolved tension between the desire to take action to prevent conflict and the unwillingness to undermine sovereignty. Detailed attention was given to the future of UN peace-keeping. The old ideals of being 'impartial','non-intrusive' and 'non-interventionist' were reaffirmed, but it was acknowledged that coercive measures could be valid as a last resort. The NAM bureau in New York was instructed to continue work on designing a Non-Aligned conflict-resolution mechanism. However, as it was to be restricted to inter-state conflicts, the mechanism would be of little relevance to most contemporary conflicts, which involved intra-state conflict. While it was not explicit, concern about these conflicts explained the increased emphasis on human rights and a new affirmation that 'tolerance is the sound foundation of any civil society and of peace'. Nevertheless, the main Cairo declaration objected to 'the tendency to intervene in the internal affairs of other states under the pretext of protecting human rights or preventing conflict'. The Malaysians also persuaded the conference to object to the UNDP's 1994 *Human Development Report* because it warned that socio-economic disparities could generate conflict in several countries.

There was intense dissatisfaction at the UN's failure to take stronger action in support of the government of Bosnia–Hercegovina (see III.1.vi; XI.1)). A special resolution at Cairo called for the current international diplomacy to be broadened to include all the countries contributing troops to the UNPROFOR force in former Yugoslavia as well as representatives of the Non-Aligned and the Islamic Conference Organization.

The momentum imparted to economic issues by the Indonesian NAM chairmanship in 1993 (see AR 1993, pp. 413–4) was not followed through in 1994. There were no meetings of either the standing ministerial committee or the committee on 'methodology', which was supposed to to review organizational questions. Nor had the 'back-up system', established in 1992 to support the NAM chairman (see AR 1992, pp. 410-11), been put into effect. There were expert group meetings on food, on debt and on project assessment, along with coordinator country activity on standardization and on the Centre for Science and Technology. In addition, ministerial meetings took place during the year on food, labour questions and health. Nevertheless, the terms of reference of the NAM–Group of 77 coordinating committee, drafted by the NAM bureau and approved in Cairo, had lost their significance, since there remained so little practical joint activity to coordinate. The failure of its own programme seemed to be recognized by the NAM in the increased emphasis at Cairo on obtaining UN support for South-South cooperation.

One initiative that was taken by the Indonesians was to invite an *ad hoc* group of 21 other countries to a consultative meeting in Jakarta in February. The main focus was on hopes for a resumption of North-South dialogue following the adoption by consensus of two resolutions by the UN General Assembly in December 1993. One had asserted the need for dialogue and the other had instructed the UN Secretary-General to finalize a report on world development. When this report (*An Agenda for Development*) came out in May (see also XI.1), it presented a broad analysis of five dimensions of development, starting with peace as the foundation, and arguing that the economy could not be separated from the environment, the search for social justice and the maintenance of democracy (as the only reliable means of achieving good governance). It called for a stronger role for the UN in promoting global norms and in coordinating policy with a new collective vision.

The Cairo NAM conference noted the report, but passed the task of reviewing it to the 30th anniversary meeting of the G-77 in New York on 24 June. The developing countries wanted a stronger stand on the need for structural adjustment programmes to tackle the eradication of poverty. They also wanted to see 'action-oriented recommendations and concrete proposals'. The UN Secretary-General produced a revised version of his report in November, containing specific proposals to strengthen UN policy-making and suggesting that UN finances should be based on compulsory assessments rather than voluntary contributions. By the end of the year the debate had not been concluded.

There were developments in 1994 on the previous year's proposal of the NAM caucus at the UN that the International Court of Justice should give an advisory opinion on whether the threat or use of nuclear weapons could ever be legal. Pressure from the NATO countries had been so intense that the Indonesians had withdrawn the draft resolution in late 1993. On the initiative of Zimbabwe, however, the Cairo conference decided to re-table the proposal and it was passed by the General Assembly on 15 December (see XI.1; XI.3; XV.1.i).

It was agreed that the 11th NAM summit would take place in 1995 in Colombia.

5. OTHER EUROPEAN ORGANIZATIONS

i. CONFERENCE ON SECURITY AND COOPERATION IN EUROPE (CSCE)

IT was a year of modest diplomatic achievements and steady organizational consolidation for the CSCE, witnessing a further redefinition of its place in Europe's institutional architecture.

In the 1970s and 1980s, the CSCE had provided a diplomatic forum for managing the East-West conflict. With the collapse of communism, the CSCE had assumed a central role in defining pan-European values and norms of behaviour in areas such as human rights, democracy, the peaceful resolution of disputes and market economics. Since the Helsinki summit in 1992 (see AR 1992, pp. 412-3), a new set of responsibilities had emerged: preventive diplomacy and crisis management. By 1994 the CSCE had become, in its own words, 'the primary instrument for early warning, conflict prevention and crisis management in the region'.

Appointed to the innovatory post of CSCE High Commissioner for National Minorities (HCNM) in 1992, Max van der Stoel (Netherlands) pursued an active diplomatic schedule in 1994, seeking to identify ethnic tensions and promote their early resolution. He visited Albania (possessing a disgruntled Greek minority—see II.3.v; III.1.vii); Ukraine, Estonia and Latvia (each with substantial Russian minorities); Romania (with a substantial Hungarian minority in Transylvania and a persecuted Roma/Gypsy community); Hungary and Slovakia (respectively containing Slovak and Hungarian minorities); Macedonia (with a large Albanian minority); and Central Asia, where he made a number of proposals on minority rights and related citizenship issues. The HCNM operated confidentially, avoiding media attention—an approach which had already proven successful in helping to promote dialogue and compromise between antagonistic communities.

As exercises in preventive diplomacy in areas of actual or potential conflict, the CSCE sent three further missions in 1994. A mission to Tajikistan began work on 19 February, aimed at promoting human rights and fostering national reconciliation after the civil war (see VIII.1.iii). One to Sarajevo began operations on 1 November with the aim of supporting the work of the three CSCE ombudsmen already in Bosnia–Hercegovina. And a mission to Ukraine started work on 24 November, seeking to promote understanding between the Russian community in the Crimea and the Ukrainian authorities (see III.2.i).

The existing CSCE mission to Georgia had its mandate significantly broadened in March: as well as being responsible for promoting inter-communal dialogue in South Ossetia, it now had the tasks of monitoring the joint peace-keeping force in the region and of promoting human rights throughout Georgia. The CSCE missions in Skopje (Macedonia), Estonia, Latvia and Moldova continued to implement their mandates, but the mission to Kosovo, Sandžak and Vojvodina—which had been expelled by the Serbian authorities in July 1993—was not permitted to resume its work. On the whole, however, the CSCE missions were regarded as having developed into a useful instrument for managing inter-communal conflict and helping to promote the CSCE's commitment to human rights, democracy and the rule of law.

These values were also the concern of the Warsaw-based Office of Democratic Institutions and Human Rights (ODIHR). In 1994 the ODIHR monitored elections in Moldova, Kazakhstan, Ukraine, Hungary, Latvia, Macedonia, Belorussia, Kyrgyzstan and Slovakia. It also provided expert advice on the drafting of new constitutions in Tajikistan, Georgia and Armenia. The ODIHR also organized two seminars in Warsaw, the first in May on local democracy and the second in September on the Roma and Sinti peoples in the CSCE region.

Throughout the year, the CSCE made concerted efforts to develop its cooperation with other relevant international organizations. Following the establishment of formal relations with the Commonwealth of Independent States (CIS) in February, the CSCE later set up links with NATO's North Atlantic Cooperation Council (NACC) with a view to possible cooperation in peace-keeping operations. On 13 September the new the secretary-general of the Council of Europe, Daniel Tarschys, visited the CSCE secretariat in Prague for talks with his counterpart, Wilhelm Höynick, and other senior CSCE officials. A meeting was also held in Austria on 23–24 September with representatives of non-governmental organizations (NGOs) in order to discuss conflict prevention.

More significantly, the CSCE deepened its relationship with the UN in 1994. The CSCE was already cooperating with the UN on the conflicts in Georgia (Abkhazia), Tajikistan and Nagorno-Karabakh. On 22 August this cooperation was extended to Bosnia when the two organizations signed a memorandum of understanding by which the UN Protection Force (UNPROFOR) agreed to supply logistical support for the CSCE mission to Sarajevo. In the same month, the UN Secretary-General had a meeting with a high-level CSCE delegation in New York to discuss further contacts and collaboration.

CSCE cooperation with other international organizations had already borne fruit in a number of areas. The CSCE and the European Union jointly ran seven 'sanctions assistance missions' (SAMs) to enforce UN sanctions against Federal Yugoslavia, involving 240 customs officers and other specialists operating in Albania, Bulgaria, Croatia, Hungary, Macedonia, Russia and Ukraine. The CSCE also sent a high-level delegation to the EU-sponsored Conference on Stability in Europe held in Paris on 26–27 May, which sought to provide a framework for managing minority disputes and border questions, and proposed anchoring a future 'pact for stability', on which it hosted round-table talks in Vienna in November.

One significant new area of CSCE activity in 1994 was the integration of the newly-participating states of Central Asia into the organization. In February-March the CSCE secretary-general visited the five Central Asian republics, his initiative leading to the creation of a CSCE liaison office in Central Asia. Another result was a series of specialized regional seminars in Central Asian locations on various themes germane to the purposes of the CSCE. These activities helped to reinforce the existing work of the HCNM and the ODIHR in the region.

There were other important CSCE meetings during the year. The third annual session of the 300-member Parliamentary Assembly met in Vienna on 4–8 July and the second meeting of the Economics Forum took place in Prague on 15–17 March. There were also regular meetings of the CSCE committee of senior officials (CSO) and the permanent committee (PC), both of which devoted much time to discussions on conflicts in the former Soviet Union and the Balkans. However, the most important meetings of the year were the Budapest review conference of 10 October–2 December, followed by the Budapest summit of heads of state and government on 5–6 December. The review conference provided the opportunity to clarify future tasks and to develop the organization's structures and decision-making procedures. The Budapest summit was marred by disputes over Bosnia, the future of NATO and Russian peace-keeping operations in the former Soviet Union. President Yeltsin warned the CSCE that an eastward expansion of NATO could plunge Europe into a 'cold peace' (see also III.2.i) and the Russians vetoed plans to subject Russian peace-keeping forces in Georgia, Moldova and Tajikistan to scrutiny by CSCE monitors.

On a more positive note, the Budapest summit endorsed a document entitled *Towards a Genuine Partnership in a New Era*, which articulated common concerns about ethno-national conflict, terrorism and nuclear proliferation. Ukraine used the occasion to renounce nuclear weapons and sign the Nuclear Non-Proliferation Treaty (see XII.2). Guidelines drawn up by the CSCE Forum for Security Cooperation (FSC) on a code of conduct on 'politico-military aspects of security' were approved. Most significantly, it was agreed (subject to UN Security Council approval) to send 3,000 CSCE peace-keeping troops to Nagorno-Karabakh once a formal cessation of armed conflict had been declared within the framework of the work of the Minsk Group (see AR 1993, p. 418). This peace-keeping force was to be multinational, with no country contributing more than 30 per cent of the total.

Finally, the Budapest summit decided to underline the CSCE's permanent status by changing its name. From 1 January 1995 the CSCE would be known as the Organization for Security and Cooperation in Europe (OSCE).

ii.   EUROPEAN BANK FOR RECONSTRUCTION AND DEVELOPMENT (EBRD)

ADDRESSING the British American Chamber of Commerce in May, the EBRD's second president, Jacques de Larosière, characterized the Bank's activities as 'project-financing where others fear to tread, or at least tread alone'. If that phrase was redolent of the adventurous policies of his predecessor (see AR 1993, p. 419), his aim was to outline the solid benefits that the Bank's financial partnership could bring to a Western investor newly entering a post-communist economy. Among these were experience in what by then had brought investment of $14,400 million (including $9,900 million from private-sector partners) to those states in 178 projects; ability to take risks underwritten by the EBRD's preferred creditor status and 'triple A' ranking; and the attraction of external finance (thus far from 26 international banks) to supplement its own government-provided equity capital.

In July the Bank launched its first bond issue in a 'country of operation', namely Hungary, in the forint equivalent of $10 million, which both tapped a new source and reduced foreign exchange risk. In the same month it made its first environmental protection loan (in Estonia). And in September it made the first large-scale equity investment by an international financial institution in a Russian bank ($35 million in Tokobank, which lent mainly to the energy sector).

As mass privatization developed throughout the 25 countries of operation, the Bank was able to find investible objectives much more widely. Whereas, by the end of 1993, 57 per cent of the portfolio had been in five countries (the Czech and Slovak Republics, Hungary, Poland and Romania), in 1994 the other 20 countries received 56 per cent of the Bank's loans. To find and assess such projects, the Bank had opened 15 resident offices by end-1994 (with two more scheduled for opening in 1995). As promised to the EBRD annual meeting held in St Petersburg on 18–19 April, these were to support a new policy of seeking out small and medium enterprises which, although riskier, promised greater dynamism than big plants that were emerging, unreconstructed and still subsidized, into the ownership of their managers and workers. The next stage, as M. Larosière said in an end-December interview, was to convince such 'insider' owners that competition was going to threaten their established position, both from home and abroad, and that alliances with Western partners could assure their future.

Restoration of the Bank's credibility, after the controversial exit of Jacques Attali in 1993, was a crucial aim. It was helped by assuring zero growth in nominal terms in the 1994 budget and planning for zero growth in real terms in 1995; administrative expenditure, which had been 5.7 per cent of accumulated commitments in late 1993, had been brought down to 2.7 per cent at the end of 1994. The cost of a resident board (12 per cent of administrative spending) and of a London base remained in question, but in-house economies became the order of the day. Two floors of the London head office were sub-let and publication was stopped of the Bank's annual and quarterly overall surveys of the 25 economies of operation. Their replacement, a meticulously-researched *Transition Report*, focused on the institutional and financial changes about which international business needed to be informed.

iii. COUNCIL OF EUROPE

FOLLOWING the rapid growth in the membership of the Council of Europe since 1991 and the first summit meeting of heads of state and government in October of the previous year (see AR 1993, p. 420), 1994 was a year of consolidation for the Council of Europe. Efforts were concentrated upon putting flesh on the bones of the final declaration of the Vienna summit and examining how far member states and candidate countries conformed to Council of Europe requirements on the maintenance of fundamental rights and freedoms.

May 1994 saw the signing of the 11th Protocol to the European Convention on Human Rights, designed to give effect to the institutional reforms agreed at the Vienna summit, most notably the establishment of a single European Court of Human Rights in place of the two-tier Court and Commission. The Protocol was to enter into force following ratification by all member states, and in May the Committee of Ministers expressed the strong wish that it be ratified in the shortest possible time. Four of the Council's 33 member states had ratified by the end of 1994. Also in pursuance of the Vienna declaration, the Committee of Ministers agreed in November the text of a Framework Convention for the Protection of National Minorities, to be opened for signature from February 1995. This set out rights and freedoms of persons belonging to national minorities and the scope for international cooperation in protecting them. The new Congress of Local and Regional Authorities, which met in Strasbourg in late May and early June, and the launching in December of the European youth campaign against racism, xenophobia, anti-semitism and intolerance were further fruits of the Vienna summit.

The concern of the Parliamentary Assembly to monitor the honouring of commitments entered into by new member countries had been sharpened in 1993 by the passage of the 'Halonen Order' (see AR 1993, p. 421). Against this background, the election in April 1994 of a Romanian judge to the European Court of Human Rights was postponed because none of the candidates was considered sufficiently free of the taint of the Ceauşescu regime. Concerns were not confined to standards in new member states: the Assembly criticized the arrest of six members of the Turkish Grand National Assembly belonging to the Kurdish Democracy Party and the subsequent effective dissolution of that parliamentary party (see II.3.vii). On 10 November the Committee of Ministers adopted a declaration on compliance with commitments accepted by member states, authorizing itself to examine the implementation of commitments on democracy, human rights and the rule of law by any member state.

In June the Parliamentary Assembly elected Daniel Tarschys of Sweden to the influential post of secretary-general of the Council of Europe, narrowly rejecting a bid for a second five-year term from Mme Catherine Lalumière of France. A Swedish Liberal, Mr Tarschys was the first Scandinavian elected to the post and a leading proponent of the expansion of the Council of Europe. Enlargement was indeed the main issue confronting the organization in the second half of 1994. Andorra was admitted as the Council's 33rd member in November, following its promulgation of a new constitution in 1993 and subsequent multi-party elections (see also II.2.viii). In May Bulgaria became the first of the new democracies to assume the chairmanship-in-office of the Committee of Ministers. The Bulgarian Foreign Minister, Stanislav Daskalov, said that his government attached high priority to furthering the accession of states of the former Soviet Union and of Albania.

The Assembly voted in October to recommend that Armenia, Azerbaijan and Georgia should be able to apply for Council of Europe membership. Nevertheless, attention within the Assembly mainly focused on the possible accession of the Russian Federation, while the Committee of Ministers sought to strengthen cooperation with Moscow. A report to the Assembly by jurists from the European Court and Commission on Human Rights, published in October, examined the extent to which the laws, constitution and practice of the Russian Federation conformed to the requirements for accession. It concluded that 'the rule of law is not established in the Russian Federation' and that its legal order 'does not, at the present moment, meet the Council of Europe standards as enshrined in the statute of the Council and developed by the organs of the European Convention on Human Rights'. This report was described by Mr Tarschys as containing an agenda for actions necessary if the Russian Federation was to be admitted in 1995.

iv.   EUROPEAN FREE TRADE ASSOCIATION (EFTA)

EFTA might well have ended the year by deciding to wind up the organization. In the event, Norway's referendum decision against joining the European Union (see II.2.iii) came as a reprieve. With Austria, Finland and Sweden moving on to EU membership on 1 January 1995, EFTA would have just four remaining members (Norway, Switzerland, Liechtenstein and Iceland) and 11 million people (just over one third of its previous total).

Similarly in question was the future of the European Economic Area (EEA), which had finally come into existence as a joint EU-EFTA structure on 1 January 1994 (see AR 1993, pp. 408–9, 421–2). Without Switzerland, whose voters had rejected the EEA in December 1992 (see AR 1992, pp. 81–2, 418), the Area was already a woefully lopsided partnership. The first EEA Council meeting, on 17 May, was long on affirmations that any talk of dismantling was premature. However, it took the Norwegian referendum 'no' to avoid the absurdity of only Iceland remaining on the EFTA side of the table. (Liechtenstein was still waiting in the wings, at least until May 1995, its participation contingent on popular approval of the revision of its ancient customs union with Switzerland.)

The EFTA ministerial meeting in Geneva on 13–14 December agreed to keep both EFTA and the EEA in existence (the latter decision being endorsed the following week by the EU). It also agreed to keep in operation, on a smaller scale, the EFTA Court in Geneva and the EFTA Surveillance Authority in Brussels, both created to oversee the operations of the EEA. The Geneva-based EFTA secretariat itself had been headed since 1 September by a new secretary-general, Kjartan Johannsson, hitherto Iceland's ambassador in Geneva. With a 1994 budget of 41.22 million Swiss francs, the secretariat faced the certainty of major cutbacks in 1995, although the December meeting deferred a decision on its future size and structure.

There was not exactly a surge of interest during 1994 in the alternative vocation sometimes touted for EFTA, as a kind of antechamber on the road to integration with the EU, through which the Central and East European countries (CEECs) might find it useful to pass. In Mr Johannsson's own words, these countries 'are focused firmly on the EU and seem to think we would only be a diversion'. Moreover, the complexities of bringing in a new member, not only to EFTA but to the EEA, might create a significant hold-up in the EEA's workings. With this in mind, the EFTA ministerial meeting in December gave little encouragement on the issue of membership to Slovenia, the only CEEC to raise the matter. The meeting stressed instead EFTA's willingness to complete the negotiations which had begun with the Slovenes in early 1994 on a non-symmetrical free trade agreement.

v.   NORDIC AND BALTIC ORGANIZATIONS

THIS was a year of uncertainty about the Nordic Council's future form and functions, as Finland, Norway and Sweden decided their relations with the European Union (EU) through membership negotiations and referendums (see II.2.iii-v). The Baltic Assembly meanwhile further strengthened its organization and clarified its sphere of activity.

In January the Nordic Council's then president, Jan P. Syse (Conservative, Norway), accused the Nordic heads of government of trying to clip the Council's wings. The former Norwegian Prime Minister claimed that they were narrowing the Council's activities to cultural cooperation by insisting that 50 per cent of its budget be devoted to this area and were transferring other important policy areas to informal inter-governmental networks. Mr Syse insisted that the Council's members—all leading national parliamentarians—should continue to focus on all the main policy areas and that these should be debated within the formal structures of inter-parliamentary and inter-governmental Nordic co-operation.

Meeting in Stockholm for its 44th session on 7–10 March, the Nordic Council called on the governments to relax their strict percentage division of budget funds between different policy areas. It also stated that parliamentary insight and control would be undermined if large areas of Nordic cooperation were transferred to informal inter-governmental cooperation. The Council's newly-elected president, Sten Andersson (Social Democrat, Sweden), asserted that such a transfer would increase the 'democratic deficit' already existing in the policy-making of the European Economic Area (EEA) and the European Union itself. Mats Nyby (Social Democrat, Finland) warned against the Council becoming a cultural discussion club, maintaining that it would play a relevant role in the later 1990s only if its work embraced all the important policy areas. Hans Engell (Conservative, Denmark) said that streamlining Nordic cooperation must be combined with retaining its role as the central forum of Nordic cooperation and policy debate.

The Council passed 16 recommendations for action by the Nordic governments. The latter were called on to draw up a programme to combat drug abuse and another for cooperation on genetic resources. Other recommendations included criminalizing the possession of child pornography; increasing the resources of the Nordic Investment Bank; formulating concrete measures for the 1994–96 Nordic environmental strategy; regulating the handling of environmentally-dangerous waste materials; and speeding up the review of Arctic resource use and environmental dangers. The governments were asked to present to the autumn Council meeting a detailed report on all sources of atomic waste in the Nordic region and to work internationally for the establishment of a nuclear-free, environmentally-protected area in the Barents Sea. The Council also decided to grant the Lapps observer status with the right to participate in the general debate.

When the Council met again in Tromsö (Norway) for its 45th session on 15–16 November, Finland and Sweden had voted to enter the EU, while Norway's referendum was due on 28 November. Although the general debate included a clash between Norway's 'yes' and 'no' supporters, there was broad consensus that the Nordic countries stood at a crossroads and that their formal cooperation needed to be re-thought if it was to remain relevant to the new situation. Such a reform, it was felt, should provide mechanisms for dealing with member states' different EU relations, for coordinating their European policies and connecting Nordic cooperation with the EU dimension. The Council decided to establish a joint parliamentary/ministerial working group to prepare proposals for the 46th session in Reykjavik in March 1995.

During the year the Nordic Council continued its active involvement in growing Baltic cooperation. On 4–5 February it organized an information seminar on Nordic cooperation for Baltic Assembly members, while in May and November Council observers attended sessions of the Baltic Assembly. In June the Council decided to open a Nordic information office in St Petersburg (Russia) in 1995, in addition to those already established in Tallinn, Riga and Vilnius, the capitals of Estonia, Latvia and Lithuania respectively.

The Baltic Assembly met for its fourth session at Kemiri (Latvia) in May. The session was devoted mainly to finalizing the new structure of inter-Baltic cooperation, designated the Baltic Council, the outline of which had been agreed at the third session at Tallinn in autumn 1993 (see AR 1993, p. 425). The Baltic Council was to have three levels: presidential summits taking initiatives and making proposals; the Council of Ministers making decisions by consensus; and the Parliamentary Assembly, composed of national delegations meeting in general sessions and committees, adopting recommendations and receiving annual reports from the Council of Ministers. The Kemiri session of the Assembly adopted a symbol for Baltic cooperation and instituted annual prizes for art, music and literature.

The fifth session of the Baltic Assembly held in Vilnius in November was attended by President Algirdas Brazauskas of Lithuania and by the three Baltic Prime Ministers. President Brazauskas proposed annual joint meetings of Presidents, Prime Ministers and parliamentary Speakers in conjunction with Assembly sessions. Latvia's Prime Minister, Maris Gailis, told the Assembly that long-term cooperation plans were in preparation with priority being given to legal harmonization, common defence planning, frontier controls, pension issues and unemployment. The Estonian Prime Minister, Andres Tarant, described security and foreign policy cooperation as the highest priority, along with adaptation to European, especially EU, structures and the creation of a Baltic common market.

6. AFRICAN, ASIA–PACIFIC, SOUTH PACIFIC AND AMERICAN REGIONAL ORGANIZATIONS

i.   AFRICAN CONFERENCES AND ORGANIZATIONS

THE 30th summit of the Organization of African Unity (OAU) met in Tunis on 13–15 June with the usual speeches calling for rejuvenation of the grouping and for continental recovery. This time they carried perhaps a little more conviction, as this was the meeting that welcomed the new non-racial democracy of South Africa as a member, after decades as an African pariah. No less than 42 of the continent's 52 heads of state assembled to hail President Nelson Mandela—a record attendance in the OAU's 31-year history, matched only by the first summits in 1963 (Addis Ababa) and 1964 (Cairo).

President Mandela, in his maiden speech as a member, referred to the decision to dissolve the OAU liberation committee and asserted that the latter body deserved congratulation for its 'remarkable achievement in throwing off the last vestige of a particularly insidious form of colonialism'. He added: 'When South Africa appears on the agenda again, let it be because we want to discuss what its contribution shall be to the making of the new African renaissance.'

The conference saw the handing-over of the OAU chairmanship to President Ben Ali of Tunisia by President Mubarak of Egypt. In his valedictory speech, President Mubarak said that Africa was increasingly taking up the reins of its own political fortune, exemplified by the setting-up in the previous year of a central 'early warning' mechanism for preventing and settling conflicts (see AR 1993, p. 427), as well as a peace fund to finance the mechanism's activities. The role of the Economic Community of West African States (ECOWAS) in Liberia, maintained the Egyptian leader, had shown that an all-African force could be set up and that African affairs need not be the province of Geneva or Washington. But the OAU secretariat should provide a 'database for the current and expected disputes of the continent'.

The need for resolving Africa's conflicts, including those internal to individual African countries, had been apparent for some time, in spite of the OAU charter's provision on non-interference in internal affairs. Conflicts like those in Angola and Somalia had deeply preoccupied African leaders, even though they had been two explosive for the OAU to handle by itself, and had thus required UN intervention. In 1994 the name of Rwanda was added to the list, and the shadow of the genocide in that country (see VII.1.ii) hung over the Tunis summit, dampening the celebration of the admission of South Africa. Although President Mandela said that Rwanda's bloody war would stand out 'as a stern and severe rebuke to us all for having failed to address inter-related matters', the summit still feebly allowed the tainted and defeated interim government to take the Rwanda seat rather than the victorious Rwandan Patriotic Front (FPR), even though the latter was virtually in control of the capital. The summit resolution called for a ceasefire and put its faith in the UN, although the latter had signally failed to do anything to prevent the April–June killings.

The impotence of the UN in Rwanda was shown two days after the OAU summit ended, when the French decided to intervene for 'humanitarian' reasons. There was unhappiness that the OAU's own mechanism had signally failed to work, perhaps because a notional UN mechanism had already been put in place. Right to the end of the year, the OAU's involvement was circumscribed, while the United Nations, in spite of replacing the French from August onwards, was still not providing adequate assistance. Similarly, the OAU could do little to remedy UN deficiencies in Angola (see VII.1.vi), while in Liberia OAU–UN Cooperation to reinforce the troubled ECOWAS peace-keeping operation had made little impact by the end of the year. A critical factor in limiting the OAU's possibilities for action was its continued budgetary problems, occasioned by tardy payments of arrears from the majority of member states: in 1994 the accumulated deficit was put at $60 million.

There was a certain ferment in some of the other African groupings, mainly those of an economic nature. In the southern part of the continent this related directly to the arrival of a newly-democratic and powerful South Africa on the scene. The first immediate question was what should happen to the Southern African Development Community (SADC), which had originally been set up as the SADCC ('Coordinating Conference') to help make South Africa's neighbours less dependent on their powerful, and in those days hostile, neighbour. The wider but related Preferential Trade Area (PTA) had suggested that the SADC should subsume itself in the wider grouping (stretching from the south up to Ethiopia and Somalia). However, after some deliberation, its ten members decided that the SADC should continue in existence, and at a special summit in Malawi in August welcomed South Africa as its 11th member. Observers said that South Africa had opted to join the SADC because the grouping provided the newly outward-looking 'giant of the south' with a ready-made sphere of influence.

The PTA, and its guiding hands at the UN Economic Commission for Africa, swallowed this disappointment and went ahead with its own plans to turn itself into a fully-fledged economic community. At a summit in Malawi in December, the 21-member Common Market for East and Southern Africa (COMESA) was launched. It included some members of SADC (because of the trade opportunities it offered) but not South Africa, at least for the time being. In a related development, the three East African countries (Tanzania, Uganda and Kenya), which had formed the East African Community (EAC) until its demise in the mid-1970s, signed a new agreement providing for the elimination of trade barriers. A secretariat was set up for this purpose in Arusha (Tanzania), the old EAC headquarters.

Similar transformations took place in the two groupings of the African franc zone, namely: the seven-member Union Monétaire Ouest-Africain (UMOA), consisting of Benin, Burkina Faso, Côte d'Ivoire, Mali, Niger, Senegal and Togo and using the franc of the Communauté Financière Africaine (CFA); and the six-member grouping (Cameroon, Central African Republic, Chad, Congo, Equatorial Guinea and Gabon) using the franc of the Coopération Financière en Afrique Centrale (also abbreviated to CFA franc). These were shaken on 11 January by a 50 per cent devaluation of the CFA franc, which had had the same parity with the French franc since 1948. The decision was taken at a summit of francophone leaders in Dakar, under strong pressure from France and the Washington financial institutions. The presence in Dakar of the IMF managing director, Michel Camedessus, and of the French Cooperation Minister, Michel Roussin, indicated that the African leaders had been given an 'offer they could not refuse'.

Although the French Treasury continued to provide some reserves and guarantees for the zone, the devaluation led to a number of bitter statements from African leaders about French 'betrayal'. However, the predicted disasters did not take place, even if some countries experienced aggravated social discontents (and the convertibility of the CFA franc became less total than before). The summit also saw the launch of a new grouping, the Union Économique et Monétaire Ouest Africain (UEMOA), to replace both the CEAO (Communauté Économique de l'Afrique de l'Ouest) and the UMOA, with encouragement and support from France. A similar change occurred in central Africa, where the six-member Communauté Économique et Monétaire de l'Afrique Centrale (CEMOC) was established. Both new bodies were officially designed to give a new boost to integration within the framework of a redynamized franc zone, but were seen at the time as evidence of France's trying to compensate for the alleged 'betrayal' of devaluation.

Against this background, the French military intervention in Rwanda in mid-1994 was seen in part as an attempt to show that France was not abandoning its African protégés. Later in the year the Franco-African summit, held on 7–9 November in the French Atlantic resort of Biarritz provided another opportunity for French efforts at reassurance and support. Rwanda itself did not figure on the agenda, if only because France studiously avoided inviting the new Rwanda government of the FPR—a decision much-criticized even by loyal francophone Presidents.

ii. SOUTH ASIAN ASSOCIATION FOR REGIONAL COOPERATION (SAARC)

HAVING succeeded to the SAARC chair at the seventh summit held in Dhaka in April 1993 (see AR 1993, p. 428), the Bangladeshi Prime Minister, Begum Khaleda Zia, found herself continuing in the office throughout 1994 and potentially into 1995. This was principally because of India's difficulties in arranging to host the eighth summit, as a result of which there was no SAARC heads of government meeting in 1994.

The annual SAARC Council of Ministers' meeting was held in Dhaka in late July, when trade and economic relations were discussed at length. But the most important SAARC meeting of the year was the first session of Finance and Planning Ministers, held in Dhaka on 10-11 July. The meeting was chaired by Begum Khaleda, who referred in her address to 'the consensus on eradication of poverty in South Asia' adopted by the 1993 summit. This had emphasized the pivotal role of national anti-poverty plans while also recognizing that 'there are real, if latent, regional linkages on the problems of poverty'. The ministers reviewed current global and regional trends and their own national economic situations in some detail. They agreed to set up a three-tier mechanism to facilitate an annual exchange of information on poverty alleviation programmes, involving both senior ministry officials and the ministers themselves.

As the occupant of the SAARC chair, Begum Khaleda visited Bhutan in October and proposed to visit the other member countries before the eighth summit, which was expected to be convened in New Delhi in mid-1995. There was no denying, however, that the organization made little impact in 1994, not least because India showed no enthusiasm for infusing it with more life.

iii.   ASIA–PACIFIC ORGANIZATIONS

The Foreign Ministers of the Association of South-East Asian Nations (ASEAN) held their 27th annual meeting in Thailand in July. In keeping with the group's efforts to incorporate the Indo-Chinese bloc in ASEAN affairs, delegations from Vietnam, Laos and Cambodia attended the meeting. It was agreed that ASEAN would admit Vietnam, which currently enjoyed observer status, as a full member at the 1995 meeting (see IX.1.viii). Members indicated that the observer status of Laos would also be upgraded to full membership in the near future. The highly controversial presence of Myanmar (Burma), invited to attend for the first time, illustrated ASEAN's pragmatic policy of 'constructive engagement' towards the military junta and an easing of Burma's diplomatic isolation (see IX.1.i).

The Foreign Ministers' meeting was followed by the first formal meeting of the ASEAN Regional Forum (ARF), the multilateral group established in 1993 to discuss regional political and security issues (see AR 1993, p. 430). The Forum brought together the six ASEAN states, their 'dialogue partners' (Australia, Canada, the European Union, Japan, South Korea, New Zealand and the USA) and China, Laos, Papua New Guinea, Russia and Vietnam. Topics discussed at the meeting included the ongoing conflict in Cambodia, North Korea's nuclear programme and the territorial dispute over the Spratly Islands. While no practical decisions were taken on these issues, it was agreed that the ARF would meet annually and optimism was expressed that concrete steps to defuse potential and actual conflicts could be taken at the 1995 meeting in Brunei.

In a move that made it clear that ASEAN was serious about stepping up economic cooperation within the grouping, the 26th meeting of Economy Ministers held in Thailand in October endorsed a decision to speed up the creation of an ASEAN Free Trade Area (AFTA) and to extend tariff cuts to unprocessed agricultural products. When the AFTA concept was first endorsed at the fourth summit in 1992, the plan had been for a 15-year programme of lower import tariffs on all goods under a two-track common effective preferential tariff (CEPT) scheme. As a result of the October decision, the AFTA was scheduled to be realized by January 2003 instead of 2008.

Heads of state and government of the 18 members of the Asia–Pacific Economic Cooperation (APEC) forum convened in Bogor, Indonesia, in mid-November (see also IX.1.vi). The leaders agreed on a potentially momentous two-step formula for freeing trade and investment among the states of the Asia–Pacific region by the year 2020. However, while the Bogor Declaration stated that a concerted liberalization process would start from 'the very date of this statement', no concrete proposals were announced. Instead, it was stated that industrialized economies would achieve the goal of 'free and open trade and investment no later than the year 2010 and developing economies no later than the year 2020'.

Prior to the Bogor meeting, there had been intense speculation over the Malaysian position on APEC's future course. In 1993 the Malaysian Prime Minister, Mahathir Mohamad, had refused to attend the forum's Seattle summit in protest at what he regarded as attempted US domination. Dr Mahathir attended the Bogor summit, but at the close his team issued a set of masterfully ambiguous 'reservations'. The target dates for APEC trade liberalization, the Malaysians stated, were 'indicative and non-binding' and liberalization should be 'undertaken on a best-endeavour basis' consistent with countries' level of economic development. Hence, Malaysia would 'only commit itself to undertaking further liberalization on a unilateral basis at a pace and capacity commensurate with our level of development'.

The 50th session of the UN Economic and Social Commission for Asia and the Pacific (ESCAP) was held in New Delhi, India, in April. The session called for greater emphasis on poverty alleviation in the Asia–Pacific region. Its final declaration suggested the development of human resources and employment-orientated activities to remove poverty.

The annual meeting of the Asian Development Bank (ADB) was held in the French Mediterranean resort of Nice in May. The ADB's governing board subsequently gave formal approval to the controversial doubling of the Bank's authorized capital base to some US$48,000 million. Asian developing countries, led by China, had expressed bitterness at the linkage between the capital increase and new lending policies. Under the new policies (which had the support of the USA and Japan), the focus of lending would be switched from infrastructural projects aimed at fostering economic growth and towards projects concerned with social and environmental development. Some reports indicated that lending would also be linked to the practice of 'good governance'.

iv. SOUTH PACIFIC REGIONAL COOPERATION

THE 25th South Pacific Forum (SPF) heads of government conference was held in Brisbane (Australia) in August. Resource management, environmental and economic cooperation issues were prominent in the discussions, which resulted in an agreement to develop a common code of conduct for indigenous forest management and timber exporting. An official Australian report released at the meeting concluded that some Pacific island countries were losing the equivalent of half their national incomes through unmonitored and underpriced logging exports.

The SPF summit also agreed to strengthen its promotion of sustainable exploitation of fishing stocks; warned that continued global warming could result in sea-level rises which threatened low-lying atolls; recommended measures to protect fragile coastal areas from tourism; and called for a rationalization of regional airline services. At the meeting, Fiji was disappointed that former President Ieremia Tabai of Kiribati was reappointed as SPF secretary-general ahead of the Fijian candidate, Filip Bole.

The SPF secretariat in Suva (Fiji) played a coordinating role in the deployment of forces from Tonga, Vanuatu and Fiji (with logistical support from Australia and New Zealand) to facilitate the peace process on the Papua New Guinean island of Bougainville (see X.1.ii). In light of its increasing regional role, the Forum was granted observer status at the United Nations.

The fourth summit of the Small Island States (a sub-group within the South Pacific Forum) was held in March on Kirimati/Christmas Island (an Australian possession). Representatives from Nauru, the Cook Islands, Kiribati, Niue and regional organizations criticized the United Kingdom's decision to withdraw from the South Pacific Commission (see AR 1993, p. 431) and applauded President Mitterrand's continued moratorium on French nuclear weapons testing in the South Pacific (see II.1.ii). The summit also welcomed Major-General Sitiveni Rabuka's re-election as Fiji's Prime Minister in February (see X.2.ii).

Meeting in October in Port Vila (Vanuatu), the annual conference of the South Pacific Commission concentrated on the organization's financial difficulties. As a main contributor, Australia warned that the budget needed to be more realistic given that total funds stood at barely US$7 million as against prospective commitments of US$22 million for 1995. As well as the chosen theme of land reform, the conference considered ways of finding new members with a view to replacing UK financial contributions for important economic, social and environmental programmes.

v.   AMERICAN ORGANIZATIONS

ON 7 March President César Gaviria Trujillo of Colombia was elected secretary-general of the Organization of American States (OAS), to take office following the expiry of his national mandate (see IV.3.v). With the support of the United States, he obtained 20 votes to 14 for Bernd Niehaus Quesada, the Foreign Minister of Costa Rica, and announced his support for the creation of a single free-trade zone in the Americas. Sr Gaviria was sworn in at OAS headquarters in Washington on 15 September.

At the annual OAS general assembly, held in Belém (Brazil) on 7–10 June, the outgoing secretary-general, João Baena Soares of Brazil, called for the reinstatement of Cuba, whose membership of the organization had been suspended since 1962. The proceedings were dominated by the issue of Haiti (see IV.3.xii). A resolution passed on 7 June was ambiguous on the question of military intervention but backed strengthened sanctions and endorsed the protracted negotiations for a return to democratic government. US officials insisted that members would in the event back intervention, however reluctantly, while then exiled President Aristide (who was unable constitutionally to back intevention) made it clear on 2 June that he favoured 'surgical' action. Brazil and Mexico remained strongly opposed to intervention, however, and Argentina, Canada and Venezuela favoured the deployment of a UN peace-keeping force. On 30 August the UN abandoned efforts to seek a political solution in Haiti. The joint UN–OAS special envoy, Dante Caputo (former Foreign Minister of Argentina), resigned on 19 September in protest against the unilateral action of the United States and what he termed 'the total absence of consultations' (see XI.1).

The eighth summit meeting of the Rio Group was held in Rio de Janeiro on 9–10 September. Members called for the lifting of the US embargo against Cuba, invited the military regime in Haiti to resign to avert armed intervention and expressed strong support for further regional integration and collaboration to fight terrorism and drug-trafficking. Panama had earlier, on 1 June, petitioned to be readmitted to the Group, from which it had been suspended in 1988.

At a ceremony held in Mexico City on 18 January, both Argentina and Chile acceded to the Treaty of Tlatelolco and became full members of the Organization to Ban Nuclear Weapons in Latin America (OPANAL). Argentina had ratified the treaty in November 1993 and Chile, having ratified in 1974, had suspended its implementation. On 30 May Brazil, too, signed the amended treaty (which was promulgated by President Franco on 16 September), while on 29 August Cuba announced its intention to sign (see also XII.1).

At the invitation of President Clinton, leaders of 34 countries in the hemisphere convened in Miami on 9–11 December for a 'Summit of the Americas', the first since 1967. In addition to discussing a draft American free trade agreement, the gathering accepted in principle a programme of biennial summit meetings which would draw together existing regional trading blocs and lead to the establishment of a Free Trade Area of the Americas (FTAA) by the year 2005. At the close of the summit, it was announced that Canada, Mexico and the USA had agreed in principle that Chile should be admitted to membership of the North American Free Trade Agreement (NAFTA).

The fifth summit meeting of the Southern Cone Common Market (Mercosur), held in Montevideo on 17 January, failed to adopt a common external tariff but confirmed that the customs union would nevertheless take effect on 1 January 1995. The leaders agreed that Bolivia, which as a member of the Andean Pact was not eligible for full membership of Mercosur, should have observer status at summit meetings. They also discussed the 'waterway' project designed to give Bolivia access to the Atlantic by way of the Paraná and Paraguay rivers. Uruguay, however, opposed an Argentinian plan to build a canal linking Rosario with the Atlantic, so that traffic on the Paraná would not have to pass through the Uruguayan port of Nueva Palmira. On 10 March Brazil secured agreement that the Mercosur member states should either form a South American Free Trade Association (ALCSA) or join NAFTA, and perhaps do both. On 5 June the government of Chile announced its intention to seek associate membership of Mercosur. Meeting in Buenos Aires on 5 August, the member states finally agreed to implement the lifting of tariffs on 85 per cent of their reciprocal trade and also expressed their hope that Bolivia and Chile would become full members in due course.

Having withdrawn from the Andean Pact (Acuerdo de Cartagena) in August 1992, Peru was readmitted at its own request on 4 April at a meeting of member states in Caracas. However, it remained an observer in the negotiations for the other members to establish a full customs union with effect from 1 January 1995.

The fourth Ibero-American summit, held at Cartagena de Indias (Colombia) on 14–15 June with the central theme of regional economic development and integration, declared its support for a commercial union stretching from Mexico to Argentina. The Prime Minister of Spain, Felipe González, expressed the view that structural adjustment policies had failed to address the twin problems of unemployment and the unequal distribution of wealth. President Franco of Brazil called for the reintegration of Cuba into the OAS and was criticized for doing so by President Carlos Menem of Argentina.

vi.   CARIBBEAN ORGANIZATIONS

RATIFICATION of the North American Free Trade Agreement (NAFTA) cast a long shadow over the vulnerable economies of the Caribbean basin. Jamaica and Trinidad & Tobago failed to gain admission to NAFTA; other states in the 13-nation Caribbean Community (Caricom), which favoured a collective application, were advised that they had some way to go in terms of free-market development. A Canada-Caricom summit was scheduled for early 1995 to discuss the issue. Meanwhile, the USA's ten–year-old Caribbean Basin Initiative (CBI) was criticized by the US General Accounting Office for providing little benefit to the USA and encouraging low-wage, export-assembly development.

On a more positive note, decisions of the 1992 and 1993 Caricom summits took effect with the creation of the Association of Caribbean States (ACS) at a summit meeting in Cartagena, Colombia, on 24 July. The ACS had 25 members spanning the Caribbean islands and littoral, a region of 200 million people: Mexico, Colombia, Venezuela, Cuba, the Dominican Republic, Suriname, Haiti and the Central American and Caricom countries. It was envisaged that 15 dependent territories would be offered associate membership; but the United States, displeased by the inclusion of Cuba in the ACS, indicated that neither Puerto Rico nor the US Virgin Islands would affiliate.

The Caricom heads of government attended a two-day inter-sessional meeting in Kingston, St Vincent, in March, prior to convening for the Community's 15th annual conference in Bridgetown, Barbados, on 4–7 July. The first meeting stressed the need for fair trade and regional integration and afforded an opportunity for the governments to lobby a high-level IMF delegation. Foreign Ministers met separately in June, pointedly choosing Belize as the venue in solidarity against Guatemalan territorial claims. A trade deal, to come into effect in January 1995, gave Caricom countries duty-free access to the Colombian market for a range of exports. The July summit endorsed military intervention in Haiti (see IV.3.xii) and welcomed the inclusion of Cuba in the nascent ACS.

Caribbean countries generally maintained a positive attitude towards Cuba, in line with a December 1993 Cuba–Caricom agreement envisaging cooperation in 24 specific economic, social, technological and cultural areas. Jamaican hotel interests, for instance, became closely involved in Cuba's burgeoning tourist trade. The socialist state was the only western-hemisphere country excluded from the 'Summit of the Americas' held in Miami in December (see XI.6.v; IV.1), when President Clinton proposed the construction by 2005 of a free trade zone encompassing the entire Americas and the Caribbean. The Caricom states, however, were economically as well as geographically peripheral to that vision. With the ascendancy of the nationalistic Republican right on Capitol Hill and the end of the Cold War, the historical conditions which gave rise to the CBI, and provided the rationale for the USA's self-interested goodwill towards the hemisphere's weaker economies, were fading fast; aid dollars were diverting to Eastern Europe and Africa, and the Caribbean countries were feeling the cold blast of free trade.

The seven smaller countries in the Organization of Eastern Caribbean States (OECS), already fiscally united in the East Caribbean Central Bank (ECCB), made progress towards the creation of a regional stock market. At the ECCB's fifth annual general meeting in St George's in September, it was noted that Grenada was the only member country currently undergoing the rigours of a structural adjustment programme. The Windward Islands (Dominica, St Lucia, Grenada and St Vincent & the Grenadines) remained under pressure to develop alternatives to their dependence on preferential markets for bananas. Their joint marketing operation Winban was replaced by Wibdeco (the Windward Islands Banana Development and Exporting Company), owned by the four governments and committed to restructuring the industry to adapt to the rigours of the free market. The European Union (EU) provided assistance to increase efficiency and develop alternative crops. Major dollar-banana producers (Colombia, Costa Rica, Nicaragua and Venezuela) withdrew their referral of the EU's import rules to a GATT panel after their tariff-free quota was raised, and the European Court of Justice dismissed a German challenge to the import regime.

Banana prices recovered somewhat, after a flood of Latin American fruit in the last pre-tariff months, but tropical storm Debbie wrought destruction across the Windward archipelago in September. More stormy weather ahead was signalled in October when the US administration announced an inquiry into complaints by American banana producers denied access to the European market.

XII DEFENCE, DISARMAMENT AND SECURITY

DURING 1994 the international security record was mixed. On the positive side, quiet progress was made in the implementation of arms reductions accords, while confrontation between Washington and Pyongyang over North Korea's nuclear programme was narrowly averted. On the negative side, the crisis on Bosnia continued to have a corrosive effect on NATO, which once again proved incapable of taking decisive action. It was also a year in which new forms of security threat were recognized as major items on the international agenda.

1. ARMS CONTROL AGREEMENTS

THE year proved to a milestone for nuclear arms control. On 14 January the United States, Russia and Ukraine signed a trilateral statement that outlined the timing of the transfer of all nuclear weapons from Ukraine to Russia within three years (see also III.2.i). The agreement specified that the estimated 50 tonnes of highly-enriched uranium from approximately 1,800 strategic warheads (1,240 on SS-19 and SS-24 missiles, 560 on bomber-launched cruise missiles) would be converted to low-enriched uranium and eventually returned to Ukraine for use in civilian power reactors. In return, Russia agreed to cancel some of Ukraine's debt for past deliveries of oil and natural gas, while the United States promised financial assistance in the amount of $700 million. Finally, the agreement established a framework within which Ukraine subsequently acceded to the Nuclear Non-Proliferation Treaty (NPT). Such action removed one of two remaining obstacles for the entry into force of the first Strategic Arms Reduction Treaty (START I).

The following month Kazakhstan removed the other obstacle by formally acceding to the NPT as a non-nuclear-weapon state on 14 February. With this action, Kazakhstan joined Belorussia (Belarus) in renouncing its possession of nuclear weapons as required by the Lisbon Protocol to START I. Finalized in May 1992, the Lisbon Protocol had specified that Belorussia, Kazakhstan and Ukraine would relinquish their nuclear weapons and accede to the NPT in the shortest time possible. There had subsequently been strong opposition to the protocol in the Ukrainian parliament (Rada), which in November 1993 had combined its conditional ratification of START I with continued resistance to Ukraine's accession to the NPT. Nevertheless, Ukraine began the process of transferring the nuclear warheads to Russia as required by the January trilateral statement. By the end of 1994 it had succeeded in deactivating all 46 of the SS-24 inter-continental ballistic missiles located in Pervomaysk.

The impasse on Ukrainian ratification of the NPT seemed to be complicated by the replacement of President Leonid Kravchuk by former Prime Minister Leonid Kuchma as a result of presidential elections in June-July. At the time, it was uncertain whether Mr Kuchma would continue his predecessor's support for Ukrainian accession, given that during the campaign he suggested that the Rada should postpone a vote on the NPT until Washington and Moscow had pledged additional financial assistance for the elimination of nuclear weapons on Ukrainian soil. Following his inauguration, however, President Kuchma on 19 August reversed his earlier opposition by announcing that he would ask the Rada to support accession to the NPT. This was accomplished on 16 November, the measure being passed by a wide 301–8 margin. On 5 December President Kuchma formally signed Ukraine's instrument of accession to the NPT at a meeting of the Conference on Security and Cooperation in Europe (CSCE). On the same day, Belorussia, Kazakhstan, Ukraine, Russia and the United States exchanged instruments of ratification of START I, thereby clearing the way for the ratification and enforcement of START II. Meanwhile, the ex-Soviet republics of Georgia, Moldova and Turkmenistan (which had not been in possession of nuclear weapons) had also acceded to the NPT.

In another significant development in nuclear arms control, Argentina and Chile on 18 January became full parties to the 1967 Treaty of Tlatelolco prohibiting the possession of nuclear weapons in Latin America and the Caribbean. Both states opted to waive the entry-into-force provisions and to accede to the treaty as full parties immediately. But expectations that Brazil would follow suit were disappointed when the upper house of the Brazilian Congress failed to act on a ratification proposal. In February, however, the Brazilian Senate ratified a quadripartite agreement between Argentina, Brazil, the International Atomic Energy Agency (IAEA) and the Argentine-Brazilian Agency for Accountancy and Control of Nuclear Materials (ABACC). This decision was significant in that the quadripartite agreement provided a basis for future arms control initiatives at the regional level (see also XI.6.v).

These achievements in nuclear arms control were supplemented by progress in the area of missile non-proliferation. In October the United States and the People's Republic of China concluded an agreement to cooperate in efforts to halt the proliferation of certain categories of missiles and related technology. Specifically, the agreement outlined an incremental approach to resolving US-Chinese differences over missile exportation. The first step of this approach involved the removal of US sanctions imposed following a determination that China had secretly transferred missile components and technology to Pakistan in 1993. In return, China reaffirmed its original commitment to adhere to the guidelines and parameters of the Missile Technology Control Regime (MTCR). Finally, the agreement stipulated that the United States would continue its discussions with China in an effort to promote the latter's membership in the MTCR.

2.   NATO AND EUROPEAN SECURITY

AMID growing international frustration over the war in former Yugo-slavia (see III.1.vi), the year began with a NATO summit meeting in Brussels on 10–11 January at which deliberations focused on threats to peace in the European continent. As expected, the discussions revealed fractious differences between the 16 members of the Alliance. On former Yugoslavia, some NATO members doubted that air strikes would be effective in deterring the Bosnian Serbs, who were accused of seeking to thwart humanitarian relief convoys to enclaves designated as safe areas by the United Nations. The Canadian Foreign Minister specifically warned that air strikes might hit the wrong targets and endanger the safety of his country's troops deployed with the UNPROFOR peace-keeping force. British officials also argued that air strikes would do little to facilitate humanitarian objectives in Bosnia–Hercegovina. Finally, on 11 January, the NATO leaders issued a warning that threatened the use air strikes if the Bosnian Serbs refused to permit the reopening of Tuzla airport, to allow the relief of UN troops in Srebrenica and to end the siege of Sarajevo.

In February the NATO warning was elevated to the status of an ultimatum. Following a mortar attack on a market-place in Sarajevo, UN Secretary-General Boutros-Ghali requested NATO to prepare for air strikes against artillery positions in and around the besieged city. In what were described as intensive consultations, member states deliberated for days over what would be the first offensive action taken in NATO's 44-year history. During these discussions, Canada continued to express concern about the possibility of retaliation against its troops serving as UN peace-keepers in Bosnia, while Greece feared that air strikes would result in an escalation of the war in the Balkans. Despite their objections, however, neither state threatened to veto a majority decision. On 9 February NATO ambassadors issued an ultimatum calling on the Bosnian Serbs to end their siege of Sarajevo and to relinquish to UNPROFOR all of their heavy weapons located within a 20-kilometre exclusion zone around Sarajevo. Shortly thereafter, the Bosnian Serbs began to withdraw their heavy weapons in accordance with the NATO ultimatum.

At the end of February, however, NATO aircraft observed six Bosnian Serb warplanes bombing a Bosnian government munitions factory in Novi Travnik, in violation of UN Security Council resolution 816 establishing an air exclusion zone over Bosnia–Hercegovina. Following two attempts to order the aircraft to land, two US F-16s engaged the six Yugoslav-made Super Galebs (on 28 February) and shot down four of them near the town Banja Luca. This action was highly significant in that it represented the first time that NATO had resorted to the use of military force in former Yugoslavia (or anywhere else in the world). It would not be the last. By the end of the year, NATO had carried out air strikes on four further occasions. On 10 April two US F-16s attacked Serb forces closing in on the Muslim enclave of Goražde, one of six sites designated as safe areas by the United Nations. In the aftermath of this action, President Clinton described it as a clear expression of the collective will of NATO and the United Nations, while inferring the possibility of future air strikes if they were requested. That request came on 5 August, when Dutch and French NATO aircraft attacked targets around Sarajevo in retaliation for the seizure by Bosnian Serbs of a tank and other heavy weapons from a UN depot.

The other two air strikes of 1994 occurred on 21 and 23 November, when NATO responded to Bosnian Serb attacks on the safe enclave of Bihać in defiance of warnings from both the Alliance and the United Nations. The first struck the Udbina airfield in the self-declared republic of Serbian Krajina, from which Serbian aircraft had bombed the Bihać enclave on three occasions despite the air exclusion zone over Bosnia–Hercegovina. Two days later a second mission destroyed three Serb surface-to-air missile sites near Bihać. Nevertheless, the entry of Bosnian Serb forces into Bihać on 24 November (in alliance with an anti-government Muslim faction) highlighted what some saw as a policy paralysis on the part of NATO, arising from the recurring debate between the United States, Britain and France over the use of force. Whereas the US government supported a show of force in response to the events in Bihać (and on 11 November announced that it would no longer enforce the UN arms embargo on former Yugoslavia), Britain and France feared that military action could prompt the Serbs to retaliate against their UN soldiers. However, in a startling reversal of its previous position, the Clinton administration in late 1994 abandoned its support for a military solution in Bosnia–Hercegovina in favour of a more conciliatory approach. In December it backed a mission to Sarajevo by former US President Jimmy Carter, who succeeded in brokering a ceasefire between the disputants that came into effect on 24 December and led to the declaration of a four-month truce on 31 December. It was widely noted that the truce was achieved without the direct involvement of NATO.

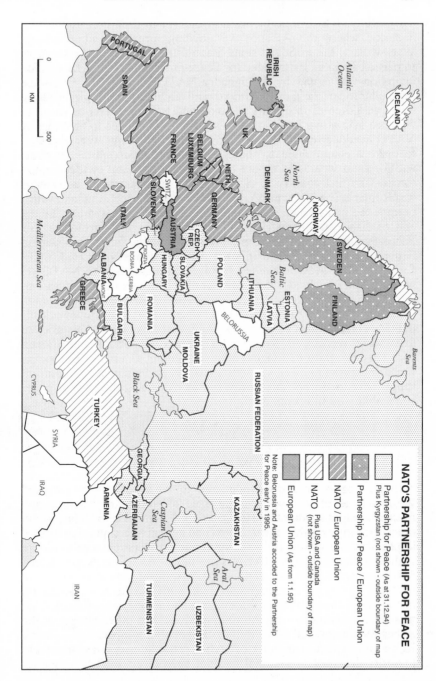

NATO'S PARTNERSHIP FOR PEACE

- **Partnership for Peace** (As at 31.12.94)
  Plus Kyrgyzstan (not shown - outside boundary of map)
- **Partnership for Peace / European Union**
- **NATO / European Union**
- **NATO**   Plus USA and Canada
  (not shown - outside boundary of map)
- **European Union** (As from 1.1.95)

Note: Belorussia and Austria acceded to the Partnership for Peace early in 1995.

Ironically, NATO's problems in former Yugoslavia occurred during a period where the Alliance was inviting former members of the Warsaw Pact, the ex-Soviet republics and the neutral European states to participate in its Partnership for Peace programme (see XIX.1). The invitation was issued by the January NATO summit (the first since the collapse of the Soviet Union) and envisaged that participating states would enter into joint planning and training exercises with the Alliance and would be entitled to send representatives to meetings at NATO headquarters in Brussels. In return, participants were expected to make a commitment to share information about military budgets and forces as well as to ensure the democratic control of their armed forces. The first country to sign a Partnership framework agreement was Romania (on 26 January), followed a day later by Lithuania, which became the first former Soviet republic to join the programme. By the end of 1994, 21 other states had signed up for the Partnership for Peace (see accompanying map), the most notable being the Russian Federation. Initially, Russia opposed any extension of NATO to Eastern Europe and in May demanded regular consultations with NATO on nuclear issues such as safety, dismantling and counter-proliferation. On 22 June, however, Russia joined the Partnership programme, while simultaneously securing NATO's agreement to a framework for political consultations going beyond military cooperation. This discrete framework recognized Russia's unique and important contribution commensurate with its weight and responsibility as a major European, world and nuclear power. Optimists saw this agreement as an important supplement to European security and as enhancing the goal of peace and stability on the continent.

3. NUCLEAR NON-PROLIFERATION ISSUES

THE year began with what appeared to be a positive step toward the resolution of the controversial issue of North Korea's suspected nuclear weapons potential (see also IX.2.v–vi). On 5 January US officials announced that North Korea had agreed to accept international inspections of all seven of its declared nuclear facilities so as to ensure that they conformed to IAEA safeguards. Although North Korea remained steadfast in its rejection of US suspicions about two of these facilities, the agreement seemed to be a prelude to the resumption of high-level talks between Washington and Pyongyang. Within days, however, differences over the timing, scope and other details of the inspection threatened to derail the negotiations. Specifically, North Korea objected to a number of IAEA procedures deemed necessary to verify that nuclear material had not been diverted since an earlier inspection in 1993. However, faced with the prospect of punitive action by the UN Security Council, North Korea announced on 15 February that it would concur with the inspection activities that the IAEA wished to carry out. On 1 March an IAEA team arrived in North Korea for an inspection that was expected to last about two weeks.

In an unexpected move, North Korean officials then prevented members of the IAEA inspection team from conducting crucial procedures at the radiochemical laboratory (reprocessing facility) at Yongbyon. These procedures had been outlined in a specific list of mutually-acceptable inspection activities agreed between North Korea and the IAEA. Inspectors were prevented from taking samples from the hot cell devices used to extract plutonium from spent nuclear fuel and were also refused permission to take certain measurements required for gamma spectrum analysis (a procedure that would have detected the recent presence of radioactive materials). Further, IAEA inspectors observed that at least one of the containment seals affixed to nuclear material inventories and equipment had been broken, this finding adding to the suspicion that the North Koreans intended to increase plutonium separation capability at the plant. As a result, the inspection team was unable to certify that there had been no diversion of weapons-grade nuclear material at the Yongbyon facility.

In response, the IAEA board of governors, convened in a special session on 21 March, adopted a resolution calling on North Korea immediately to allow the IAEA to complete all requested inspection activities and to comply fully with its safeguards agreement. The US government reacted by abruptly cancelling imminent high-level talks with North Korea and by announcing the deployment of six Patriot air defence missile batteries in South Korea. But a US move for the authorization of economic sanctions on North Korea by the United Nations was opposed in the Security Council as likely to be counter-productive to a peaceful resolution of the crisis. China was concerned that undue pressure on North Korea would only encourage it to stiffen its negative attitude and possibly to launch a military attack on South Korea (and even on Japan)—North Korea having threatened to turn Seoul into 'a sea of fire' if any direct punitive action were undertaken. Russia also appeared to favour diplomatic alternatives to the imposition of economic sanctions (as did the South Korean and Japanese governments). In the event, the UN Security Council on 31 March adopted a Chinese-proposed statement which demanded that North Korea should allow the completion of the blocked IAEA inspections and honour its obligations under its safeguards agreement with the IAEA.

The crisis intensified in April when the North Korean regime announced that it was preparing to shut down the Yongbyon reactor so that it could remove spent nuclear elements and refuel the reactor. It also rejected a further IAEA request for a proper inspection of the reactor and the refuelling process, suggesting instead that a limited inspection would be sufficient to deter future diversion of nuclear material. On 19 May the IAEA confirmed that North Korea had broken the seals on the reactor and had begun to move the fuel rods from the reactor, despite the absence of IAEA inspectors, who were at that point on their way to Yongbyon. Subsequent efforts by the inspectors to sample the fuel rods were hampered by the North Koreans' acceleration of the removal process. On 3 June the IAEA director-general, Hans Blix, informed the UN Secretary-General that his agency's ability to ascertain with confidence whether nuclear material from the reactor had been diverted in the past 'has been lost'. On 13 June North Korea withdrew from the IAEA.

Amidst growing tensions between Washington and Pyongyang, the US government dispatched former President Jimmy Carter to North Korea on what was described as a 'private trip'. On 15 June talks between Mr Carter and President Kim Il Sung resulted in an agreement on a framework for future discussions to resolve the crisis through diplomatic means. In exchange for a US commitment to engage in high-level political talks with North Korea, the latter agreed to a freeze of its nuclear weapons programme. Initially scheduled to begin on 8 July, these talks were postponed because of the death of Kim Il Sung that day (see XX: Obituary). When talks resumed in the first week of August, the two sides quickly signed an agreed statement intended to serve as the basis for 'a final resolution of the nuclear issue'. Finalized at Geneva on 21 October, the agreement required the cessation of all reprocessing and construction activities at Yongbyon and North Korea's submission to unhindered international nuclear inspection. In exchange, the United States offered the prospect of diplomatic recognition of the Pyongyang regime and undertook to provide North Korea with new, more proliferation-resistant light-water reactors to replace the latter's graphite-moderated reactors. The two sides also pledged to work together to strengthen the international nuclear non-proliferation regime and to promote peace and security on a nuclear-free Korean peninsula.

The resolution by diplomatic means of the crisis with North Korea over its nuclear weapons potential was widely welcomed in the international community, especially by Western governments. At the same time, the worldwide diffusion of advanced weapons technology, and the apparent aim of certain states and groups to acquire nuclear weapons (see below), was seen, in the West at least, to require collective approaches and strategies designed to enhance international security in such areas.

4.   TRANSNATIONAL ORGANIZED CRIME

IF 1994 was a year in which traditional security problems seemed to be intractable but containable, it was also a year in which new security problems were acknowledged by the international community. Foremost among these was the challenge associated with the rise of transnational organized crime. Although not an entirely new phenomenon, the problem became much more pressing during 1994, largely because of an upsurge in illicit trafficking in nuclear materials. There were several dramatic seizures and arrests that helped to underline the danger that weapons-grade material might fall into the hands of nuclear terrorists, pariah states or organized criminals intent on large-scale extortion.

Incidents of trafficking in nuclear material had been recorded with increasing frequency since 1991. Until 1994 such trafficking had been characterized by fraudulent activities—especially involving the sale of 'red mercury'—and by trade in non-weapons-grade materials. But the resultant rather complacent assessment of the problem was completely dispelled in 1994. Three incidents, in particular, underlined the urgency of the problem: the seizure of enriched plutonium in Tengen (Germany) in May; the arrest in August of three men disembarking from a flight from Moscow to Munich and the confiscation of materials in their possession; and the arrest of three men in Prague in December.

The most disturbing aspect of the Tengen case was that six grams of plutonium-239 were discovered fortuitously when law enforcement authorities were searching for counterfeit material in the home of a German businessman. In the ensuing investigation, it emerged that the businessman had links with former KGB officers and with Kintex, a Bulgarian arms sales company. Initially, there was considerable speculation that he was involved in a nuclear materials deal on behalf of North Korea. Gradually, however, this gave way to reports that he was part of a Russsian–Bulgarian–Iraqi supply network for such materials. Whatever the precise details, the case revealed that illicit nuclear trafficking was a more serious problem than had hitherto been believed.

This assessment was reinforced in August when a Colombian dentist and two Spaniards were arrested at Munich airport in possession of 330 grams of enriched plutonium and a quantity of lithium-6. Superficially, this incident was more serious than the previous one, in that the amount of material was much greater. On the other hand, it was revealed that the three men all had financial problems and had been induced to bring the materials to Munich by German undercover agents. The nature of this 'sting' operation generated complaints that German law enforcement and intelligence operatives were creating a market for nuclear material. However, the fact that three men who were essentially amateurs in the nuclear trafficking business had been able to obtain a significant amount of high-grade plutonium gave pause for thought.

The potential threat was reinforced on 14 December when three kilograms of highly-enriched (87 per cent) uranium-235 was seized in Prague by the Czech Security and Information Service (BIS). Discovered in two cylindrical containers, the material was accompanied by Russian certificates. The three men arrested were a Belorussian, a Ukrainian and a Czech nuclear physicist. According to a Czech Interior Ministry spokesman, the enriched uranium was worth 'several dozen million dollars'. In addition to heightening earlier concerns about trade in weapons-grade material, the episode highlighted the danger that scientists themselves would become involved in illicit trafficking in nuclear materials. All three of the men arrested had worked in the nuclear industry, and the Czech scientist had specialized in heavy-water reactors.

If nuclear-materials smuggling was a major concern for responsible governments, it was far from being the only one. That burgeoning activity was accompanied by some disquieting trends in drug-trafficking, including an upsurge of heroin abuse in the United States and the establishment of a European cocaine-distribution network by the Colombian Calí cartel, working in close cooperation with the Sicilian Mafia. The rise of organized crime in Russia was also seen as a particularly dangerous development, not least because it raised the possibility that the most powerful successor to the Soviet Union would be not a democratic state but one dominated by organized crime. Other concerns were expressed about the extent of money-laundering (and its impact on the global financial system) and the growth of linkages or strategic alliances among transnational criminal organizations.

Against this background, there was increasing awareness of the need for a coordinated international response, both on the specific problems of nuclear-materials trafficking and on the broader challenge posed by transnational organized crime. Measures taken to combat illicit trade in nuclear materials included an agreement between Germany and Russia to share information on the issue; joint US and French efforts to assist Russia in the creation of stricter inventory and control measures; and a decision by the IAEA to establish a database on incidents of nuclear smuggling.

There were also broader moves to deal with the growing phenomenon of transnational organized crime. In the United States, for example, President Clinton categorized international crime as a threat to national security. Perhaps most important of all, however, was the World Ministerial Conference on Organized Transnational Crime, held in Naples (Italy) on 21–23 November. This conference was convened to assess the dangers posed by the phenomenon and to identify possible forms of international cooperation for its prevention and control. Bringing together Justice and Interior Ministers, the conference concluded with the adoption of a declaration and action plan designed to initiate more effective measures to prevent and control cross-border criminal activities. The key components of the plan included the need to acquire greater knowledge about transnational organized crime, the need for substantive legislation at the national level imposing penalties for participating in criminal associations and conspiracies, and the development of better evidence-gathering and witness-protection schemes, It was further agreed that these measures needed to be accompanied by bilateral and multilateral cooperative arrangements, including provision for extradition and mutual legal assistance treaties, as well as by greater efforts to control money-laundering and to confiscate the proceeds of crime.

The Naples action plan also included an agreement to study the merits of a convention against transnational organized crime, along the lines of the existing global convention against drug-trafficking. That it did not include the draft text of an actual convention suggested that the international community still had a long way to go before it would be able to develop a comprehensive strategy against transnational organized crime. Nevertheless, the Naples conference was a major step towards a general recognition that transnational organized crime had become a global problem and one that jeopardized international security and stability.

XIII RELIGION

ANGLICAN DIVERSITY. The first women priests in the Anglican Church in England (see AR 1993, pp. 447–8) were ordained in Bristol Cathedral by Bishop Barry Rogerson on 12 March before a packed congregation. Bristol, where 32 women deacons were priested, was followed by Sheffield, Winchester, London and other dioceses: by the end of the year around 1,000 women had become priests. There was dismay among the minority opponents, among whom John Selwyn Gummer, Environment Secretary and Synod member, gave up the fight and entered the Roman Catholic Church on 27 February, followed in July by Sir George Gardiner MP. In a separate conversion, the Duchess of Kent was received into the Roman Church by Cardinal Basil Hume in January. The former Bishop of London, Graham Leonard, was ordained into the Roman Catholic priesthood on 23 April, conditionally on the validity of his previous Anglican ordination. But a series of High Court actions aimed at invalidating the female ordinations were unsuccessful. Seven retired or suffragan Anglican bishops, together with 712 priests and deacons, signed a declaration accepting the Pope as 'Supreme Pastor of the Universal Church'. Nevertheless, by the end of the year Anglican defections were not as numerous as had been feared, many bishops and clergy welcoming the change and others preferring to work against it from within the establishment. Two 'provincial visitors', or 'flying bishops', were appointed to encourage clergy opposed to women priests to 'remain with dignity' within the Church of England.

Clergy in the Anglican Church in Wales voted narrowly against women's ordination in April, though bishops and laity cast majorities in favour. In the USA, former Dominican theologian Matthew Fox was received into the Anglican Episcopal Church in April, attracted by its 'common sense', while in Belgium a professor at Louvain University became an Anglican because of the Pope's ruling against women's ordination. In July Rev Anthony Freeman was dismissed as vicar of Stapleford in Sussex by the Anglo-Catholic Bishop of Chichester, for teaching that there was no objective deity (see AR 1993, p. 452). The appointment of a prominent evangelical, Michael Marshall, as Bishop of Durham was criticized when the popular press discovered that he had been convicted for indecency 26 years previously. He protested that he had never been a homosexual and opposed homosexuals serving as full-time clergy. The Lesbian and Gay Christian Movement accused the bishop of inconsistency, and in November the pressure group Outrage named ten Anglican bishops, including Dr Marshall, alleged to be 'gay'. The General Synod in December asked the House of Bishops to reconsider the ban on remarriage of divorcees in church.

Jim Thompson, Bishop of Bath and Wells, who himself remarried divorcees, nevertheless urged caution in changing the rules.

The introduction of a national lottery in Britain in November brought condemnation from the Methodist Church and the largest black church, the New Testament Church of God, for 'luring poor people with the bait of quick rewards'. They said that they would sell their shares in companies involved in the lottery. In December the largest lottery jackpot so far, £17.8 million, was won by an Indian Muslim from Bradford, whose religion forbade gambling.

VATICAN MANOEUVRES. At a UN-sponsored International Conference on Population and Development in Cairo in September (see also XI.1), the Vatican joined with Muslim fundamentalists in attacking abortion and contraception and in opposing 'the individualist approach toward life'. Critics complained of undue concentration on these two issues, to the neglect of family needs and women's rights. But eventually the Vatican adopted nine of 16 chapters in a programme of action issued by the conference.

In November Pope John Paul II created 30 new cardinals, making a total of 167, bringing fears of conservative dominance in choosing his successor (see also II.2.viii). In a letter to bishops in May the Pope affirmed that the Church had 'no authority whatsoever' to ordain women and that this judgement was to be 'definitively held' by all the faithful. There were strong protests, especially in Germany, Belgium, Switzerland and the USA, pointing out that this ruling was not 'infallible'. A German bishops' conference in September took the view that divorced and remarried Catholics should receive care and not be barred from the sacraments, but the Vatican ruled this inadmissible. Sex scandals in Ireland, which helped to bring down the government in November (see II.1.vii), highlighted the problems of a celibate priesthood. Meanwhile, the Old Catholic Church decided by 124 votes to 10 to ordain women.

The Pope's health aroused increasing concern. In April he broke his hip in a fall and had to undergo surgery. In September he was unable to fulfil a promised visit to Sarajevo, partly for security reasons. A new *Catechism of the Catholic Church* (running to 680 pages in the English text), the first for 400 years, recapitulated traditional precepts, for which reason critics described it as 'yesterday's document'. The Vatican's central statistics office claimed that there were 958 million Catholics in the world (18 per cent of the total population), the highest number being in Brazil (137 million), followed by Mexico (85 million), Italy (55 million) and the USA (55 million). The number of Catholic priests worldwide was given as 404,641, the statistics showing an increase of 29 per cent in Africa but decreases of 9.9 per cent in Europe and of 10 per cent in North America.

ORTHODOX RECOVERY. The first statistics published in 80 years showed that the Russian Orthodox Church had more than doubled its numbers of priests and parishes from 6,800 parishes at the Millenium in 1988 (see AR 1988, p. 435) to 15,810. There were 12,707 priests, 269 monasteries and 2,548 candidates studying at 13 seminaries. But the latest figures still contrasted sharply with pre-revolutionary times, when there were 54,000 parishes, 40 seminaries and over 1,000 monasteries. During the communist period 140,000 priests, monks and nuns were executed and at least 45,000 churches closed or destroyed.

In Ukraine, Orthodox and Catholic continued to dispute the ownership of hundreds of churches (see AR 1989, p. 427), as state officials also claimed rights to church buildings. The Orthodox community was divided: the largest number was loyal to the Moscow Patriarchate (with 5,763 registered parishes), while the Ukrainian Orthodox (Kiev Patriarchate) had 1,892 parishes and the Ukrainian Autocephalous Orthodox 282.

In December an assembly of bishops of the Russian Orthodox Church confirmed that former dissident priest Fr Gleb Yakunin (see AR 1991, p. 439) was unfrocked for standing in 1993 parliamentary elections and entering the State Duma. Fr Yakunin, who was still recognized as a priest by the Kiev Patriarchate, maintained that since the Church had often collaborated with the previous undemocratic regime it should now help in building up democracy. A number of other senior clerics were politically active, including Metropolitan Filaret of Minsk, who was a member of the Belorussian parliament. It was therefore asked why the latter could be in parliament but not Fr Yakunin. In an open letter to Patriarch Aleksi II, Fr Yakunin warned against right-wing extremism in the Church. He declared that the Church's new statutes were copied from those of the KGB and remarked that attempts to regain all church buildings and land were 'unrealistic'.

AFRICAN GROWTH. At the end of the colonial period, it had often been assumed that Christianity in Africa would decline with the disappearance of imperial links. However, as with use of the English language, the opposite had happened. In the three decades since the achievement of independence, there had been a huge increase in Christianity south of the Sahara, comparable to that in Latin America. An essential part of black African society, the Christian Churches played vital roles in public affairs, President Mandela, himself a churchman, praised their activities in the struggle against apartheid. In Kenya, Uganda and Malawi, criticism of government came in large part from Anglican and Roman Catholic bishops and national councils of Churches (see AR 1992, p. 442). In francophone Africa, Catholic bishops were asked to preside over national conferences discussing the political future in Togo, Benin, Gabon, Congo and Zaïre.

It was estimated that, by the year 2000, 48 per cent of all Africans would be Christian and 42 per cent Muslim. Official Vatican figures claimed that there were 89 million African Catholics in 1992 (14 per cent of the total population). The Church appeared to be Africanized (most bishops in Africa were black), yet they continued to be appointed from abroad. The first Synod of the whole Roman Catholic African Church was held in May, not in Africa but in Rome, where Cardinal Hyacinthe Thiandom of Senegal pleaded for African theology, liturgy and moral teaching, and for dialogue with African traditional religion and Islam. Discussion on priestly celibacy was ruled out, though referred to indirectly in discussions on seminaries and the need for women teachers.

While traditional Protestant churches had reduced the number of foreign missionaries, Catholics increased theirs. The latest figures showed that in 1993 Nigeria had 923 Catholic missionaries compared to 768 Protestants, Cameroon 1640 to 689 and in Malawi 578 to 366. Most missionaries were involved in education, health and general development and many were laity trained by religious congregations. Near Nairobi 30 religious houses were training European recruits, and similar houses flourished near to universities at Yaoundé in Cameroon and Ibadan in Nigeria. The Catholic strength enabled Rome to block attempts to introduce 'human life' education in schools, in light of the official Catholic ban on contraception. But both the Catholic Church and traditional Protestants lost members to a Pentecostal invasion of Africa.

Independent of mission foundations, tropical and southern Africa had countless churches, already estimated at over 6,000 organizations in 1968. Some were fairly orthodox, following the pattern of their mother-churches although with independent rule; others had developed new practices and had become great communities. In Zimbabwe, for example, the Assemblies of God Africa claimed to be the largest church in the country, surpassing Catholics and Anglicans. From the 1980s a new wave of Pentecostal missionaries, chiefly North American, had flooded over Africa, engaging in proselytism rather than education and health. Even in Guinea, where only Catholics and Anglicans had been tolerated, there was one Anglican missionary in 1991 compared with over 100 Pentecostals. American Protestant missionaries in Africa had increased in numbers generally: in Malawi from 155 in 1989 to 199 in 1993; in Zimbabwe from 232 to 309; in Ghana from 158 to 184. Then a new strategy had been adopted, of training local missionaries supported by US agencies. Some 40,000 were fully or partially financed from abroad in 1992, while evangelical colleges in the USA sent students on part-time missions to Africa.

New missionaries, charismatic or fundamentalist, were often linked to the 'religious right' of the southern states of USA. They attacked the 'perverted, unbelieving Christianity' of the World Council of Churches as well as churchmen like Archbishop Desmond Tutu for his political involvement in South Africa. They opposed ecumenism and inter-religious tolerance, regarding Islam as part of the empire of Satan, a stance which fostered religious conflict (see AR 1991, p. 443). Traditional evangelicals, who had opposed Pentecostal practices, were divided and alarmed at the loss of young people (the United Church of Zambia having split on the Pentecostal issue in 1993). The Pentecostals looked towards a Second Advent in the millenial year 2000, while traditional Protestants and Catholics hoped that their organizations and work would carry them through to calmer times.

In the humanitarian effort in Rwanda in 1994 (see VII.1.ii), 100 church-related agencies were registered. Some, like Operation Blessing organized by US television preacher Pat Robertson (see AR 1985, p. 381), were accused of using medical care as a cover to push religion. Others were charged with manipulating children for fund-raising campaigns.

PERSECUTION. In Rwanda, where 70 per cent of the population were Catholics, eight Tutsi priests were killed in April, followed by ten more in June along with the Archbishop of Kigali and two other bishops. In Algeria, two elderly French religious were shot dead in May by Muslim fundamentalists, and the Armed Islamic Group (GIA) murdered four Catholic priests in revenge killings on 27 December (see also II.1.ii). The latter were White Fathers, of the Society of Missionaries of Africa, fluent Arabic speakers and engaged in dialogue with Islam, eschewing proselytism. On the day of their funeral, every shop and business in Tizi-Ouzou, where they died, was closed in respect. Ten Lebanese Christians were killed and 60 injured in February by mortar bombs in a church near Beirut. In Pakistan one Christian was killed and two injured by gunmen in April, and three Christian leaders were murdered in Iran, all having been involved in issues of religious liberty. In South Africa, Johan Heyns, a prominent churchman who had helped to lead the Dutch Reformed Church away from apartheid, was murdered by an unknown assailant in November. Over 30 Catholic and Protestant leaders were arrested in China in April for activities outside officially recognized churches.

JEWISH PROBLEMS. The latest figures showed that the number of Jews in Britain had dropped by 10 per cent over 15 years, to 300,000. Chief Rabbi Jonathan Sacks responded by launching a rescue plan called 'Jewish Continuity', intended to rebuild a community on the basis of its great past. Critics saw this as religious conservatism and as 'alienating women', who had only a marginal part in orthodox synagogue life.

Liberal leaders were meanwhile working on new liturgies using inclusive language.

The massacre of 29 Muslim Arabs in a Hebron mosque on 25 February by an Israeli Jew (see V.1) was condemned as 'shame to Judaism' by Dr Sacks and other religious leaders. It was followed by bomb attacks on Jews in Europe and America, almost 100 people being killed in an explosion at the main Jewish organization in Buenos Aires. The death in June of Rabbi Menachem Schneerson (see XX: Obituary) brought crisis to the Lubavitch movement of mystical Hasidism, of which he was the Rebbe or spiritual head in Brooklyn. He had taught the imminent coming of the Messiah, but never claimed to be Messiah himself. The ultra-orthodox Lubavitch movement published works in many languages, its zeal having built up a network of religious institutions across the world, with 1,400 schools, centres and summer camps, and an annual budget of $200 million. It had revitalized many orthodox groups and was admired for its activities, but criticized by reformers for literal interpretations of scripture and for idolatry in believing in a false Messiah.

ISLAMIC TENSIONS. In October the School of Oriental and African Studies in London banned an Islamic fundamentalist group for making threats against Jews and gays. In France, where the policy was assimilation rather than the British line of accepting that immigrants were different, 17 schoolgirls were excluded from their schools in Lille in October for refusing to remove Islamic headscarves. There were 3 million Muslims in France, but surveys found that only 22 per cent were in favour of the headscarf and that 95 per cent believed in total integration, while having their own mosques. As regards the civil war in Algeria, assassinations of French nationals by Islamist militants were not supported by most French Muslims, who were politically moderate.

In the war in Bosnia, Islamic, Jewish and Christian groups were among those providing relief, the Islamic Relief Agency (ISRA) from Khartoum claiming to practise 'charity without distinction of race or religion'. In Kosovo, many mosques had been destroyed and new Orthodox churches were being built by the Serbs. In Egypt, attacks continued on the Coptic Christian community and on Western tourists by Islamic extremists (see V.2.ii). In Sudan, the dominant National Islamic Front imposed its own interpretation of Islam on Muslim and non-Muslim alike and was responsible for attacks on churches, although moderate Muslims and Christians generally got on well together. Some 2.5 million Muslims made the annual pilgrimage to Mecca in May, but over 250 died in a crowd stampede. Five years after the issuing of a *fatweh* against Salman Rushdie in February 1989, the Iranian news agency insisted that there could be no reprieve of the death sentence imposed on the British novelist for alleged blasphemy against Islam.

BOOKS OF THE YEAR. The religious best-seller was the Pope's *Crossing the Threshold of Hope*, a series of answers to questions, with an initial print-run of 20 million copies, in 20 languages and released in 36 countries. Raymond Brown's *The Death of the Messiah* was the result of ten years' work and referred to 2,250 other scholars, differently from Enoch Powell's *The Evolution of the Gospel*, which blithely disregarded two centuries of research. In *A Tale of Two Missions*, Michael Goulder stressed the conflict between Petrines and Paulines in the early church, while Otto Betz and Rainer Riesner, in *Jesus, Qumran and the Vatican*, defended the slow deciphering of the Dead Sea Scrolls. *William Tyndale* by David Daniell celebrated the quincentenary of the birth of the great bible translator, and Andrew Linzey in *Animal Theology* criticized the Catholic catechism for undermining the better treatment of animals. *Looking for God in Brazil* by John Burdick described progressive Catholicism in Latin America; Paul Gifford in *Christianity and Politics in Doe's Liberia* discussed Pentecostalism; and Lamin Sanneh considered the effect of translations of the Bible in Africa in *Encountering the West*. In *Russian Revolution*, Michael Rowe depicted the travails of Evangelical churches. In *Will We Have Jewish Grandchildren?*, British Chief Rabbi Jonathan Sacks faced the problem of marriage outside the faith, while *Judaism and Other Faiths* by Dan Cohn Sherbok was a rare examination of Jewish approaches to different religions. *Islam in the Balkans* by H.T. Norris described the history and present struggles of mixed communities. Leo Lefebvre gave a model of inter-faith dialogue in *The Buddha and the Christ*. Bill Porter in *Road to Heaven* described the pressures on Buddhist and Taoist monastics in China. *Protestantism in Contemporary China* by Alan Hunter and Chan Kim-Kuong estimated that there were over 25 million practising Christians in China.

XIV THE SCIENCES

1. SCIENTIFIC, MEDICAL AND INDUSTRIAL RESEARCH

SPACE, ASTRONOMY AND PHYSICAL SCIENCES. In July astronomers had ringside seats for a cosmic spectacular: the impacts of at least 21 fragments of comet Shoemaker Levy 9 with the planet Jupiter, which had been predicted in 1993 (see AR 1993, p. 454). There were fears that nothing would be seen at all, since the impacts actually all took place out of sight, over the Jupiter horizon. But the reality far exceeded expectations. The initial flash of each impact was visible at infra-red wavelengths high in the Jovian atmosphere, above the horizon. Less than an hour later, the impact site rotated into view, revealing large and rapidly expanding dark patches which, in many cases, became larger than the Earth. Between 16 and 22 July the bombardment continued, creating a string of dark patches in Jupiter's southern hemisphere, visible even in small telescopes. By the end of the year, they had spread out but were still visible as a broad band and astronomers were studying them to understand better the composition of the comet and of Jupiter's atmosphere and its circulation.

The energies unleashed on Jupiter, equivalent to multi-megaton nuclear explosions, reminded scientists on Earth of the danger of potential impacts with our own planet. Evidence continued to mount that a major asteroid impact 65 million years ago in the Caribbean, off the Yucatan peninsula in Mexico, had been responsible for the multiple extinctions at that time, including the last of the dinosaurs. On 15 March a rocky object 20 metres across and travelling at 70,000 kilometres per hour passed closer to the Earth than the Moon. Early in the morning of 1 February two Micronesian fishermen saw, for a few seconds, an object above the Pacific ten times brighter than the Sun. The only other witnesses were US spy satellites, data from which led scientists to conclude that it was probably part of a comet exploding in the atmosphere. The danger that larger objects could reach the surface, with serious consequences, was considered real enough to warrant a network of telescopes called Spaceguard and discussions on the feasibility of deflecting objects by using nuclear missiles or even reflected sunlight.

Elsewhere in the Solar System, an American rocket took the first close-up pictures of the Moon for 21 years. The *Clementine* rocket was a joint project between the civilian National Aeronautics and Space Administration (NASA) and the US Defence Department. It tested military targeting systems and carried scientific instruments, including the first spectral scanner able to determine the composition of surface rocks across the Moon. It also surveyed the south polar region of the Moon for the first time, its radar measurements suggesting that this area might have potential for prospecting for frozen water underground. On 13 September the European Space Agency (ESA) probe *Ulysses* became the first man-made object to fly over the south pole of the Sun, surveying the magnetic field and the wind of particles streaming out from the star. On 12 October ground controllers at NASA's Jet Propulsion Laboratory lost contact with the *Magellan* space probe as it burned up in the atmosphere of Venus. Its planned demise was the culmination of a highly-successful five-year mission during which it had observed the gravitational field and upper atmosphere of Venus.

In January US astronomers were relieved to be able to announce that the repair mission to the *Hubble Space Telescope* (HST) in December 1993 (see AR 1993, p. 453) had been a complete success. The corrective optics produced far sharper images of stars and captured far more light from distant galaxies than had been possible before. The HST was able to provide spectacular images of the impact sites on Jupiter in July, to reveal planets forming around stars in the Orion Nebula and to image the region close to suspected super-massive black holes in distant galaxies. The HST's most important result of the year, supported by ground-based telescopes, was to observe variable stars in the galaxy M100 in the Virgo cluster, these being stars of known absolute brightness used by astronomers to estimate cosmic distances. If this distance scale were extended to inter-galactic scales, it would allow estimates of the expansion rate of the Universe and hence its age. The values for M100 suggested an age for the Universe of only 8,000 to 12,000 million years, far less than many cosmologists had preferred to believe and making the Universe younger than the prevailing estimates of the ages of many stars in globular clusters. It being unlikely that stars could be older than the Universe containing them, astronomers were faced with a dilemma.

Astronomers on the ground used microwave telescopes on the island of Tenerife and in Cambridge to begin mapping minute fluctuations in the cosmic microwave background radiation, the cooled glow of the Big Bang itself. Evidence for such 'ripples' was first found by the COBE satellite in 1992 (see AR 1992, p. 447). The measurements confirmed the reality of the ripples, on a scale that might link quantum fluctuations in the first fraction of a second of the Universe with the large-scale clustering of galaxies seen today. They tended to support the inflation hypothesis for the expansion of the early Universe and could be evidence for gravitational waves in the early Universe as predicted by Einstein's theory of general relativity.

Activities in near-Earth space continued throughout 1994 with a mixture of failures, delays and successes. Two successive launches of *Ariane IV* rockets failed during the third stage, but test firings on the ground of the new *Ariane V* continued successfully. On 19 August a launch of the US space shuttle *Endeavour* was called off just 1.8 seconds before lift-off when computers detected a fault in a fuel pump. On 2 September Russian cosmonauts finally succeeded, using manual controls, in docking a *Progress* supply craft with their *Mir* space station after two automatic attempts had failed. And a home-made space experiment produced the first extended man-made object visible to the naked eye in space when a *Delta* rocket released a polyethylene space tether 20 kilometres long. It tested technologies that might help to position satellites and generate electrical power in space.

An earthquake rocked southern California on 17 January, damaging buildings and freeways just north of Los Angeles (see also IV.1). The rupture was in the Northridge fault and probably did not ease the stresses and reduce the risk of a severe quake on the San Andreas fault. The world's most powerful earthquake for 30 years took place beneath Bolivia in June. Although the magnitude was 8.3 on the Richter scale, and it was felt from Canada to West Africa, the fact that it took place 630 kilometres underground in the Earth's mantle meant that damage on the surface was not severe. It did, however, reverberate through the planet, allowing seismologists to build up a clearer picture of the Earth's interior and confirming an anisotropy in the Earth's core that some geologists interpreted to mean that the inner core was formed of a single crystal of iron the size of the Moon.

Fossil bones 80 million years old believed to be from a dinosaur were discovered in a coal mine in Utah and yielded short fragments of DNA; but most geologists insisted that it would never be possible to find enough DNA intact to recreate any features of dinosaurs. Two teams did, however, succeed in cloning more substantial extracts of DNA from mammoths frozen in the Siberian tundra for more than 100,000 years. A living fossil was found growing in a forest gorge 200 kilometres west of Sydney. The trees, up to 40 metres high and called Wollemi pines, were similar to fossil species last recorded in rocks 150 million years old. Methane-eating bacteria were found alive 500 metres below the floor of the Pacific in sediments four million years old.

An important discovery of what was believed to be an early human ancestor was made in Ethiopia. Seventeen bone fragments, including teeth, were found near the village of Aramis by anthropologists under Professor Tim White of the University of California at Berkeley. The creature, named *Australopithecus ramidus* (from the word meaning 'root' in the local language) could have looked rather like a chimpanzee, but details of its bones made anthropologists believe that it was a direct ancestor of modern humans. Dated as being 4.4 million years old, it pushed the human family tree back by nearly a million years. The shin bone of an adult human, discovered at an archaeological site at Boxgrove in southern England, was dated at about 500,000 years old, making it the oldest human bone found in Europe so far.

Physicists at the Fermilab particle accelerator near Chicago announced that they believed that they had completed a 100-year search for the fundamental constituents of the Universe. In somewhat cautious terms, they presented evidence from their particle collisions that they had identified the so-called 'top quark'. This had been predicted as the final and heaviest member of the family of six leptons and six quarks, but it was so massive (174 GeV) and short-lived that the researchers could not be certain they had found it in the particle debris from their experiments. Final confirmation might not come until after the year 2004, the estimated completion date of the European Large Hadron Collider to be built at the CERN site near Geneva. The CERN Council gave its final approval to this project in December.

German scientists, working at a heavy ion research facility in Darmstadt, announced in November that they had created a new element with atomic number 110. A month later they reported that they had also created element 111 by smashing together nickel and bismuth nuclei. In theory, element 111 fitted into the chemical family including gold and silver; however, in view of its unstable nature and existence of only a fraction of a second, no-one was likely to see it glisten.

Research towards more useful new materials continued on several fronts. New conducting and semi-conducting polymers were developed, including ones that could be printed in thin films in electronic circuits. Another new polymer had the potential to enable a single light-emitting diode to glow in different colours. Also in 1994, a way of cross-linking polymer molecules was developed, potentially allowing the design of forms of polyethylene with rubber-like properties. Among many research projects on high-temperature ceramic superconductors, one at the University of Missouri suggested that the materials might be made at room temperature and in aqueous solution using electro-deposition techniques. A team of chemists at Oxford devised a way of making the carbon lattice compounds known as fullerenes in the form of molecular tubes closed at one end, like molecular test tubes, each able to hold individual atoms so that they might take part in carefully-controlled chemical reactions such as catalysis.

MEDICINE AND MOLECULAR BIOLOGY. Harsh statistics continued to emerge on the health risks of smoking. Britain's Imperial Cancer Research Fund announced the results of a 40-year study of the fate of more than 34,000 British doctors, showing that cigarette smoking accounted for the death of half of all regular smokers. In middle age, the total death rate among smokers was found to be three times greater than among non-smokers; on average, each cigarette reduced life expectancy by about six minutes. During 1994 smoking killed an estimated three million people worldwide, approximately one every ten seconds. According to global trends in smoking, the habit was predicted to kill ten million a year by the year 2020, making it the biggest single cause of adult death in the world. Better news from the same study showed that middle-aged men who had one or two alcoholic drinks a day lived longer on average than men who did not drink at all. Another study of 11,000 people in Britain compared the death rates of meat eaters and vegetarians over a 12-year period and found that the latter were 40 per cent less likely to die of cancer.

It was clear, however, that smoking was not the only cause of cancer. Two teams in the USA announced in September that they had found a gene (known as BRCA-1) which normally provided protection against cancer and that women in whom the gene was defective stood an up to 85 per cent chance of developing breast or ovarian cancer. Though the gene defect was rare, its discovery attracted great interest from those trying to understand the molecular mechanisms of cancer. It also raised ethical dilemmas about developing a test for the defect, since a positive result would not only seem like a death sentence but might also affect health insurance and employment prospects.

BRCA-1 was one of many genes attracting attention during 1994 for their role in cell death or apoptosis. Research showed that cells frequently divided naturally but that this process was normally controlled by the programmed suicide of surplus cells; only where things went wrong did cancer result. Another gene involved in programmed cell death and thus in tumour supression, called p53, had been implicated in a wide variety of human cancers. It was thought to be involved in recognizing damaged genes and in making cells containing them either die or stop dividing until the damage was repaired. Researchers at Dundee University found a way of repairing the function of defective p53 genes and predicted that it might lead to treatments for up to half of human cancers. Meanwhile, research continued on the natural mechanisms by which cells repaired their damaged genes, central to these bing a suite of natural DNA repair enzymes. During 1994 there were so many advances in the understanding of their form and function in many organisms that *Science* magazine declared them to be collectively the 'Molecules of the Year'.

Infectious diseases continued to take their toll around the world, even though many were treatable. Cholera broke out in a number of places, notably in Zaïre at Rwandan refugee camps (see VII.1.ii). An outbreak of disease around Surat in India was attributed to bubonic plague (see VIII.2.i), though some doubts were raised about this diagnosis. Cases of tuberculosis continued to rise, an estimated three million people dying of the disease during the year. The World Health Organization (WHO) reported cases of resistance in the schistosomiasis parasite to the drug praziquantel most commonly used to treat it. However, continued use of the drug ivermectin against the river blindness parasite led the WHO officials to hope that the disease might be eliminated from wide areas within ten years. They hoped the same would be true of tetanus within two years.

Malaria continued to take a toll, particularly the severe form, cerebral malaria. Research into what caused about 1 per cent of malaria victims develop the cerebral form found that a molecule called tumour necrosis factor (TNF) might be involved. TNF was also implicated in rheumatoid arthritis cases, where drugs to block it proved successful in early trials. Trials of a herbal extract called artemether, from a plant called qinghaosu, a Chinese malaria remedy, showed that it was indeed effective against that disease. Trials of a malaria vaccine developed in Colombia by Dr Manuel Patarroyo proved that it gave at least 40 per cent protection in South America and 31 per cent protection in southern Tanzania. Dr Patarroyo donated all rights to the vaccine to the WHO.

By the end of 1994 an estimated 17 million people were infected with the AIDS virus worldwide. Statistics suggested that Asia would soon rival Africa for prevalence of the disease. In spite of intensive research, the prospect of effective vaccines or cures still seemed remote. The drug AZT continued to delay the onset of symptoms but, by itself, seemed unable to postpone them forever. It did reduce considerably transmission of the virus from mother to baby, however. Several lines of research gave hope of better treatments and vaccines in the future, including the discovery that some prostitutes in West Africa had developed natural resistance to the virus.

Bacteria causing the disease necrotising faciitis caught headlines in Britain due to the alarming speed at which they spread through human tissue. But the so-called 'flesh-eating bug' claimed only a few lives. More serious was the continued spread of bacteria resistant to antibiotics, the WHO receiving reports of bacteria which, between them, were resistant to all known drugs. Procedures were recommended to prevent their spread, particularly in hospitals and through the excessive use of antibiotics.

Heart disease continued to be the biggest single cause of death in the developed world, much of it triggered by smoking and poor diet. British doctors predicted an epidemic of heart disease among women unless many more stopped smoking. Genetic engineers proposed one way in which they might boost the effects of a good diet: genetically engineered tomatoes with extra-high levels of carotenoids, the anti-oxidants known to ward off heart disease and cancer. Genetic engineers at London's St Mary's Hospital, using replacement human genes in a nasal spray of fatty droplets, announced a successful outcome for their first trial with 15 cystic fibrosis patients.

Potential new fertility treatments raised ethical issues in 1994. Thanks to the test-tube-baby procedure, a black Italian woman gave birth to a white baby, while another Italian woman became pregnant at the age of 62. Since baby girls already had a full complement of eggs in their ovaries before birth, doctors researched the possibility of using eggs from aborted foetuses to enable sterile women to have babies; but many people were shocked at the possibility of babies whose genetic mothers had never been born. In the USA, scientists successfully transplanted, from one mouse to another, testicle tissue which continued to function. In humans such a procedure could cure infertility, or allow more sinister selective breeding.

Genetic engineering made several advances for agriculture in 1994. British scientists found a gene used by plants to compete against each other for light by growing taller. Disabling it might allow crops to grow strong in the shade instead of becoming tall and weedy. Tests of an insect virus engineered with the scorpion venom gene to make it kill pests more quickly were conducted in fields in Oxfordshire, but were inconclusive and raised fears of the gene getting into other species. Fisheries scientists in the USA and Canada engineered salmon with extra growth hormone genes which grew 37 times the normal size in their first two years. Scientists at the International Rice Research Institute in the Philippines developed a breed of rice which could produce 25 per cent more grain on the same area of land.

NOBEL PRIZES. The 1994 Nobel Prize for Medicine or Physiology was awarded jointly to Alfred Gilman and Martin Rodbell of the USA for their discovery in the 1960s and 1970s of a family of natural proteins called G-proteins. These molecules switch cells into action in response to chemical messages from elsewhere in the body and their discovery led to insights into the mechanisms of many diseases.

The Chemistry Prize was awarded to the Hungarian-born US resident George Olah for research which showed how hydrocarbons could be made more reactive. It led the way to the manufacture of lead-free petrol. The Physics Prize was shared by Bertram Brockhouse of Canada and Clifford Shull of the USA for the development of neutron-scattering techniques used in the study of the properties of many different materials.

2. INFORMATION TECHNOLOGY

CONSUMER-orientated products/services and associated issues came into greater prominence in 1994—that is, products/services aimed at the general public rather than at specific groups of 'professionals' in the broadest sense, such as academics, researchers or business people. It was not that such services were new, for the 'mission' of the information technology industry had been articulated by the US software company, Microsoft, as long ago as 1975: a personal computer on every desk and

in every home. Moreover, attempts to attain this holy grail had been
evident in the early 1980s. For example, the Prestel service, launched
in 1979 by the then still state-owned British Telecommunications (BT),
had originally been popularist in concept, as was the Télétel service
initiated by France Télécom in 1984. Whilst the former changed its
focus after being launched, the latter achieved a measure of success,
with well over six million terminals in place by 1994, although the
principal use of the service remained the electronic telephone directory.
If not new, therefore, certainly the visibility of consumer-orientated
products/services was enhanced by various developments in 1994.

CONSUMER ONLINE INITIATIVES. Online information and communication services aimed at the general public had been available for some
years in North America, the three largest operators being Prodigy,
CompuServe and America Online. Even so, and despite dramatic
growth, the aggregate revenues of consumer online services were
reported to have reached no more than about $550 million in 1993.
In Europe, in contrast, consumer online had hitherto been the domain
of enthusiasts, with only one of the major US players being represented
in the market-place, namely CompuServe, whose subscriber base in the
UK was estimated as only about 70,000 at the end of 1994. In the course
of the year, however, several new services were announced.

In mid-1994 a German-led consortium, which included participation by
one of the founders of America Online, announced Europe Online
(EOL), with plans to offer electronic mail (e-mail), special-interest
bulletin boards, magazines, news, remote shopping and gateway access
to other online services. Later in the summer, the fifth largest US
operator, Delphi, which had been purchased in late 1993 by Rupert
Murdoch's News Corporation, became the first US service after Compu-
Serve actually to commence operations in Europe. Based in the UK,
Delphi aimed to offer, alongside e-mail and full Internet access, a
range of information and entertainment with a more local flavour
than had hitherto been available from CompuServe, including news
material from News International's UK portfolio, such as *The Times*
and the *Sunday Times*, and a facility for remote sampling ('try before
you buy', achieved by selective downloading of text) and ordering for
books published by HarperCollins. Subsequently, consortia headed by
the Italian company Olivetti Telemedia announced first Italia Online
and then, in December, UK Online (UKOL). Again, the new services
planned to emphasize their local information and entertainment content,
together with transactional services like home shopping and theatre
booking.

Meanwhile, in the USA, moves towards the commercialization of the
Internet continued, despite the difficulties of security still presented
by the system and despite the fact that such developments remained

contentious and were opposed by some academics (see AR 1993, pp. 461). One noteworthy and symptomatic event was the purchase in summer 1994 of Internet Shopping Network (ISN) by Home Shopping Network (HSN), proprietor of the largest cable television shopping channel in the USA. The most remarkable aspect of the transaction was that ISN, set up in June 1993, had commenced selling activity over the Internet only about three months before it was swallowed up by HSN in what looked like an eager attempt to gain the initiative in this area. Preparations also continued in the USA for the introduction by Time Warner, the country's second largest cable television operator, of a 'full service network'—a multimedia interactive television service featuring home shopping, games and information. BT in the UK was reported to be laying similar plans and during 1994 commenced trials, in a small number of selected homes, of a video-on-demand service delivered via the telephone network.

OTHER ONLINE INITIATIVES. Apple eWorld and The Microsoft Network (TMN) were also announced during 1994. Although the focus of these online services was neither specific to Europe nor to consumers, both were expected to have a worldwide impact and to extend quickly to users in all parts of the spectrum. Microsoft's initiative, in particular, had major implications, because of the company's position as the supplier of an estimated 85 per cent of all personal computer operating systems and because access to TMN was to be incorporated in the next generation of the 'Windows' operating system, due to come on to the market in summer 1995. TMN was not intended to be a proprietary online publishing operation for Microsoft alone, but rather a generic electronic trading environment in which all types of 'content providers' (i.e. companies offering information or entertainment software) could participate. Accordingly, in late 1994 Microsoft embarked upon a major publisher relations programme aimed at attracting the participation of publishers in TMN. A key element of the Microsoft approach was to offer publishers charging mechanisms which would permit them to enjoy more than the 20–30 per cent typically available from other online services. Interactive advertising was also to be built into the network.

Ambition on the part of Microsoft to reach into the consumer market had also been underlined by its acquisition during the year, subject to regulatory approval, of Intuit, a software house which developed personal and small-business financial software, notably a product known as 'Quicken'. It was anticipated that the move would facilitate the introduction on Microsoft's network of a range of financial services.

DIGITAL VIDEO AND TELEVISION. Towards the end of the year the Dutch consumer electronics company Philips and the Japanese company Sony, which had worked together in developing CD-I (Compact Disc–

Interactive—see AR 1993, pp. 462–3), announced their specification for a high-density CD-ROM (Compact Disc Read Only Memory) format, still based upon the standard 12-centimetre disc size. The new disc format offered a storage capacity of 3.7 gigabytes (3,700 megabytes), plus the option to double that capacity by providing a second layer of data which could be read by altering the focus of the laser used to read the disc.

At the time, standard CD-ROMs had a capacity of 650 megabytes (650 million bytes), which was adequate for a very wide range of purposes, including 'multimedia' applications involving a combination of text, graphics, sound, still photography and moving pictures. However, because of the substantial storage needs of full-motion video (even using compression technology), the playing-time of a single disc (approximately 75 minutes) was insufficient for most full-length feature films. Using the latest compression standard for motion pictures in digital form promulgated by the Moving Pictures Experts Group (MPEG-2), the Philips/Sony system, scheduled to be launched commercially in late 1996, made possible the distribution on disc of even the longest feature films with a quality of picture and sound at least as good as the best available analogue systems.

Since several companies in the sector had been working on higher density CD storage, the announcement by Philips and Sony was to some extent pre-emptive, in that they clearly hoped to establish their specification as a worldwide standard. They were well-placed to achieve this ambition, given the position already held by VideoCD, developed by Philips and already accepted as a *de facto* standard by leading film distribution companies (see AR 1993, p. 462). Earlier in the year, International Business Machines (IBM) had revealed that it had obtained a ten-fold increase in storage capacity by laminating together ten CD-ROMs and using a CD-ROM drive with a variable-focus laser. The Japanese companies Pioneer and Toshiba, together with Time Warner of the USA, had also publicized work on a high-density disc format. Their format promised a capacity of 4.8 gigabytes, with the option to double that figure by using both sides of the disc. The development of high-density CD storage foreshadowed the demise not only of the 12-inch analogue videodisc, which had hitherto offered superior picture quality, but also, in the medium term, of the widely-used VHS video cassette.

Meanwhile, quite early in the year, it had become clear that consensus in the USA amongst television manufacturers, including the two European-based giants (Philips of the Netherlands and Thomson of France), meant that the US standard on digital high-definition television (HDTV) would be likely to prevail internationally. Previous European initiatives aimed at establishing a European analogue HDTV standard had come to naught. Furthermore, at much the same time, the Japanese Ministry of

Posts and Telecommunications indicated that it was willing to consider digital technology as an alternative to the analogue HDTV system already in operation, known as Hi-Vision.

EUROPEAN UNION ACTIVITY. In December 1993 the EU Council of Ministers had debated and approved the European Commission's White Paper entitled *Growth, Competitiveness, Employment—The Challenges and Ways Forward into the 21st Century* (see AR 1993, p. 405). This was followed in mid-1994 by a paper focusing more specifically on information technology, entitled *Europe and the Global Information Society*, commonly referred to as the Bangemann Report, since the group which had prepared the recommendations had been chaired by Commissioner Martin Bangemann. The report was endorsed at the EU's Corfu summit in June (see also XI.3) and prompted a swift response from the Commission, entitled *Europe's Way to the Information Society: An Action Plan*. These various documents served to raise levels of consciousness. Information super-highways and multimedia passed into everyday EU vocabulary, and high-profile attention at Commission and ministerial level enhanced expectations in this area.

Specific action ensued in the shape of the detailed work-plans set out in the 'fourth framework programme' of activity in the field of research and technological development (covering the period 1994–98), which were developed and approved during the course of 1994. Three important programmes within the very broad category 'information and communications technologies' were worthy of note, namely the information technology (IT) programme, with a budget of 1,930 million ecu, the telematics applications programme (TAP), with a budget of 843 million ecu, and the advanced communications technologies and services (ACTS) programme, with a budget of over 600 million ecu.

LEGAL AND REGULATORY AFFAIRS. The upheaval in the industry caused by the granting to US CD-ROM publisher Compton's NewMedia of a patent with particularly wide scope (see AR 1993, pp. 463–4) continued for a good part of the year. In a most unusual move, the US Patent Office reviewed its original decision on the patent and reversed it in March, but the matter did not rest there, as Compton's made some modifications to its claims and filed a revised application during the summer.

Microsoft, which had been under investigation in 1993 by the US Justice Department (see AR 1993, pp. 464), succeeded in reaching an accommodation in the form of a consent decree, subject to court approval, in which the company agreed to modify some of its licensing practices relating to personal computer operating systems.

Finally, the Financial Times Group emerged relatively unscathed from a year-long inquiry initiated by the UK Monopolies and Mergers Commission (MMC) during 1993 (see AR 1993, pp. 464), which probed its policies concerning online access and the licensing of electronic rights relating to the *Financial Times* newspaper. The MMC found that the *FT*—and indeed DataStar-Dialog, which had not been cited in the referral by the director-general of fair trading—did have a monopoly position in relation to the market for online databases containing archival business and financial information; but it did not regard this as an unassailable advantage in a highly competitive market.

3.   THE ENVIRONMENT

THE environment continued to decline as a major political issue in 1994, despite some unseasonable weather which focused people's attention on the possibility of a change in climate driven by pollution. Globally, the year was either the third or the fourth warmest year on record, according to the UK Meteorological Office, which needed more statistics before making a final decision. It was cooler than 1990 (warmest ever) and 1991 (second warmest), about equal to 1988 and warmer than 1992 and 1993. The Met Office noted that the planet seemed to be warming up again after the cooling effect of the eruption of Mount Pinatubo in the Philippines in June 1991 (see AR 1991, pp. 339, 457). This had injected millions of tonnes of dust into the atmosphere, blocking sunlight and cooling the surface of the planet by up to 0.5 C for a period in 1992. Central and Eastern Europe had especially hot summers in 1994, and November was the hottest in the 336-year-old Central England Temperature record for that month.

The 1994 warmth was also associated with the continuing El Niño event in the tropical Pacific, resulting in the warming of the Indian Ocean and western North America (see also IV.2). This syndrome had been accompanied by drought in Australia and floods in California, and had lasted since late 1990, considerably longer than the usual span of one or two years. A warmer climate was consistent with computer models suggesting that rising amounts of carbon dioxide and other 'greenhouse gases' would raise average global temperatures and cause more weather events associated with increased energy in the atmosphere, such as typhoons and hurricanes. But there was no proof that current weather was caused by such pollution.

Meanwhile, a number of important environmentalist groups continued to experience falls in membership, financial contributions and influence. This trend had begun during, and had been blamed on, the 1990–91 recession, but had continued since then. Greenpeace International, having lost almost a third of its membership since 1990, announced plans in 1994 to cut its international operating budget by $3 million and to decrease its staff by 8 per cent. It also announced a split approach under which it would henceforth work in partnership with the business sector, where appropriate, while continuing to mount publicity-seeking demonstrations against specific businesses, where appropriate.

Groups in the United States suffered similar problems. The Wilderness Society lost a third of its members over 1990–94, while membership of the conservative Sierra Club dropped from 600,000 to 500,000. Membership in the US groups had increased rapidly during the years of the 'anti-environment' Reagan presidency, but had begun to decline following the advent of the avowedly more environment-friendly Clinton administration in January 1993.

In January 50 countries involved in the tropical timber trade signed a new International Tropical Timber Agreement (ITTA), 27 of the signatories being consumers and 23 producers. Requiring formal ratification, the pact recorded that the need to conserve the world's forests was equal to the need to profit by them. The negotiators described this statement as a first for a commodity treaty. But many environmental groups charged that the document dodged important issues related to deforestation. The consumer countries, mainly in the North, defeated the efforts of tropical countries to expand the agreement to cover all productive forests, North and South. Signed in Geneva, the new ITTA replaced the 1983 agreement of the same name, which expired in March 1994.

In March the 64 nations which had signed the 1989 Basle Convention on the Trans-boundary Movement of Hazardous Waste agreed on a ban on the export of all such wastes from industrial to developing nations. The ban on exporting waste for disposal was to take effect immediately; a ban on waste 'for recycling' was to come into force from the end of 1997. Australia, Britain, Canada, Germany and Japan had initially opposed the move, as had the United States, which was not a signatory to the Basel Convention. Greenpeace and other environmental groups had campaigned for the total ban.

In June delegates from 25 European countries and Canada signed a pact to reduce sulphur emissions (a key cause of acid rain). The agreement was a protocol of the 1979 Convention on Long-range Trans-boundary Air Pollution and replaced a 1985 protocol by which the signatories had agreed to cut emissions by 30 per cent by the end of 1993. Most had achieved this goal. Under the latest pact, governments set their own targets. Austria, Denmark, Finland and Sweden set targets of 80 per cent reductions (from 1980 levels) by the year 2000; Britain chose 80 per cent by 2010. The most ambitious target was Germany's (87 per cent by 2000) and the least ambitious was Canada's (30 per cent by 2000). The United States declined to sign the agreement, arguing that its Clean Air Act was adequate.

In October the world discovered that oil was leaking from a 20-year-old pipeline in the Komi republic of the Russian Federation (see also III.2.i). The leak reportedly began in February but was contained by dams until heavy rains in August. There was considerable disagreement about the scale and damage of the pollution, some US estimates putting the oil lost at two million barrels, while Russian estimates were closer to 200,000 barrels.

In May delegates to the 46th annual meeting of the International Whaling Commission (IWC) in Puerto Vallarta (Mexico) voted by the necessary three-quarters majority to establish an Antarctic whale sanctuary south of the 40th parallel, to be overseen by Australia. The move had been proposed by France and, being connected to a refuge in the Indian Ocean, was thought likely to afford protection to 80–90 per cent of the world's whale population. As whaling nations, Japan and Norway denounced the move. Norway did not attend the Mexico meeting and Japan was the only nation to vote against the move. Norway had decided in 1993 to break the moratorium on commercial whaling, while Iceland (the other main whaling nation) had withdrawn from the IWC in 1992 (see AR 1993, pp. 72, 75).

Florida was the location of a meeting in November of the signatories of the Convention on International Trade in Endangered Species (CITES), under which animal and plant species were placed on various lists determining the extent to which they could be traded internationally. Environmentalists fought before and at the meeting for some limit on exports of broadleaf mahogany, but were defeated. South Africa withdrew a proposal to allow trade in elephant parts such as hides and meat (but not ivory), but was successful in a bid to allow the export of live white rhino and to allow hunters to take trophies out of the country. China, India and eight other Asian countries agreed to enact legislation to ban trade in tiger organs and to improve the protection of tiger habitats. The meeting approved a US proposal for studies of shark species with a view to placing limits on the numbers that could be taken for the growing trade in shark fins and other products.

In October delegates from 100 nations meeting in Paris signed the UN Convention on Desertification, agreed at the UN Conference on Environment and Development (the 'Earth Summit') in 1992 (see AR 1992, pp. 458-60). The convention committed governments to repair and prevent land degradation, largely in the drier tropics, and envisaged that the work would be paid for mainly by the richer, temperate nations, particularly through their contributions to the Global Environment Facility. UNESCO (which hosted the signing meeting) and other UN bodies estimated that it would cost between $10,000 million and $22,000 million annually over the next two decades to arrest desertification, currently affecting about a fifth of the planet's land mass. No-one expected anywhere near these amounts to become available.

In early March the High Court in London rejected an application for a judicial review of the government's approval in 1993 of the start-up of operations at the Thorp nuclear reprocessing plant at Sellafield in Cumbria (see AR 1993, pp. 467-8). Operated by British Nuclear Fuels, the Thorp plant was capable of reprocessing 7,000 tonnes of spent nuclear fuel a year and had already accepted shipments from Japan for reprocessing into uranium and plutonium for nuclear power plants. Protesters had argued that there should have been a public inquiry on the plant, while environmentalists claimed that the facility increased the dangers of nuclear proliferation.

The British Prime Minister, John Major, announced in June that his government would ratify the international Biodiversity Convention, which had also been agreed at the 1992 Earth Summit and had entered into force in late 1993 (see AR 1993, p. 465). In late November the first conference of the parties (COP) to this convention began a two-week meeting in Nassau (Bahamas) with about 1,000 government and environmental group delegates present. Little was decided, other than that the UN Environment Programme (UNEP) should provide a permanent secretariat for the convention and that another COP would be held in late 1995. The developing countries (tending to have the biodiversity) accused the industrial countries (tending to have the money) of not being willing to spend money on protecting biodiversity.

In October the first-ever Central American summit on ecological issues was held in Managua (Nicaragua), attended by the Presidents of Costa Rica, El Salvador, Guatemala, Honduras, Nicaragua and Panama, with US Vice-President Al Gore present as an observer. The meeting created a special fund for environmental projects, agreed to establish a 'biological corridor' in Central America and decided to set up an inventory of endangered species. They also signed an 'alliance for sustainable development'.

In a referendum held in February Swiss voters approved a ban on foreign lorry transit through Switzerland within ten years as well as a ban on the construction of more transit motorways (see also II.2.vii). International freight would have to be shifted to rail at the borders, the aim being to protect the Alpine region against pollution from motor traffic. The vote caused concern among Switzerland's neighbours, particularly Italy and Germany, in view of the large (and growing) amount of road freight traffic passing through Switzerland, concentrated on the St Gotthard Pass route.

Most environmental groups welcomed the results of September's International Conference on Population and Development, organized in Cairo by the UN Fund for Population Activities (see also XI.1). The gathering of over 20,000 delegates agreed a 113-page programme of action aimed at stabilizing global population in the 21st century. Its proposals, some of which were opposed by the Vatican and by many Catholic and Muslim countries (see also II.2.viii; Pt. XIII), featured increased education and empowerment of women. Environmentalists felt that this approach would also result in more effective management of environmental resources.

On 16 November the 1982 UN Convention on the Law of the Sea finally entered into force, a year after its ratification by 60 states. Much of the treaty had been essentially in effect, through national laws, before the treaty came into force, including the 200-nautical-mile exclusive economic zones. In theory, at least, these gave nations more control over their fish stocks and pollution from ships.

XV THE LAW

i. INTERNATIONAL LAW

THE International Court of Justice (ICJ) delivered two judgments, both about boundary delimitation, the largest single category of cases decided by the Court. In *Qatar* v. *Bahrain*, the Court pronounced on jurisdiction and admissibility. Qatar had filed an application instituting proceedings about sovereignty over the Hawar Islands and sovereign rights over the shoals of Dibal and Qitat Jaradah, and also seeking the delimitation of the maritime areas of the two states. It founded the Court's jurisdiction on two agreements concluded in 1987 and 1990. Bahrain contested jurisdiction, saying that the 1990 agreement was merely the minutes of a meeting and thus not legally binding, and that anyhow neither agreement enabled Qatar to seise the Court unilaterally. Bahrain also argued that the subsequent conduct of the parties showed that they did not consider the 1990 minutes to be binding. But the Court held that the 1990 agreement did create rights and obligations in international law; non-registration or late registration of a treaty with the United Nations and the Arab League did not affect its validity.

The Court then considered the content of the two agreements. The 1987 agreement provided that 'all disputed matters' should be referred to the ICJ; these were determined in the 1990 minutes to be any matter of territorial rights and interests. But Bahrain argued that Qatar's application did not cover all the matters in dispute and was therefore inadmissible. The Court consequently decided to afford the parties the opportunity to ensure submission of the entire dispute. The parties made further submissions and on 12 December the Court declared itself ready to resume dealing with the case.

In *Libya* v. *Chad*, the Court on 3 February decided the merits of the longstanding dispute concerning the boundary between the two states and sovereignty over the Aouzou Strip (see also V.4.ii; VI.3.x). Libya argued that there was no existing boundary and that the case involved attribution of territory; Chad said that there was an existing boundary, determined by the 1955 France–Libya Friendship Treaty, and that the dispute was over the location of this boundary. The Court found that both states accepted the validity of the 1955 treaty and that they had in this treaty recognized the frontiers set out in various instruments contained in an annex. Libya argued that these instruments were no longer in force and therefore could not now establish a boundary. But the Court rejected this, saying that the effectiveness principle of treaty interpretation, the object and purpose of the treaty and the context of its conclusion all showed that it had established a boundary.

The Court then accepted Chad's claim as to the actual line of the boundary established by the treaty, and confirmed this finding on the basis of the subsequent attitudes of the parties. Finally, the Court held that the 1955 treaty did establish a permanent frontier even though the treaty itself was concluded for 25 years only and was subject to unilateral denunciation. Nothing in the treaty indicated that the boundary agreed was to be provisional or temporary. The boundary had a legal life of its own independent of the fate of the 1955 treaty; any other approach would vitiate the fundamental principle of the stability of boundaries. The Court thus recognized Chad's sovereignty over the Aouzou Strip (from which Libya withdrew in May).

Two new cases were brought to the Court. The Federal Republic Yugoslavia (Serbia and Montenegro) claimed that the member states of NATO, by their decision of 9 February to respond to the UN request for air strikes to protect Sarajevo (see also III.1.vi; XI.1; XII.2), had breached the UN Charter by threatening to use force without the authorization of the Security Council and in the form of an ultimatum. However, this was a unilateral application and the defendant states did not consent to the Court's jurisdiction. Cameroon brought an action against Nigeria on 29 March, not only claiming sovereignty over the oil-rich Bakassi peninsula and asking the Court to determine part of the maritime boundary, but also seeking a declaration that Nigeria had illegally used force and occupied the peninsula (see also VI.3.ix). On 6 June Cameroon made an additional application asking the Court to specify definitively the frontier from Lake Chad to the sea.

On 23 December the UN General Assembly made a request for an advisory opinion by the ICJ on the question, 'Is the threat or use of nuclear weapons in any circumstances permitted under international law?'. This request supplemented that made by the WHO in 1993 (see AR 1993, p. 469).

Judge *ad hoc* Ruda and Judge Tarassov (a member of the Court since 1985) both died during the year. On 7 February Judge Mohammed Bedjaoui (Algeria) was elected president of the ICJ, in succession to Sir Robert Jennings (UK), and Judge Stephen M. Schwebel (USA) was elected as vice-president, both to serve three-year terms.

The law of the sea saw two crucial developments in 1994: the coming into force of the 1982 UN Convention on the Law of the Sea on 16 November and the adoption by the UN General Assembly (by 121 votes to none with seven abstentions) of an 'agreement relating to the implementation of Part XI' of the convention. The former codified the whole law of the sea and had already had a substantial impact on the development of customary international law (see also XI.1; XIV.3). It created new treaty rules on the exclusive economic zone, straits, archipelagoes and conservation and identified new boundaries for the territorial sea, contiguous zone and continental shelf. Most controversially, in Part XI it created an elaborate regime on the deep seabed. This last part had proved unacceptable to the USA and to other developed states, and they had refused to ratify the convention. In order to secure universal participation, the UN Secretary-General had initiated consultations in July 1990 which led to the 1994 agreement, fundamentally modifying the seabed regime of Part XI. In adopting the agreement, the General Assembly said that political and economic changes, including a growing reliance on market principles, had shown the need to re-evaluate the 1982 regime.

The 1994 agreement addressed all the concerns of the USA, while preserving the principle of the common heritage of mankind and a UN-administered system of mining. It also preserved the institutional structure of Part XI but scaled it down and gave the USA and other developed states stronger representation on the decision-making Council. The 1982 provisions on mandatory technology transfer, on the financing of the new institutions and on production limits were all modified; levies payable by deep-sea mining companies were reduced; and licences granted to companies by developed states were given protection. The 1982 convention and the 1994 agreement were to be interpreted and applied as a single instrument; in the event of inconsistency, the agreement was to prevail. The latter was to come into force when 40 states which were also parties to the convention had consented. By the end of 1994, over 50 states, including the USA and almost all developed states, had signed the agreement.

States continued to build on the achievements of the 1992 Rio Earth Summit (see AR 1992, pp. 458–60, 546–52). Following the entry into force of the UN Convention on Biological Diversity on 29 December 1993 (see AR 1993, p. 465), the UN Convention on Climate Change came into force on 21 March. The International Tropical Timber Agreement (the first international instrument to stress the sustainable management of forests) and the UN Convention to Combat Desertification were also opened for signature, in April and October respectively (see XIV.3).

Other international treaty-making included the Convention to Ensure the Safety and Security of UN and Associated Personnel, which was opened for signature on 9 December. It obliged states to establish jurisdiction over crimes against UN personnel and defined the duties of states to ensure the safety and security of personnel. The Organization of American States (OAS) adopted two human rights treaties on 9 June, on 'the forced disappearance of persons' and on 'the prevention, punishment and eradication of violence against women'.

In the area of international criminal jurisdiction, the UN Tribunal for the former Yugoslavia (see AR 1993, p. 469) held its first public hearing and issued its first indictment; it requested Germany to extradite a Bosnian Serb. The UN Security Council also agreed on 8 November to establish another tribunal, to try crimes of genocide, crimes against humanity and violations of humanitarian law committed in 1994 in Rwanda and neighbouring states (see also VII.1.ii; XI.1).

The reform of the European Convention on Human Rights system for the protection of human rights continued with the opening for signature of the 11th Protocol on 11 May (see also XI.5.iii). This streamlined the protection mechanisms by replacing the present part-time Commission and Court with a single, full-time Court, with new powers, functions and composition. The Court was to consist of one judge from each member state, elected by the respective national parliaments; but the full plenary Court would deal only with matters of procedure and administration, the majority of cases being heard by chambers consisting of seven judges. The Grand Chamber of 17 judges would hear cases sent to it by chambers where the case involved a serious question affecting the interpretation of the convention or where a judgment might be inconsistent with earlier jurisprudence. The Grand Chamber would also decide cases referred to it by one of the parties for rehearing in the event of there being a serious question affecting the interpretation or application of the convention or a serious issue of general importance. This unusual provision was adopted as a political compromise in order to induce states to accept the mandatory right of individual and inter-state petition and the mandatory jurisdiction of the Court. The 11th Protocol would come into force on ratification by all states parties (currently 28) to the convention. Meanwhile, the more limited procedural reforms of the 9th Protocol, allowing individuals increased access to the Court, came into force on 1 October.

ii.   EUROPEAN COMMUNITY LAW

THIS was a strange year for the European lawyer, a year of change and yet not of finality. Much of the change was temporary, looking forward to further change, and yet more beyond that. Problems with the Maastricht Treaty itself—officially the Treaty on European Union (TEU)—emerged immediately as a result of technical confusion over nomenclature. What was the Union? Did the Communities/Community survive or had they become absorbed? What now was the grouping's law to be called? And what was the law itself? Eventually, some sort of consensus emerged (with, however, some persistent dissidents): to retain 'Community' for the law but to use 'European Union' (EU) for the organization and for politics. Even more importantly, Community law remained what it was and continued to develop as before.

The year opened not only with the TEU effectively beginning its life (it had actually come into force two months earlier, in November 1993) but also with the advent of the European Economic Area (EEA). As a consequence, five of the seven EFTA countries (the exceptions being Switzerland and Liechtenstein) were brought within the territorial coverage of Community law. That in itself required lawyers in the Union to extend their horizons and apply their rules (particularly those on free movement) to situations in which EFTA nationals and companies appeared. For the EFTA/EEA states themselves, the change was much more traumatic. They were now confronted with the new EEA institutions, and especially the two major new EFTA bodies: the EFTA Court and the EFTA Surveillance Authority (ESA). These both opened their doors on 1 January and had got fully into their stride by the spring. Throughout the year the ESA showed a vigour and efficacy in applying Community competition law which was worthy of the Commission's competition directorate itself; it also exercised its general law enforcement powers by instituting proceedings against some EFTA states before the EFTA Court. The EFTA Court quickly settled down too. It was a small court with only five bench members (a Finnish president and Norwegian, Swedish, Austrian and Finnish judges), supported by a Swedish registrar, a Finnish librarian and an English press officer. Being such a small court, it did not sit in chambers or use an advocate-general. Also, like all other EFTA institutions, it used English as its only official language, and so had no need of translators or interpreters. By the end of the year it had delivered its first judgment—on the Finnish state alcohol monopoly, on reference by a Finnish court—and had several others on its register.

It looked, therefore, as though the virtual enlargement of the Community/Union by means of the EEA was going to proceed smoothly. But the process was put in question by the actual enlargement. Four of the EFTA/EEA states successfully concluded their negotiations for accession to the EU. Of these, Norway produced a negative referendum result (as it had in 1972) and withdrew from its accession treaty (see II.2.iii; XI.3). The other three applicants (Austria, Sweden and Finland) all obtained positive referendum verdicts (see II.2.iv–vi) and so, at midnight at the end of 1994, transferred from the EFTA side to the EU side of the EEA. That meant that they also withdrew from the EFTA institutions, including the Court and the Surveillance Authority, leaving those bodies with only Iceland and Norway as members. The question was whether that would be enough to keep them viable.

Towards the year's end Liechtenstein—whose referendum vote had been in favour of joining the EEA but which had had to hold back because of its monetary union with Switzerland—was able to negotiate a means of joining the EEA nonetheless. This would bring the number of EFTA/EEA members to three, perhaps enough to keep the Court and the ESA in operation. It was originally expected that the Swedish, Finnish and Austrian judges would immediately leave the EFTA Court and transfer to the European Court of Justice (ECJ) in Luxembourg. In the event, only the Finnish president, Leif Sevon, made the move, to become the Finnish judge on the ECJ. Otherwise, the new EU member states all appointed different jurists to the ECJ, leaving the EFTA Court with a Norwegian president, a new Finnish judge and a prospective nominee from Liechtenstein.

The political aspects of the EEA did not cause any problems, the updating of the *acquis communautaire* being duly accomplished by the EEA Joint Committee. This was necessary because the EFTA/EEA states had undertaken to adopt Community law only as it was at the date of signature of the EEA in May 1992. It was necessary, therefore, to include any Community legislation adopted after that date by means of an addendum to the EEA. This addendum took the form of a decision of the Joint Committee amending the annexes to the EEA containing the lists of current Community legislation which constituted the *acquis* for EEA purposes.

Because the three prospective EU member states were already members of the EEA, their accession to the Union was straightforward, since most Community law was already applicable internally. It did, however, give rise to one somewhat Byzantine affair, relating to the changed majority voting figures in the enlarged Council. The United Kingdom somewhat tetchily insisted on maintaining the existing blocking minority vote in absolute terms, even if that meant a reduction of the blocking percentage (see I.1). A fudged solution was cobbled together and adopted as the so-called 'Ioannina compromise', named after the Greek town in which it was reached. The UK government yielded on an increase in the post-enlargment blocking vote, on the basis that a minority vote at the previous level would delay legislation for a 'reasonable period' in which consensus would be sought.

Judicial activity showed some interesting developments, particularly on the management level. There had been much concern within the administration of the ECJ about the delay in reporting its judgments, which was partly due to the overloading of the Court's translation department. To cut through this, two remedies were introduced. As from January 1994, the ECJ was no longer required to report (and so no longer had to translate) the 'report for the hearing' containing a summary of the facts of, and arguments in, cases before it. The 18-month backlog of unreported cases from 1992–93 was put out to private translators. These measures allowed the Court to put its reports onto a normal publication schedule: for the first time, *European Court Reports* (the English title) came out promptly in its various language versions. The January 1994 issue (covering judgments delivered in January) appeared in April, and the same efficiency was maintained throughout the year (as compared with the previous standard delay of 18–24 months). The Court of First Instance, which had never published a 'report for the hearing', chose another solution for its contribution to the speed-up. In view of the very slight public interest among lawyers in its judgments on staff disputes within the Community institutions (for which it acted as a sort of labour tribunal), it took the radical step of omitting most of these cases altogether and reporting only the more significant, thereby saving an immense translation resource. But as if to undermine the effect of this valiant effort by the European courts, the EU publications office decided to raise the annual subscription price by 76 per cent.

Judicial highlights of the year included an August judgment striking down an executive agreement between the European Commission and the US Justice Department on cooperation in anti-trust procedures, on the ground that it was an inter-state treaty and therefore required the full Community treaty-making procedure to be followed (under the control of the Council). In the *Heiztechnik* case, the ECJ clarified very elegantly the new basis for handling free movement of trade-marked goods where the mark itself was fragmented under different owners in different member states—an issue which had not been fully resolved by the *Cafe HAG II* judgment of 1990 (see AR 1990, p. 474). The English Court of Appeal produced a curious but potentially revolutionary pair of judgments. In *Chiron Corp.* v. *Murex Diagnostics Ltd.*, it first said (following its previous case law) that it was not bound by Article 177(3) EC to refer questions to the ECJ because its superior court was the House of Lords (even if it refused leave to go there). A month later, however, it held in *Lloyd's* v. *Clementson* that it would consistently exercise its discretion under paragraph (2) of the article to make such references to the ECJ unless the case was *acte clair*. The effect was that, although the Court of Appeal did not feel obliged to make references to the ECJ under Article 177(3), it would in fact behave as though it were, as a matter of its own judicial policy. This approach, if maintained, would solve decades of argument over the position of the Court of Appeal in matters of Community law.

2.   LAW IN THE UNITED KINGDOM

IN a potentially very sensitive constitutional decision, the Divisional Court refused to accept jurisdiction to prevent the Crown acceding to the Maastricht Treaty.[1] In other important rulings, the House of Lords held that the rules providing for less generous payments for unfair dismissal or redundancy for part-time workers than for full-time workers were incompatible with the relevant provisions of European Community law.[2] Greater control over state agencies—in this

case previously unregulated branches of the intelligence services—was
achieved by the *Security Services Act*. The Home Secretary was held
by the Court of Appeal to have abused his powers in purporting to
implement a scheme for the compensation of criminal injuries which
was inconsistent with the existing statutory scheme,[3] while the Divisional
Court held that the Foreign Secretary had acted improperly in spending
money on the Pergau Dam project.[4]

Freedom of newspaper reporting was considered on a number of
occasions by the courts. The Court of Appeal refused to prohibit reports
of the trial of a man charged with the abduction of a ward of court,[5] or of
a man charged with paedophiliac offences, even though the publication
of such reports might cause embarrassment to his children.[6] A mother
failed to obtain an injunction against her former husband, a trans-
sexual, to prevent him giving interviews to a newspaper when she feared
that this would have adverse effects on the children.[7] The provisions
of the *Contempt of Court Act 1981* preventing the disclosure of jury
deliberations were held to apply to the publication by a newspaper
of information relating to the conduct of a jury, even though that
information might have been disclosed previously.[8] But reports of the
use by jurors of an ouija board in an attempt to determine the truth
of a case attracted no prosecution; the jurors' conduct was held to be
sufficiently irregular to demand that there should be a retrial.[9] The
boundaries of public interest immunity were prospectively explored in
a court decision that a chief constable had acted properly in refusing
to give an undertaking to complainants of police misconduct that the
details of their complaints would not be disclosed in any subsequent
legal proceedings.[10]

A number of important statutes were passed in the interests of
consumers. Many of the restrictions which had formerly applied to
the retail trade were removed: the *Sunday Trading Act* allowed shops
to open on Sundays, although the opening of most large stores was
limited to six hours; trading freedom was further enhanced by the
Deregulation and Contracting Out Act, which abolished a wide range
of minor regulatory provisions. The *Sale of Goods (Amendment) Act*
abolished the old rules on the passing of title to goods sold in market
overt, while the *Sale and Supply of Goods Act* updated the law relating
to the implication of terms in consumer contracts. Developments in the
law of commercial contracts was more the preserve of the courts: the
Privy Council held that cargo owners were bound by the terms of a
sub-bailment which had been made with their approval;[11] and the legal
rules determining the passage of title in goods were upheld by the Privy
Council in *re Goldcorp Exchange*,[12] despite a strong argument that the
rules of equity might have justified some variation in them.

Among other statutes were three measures regulating very different
concerns: the coal industry was put on a new statutory footing in

the *Coal Industry Act*, enabling it to move into the private sector; governmental regulation of the educational services was yet further increased by the *Education Act*, introducing new provisions for the training of teachers and imposing restrictions on the powers of student unions; and the chiropractic profession was regulated for the first time.[13] Three statutes were passed to give effect to significant new international obligations: the *Trade Marks Act*, following a European directive for the harmonization of the laws on the subject in member states; the *Merchant Shipping (Salvage and Pollution) Act*; and the *Drug Trafficking Act*. The *Social Security (Incapacity for Work) Act* abolished sickness benefit and invalidity benefit, replacing them with a streamlined, though less generous, incapacity benefit. Improved remedies for racial discrimination were introduced in the *Race Relations (Remedies) Act*.

The Court of Appeal held that administrators of an insolvent company might impliedly adopt employment contracts of the company, and in such cases claims might gain priority in the administration or (in some situations) lie against the administrators personally.[14] The potentially undesirable effects of this decision were rapidly mitigated by the *Insolvency Act*. A contract between the liquidators of a company with undisclosed backers whereby the backers would finance litigation on behalf of the company in exchange for half of the proceeds of any successful lawsuits was held to be champertous, and the Chancery Division ordered a stay of the actions so financed.[15]

A number of changes in the law of civil procedure were introduced. The House of Lords overruled an earlier decision of the Divisional Court, holding that a nuisance abatement notice continued to be enforceable after the statute under which it had been issued had been repealed; but in another case they stressed that any retroactive effect of a statute had to be assessed by standards of fairness.[17] The Court of Appeal gave guidance on the procedure for expediting appeals[18] and the circumstances in which a wasted costs order, imposing liability for costs on a party's legal adviser, could be made;[19] and the Divisional Court provided guidelines for the award of costs against justices personally.

Far more important were the changes concerning the rules of criminal practice and procedure. The *Criminal Justice and Public Order Act* introduced wholesale reforms of the administration of justice and the rules of criminal evidence and procedure. Among other reforms of the prison service, it made provision for the introduction of a new system of punishment of young offenders;[21] increased the powers of the police to take bodily samples,[22] and to stop and search vehicles;[23] and gave to courts and juries the power to make adverse inferences from an accused person's silence during investigation or trial.[24] The act introduced a number of new criminal offences relating to public order, including a widely-drawn offence of aggravated trespass,[25] and significantly increased the powers of the police to control potentially disruptive assemblies.[26] The act further reformed the law relating to sexual offences, introducing an offence of rape on a man,[27] and lowering the age of consent to private homosexual acts from 21 to 18.[28] The passing of the act was itself the cause of considerable public disorder.[29]

The Divisional Court abolished the (rebuttable) presumption that a child aged between ten and 14 did not know that what he or she was doing was seriously wrong, holding that it was no longer necessary for the prosecution to provide evidence that the child was so aware.[30] It reinforced the principle that a person held in custody was entitled to consult a solicitor, and laid down ground rules for the operation of this principle.[31] In a series of cases, the Court of Appeal clarified the rules relating to the admissibility of evidence that might have been obtained by collusion.[32] Evidence obtained by tapping conversations on a mobile telephone was held to be admissible, and not governed by the rules laid down in the *Interception of Communications Act 1985*.[33]

The courts were also very active in the field of substantive criminal law. The Court of Appeal reiterated that in imposing liability for attempted crimes, while it was necessary for the prosecution to prove an intention to bring about the illegal result, simple recklessness as to the surrounding circumstances was sufficient.[34] The offence of assault occasioning actual bodily harm was held to apply to the infliction of psychological damage, so long as some clinically identifiable effect on the victim could be discerned;[35] and the House of Lords restated that a broad approach would be taken to the circumstances in which a person charged with one offence could be convicted of another.[36] The House of Lords gave some much-needed clarification of the law of manslaughter,[37] and the Court of Appeal stressed that the determination of whether a person accused of murder had been acting under provocation was properly a matter for the jury.[38] The traditional rules for the operation of the defence of involuntary intoxication were reimposed by the House of Lords, reversing a decision of the Court of Appeal;[39] and it was held to be no defence to a charge of conspiracy that the accused might have been acting with laudable motives and with no intention that the agreed offence should ever have been committed.[40]

The boundaries of the tort of negligence continued to be explored. The Court of Appeal held that children had no right of action in negligence against local authorities who had failed adequately to carry out their social service duties; leave was given to appeal to the House of Lords.[41] A local authority was similarly held not liable for the inadequate supervision of child minders, although it was suggested that the authority might be liable if it had informed a mother that a particular individual was an appropriate person to look after her child.[43] In both situations it was thought that the regulatory machinery was self-sufficient. The Court of Appeal reached a different conclusion in *E* v. *Dorset County Council*, holding that the ordinary rules of liability for negligence and breach of statutory duty were not displaced by the statutory regime applicable to the education of children with special educational needs. A person who had carelessly given an unfavourable reference for a former employee was held liable to the employee in negligence.[44] Litigation stemming from the losses suffered by the Lloyd's insurance market reached the House of Lords, which held that plaintiffs' causes of action in contract and tort might overlap with each other.[45] The Court of Appeal held that the test of the existence of a duty of care, developed in the context of cases imposing liability for pure economic loss, was of general application.[46] A person injured in a road accident was held by the House of Lords not to be entitled to recover as a head of damages the value of services voluntarily provided by the defendant in looking after her.[47] Elsewhere in the law of tort, the House of Lords applied a test of foreseeability of harm in determining whether damage was recoverable under the rule in *Rylands* v. *Fletcher*, generalizing the test of remoteness of damage found in the torts of nuisance and negligence.[48]

The Family Division gave much-needed guidance on the proper use of experts in proceedings under the *Children Act*.[49] The legal requirement to give priority to 'the interests of the child' was held by the House of Lords not to force the courts to give preference to the interests of a baby over those her mother when the mother was herself a child.[50] Regulations were made under the *Human Fertilization and Embryology Act 1990* to allow for legal parenthood to be transferred from a surrogate mother to a commissioning couple.[51]

The Court of Appeal had recourse to fundamental principles of the law of trusts in holding that a declaration of trust of generic property was valid; the House of Lords refused leave to appeal.[52] Morritt J approved an order varying the statutory rules for the devolution of the Duke of Marlborough's estate.[53] The House of Lords refused to overrule the longstanding law that positive covenants could not be enforced against the covenantor's successor in title.[54] The Law Commission put forward proposals for the reform of the rules applying to the forfeiture of leases;[55] and an earlier report of the Law Commission formed the basis of the *Law of Property (Miscellaneous Provisions) Act*, streamlining the practice of property conveyancing.

1   *R* v. *Secretary of State for Foreign and Commonwealth Affairs, ex parte Rees Mogg* [1994] 2 WLR 115

2. *R* v. *Secretary of State for Employment, ex parte Equal Opportunities Commission* [1994] 2 WLR 409

3. *R* v. *Secretary of State for the Home Department, ex parte Fire Brigades Union*, *The Times*, 10 November

4. *R* v. *Secretary of State for Foreign Affairs ex parte the World Development Movement Ltd*, *The Times*, 27 December

5. *re R (Wardship: Restriction on Publication)* [1994] 3 WLR 36

6. *R* v. *Central TV* [1994] 3 WLR 20

7. *re H.-S. (Minors)(Protection of Identity)* [1994] 1 WLR 1141 (Court of Appeal)
8. *Attorney-General* v. *Associated Newspapers* [1994] 2 WLR 277 (House of Lords)
9. *R* v. *Young, The Times,* 30 December
10. *R* v. *Chief Constable of the West Midlands Police Authority ex parte Wiley* [1994] 3 WLR 433
11. *The Pioneer Container* [1994] 3 WLR 1
12. [1994] 3 WLR 199; cf *re Stapylton Fletcher Ltd* [1994] 1 WLR 1183 (Chancery Division)
13. *Chiropractors Act*
14. *Powdrill* v. *Watson* [1994] ICR 395; and see *re Ferranti International plc, The Times,* 11 August (Lightman J)
15. *Grovewood Holding plc* v. *James Capel & Co Ltd, The Times,* 15 August (Lightman J)
16. *Aitken* v. *South Hams District Council* [1994] 3 WLR 333
17. *L'Office Chérifien des Phosphates* v. *Yamashita-Shinnihon Steamship Co* [1994] 2 WLR 39
18. *Unilever plc* v. *Chefaro Proprietaries Ltd, The Times,* 28 November
19. *Ridehalgh* v. *Horsfield* [1994] 3 WLR 462
20. *R* v. *Newcastle under Lyme Justices ex parte Massey* [1994] 1 WLR 1684
21. Part I (not brought into force)
22. ss.54–59 (not brought into force)
23. s.60 (not brought into force), s.81
24. ss.34–39 (not brought into force)
25. s.68
26. ss.63–80 (not all brought into force)
27. s.143
28. s.145
29. *The Times,* 10 October
30. *C* v. *Director of Public Prosecutions* [1994] 3 WLR 888
31. *R* v. *Chief Constable of South Wales ex parte Merrick* [1994] 1 WLR 663
32. *R* v. *Ananthanarayanan* [1994] 1 WLR 788; *R* v. *W* [1994] 1 WLR 800; *R* v. *H* [1994] 1 WLR 809
33. *R* v. *Effik* [1994] 3 WLR 583
34. *Attorney-General's Reference (No 3 of 1992)* [1994] 1 WLR 409
35. *R* v. *Chan-Fook* [1994] 1 WLR 689
36. *R* v. *Mandan* [1994] 2 WLR 700
37. *R* v. *Adomako* [1994] 3 WLR 288
38. *R* v. *Cambridge* [1994] 1 WLR 971
39. *R* v. *Kingston* [1994] 3 WLR 519
40. *Yip Chiu-Cheung* v. *R* [1994] 3 WLR 514
41. *M* v. *Newham* [1994] 2 WLR 554
42. *T* v. *Surrey County Council, The Independent,* 21 January (Scott Baker J)
43. [1994] 3 WLR 853
44. *Spring* v. *Guardian Assurance* [1994] 3 WLR 354
45. *Henderson* v. *Merrett Syndicate Ltd* [1994] 3 WLR 761
46. *Marc Rich & Co AG* v. *Bishop Rock Marine Co Ltd* [1994] 1 WLR 1071
47. *Hunt* v. *Severs* [1994] 2 AC 350
48. *Cambridge Water Company* v. *Eastern Counties Leather plc* [1994] 2 WLR 53
49. See (1994) 144 *New Law Journal* 501
50. *Birmingham City Council* v. *H* [1994] 2 WLR 31
51. *Human Fertilization and Embryology Act 1990 (Commencement No. 5) Order No. 1776 (C.33)*
52. *Hunter* v. *Moss* [1994] 1 WLR 452
53. *Hambro* v. *Duke of Marlborough* [1994] 3 WLR 341
54. *Rhone* v. *Stephens* [1994] 2 WLR 429
55. *Termination of Tenancies Bill,* based on Law Commission Report no. 221

3.   UNITED STATES LAW

Two record-breaking punitive damage judgments were awarded in 1994. A federal court in Alaska awarded $5,000 million in favour of tens of thousands of plaintiffs in Alaska in a case against Exxon Corporation for the damage caused by the *Exxon Valdez* oil spill in 1989 (see AR 1989, pp. 45–6), setting a new record in punitive damages. A judgment in 1986 of $10,530 million in damages in favour of Pennzoil Company against Texaco Inc. was the highest-ever judgment, but it included only $3,000 million in punitive damages. A San Francisco court awarded $7.1 million in punitive damages against the Chicago-based international law firm Baker & McKenzie and one of its partners, for the partner's sexual harassment of a female employee. It was more than double the highest previous award in a sexual harassment case.

On the other hand, trial judges and appellate courts also continued to reduce and reverse punitive damages awarded by juries. A $124 million judgment awarded by a jury in an Illinois court against the manufacturer of a prescription drug, for failure to warn of the risk of loss of vision associated with the injection of the drug, was reduced by the trial judge to $35 million; the Illinois appellate court, in turn, reduced the award to $3 million, finding that punitive damages more than 11 times higher than the compensatory damages were excessive. An Ohio appellate court reduced to $1 million a $3 million award of punitive damages against a physician who failed to make a timely diagnosis of a malignant tumor on a patient's leg, where the aggregate compensatory damages were $3.25 million; the court found that the punitive damages were excessive in light of the physician's net worth of $2.1 million.

Tort liability was expanded for infliction of emotional distress and for subjection to second-hand cigarette smoke. The New Jersey and Wisconsin supreme courts held that a bystander did not have to witness an accident involving a member of a family, nor have to be a member of the immediate family of the victim, to have a cause of action for emotional distress resulting from witnessing the accident or the aftermath. The law in those and other states had hitherto limited such a cause of action to bystanders witnessing an accident that injured immediate family members. A California court awarded $500,000 to a man who alleged that two psychotherapists planted false memories of childhood sexual abuse in his daughter's mind. This case was the first in which a person other than a patient successfully sued a psychotherapist for so-called 'recovery memory therapy'. An Ohio appellate court held that a bystander had a cause of action for assault and battery against a smoker who intentionally exhaled smoke on him. A Georgia appellate court held that a person might have a cause of action against another for injuries incurred as a result of the latter's smoking tobacco in the presence of the former.

Verdicts in two product-liability cases were signals for the likely direction of litigation for similar cases. Compaq Computer Corporation won what was believed to be the first trial in which a computer manufacturer was alleged to have caused 'carpal tunnel syndrome' (crippling wrist injuries allegedly associated with repetitive use of computer keyboards). As several thousand similar cases were pending, the verdict in favour of Compaq was regarded as a significant indicator. A federal appellate court upheld awards of compensatory damages of $840,000 and punitive damages of $6.5 million against a manufacturer of breast implants for injuries suffered by a patient who underwent breast reconstruction surgeries. Numerous other such suits had been filed against the manufacturer.

A California state trial court held valid an agreement included by Bank of America in a mailing to its customers requiring them to submit their claims against the bank to arbitration. The case was the first ruling in the United States on the legality of a bank's policy requiring its customers to submit claims to arbitration, which was generally believed to be a way for banks to avoid mass claims concerning its fees, charges and interest rates.

The US Supreme Court expanded the protection of the rights of property owners against local planning requirements that might burden developers with additional costs. It ruled that a requirement that a property owner must dedicate land for a pedestrian and bicycle path and for a storm-water drain, as a condition for a granting him a construction permit, was a deprivation of his right to property; as such, he had to be compensated. The decision was believed to be applicable to fees, charges and similar requirements frequently imposed on developers as conditions of the grant of permission to develop projects.

The courts applied the conventional distinction between speech and symbolic speech, or actions, in upholding penal statutes prohibiting obstruction of persons trying to enter abortion clinics and to hunt game. Federal courts upheld a federal law prohibiting the former actions and a Montana court held that a Montana statute prohibiting the latter did not violate the obstructionists' rights to freedom of expression, such expressions being symbolic and subject to greater restriction by government.

Efforts to control urban crime by searches for evidence of crime without a search warrant (or a warrant for inspection for health and building-code violations) were held illegal. A federal court in Chicago held that a four-day search for firearms of more than 1,500 apartments in a public housing complex (in response to persistent shooting in the area) was illegal because no prior search warrant had been obtained. In San Francisco a federal court held that the 'storming' by the police of an apartment in order to arrest a suspect was illegal even though they had a warrant to inspect for health and building-code violations.

The California supreme court held that homeowners' associations (the entities owning common areas in development areas and managed by committees of homeowners) could not restrict access on public streets in their areas.

XVI THE ARTS

1. OPERA—MUSIC—DANCE/BALLET—THEATRE—CINEMA —TELEVISION & RADIO

i. OPERA

THE major event of the year in Britain was the opening in June of Glyndebourne's new opera house, a magnificent theatre constructed from local materials and endowed with a traditional horseshoe-shaped auditorium with excellent acoustics and an atmosphere producing, in the words of the editor of *Opera*, 'a sense of community, of belonging to something larger than the sum of a random group of visitors, something you never quite got from the straight, serried rows of the old theatre'. The new opera house opened with a revival of Peter Hall's production of Mozart's *Le Nozze di Figaro*, the work with which Glyndebourne first began in 1934. The performance was more than worthy of the occasion, with Renée Fleming a creamy-voiced Countess, Gerald Finley a sturdy Figaro and Alison Hagley as attractive a Susanna as one could hope to encounter.

The first new production of the Glyndebourne Festival was Tchaikovsky's *Eugene Onegin*, brilliantly staged by Graham Vick and with an excellent cast headed by Wojciech Drabowicz as an elegantly melancholy Onegin and Elena Prokina an affecting Tatyana. Later in the season, Deborah Warner's determinedly modish *Don Giovanni* was a serious disappointment, its action taking place neither in Seville nor anywhere else in the world but in a stage designer's abstract no-man's-land. However, a revival of Trevor Nunn's exemplary production of Britten's *Peter Grimes* in John Gunter's evocative decor was most welcome, its title role movingly sung by Anthony Rolfe Johnson.

The Royal Opera had its ups and downs. Trevor Nunn's first production for the company was Janáček's *Katya Kabanova*, which had not previously been performed at Covent Garden. Nunn's staging made the most of this dramatically taut and musically lyrical work, offering great opportunities for singers who could act. These were seized upon by a fine cast headed by Elena Prokina as Katya and Eva Randova as her grimly oppressive mother-in-law. Unfortunately, Maria Bjornson's Expressionist decor failed to convey the atmosphere of a small town on the banks of the Volga and tended to detract from the claustrophobic intensity of Janáček's opera.

Another work new to the Royal Opera House was the original version of Rossini's *Mosé in Egitto*, staged conventionally but effectively, with Ruggero Raimondi as Moses, a new young Italian soprano Anna

Caterina Antonacci as Elcia, and Bruce Ford superb in the immensely exacting role of Osiride. Verdi's *Aida* returned after a ten-year absence in a disappointingly nondescript production, while a second-rate piece, Giordano's *Fedora*, was lavishly staged and glamorously cast with Mirella Freni and José Carreras in the leading roles.

A new *Ring* cycle was begun which turned out to be a childish, comic-strip send-up of Wagner's masterpiece. The consecutive first nights of *Das Rheingold* and *Die Walküre* were greeted with a prolonged outburst of booing and cries of 'rubbish' from all parts of the theatre, to which the production team responded with self-satisfied smirks. The Royal Opera's year ended more happily with Gounod's *Roméo et Juliette*. Romeo was the young Sicilian tenor, Roberto Alagna, who on the first night was accorded a prolonged ovation which he thoroughly deserved. Here was one of the leading lyric tenors of the next 20 years.

English National Opera's new productions included a *Tosca* heavily dripping with symbolism, some of it dauntingly obscure, played in decor which rarely stayed still for more than a few minutes at a time; Massenet's sub-standard *Don Quixote*; and *Cosi Fan Tutte*, splendidly sung but updated to the 1950s with vacuum-cleaners much in evidence. More successful were Jonathan Miller's production of Richard Strauss's most popular opera, *Der Rosenkavalier*; the first ENO staging of Mussorgsky's *Khovantschina*; and a new opera, *Blond Eckbert*, by the Scottish composer Judith Weir, only some weeks after she had received the Critics' Circle Award for having made the most outstanding contribution to musical life in Britain in the preceding year.

New regional productions of interest included Scottish Opera's *L'Elisir d'Amore*, *Peter Grimes*, *The Turn of the Screw* and *Maria Stuarda*; Welsh National Opera's *Turandot*; and Opera North's *La Rondine* and *Die Zauberflöte*. Opera North's new opera, *Playing Away*, an ephemeral piece about soccer, with instantly disposable music by Benedict Mason and an over-wordy text by Howard Brenton, was not likely to be seen again, but Harrison Birtwistle's *The Second Mrs Kong*, the product of its composer's obsession with the 1933 movie *King Kong*, intrigued and delighted Glyndebourne Touring Opera's audiences.

There was interesting operatic fare at the Edinburgh Festival, whose programme included a visit from Australian Opera on its first tour abroad. The Australians' staging of Britten's *A Midsummer Night's Dream* placed the action of the opera in India under the British Raj, with the stage area dominated by an enormous bandstand. At Aldeburgh, the festival begun by Benjamin Britten and Peter Pears revived Britten's *Noyes Fludde*, not in the church for which it was composed but inappropriately at the Maltings. The engaging Garsington Festival had a success with Strauss's *Capriccio*.

Several enterprising American festivals did fine work, among them Santa Fe which added Judith Weir's *Blond Eckbert* to a programme of old favourites such as *Tosca* and *Il Barbiere di Siviglia*; Colorado Springs, with its lavish *Turandot*; and Ohio Light Opera with its marvellous array of operettas. Glimmerglass Opera, in upstate New York on the banks of the enchanting Lake Otsego, offered Monteverdi's *L'Incoronazione di Poppea* directed by Jonathan Miller, *Iolanthe*, and *Ariadne auf Naxos*.

Among those who died in 1994 were Irene Jessner, the Austrian soprano who, after the 1938 Anschluss, joined the Metropolitan Opera, New York, where she was greatly admired in a number of Wagner, Verdi and Strauss roles; Ivan Kozlovsky, the Russian tenor who possessed one of the century's most sheerly beautiful voices; Tiana Lemnitz, the German soprano who was an unsurpassed Pamina, Elsa and Eva in the thirties; Jarmila Novotna, the Czech-born soprano who reigned as prima donna at the opera houses of Prague, Berlin, Vienna and New York in succession; Gottlob Frick, the German bass whose black, saturnine voice was perfectly suited to such Wagner roles as Hagen and Hunding; Karl Dönch, one of the most adept and best-loved baritones at the Vienna State Opera for more than 30 years; and Hans Gabor, the Hungarian-born conductor and administrator who founded and led the Vienna Chamber Opera.

ii. MUSIC

FOR Western music generally, it was a backward-looking year. The lack of an accepted aesthetic standard had become all too plain after the rejection of serialism, and the complexities associated with it, during the 1980s. Nowhere was this more starkly demonstrated than in the record industry. The technological sophistication of the compact disc (CD) far outstripped the artistic integrity of a divided culture. It was a cruel twist of fate that such opportunities should occur just at the time when Western musicians had lost their sense of aesthetic direction. When it became clear that total serialism did not represent the future in the way that its advocates had claimed, this meant the collapse of one of the prime creative movements of the twentieth century (jazz was the other main one). The resulting vacuum in contemporary music, added to the greatly increased audience antipathy to it, led to nostalgia for the past.

In view of such a trend away from the discovery of the new, one might have expected the exploitation of the classics to have risen to new heights. This was not the case. The CD market proved to be particularly vulnerable to commercial pressures, and in fact classical sales plummeted. In 1994 they amounted to just 9 per cent of total CD sales; or to put it another way, 91 per cent consisted of pop, rock or jazz. Innovative marketing was clearly necessary if commercial difficulties were to be avoided. But the figures for 1994 showed just how unpredictable and fickle a thing the popularity of the mass market was. In 1994 12 per cent of all classical sales went to just one project: the reunion in Los Angeles of the Three Tenors (Carreras, Domingo and Pavarotti) and a subsequent repackaging of their 1990 Rome concert. A further sizeable slice of the total market, with sales of seven million, was accounted for by just three other 'hits'—*Canto Gregoriano* performed by Spanish monks, Vivaldi's *Four Seasons* with Nigel Kennedy, and the *Third Symphony* of Gorecki.

In 1994 a leaf was taken out of the show-business books by the institution of the Classical Music Awards. An international jury gave awards, like Oscars, for different categories of performers; just one award was reserved for 'best composition', and this went to Witold Lutoslawski for his *Fourth Symphony*, which had been first heard in Los Angeles in 1993. Indeed, the death of Lutoslawski in February (see XX: Obituary) robbed music of the leading symphonist of the late twentieth century.

Against such a volatile background, some notable recordings of the year included music by Elliott Carter (*Cello Sonata* 1948, *Duo* 1974), Philip Glass (*Einstein on the Beach*), and in particular Messiaen's last work, which had made such an impression when it was performed posthumously for the first time in Florence in 1993 (see AR 1993, p. 487), *Éclairs sur l'Au Delà*. Seventy discs of the complete piano works of Liszt were begun, with pianist Leslie Howard. The music of unknown composers which began the long resurrection process on CD in 1994 included the eight symphonies of Benjamin Frankel, selected pieces by Alan Bush and the complete works of Dmitri Kabalevsky.

The CD still seemed to be a means of survival to the hard-pressed London orchestras, who confined their repertoire to the well-worn music of the past. The Royal Philharmonic issued the first ten of a projected series of 120, all popular classics. The London Symphony marked its 90th anniversary with 15 in similar vein. The pick of the year went to the Bournemouth Symphony, who issued an excellent Tippett disc (*Fourth Symphony, Fantasia Concertante, Fantasia on a Theme of Handel*) under Richard Hickox. As well as familiar classics, there was a spate of 'early music' recordings; among the most notable was a disc of Purcell's secular songs arranged by the King's Consort. Also, a small corner of the record industry was reserved for 'ethno-musicolgy', the year featuring examples of music from North Africa, Japan, Ethiopia, Georgia, India and Bangladesh.

Those reaching the age of 60 in 1994 included Alfred Schnittke, whose works were widely performed; Vinko Globokar; the American Roger Reynolds, and the Tweedle Dum and Tweedle Dee of British music, Harrison Birtwistle and Peter Maxwell Davies. Both had a busy year. Birtwistle's *Gawain* was heard, in spite of some organized booing, at Covent Garden; and *The Second Mrs Kong* was given by the Glyndebourne touring company. Both works were characteristic examples of his nihilism seen through the filter of myth and ritual. Davies was more active, more in the public eye. Performances included the new *Fifth Symphony*, the overture *Cross Lane Fair*, for Northumbrian pipes and orchestra, and the opera *Resurrection*. A book was published about him, and recordings of the year included the early *Worldes Blis*, and *Symphonies 1 and 2*. The St Magnus Festival in the Orkneys continued much the same as in previous years, encouraging as it did the active participation of young local musicians. The festival was mainly the vehicle for Davies's own work, though his conducting was particularly successful with the choral performance (Beethoven's *Mass in C*).

The St Magnus Festival was unique in the United Kingdom in being directed by a composer. In this respect, though smaller in scale, it was the British equivalent of the Munich Biennale, for which the composer Hans Werner Henze assembled all sorts of music-theatre and spectacle, including puppet theatre and street theatre, which he interspersed with some concerts. In 1994 the net was cast wide, with variable results and attendances. *The Scourge of Hyacinths* by the Cuban composer Tania Leon could be called opera; *Report of the Death of the Musician Jack Tiergarten* by Johannes Kalitzke was music-theatre; *Freeze* by Robert Zuidam was a morality play, with a distinctly ambiguous message. In recognition of his longstanding links with England, Henze was in the habit of inviting a contribution by an English composer. In 1994 this invitation was extended to Benedict Mason, a young composer for whom music was a 'dead language'. This did not prevent him from writing, with librettist Howard Brenton, *Playing Away*, which was a re-working of the Faust story in the context of English football culture, and for which he made use of sampling technique used by pop musicians. As in previous years (see AR 1992, p. 483), Henze chose to revive existing work—in this case his *Cantata Novae de Infinito Laudes*, to a text by the sixteenth-century dissident Giordano Bruno. Against this, Wladimir Tamopolski's *Der Atem der Erschöpften Zeit* (The Breath of an Exhausted Time) was darkly disturbing.

Avant-garde chamber works were the feature of the Witten Festival, such as György Ligeti's *Aventures et Nouvelles Aventures*, and Klaus Huber's *The Earth Moves on the Horns of an Ox*. A directly political message was contained in the programmes of the Schleswig-Holstein Festival, when for the first time since the 1930s the music of Israel was introduced to a German public. The orchestras were the Israel Philharmonic, with Pinchas Zuckerman, the Jerusalem Symphony and the Israel Symphony, and the concerts were entitled 'Prohibited Music in Nazi Germany'.

Notable premières in the United States during the year included, in Chicago, a performance by the Chicago Symphony of *Partita* by Elliott

Carter, by which the 85-year-old composer intended his audience to understand that he meant 'orchestral games'; and certainly the new score was much more sprightly and quick moving than most of his recent works. There was also, in Minneapolis, a first performance by the Minnesota Orchestra and Jorja Fleezanis of the new *Violin Concerto* by the minimalist John Adams.

The London concert scene in 1994 was diverse and variable, starting in January with a series of performances of works by John Tavener. His big new work, *The Apocalypse*, was heard later in the year. His choosing to forge a musical language from the litany of the Orthodox Church, with its repetitive features and its primitive use of tonality, was an attempt to carry out a sort of artistic transplant from one musical tradition to another. Unfortunately, it ignored the positive characteristics of each. Spirituality was not something to be packaged and processed. Tavener's real if slender talent was overstretched.

The 'Meltdown Festival', the South Bank's answer to the BBC's Promenade Concerts during the summer, celebrated the work of Louis Andriessen, along with that of 26 others, and included the UK première of his *De Materie*. A series of concerts, 'Renderings', devoted to Berio in April/May had greater impact, with as its highlight *La Vera Storia*, to a libretto by Italo Calvino. Several other events helped to avert the overhanging threat of a grey monotony on the London scene. The Almeida Theatre had two interesting seasons, the first of Spanish Arts, the second of music from the newly-independent states of the former USSR; another highlight was the contribution of the Latin American and Caribbean Cultural Society, under the direction of Juan Monroy. The latter gave vivid performances of national music, tending to focus on guitarists, chief among them the composer Eduardo Falu. Equally colourful and distinctive concerts were given by the Guatemalan Ensemble (three guitars and marimba) and a company from Chile, Bafochi, who gave national songs and dances to the delight of their cosmopolitan London audience.

Apart from Lutoslawski, others who died in 1994 included the composers Nikolai Karetnikov and Elizabeth Maconchy, and the pianist/teacher Soulima Stravinsky.

BOOKS OF THE YEAR. *Olivier Messiaen: Music and Colour*, by Claude Samuel; *Max: The Life and Music of Peter Maxwell Davies*, by Mike Seabrook; *Soundpieces 2*, by Cole Gagne (interviews with American composers); *Music since 1945: Issues, Materials and Literature*, by Elliott Schwartz and Daniel Godfrey; *Essays on Music*, by Hans Keller; *Peter Warlock: The Life of Philip Heseltine*, by Barry Smith; *Sondheim's Broadway Musicals*, by Stephen Banfield; *Leonard Bernstein*, by Humphrey Burton.

iii.   BALLET & DANCE

IT was a disappointing year for new choreography and a much happier one for reconstructions and revivals. Star dancers seemed to be searching for new repertories. Sylvie Guillem guested with the Kirov/Maryinsky Ballet, justifying their revival of the Soviet ballet based on the poem by Pushkin, *The Fountain of the Bakhchisaray*. This had not been seen in the West for many years but became the centre-piece of the autumn Saison Russe at the Théâtre des Champs-Elysées in Paris. They also performed a new version of *Coppélia*, choreographed by Oleg Vinogradov, which proved to be a travesty of the original nineteenth-century work.

Irek Mukhamedov turned to Kim Brandstrup to create a new *Othello*, condensing Shakespeare's tragedy into one act. This enabled Brandstrup's company, Arc, to play to packed houses and gave his star an anguished and tortured role in which to display his acting abilities. Later in the year Mukhamedov faced greater challenges technically in Ashley Page's highly-charged *Fearful Symmetries* for the Royal Ballet.

After an unmemorable first half, Michael Clark's *O* developed into a stunningly beautiful reinterpretation of Stravinsky's *Apollo* with Clark himself dancing the central role. Nevertheless, his eagerly-awaited work for the Royal Ballet was abandoned before its première.

New York City Ballet presented its second Diamond Project— festivals of new ballet giving choreographers of classical works a showcase using the company's highly-skilled dancers. James Kudelka created new ballets for both the National Ballet of Canada (*Spring Awakening* based on Frank Wedekind's play of sexual initiation) and for American Ballet Theatre (*Cruel World*, depicting unspecified human turmoil to the accompaniment of Tchaikovsky's *Souvenir de Florence*). More significant than ABT's new works (including the ballet sequence from the short-lived Broadway musical *The Red Shoes* and a *Nutcracker* with scenario adapted by playwright Wendy Wasserstein) was the revival of Antony Tudor's portrayal of a community torn apart by war, *Echoing of Trumpets*.

In America regional companies generated most interest both at home and abroad. Miami City Ballet had made its mark as a custodian of George Balanchine's choreography, and the company's two ambitious programmes at the Edinburgh Festival (*Jewels* and a mixed bill including the company's première of *Western Symphony*) revealed Balanchine's reputation was safe in the hands of Edward Villella, their artistic director. San Francisco Ballet premièred a lavish, if not entirely satisfying, *Romeo and Juliet* by their artistic director, Helgi Tomasson. On tour they performed mixed programmes including Mark Morris's new, complex but apt interpretation of Beethoven's 'Ghost' trio, *Maelstrom*.

Morris continued to create some of the most interesting contemporary work, often undertaking his choreography while resident at universities. His company was an attraction at both the Adelaide and Edinburgh Festivals. Thanks to the opening of the new Festival Theatre in

Edinburgh (the closest in Britain to an acknowledged dance house) we could at last see Morris's masterwork of optimism and joy, *L'Allegro, il Penseroso ed il Moderato*, inspired by the music of Handel and the poems of John Milton.

Other Americans who visited Britain and toured in Europe included Twyla Tharp, whose dancers energized the restricted space of London's Riverside Studios; Merce Cunningham, who showed his gentle, computer-inspired *Enter*; and Lucinda Childs, seen twice, who in addition to new work revived her 1979 *Dance*, in which live performers interact with filmed images. Washington Ballet was only a little better than the Australian Perth City Ballet and quite unready for international exposure. Neither was helped by using recorded music.

Audiences and critics were more sympathetic to Cape Ballet after years of isolation in South Africa, but it had not maintained its fine early reputation. Its new ballets, *Hamlet* and *Orpheus in the Underworld*, were old-fashioned and the one familiar work included for its London performances, John Cranko's *The Lady and the Fool*, was miscast. Reports of NAPAC, the Durban-based company, suggested that it was better received at the Basle Dance Festival.

Bill T. Jones attracted enormous coverage on television and stage but his company's programme at Sadler's Wells Theatre was self-indulgent. He premièred his *Still/Here*, based on workshops with the terminally ill, at the Biennale de la Danse in Lyon at the start of a world tour. This, like much of his recent work, was based on anger and his obsessions with being black, homosexual and HIV-positive.

The most interesting British choreography came from Jonathan Burrows with *Our*; from Mark Baldwin with a lively and witty repertory for his own company; and from the new Richard Alston and Dancers. The latter emerged from the remains of London Contemporary Dance Theatre, which closed in July. Before its demise it mounted two glorious programmes: a gala tribute to its founder, Robin Howard, reviving memorable productions from its past, and a special Britten and Stravinsky programme choreographed by Alston for the Aldeburgh Festival. From this, *Movements from Petrushka*, a portrayal of an individual allienated from society, continued into the new company's exciting repertory.

Britain's other leading contemporary ensemble, the Rambert Dance Company, was re-launched under the direction of Christopher Bruce. Now a deliberately middle-of-the-road company and employing 25 superb dancers, its productions ranged from Martha Clarke's Bosch-inspired music-theatre, *The Garden of Earthly Delights*, to the virtuoso dance of Jiri Kylian's *Petite Mort*. They also presented a selection of new and popular works by Bruce but had yet to establish their own identity necessary to fill the large venues in which they were performing.

Well-known ballets and narratives were revised, most notably with

Adventures in Motion Pictures continuing to work their way through the nineteenth-century repertory. This year they focused on *La Sylphide*, which, as *Highland Fling*, was relocated to a Glaswegian tenement and used-car dump with new-age sylphs luring James to his doom. Their choreographer, Matthew Bourne, appeared to be stronger on ideas than dance, a criticism that also applied to Northern Ballet's new *Cinderella*.

English National Ballet's *Giselle* (now set in Austria immediately after the 1914–18 war) showed, particularly in the romantic Act II, just how their corps de ballet had improved. Their repertory was enhanced by Mauro Bigonzetti's chic *X.N. Tricities* and excellent performances of Balanchine's *Square Dance* with a young cast led by the Italians, Ambra Valla and Giuseppi Picone.

The centrepiece of the Royal Ballet's year was Anthony Dowell's staging of *The Sleeping Beauty*. After a gala première in Washington it was seen in New York before opening in London. The production was swamped by Maria Björnson's capricious designs and the dancers seemed less at home in Petipa's choreography than in the contemporary ballets in their repertory. The highlight of the Royal's year was their mini-season of Ashton's choreography to honour the 90th anniversary of Sir Frederick's birth. *Daphnis and Chloë* was particularly well performed, especially by guest artist Trinidad Sevillano, and had new designs evoking the Greek landscape by Martyn Bainbridge. *La Valse, Symphonic Variations* and *The Dream* were meticulously revived and well danced but the *divertissement* proved more challenging. Some dancers were defeated by the complexity of Ashton's style, although Lesley Collier, Adam Cooper, Bruce Samson, Miyako Yoshida, Stephen Jefferies (as the comic Dago in *Facade*) and Fiona Chadwick (in *Cinderella*) showed a real understanding of the choreographer's intentions.

Birmingham Royal Ballet also paid tribute to Ashton with a superb staging of *Enigma Variations* mounted with loving care by Michael Somes just before his death. In this elegiac portrait of Elgar and his friends, the cast stood comparison with the original. This was the pinnacle of Peter Wright's valuable programme of revivals. Earlier in the year Marion Tait presented a harrowing Lizzie Bordon in Agnes de Mille's *Fall River Legend*, but Léonide Massine's *Le Tricorne* was disappointing for its lack of detail.

Massine's choreography was better shown by Nice Opéra Ballet, which ended the year with an excellent programme contrasting his witty, Viennese *Le Beau Danube* with the cubist *Parade* and ritualistic *Le Sacre du Printemps*. The dancers had been coached by Tatiana Leskova, Susanna Della Pietra and Enrico Sportiello, custodians of Massine's style, and the company was strengthened by two dancers from the Paris Opéra. Agnès Letestu danced both the Chosen Maiden and the flirtatious Street Dancer, and José Martinez, possessing stage presence as well as dancing skills, assumed Massine's own role of the Hussar. Martinez was also one of the dancers to take the title role in the Paris Opéra's *Tyl Eulenspiegl* by Vaslav Nijinsky. This fast-moving, colourful character-work, reconstructed by Millicent Hodson and Kenneth Archer, was receiving its European première 78 years after its creation!

Aside from productions and festivals, 1994 would be remembered as the year in which two overseas tours by the Bolshoi collapsed. Even in Britain, audiences refused to pay the high ticket-prices demanded by promoters. With the Bolshoi Theatre in Moscow physically crumbling and amid new competition for contracts where jobs were once secure, a question-mark hung over the future of this once-great company.

iv. THEATRE

FIFTEEN West End shows that were playing at the start of 1994 were still packing their theatres 12 months later. Eleven of these long-runners were musicals, four of them from Sir Andrew Lloyd Webber, whose reworked *Sunset Boulevard*, sharper and darker, reopened with Betty Buckley in magnificent voice as the fading screen diva and John Barrowman as her puppyish gigolo.

With production costs continuing to spiral upwards, no new plays made it to the West End that had not already proved their worth elsewhere in smaller theatres, outside London or abroad. Terry Johnson's *Dead Funny*, a perceptive analysis of a group of men concealing social inadequacy behind their veneration of old comedians, transferred from Hampstead for a successful run at the Vaudeville; Zoe Wanamaker gave an icily funny performance as a wife loathing her husband's antics. Hampstead turned down Kevin Elyot's *My Night With Reg*, which the Royal Court then put on at its Theatre Upstairs, from where it transferred directly to the Criterion. Wise and desperately funny, about a group of AIDS-generation gays knocking themselves askew in the search for companionship, Elyot's cunningly-crafted play won a cluster of awards. Its arrival in the same month as Jonathan Harvey's touching portrayal of gay adolescent love on a housing estate, *Beautiful Thing* (Duke of York's), prompted distasteful warnings in some newspapers that a 'gay plague' threatened the West End. By coincidence, several accomplished plays with gay themes were being mounted at this time in outlying theatres, including a revival of Noël Coward's swansong *A Song at Twilight* at Greenwich.

The Royal Shakespeare Company, not always wise in its choice of new plays, came up with two winners in its Stratford season. Anne Devlin's brutally honest *After Easter* depicted the strains of surviving as an Ulster

Catholic woman, where the only solution appeared to be exile, either
to another country or internally into numb selfishness. David Edgar's
Pentecost, set in an unnamed East European country and centred on
the discovery of an ancient fresco in a crumbling church, hit upon an
arresting metaphor for numerous contemporary concerns: the function
of art, tourism, the cult of the past, national self-respect and the needs
of suffering humanity. Both plays were superbly acted, and directed in
each case by Michael Attenborough.

Another new British play, Sue Townsend's adaptation of her novel
The Queen and I (Royal Court and Vaudeville), appealed to the public's
seemingly insatiable interest in the royals; but as a play her fantasy about
Mr and Mrs Windsor banished to a Leicester housing estate was not a
patch on her original, socially-observant book.

The year was remarkable for the quantity of new work arriving
from across the Atlantic. From Canada came two Brad Fraser plays:
The Ugly Man (Battersea Arts Studios), a sexy, thoroughly blood-
spattering rework of Middleton's Jacobean tragedy *The Changeling*;
and the excellent *Poor Super Man* (Edinburgh and Hampstead), in
which a gay seduction worked wonders for a painter suffering from
artist's block. Fraser's announcement that he was giving up the stage
in order to write film scripts for Disney (of all companies) was one of
the year's more bizarre pieces of news. From the United States, Arthur
Miller's *Broken Glass* (National Theatre) explored the traumatic effects
on a Jewish family, safely living out the thirties in New York, of ignoring
contemporary events in Nazi Germany. Now in his 80th year, and with
the peaks of his creative achievements behind him, Miller could still
come up with strong dramatic metaphors for people's refusal to be
involved in the society of which they are a part.

David Beaird's astonishing piece of Southern Gothick shock-horror
900 Oneonta moved from the Lyric, Hammersmith, to the Old Vic
and then to the smaller Ambassadors. It was brought in by the
West End Producers Alliance, a new management cooperative and
the brainchild of Frank and Woji Gero, who gathered together 16
like-minded independent managements to share the costs of mounting
imaginative work that might otherwise be staged only briefly or not at all.
As an inducement to audiences, ticket prices were kept to a maximum
of £7.50.

After a dodgy start, Wendy Wasserstein's cute and sentimental *The
Sisters Rosensweig* (Greenwich and Old Vic) enjoyed an unexpected run,
presumably due to the presence of Janet Suzman, Maureen Lipman and
Lynda Bellingham as the Brooklyn-born trio. Tony Kushner introduced
interesting ideas and effects into *Slavs* (Hampstead), a glimpse at the
nastiness of Russian life before and after the fall of communism, but the
play seemed hardly more than an appendage to his *Angels in America*.
Richard Nelson's *New England* (RSC: The Pit) reversed the basic

situation of his *Some Americans Abroad* and showed English exiles behaving badly. *Butterfly Kiss* (Almeida), Phyllis Nagy's rich and acute study of parental exploitation, added to her growing reputation in Britain: the American actress Elizabeth Berridge gave a haunting performance as the reluctant Lolita turned mother-killer in an expertly-handled production by Stephen Pimlott.

As regards new work, the event of the year was *Three Tall Women* (Wyndhams), marking Edward Albee's return to the ranks of the Pulitzer Prize-winners after decades of indifferent plays. Inspired by his own complex feelings towards his adopted mother, it drew a portrait of extreme and bitter old age. Maggie Smith triumphed with her portrait of the autocratic horror, and in the second half, where Albee had divided the character into three, Frances de la Tour and Anastasia Hille played her in resigned middle-age and in her still-hopeful youth respectively. These excellent performances drew wide praise, although the play itself divided critics into those who saw it as a humane meditation upon change and death, and others who found it cold and specious. The London *Evening Standard* named it Play of the Year.

The National Theatre opened its year with Caryl Churchill's *The Skriker*, a verbally and visually fascinating account of a demon inserting herself into the modern world. Kathryn Hunter gave another of her extraordinary shape-shifting performances (spider, child, raucous American), but the play's angle on life was obscure. Sam Mendes's gripping revival of Harold Pinter's *The Birthday Party* followed, on a cosily boxed-in set by Tom Piper that finally receded into a terrace of blank-windowed suburban houses; in every such place, we were left to suppose, fear, guilt and deception might be present. First-class performances came from Dora Bryan, Trevor Peacock and Anton Lesser.

Johnny on a Spot, a 1942 political farce by Charles MacArthur (co-author of *The Front Page*), was not a success, nor was Phyllida Lloyd's opulent and operatic *Pericles*. Sean Matthias showed that there was strength as well as campness in Jean Cocteau's *Les Parents Terribles*, one of the National's all-too-rare forays into continental European drama. As the raddled, incestuous mother, Sheila Gish came up with an all-stops-out performance that stopped only just short of chewing the scenery.

John Caird staged a muddled version of *The Seagull* and Christopher Morahan a decent-enough revival of Shaw's *The Devil's Disciple*, neither of which came near the excitement generated by Katie Mitchell's rediscovery of Gina Sowerby's *Rutherford and Son*. Written in 1912, a rare example for the time of a play set in the industrial world (and by a woman), the play was superbly acted, notably by Bob Peck as the flinty patriarch Rutherford.

Two American classics were lavishly mounted in the second half of the year: Tennessee Williams's *Sweet Bird of Youth*, directed by Richard Eyre (the National's artistic director), showed itself to be a near-masterpiece, and Clare Higgins gave a knock-out performance as the ageing movie queen. Howard Davies's revival of *The Children's Hour*, Lillian Hellman's 1934 melodrama, long banned in Britain because of its lesbian content, proved to be a worthy piece, remarkable for its period, but flawed by the simplicities of melodrama. Higgins and Harriet Walter played the two accused women.

Jonathan Kent, joint artistic director of Islington's adventurous Almeida Theatre, came to the National for the first time to reveal the power in Corneille's *Le Cid*. On a sumptuously-designed set of mirrors and horses frozen in mid-charge, and with notable playing by two young actresses, Samantha Bond and Susan Lynch, the tragedies of love almost triumphed over the quaintness of Old Castilian honour. The National also opened its stages to a few visiting companies, the most eagerly-awaited being Peter Brook's return to London (after 20 years) with *The Man Who*—comic, sad and bracingly acted by four actors playing scenes from the book by Oliver Sacks, *The Man Who Mistook His Wife for a Hat*.

Foreign companies came to the Barbican as well but brought little to admire. The charismatic Michael Sheen fought valiantly against electronic games in Yukio Ninagawa's multinational, multimedia *Peer Gynt*. Worse than this was the season grandiloquently entitled 'Everybody's Shakespeare', headed by Peter Sellars's *The Merchant of Venice* (from the Goodman Theater, Chicago), ridiculously relocated to Venice Beach, California, and endeavouring to suggest a parallel between Shylock's resentment of Christians and the black rioters of Los Angeles.

At Stratford, however, the RSC enjoyed a good year. A mesmeric Alex Jennings created a trio of virtuoso performances: in the title role of *Peer Gynt*, as the tormented Angelo in *Measure for Measure* and as a chilling, imperious Oberon in *A Midsummer Night's Dream*, a production by Adrian Noble that in some respects paid homage to Brook's mould-breaking achievement a quarter of a century before. Toby Stephens established himself as a riveting young actor with his bullyboy Coriolanus, as did Iain Glen in *Henry V*. At the RSC's London studio, The Pit, Nicholas Wright's exquisite production of Euripedes' *Ion*, ignored for a century, delighted audiences with its irony, dignity and moral ambiguity, truly a play that crossed the millenia.

Other impressive rediscoveries included *The Case of Rebellious Susan*, an 1894 moral comedy by Henry Arthur Jones, in which the heroine questions the iron law that what is all right for a husband (i.e. adultery) is all wrong for a wife. The play was staged by the Orange Tree, the Richmond theatre making a speciality of exploring forgotten corners of British drama. Greenwich came up with a powerful revival of Rattigan's *The Browning Version*, and Nigel Hawthorne mounted a warm-hearted production of the eighteenth-century comedy *The Clandestine Marriage*, which he directed himself as well as playing the dilapidated Lord Ogleby.

At the Royal Court, Stephen Daldry (a possible successor to Eyre at the National) achieved a *coup de théâtre* with his amazing staging of *The Kitchen*, Arnold Wesker's fifties' vision of the exploitation of a workforce. Daldry and designer Mark Thompson ripped out the stalls, reducing the theatre's seating by a third, and constructed a full-scale commercial kitchen in its place, where the audience watched the mimed frenzy from circle level. At £150,000 the most expensive production in the Royal Court's history, it became an astounding theatrical experience.

Deborah Warner also rearranged a theatre, the Garrick, for twice-nightly performances of Beckett's 20-minute-long *Footfalls*. Instead of relentlessly walking across a stage, Fiona Shaw paced a platform slung out from the front of the circle and, by thus altering Beckett's stage directions, broke the restrictions imposed on all performances by the officers of his estate. No matter that a fine actress and talented director brought Beckett's image of female sensuality and despair to the heart of the West End: Warner was banned from taking the production to Paris and might never be allowed to direct Beckett again, or not until he had been dead 50 years (in 2039).

In October the Globe Theatre on Shaftesbury Avenue was renamed the Gielgud in honour of Sir John, who celebrated his 90th birthday earlier in the year. Appropriately, the first production following the rechristening was *Hamlet*, the play in which Gielgud secured his reputation 64 years before. Peter Hall directed a relative newcomer, Stephen Dillane, whose volatile, quick-thinking interpretation was widely praised. At the start of the year, and at the same theatre before its change of name, Hall directed Griff Rhys Jones in a deliriously funny production of Feydeau's farce *Le Dindon*, retitled *An Absolute Turkey*.

Theatre de Complicité, nowadays a British flagship company permanently touring the world, mounted three productions: *Street of Crocodiles*, based on stories by Bruno Schulz, was revived at the Young Vic; *Out of a House Walked a Man*, from writings by the Russian absurdist Danil Kharms, enjoyed a good run at the National; best of the three, also drawn from a book, by John Berger, *The Three Lives of Lucie Cabrol*, was superlatively staged at Riverside Studios and was due in the West End early in 1995. A similarly successful use of mime and heightened gesture characterized Tim Supple's *Grimm Tales* (Young Vic). Indeed, some of the company had previously worked with Complicité.

The year was festooned with tribute musicals: *Patsy Cline* (Whitehall); *Noël/Cole* (Chichester); *Let There Be Love* (Stratford East), venerating

Nat King Cole; and *Only the Lonely* (Piccadilly), turning Roy Orbison, the 'Big O', into a big zero. For *Once On This Island* the Royalty Theatre was temporarily renamed Island and the front of house transformed into a Caribbean festival. *Copacabana* (Prince of Wales) gave pleasure to Barry Manilow fans, and Topol starred yet again in the umpteenth revival of *Fiddler on the Roof* (Palladium). Ruthie Henshall and John Gordon-Sinclair gave charming, not-too-cute performances at the sentimental heart of *She Loves Me* (Savoy), an earlier work by the creators of *Fiddler*, unashamedly celebrating romantic love.

Two visions of London's underworld brought the year to a close: Phyllida Lloyd's *The Threepenny Opera* (Donmar Warehouse), updated to 2001, the year of King William V's coronation, added contemporary vices to Brecht's text but thereby caused Weill's haunting music to seem anachronistic. At the other extreme, a sugary *Oliver!* (Palladium), though set to make a fortune, exposed the false optimism of Bart's admittedly tuneful score.

NEW YORK THEATRE. In New York *Three Tall Women* continued to play to full houses Off-Broadway. Destined for a transfer to Broadway from the Public Theater was Anna Devere Smith's one-woman show *Twilight: Los Angeles*, based on interviews with observers of the Rodney King riots. Terence McNally continued his string of successes with a study of the different lifestyles enjoyed by a group of gay men, *Love! Valor! Compassion!* (Manhattan Theatre Club). The highlight of George C. Wolfe's first full season in charge of the New York Shakespeare Festival proved to be Sam Shepard's *Simplicité*, his first play for several years.

On the musical front, the big three of 1994 were *Sunset Boulevard* (Marquis), with Glenn Close outstanding in the central role; the kitschy but immensely popular *Beauty and the Beast* (Palace), adapted from the Disney film; and the latest Sondheim/Lapine collaboration, *Passion*, a variation on the Cyrano de Bergerac theme where a plain, if not actually large-nosed, woman eventually touches the heart of an unobservant young man. *Perestroika*, the second half of Tony Kushner's *Angels in America*, won most of the Tony awards.

v. CINEMA

HOLLYWOOD, whose films continued to be one of America's most successful exports and whose tentacles now reached throughout the world, had the kind of year in 1994 which proved that you could transcend any number of failures if you had several mega-successes. The failures of a tumultuous year included the fact that the Japanese electronics giants controlling several of the major companies found themselves at the losing end of the profits gamble. As a direct result, three powerful industry figures—Steven Spielberg, Jeffrey Katzenberg and David Geffen—decided to start a new studio, as yet untitled, which would make films and control their distribution and exhibition.

The two American films which did hit the jackpot were Disney's animated *The Lion King*, a jungle fable elaborated with music by Elton John, and Paramount's historical fable *Forrest Gump*. Between them, these two took some $600 million at the American box-office alone and were expected to achieve similar figures on international screens. Considering the further revenue that would accrue when television and video rights were sold, no amount of money spent on making such projects seemed excessive. In fact, neither of these movies was among the most expensive of the year, though each had large budgets. The average American film was currently costing $30 million, and both *The Lion King* and *Forrest Gump* ran to $40 million. The accolade for spending money on production was probably won by James Cameron's *True Lies*, an Arnold Schwarzenegger action thriller rumoured to have cost over $100 million to complete. It earned almost exactly half of the returns achieved by the first two films in America. But its success, as number three on the 1994 list, gave much-needed succour to Twentieth Century Fox, one of the few Hollywood studios not owned or part-owned by the Japanese.

By the end of the year a dozen American films had reached the $100 million mark in the USA, which was about average. Perhaps the biggest surprise was another Fox film, also an action adventure, called *Speed*, starring Keanu Reeves, which made $121 million in its home territory—double the expected return. No-one was much surprised that Disney continued to cater for family audiences so well, since *Aladdin*, *Beauty and the Beast* and *The Little Mermaid* had proved in recent years that animated features, though expensive and time-consuming to make, were once again fashionable. Even in its founder's glory days, when classic after classic was produced, the studio did not have such resounding hits. *Forrest Gump* was certainly more of a surprise success than *The Lion King*, even though it starred Tom Hanks, the year's Oscar winner for his part as a gay man dying of AIDS in Jonathan Demme's *Philadelphia*. The new Hanks film, an overview of America's recent history as seen through the eyes of an idiot savant, had not been expected to do more than average business and was possibly the year's most intelligently-made hit movie.

Steven Spielberg's *Schindler's List*, the director's most risk-taking film (see AR 1993, p. 499), almost reached the magic figure of $100 million at the American box-office, despite the fact that it was nearly three hours long, made in black and white and about the Holocaust. The fact that it swept the board at the 1994 Oscars, winning best film and best director awards, aided it in the world at large to gross over $300 million. It was the first time that Spielberg, Jewish himself, had won the Oscar and he considered it to be his greatest triumph.

Critically speaking, though, Spielberg's film vied with two other American films as the best of the year: Robert Altman's *Short Cuts*, a stunning adaptation of several Raymond Carver stories, which attempted to chart the present mood of America; and Quentin Tarantino's *Pulp Fiction*, a talented if modish exploration of low-life violence in Los Angeles. The controversy surrounding the latter film contributed to its considerable box-office success and made Tarantino the most heavily-hyped young talent of the year. Abroad, *Pulp Fiction* won the Palme d'Or at Cannes, which added to its artistic credentials. Sadly, the critically-acclaimed *Short Shorts* was much less of a financial success. The other major controversy of the year concerned Oliver Stone's *Natural Born Killers*, a violent tale of two young killers on the loose in America and of the media circus pursuing them. The film was briefly banned in Britain because of claims that copy-cat killings had taken place in America and France, but shown everywhere else, without producing the expected profits.

Away from America, European film-makers still found it a hard row to hoe attempting to compete with Hollywood on anything like even terms. But Krzysztof Kieslowski's *Three Colours: Red*, the last of a fine trilogy based on the colours of the French flag and the precepts of the French Revolution, kept Europe's reputation from falling further, even if the Cannes jury, presided over by Clint Eastwood, unaccountably refused to give it a prize. The news that this accomplished Polish director had decided to make no further films was treated with a pinch of salt and it was to be hoped he would eventually change his mind. The most successful European film by far in 1994 was British—Mike Newell's *Four Weddings and a Funeral*, a shrewd and entertaining comedy of middle-class manners which made Hugh Grant into an international star, fêted all over the world. By year's end it had earned well over $250 million worldwide—£29 million coming from Britain alone, where it became the second most successful film ever shown, beaten only by *Jurassic Park*.

Other European films to make their mark included two by Italian directors—Nanni Moretti's delightfully personal commentary on life, *Dear Diary*, and Gianni Amelio's *Lamerica*, set in Albania just after the communist regime was overthrown. Amelio won the European Felix award for the third time in five years for his large-scale European epic. Otherwise, American films took 74 per cent of European audiences, with domestic films accounting for only 17 per cent—a sorry state of affairs. Only the British managed to sell regularly to America, though finding it difficult to show on screens in Britain, where 86 per cent of the audience market share was taken by American films. Added to that disadvantage, the British government still held back from giving the tax concessions available elsewhere in Europe, so that most British films had to be co-produced with Europe or financed with American money. This was true of Ken Loach's remarkable *Ladybird Ladybird*, the story of a mother fighting to keep her children from being taken into care because of her irregular lifestyle. The film won several festival prizes and managed to go into profit despite a poorly-attended British release.

Towards the end of the year, another British film, Danny Boyle's Edinburgh thriller *Shallow Grave* proved as successful outside Britain as at home, whereas Kenneth Branagh's big budget *Mary Shelley's Frankenstein*, made for an American company in England and starring Robert De Niro, deservedly failed to do much business. This contrasted with the success of Neil Jordan's *Interview with a Vampire*, a British-directed American film starring Tom Cruise, which had considerable success. A point in Britain's favour was the fact that its few remaining studios were fully-booked, mostly by American productions, thus giving employment to its much-admired technicians and craftsmen.

Outside Europe and America, the Latin American cinema made only some 30 films in the entire continent in 1994, thanks to Hollywood domination. Africa produced very little of note, except films co-produced in France and made in French-speaking Africa, and African audiences, deluged by films from India and Hong Kong rather than Hollywood output, did not seem eager to see the continent's own product. Nevertheless, two North African films made their mark at festivals—the Tunisian *Silence of the Palaces* and the Algerian *Bad-El-Oued City*, both with French money and technical resources behind them.

The huge Indian film industry, much larger than Hollywood, made some 750 films in 1994, despite a new American invasion that saw *Jurassic Park* dubbed into Hindi and becoming very successful at the box-office. The problem in India was that the three biggest centres of film-making—Madras, Bombay, and Calcutta—were beginning to feel the draught of inadequate production funds and out-of-date technology. Hits seemed to be getting rarer and there was considerable controversy over one film that could have been a success. This was Shakhur Kapoor's excellent *The Bandit Queen*, an account of the life of Phoolan Devi, India's most prominent woman outlaw, now out of gaol and responsible for a high court injunction banning the film's screening in India. Nominated as India's candidate for the US Academy awards and highly praised at Cannes, the film nevertheless faced severe problems in demonstrating its worth at the international box-office. Oddly, it was financed not by Indian interests but by Britain's Channel Four television station.

China's film industry, still beset by political censorship, produced several outstanding films which came up against the wrath of the authorities. Particularly notable was Zhang Yimou's *To Live*, an account of Chinese history over the last 40 years through the eyes of one family and their struggles to survive. This caused Zhang to be banned from making any further films in his homeland for five years. The harsh decision gave warning that the Chinese revival of recent years, celebrated as much abroad as at home, might be short-lived. The rest of the films of the Chinese-speaking world fared better, with several outstanding productions emanating from Taiwan, including Tsai Ming Liang's *Vive l'Amour*, the joint Golden Lion winner at the prestigious Venice Festival.

The Japanese cinema, fighting American domination, had several domestic successes but rather more failures. Few of the films of a once-great and much-admired industry reached international audiences.

Deaths in 1994 included those of Burt Lancaster (Hollywood actor), Melina Mercouri (Greek actress turned politician), Mai Zetterling (Swedish/British actress and director), Ivan Reisman (Soviet director), Lindsay Anderson (British director), River Phoenix (Hollywood actor), Peter Cushing (British actor) and Jessica Tandy (American actress). (For Lancaster, Mercouri, Zetterling, Cushing and Tandy, see XX: Obituary.)

vi.   TELEVISION & RADIO

ON the small screen it was year of contrasts, with both the BBC and ITV being simultaneously praised and vilified for the quality of their programmes. The BBC won numerous plaudits for its excellent adaptation of George Eliot's *Middlemarch*, which was seen as a sure sign that the corporation was once again being true to its public-service purpose rather than straining to win the largest audiences possible. At the same time, the BBC was roundly condemned for the crass and populist nature of *National Lottery Live*, its coverage of the weekly choosing of the six winning balls in Britain's new competition launched in November. It was a similiar story in the independent television network, where awards were won for off-beat crime series such as *Cracker* and *Prime Suspect*, both produced by Granada Television. Yet in its review of the first year of the new ITV licences that began in 1993 (see AR 1993, p. 503), the Independent Television Commission (ITC) strongly criticized the lack of adventure and daring in much of ITV's output.

Published on 26 May, the ITC report singled out Carlton Television and GMTV, new holders of the London weekday and the national breakfast franchises respectively, for particular attack. Carlton's network performance was described as 'well below expectations' and Carlton programmes such as the *Hollywood Women* series were denounced as 'glib and superficial'. GMTV fared even worse, being given a formal warning in view of its 'unsatisfactory performance over 1993 as a whole'. There was not universal agreement with the ITC's verdict (some critics and a sizeable audience liked *Hollywood Women*), and the ITC was itself criticized for moving beyond regulation and appearing to want to act as critic of the style of individual programmes. Nevertheless, the ITC again showed its teeth later in the year when it imposed an unprecedented £500,000 fine on Granada Television for repeated breaches by the *This Morning* programme of the rules designed to prevent 'undue prominence of products'.

Despite the criticisms, there was general ITC praise for ITV for maintaining its 10 per cent ratings lead over BBC1, and also for Channel 4, which continued to prosper by selling its own advertising. Channel 4 was disappointed, though, when it failed to persuade the government to change the prevailing funding formula, originally designed as an insurance policy for the new channel. According to Channel 4's calculations, the formula would mean the channel's paying ITV as much as £500 million over ten years—money it would have used for British programme production.

As usual, what was going on 'behind the box' often merited more attention and interest than what was actually shown on the television screen itself. It was the year when the electronic super-highway—capable, in theory at least, of delivering all the images, moving and still, and all the information in the world to every home—really began to seize the imagination (see XIV.2). There was, however, more talk about information super-highways than evidence of willingness to fund them, although the Internet, the informal network linking more than 30 million subscribers with thousands of databases around the world, made great strides. For those with the necessary receiving equipment, the first moving pictures of a regular 'television service' travelled through the Internet 'cyberspace' just before Christmas.

Amid all the hype, it was very noticeable that a number of the huge corporate deals agreed in 1993 between cable and telecommunications companies to launch the super-highway collapsed in 1994. TCI of Denver, the largest US cable operator, was supposed to create a $60,000 million giant in a merger with the Bell Atlantic telephone corporation. In the end, both companies decided that they had little in common and went their separate ways, casting more than an element of doubt over how soon, or even if, the digital revolution was going to transform the world of broadcasting.

In the United Kingdom, the most significant developments were the consolidation of ITV through enormous takeovers and the publication of the government's White Paper on the future of the BBC on 6

July. In this document the BBC emerged virtually unscathed from three years of intense government scrutiny. The BBC's structure, its financing by universal licence fee and its public-service purpose were left intact; indeed, it was encouraged to develop a new role by expanding its commercial activities in Britain and around the world. The corporation's new Royal Charter was to run for ten years from 1997, although the future of the licence fee would be reviewed in 2001 in the light of changing technology. On actual BBC output, the government merely said that it wanted to see more programmes featuring science and engineering, more programmes reflecting life in the UK regions and greater audience sensitivity in matters of taste and decency. The White Paper did warn, however, that the government intended to look at ways of introducing private capital into the running of BBC transmitters.

The outcome of the White Paper debate underpinned the position of John Birt, the BBC director-general, who had caused further controversy by introducing market mechanisms into the relationships between programme producers and staff under the 'producer choice' plan. The first fruits of the new commercialism came in November when the BBC, in partnership with the Pearson media and entertainment group, announced that it would launch two 24-hour European satellite television channels in January. One, BBC Prime, would be a sub-scription channel devoted to entertainment and the other, BBC World, would be financed by advertising and would offer news, current affairs and documentaries.

Rupert Murdoch, chairman of the News Corporation, admitted in a June interview that he had asked for the BBC's existing 24-hour news service to be removed from his Hong Hong-based Star satellite system to appease the sensitivities of the Chinese government. Nevertheless, the BBC service continued to be available in the Indian sub-continent. During the year the BBC also launched a 24-hour television news service in Arabic aimed at the Middle East as well as a service aimed at Japan, partially in Japanese.

The government's decision to allow one ITV company to own two broadcasting licences (except if both were in London) led to the almost immediate restructuring of ITV through three large takeovers followed by the inevitable redundancies. In January, no sooner had Carlton Communications been able to bid for Central (the second largest ITV company) than MAI, the media and financial services group controlling Meridian Broadcasting, bid £292 million for Anglia Television. In February Granada finally won London Weekend Television in a hostile takeover battle that finally valued the London company at £776 million. Sir Christopher Bland (the LWT chairman) and Greg Dyke (chief executive) both resigned following the change of ownership.

After considerable delay, mostly caused by the government, the ITC was finally able (in November) to readvertise for tenders for Channel 5, the new national commercial television station. Despite the setting aside of frequencies for future digital terrestrial services, the new channel was still expected to be able to reach about 70 per cent of the UK population.

One of the most dramatic broadcasting developments of 1994 was the continued growth of commercial radio. The launch of new local, regional and national commercial stations meant that in October, for the first time since the launch of commercial radio in Britain 21 years previously, the commercial sector won a larger share of the audience than the BBC. The launch of a third national commercial station, Talk Radio UK, was scheduled for February 1995 and was likely to result in a further increase of radio revenues. One of the commercial success stories, Classic FM, began to export its concept and won licences in The Netherlands and Finland. Meanwhile, the BBC announced plans to launch network radio transmissions of digital audio broadcasting in September 1995, providing interference-free CD-quality sound everywhere, including in a moving car.

Cable and satellite television made considerable progress during the year—progress that could be financially quantified because leading cable operators such as TeleWest and British Sky Broadcasting (BSkyB) were floated on the London Stock Exchange. The most spectacular float was that of BSkyB, which by the end of the year had more than 3.7 million subscribers via dishes and cable television networks. Although there were dissenting voices from the investment community, BSkyB was valued in December at £4,400 million—more than double the current market value of Carlton, the largest ITV group. TeleWest, a 50–50 joint venture between TCI and US West, the American telecommunications group, was valued at £1,800 million.

The share price of both groups came under pressure after their flotations. The reason was a degree of scepticism about just how robust and reliable the earnings of the new media would be. The so-called 'churn' factor—the level of disconnection by dissatisfied subscribers— remained high in cable. Moreover, although hundreds of millions of pounds were being invested in building cable networks in the UK, the actual number of subscribers remained modest. By the end of 1994 the total had topped 800,000 and was expected to pass one million during 1995. But the cable penetration rate—actual subscribers as a percentage of those who could subscribe—remained stubbornly low at just under 22 per cent.

In homes choosing to have the new media channels of cable and satellite, the four national channels still accounted for two-thirds of total viewing, the remaining third being fragmented among 20 or 30 channels. Cable did, however, encourage the creation of 'cable-only' channels to try to differentiate the service from the offerings of the satellite stations. This development provided an opening for national newspapers long ambitious to get into television but prevented by current broadcasting legislation from owning more than 20 per cent of an ITV company. In November Associated Newspapers, publishers of the *Daily Mail*, launched Channel One, a 24-hour news channel for London which it hoped would spread to the rest of the country. Not to be outdone, the Mirror Group announced that it intended to launch its own cable channel, LiveTV, in 1995. It then, as part of an expansion into the elecronic media, bought a 19.9 per cent stake in Scottish Television. Meanwhile, the most positive aspect of cable so far, at least in the UK, was the rapid spread of cable telecommunications services, more than 600,000 lines being installed by late 1994.

In the United States, the move to digital satellite television meant that for the first time the entire continental USA had a 150-channel satellite system, using newly-developed digital compression technology. Plan were already being laid to launch a similiar system in Europe during 1995, using technology which at least promised as many as 500 channels. Apart from minority thematic channels, the main practical service on offer to viewers would be 'near-video-on-demand', under which as many as 60 channels would be reserved to show the top ten movies. The start of each movie would staggered so that the viewer was rarely more than 20 minutes away from the start of a popular film. No-one yet knew, however, whether the audience would pay enough for the extra convenience to justify the extra cost.

Apart from the prospect of a proliferation in the number of channels available, there was also a continuing trend towards taking existing channels around the world. VH1, the Viacom channel for those too old for MTV (the teenagers' music television channel), came to Europe for the first time, while the Disney Channel spread into Germany and announced that in September 1995 it would become part of the BSkyB package.

At the European Union (EU), there was further delay over plans to introduce EU-wide regulations on non-European programming. Many thought that plans to force broadcasters to ensure that at least 50 per cent of programmes shown were European-made were too restrictive.

Amid attempts to restrict the power of Hollywood, one very small David did well against the US Goliath. S4C, the Welsh fourth television channel, received a 'best foreign film' Oscar nomination for its £700,000 Welsh-language production *Hedd Wyn*, the story of a poet from Trawsfyndd who died in the trenches in World War I (see also I.7). The Welsh came home without an Oscar, but the retiring S4C director-general, Geraint Stanley Jones, said that the nomination proved that 'small can be quite good' and that 'a funny language may not be that restrictive'.

2. ART—ARCHITECTURE

i. ART

THE year's most significant occurrence for the long-term future of the visual arts in Britain, as perhaps for all the arts, was the introduction of the national lottery in November. The allocation of up to 30 per cent of the proceeds to five 'good causes', including the arts, was expected to have major implications for the funding of capital projects such as museum development. It was also anticipated—and in certain quarters feared—that the lottery dividend would come to affect the Treasury's approach to revenue funding for the arts.

A government lottery two centuries previously had ended in corruption and scandal, but its lasting legacy was the British Museum (BM). That same institution now planned, with aid from the lottery-funded Millenium Fund, to increase its floor space by a staggering 40 per cent at a cost of $110 million. A great deal of space would become available when the British Library (BL) accomplished its long-planned move from Bloomsbury to its new headquarters on the Euston Road. The move was currently scheduled for 1996, but the new library had such a chequered history (having been nearly 20 years in the building, at a cost so far of £450 million) that this date hardly seemed to be guaranteed. Meanwhile, in 1994, the BM opened its new Mexican Gallery with artefacts from the Museum of Mankind, which was soon to vacate its premises in Burlington House to join the other collections in Bloomsbury. The BM's year also included the 'Greek Gold' exhibition, featuring works from the Metropolitan Museum in New York and the Hermitage in St Petersburg as well as the BM itself.

As the BL and BM celebrated their impending divorce, the Tate Gallery was also contemplating a split as it campaigned for the establishment of a Museum of Modern Art for London at the disused Bankside power station site in Southwark (on the south side of the Thames) by the year 2000. Once a branch of the National Gallery, the Tate had for historical reasons come to consist of two discrete, though chronologically overlapping, collections: of British art since 1600 and of Modern foreign art. It also housed the Turners given to the nation by the artist in the Clore Gallery at Millbank. Under the proposals drawn up by the Tate's director, Nicholas Serota, Millbank would remain the home of the British Collection but twentieth-century British works would be divided between the two sites. There were enough of the latter for it then to be possible, for instance, to see Francis Bacon in the company of Giacometti in one venue and of Fuseli in the other.

While national collections were planning splits, the world of contemporary art showed increasing signs of polarization. The self-consciously controversial Turner Prize, administerd by the Patrons of New Art at the

Tate and sponsored by Channel 4 Television, awarded the £20,000 prize to sculptor Antony Gormley. His most familiar work involved having casts of himself made in segments of lead, revealing a preoccupation with 'the body' in harmony with international avant-garde concerns. Another series of his work exhibited at the Tate Gallery Liverpool in the spring consisted of rectangular slabs of concrete with holes intimating where a body (in fact the artist's) had been lying, or standing, or kneeling. The series was markedly similar in ethos to work by the 1993 Turner Prize winner, Rachel Whiteread, who won the prize with a cast of an East London house (see AR 1993, p. 509).

The Turner Prize found itself with a direct competitor in 1994 in the shape of the Jerwood Prize for Painting, signalling in its designation more traditional aesthetic criteria. For although the first Turner Prize had been won by a painter (Malcolm Morley), the awards had recently shown a bias towards three-dimensional and multi-media works. The Jerwood shortlist of five included abstractionists John Hoyland and Yuko Shiraishi, rigorously observational figure painters Euan Uglow and John Lessore, and Maurice Cockrill, who painted in a landscape-influenced romantic expressionism. The winner was Craigie Aitchison, a painter of portraits and religiously-inspired landscapes in an ethereal, pared-down decorative style. As if sensing competition, the Turner jury included on its shortlist a young Canadian painter, Peter Doig, who would not have been out of place among the Jerwood contenders.

One of the more notorious exhibitions of the year was curated by neo-conceptualist Damien Hirst at the Serpentine Gallery. Under the enigmatic title 'Some Went Mad, Some Ran Away', the exhibition included such novelties as a blow-up replica in rubber of Rodin's statue of Balzac suspended from the ceiling, as well as a typical piece by Hirst himself consisting of a sheep suspended in formaldehyde. A great deal of press coverage focused on the vandalism of this piece by a disaffected young artist who poured black ink into the vitrine, and was prosecuted for his action.

While the international reputations of artists such as Whiteread and Hirst continued to soar, their high-profile patron Charles Saatchi indicated a shift in his collecting of young British artists with a show of three *painters*: Simon Callery, Simon English and Jenny Saville. The previous year the collector had made headline news when he purchased the entire debut show of Callery's minimalist landscapes. Saville received widespread critical acclaim for her monumental canvases depicting obese women in a realist style upon which feminist slogans were scratched. The artist objected when a mirror which was supposed to accompany one work, to enable the viewer to read the reversed writing on the canvas, was left out of the display by Charles Saatchi.

The year began with an impassioned outburst of critical polarization when 35 prominent art-world figures pubished a letter in the London

Evening Standard condemning the paper's vituperative art critic Brian Sewell and calling for his dismissal. The signatories took particular offence at what they described as his 'homophobia' and 'misogyny', being moved by his recent—and typical—dismissal of a Vanessa Bell nude as being unlikely to excite even 'a purblind lesbian'. The letter only served to bolster Sewell's wide popularity with readers. Along with television star Sister Wendy Beckett, Sewell became the most talked-about art critic of the day, the engaging nun being as notoriously enthusiastic about contemporary artists as Sewell was cutting. Later in the year Sewell published an anthology of his articles under the title *The Reviews That Caused the Rumpus*, reprinting the letter and its list of signatories in his introduction, but failing to mention a follow-up letter signed by 20 equally distinguished art-world personalities criticizing the 'sanctimonious attitudes' of the first petition.

Newspaper critics also caused consternation and surprise among art-world colleagues with their antagonism towards the retrospective of the expatriate American painter R.B. Kitaj at the Tate. Although Kitaj was held in high esteem by scholars and fellow painters (having been a leading force in the return to figuration in the mid-1970s), his ambitious narrative paintings dealing with major themes such as the Holocaust were viewed as portentous and crudely-executed by most critics. The exhibition was more graciously received in Los Angeles, where it began its subsequent US tour. In interviews with the American press, Kitaj accused his critics of philistinism and prejudice.

The year was a significant one for British sculpture. Sir Anthony Caro celebrated his 70th birthday with small exhibitions in London, Cambridge and Halifax, while a model of his forthcoming 1995 retrospective in Tokyo, which would be the largest display ever of his work, was unveiled by the British Council. Several exhibitions cast new light on neglected modernists: Barbara Hepworth was given a centenary show in Liverpool; the major pre-war sculptor Frank Dobson was the subject of an exhibition in Leeds; and Geoffrey Clarke, a prominent publicly-commissioned artist in the 1950s and 1960s, was shown in a regional touring exhibition. Meanwhile, the first public sculpture garden in the south of England was opened by Lord Gowrie, chairman of the Arts Council. Called 'Sculpture at Goodwood', the show was located at the Sussex home of collectors Wilfrid and Jeannette Cass, who initiated the project through their Goodwood Sculpture Foundation. Forty sculptures loaned by the artists were imaginatively sited in the landscaped, wooded park. The foundation also helped artists with the costs of making original works for display in the park, the first example of such patronage being Nigel Hall's monumental open-form steel construction *Soglio (Goodwood)*.

More complicated and fraught patronage was required in the case of Antonio Canova's *Three Graces* of 1819, which was acquired jointly by

the Victoria and Albert Museum in London and the Scottish National
Gallery in Edinburgh. The statue, a second version of an original in the
Hermitage, was made especially for the Duke of Bedford at Woburn
Abbey, where it was housed in its own domed temple. Rejected by the
nation when offered for £1 million in 1982, the statue became the subject
of heated debate when purchased by the Getty Museum in California
for £6.7 million. Export was delayed by the National Heritage Secretary
to give British institutions the chance to raise the money. Timothy
Clifford, director of the National Gallery in Edinburgh, masterminded
the successful operation, securing donations from John Paul Getty II
(nephew of the American museum's benefactor) and Baron Thyssen-
Bornemisza. This triumph contrasted with Clifford's ill-fated effort to
open a Museum of Scottish Art in Glasgow, which was refused a licence
by the Scottish Office because of its unpopularity with informed Scotish
opinion.

Major British exhibitions of 1994 included 'The Glory of Venice',
a survey of such eighteenth-century painters as Canaletto, Guardi,
the Tiepolos and Belloti, organized by the Royal Academy in the
spirit of their memorable 1983 'Genius of Venice' exhibition devoted
to the Renaissance period. The Academy also took a show of small
paintings by Goya from the Prado and was due, in January 1995, to
repeat the mammoth Poussin centenary exhibition first seen in Paris
in the autumn. The latter was arguably the most significant exhibition
of the year, its closest rival being the Memling exhibition in Bruges
commemorating the 500th anniversary of the Flemish master's death.
Meanwhile, Poussin's friend Claude was the subject of a satisfying
display at London's National Gallery. Other foreign shows of note
included Derain in Paris, Léger in Basel, Schiele in Washington DC
and Redon in Chicago.

The Royal Academy elected architect Sir Philip Dowson as president
in succession to Sir Roger de Grey, who at 75 had reached the
compulsory age of retirement. Sir Roger's long tenure was widely judged
a success, leaving the institution on a sounder financial footing. Although
he was severely criticized for his handling of the controversy surrounding
the 1993 'American Art in the Twentieth Century' exhibition, his more
lasting monument was the impressive Sackler Galleries, designed by Sir
Norman Foster, which had opened in 1991.

Notwithstanding the Canova sale, which bypassed the auction houses,
the international art market showed signs of renewed recession in 1994,
despite the modest recovery of the previous autumn. The *International
Art Index*'s authoritative equivalent of the *Financial Times* 100-share
index—a sampling of 100 artists of different nationalities and periods—
showed a slide of 11 per cent in the first half of the year, a trend which
continued in the second six months.

Among those who died in 1994 were Paul Delvaux, French surrealist painter; Sandra Fisher, London-based American figurative painter; Nikos Ghika, influential Greek painter, sculptor and architect; Felix Kelly, New Zealand-born British painter and illustrator; and Sir John Pope-Hennessy, British art historian and museum director (for all of whom, see XX: Obituary). Other deaths included those of Clement Greenberg, doyen of modern American art criticism; Sam Francis, Californian-born abstract expressionist; Donald Judd, pioneer minimalist; Edward Keinholz, installation artist and sculptor; Fabrizio Mancinelli, restorer of Michelangelo's Sistine Chapel Ceiling; Henry Geldzahler, former curator of the Metropolitan Museum in New York; and Helen Lessore, British realist painter and prominent 1950s dealer.

ii. ARCHITECTURE

THE year was marked for architects by increasing interest in the possible funding of new buildings by the national lottery, launched. in November. Many institutions became involved in the organizing of competitions for new buildings, or extensions to existing ones, which might be funded by one of the lottery's beneficiaries, particularly the Millennium Commission. This latter body, chaired by the Secretary of State for National Heritage, spelled out its aim of promoting buildings (among other things) which would mark the advent of the 21st century in appropriate ways.

Large projects for London were early examples of major bidders for such funding, two of them involving the country's best-known architects. Sir Norman Foster & Partners won a competition to extend and upgrade the British Museum, opening up the Reading Room for public use for the first time. Another example of improving on the past occurred at the South Bank arts complex on the Thames, where Sir Richard Rogers won a competition to improve the facilities there. His winning design envisaged a giant glass roof covering part of the existing complex, providing an element of weathering and raising the ambient temperature to that of Bordeaux.

Also on the South Bank, the Tate Gallery announced an international competition to create a Gallery of Modern Art within the redundant Bankside power station, itself only 40 years old (see also XVI.2.i). A shortlist of six firms had been identified by the year's end, one British. The prospect was thus raised of the first major London cultural building to be procured by competition in living memory. Outside the capital, Glasgow won a three-city race to become the Arts Council's 1999 City of Architecture.

The most controversial competition of 1994 was the one for a new opera house in Cardiff. The London-based architect Zaha Hadid

(Iraqi by birth but trained at the Architectural Association) won a two-stage competition, being shortlisted at the first stage and then competing against four invited international firms, including Sir Norman Foster. To general acclaim amongst the architectural community, but to the shock of some in Wales, Hadid convinced the judges with an uncompromisingly deconstructivist design. A campaign was immediately launched against her design by the local media, some MPs and many Cardiff businessmen. The result was that the controversy became a *cause célèbre*, opinion being deeply divided not only over her scheme but also over the ethics of the competition system in general and of this one in particular. Battle-lines were still drawn as the year ended, with the architectural establishment set to support Hadid in the face of undiminished opposition to her design (see also I.7).

Two other buildings by prominent British architects, both the result of competitions, opened to general approval and were a reminder that, whatever their faults, competition encouraged the best designs, often by younger architects. The best example was the Hôtel du Département in Marseilles (France), by Will Alsop. His spectacular design, which had been preferred to Sir Norman Foster's shortlisted alternative, was the largest building by a British architect to be completed in 1994. Continuing the European theme, Nicholas Grimshaw's splendid Waterloo International Terminal in London, for passengers taking the Eurostar train service through the Channel Tunnel to Paris and Brussels, was opened to general approval and won the Building of the Year award of the Royal Institute of British Architects (RIBA). And there were other 'European' successes for British architects. Grimshaw's old partner, Terry Farrell, was commissioned to produce a study for the upgrading of the Lisbon Docks and to design various transport schemes for the Portuguese capital. In Moscow, ABK unveiled their new designs for a riverside British embassy, the foundation stone of which was laid by the Queen during her state visit to Russia in November.

In Britain, the new Glyndebourne opera house, by Michael and Patty Hopkins, won rave reviews from audiences, performers and critics alike (see also XVI.1.i). A replacement of the existing complex, the building used traditional materials in a contemporary fashion, suggesting that the architectural trend was away from a high-tech image towards becoming the standard-bearer for 'adapted tradition'. The award of the RIBA's Royal Gold Medal to the Hopkinses was an official seal of approval for architecture's leading couple: not since Charles and Ray Eames had a husband-and-wife team received this accolade. There was no sign of their practice slowing down: work was nearly finished on a new headquarters for the Inland Revenue in Nottingham (arguably the tax-man's most important building since Somerset House) and on a new office building for MPs in Westminster, plus Underground station, opposite the Big Ben tower.

The government did little to help the fortunes of architects during
the year, which were almost uniformly difficult in terms of workload
and prospects for young graduates entering the profession. Instead,
some attention was paid to improving the efficiency of the construction
industry as a whole, following a report commissioned from Sir Michael
Latham, the former Conservative MP. His ideas, while not necessarily
hostile to architects, suggested new forms of contract which would
have to be negotiated toughly if they were not to result in even more
powers being given to project managers and contractors, rather than
to designers. Legislation to revise the procedure for registration of
professionals seemed to be put on the government backburner, although
action was promised for 1995.

In a busy year for royalty, proposals for upgrading fire-damaged
Windsor Castle, by architects Siddell Gibson, were criticized as 'too
safe' by the architectural magazines, but welcomed by most of the
newspapers. The Prince of Wales launched his polemical magazine
Perspectives, partly intended to promote the views of his institute of
architecture. Several supporters of the Prince's views found significant
new roles. Liam O'Connor was appointed special adviser on architecture
to the Secretary of State for the Environment, while Dr Richard John
became the new head of the Prince's Institute. Three new Royal Fine
Art Commissioners could also be said to share the values of the Prince:
developer Trevor Osborne, architect Quinlan Terry and critic Giles
Worsley (who became the second editor of *Perspectives* before the year
was out).

At the RIBA, a surprise winner emerged in a contested election for
the institute's presidency, namely Owen Luder, who had been president
in the early 1980s. He expressed scepticism during his election campaign
about the idea of the RIBA becoming a populist 'architecture centre'.
Such plans nevertheless continued apace, involving an expanding programme of exhibitions and events. Meanwhile, the institute concluded
a study into the profession's future which contained some harsh criticism
about the need for change with a view to becoming more competitive
and responsive to the needs of clients.

Well-known architects who died during the year included Hidalgo
'Jacko' Moya of Powell & Moya, designer of the 1951 Festival of Britain
Skylon structure; Gordon Cullen, deviser of the idea of 'townscape' in
the 1950s; Theo Crosby , whose last job, the re-creation of Shakespeare's
Globe Theatre on the South Bank, neared completion during the year;
and Ron Herron, co-founder of the Archigram group and influential
architect and teacher for more than 30 years (see XX: Obituary).

Two major international architectural prizes awarded in 1994: Christian de Portzamparc of France won the Pritzker and Charles Correa of
India won the Japanese Praemium Imperiale.

3. LITERATURE

As in previous years, the Booker Prize for fiction afforded the only
moment in the British cultural calendar when the arts could be certain
of a place on the front pages of the newspapers. In 1994 it did so
for what seemed like weeks on end. There were several stories of
limited importance: the judge who neglected to mention that one of the
books submitted was by his wife; the chairman, Professor John Bayley,
announcing that modern British fiction was humourless and not much
good; and the selection for the shortlist of a self-published book. They
were eclipsed by the storm surrounding the final verdict. The admirable
Scottish writer James Kelman, with *How Late It Was, How Late*,
emerged as the winner, but the jury nearly fell apart in the process
and the choice was roundly condemned by self-appointed guardians of
pure language who objected to the proliferation of four-letter words in
this study of a Glaswegian alcoholic going blind and living a derelict life
at other people's mercy. Serious critics of literature praised the choice,
if not the shortlist of fairly unfamiliar authors from which it was taken.
In sales terms it proved a far less marketable winner than its Irish
predecessor, *Paddy Clarke Ha Ha Ha* by Roddy Doyle, which ended
the year with possibly the highest sales of any Booker Prize winner.

In the field of fiction the year produced the customary crop of
guaranteed best-sellers by household names. P.D. James's *Original
Sin*, in which she returned to familiar territory with Adam Dalgleish as
her hero, was universally praised as one of her strongest murder stories
with its disturbing insights into the world of publishing. Within the limits
of their genres, Len Deighton, Frederick Forsyth and Mary Wesley
(who was honoured with a CBE at the end of the year and who
in her eighties defied the creative sterility assumed of old age) all
proved their recurring popularity. One of the joys of fiction, however,
remained the phenomenon of an experienced writer coming up with
something unexpectedly outside his or her normal range. This was
true of several authors in 1994: Peter Ackroyd, for example, with *Dan
Leno and the Limehouse Golem*, in which George Gissing, Karl Marx,
Charlie Chaplin's father and other Victorian personalities, headed by the
music-hall artist Dan Leno, were caught up in a celebrated murder of the
period. In the year of South Africa's freedom, its two most distinguished
white novelists, Nadine Gordimer with *None To Accompany Me* and
J.M. Coetzee with *The Master of Petersburg*, were in good form, the
one staying within South African subject-matter and the other exploring
hidden aspects of Dostoyevsky's personality.

The most startling success of the year was Jill Paton Walsh's meta-
physical novel *Knowledge of Angels*, an enthralling investigation into
the existence of God. Based on the true story of a wolf-reared child
found in France and brought up within the confines of a convent,

the novel transposed this tale to a Mediterranean island around 1450. Initially overlooked by most critics, it leapt to prominence on the Booker shortlist and very nearly won the prize. This was a remarkable achievement considering its provenance as a book for which the author, previously known mainly for children's fiction, had to arrange her own publication in Britain, despite the modest reputation it had already acquired in the United States.

Outstanding novels came from James Hamilton-Paterson (*Ghosts of Manila*) and Louis de Bernières (*Captain Corelli's Mandolin*). Alan Hollinghurst's *The Folding Star* was regarded by many as a breakthrough work which placed overt homosexuality in the mainstream of English fiction, where previously it had tended to be sublimated or unacknowledged. John Updike and John Irving did not disappoint students of American literature. V.S. Naipaul's *A Way in the World* was an exploratory text midway between fiction and history, as confusing to the cataloguer as Craig Raine's *History: The Home Movie*, a verse novel on a scale rarely attempted in modern times. Newer names arousing great interest included Fred D'Aguiar, Adbulrazak Gurnah and Romesh Gunesekera, the common factor being their origins in post-colonial Commonwealth societies whose political and cultural roots they wished to examine.

Short stories, so long regarded as a *passé* form of writing, continued their return to favour with serious authors—and, indeed, with writers of formulaic potboilers like Jeffrey Archer, whose *Twelve Red Herrings* was a collection of short stories which quickly established itself as the fastest-selling fiction of the year. At a rather higher level, A.S. Byatt, Salman Rushdie and Rose Tremain all produced significant collections of short fiction.

For many people, however, 1994 was a year of poetry. Whether there really was a poetry boom (and the truth or otherwise of a report by the *The Times* that the reading and writing of poetry were more of a national obsession than football) was to be tested out by a National Poetry Survey announced during the year by the Arts Council of England. Certainly there were signs of a new maturity in the marketing and public perception of poetry. On 6 October Britain had its first National Poetry Day, which made extraordinary breakthroughs in unexpected places. Poetry appeared on the departures notice board at Waterloo Station, on the platform of the Labour Party conference, in committee meetings, schools and social gatherings up and down the country, on the radio and in the papers. There could have been few people in Britain unaware of the existence of poetry on that day, which was likely to become an annual event as accepted as Poppy Day and Red Nose Day.

Though other initiatives to encourage poetry were less populist, they nevertheless showed signs of taking root. Two major awards were introduced. The T.S. Eliot Prize for the best volume of poetry from the

preceding year was set up by the Poetry Book Society and partly funded
by the poet's widow, Valerie Eliot; it was won by the Northern Irish
writer Ciarán Carson with *First Language*. The Forward Poetry Prize
was won by Alan Jenkins, with a 'best first-time published' category
going to a young black writer, Kwame Dawes. This prize, like National
Poetry Day, owed everything to the inspirational drive of an energetic
publishing entrepreneur, William Sieghart. Most adventurous of all the
ploys to propagate poetry was the promotion of 20 'new generation
poets', all of them under the age of 40. Their work was seen and heard
all over the country and their booksales inevitably increased. Amid all
this raising of the profile of poetry, however, was a continuing concern
that overall it was struggling for attention in the bookshops and literary
columns of journals and newspapers.

Among poetry books published during the year, new volumes by
Dannie Abse, Paul Durcan, Paul Muldoon and Peter Reading stood
out. Carol Ann Duffy, having scooped most of the available literary
awards the previous year with *Mean Time* (see AR 1993, p. 515),
confirmed her pre-eminence among younger poets (she was one of
the 'new generation') with her first *Selected Poems*.

Within the publishing world as a whole there were continuing
convulsions. The takeover by Headline of Hodder & Stoughton was
the latest in a long line of acquisitions which threatened the survival of
independent publishing. With profitability becoming the main motive,
there was growing concern that not only poetry but also new fiction
and certain kinds of biography and documentary would not so easily be
published in future years. As nearly 70,000 new titles were published
in Britain in 1994, too many to be displayed in even the largest
bookshops, any anticipated reduction might not seem too serious; but
the fear was that quality literature would be sacrificed to increasing
numbers of travel, do-it-yourself and cookery books. The outstanding
individual seller of the year was in fact a new book by the veteran
cook Delia Smith, *Delia Smith's Summer Collection*. With challenges
to the Net Book Agreement now more overt than ever—during the year
several shops took the unprecedented step of discounting lead titles by
up to 25 per cent—and with European legislation pointing the way to
the eventual introduction of value-added tax on publications (though
the Chancellor managed to resist it this year), there was much debate
during 1994 about future strategies in the transformed publishing and
bookselling worlds which many people said would be inevitable by
the end of the century. As 1994 was also the year in which access to
Internet and usage of CD-ROM technology became significantly more
inclusive (see XIV.2; XVI.1.vi), it was inevitable that prognostications
of the death of the book should be rife. Continuing public dismay at
further delays to the opening of the new British Library did not help
(see also XVI.2.i).

Public concerns about reading standards among young people were addressed by a number of new initiatives, of which the adoption of an agreed National Curriculum for English in schools was especially momentous. After three years of often acrimonious discussion about the syllabus, it was a relief to everyone that a mature balance between prescription and teachers' choice seemed to have been struck, with equal emphasis put on authors of the past and present. In the publishing world, the year saw the re-launching of Young Book Trust, a revamped version of the Children's Book Foundation, and the success of a film called *The Pagemaster*, which imaginatively exhorted children to inhabit a world of books. The death at an early age of Janet Ahlberg—with her husband Allan the most successful children's illustrator-author of her generation—cast a shadow over the world of young people's literature. For many years the most successful British author for young people, Roald Dahl was overtaken in 1994 by Terry Pratchett as the most-sold writer in this category. Jeremy Treglown's long-awaited biography aroused controversy by portraying Dahl (who died in 1991) as a misanthrope.

Elsewhere, the runaway best-sellers of the year were by Dick Francis, Roddy Doyle, Stephen Fry (showing the power of television celebrity to sell indifferent books), Catherine Cookson and Jeffrey Archer in the world of fiction, with Jung Chang's *Wild Swans* continuing its paperback odyssey as the most commercially-successful book of its time. The fact that such books made their authors and publishers huge sums of money, and in many cases drew critical plaudits too, tended to distort public opinion about the literary world. The great success of a few was taken to typify the rest, whereas almost any publisher (and most authors) could testify that there had not been any overall increase authors' receipts in modern times, taking inflation into account.

One of the growth areas in literature continued to be biographical and autobiographical writing. The latter was led in 1994 by Alan Bennett's *Writing Home*, a collection of diary extracts and other writings which propelled this unassuming playwright into a new category of popular recognition. The first volume of Doris Lessing's autobiography, *Under My Skin*, aroused great interest, and there was commercial success for John Mortimer with a book of reminiscences called *Murderers and Other Friends*. Political memoirs poured off the press, including books by Sir Geoffrey Howe and one by Terry Major-Ball, brother of the British Prime Minister, which gave rise to a certain amount of slightly patronizing national ribaldry. Much the most important political autobiography of the year was Nelson Mandela's *Long Walk to Freedom*. Even though parts of it were written for him, it was potentially the most enduring publication of the year, likely still to be read a century hence.

Among biographies of lasting value, the second volume of Norman Sherry's *The Life of Graham Greene* stood out. Christopher Fitz-Simon's

The Boys, a study of the partnership of the Dublin theatre couple Micheal MacLiammoir and Hilton Edwards, was the best of the annual crop of show business biographies, though Robert Lacey's *Grace*, a life of Grace Kelly, caused interest because of the Monegasque royal family's lack of enthusiasm for it. Claire Tomalin's *Mrs Jordan's Profession*, on the subject of the actress-mistress of King William IV, and Michael Holroyd's revised life of Lytton Strachey were the best of the historical lives published in the year.

Unlikely to have the same enduring value, but arousing ephemeral interest all the same, was Barbara Cartland's *I Reach For the Stars*, her fifth autobiography, published in the year of her 600th book! As the Princess of Wales's ex-step-grandmother—the gradations of such relationships were minutely documented in the press—Dame Barbara perhaps benefited from the popularity in the publishing world of royal subjects. Yet somehow in 1994 there was a sense that this particular bubble might have burst and that the public felt glutted by such books, which of their nature were often overtaken within days of their publication by tabloid reports of new royal activities. Anna Pasternak's *Princess in Love* was generally thought to be the most intrusive of the 1994 'royal' books, and Jonathan Dimbleby's *The Prince of Wales* the most considered, accompanied as it was by a hagiographical television documentary in which Prince Charles confessed to adultery. By the end of the year, however, evidence was apparent of public indifference to books about royal shenanigans. Certainly Andrew Morton's second book about Princess Diana failed to make anything like the mark of his first, seen by many as the catalyst of the royal separation.

Internationally, the award of the 1994 Nobel Prize for Literature was another case of an author being introduced to a world stage who had previously been known only in his own country. The chosen Japanese writer, Kenzaburo Oe, had been little translated and his work was not regarded as typifying any stereotype of Japan, but the unique prestige of the Nobel Prize was likely to ensure that his work and that of his country as a whole would be much more widely read. The most-sold book internationally was said to be *Crossing the Threshold of Hope* by Pope John Paul II, which was reputed to be the first book written by a reigning Supreme Pontiff.

A book by the Pope was, of course, more of a media event than a serious literary or religious occasion. Much of the publishing industry continued to be celebrity-focused. New novels were marketed on the strength of famous names, as perfumes once were, and gained more review coverage, even in the quality press, than more worthwhile books. In 1994 new 'novels' by tennis champion Martina Navratilova and by international model Naomi Campbell both became best-sellers, even though no critic had a good word to say for them. Perhaps, however, this causal link between publicity and sales could work to the benefit of good writing too. One of the best-selling books of the year was *Middlemarch* by George Eliot, first published in 1871 and now a successful television serial. Dickens's *Martin Chuzzlewit*, adapted for television by the fine novelist David Lodge, and Edith Wharton's *The Age of Innocence*, a hit in the cinema, were also good sellers in the bookshops. If the Princess of Wales could be photographed reading the collected works of Proust, no doubt he too would be as widely read as Navratilova. There was hope for literature yet.

Among the new books published in 1994 in Britain, the following deserve mention:

FICTION. Peter Ackroyd, *Dan Leno and the Limehouse Golem* (Sinclair-Stevenson); Allan Ahlberg, *The Giant Baby* (Viking); Kingsley Amis, *You Can't Do Both* (Hutchinson); Jeffrey Archer, *Twelve Red Herrings* (Harper Collins); Iain M. Banks, *Feersum Endjinn* (Orbit); Louis de Bernières, *Captain Corelli's Mandolin* (Secker); Alain de Botton, *Essays in Love* (Macmillan); Paul Bowles, *Too Far From Home* (Peter Owen); Anita Brookner, *A Private View* (Cape); George Mackay Brown, *Beside the Ocean of Time* (John Murray); A.S. Byatt, *The Djinn in the Nightingale's Eye* (Chatto); Naomi Campbell, *Swan* (Heinemann); Peter Carey, *The Unusual Life of Tristan Smith* (Faber); Jonathan Coe, *What A Carve Up!* (Viking); J.M. Coetzee, *The Master of Petersburg* (Secker); Andrew Cowan, *Pig* (Michael Joseph); Jim Crace, *Signals of Distress* (Viking); Fred D'Aguiar, *The Longest Memory* (Chatto); Stevie Davies, *Closing the Book* (The Women's Press); Len Deighton, *Faith* (Harper Collins); Jenny Diski, *Monkey's Uncle* (Weidenfeld); Suzannah Dunn, *Blood Sugar* (Flamingo); Shusaku Endo, translated Van C. Gessel, *Deep River* (Peter Owen); Elaine Feinstein, *Dreamers* (Macmillan); Margaret Forster, *Mothers' Boys* (Chatto); Frederick Forsyth, *The Fist of God* (Bantam); Dick Francis, *Wild Horses* (Michael Joseph); Janice Galloway, *Foreign Parts* (Cape); Maggie Gee, *Lost Children* (Flamingo); Lesley Glaister, *Partial Eclipse* (Hamish Hamilton); Nadine Gordimer, *None To Accompany Me* (Bloomsbury); David Grossman, translated Betsy Rosenberg, *The Book of Intimate Grammar* (Cape); Romesh Gunesekera, *Reef* (Granta); Abdulrazak Gurnah, *Paradise* (Hamish Hamilton); James Hamilton-Paterson, *Ghosts of Manila* (Cape); Joseph Heller, *Closing Time* (Simon and Schuster); Alan Hollinghurst, *The Folding Star* (Chatto); Angela Huth, *Land Girls* (Sinclair-Stevenson); John Irving, *A Son of the Circus* (Bloomsbury); James Kelman, *How Late It Was, How Late* (Secker); Thomas Keneally, *Jacko, The Great Intruder* (Hodder); Francis King, *The One and Only* (Constable); Hilary Mantel, *A Change of Climate* (Viking); Simon Mason, *Death of a Fantasist* (Constable); Ian McEwan, *The Daydreamer* (Cape); Claire Messud, *When the World Was Steady* (Granta); V.S. Naipaul, *A Way in the World* (Heinemann); Martina Navratilova, *The Total Zone* (Hodder); Kenzaburo Oe, translated Michiko N. Wilson and Michael N. Wilson, *The Pinch Runner Memorandum* (M.E. Sharpe); William Riviere, *Eros and Psyche* (Hodder); Michele Roberts, *Flesh and Blood* (Virago); Salman Rushdie, *East, West* (Cape); Edward St. Aubyn, *Some Hope* (Heinemann); Mark Salzman, *The Soloist* (Bloomsbury); Iain Sinclair, *Radon Daughters* (Cape); D.M. Thomas, *Eating Pavlova*); William Trevor, *Felicia's Journey* (Viking); John Updike, *Brazil* (Hamish Hamilton); Jill Paton Walsh, *Knowledge of Angels* (Green Bay); Fay Weldon, *Affliction* (Harper Collins); Mary Wesley, *An Imaginative Experience* (Bantam); Nigel Williams, *Scenes From A Poisoner's Life* (Faber).

POETRY. Dannie Abse, *On the Evening Road* (Hutchinson); Alan Brownjohn, *In the Cruel Arcade* (Sinclair-Stevenson); Ciaran Carson, *First Language* (Gallery);

Jonathan Davidson, *The Living Room* (Arc); Carol Ann Duffy, *Selected Poems* (Penguin); Paul Durcan, *Give Me Your Hand* (Macmillan); Vicki Feaver, *Handless Maiden* (Cape); Roy Fisher, *Birmingham River* (OUP); Kathleen Jamie, *The Queen of Sheba* (Bloodaxe); Sylvia Kantaris, *Lad's Love* (Bloodaxe); Medbh McGuckian, *The Flower Master and Other Poems* (Gallery); James Michie, *Collected Poems* (Sinclair-Stevenson); Edwin Morgan, *Sweeping Out the Dark* (Carcanet); Paul Muldoon, *The Annals of Chile* (Faber); Tom Paulin, *Walking a Line* (Faber); Craig Raine, *History: The Home Movie* (Penguin); Peter Reading, *Last Poems* (Chatto); Hugo Williams, *Dock Leaves* (Faber).

BIOGRAPHY AND AUTOBIOGRAPHY. Peter F. Alexander, *Alan Paton: A Biography* (OUP); Juliet Barker, *The Brontes* (Weidenfeld); Nina Bawden, *In My Own Time* (Virago); Alan Bennett, *Writing Home* (Faber); Ian Botham, *Botham: My Autobiography* (Collins Willow); Joan Brady, *Prologue: Her Unconventional Life* (Deutsch); Humphrey Burton, *Leonard Bernstein* (Faber); Barbara Cartland, *I Reach For the Stars* (Weidenfeld); Roy Castle, *Now and Then* (Robson); Jonathan Dimbleby, *The Prince of Wales* (Little, Brown); Christopher Fitz-Simon, *The Boys: A Biography of Micheal MacLiammoir and Hilton Edwards* (Viking); David Gilmour, *Curzon* (John Murray); Richard Perceval Graves, *Richard Hughes* (Deutsch); Bob Hawke, *The Hawke Memoirs* (Heinemann); Michael Holroyd, *Lytton Strachey: The New Biography* (Chatto); Richard Hough, *Captain James Cook* (John Curtis/Hodder); Geoffrey Howe, *Conflict of Loyalty* (Macmillan); Peter Jackson, *Frieda Lawrence* (Pandora); Derek Jarman, *Chroma* (Century); Mervyn Jones, *Michael Foot* (Gollancz); Peter Keating, *Kipling the Poet* (Secker); Robert Lacey, *Grace* (Macmillan); Doris Lessing, *Under My Skin* (Harper Collins); Roger Lewis, *The Life and Death of Peter Sellars* (Century); Brenda Maddox, *The Married Man: A Life of D.H. Lawrence* Sinclair-Stevenson); Terry Major-Ball, *Major Major: Memories of an Older Brother* (Duckworth); Nelson Mandela, *Long Walk to Freedom* (Little, Brown); Jan Marsh, *Christina Rossetti* (Cape); John Mortimer, *Murderers and Other Friends* (Viking); Peter T. Marsh, *Joseph Chamberlain: Entrepreneur in Politics* (Yale); Sara Parkin, *The Life and Death of Petra Kelly* (Pandora); Clive Ponting, *Churchill* (Sinclair-Stevenson); Stacy Schiff, *Saint-Exupery: A Biography* (Chatto); Mike Seabrook, *Max: The Life and Music of Peter Maxwell Davies* Gollancz); Martin Seymour-Smith, *Hardy* (Bloomsbury); Norman Sherry, *The Life of Graham Greene, Vol. 2, 1939–55* (Cape); Julian Symons, *Playing Happy Families* (Macmillan); Claire Tomalin, *Mrs. Jordan's Profession* (Viking); Jeremy Treglown, *Roald Dahl* (Faber); Alexander Walker, *Audrey: Her Real Story* ([Audrey Hepburn] Weidenfeld); Keith Waterhouse, *City Lights* (Hodder); George Weidenfeld, *Remembering My Good Friends* (Harper Collins); Elizabeth Wilson, *Shostokovich: A Life Remembered* (Faber).

ESSAY WRITINGS, HISTORY AND CRITICISM. Saul Bellow, *It All Adds Up: From the Dim Past to the Uncertain Future* (Cape); Stephen Brook (ed.), *The Penguin Book of Infidelities* (Viking); Robert Giroux (ed.), *Elizabeth Bishop, One Art: The Selected Letters* Chatto); Pope John Paul II, *Crossing the Threshold of Hope* (Cape); Candida Lycett Green (ed.), *John Betjeman, Letters, Vol. 1, 1926–51* (Methuen); John Osborne, *Collected Prose* (Faber); Ben Pimlott, *Frustrate Their Knavish Tricks* (Harper Collins); William Scammell (ed.), *Winter Pollen: Occasional Prose by Ted Hughes* (Faber); Delia Smith, *Delia Smith's Summer Collection* (BBC); Colin Thubron, *The Lost Heart of Asia* (Heinemann); Colm Toibin, *The Sign of the Cross: Travels in Catholic Europe* (Cape); Marina Warner, *From the Beast to the Blonde: On Fairy Tales and Their Tellers* (Chatto).

XVII SPORT

WINTER OLYMPICS. International Olympic Committee president Juan Samaranch congratulated Norway on staging the best Winter Olympics ever. He added that their special care for the environment—taken to the lengths that even the canteen plates and cutlery were made from potato or corn starch—had set an example for others to follow. Despite the modern commercialization and professionalization of the Games, the true Olympic spirit was still evident in the raising of funds to restore sporting facilities in Sarajevo, where the 1984 Winter Games were held, with Sr Samaranch himself visiting that suffering city.

Norway were also to be congratulated on winning more medals than any other country, though Russia had ten golds to Norway's nine. Germany, Italy and the USA, in that order, also had big hauls of medals. It was not all light and joy, however. A shadow had been cast over the Alpine events when, a few weeks earlier, Austria's outstanding woman skier, Ulrike Maier, was killed during the Garmisch downhill race. The whole media publicity at the Games then centred relentlessly on a feud between the USA's two top women skaters. Nancy Kerrigan had been injured some months earlier in a violent attack by Tonya Harding's ex-husband, who implicated Harding following his arrest. With her trial looming, Harding had to threaten legal action to be allowed to compete in Norway. But this particular pantomine had a suitably moral ending when the statuesque ice queen, Kerrigan, skated gracefully to silver and riches, while Harding finished a poor eighth.

There was much concern, especially in Britain, about the perceived error or bias of the ice dance judges in placing former champions Jayne Torvill and Christopher Dean of Britain third instead of first, as many people thought they richly deserved. Concern over judging was aggravated in the short-track speed skating, in which there was a string of disqualifications and a bronze medal was awarded to a skater who had not even reached the four-man final. Britain's Nicholas Gooch was one of those controversially disqualified when he appeared to have won silver in the 1,000-metre final. Undaunted, he took bronze in his worst event, the 500 metres.

The good, however, far outweighed the controversial in the shape of many fine performances. America's Tommy Moe gave the Games a racing start with an unexpected win in Alpine skiing's most prestigious race, the men's downhill. The favourite, Norway's Kjetil Andre Aamodt, came second, and was second again in the combined as Norway filled the first three places. In the women's combined Pernilla Wiberg of Sweden took gold. Outstanding for Norway in other events was Johann Olav Koss, who won three speed skating golds in the 1,500,

5,000 and 10,000 metres, all in world record times. Russia's Lyubov Ergorova won three golds in cross-country racing, with Italy's Manuela de Centa also outstanding in this discipline. Following Moe's unexpected downhill win, Dianne Roffe was a surprise winner of the women's giant slalom. Other American successes included Bonnie Blair's two gold medals in the women's speed skating, while Dan Jansen at last won a gold in the men's events. German successes included two golds for the experienced Markus Wasmeier in the 'super G' and giant slaloms and Jens Weissflog's individual and team golds in high hill ski jumping.

The happiest of Winter Olympics was climaxed by the most delightful of closing ceremonies, following an intriguing ice-hockey final. With the Russian red machine no longer dominant, Sweden beat Canada in a shoot-out following extra time.

POLITICS AND PASSION IN SPORT. There were still a significant number of drug test failures among high-profile sporting personalities. The most notable was Argentina's most famous footballer, Diego Maradona, who was ignominiously ejected from the World Cup finals in America (in which his team failed to make their expected progress). The different approaches in different sports was emphasized when Maradona was only suspended for 15 months, despite earlier offences, while an athlete found taking a similar cocktail of drugs would have received an automatic four-year ban.

The two most newsworthy athletics cases both came to light during the Commonwealth Games in Canada. Sierra Leone's first medal winner, Horace Dove-Edwin, became a folk hero by finishing second to world champion Linford Christie in the 100 metres, only to be sent home in shame after testing positive. England's 800-metre runner, Diane Modahl, had tested positive in a race in Portugal nine weeks before. There were many odd features about this, not least that notification came outside the time required by standard procedures and that Russian newspapers had announced that she had tested positive within days of the event. The International Athletics Federation asked Britain to withdraw its women's team from the World Cup because Modahl had taken part in the European qualifier after the race in Portugal. The British declined to do so on the basis that her appeal had not yet been heard and that she was entitled not to be pre-judged. The IAF responded with a threat to withdraw any team medal won by the British women, but this was not tested because the team finished last.

The Modahl case, like that of America's 'Butch' Reynolds earlier, called into question the fairness of drugs-testing procedures as well as the complex list of banned substances, some of them not performance-enhancing. There was also the case of club athlete, Peter Gordon, who was banned for four years when his testicular cancer prevented him from giving an adequate sample within the required period.

The ease with which the passion engendered by sport could be taken to excessive lengths was tragically emphasized by the death of the Colombian footballer Andrés Escobar. His 'own goal' when facing the USA in the World Cup finals (see below) was primarily responsible for America qualifying from their group and Colombia failing to do so. On his return home he was gunned down in a reprisal even more brutal than the previous year's knifing of the Czech tennis player, Monica Seles, by a German spectator. The latter's confessed aim of helping Steffi Graf to regain the number one spot was all too successful, as Seles remained unable to compete again at top level in the new season.

ASSOCIATION FOOTBALL. There were many pluses in a World Cup championship much more highly acclaimed than the previous one in Italy, which had ended with a boring and bad-tempered final. Not least of these was the splendid organization of the American hosts and the joyful spirit generated in the many impressive stadia. In a country not noted for its soccer (though it was a past semi-finalist), public interest was sustained by the excellent performance of the American team.

Use of the English League system of three points for a win and only one for a draw encouraged more adventurous attacking football in the group matches. Instructions to referees to be harsh in punishing fouls, coupled with various law changes, gave some advantage to skilful players. That outweighed the adverse effects. Referees appeared to be so intimidated that they gave out red and yellow cards like confetti, often for trivial offences (15 red, 227 yellow). The final assessment was that the changes had brought some brighter attacking play, particularly in the group matches; yet the average of 2.7 goals per game was not a huge advance on the 2.2 in 1990. As in the past, after all the hype about brilliant attacking play, the two best defensive teams reached the final, namely Brazil (three goals conceded in seven matches) and Italy (five in seven). Italy also had one of the poorest scoring records: just five goals during ordinary time compared with Russia's eight in failing to qualify from group B.

Despite advance publicity anticipating a final of flair and attack, the match was predictably even duller than that of 1990. No goals were scored in full or extra time, so the match went to the very unsatisfactory ending of a penalty shoot-out. This was settled by an horrendous miss by the brilliant Roberto Baggio, who had done much to get Italy to the final after defeat in their first group match and some remarkable escape acts when down to ten men. That defeat was by Ireland (managed by Englishman Jack Charlton), who duly qualified for the play-offs but were immediately defeated by Holland. Maradona's suspension on drug charges (see above) unsettled fancied Argentina, who lost to Romania in one of the most entertaining matches. Nigeria too showed great flair and were within a couple of minutes of knocking out Italy. But it was Europeans who dominated, providing seven of the eight quarter-finalists. However, the odd-one-out, Brazil, was unquestionably the best since the goal-scoring skills of Romario and Bebeto were backed by such an unyielding defence. Bulgaria reached the semi-final by knocking out holders Germany, only to be beaten by Roberto Baggio's two brilliant goals. Brazil came through to the uninspiring final with a late winner from Romario against Sweden.

The English domestic football scene was dominated by Manchester United. Managed by Alex Ferguson and inspired by Frenchman Eric Cantona, they completed the double—only the fourth team to do so this century—and nearly made it a triple, unexpectedly losing to Aston Villa in the final of the Coca-Cola Cup. They won the League by eight points while in the Cup Final unhappy Chelsea conceded two penalties and United cantered away to win 4-0. United's patriarchal figure, Sir Matt Busby, never achieved the 'double' and sadly died in the team's year of triumph (see XX: Obituary). Sir Matt's successes in Europe were not, however, matched by Ferguson's United: in the revamped European Champions League, heavy defeats by Barcelona and Gottenburg eliminated them from the later stages of the 1994/95 competition. Arsenal did better in the 1993/94 Cup Winners Cup, beating Italy's Parma 1-0 to give George Graham a sixth trophy in eight years, while AC Milan beat Barcelona 4-0 in the 1993/94 European Cup Final.

ATHLETICS. The European Cup was staged in June at Birmingham, where the British men and women both qualified for the world championship at Crystal Palace in September by finishing second. This was the first time the women's team had qualified, and captain Sally Gunnell led from the front by winning the 400-metre hurdles and bringing the 4 × 400-metre relay team home for another impressive win. Another outstanding performance was by Diane Modahl, who came first in the 800 metres after finishing fifth in the previous Cup match. In the end, the British team finished only one point behind Germany, a deficit largely due to javelin thrower Shelley Holroyd having to withdraw on the day with an asthma attack. Unusually, Russia was run out of it, finishing three points behind the British women. For Britain, however, success turned sour when Modahl's drug test at a previous meeting proved positive (see above). In the men's event, Linford Christie won the 100 metres in his usual dominant style, while a rejuvenated Roger Black had an even more emphatic success in the 400 metres. But in the men's case the luck was with them. Germany were comfortably first with 121 points, but Britain were only five points ahead of Russia when Russian pole vaulter Rodion Gataullin, one of only two men ever to clear six metres, failed at 5.6 metres and ended pointless.

In the European championship in Helsinki, Britain's athletes remained on the gold standard. Christie won his third European title, while Gunnell was even more dominant and Colin Jackson triumphed in the 100-metre hurdles. Steve Backley recovered his form to beat two other world champions in winning the javelin. Roger Black's eight-year reign as European 400-metre champion was ended as team-mate Du'aine Ladejo beat him into second place, both then winning gold in the relay. In the medal count, Russia was easily first in golds, Germany and Britain coming equal second with five each.

The Commonwealth Games had an unhappy start when the Australian team manager said that the integration of some disabled athletes into the full Games was an 'embarrassment'. There was no embarrassment for Australia's sportsmen, who collected double the medals of any other country, including hosts Canada, and England who finished well ahead of the rest. The Games were as friendly as ever (and marked the return of South Africa to Commonwealth competition), but were overshadowed by drug controversies, especially those involving Dove-Edwin and Modahl.

CRICKET. West Indian Brian Lara bestrode the cricket scene at many levels. In the final Test in the West Indies he ensured that England lost the series with a world record individual score of 375. That was only the start of a sequence of records. The young left-hander then began his first season with Warwickshire by scoring seven centuries in eight consecutive innings. That was promptly topped by his remarkable 501 not out against Durham, the highest-ever first-class score, two more than Hanif Mohammed's previous record.

To add to his individual records, Lara then played a significant part in Warwickshire's victories in the championship, the Sunday League and the Benson and Hedges Cup—a triple never before achieved. For good measure, Warwickshire also reached the other one-day final, only to lose to Worcestershire, for whom Graeme Hick and Australian Tom Moody were outstanding. Lara was the only Test star in the Warwickshire side, but their success was a genuine team effort inspired by coach Bob Woolmer, whom the South Africans then recruited in the hope that he would do the same for them. Dermot Reeve and Tim Munton, captain and vice-captain, were also outstanding in a side known as 'the unlikely lads' as they surprised everyone with their sweeping success.

England had mixed fortune at Test level. Just as all the critics were condemning them as total failures in the West Indies, they achieved a memorable success in the fourth Test at Kingston, becoming the first team to win there for 35 years. That was due to a century in each innings by Alec Stewart and fine bowling from Andrew Caddick and Angus Fraser. Uncowed by Lara's record score, they then drew the final Test by matching the West Indies' huge first innings total, Robin Smith contributing 175. The fight-back there was much influenced by the young captain, Michael Atherton, who proved a tough and resilient leader. He was rewarded with success in England against New Zealand, who lost by an innings in the first Test and were saved by rain from a second defeat in the third and final match. Atherton then needed all his resilience as the South Africans, welcomed back to Lord's, overwhelmed England in the first Test, while Atherton was fined £2,000 and held up to ridicule in the media for having dirt in his pocket while on the field. He said that the dirt was to help dry the ball, but its presence inevitably attracted fashionable charges of ball-tampering. Since the umpires agreed that the dirt had not changed the ball's condition, many saw Atherton's fine as excessive. Atherton showed his courage by scoring 99 in the next Test, in which England had much the best of a draw, and then led his team to an eight-wicket victory at the Oval, where Devon Malcolm took 9 for 57 and destroyed South Africa's second innings, allowing England to square the series.

South Africa had had a similar result against Australia, ending one-all after winning the first Test. With the fine Pakistan team beating Australia 1-0 in a close three-match series, there were expectations that the Ashes contest starting in Australia in November would find the hosts and England evenly matched. After the first two Tests, England were looking outclassed and out of form, before staging a remarkable comeback to take a comfortable victory in the third in December.

GOLF. The world order changed dramatically in 1994, as new players took over at the top and for the first time no American won any of the majors. Nick Faldo had a disappointing season and for much of it looked far from being one of the world's best golfers. A resurgence of form at the season's end was marred by disqualification on a technical point of which he was unaware when leading in Bali by six strokes. If those who kept backing him to win had an expensive year, his own accounts were then put in good shape by an end-of-season victory in the million-dollar Sun City event in South Africa.

There was no doubt who qualified as number one, or of the year's other three top performers. The 37-year-old Zimbabwean, Nick Price, turned an up-and-down year into a dramatically successful one as July warmed him to his work. Until then he had had three wins, but had missed four cuts. Winning the Western Open made him one of the favourites for the British Open at Turnberry. Jasper Parnevik of Sweden appeared to have it won as he stood on the 18th fairway two strokes ahead and with a simple approach shot to play; but the Swede bogeyed the hole, while at the 17th Price sank a 20-yard putt for an eagle, the stroke of the season. That three-stroke swing left Price through to win the Open. After coming a respectable fourth in the St Jude Classic, Price then won the US PGA championship at Southern Hills by six strokes from Corey Pavin. Price's victory was the first time anyone had won consecutive majors since 1982, when Tom Watson was gifted the second at Troon (Scotland) by the collapse of a certain Nick Price.

Apart from his two majors, Price had another five wins and two seconds and not surprisingly headed the US PGA Tour money list, a few dollars short of a million and a half. Greg Norman did not have the most successful year by his high standards, but still came second on that list. Mark McCumber was third and another American, Loren Roberts, not only came sixth but to general surprise headed their Ryder Cup points list.

The three golfers closest to Price's rating for the year were South Africa's Ernie Els, Scotland's Colin Montgomerie and Spain's José Maria Olazabal. Els bettered Montgomerie by beating him and Roberts in a play-off to win the US Open at Oakmont and again in the World Matchplay final at Wentworth. But Montgomerie again headed the Volvo Order of Merit for Europe, with Bernhard Langer second and Seve Ballesteros third. Olazabal finished fourth in that table, but the highlight for him was winning the other major, the Masters at Augusta.

The surprise of the season was 66-1 outsiders Canada winning the Dunhill Nations Cup by beating England in the final. In Ladies' golf, England's Laura Davies reigned supreme. Apart from heading the LPGA money list, this powerful player won her second major when she took the LPGA title in May. One of Sweden's growing number of outstanding players in both men's and ladies' golf was Liselotte Neumann, who came third in the money list behind Beth Daniel (USA). In a year when overall America had less than its usual quota of success, consolation came with their ladies' comprehensive defeat of Europe in the professional Solheim Cup.

MOTOR SPORT. For Grand Prix racing, it was a season of tragedy and controversy lightened by the duel between the charismatic German Michael Schumacher and the determined Briton Damon Hill. Partly due to a two-race suspension imposed on Schumacher for ignoring a black flag and Benetton's disqualification on a technical offence after he had finished first in Portugal, the German led Hill by only 92 points to 91 at the start of the final Grand Prix in Australia. Then came the most controversial incident of a controversial season. As Hill challenged Schumacher for the lead, the German made an error, hit the safety-rail and damaged his car. He then swerved back to collide with Hill and put both of them out of the race, which meant that Schumacher won the championship by a single point.

Schumacher had won the first four Grand Prix races of 1994, including one marred by a double tragedy. On the first practice day of the San Marino race Brazilian Rubens Barrichello had an horrific accident but survived with minor injuries. On the second, Austrian

Roland Ratzenberger was killed when his Simtek car struck a wall at 200 mph. In the race itself, Ayrton Senna, still pointless, was at his most determined to beat Schumacher, He took an early lead, only for his car to plough straight on at a gentle corner. In the crash a piece of flying metal pierced his visor, killing him and leaving Grand Prix racing and the Brazilian public in deep shock. There had been no death in Grand Prix racing for 12 years, so the double disaster brought immediate changes to improve safety. A contravention of the new downforce regulation then cost disqualification in the Portuguese Grand Prix for Benetton, who were also criticized for a pit fire-storm which driver Jos Verstappen was fortunate to survive.

Taking over from Senna as the senior Williams Renault driver, Hill began to drive with such consistency that he was only one point behind the suspension-affected Schumacher with three races to go. Schumacher won the first mainly through better work in his pits. In dangerously wet conditions, the results were reversed in Japan. So all was set for that sour climax in Australia. Nigel Mansell, recalled by Williams Renault for occasional drives in place of the promising David Coulthard, profited from the Hill-Schumacher collision to win the race, helping Williams Renault to take the constructors' championship.

RUGBY UNION. In the Five Nations Championship, the Welsh dragon at last breathed fire after a series of limp performances and a recent humiliating defeat by Canada. For the first time in years, they ended as champions, equal on points with England, but with a better scoring record. Wales began by overwhelming Scotland at Cardiff, while England's win at Murrayfield depended on the last kick of the game deep into injury time. A narrow Welsh win in Ireland owed something to Eric Elwood for once being off-target with his penalty kicks, although Wales dominated much of the game. Playing with great spirit, the Irish then won at Twickenham, England's first home defeat for six years. A rousing Welsh win over France was largely due to the brilliance of Scott Quinnell on his final international appearance at the National Stadium in Cardiff before transferring to Rugby League. England countered with an outstanding performance in Paris, Rob Andrew kicking five penalties as well as dropping a goal. So all depended on the final game at Twickenham, the 100th meeting between England and Wales. England needed to win by 16 points to take the championship. Win they did, but the required margin was beyond them.

In June England played an historic match in South Africa, venue for the forthcoming world championship. Watched by Nelson Mandela, they scored a record win in which Andrew's kicking brought him 27 points. But a tour that began so brightly was turned sour by brutality, poor refereeing and defeat in the other Test. At the season's end, England demolished Romania (captain Will Carling scoring a try in his 50th international) as well as Canada, against whom Andrew scored a record 30 points. The touring South Africans overran Scotland, then beat Wales in a better-contested match. Their last-match defeat by the Barbarians was the only significant setback in a morale-enhancing visit.

Before taking over from Geoff Cooke as England manager, Jack Rowell ended his 17-year reign at Bath with a suitable leaving present in the form of yet another Courage League and Pilkington Cup double, despite a fierce challenge from Leicester. In Scotland Melrose won the McEwan League, while Swansea were the Welsh champions and Cardiff won the Welsh Cup.

RUGBY LEAGUE. World champions Australia came over for an 'Ashes' series against Great Britain, who had last won in 1959. In the first Test at Wembley the British team, now coached by Ellery Hanley, looked likely to change that dismal record. Despite having captain Shaun Edwards sent off in the first half, Great Britain held on to win after a brilliant try by Jonathan Davies had given them the lead. Davies was injured later in the game and was unable to play in the final two Tests, which were both won convincingly by Australia.

Wigan's supremacy at club level came under threat when Castleford beat them 24-20 in the Regal Trophy final. Thereafter, however, they won everything. The highlight of their seventh successive Challenge Cup win at Wembley was a try against Leeds by Martin Offiah, for which he ran the length of the pitch. That completed a triple for Wigan, who won the League Championship for the fifth successive time and also the Premiership. To round off a splendid season, Wigan went to Australia and won the World Club title by defeating Brisbane Broncos.

TENNIS. Pete Sampras began and ended the year as undisputed number one. He started by winning the final of the Australian Open in straight sets against fellow American Todd Martin. He had less success in Paris, where the Spanish clay court specialists dominated the championship, with Sergi Bruguera defeating Alberto Barasategui in the final. But at Wimbledon Sampras was back to his best. In a final of blistering serves and power tennis, Sampras beat the Croatian Goran Ivanisevic in straight sets. The first two were decided by tie-breaks, but Ivanisevic was then overwhelmed 6-0 by Sampras's power and skill. In the US Open a tired Sampras made little impact, and it was the popular and flamboyant Andre Agassi who won it for the first time to record his second Grand Slam victory. But Sampras finished the year as he began it by beating Boris Becker in the final of the World Championship in Frankfurt.

There was no such clear leader in women's tennis. At first Steffi Graf reasserted her number one status, brushing aside Spain's Arantxa Sanchez Vicario in the final of the Australian Open. That changed rapidly in Paris. After four successive wins, Graf was out-gunned in the semi-final by the power of Mary Pierce, once an American player but now French, who lost out in the final to Sanchez Vicario. Graf still came to Wimbledon as the hot favourite, but went out in the first round to Lori McNeil, achieving the unwelcome record of becoming the first reigning ladies' champion to lose her opening match. The emotional atmosphere at Wimbledon was heightened with each of Martina Navratilova's victories as she swept on to the final. This was her last year and a record tenth win was the popular hope. But on the day, Spain's Conchita Martinez proved that her clay court skills could be adapted to grass, as she beat Navratilova; but the great Czech/US player could look back on a total of 18 championship wins, nine in the singles. Sanchez Vicario then won the US Open title, and as the season ended looked set to take over as number one.

The Davis Cup final in Moscow was won with ease by Sweden by three matches to nil. Boris Yeltsin's appearance among the spectators was no help to Russia. Coming at a critical stage, the disturbance of the Russian President's arrival proved more unsettling to the Russian than the Swede on court at the time.

THE TURF. The Grand National was back to normal after the disaster of the previous year (see AR 1993, p. 527). The new starting mechanism worked smoothly and there were no bad injuries to horses or jockeys. Yet the race still lived up to its reputation as the most gruelling in the world, only five horses finishing. Three of them were close together in the final run-in but Miinnehoma held on to win from Just So. Fifth home was the only woman rider, 52-year-old Rosemary Henderson. It was jockey Richard Dunwoody's second National win, and to cap a triumphant year he beat Adrian Maguire by the narrowest of margins for the jockeys' championship. At one stage Maguire was 43 winners ahead, but Dunwoody finished better to end with 198 winners from 891 rides, compared with Maguire's 194. No-one had ever ridden so many winners without being a champion, but Maguire had the consolation of topping a million pounds in prize money.

On the flat, Frankie Dettori was champion jockey by many lengths. To round off a wonderful season, he won the Breeder's Cup mile in Kentucky on Barathea, only the third time a British-trained horse had done so. Barathea was voted horse of the year, but two others were special favourites with Frankie. Lochsong's sprint to victory was a highlight of Royal Ascot, while Ballantine won the Oaks and the Irish Derby. 51-year-old Willie Carson won the Derby for the fourth time with a late dash on Erhaab. Celtic Swing was rated as outstanding after spectacular wins at Doncaster and Ascot. As usual there were falls and injuries aplenty in National Hunt racing, but one of the saddest events of the year was the death of Steve Wood in a flat race at Lingfield.

AMERICAN ASPECTS. In Atlanta's Georgia Dome, the 1994 Super Bowl proved to be a repeat of the previous year. Having beaten the San Francisco 49ers in the semi-final, the Dallas Cowboys were again too strong for the Buffalo Bills, who had demolished the Kansas City Chiefs to reach their fourth successive Super Bowl final. That was in itself a remarkable record, though tarnished by their losing in each. For Atlanta, the Bills were billed as such underdogs that the game was branded as likely to be the 'Stupor Bowl'. In fact, the Bills made such a brave fight that they led 13-6 at half-time. Running-back Thurman Thomas, having scored the touchdown which put the Bills ahead, then made the fumble which led directly to an equalizing touchdown for the Cowboys. That turnover and touchdown prompted Dallas to a powerful offensive, with Emmitt Smith scoring two more touchdowns, in the Cowboys' 30-13 victory. Thomas's opposite number, the outstanding Emmitt Smith, won the Most Valuable Player award. This was a tenth time in succession that the champions of the American Conference had lost out in the Super Bowl to the champions of the National Conference.

Owners collectively were left without baseball teams to run when the players, despite average annual earnings of some $900,000 per man, went on prolonged strike over pay. What became known as the battle of the billionaires against the millionaires left stadia empty and the World Series abandoned. Money was indeed becoming the root of a lot of evil in many sports, the devotee followers of America's national game being the sufferers in this case.

George Foreman struck a blow for heavyweight grandfathers by winning back one version of the WBA and IBF versions of the world boxing title he had lost 21 years earlier.

XVIII ECONOMIC AND SOCIAL AFFAIRS

1. THE INTERNATIONAL ECONOMY

THE economy of the whole world expanded by just over 3 per cent in 1994, compared with 2.3 per cent in 1993 and 1.7 per cent in 1992. This marked the third successive expansion since the recession of 1991, when world growth was less than 1 per cent. Once again, the average rate of global growth concealed a wide variety of individual experiences, ranging from expansion of 10 per cent for Singapore to a contraction (−12 per cent) in Russia. Developing economies continued to set the pace with average growth of 5.6 per cent, but this was a rather misleading figure because it included growth of 8 per cent (for the third year running) for Asia, many of whose economies had really outgrown the label 'developing'.

Most of the poorest countries of the world were still located in Africa, which managed to grow by 3.3 per cent in 1994. This was disappointing by world standards, but it did mark an improvement of over 300 per cent on the 1 per cent growth recorded in 1993. It also looked as though economic growth would continue to accelerate in 1995. The economies of the 25-nation OECD (accounting for 54 per cent of the world economy) grew by 2.8 per cent in 1994 compared with only 1.3 per cent the previous year (see also XI.4.i). They were propelled by an unexpectedly sharp resurgence of world trade. OECD exports rose by almost 8 per cent in 1994 compared with 3 per cent the previous year. Over the same period, OECD imports rose by 9 per cent against 4.2 per cent in 1993. The volume of total trade in the industrialized countries was 7.2 per cent higher in 1994 compared with a 4.0 per cent increase in 1993 (the latter figure having been revised upwards from 2.5 per cent following the discovery of errors made when the European Union changed the way it recorded trade transactions).

At the end of 1994 world trade looked as though it was entering a period of stronger-than-usual growth. During the previous two decades world growth had averaged about 5 per cent a year; in each of the next two years, at least, it was expected to grow by 6 to 7 per cent by most international forecasters. The reason was that strong growth in East Asia was coinciding with a revival among developing countries and in Europe, North America and Japan. Also contributing to this simultaneous cyclical growth was the relatively strong expansion in a number of East European countries. Although these so-called 'countries in transition' were still, on average, expected to contract by 1 per cent in 1995, this forecast represented a major improvement on the 8.3 per cent fall recorded in 1994. Moreover, the average figure of 1 per cent itself covered sharply-contrasting performances by individual nations. While Russia was expected to contract by 4 per cent in 1995, the countries of Central and Eastern Europe (excluding Belorussia and Ukraine, which contracted by 17 and 25 per cent respectively in 1994) were expected to expand by a creditable 3 per cent.

The most encouraging recovery story in Eastern Europe was probably that of Albania (see III.1.vii). This former hardline communist dictatorship saw its economy collapse by 28 per cent in 1991 and by another 10 per cent in 1992. In 1993 it grew by 11 per cent and in 1994 by 8 per cent, becoming one of the strongest-growing economies in the world (admittedly from an extremely low base). The worst performing country in Eastern Europe, and almost certainly in the whole world, was Georgia, which in the years 1991 to 1994 contracted by 20.6, 42.7, 39.1 and 10 per cent respectively. In other words, Georgia's economy shrank to 24.9 per cent of its pre-1991 size.

The cyclical recovery in trade for most of the world was sufficient to give a boost to all the major OECD economies, with the exception of Japan, which was taking an unusually long time to emerge from an exceptionally deep (for Japan) recession. This had been exacerbated by a depression of asset prices (mainly property and shares). However, towards the end of 1994 there were signs of an upturn and growth of 1 per cent in 1994 was expected to accelerate in future years, although with little prospect of getting back to the super-growth of the 1970s.

The economy of the United States continued its voyage out of recession with growth of 4 per cent in 1994 accompanied by consumer inflation of only 2.7 per cent (see also IV.1). This marked the third year of positive growth since the recession of 1990–91. It was a more orderly recovery compared with the revival of the early 1980s (when growth and inflation were stronger), thanks partly to the vigilance of the Federal Reserve, which raised short-term interest rates by 3 percentage points in 1994 in seven separate stages. This brought the federal funds rate to 6 per cent. The motive for the increases seemed to be to prevent a possible overheating of the economy rather than to dampen down inflation, which was remarkably subdued. By the end of the year the annual rate of 'core' inflation (excluding volatile food and energy prices) was down to 2.6 per cent from 3.2 per cent a year earlier. Although private consumption expanded quite fast (at 3.4 per cent), the main engines of growth in 1994 were private fixed investment (up 11.5 per cent) and exports (up almost 8 per cent). Unfortunately, imports rose even faster at 12.5 per cent to increase the trade deficit from $133,000 million to $170,000 million. Unemployment dropped from 6.7 per cent in January to 5.4 per cent in December, while productivity was up (by at least 1.5 per cent) for the fourth year running. Monetary policy started the year by being gently restrictive—interest rates were raised by only

0.25 per cent each time—in order not to upset the financial markets. But fiscal policy remained tough because of the effects of the previous year's Omnibus Budget Reconciliation Act. As a result, the 1994 deficit (as measured by the Congressional Budget Office) was reduced by $52 billion to $202 billion.

In Central and South America the total economy grew by 4.4 per cent in 1994. The strongest performers were Argentina (4.5 per cent after 6 per cent or more for the two previous years), Brazil (where a second-half recovery coinciding with the introduction of a new currency, the real, took growth to 6 per cent) and Peru (9 per cent). These were offset by continuing problems in Venezuela (–5.5 per cent) and in Mexico, whose escalating economic problems in December, mainly induced by too much short-term debt, necessitated a US-orchestrated international rescue operation. Mexico's crisis broke six months after it had achieved the apparent respectability of becoming the 25th member of the OECD, the first former 'developing' country to do so.

The economies of the Middle East failed to reach the optimistic expectations of a year earlier. This was mainly because the sharp fall in oil prices in the year to mid-1994 offset the favourable impact of the Arab-Israeli peace process. According to the Economist Intelligence Unit, ten of the region's 16 countries were in recession in 1994, although six managed to record positive growth, namely Jordan (5.5 per cent), Lebanon (8.5 per cent), Israel (6.3 per cent), Syria (5.5 per cent), Egypt (1.5 per cent) and Kuwait (4 per cent). Among the economies which contracted were those of Saudi Arabia (–3 per cent), Qatar (–2.8 per cent) and the UAE (–0.9 per cent).

The most dynamic area of the world economy was, once again, the broad region of East Asia. China—now elevated to the status of third largest economy in the world in absolute terms—expanded by almost 12 per cent following a 13 per cent increase the previous year (see also IX.2.i). Although China showed signs of monetary overheating in 1994 (during which inflation rose by 21.5 per cent), its pace of economic growth was expected by the OECD to moderate only slightly to 10 per cent in 1995. But if one country deserved to be singled out for special mention in 1994 it was Singapore, a former British colony which in 1994 overtook Britain in the league table of living standards as measured by gross domestic product (GDP) per capita.

Founded by Sir Stamford Raffles in 1819 as a servicing post for Britain's empire in the Far East, Singapore had progressed from being a barren piece of land to becoming one of the success stories of the world. Its growth rate had been averaging 10 per cent for several years, partly by means of an open door policy towards any multinationals that wanted to build factories there. In 1994 unemployment was under 3 per cent (mainly people moving between jobs), the consistently low rate being partly due to having a migrant labour force (accounting for nearly 40 per cent of the total) whose permits could be cancelled if unemployment rose. Inflation was also kept at a remarkably low level (3.4 per cent in the year to December) considering the speed of economic expansion and the low level of unemployment. Singapore also claimed to be the most advanced information technology economy in the world, and had ambitious plans for the future. Just as their forefathers had grown rich by adding value to goods coming from Europe to the Far East, so present-day Singaporeans hoped to gain from 'knowledge arbitrage', adding value to the products of the digital revolution.

Most of the other Asian economies (including Hong Kong, Indonesia, Malaysia, Taiwan, South Korea and Thailand) managed growth of 6 per cent or more in 1994. The two countries with the largest foreign exchange reserves in the world continued to be Japan ($124,000 million) and Taiwan ($90,000 million), while Singapore's reserves of $55,000 million gave it a much higher per capita rate, in view of its tiny population of less than three million.

ECONOMIC SUMMITS. There were two important summit conferences of the Group of Seven (G-7) leading industrialized nations during the year. The first was the 'jobs summit' convened by President Clinton in Detroit in March. This was intended to be a forum at which member nations could put forward new ways to tackle the problem of 35 million unemployed people in the OECD countries as a whole. Its importance was not that any panaceas were suddenly produced, but that it acted as a catalyst for new ideas which would subsequently be debated by think-tanks and governmental bodies. The OECD itself embarked on a major study of unemployment, including its links with drugs, crime and other social diseases.

The main G-7 summit was held on 8–10 July in Naples (Italy). It sanctioned a number of projects, including aid of $3,000 million for Ukraine and $200 million to decommission dangerous reactors at the Chernobyl nuclear power station. But the main initiative to emerge was an attempt to examine the need for change in international institutions such as the IMF, the United Nations and the World Bank in the light of the end of the Cold War and the burgeoning power of international financial flows. Russia was brought into the inner sanctum of the G-7, which became the G-8 for political purposes, while remaining G-7 for economic decisions. Recent economic summits had tried to accelerate a successful end to the GATT Uruguay Round of tariff reductions, the final deal being concluded in December 1993 (see AR 1993, pp. 406–8, 534, 574–86). However, a year later the proposed successor body to GATT—the World Trade Organization—was still without a head as world leaders could not agree on a mutually acceptable candidate.

NOBEL ECONOMICS PRIZE. The 1994 Nobel Prize for Economics was won by three men—John Nash (USA), John Harsanyi (USA) and Reinhard Selten (Germany)—who were the leading proponents of games theory as applied to economics. The idea is that bridge and poker are games in which the outcome depends not only on what you do, but also on the actions of other players: what you do is a function of what you think other players will do. Applied to the real world this means, for example, that General Motors needs to predict what competitors like Ford and Toyota will decide to produce (bearing in mind that they will be making their own predictions about GM) before deciding on its own production plans.

2.   ECONOMIC AND SOCIAL DATA

The statistical data on the following pages record developments from 1989 to the latest year, usually 1994, for which reasonably stable figures were available at the time of going to press. Year headings 1989 to 1994 are printed only at the head of each page and are not repeated over individual tables unless the sequence is broken by extending series of figures over a longer period than elsewhere on the page.

Pages to which the point is relevant include a comparative price index, allowing the current-price figures to be adjusted in accordance with changing values of money.

Unless figures are stated as indicating the position at the *end* of year, they should be taken as annual *totals* or *averages*, according to context.

Tables 2, 3, 4 and 5. Statistics which are normally reported or collected separately in the three UK home jurisdictions (England and Wales, Scotland, and Northern Ireland) have been consolidated into UK series only to show general trends. As the component returns were made at varying times of year and in accordance with differing definitions and regulatory requirements, the series thus consolidated may therefore be subject to error, may not be strictly comparable from year to year, and may be less reliable than the remainder of the data.

Symbols: — = nil or not applicable .. = not available at time of compilation.

SOURCES

A. **UNITED KINGDOM**
GOVERNMENT SOURCES
Annual Abstract of Statistics: Tables 1, 2, 3, 4, 5.
Monthly Digest of Statistics: Tables 1, 11, 17, 18, 23, 24, 25.
Financial Statistics: Tables 9, 11, 12, 13, 14, 15, 16, 26.
Economic Trends: Tables 6, 7, 8, 9, 11, 26.
Social Trends: Tables 2, 3, 4, 5.
Department of Employment Gazette: Tables 19, 20, 21, 22.
Housing and Construction Statistics: Table 5.
UK National Accounts: Tables 8, 10.
ADDITIONAL SOURCES
National Institute of Economic and Social Research, *National Institute Economic Review*: Tables 6, 7, 8.
United Nations, *Monthly Bulletin of Statistics*: Table 1.
Financial Times: Tables 13, 15.

B. **UNITED STATES**
GOVERNMENT AND OTHER PUBLIC SOURCES
Department of Commerce, *Survey of Current Business*: Tables 27, 28, 29, 30, 31, 32, 37, 38, 40.
Department of Commerce, Bureau of the Census, *US Industrial Outlook*: Table 40.
Council of Economic Advisers, Joint Economic Committee, *Economic Indicators*: Tables 30, 36.
Federal Reserve Bulletin: Tables 33, 34, 35.
ADDITIONAL SOURCES
A. M. Best Co.: Table 35.
Insurance Information Institute, New York: Table 35.
Monthly Labor Review: Tables 38, 39.
Bureau of Economic Statistics, *Basic Economic Statistics*: Table 39.

C. **INTERNATIONAL COMPARISONS**
United Nations, *World Economic Survey*: Table 44.
UN, *Monthly Bulletin of Statistics*: Tables 41, 42.
World Bank, *World Development Report*: Table 41.
IMF, *International Financial Statistics*: Tables 41, 43, 45, 46, 47, 48, 49.
OECD, *Main Economic Indicators*: Table 42.
Stockholm International Peace Research Institute, *Yearbook:* Table 50.
OECD, *Labour Force Statistics*: Table 51.

ECONOMIC AND SOCIAL DATA

2A. THE UNITED KINGDOM

SOCIAL

1. Population	1989	1990	1991	1992	1993	1994
Population, mid-year est. ('000)	57,236	57,411	57,808	58,006	58,191	..
Crude birth rate (per 1,000 pop.)	13·6	13·9	13·7	13·5	13·1	..
Crude death rate (per 1,000 pop.)	11·5	11·2	11·3	11·0	11·3	..
Net migration ('000)	+44	+36	+28	−11	..	

2. Health

Hospitals:						
staffed beds, end-year ('000)	372·9	362·5	337·0	313·0	..	..
waiting list, end-year ('000)(1)	828	827·0	841·2	830·1	..	..
Certifications of death ('000)(2) by:						
ischaemic heart disease	153·1	150·8	148·2	150·1	145·9	
malignant neoplasm, lungs and						
bronchus	35·3	34·6	34·4	34·2	33·7	..
road fatality	4·6	4·9	5·0	4·5	4·1	..
accidents at work (number)(3)	610	475	433	368	..	..
(1) end-Sept. except 1991, March						
(2) England and Wales						
(3) UK						

3. Education

Schools ('000)	34·9	34.8	34·6	34·3	34·1	..
Pupils enrolled ('000) in schools	9,023	9,010	9,062	9,162	..	..
Primary	4,663	4,747	4,812	4,849	4,923	..
Secondary	3,552	3,492	3,473	3,534	3,606	..
Pupils per teacher	17·1	16·9	17·0	17·1	17·3	..
Universities	46	46	48	48	48	..
Polytechnics(1)	30	30	32	34	32	..
Other HE/FE	726	675	666	660	656	..
Full-time students ('000)(2)	334	351	370	402	..	..
First degrees awarded(2)	74,953	77,163	79,637	84,900	..	..
(1) achieved university status in 1992						
(2) excluding Open University and former polytechnics						

4. Law and Order

Police ('000)						
Full-time strength(1)	137·3	138·0	139·6	139·2	140·9	..
Ulster, full-time strength	8·2	8·3	8·2	8·2	8·5	
Serious offences known to police ('000)(2)	4,241·7	4,419·4	5,090·1	5,879·1	6,248·8	..
Persons convicted, all offences ('000)(2)	1,777	1,744	1,731	1,676	..	..
Burglary or robbery(3)	54·5	49·6	49·9	52·3	50.7	..
Handling stolen goods/receiving, theft	167	138	137·7	136·8	131.1	
Violence against person	64	57·1	54·3	48·7	45.2	..
Traffic offences	774	760	788	744	755	
All summary offences	1,204	1,224	1,203	1,192	1,220	..
Prisons: average population ('000)	57·1	55·41	52·15	52·4	52·9	..

(1) Police full-time strength: Great Britain only. (2) Because of differences in juridical and penal systems in the three UK jurisdictions, totals of offences are not strictly comparable from year to year: they should be read only as indicating broad trends. (3) Specific offences: England, Wales and N. Ireland.

Overall price index (1990=100)	92·8	100·0	105·8	110·6	114·8	116·9

	1989	1990	1991	1992	1993	1994

5. Housing

Dwellings completed ('000)

	1989	1990	1991	1992	1993	1994
by and for public sector(1)	32	33	30	30	37	36
by private sector	180	160	154	141	139	143
Homeless households ('000)(2)	129	151	161	167	154	..
Housing land, private sector, weighted average price (£/hect.)	435,658	394,056	405,107	343,087	..	..
Dwelling prices, average (£)(3)	54,846	59,785	62,455	60,821	61,223	..

(1) Including government departments (police houses, military married quarters, etc.) and approved housing associations and trusts Great Britain. (2) Accepted by local authorities as in priority need. (3) Of properties newly mortgaged by building societies.

PRICES, INCOME AND EXPENDITURE

6. National Income and Expenditure
(£ million, 1990 prices)

	1989	1990	1991	1992	1993	1994
GDP at factor cost	476,226	478,886	468,913	466,564	476,162	495,000
GDP at market prices (1)	515,957	551,118	575,321	597,121	630,235	667,896
Volume index (1990 =100)	99·4	100·0	97·9	97·4	99·4	103·3
Components of gross domestic product:						
Consumers' expenditure	345,406	347,527	339,915	339,946	348,753	357,800
General government consumption	110,139	112,934	115,845	115,842	116,910	118,400
Gross fixed investment	110,503	107,577	97,403	96,280	96,611	99,700
Total final expenditure	696,553	699,403	680,715	686,684	702,642	732,900
Stockbuilding	3,669	−1,800	−4,631	−1,697	−185	3,500
Adjustment to factor cost	72,712	72,232	71,395	70,989	72,501	75,100

(1) Current prices, £ '000 million: 'money GDP'

7. Fixed Investment
(£ million, 1990 prices, seasonally adjusted)

	1989	1990	1991	1992	1993	1994
Total, all fixed investment	111,470	107,577	97,403	96,280	96,611	99,700
Dwellings	24,789	21,439	17,919	18,280	19,238	19,900
Private sector	95,745	89,963	80,896	77,970	78,189	..
manufacturing	14,984	14,227	12,803	11,590	10,989	11,100
other	80,761	75,736	68,093	66,380	67,200	..
Government and public corporations	15,725	17,614	16,507	18,310	18,422	..

8. Personal Income and Expenditure
(£ million, seasonally adjusted, current prices unless otherwise stated)

	1989	1990	1991	1992	1993	1994
Wages, salaries and forces' pay	249,103	275,016	289,406	300,891	308,237	..
Current grants	54,033	58,939	69,287	80,066	88,574	..
Other personal income(1)	104,934	115,393	119,487	129,230	132,255	..
Personal disposable income	351,438	383,020	407,226	437,330	437,100	..
Real personal disposable income(2)	372,356	380,092	378,189	388,563	392,700	..
Consumers' expenditure	327,363	347,527	364,972	382,240	405,788	..
Personal savings ratio(3)	7·2	8·4	10·5	12·8	11·8	

(1) From rent, self-employment (before depreciation and stock appreciation provisions), dividend and interest receipts and charitable receipts from companies. (2) At 1990 prices. (3) Personal savings as % of personal disposable income.

Overall price index (1990=100)	92·8	100·0	105·8	110·6	114·8	116·9

	1989	1990	1991	1992	1993	1994
9. Government Finance(1) (£ million)						
Revenue(2)	191,512	206,199	220,226	225,523	222,981	230,436
taxes on income	62,887	71,296	77,302	75,963	72,213	73,760
corporation tax	18,537	21,495	21,495	18,263	15,783	14,887
taxes on expenditure	77,153	81,200	77,176	87,786	88,082	91,788
value added tax	27,328	29,483	30,991	35,626	37,340	38,865
taxes on capital(3)	4,373	4,273	4,027	3,073	2,548	2,419
Expenditure(4)	185,371	207,105	224,820	244,174	267,074	281,718
net lending(5)	−5,354	−6,172	−6,703	−7,983	−6,876	−3,978
Deficit(−) or surplus	+6,436	−805	−4,616	−18,728	−44,137	−51,137

(1) Financial years ended 5 April of year indicated. (2) Total current receipts, taxes on capital and other capital receipts. (3) Capital gains, capital transfer tax, estate duty. (4) Total government expenditure, gross domestic capital formation and grants. (5) To private sector, public corporations, and overseas.

10. Public Expenditure
(£ '000 million, current prices)

Health	25·2	27·8	31·1	34·9	36·9	..
Social Security	57·3	62·9	73·8	84·5	93·2	..
Education	24·8	26·7	29·4	31·9	33·9	..
Housing	4·3	5·3	6·0	6·1	6·4	..
Defence	21·0	22·9	23·2	24·5	24·4	..
Law and order	9·4	10·9	12·9	13·8	15·0	..

11. Prices and Costs (index 1990=100)

Total UK costs per unit of output(1)	92·8	100·0	105·8	110·6	114·8	116·9
Labour costs per unit of output	91·2	100·0	107·6	111·8	112·9	..
Mfg. wages/salaries per unit of output	93·2	100·0	107·0	109·1	109·7	
Import unit values	97·7	100·0	101·2	102·1	110·5	114·4
Wholesale prices, manufactures	94·1	100·0	105·4	108·7	113·0	115·8
Consumer prices	91·3	100·0	105·9	109·8	111·6	114·3

(1) Used as 'Overall price index' on all pages of UK statistics.

FINANCIAL

12. Monetary Sector(1)
(£ million, amounts outstanding at end of period)

Notes and coins in circulation	15,362	15,253	15,690	16,770	17,795	18,585
M_0(2) (average)	17,312	18,293	18,850	19,380	20,507	21,278
M_2(3)	236,257	255,202	278,272	374,115	395,408	411,362
M_4(4)	424,017	477,567	504,352	519,907	546,167	568,820
Deposits						
domestic	336,108	372,783	366,509	386,896	412,320	433,243
overseas	610,069	588,277	562,109	678,886	702,269	749,600
Domestic lending						
private sector	432,941	470,461	467,441	475,930	492,407	511,062
public sector	15,140	14,252	14,499	19,584	23,700	27,819
Overseas lending	566,377	545,186	516,640	646,934	682,181	736,426

(1) Institutions recognized as banks or licensed deposit-takers, plus Bank of England banking dept. and other institutions adhering to monetary control arrangements. (2) M_0=Notes and coins in circulation plus banks' till money plus bankers' balance with Bank of England. (3) M_2=Notes and coin plus sterling retail deposits with banks and building societies. From 1992, retail deposits and cash in M_4 (4) M_4= Notes and coin plus all sterling deposits held with UK banks and building societies.

Overall price index (1990=100)	92·8	100·0	105·8	110·6	114·8	116·9

	1989	1990	1991	1992	1993	1994
13. Interest Rates and Security Yields(1)						
(% per annum, end of year)						
Treasury bill yield	14·63	13·44	11·00	6·54	5·00	6·06
London clearing banks base rate	15·00	14·00	10·50	7·00	5·50	6·25
21/2% consols, gross flat yield(2)	9·22	10·84	9·98	9·17	7·72	8·09
10–year government securities(2)	10·18	11·80	10·11	9·07	7·47	8·17
Ordinary shares, dividend yield(2)	4·24	5·03	4·93	4·85	3·90	3·76
Interbank 3–month deposits	15·13	14·03	10·94	7·00	5·38	6·63
Clearing bank 7–day deposits(3)	6·59	5·11	4·00	4·74	3·41	3·73

(1) Gross redemption yields, unless stated otherwise. For building societies see Table 16. (2) Average during year. (3) From 1992, instant access, medium balance accounts.

14. Companies
(£ million unless stated)

	1989	1990	1991	1992	1993	1994
Total income	110,757	113,384	105,376	103,670	113,689	..
Gross trading profit in UK	79,892	74,405	73,764	83,971	..	
Total overseas income	18,124	18,033	15,005	14,577	15,809	..
Dividends	16,212	17,496	18,738	20,818	21,711	..
Net profit	40,576	37,603	36,241	37,708	52,340	..
Companies taken over (number)	1,337	779	506	432	526	..
Total take-over consideration	27,250	8,329	10,354	5,941	7,063	..
Company insolvencies (number)(1)	10,456	15,051	21,827	24,424	20,708	16,728
Individual insolvencies (number)(1)	9,365	13,987	25,640	36,794	36,703	30,739

(1) England and Wales.

15. The Stock Market
(£ million unless stated)

	1989	1990	1991	1992	1993	1994
Turnover (£ '000 million)	1,627·3	1,655·0	1,814·0	2,089·0	2,830·1	2,951.9
ordinary shares (£000 mn.)(4)	564·6	316·0	360·5	433·9	564·0	606.0
New issues, less redemptions (value)						
Government securities	−14,113	−8,824	6,384	18,480	51,662	22,564
Local authority issues(1)	−10	−37	1	−38	−76	..
UK companies	7,443	6,285	15,113	8,346	16,334	13,073
FT ordinary share index (1935=100)(2)	1,781·41	1,749·4	1,921·9	1,951·9	2,287·9	2,445·2
FT-Actuaries index All-share(3)	1,110·29	1,092·4	1,187·3	1,224·2	1,457·3	1,574·5
FTSE-Actuaries Indices(5)						
Gen. Manufacturing	1,639·3	1,480·4	1,518·1	1,490·9	1,808·4	2,004·6
Financial	1,484·4	1,460·8	1,506·6	1,490·9	1,808·4	2,004·6

(1) Includes public corporation issues. (2) Average during year. (3) 1962=100 (4) From 1990, UK and Irish only (5) Dec 31 1985=1000.

16. Building Societies

	1989	1990	1991	1992	1993	1994
Interest rates (%): end year:						
Paid on shares, ave. actual	9·96	10·06	7·27	4·72	3·99	4·20
Mortgages, ave. charged	14·44	14·34	11·39	8·98	7·94	7·84
Basic rate	14·42	14·48	11·52	8·98	7·99	8·14
Shares and deposits, net acq.(£ min.)	17,558	18,213	17,614	11,696	10,243	8,500
Net advances, (£ min.)	26,460	26,338	22,203	14,748	11,162	14,371

| *Overall price index (1990=100)* | 92·8 | 100·0 | 105·8 | 110·6 | 114·8 | 116·9 |

	1989	1990	1991	1992	1993	1994
17. Industrial Production						
(Index, average 1990=100, seasonally adjusted)						
All industries	100·3	100·0	96·1	95·9	97·9	103·0
Electricity, gas and water	97·3	100·0	105·6	105·6	109·9	111·9
Manufacturing industries	100·2	100·0	94·6	94·0	95·2	99·1
Food, drink and tobacco	98·7	100·0	99·6	100·9	101·2	103·7
Chemicals	100·3	100·0	102·6	104·8	107·4	113·5
Metal manufacture	102·8	100·0	90·1	86·4	86·0	85·9
Engineering and allied	99·8	100·0	92·9	90·7	91·6	96·9
Textiles	102·5	100·0	89·8	89·6	89·7	90·7
Intermediate goods	101·2	100·0	97·7	97·7	100·7	107·1
Consumer goods	97·7	100·0	100·0	95·2	96·2	97·8
Investment goods	98·6	100·0	93·9	91·5	92·6	96·5
Construction, gross output	97·7	100·0	92·0	88·3	87·2	..
Crude steel (million tonnes)	18·7	17·8	16·5	16·2	16·6	17·3
Man-made fibres (million tonnes)	0·27	0·27	0·27	0·26	0·24	..
Cars ('000)	1,299	1,296	1,237	1,292	1,375	1,466
Motor vehicles, cars imported ('000)(1)	1,250	1,310	1,190	821	..	..
Commercial vehicles ('000)	327	270	217	248	193	228
Merchant ships(2) completed ('000 gr.t)	106	133	110	229	..	

(1) Including imported chassis. (2) 100 gross tons and over.

	1989	1990	1991	1992	1993	1994
18. Energy						
Coal, production (mn. tonnes)	100·6	93·5	94·9	84·5	68·2	..
Power station consumption (mn. tonnes)	82·6	84·6	84·0	78·5	66·2	..
Electricity generated ('000 mn. kwh.)	292·9	298·5	301·2	300·2	300·5	..
by nuclear plant ('000 mn. kwh.)	59·3	55·0	59·3	66·3	76·9	..
Natural gas production (GWh)	477,544	527,583	587,825	597,854	703,884	..
Crude oil output ('000 tonnes)(1)	91,800	91,600	91,300	94,200	100,100	..
Oil refinery output (mn. tonnes)(2)	73·0	73·9	74·5	75·5		

(1) Including natural gas liquids. (2) All fuels and other petroleum products.

LABOUR

	1989	1990	1991	1992	1993	1994
19. Employment						
(millions of persons, in June each year)						
Workforce(1)	28·48	28·55	28·55	28·39	28·16	27·91
Workforce in employment(2)	26·69	26·94	26·25	25·66	25·24	25·26
Employees: production industries	5·56	5·46	5·05	4·82	4·62	4·56
Manufacturing	5·10	5·01	4·61	4·42	4·27	4·23
Transport and communications	1·34	1·36	1·33	1·29	1·24	1·21
Distributive trades	3·47	3·52	3·44	3·40	3·32	3·38
Education and health	3·13	3·18	3·20	3·39	3·37	3·40
Insurance, banking, financial	2·59	2·70	2·63	2·60	2·66	2·67
Public service	1·86	1·93	1·95	1·79	1·79	1·76
Total employees	22·14	22·35	21·67	21·30	20·95	20·88
of whom, females	10·53	10·81	10·44	10·40	10·32	10·35

(1) Including claimant unemployed and employed workforce.
(2) Comprises employees in employment, the self-employed, the armed forces and those on work-related government training schemes.

	1989	1990	1991	1992	1993	1994
Overall price index (1990=100)	92·8	100·0	105·8	110·6	114·8	116·9

	1989	1990	1991	1992	1993	1994
20. Demand for Labour						
Average index of weekly hours worked,						
manufacturing industry, 1985=100	97·1	90·3	78·4	73·9	72·7	..
Manufacturing employees:						
Total overtime hours worked ('000)(1)	13,440	12,440	9,630	9,460	9,090	..
Short time, total hours lost ('000)(1)	302	395	800	597	381	..
Unemployment, claimants over 18						
(monthly ave. '000)(2)	1,782·2	1,660·8	2,286·1	2,765·0	2,900·6	2,654·0
Percentage of workforce	6·2	5·8	8·0	9·7	10·3	9·4
Unfilled vacancies, average ('000)	219·5	173·6	117·9	117·1	127·9	157·9
Work-related training programmes ('000)	343	450	418	354	334	..

(1) Great Britain. (2) Seasonally adjusted.

21. Industrial Disputes						
Stoppages (number)(1)(2)	693	620	357	240	203	168
Workers involved ('000)(3)	727	285	175	142	383	93
Work days lost ('000), all inds., services	4,128	1,903	761	528	649	238

(1) Excluding protest action of a political nature, and stoppages involving fewer than 10 workers and/or lasting less than one day except where the working days lost exceeded 100. (2) Stoppages beginning in year stated. (3) Directly and indirectly, where stoppages occurred; lay-offs elsewhere in consequence are excluded.

22. Wages and Earnings						
Average earnings index (1990=100)						
Whole economy	91·1	100.0	108.0	114.8	118.5	123·2
Manufacturing	91·4	100.0	108·2	115·3	120·5	126·0
Average weekly earnings(1)(2)						
Men						
Manual	217·8	237·2	253·1	268·3	274·3	..
Non-manual	323·6	354·9	375·7	400·4	418·2	..
All occupations	269·5	295·6	318·9	340·1	353·5	362·1
Women						
Manual	134·9	148·0	159·2	170·1	177·1	..
Non-manual	195·0	215·5	236·8	256·5	268·7	..
All occupations	182·3	201·5	222·4	241·1	252·6	261·5
Average hours(3)	40·7	40·5	40·0	39·9	39·8	40·1

(1) In all industries and services, full time. From 1991, manual and non-manual based on new standard occupational classification. (2) April. (3) All industries and services, all occupations, men and women over 18 years.

23. Productivity
(Index of output per head 1990=100)

	1989	1990	1991	1992	1993	1994
All production industries(1)	98·2	100·0	102·6	108·0	113·6	121·6
Manufacturing	98·1	100·0	101·2	105·3	109·8	115·1
Food, drink and tobacco	97·8	100·0	99·1	104·6	107·3	..
Metal manufacture	101·7	100·0	99·9	102·6	105·0	..
Engineering	97·9	100·0	100·3	105·0	111·9	..
Textiles	94·6	100·0	99·3	101·2	98·4	..
Chemicals	99·2	100·0	107·2	110·2	115·0	..

(1) Excluding extraction of mineral oil and natural gas.

Overall price index (1990=100)	92·8	100·0	105·8	110·6	114·8	116·9

TRADE

24. Trade by Areas and Main Trading Partners

(£ million; exports fob; imports cif)	1989	1990	1991	1992	1993	1994
All countries: *exports*	93,771	103,882	104,816	107,407	120,862	..
All countries: *imports*	121,888	126,135	118,867	124,998	138,369	..
European Union: *exports*	47,540	55,071	59,412	60,703	63,830	..
European Union: *imports*	63,807	65,955	61,308	65,609	68,913	..
Other Western Europe: *exports*	7,987	9,041	8,608	8,547	10,224	..
Other Western Europe: *imports*	15,155	15,745	14,306	14,512	16,296	..
North America: *exports*	14,437	14,973	13,983	13,971	17,384	..
North America: *imports*	15,929	16,751	15,740	15,718	18,297	..
Other OECD countries: *exports*	4,519	4,824	3,986	3,991	4,699	..
Other OECD countries: *imports*	8,514	8,414	8,104	8,970	10,064	..
Oil exporting countries: *exports*	5,831	5,575	5,717	6,014	6,526	..
Oil exporting countries: *imports*	2,313	2,974	2,786	3,078	3,801	..
Other countries: *exports*	11,185	12,189	12,063	12,477	15,875	..
Other countries: *imports*	13,557	13,855	14,165	15,465	18,710	..
E. Eur. & former USSR: *exports*	1,473	1,480	1,253	1,704	2,324	..
E. Eur. & former USSR: *imports*	1,781	1,797	1,691	1,646	2,288	..
Balance of trade in manufactures	−19,567	−13,722	−6,045	−10,057	−8,103	−7,519

25. Terms of Trade
(Index 1990=100)

	1989	1990	1991	1992	1993	1994
Volume of exports(1)	94·2	100·0	101·2	103·7	106·9	118·2
manufactures	93·3	100·0	101·8	103·6	107·0	117·0
Volume of imports(1)	99·9	100·0	94·7	100·9	104·6	110·6
Unit value of exports(1)	96·5	100·0	101·4	103·5	114·8	117·0
manufactures	98·0	100·0	102·3	104·4	117·0	120·0
Unit value of imports(1)	97·7	100·0	101·2	102·1	110·7	114·5
Terms of trade(2)	98·8	100·0	100·2	101·4	103·7	102·2

(1) Volume: seasonally adjusted; value: unadjusted. Balance of Payments basis. (2) Export unit value index as percentage of import value index, expressed as an index on the same base.

26. Balance of Payments
(£ million: current transactions seasonally adjusted; remaining data unadjusted)

	1989	1990	1991	1992	1993	1994
Exports (f.o.b.)	92,154	101,718	103,413	107,343	121,414	..
Imports (f.o.b.)	116,837	120,527	113,697	120,447	134,623	..
Visible balance	−24,683	−18,809	−10,284	−13,104	−13,209	..
Invisible balance	+2,171	−226	+2,108	+3,273	+2,029	..
Current balance	−22,512	−19,035	−8,176	−9,831	−11,180	..
Direct investment overseas	−21,503	−10,492	−9,110	−11,077	−17,292	..
Portfolio investment overseas	−36,524	−17,214	−29,353	−27,435	−85,603	..
Bank lending abroad	−29,041	−40,019	+30,891	−27,178	+4,428	..
Direct investment in UK	+18,567	+18,516	+8,971	−9,370	+9,502	..
Portfolio investment in UK	+16,079	+12,445	+17,776	+23,684	+40,009	..
UK overseas bank borrowing	+45,467	+47,304	−21,311	+22,150	+24,418	..
Net change in assets/liabilities	+19,636	+18,193	+8,619	+3,369	+8,313	..
Balancing item	+2,876	+842	−443	+6,462	+1,998	..
Official reserves, end of year	26,281	22,673	26,291	27,894	29,914	28,059

	1989	1990	1991	1992	1993	1994
Overall price index (1990=100)	92·8	100·0	105·8	110·6	114·8	116·9

2B. THE UNITED STATES

27. Population	1989	1990	1991	1992	1993	1994
Population, mid-year est. (mn)	247·3	249·9	252·6	255·4	258·2	..
Crude birth rate (per 1,000 pop.)	16·0	16·7	16·3	16·0	..	..
Crude death rate (per 1,000 pop.)	8·7	8·7	8·6	8·5	..	..

28. Gross Domestic Product
($000 million current)

Gross domestic product	5,251	5,522	5,677	6,038	6,343	6,737
Personal consumption	3,523	3,748	3,888	4,140	4,391	4,627
Gross private domestic investment	832	799	721	796	882	1,037
Net exports, goods and services	−80	−69	−22	−30	−65	−102
Government purchases	975	1,043	1,090	1,132	1,148	1,174

29. Government Finance
($000 million, seasonally adjusted)

Federal government receipts	1,053	1,105	1,121	1,183	1,266	..
from personal taxes(1)	464	482	473	491	520	566
Federal government expenditure	1,187	1,270	1,333	1,459	1,507	1,538
Defence purchases	301	314	324	313	303	292
Grants to state/local govts.	118	131	153	172	186	198
Federal surplus or (−) deficit	−134	−166	−210	−276	−241	..
State and local govt. receipts	750	724	778	838	891	..
from indirect business tax(1)	356	373	397	421	441	463

(1) Includes related non-tax receipts on national income account.

30. Balance of Payments
($ million)

Merchandise trade balance	−115,249	−109,033	−74,068	−96,097	−132,575	..
Balance on current account(1)	−101,624	−91,861	−6,952	−67,886	−103,896	..
Change in US private assets abroad(2)	105,297	44,280	60,175	63,759	146,213	..
Change in foreign private assets in US(2)	205,068	70,975	80,935	105,646	159,017	..

(1) Includes balance on services and remittances and US government grants other than military.
(2) Includes reinvested earnings of incorporated affiliates.

31. Merchandise Trade by Main Areas
($ million)

All countries: *exports* (f.o.b.)	362,116	389,803	416,937	440,138	456,866	..
All countries: *imports* (f.o.b.)	477,365	498,336	490,739	536,276	589,441	..
Western Europe: *exports*	98,397	111,382	116,813	114,454	111,257	..
Western Europe: *imports*	102,387	109,162	101,885	111,287	120,947	..
Canada: *exports*	81,076	83,464	85,915	91,146	101,194	..
Canada: *imports*	89,935	93,099	93,022	100,871	113,310	..
Latin America						
exports	48,842	54,285	63,252	75,379	78,198	..
imports	57,501	64,355	62,990	69,179	75,173	..
Japan: *exports*	43,865	47,808	47,212	46,874	46,684	..
imports	93,531	90,372	92,252	97,387	107,228	..

Dollar purchasing power (1982–84=100)	80·7	76·5	73·4	71·3	69·2	67·5

32. Merchandise Trade by Main Commodity Groups

($ million)	1989	1990	1991	1992	1993	1994
Exports:						
Food,feed and beverages	37,400	35,100	35,800	40,300	40,700	..
Industrial supplies, inc. energy	99,900	105,700	109,800	109,600	111,900	..
Capital goods	139,600	153,300	166,500	176,100	182,200	..
Automotive	34,900	36,500	40,000	47,000	52,400	..
Consumer goods	36,600	42,800	46,900	51.400	54,700	..
Imports:						
Food,feed and beverages	25,100	26,700	26,200	27,600	27,900	..
Industrial supplies,inc. energy	135,100	144,800	133,000	140,600	157,400	
Capital goods	112,300	116,000	120,800	134,300	152,400	
Automotive	87,400	88,500	85,700	91,800	102,400	..
Consumer goods	103,500	105,300	107,800	122,900	134,000	..

33. Interest Rates

(per cent per annum, annual averages, unless otherwise stated)

Federal Funds rate(1)	9·21	8·10	5·69	3·52	3·02	4·20
Treasury bill rate	8·11	7·50	5·38	3·43	3·02	4·27
Government bond yields: 3–5 years	8·55	8·26	6·82	5·30	4·44	6·27
Long-term (10 years or more)	8·55	7·86	7·01	5·82	7·10	..
Banks' prime lending rate(2)	10·87	10·00	8·46	6·25	6·00	7·01

(1) Effective rate. (2) Predominant rate charged by commercial banks on short-term loans to large business borrowers with the highest credit rating.

34. Banking, money and credit

($000 million, outstanding at end of year, seasonally adjusted)

Money supply M1(1)	783·4	812·0	860·4	966·5	1,078·7	..
Money supply M2(2)	3,130·3	3,298·3	3,402·7	3,473·8	3,509·5	..
Money supply M3(3)	3,990·8	4,093·0	4,160·5	4,177·7	4,163·3	..
Currency	217·6	235·5	259·5	279·6	308·4	..
Demand deposits of commercial banks	248·3	278·7	255·0	301·8	322·3	..
Loans of commercial banks	994·1	1,072·2	1,027·0	1,007·1	1,060·3	..
Instalment credit	718·9	738·8	733·5	756·9	807·3	..
Motor vehicle contracts	290·8	284·8	260·9	259·9	278·7	..
Mortgage debt	3,556	3,761	3,923	4,049	4,210	..

(1) Currency plus demand deposits, travellers cheques, other checkable deposits. (2) M1 plus overnight repurchase agreements, eurodollars, money market mutual fund shares, savings and small time deposits. (3) M2 plus large time deposits and term repurchase agreements.

35. Insurance

($ billion, unless otherwise stated)

Property-liability, net premiums written	208·4	217·8	223·0	227·5	235·5	244·9
Automobile(1)	73·6	78·4	82·8	88·4		
Underwriting gain/loss(2)	−19·2	−20·9	−19·4	−35·5	..	..
Net investment income(3)	31·2	32·9	34·2	33·7	..	..
Combined net income(3)	+12·0	+12·0	+1·8	−1·8	..	..
Life insurance, total assets, end-year	1,299·8	1,408·2	1,551·2	1,664·5	1,789·3	1,914·6

(1) Physical damage and liability, private and commercial. (2) After stockholder and policy-holder dividends and premium rebates. (3) Property, casualty.

Dollar purchasing power (1982–84=100)	80·7	76·5	73·4	71·3	69·2	67·5

36. Companies(1) ($000 million)	1989	1990	1991	1992	1993	1994
Net profit after taxes	136·5	111·3	68·0	93·4	..	..
Cash dividends paid	65·2	62·2	60·2	63·1	..	..

(1) Manufacturing corporations, all industries.

37. The Stock Market
($million, unless otherwise stated)

	1989	1990	1991	1992	1993	1994
Turnover (sales), all exchanges	1,844,768	1,611,687	1,776,770	2,033,200	..	..
New York Stock Exchange	1,576,899	1,389,084	1,532,979	1,757,494	..	..
Stock prices (end-year):						
Combined index (500 stocks)(1)	353·4	330·22	376·18	435·71	466·45	459·27
Industrials (30 stocks)(2)	2,753·2	2,633·7	3,168·8	3,301·11	3,754·09	3,834·44

(1) Standard and Poor Composite 1941–43=10. (2) Dow-Jones Industrial (Oct. 1928=100).

38. Employment
('000 persons)

	1989	1990	1991	1992	1993	1994
Civilian labour force(1)	123,869	124,787	125,303	126,982	128,040	130,959
in non-agricultural industry	114,142	114,728	113,644	114,391	116,232	119,503
in manufacturing industry	19,612	19,063	18,427	18,040	17,802	..
in agriculture	3,199	3,186	3,233	3,207	3,074	..
unemployed	6,528	6,874	8,426	9,384	8,734	8,080
Industrial stoppages(2) (number)	51	44	40	35	35	..
Workers involved ('000)	452	185	392	364	182	..

(1) Aged 16 years and over. (2) Beginning in the year & involving 1,000 workers or more.

39. Earnings and Prices

	1989	1990	1991	1992	1993	1994
Average weekly earnings per worker						
(current dollars): mining	569·7	602·0	629·6	638·3	646·8	..
contract construction	512·4	526·4	533·0	537·7	551·0	..
manufacturing	430·1	442·3	455·0	469·9	486·9	..
Average weekly hours per worker						
in manufacturing	41·0	40·8	40·7	41·0	41·4	..
Farm prices received (1977=100)	147·0	149·0	145·0	139·0	143·0	..
Wholesale prices (1982=100)	113·6	119·2	121·7	123·2	124·7	126·3
Fuels and power	75·9	85·9	81·2	80·4	80·0	..
Consumer prices (1982–4=100)	124·0	130·7	136·2	140·3	144·5	148·2
Food	125·1	132·4	136·3	137·9	140·9	..
Dollar purchasing power (1982–84=100)(1)	80·7	76·5	73·4	71·3	69·2	67·5

(1) Based on changes in retail price indexes.

40. Production

	1989	1990	1991	1992	1993	1994
Farm production (1977=100)	114·0	119·0	120·0	..	..	..
Industrial production (1977=100)	108·1	109·2	107·0	106·6	110·9	117·7
Manufacturing	108·9	109·9	107·4	106·9	111·7	118·6
Output of main products and manufacturers						
Coal (million tons)	979·6	1,029	994·1	1,015·0	992·4	1,033·3
Oil, indigenous (000 barrels/day)	7,613	7,355	7,417	7,199	6,870	6,670
Oil refinery throughput (000 barrels/day)	15,170	15,260	15,230	15,150	15,670	15,770
Natural gas ('000 mn. cu. ft.)	17,310	17,810	17,750	17,780	18,410	18,780
Electricity generated ('000 mn. kwh)	2,784	2,807	2,826	2,797	..	..
Steel, crude (million tonnes)	89·7	79·7	84·3	88·0	90·0	..
Aluminium ('000 tonnes)	4,030	4,048	4,121	4,042	3,700	3,750
Cotton yarn shipments (1987$m)	5,313	5,110	5,398	5,506	5,448	..
Man-made fibres shipments (1987$m)	8,160	9,928	7,735	7,782	7,700	..
Plastics/resins shipments(1987$m)	27,622	27,870	27,100	27,642	28,748	30,473
Motor cars, factory sales ('000)	6,639	6,050	5,407	5,684	..	..

2C. INTERNATIONAL COMPARISONS

	Area '000	Population (millions) mid-year estimate		Gross Domestic Product(1) US $ millions(2)	
41. Population and GDP, Selected countries	sq. km.	1992	1993	1992	1993
Argentina	2,767	33·37	33·78	237,676	257,895
Australia(3)	7,687	17·48	17·66	290,510	281,895
Belgium	31	9·98	10·05	208,554	203,255
Canada	9,976	28·43	28·75	569,530	551,632
China	9,561	1,183·6	1,196·4	435,571	544,603
Denmark	43	5·17	5·19	141,037	134,670
France	552	57·37	57·66	1,322,100	1,252,600
Germany(4)	357	80·59	81·19	1,797,900	1,722,900
India (incl. India-admin. Kashmir)	3,287	870·0	901·5	272,232	..
Irish Republic	70	3·55	3·56	51,137	47,373
Israel (excl. occupied areas)	22	5·19	5·26	65,585	65,043
Italy	301	56·86	57·07	1,157,400	957,743
Japan	378	124·32	124·54	3,662,456	4,215,549
Kuwait(5)	18	1·40	1·43	18,809	22,427
Netherlands	34	15·18	15·30	321,737	308,997
New Zealand(5)	270	3·41	3·46	40,955	43,691
Norway	324	4·29	4·31	113,114	103,418
Portugal	92	9·86	9·86	84,022	..
Saudi Arabia	2,200	16·82	17·12	121,530	..
South Africa	1,220	38·78	39·66	119,651	117,377
Spain	505	39·08	39·14	576,340	478,579
Sweden	450	8·69	8·75	247,234	186,225
Switzerland	41	6·90	6·94	240,933	232,133
Turkey	781	58·78	60·23	..	..
UK	244	58·00	57·92	1,054,215	946,621
USA	9,372	255·02	257·59	6,020,200	6,343,300

(1) Expenditure basis. (2) Converted from national currencies at average exchange rates. (3) Years beginning 1 July. (4) Combines East and West Germany. (5) Years beginning 1 April.

42. World Production
(Index 1980=100)

	1989	1990	1991	1992	1993	1994
Food(1)	123·0	126·0	126·0	128·0	127·0	..
Industrial production(2)	125·2	123·8	122·7	122·7	124·3	..
Crude petroleum, nat. gas	92·9	93·2	90·4	95·8	103·5	..
Manufacturing	128·5	128·0	126·6	125·6	126·0	..
Chemicals	134·8	133·5	133·5	137·1	139·1	..
Paper, printing, publishing	135·9	138·8	139·5	139·5	138·0	..
Textiles	108·9	103·4	100·9	99·8	97·9	..
Developed countries(3)	124·4	123·1	121·3	119·7	117·9	..
European Union	118·3	114·5	113·0	110·9	105·8	..
Developing market economies(4)	158·9	172·3	189·0	209·0	..	..
Caribbean, C. & S. America	109·2	108·6	112·1	113·7	120·0	..
Asia(5)	202·7	221·9	232·7	247·2	265·2	..
France	112·0	114·0	114·0	114·0	109·6	..
Germany	117·0	123·0	126·0	124·0	115·7	..
Italy	114·0	114·0	112·0	115·0	111·7	..
UK	119·0	118·0	115·0	114·0	116·4	..
Japan	142·0	149·0	152·0	142·0	136·2	..
Sweden	120·0	121·0	110·0	107·0	115·2	..
USSR	136·0	135·0	124·0	..	..	..

(1) Excluding China. (2) Excluding former USSR and Yugoslavia. (3) N. America, Europe (excluding former Czechoslovakia and the European countries of former USSR), Australia, Israel, Japan, N. Zealand and S. Africa. (4) Manufacturing. (5) Excluding Japan and Israel.

43. World Trade
$million. Exports f.o.b.,
imports c.i.f.)

	1989	1990	1991	1992	1993	1994
World(1): exports	2,906,300	3,324,600	3,442,200	3,755,800	3,772,700	..
imports	3,005,300	3,447,800	3,555,000	3,779,500	3,733,900	..
Industrial Countries: exports	2,126,300	2,452,600	2,502,300	2,651,900	2,583,800	..
imports	2,238,800	2,579,200	2,591,700	2,706,100	2,555,700	..
USA: exports	363,812	393,592	421,730	448,164	464,773	..
imports	492,922	516,987	508,967	553,923	603,438	..
Germany: exports	341,231	410,104	402,843	422,271	380,154	..
imports	269,702	346,153	389,908	402,441	348,631	..
Japan: exports	273,932	287,581	314,786	339,885	362,244	..
imports	209,715	235,368	236,999	233,246	241,624	..
France: exports	179,397	216,588	217,100	235,871	209,349	..
imports	192,986	234,436	231,784	239,638	202,271	..
UK: exports	152,344	185,170	184,962	190,003	180,180	..
imports	197,730	222,975	209,946	221,549	205,390	..
Other W. Europe: exports	708,673	855,393	845,800	828,611	..	..
imports	767,342	929,431	924,306	870,654	..	..
Australia, NZ, S. Afr: exports	68,757	72,953	75,672	76,071	77,521	..
imports	71,550	69,005	68,872	72,770	75,230	..
Developing Countries(2): exports	845,760	948,571	1,014,800	1,080,457	1,164,609	..
imports	757,922	850,761	948,296	1,053,629	1,158,113	..
W. Hemisphere: exports	117,850	128,400	125,840	130,890	136,470	..
imports	101,580	112,880	130,510	158,170	170,950	..
Middle East: exports	..	..	..	..	..	..
imports	101,930	115,310	135,140	147,610	..	..
Asia: exports	405,930	451,100	515,360	580,360	644,090	..
imports	418,030	470,840	539,640	604,420	683,160	..
Africa: exports	70,420	86,150	83,580	81,710	72,050	..
imports	69,200	76,750	76,470	83,650	74,130	..

(1) IMF members.
(2) Excluding S. Africa.

	1989	1990	1991	1992	1993	1994
Unit value index of world exports (US$) (1990=100)	91·3	100·0	97·4	98·3	93·9	..

44. Volume of World Trade
annual percentage changes

	1989	1990	1991	1992	1993	1994
World	8·0	5·6	4·6	5·5	2·7	6·4
Developed market economies	7·3	5·1	3·8	4·2	1·3	5·0
Developing countries	11·8	8·7	8·7	8·5	8·3	7·4
Economies in transition	−1·5	−9·5	−18·8	−11·3	..	..
-E. Europe	−2·9	−6·2	−9·3	−0·1	−5·0	..
-Former USSR	0·1	−13·0	−31·0	−22·7	..	..

45. Prices of Selected Commodities
(Index 1990=100)

	1989	1990	1991	1992	1993	1994
Aluminium, All origins (London)	108·4	100·0	95·6	95·4	91·8	103·2
Beef, Australia-N	Z100·2	100·0	103·9	95·8	102·1	91·0
Copper (London)	107·0	100·0	87·9	85·9	72·0	86·6
Cotton, Egyptian (L'pool)	96·4	100·0	92·9	70·9	67·0	57·2
Gold (London)	99·4	100·0	96·4	89·5	93·8	100·2
Newsprint (New York)	102·5	100·0	101·1	91·8	93·7	..
Rice, Thai (Bangkok)	111·5	100·0	108·8	100·1	93·3	124·7
Rubber, Malay (Singapore)	112·2	100·0	95·5	99·6	96·1	130·26
Soya Beans, US (R'dam)	111·4	100·0	97·1	95·4	103·4	102·5
Sugar, fob (Caribbean)	102·4	100·0	71·8	72·5	80·1	96·8
Tin, spot (London)	140·5	100·0	90·3	98·5	83·4	88·1
Wheat (US Gulf Ports)	124·9	100·0	94·9	111·6	103·5	110·5
Wool, greasy (Sydney)	114·7	100·0	68·8	61·7	47·6	76·6

46. Consumer Prices, Selected Countries
(Index 1990=100)

	1989	1990	1991	1992	1993	1994
Argentina	100	272	339	375	..	..
Australia	93·2	100·0	103·2	104·2	106·1	..
France	96·7	100·0	103·2	105·7	107·9	109·7
Germany(1)	97·4	100·0	103·5	107·6	112·0	115·4
India	91·8	100·0	113·5	127·0	136·4	..
Japan	97·0	100·0	103·3	105·1	106·4	107·2
South Africa	87·4	100·0	115·3	131·3	146·0	157·0
Sweden	91·0	100·0	109·0	112·0	117·0	119·5
UK	91·3	100·0	105·9	109·8	111·6	114·3
US	94·9	100·0	104·2	107·4	110·6	113·5

(1) To 1990, West Germany.

	1989	1990	1991	1992	1993	1994
Unit value index of world exports (US$) (1990=100)	91·3	100·0	97·4	98·3	93·9	..

47. Industrial Ordinary Share Prices
(Index 1990=100) average

	1989	1990	1991	1992	1993	1994
Amsterdam	103·5	100·0	100·1	107·0	125·4	152·2
Australia, all exchanges	105·7	100·0	100·8	120·9	138·2	
Canada, all exchanges	111·1	100·0	101·4	99·5	114·1	..
Germany, all exchanges(1)	87·3	100·0	89·1	86·2	87·8	106·0
Hong Kong (31 July 1968=100)(2)	2,836	3,053	4,297	5,512	11,888	8,191
Johannesburg	95·4	100·0	133·2	149·3	..	..
New York	94·7	100·0	114·0	125·5	137·7	..
Paris	103·7	100·0	97·5	107·8	116·2	..
Tokyo	117·8	100·0	84·5	62·6	69·9	73·1
UK	101·9	100·0	109·8	114·7	131·7	..

(1) To 1990, West Germany.
(2) Hang Seng index for Hong Kong Stock Exchange only: last trading day of year.

48. Central Bank Discount Rates
(per cent per annum, end of year)

	1989	1990	1991	1992	1993	1994
Canada	12·47	11·78	7·67	7·36	4·11	6·00
France	9·50	9·50	9·50	9·50	9·50	9·50
Germany(1)	6·00	6·00	8·00	8·25	5·75	4·50
Italy	13·50	12·50	12·00	12·00	8·00	7·50
Japan	4·25	6·00	4·50	3·25	1·75	1·75
Sweden	10·50	11·50	8·00	10·00	5·00	5·50
Switzerland	6·00	6·00	7·00	6·00	4·00	3·50
UK	15·00	14·00	10·50	7·00	5·50	6·25
USA (Federal Reserve Bank of N.Y.)	7·00	7·00	3·50	3·00	3·00	4·75

(1) To 1990, West Germany.

49. Exchange Rates   *Currency units per US dollar*   *per £*
(Middle rates at end of year)   (US$)   (£)

	1990	1991	1992	1993	1994	1993	1994
Australia (Australian dollar)	1·2965	1·3165	1·4540	1·4733	1·2892	2·1798	2·0170
Belgium-Luxembourg (franc)	30·95	31·36	33·25	38·15	31·83	53·49	49·80
Canada (Canadian dollar)	1·1605	1·1593	1·2715	1·3239	1·4026	1·9588	2.1945
China (yuan)	5·1974	5·3893	5·7312	5·8000	8·4462	8·5812	13·2141
France (franc)	5·0855	5·1901	5·5250	5·9044	5·3367	8·7357	8·3494
Germany (Deutschmark)	1·4950	1·5198	1·6195	1·7365	1·5500	2·5692	2·4250
Italy (lire)	1,128·0	1,151·4	1,473·5	1,712·0	1,622·3	2,532·9	2,538·0
Japan (yen)	135·65	125·74	124·85	111·61	99·77	165·12	156·09
Netherlands (guilder)	1·6865	1·7126	1·8190	1·9422	1·7353	2·8736	2·7149
Portugal (escudo)	134·05	134·76	146·45	176·7	159·20	261·43	249·07
South Africa (rand)	2·5635	2·7518	3·0525	3·3977	3·5442	5·0270	5·5450
Spain (peseta)	95·55	96·76	114·55	142·93	131·63	211·46	205·94
Sweden (krona)	5·6250	5·5543	7·0725	8·3352	7·434	12·3320	11·6306
Switzerland (franc)	1·2750	1·3564	1·4655	1·4850	1·3086	2·1971	2·0474
CIS (rouble)(1)	0·5655	0·5511	0·5719	0·5851	0·6662	0·8658	1·0423
UK (£)(2)	1·9300	1·8671	1·5140	1·4795	1·5645	..	..

(1) Official rate. (2) US$ per £.

50. Defence Expenditure

Expenditure or budget (US$ million)

	1989	1990	1991	$ per capita 1992	% of GDP 1992	1991
France	35,264	42,675	42,433	45,604	795	3·5
Germany	33,605	42,320	39,517	42,353	661	2·8
Greece	3,097	3,813	3,807	4,246	412	5·5
Iran	5,747	5,133	6,125	..	..	..
Israel	3,830	3,807	3,909	..	..	..
Japan	28,413	28,726	32,559	35,940	289	0·95
Saudi Arabia	14,522	15,213	26,227	..	..	..
South Africa	3,808	3,407	3,081	..	..	..
Sweden	4,560	5,499	5,802	6,221	716	2·4
Turkey	3,374	5,316	5,671	3,484	59	3·9
USSR(1)	77·3	71·0	96·6	..	..	..
UK	33,542	39,420	42,422	42,293	729	4·2
USA	304,607	299,701	288,791	308,489	1,209	5·1

(1) Official figures ('000 million roubles). Before 1989, military personnel and operations and maintenance only.

51. Employment and Unemployment

Civilian Employment ('000)	1989	1990	1991	1992	1993	1994
USA	117,342	117,914	116,377	..	..	
Japan	61,280	62,490	63,690	..	..	
W. Germany	27,209	27,997	28,533	..	..	
France	21,455	21,684	21,785	..	..	
UK	26,376	26,620	25,957	25,371	24,970	..
Unemployment (%)						
OECD	6·1	6·0	6·7	7·3	7·7	..
European Union	8·8	8·1	8·3	9·0	10·2	..
USA	5·2	5·4	6·6	7·3	6·7	..
Japan	2·3	2·1	2·1	2·1	2·5	..
UK	7·1	6·8	8·7	9·9	10·3	..

XIX DOCUMENTS AND REFERENCE

1. NATO PARTNERSHIP FOR PEACE

Meeting in Brussels on 10–11 January 1994, the heads of state and government of the 16 member states of the North Atlantic Treaty Organization (NATO) issued an invitation to the neutral and ex-communist states to the east and north of the NATO area to join a Partnership for Peace (PFP) with NATO, setting out details of how the arrangement would work, as given below. By end-1994 22 states had become PFP full signatories, namely Albania, Armenia, Azerbaijan, Bulgaria, the Czech Republic, Estonia, Finland, Georgia, Hungary, Kazakhstan, Kyrgyzstan, Latvia, Lithuania, Moldova, Poland, Romania, Slovakia, Slovenia, Sweden, Turkmenistan, Ukraine and Uzbekistan, while the Russian Federation had acceded to the PFP's general principles without signing an individual partnership agreement. (Text supplied by NATO Office of Information and Press, Brussels.)

INVITATION

We, the heads of state and government of the member countries of the North Atlantic Alliance, building on the close and longstanding partnership among the North American and European allies, are committed to enhancing security and stability in the whole of Europe. We therefore wish to strengthen ties with the democratic states to our east. We reaffirm that the Alliance, as provided for in Article 10 of the Washington Treaty, remains open to the membership of other European states in a position to further the principles of the treaty and to contribute to the security of the North Atlantic area. We expect and would welcome NATO expansion that would reach to democratic states to our east, as part of an evolutionary process, taking into account political and security developments in the whole of Europe.

We have today launched an immediate and practical programme that will transform the relationship between NATO and participating states. This new programme goes beyond dialogue and cooperation to forge a real partnership—a Partnership for Peace. We therefore invite the other states participating in the NACC [North Atlantic Cooperation Council] and other CSCE [Conference on Security and Cooperation in Europe] countries able and willing to contribute to this programme, to join with us in this partnership. Active participation in the Partnership for Peace will play an important role in the evolutionary process of the expansion of NATO.

The Partnership for Peace, which will operate under the authority of the North Atlantic Council, will forge new security relationships between the North Atlantic Alliance and its Partners for Peace. Partner states will be invited by the North Atlantic Council to participate in political and military bodies at NATO headquarters with respect to Partnership activities. The Partnership will expand and intensify political and military cooperation throughout Europe, increase stability, diminish threats to peace, and build strengthened relationships by promoting the spirit of practical cooperation and commitment to democratic principles that underpin our Alliance. NATO will consult with any active participant in the Partnership if that partner perceives a direct threat to its territorial integrity, political independence or security. At a pace and scope determined by the capacity and desire of the individual participating states, we will work in concrete ways towards transparency in defence budgeting, promoting democratic control of defence ministries, joint planning, joint military exercises, and creating an ability to operate with NATO forces in such fields as peace-keeping, search and rescue and humanitarian operations, and others as may be agreed.

To promote closer military cooperation and interoperability, we will propose, within the Partnership framework, peace-keeping field exercises beginning in 1994. To coordinate joint military activities within the Partnership, we will invite states participating in the Partnership to send permanent liaison officers to NATO headquarters and a separate Partnership Coordination Cell at Mons (Belgium) that would, under the authority of the North Atlantic Council, carry out the military planning necessary to implement the Partnership programmes.

Since its inception two years ago, the NACC has greatly expanded the depth and scope of its activities. We will continue to work with all our NACC partners to build cooperative relationships across the entire spectrum of the Alliance's activities. With the expansion of NACC activities and the establishment of the Partnership for Peace, we have decided to offer permanent facilities at NATO headquarters for personnel from NACC countries and other

Partnership for Peace participants in order to improve our working relationships and facilitate closer cooperation.

FRAMEWORK DOCUMENT

1. Further to the invitation extended by the NATO heads of state and government at their meeting on 10–11 January 1994, the member states of the North Atlantic Alliance and the other states subscribing to this document, resolved to deepen their political and military ties and to contribute further to the strengthening of security within the Euro-Atlantic area, hereby establish, within the framework of the NACC, this Partnership for Peace.

2. This Partnership is established as an expression of a joint conviction that stability and security in the Euro-Atlantic area can be achieved only through cooperation and common action. Protection and promotion of fundamental freedoms and human rights, and safeguarding of freedom, justice, and peace through democracy are shared values fundamental to the Partnership. In joining the Partnership, the member states of the North Atlantic Alliance and the other states subscribing to this document recall that they are committed to the preservation of democratic societies, their freedom from coercion and intimidation, and the maintenance of the principles of international law. They reaffirm their commitment to fulfil in good faith the obligations of the Charter of the United Nations and the principles of the Universal Declaration on Human Rights; specifically, to refrain from the threat or use of force against the territorial integrity or political independence of any state, to respect existing borders and to settle disputes by peaceful means. They also reaffirm their commitment to the Helsinki Final Act and all subsequent CSCE documents and to the fulfilment of the commitments and obligations they have undertaken in the field of disarmament and arms control.

3. The other states subscribing to this document will cooperate with the North Atlantic Treaty Organization in pursuing the following objectives:

(a) facilitation of transparency in national defence planning and budgeting processes;

(b) ensuring democratic control of defence forces;

(c) maintenance of the capability and readiness to contribute, subject to constitutional considerations, to operations under the authority of the UN and/or the responsibility of the CSCE;

(d) the development of cooperative military relations with NATO, for the purpose of joint planning, training, and exercises in order to strengthen their ability to undertake missions in the fields of peacekeeping, search and rescue, humanitarian operations, and others as may subsequently be agreed;

(e) the development, over the longer term, of forces that are better able to operate with those of the members of the North Atlantic Alliance.

4. The other subscribing states will provide to the NATO authorities presentation documents identifying the steps they will take to achieve the political goals of the Partnership and the military and other assets that might be used for Partnership activities. NATO will propose a programme of partnership exercises and other activities consistent with the Partnership's objectives. Based on this programme and its presentation document, each subscribing state will develop with NATO an individual Partnership programme.

5. In preparing and implementing their individual Partnership programmes, other subscribing states may, at their own expense and in agreement with the Alliance and, as necessary, relevant Belgian authorities, establish their own liaison office with NATO headquarters in Brussels. This will facilitate their participation in NACC/Partnership meetings and activities, as well as certain others by invitation. They will also make available personnel, assets, facilities and capabilities necessary and appropriate for carrying out the agreed Partnership programme. NATO will assist them, as appropriate, in formulating and executing their individual Partnership programmes.

6. The other subscribing states accept the following understandings:

• those who envisage participation in missions referred to in paragraph 3(d) will, where appropriate, take part in related NATO exercises;

• they will fund their own participation in Partnership activities, and will endeavour otherwise to share the burdens of mounting exercises in which they take part;

• they may send, after appropriate agreement, permanent liaison officers to a separate Partnership Coordination Cell at Mons (Belgium) that would, under the authority of the North Atlantic Council, carry out the military planning necessary to implement the Partnership programmes;

• those participating in planning and military exercises will have access to certain NATO technical data relevant to interoperability;

• building upon the CSCE measures on defence planning, the other subscribing states and NATO countries will exchange information on the steps that have been taken or are being taken

to promote transparency in defence planning and budgeting and to ensure the democratic control of armed forces;
• they may participate in a reciprocal exchange of information on defence planning and budgeting which will be developed within the framework of the NACC/Partnership for Peace.
7. In keeping with their commitment to the objectives of this Partnership for Peace, the members of the North Atlantic Alliance will:
• develop with the other subscribing states a planning and review process to provide a basis for identifying and evaluating forces and capabilities that might be made available by them for multinational training, exercises, and operations in conjunction with Alliance forces;
• promote military and political coordination at NATO headquarters in order to provide direction and guidance relevant to Partnership activities with the other subscribing states, including planning, training, exercises and the development of doctrine.
8. NATO will consult with any active participant in the Partnership if that partner perceives a direct threat to its territorial integrity, political independence, or security.

2.   ISRAEL-PLO AGREEMENT ON PALESTINIAN SELF-RULE

Printed below are the substantive passages of the Agreement on the Gaza Strip and the Jericho Area signed in Cairo on 4 May 1994 by the Israeli Prime Minister, Yitzhak Rabin, and the Chairman of the Palestine Liberation Organization (PLO), Yassir Arafat, and witnessed by US, Russian and Egyptian representatives. Providing for qualified Palestinian self-rule in some parts of the territories occupied by Israel since 1967, the agreement was the delayed product of the Israel-PLO peace declaration of September 1993 (see AR 1993, pp. 557–63). (Text supplied by Israeli embassy, London.)

The government of the State of Israel and the Palestine Liberation Organization (hereinafter 'the PLO'), the representative of the Palestinian people

Preamble

Within the framework of the Middle East peace process initiated at Madrid in October 1991;
Reaffirming their determination to live in peaceful coexistence, mutual dignity and security, while recognizing their mutual legitimate and political rights;
Reaffirming their desire to achieve a just, lasting and comprehensive peace settlement through the agreed political process;
Reaffirming their adherence to the mutual recognition and commitments expressed in the letters dated 9 September 1993, signed by and exchanged between the Prime Minister of Israel and the Chairman of the PLO;
Reaffirming their understanding that the interim self-government arrangements, including the arrangements to apply in the Gaza Strip and the Jericho Area contained in their agreement, are an integral part of the whole peace process and that the negotiations on the permanent status will lead to the implementation of Security Council Resolutions 242 and 338;
Desirous of putting into effect the Declaration of Principles on Interim Self-Government Arrangements signed at Washington, DC on 13 September 1993 and the Agreed Minutes thereto (hereinafter 'the Declaration of Principles'), and in particular the Protocol on withdrawal of Israeli forces from the Gaza Strip and the Jericho Area [see AR 1993, pp. 557–63];
Hereby agree to the following arrangements regarding the Gaza Strip and the Jericho Area:

Art. I: Definitions

For the purpose of this agreement:
(a) the Gaza Strip and the Jericho Area are delineated on map Nos. 1 and 2 attached to this agreement [see maps in V.1];
(b) 'the settlements' means the Gush Katif and Erez settlement areas, as well as the other settlements in the Gaza Strip, as shown on attached map No. 1;
(c) 'the Military Installation Area' means the Israeli military installation area along the Egyptian border in the Gaza Strip, as shown on map No. 1; and
(d) the term 'Israelis' shall also include Israeli statutory agencies and corporations registered in Israel.

Art. II: Scheduled Withdrawal of Israeli Military Forces

1. Israel shall implement an accelerated and scheduled withdrawal of Israeli military forces from the Gaza Strip and from the Jericho Area to begin immediately with the signing of this agreement. Israel shall complete such withdrawal within three weeks from this date.

2. Subject to the arrangements included in the Protocol Concerning Withdrawal of Israeli Military Forces and Security Arrangements attached as Annex I, the Israeli withdrawal shall include evacuating all military bases and other fixed installations to be handed over to the Palestinian Police, to be established pursuant to Article IX below (hereinafter 'the Palestinian Police').

3. In order to carry out Israel's responsibility for external security and for internal security and public order of settlements and Israelis, Israel shall, concurrently with the withdrawal, redeploy its remaining military forces to the settlements and the Military Installation Area, in accordance with the provisions of this agreement. Subject to the provisions of this agreement, this redeployment shall constitute full implementation of Article XIII of the Declaration of Principles with regard to the Gaza Strip and the Jericho Area only.

4. For the purposes of this agreement, 'Israeli military forces' may include Israel police and other Israeli security forces.

5. Israelis, including Israeli military forces, may continue to use roads freely within the Gaza Strip and the Jericho Area. Palestinians may use public roads crossing the settlements freely . . . .

6. The Palestinian Police shall be deployed and shall assume responsibility for public order and internal security of Palestinians . . . .

Art. III: Transfer of Authority

1. Israel shall transfer authority as specified in this agreement from the Israeli military government and its civil administration to the Palestinian Authority, hereby established, in accordance with Article V of this agreement, except for the authority that Israel shall continue to exercise as specified in this agreement.

2. As regards the transfer and assumption of authority in civil spheres, powers and responsibilities shall be transferred and assumed as set out in the Protocol Concerning Civil Affairs attached as Annex II.

3. Arrangements for a smooth and peaceful transfer of the agreed powers and responsibilities are set out in Annex II.

4. Upon the completion of the Israeli withdrawal and the transfer of powers and responsibilities as detailed in paragraphs 1 and 2 above and in Annex II, the civil administration in the Gaza Strip and the Jericho Area will be dissolved and the Israeli military government will be withdrawn. The withdrawal of the military government shall not prevent it from continuing to exercise the powers and responsibilities specified in this agreement.

5. A Joint Civil Affairs Coordination and Cooperation Committee [hereinafter 'the CAC') and two joint regional civil affairs subcommittees for the Gaza Strip and the Jericho Area respectively shall be established in order to provide for coordination and cooperation in civil affairs between the Palestinian Authority and Israel . . . .

6. The offices of the Palestinian Authority shall be located in the Gaza Strip and the Jericho Area pending the inauguration of the Council to be elected pursuant to the Declaration of Principles.

Art. IV: Structure and Composition of the Palestinian Authority

1. The Palestinian Authority will consist of one body of 24 members which shall carry out and be responsible for all the legislative and executive powers and responsibilities transferred to it under this agreement, in accordance with this article, and shall be responsible for the exercise of judicial functions in accordance with Article VI, subparagraph 1(b) of this agreement.

2. The Palestinian Authority shall administer the departments transferred to it and may establish, within its jurisdiction, other departments and subordinate administrative units as necessary for the fulfillment of its responsibilities. It shall determine its own internal procedures.

3. The PLO shall inform the government of Israel of the names of the members of the Palestinian Authority and any change of members. Changes in the membership of the Palestinian Authority will take effect upon an exchange of letters between the PLO and the government of Israel.

4. Each member of the Palestinian Authority shall enter into office upon undertaking to act in accordance with this agreement.

Art. V: Jurisdiction

1. The authority of the Palestinian Authority encompasses all matters that fall within its territorial, functional and personal jurisdiction, as follows:

(a) The territorial jurisdiction covers the Gaza Strip and the Jericho Area territory, as defined in Article I, except for settlements and the Military Installation Area. Territorial jurisdiction shall include land, subsoil and territorial waters, in accordance with the provisions of this agreement.

(b) The functional jurisdiction encompasses all powers and responsibilities as specified in this agreement. This jurisdiction does not include foreign relations, internal security and public order of settlements and the Military Installation Area and Israelis, and external security.

(c) The personal jurisdiction extends to all persons within the territorial jurisdiction referred to above, except for Israelis, unless otherwise provided in this agreement.

2. The Palestinian Authority has, within its authority, legislative, executive and judicial powers and responsibilities, as provided for in this agreement.

3. *(a)* Israel has authority over the settlements, the Military Installation Area, Israelis, external security, internal security and public order of settlements, the Military Installation Area and Israelis, and those agreed powers and responsibilities specified in this agreement.

(b) Israel shall exercise its authority through its military government, which, for that end, shall continue to have the necessary legislative, judicial and executive powers and responsibilities, in accordance with international law. This provision shall not derogate from Israel's applicable legislation over Israelis *in personam.*

4. The exercise of authority with regard to the electromagnetic sphere and airspace shall be in accordance with the provisions of this agreement.

5. The provisions of this article are subject to the specific legal arrangements detailed in the Protocol Concerning Legal Matters attached as Annex III. Israel and the Palestinian Authority may negotiate further legal arrangements.

6. Israel and the Palestinian Authority shall cooperate on matters of legal assistance in criminal and civil matters through the legal subcommittee of the CAC.

Art. VI: Powers and Responsibilities of the Palestinian Authority

1. Subject to the provisions of this agreement, the Palestinian Authority, within its jurisdiction:

(a) has legislative powers as set out in Article VII of this agreement, as well as executive powers;

(b) will administer justice through an independent judiciary;

(c) will have, *inter alia*, power to formulate policies, supervise their implementation, employ staff, establish departments, authorities and institutions, sue and be sued and conclude contracts; and

(d) will have, *inter alia*, the power to keep and administer registers and records of the population, and issue certificates, licenses and documents.

2. *(a)* In accordance with the Declaration of Principles, the Palestinian Authority will not have powers and responsibilities in the sphere of foreign relations, which sphere includes the establishment abroad of embassies, consulates or other types of foreign missions and posts or permitting their establishment in the Gaza Strip or the Jericho Area, the appointment of or admission of diplomatic and consular staff, and the exercise of diplomatic functions.

(b) Notwithstanding the provisions of this paragraph, the PLO may conduct negotiations and sign agreements with states or international organizations for the benefit of the Palestinian Authority in the following cases only:

(i) economic agreements, as specifically provided in Annex IV of this agreement;

(ii) agreements with donor countries for the purpose of implementing arrangements for the provision of assistance to the Palestinian Authority;

(iii) agreements for the purpose of implementing the regional development plans detailed in Annex IV of the Declaration of Principles or in agreements entered into in the framework of the multilateral negotiations; and

(iv) cultural, scientific and educational agreements.

(c) Dealings between the Palestinian Authority and representatives of foreign states and international organizations, as well as the establishment in the Gaza Strip and the Jericho Area of representative offices other than those described in subparagraph 2*(a)* above, for the purpose of implementing the agreements referred to in subparagraph 2*(b)* above, shall not be considered foreign relations.

Art. VII: Legislative Powers of the Palestinian Authority

1. The Palestinian Authority will have the power, within its jurisdiction, to promulgate legislation, including basic laws, laws, regulations and other legislative acts.

2. Legislation promulgated by the Palestinian Authority shall be consistent with the provisions of this Agreement.

3. Legislation promulgated by the Palestinian Authority shall be communicated to a legislation subcommittee to be established by the CAC (hereinafter 'the legislation subcommittee'). During a period of 30 days from the communication of the legislation, Israel may request that the legislation subcommittee decide whether such legislation exceeds the jurisdiction of the Palestinian Authority or its otherwise inconsistent with the provisions of this agreement.

4. Upon receipt of the Israeli request, the legislation subcommittee shall decide, as an initial matter, on the entry into force of the legislation pending its decision on the merits of the matter.

5. If the legislation subcommittee is unable to reach a decision with regard to the entry into force of the legislation within 15 days, this issue will be referred to a board of review. This board of review shall be comprised of two judges, retired judges or senior jurists (hereinafter 'judges'), one from each side, to be appointed from a compiled list of three judges proposed by each. In order to expedite the proceedings before this board of review, the two most senior judges, one from each side, shall develop written informal rules of procedure.

6. Legislation referred to the board of review shall enter into force only if the board of review decides that it does not deal with a security issue which falls under Israel's responsibility, that it does not seriously threaten other significant Israeli interests protected by this agreement and that the entry into force of the legislation could not cause irreparable damage or harm.

7. The legislation subcommittee shall attempt to reach a decision on the merits of the matter within 30 days from the date of the Israeli request. If this subcommittee is unable to reach such a decision within this period of 30 days, the matter shall be referred to the Joint Israeli-Palestinian Liaison Committee referred to in Article XV below (hereinafter 'the Liaison Committee'). This Liaison Committee will deal with the matter immediately and will attempt to settle it within 30 days.

8. Where the legislation has not entered into force pursuant to paragraphs 5 or 7 above, this situation shall be maintained pending the decision of the Liaison Committee on the merits of the matter, unless it has decided otherwise.

9. Laws and military orders in effect in the Gaza Strip or the Jericho Area prior to the signing of this agreement shall remain in force, unless amended or abrogated in accordance with this agreement.

Art. VIII: Arrangements for Security and Public Order

1. In order to guarantee public order and internal security for the Palestinians of the Gaza Strip and the Jericho Area, the Palestinian Authority shall establish a strong police force, as set out in Article IX below. Israel shall continue to carry the responsibility for defence against external threats, including the responsibility for protecting the Egyptian border and the Jordanian line, and for defence against external threats from the sea and from the air, as well as the responsibility for overall security of Israelis and settlements, for the purpose of safeguarding their internal security and public order, and will have all the powers to take the steps necessary to meet this responsibility.

2. Agreed security arrangements and coordination mechanisms are specified in Annex I.

3. A Joint Coordination and Cooperation Committee for mutual security purposes (hereinafter 'the JSC'), as well as three joint district coordination and cooperation offices for the Gaza district, the Khan Yunis district and the Jericho district respectively (hereinafter 'the DCOs') are hereby established . . . .

4. The security arrangements provided for in this agreement . . . may be reviewed at the request of either party and may be amended by mutual agreement of the parties . . .

Art. IX: The Palestinian Directorate of Police Force

1. The Palestinian Authority shall establish a strong police force, the Palestinian Directorate of Police Force (hereinafter 'the Palestinian Police'). The duties, functions, structure, deployment and composition of the Palestinian Police, together with provisions regarding its equipment and operation, are set out in Annex I, Article III . . . .

2. Except for the Palestinian Police referred to in this article and the Israeli military forces, no other armed forces shall be established or operate in the Gaza Strip or the Jericho Area.

3. Except for the arms, ammunition and equipment of the Palestinian Police . . . and those of the Israeli military forces, no organization or individual in the Gaza Strip and the Jericho Area shall manufacture, sell, acquire, possess, import or otherwise introduce into the Gaza Strip

or the Jericho Area any firearms, ammunition, weapons, explosives, gunpowder or any related equipment, unless otherwise provided for in Annex I . . . .

Art. XII: Relations Between Israel and the Palestinian Authority

1. Israel and the Palestinian Authority shall seek to foster mutual understanding and tolerance and shall accordingly abstain from incitement, including hostile propaganda, against each other and, without derogating from the principle of freedom of expression, shall take legal measures to prevent such incitement by any organizations, groups or individuals within their jurisdiction.

2. Without derogating from the other provisions of this agreement, Israel and the Palestinian Authority shall cooperate in combating criminal activity which may affect both sides, including offences related to trafficking in illegal drugs and psychotropic substances, smuggling, and offences against property, including offences related to vehicles . . . .

Art. XIV: Human Rights and the Rule of Law

Israel and the Palestinian Authority shall exercise their powers and responsibilities pursuant to this agreement with due regard to internationally-accepted norms and principles of human rights and the rule of law.

Art. XV: The Joint Israeli-Palestinian Liaison Committee

1. The Liaison Committee established pursuant to Article X of the Declaration of Principles shall ensure the smooth implementation of this agreement. It shall deal with issues requiring coordination, other issues of common interest and disputes.

2. The Liaison Committee shall be composed of an equal number of members from each party. It may add other technicians and experts as necessary.

3. The Liaison Committee shall adopt its rules of procedure, including the frequency and place or places of its meetings.

4. The Liaison Committee shall reach its decisions by agreement.

Art. XVI: Liaison and Cooperation with Jordan and Egypt

1. Pursuant to Article XII of the Declaration of Principles, the two parties shall invite the governments of Jordan and Egypt to participate in establishing further liaison and cooperation arrangements between the government of Israel and the Palestinian representatives on the one hand, and the governments of Jordan and Egypt on the other hand, to promote cooperation between them. These arrangements shall include the constitution of a Continuing Committee.

2. The Continuing Committee shall decide by agreement on the modalities of admission of persons displaced from the West Bank and the Gaza Strip in 1967, together with necessary measures to prevent disruption and disorder.

3. The Continuing Committee shall deal with other matters of common concern.

Art. XVII: Settlement of Differences and Disputes

Any difference relating to the application of this agreement shall be referred to the appropriate coordination and cooperation mechanism established under this agreement. The provisions of Article XV of the Declaration of Principles shall apply to any such difference which is not settled through the appropriate coordination and cooperation mechanism, namely:

1. Disputes arising out of the application or interpretation of this agreement or any subsequent agreements pertaining to the interim period shall be settled by negotiations through the Liaison Committee.

2. Disputes which cannot be settled by negotiations may be settled by a mechanism of conciliation to be agreed between the parties.

3. The parties may agree to submit to arbitration disputes relating to the interim period, which cannot be settled through conciliation. To this end, upon the agreement of both parties, the parties will establish an Arbitration Committee.

Art. XVIII: Prevention of Hostile Acts

Both sides shall take all measures necessary in order to prevent acts of terrorism, crime and hostilities directed against each other, against individuals falling under the other's authority and against their property, and shall take legal measures against offenders. In addition, the Palestinian side shall take all measures necessary to prevent such hostile acts directed against the settlements, the infrastructure serving them and the Military Installation Area, and the Israeli side shall take all measures necessary to prevent such hostile acts emanating from the settlements and directed against Palestinians.

Art. XIX: Missing Persons

The Palestinian Authority shall cooperate with Israel by providing all necessary assistance in the conduct of searches by Israel within the Gaza Strip and the Jericho Area for missing Israelis, as well as by providing information about missing Israelis. Israel shall cooperate with the Palestinian Authority in searching for, and providing necessary information about, missing Palestinians.

Art. XX: Confidence-building Measures

With a view to creating a positive and supportive public atmosphere to accompany the implementation of this agreement, and to establish a solid basis of mutual trust and good faith, both parties agree to carry out confidence-building measures as detailed herewith.

1. Upon the signing of this agreement, Israel will release, or turn over, to the Palestinian Authority within a period of five weeks, about 5,000 Palestinian detainees and prisoners, residents of the West Bank and the Gaza Strip. Those released will be free to return to their homes anywhere in the West Bank or the Gaza Strip. Prisoners turned over to the Palestinian Authority shall be obliged to remain in the Gaza Strip or the Jericho Area for the remainder of their sentence.

2. After the signing of this agreement, the two parties shall continue to negotiate the release of additional Palestinian prisoners and detainees, building on agreed principles.

3. The implementation of the above measures will be subject to the fulfilment of the procedures determined by Israeli law for the release and transfer of detainees and prisoners.

4. With the assumption of Palestinian Authority, the Palestinian side commits itself to solving the problem of those Palestinians who were in contact with the Israeli authorities. Until an agreed solution is found, the Palestinian side undertakes not to prosecute these Palestinians or to harm them in any way.

5. Palestinians from abroad whose entry into the Gaza Strip and the Jericho Area is approved pursuant to this agreement, and to whom the provisions of this article are applicable, will not be prosecuted for offenses commited prior to September 1993.

Art. XXI: Temporary International Presence

1. The parties agree to a temporary international or foreign presence in the Gaza Strip and the Jericho Area (hereinafter 'the TIP'), in accordance with the provisions of this article.

2. The TIP shall consist of 400 qualified personnel, including observers, instructors and other experts, from five or six of the donor countries.

3. The two parties shall request the donor countries to establish a special fund to provide finance for the TIP.

4. The TIP will function for a period of six months. The TIP may extend this period, or change the scope of its operation, with the agreement of the two parties.

5. The TIP shall be stationed and operate within the following cities and villages: Gaza, Khan Yunis, Rafah, Deir El Ballah, Jabaliya, Absan, Beit Hanun and Jericho.

6. Israel and the Palestinian Authority shall agree on a special protocol to implement this article, with the goal of concluding negotiations with the donor countries contributing personnel within two months.

Art. XXII: Rights, Liabilities and Obligations

1. *(a)* The transfer of all powers and responsibilities to the Palestinian Authority includes all related rights, liabilities and obligations arising with regard to acts or omissions which occurred prior to the transfer. Israel will cease to bear any financial responsibility regarding such acts or omissions and the Palestinian Authority will bear all financial responsibility for these and for its own functioning.

(b) Any financial claim made in this regard against Israel will be referred to the Palestinian Authority.

(c) Israel shall provide the Palestinian Authority with the information it has regarding pending and anticipated claims brought before any court or tribunal against Israel in this regard.

(d) Where legal proceedings are brought in respect of such a claim, Israel will notify the Palestinian Authority and enable it to participate in defending the claim and raise any arguments on its behalf.

(e) In the event that an award is made against Israel by any court or tribunal in respect of such a claim, the Palestinian Authority shall reimburse Israel the full amount of the award.

(f) Without prejudice to the above, where a court or tribunal hearing such a claim finds that liability rests solely with an employee or agent who acted beyond the scope of the powers assigned to him or her, unlawfully or with willful malfeasance, the Palestinian Authority shall not bear financial responsibility.

2. The transfer of authority in itself shall not affect rights, liabilities and obligations of any person or legal entity, in existence at the date of signing of this agreement.

Art. XXIII: Final Clauses

1. This agreement shall enter into force on the date of its signing.

2. The arrangements established by this agreement shall remain in force until and to the extent superseded by the Interim Agreement referred to in the Declaration of Principles or any other agreement between the parties.

3. The five-year interim period referred to in the Declaration of Principles commences on the date of the signing of this agreement.

4. The parties agree that, as long as this agreement is in force, the security fence erected by Israel around the Gaza Strip shall remain in place and that the line demarcated by the fence, as shown on attached map No. 1, shall be authoritative only for the purpose of this agreement.

5. Nothing in this agreement shall prejudice or pre-empt the outcome of the negotiations on the Interim Agreement or on the permanent status to be conducted pursuant to the Declaration of Principles. Neither party shall be deemed, by virtue of having entered into this agreement, to have renounced or waived any of its existing rights, claims or positions.

6. The two parties view the West Bank and the Gaza Strip as a single territorial unit, the integrity of which will be preserved during the interim period.

7. The Gaza Strip and the Jericho Area shall continue to be an integral part of the West Bank and the Gaza Strip, and their status shall not be changed for the period of this agreement. Nothing in this agreement shall be considered to change this status.

8. The Preamble to this agreement, and all annexes, appendices and maps attached hereto, shall constitute an integral part hereof.

Done in Cairo this fourth day of May, 1994.

3.   NORTHERN IRELAND CEASEFIRE DECLARATIONS

Printed below are the 'cessation of hostilities' statements issued in Northern Ireland by the Irish Republican Army (IRA) on 31 August 1994 and by the Combined Loyalist Military Command (CLMC), representing the Ulster Defence Association (UDA), the Ulster Volunteer Force (UVF) and the Red Hand Commandos, on 13 October 1994. (Texts taken from the Belfast Telegraph.*)*

IRA STATEMENT

Recognizing the potential of the current situation and in order to enhance the democratic peace process and to underline our definitive commitment to its success the leadership of Oglaigh na hEireann have decided that as of midnight Wednesday, 31 August, there will be a complete cessation of military operations.

All our units have been instructed accordingly. At this historic crossroads the leadership of Oglaigh na hEireann [the IRA] salutes and commends our volunteers and other activists, our supporters and the political prisoners who have sustained this struggle against all odds for the past 25 years.

Your courage, determination and sacrifice have demonstrated that the spirit of freedom and the desire for peace based on a just and lasting settlement cannot be crushed. We remember all those who have died for Irish freedom and we reiterate our commitment to our republican objectives.

Our struggle has seen many gains and advances made by nationalists and for the democratic position. We believe that an opportunity to secure a just and lasting settlement has been created.

We are therefore entering a new situation in a spirit of determination and confidence, determined that the injustices which created this conflict will be removed and confident in the strength and justice of our struggle to achieve this.

We note that the Downing Street Declaration [of December 1993—see AR 1993, pp. 572–4] is not a solution, nor was it presented as such by its authors. A solution will only be found as a result of inclusive negotiations. Others, not least the British government, have a duty to face up to their responsibilities. It is our desire to significantly contribute with energy, determination and patience.

LOYALIST STATEMENT

After a widespread consultative process initiated by representations from the Ulster Democratic and Progressive Unionist parties, and after having received confirmation and guarantees in relation to Northern Ireland's constitutional position within the United Kingdom, as well as other assurances, and, in the belief that the democratically—expressed wishes of the greater number of people in Northern Ireland will be respected and upheld, the Combined Loyalist Military Command (CLMC) will universally cease all operational hostilities as from 12 midnight on Thursday 13 October 1994.

The permanence of our ceasefire will be completely dependent upon the continued cessation of all nationalist/republican violence, the sole responsibility for a return to war lies with them.

In the genuine hope that this pease will be permanent, we take the opportunity to pay homage to all our fighters, commandos and volunteers who have paid the supreme sacrifice. They did not die in vain. The Union is safe.

To our physically and mentally wounded who have served Ulster so unselfishly, we wish a speedy recovery, and to the relatives of these men and women we pledge our continued moral and practical support.

To our prisoners who have undergone so much deprivation and degradation with great courage and forbearance, we solemnly promise to leave no stone unturned to secure their freedom.

To our serving officers, NCOs and personnel, we extend our eternal gratitude for their obedience of orders, for their ingenuity, resilience and good humour in the most trying of circumstances, and, we commend them for their courageous fortitude and unshakeable faith over the long years of armed confrontation.

In all sincerity, we offer to the loved ones of all innocent victims over the past 25 years, abject and true remorse. No words of ours will compensate for the intolerable suffering they have undergone during the conflict.

Let us firmly resolve to respect our differing views of freedom, culture and aspiration and never again permit our political circumstances to degenerate into bloody warfare. We are on the threshold of a new and exciting beginning with our battles in future being political battles, fought on the side of honesty, decency and democracy against the negativity of mistrust, misunderstanding and malevolence, so that, together, we can bring forth a wholesome society in which our children, and their children, will know the meaning of true peace.

4. ISRAEL–JORDAN PEACE TREATY

Below are the substantive passages of the Treaty of Peace signed at Araba/Arava on the Israel-Jordan border on 26 October 1994 by Yitzhak Rabin and Abdul Salam Majali (Prime Ministers of Israel and Jordan respectively) and witnessed by President Clinton of the United States. Its signature followed the conclusion on 25 July, by King Husain of Jordan and Mr Rabin, of the Washington Declaration ending the state of belligerency between the two countries. (Text supplied by Israeli embassy, London.)

Preamble

The government of the State of Israel and the government of the Hashemite Kingdom of Jordan:

Bearing in mind the Washington Declaration, signed by them on 25 July 1994, and which they are both committed to honour;

Aiming at the achievement of a just, lasting and comprehensive peace in the Middle East based on Security Council resolutions 242 and 338 in all their aspects;

Bearing in mind the importance of maintaining and strengthening peace based on freedom, equality, justice and respect for fundamental human rights, thereby overcoming psychological barriers and promoting human dignity;

Reaffirming their faith in the purposes and principles of the Charter of the United Nations and recognising their right and obligation to live in peace with each other as well as with all states, within secure and recognized boundaries;

Desiring to develop friendly relations and cooperation between them in accordance with the principles of international law governing international relations in times of peace;

Desiring as well to ensure lasting security for both their states and in particular to avoid threats and the use of force between them;

Bearing in mind that in their Washington Declaration of 25 July 1994 they declared the termination of the state of belligerency between them;

Deciding to establish peace between them in accordance with this Treaty of Peace;

Have agreed as follows;

Article 1: Establishment of Peace

Peace is hereby established between the State of Israel and the Hashemite Kingdom of Jordan (the 'parties') effective from the exchange of the instruments of ratification of this treaty.

Article 2: General Principles

The parties will apply between them the provisions of the Charter of the United Nations and the principles of international law governing relations among states in times of peace. In particular:

1. They recognize and will respect each other's sovereignty, territorial integrity and political independence;

2. They recognize and will respect each other's right to live in peace within secure and recognized boundaries;

3. They will develop good neighbourly relations of cooperation between them to ensure lasting security, will refrain from the threat or use of force against each other and will settle all disputes between them by peaceful means;

4. They respect and recognize the sovereignty, territorial integrity and political independence of every state in the region;

5. They respect and recognize the pivotal role of human development and dignity in regional and bilateral relationships;

6. They further believe that within their control, involuntary movements of persons in such a way as to adversely prejudice the security of either party should not be permitted.

Article 3: International Boundary

1. The international boundary between Israel and Jordan is delimited with reference to the boundary definition under the Mandate as is shown in Annex I(a), on the mapping materials attached thereto and coordinates specified therein.

2. The boundary, as set out in Annex I(a), is the permanent, secure and recognized international boundary between Israel and Jordan, without prejudice to the status of any territories that came under Israeli military government control in 1967.

3. The parties recognize the international boundary, as well as each other's territory, territorial waters and airspace, as inviolable, and will respect and comply with them.

4. The demarcation of the boundary will take place as set forth in Appendix (I) to Annex I and will be concluded not later than nine months after the signing of the treaty.

5. It is agreed that where the boundary follows a river, in the event of natural changes in the course of the flow of the river as described in Annex I(a), the boundary shall follow the new course of the flow. In the event of any other changes the boundary shall not be affected unless otherwise agreed.

6. Immediately upon the exchange of the instruments of ratification of this treaty, each party will deploy on its side of the international boundary as defined in Annex I(a).

7. The parties shall, upon the signature of the treaty, enter into negotiations to conclude, within nine months, an agreement on the delimitation of their maritime boundary in the Gulf of Aqaba.

8. Taking into account the special circumstances of the Naharayim/Baqura area, which is under Jordanian sovereignty, with Israeli private ownership rights, the parties agreed to apply the provisions set out in Annex I(b).

9. With respect to the Zofar/Al-Ghamr area, the provisions set out in Annex I(c) will apply.

Article 4: Security

1(a) Both parties, acknowledging that mutual understanding and cooperation in security-related matters will form a significant part of their relations and will further enhance the security of the region, take upon themselves to base their security relations on mutual trust, advancement of joint interests and cooperation, and to aim towards a regional framework of partnership in peace.

(b) Towards that goal the parties recognize the achievements of the European Community and European Union in the development of the Conference on Security and Cooperation in Europe (CSCE) and commit themselves to the creation, in the Middle East, of a Conference on Security and Cooperation in the Middle East (CSCME). This commitment entails the adoption of regional models of security successfully implemented in the post-World War era (along the lines of the Helsinki process) culminating in a regional zone of security and stability.

2. The obligations referred to in this article are without prejudice to the inherent right of self-defence in accordance with the United Nations Charter.

3. The parties undertake, in accordance with the provisions of this article, the following:

(a) to refrain from the threat or use of force or weapons, conventional, non-conventional or of any other kind, against each other, or of other actions or activities that adversely affect the security of the other party;

(b) to refrain from organizing, instigating, inciting, assisting or participating in acts or threats of belligerency, hostility, subversion or violence against the other party;

(c) to take necessary and effective measures to ensure that acts or threats of belligerency, hostility, subversion or violence against the other party do not originate from, and are not committed within, through or over their territory (hereinafter the term 'territory' includes the airspace and territorial waters).

4. Consistent with the era of peace and with the efforts to build regional security and to avoid and prevent aggression and violence, the parties further agree to refrain from the following:

(a) joining or in any way assisting, promoting or cooperating with any coalition, organization or alliance with a military or security character with a third party, the objectives or activities of which include launching aggression or other acts of military hostility against the other party, in contravention of the provisions of the present treaty;

(b) allowing the entry, stationing and operating on their territory, or through it, of military forces, personnel or *matériel* of a third party, in circumstances which may adversely prejudice the security of the other party.

5. Both parties will take necessary and effective measures, and will cooperate in combating terrorism of all kinds. The parties undertake:

(a) to take necessary and effective measures to prevent acts of terrorism, subversion or violence from being carried out from their territory or through it and to take necessary and effective measures to combat such activities and all their perpetrators;

(b) without prejudice to the basic rights of freedom of expression and association, to take necessary and effective measures to prevent the entry, presence and cooperation in their territory of any group or organization, and their infrastructure, which threatens the security of the other party by the use of or incitement to the use of, violent means;

(c) to cooperate in preventing and combating cross-boundary infiltrations.

6. Any question as to the implementation of this article will be dealt with through a mechanism of consultations which will include a liaison system, verification, supervision, and where necessary, other mechanisms, and higher level consultations. The details of the mechanism of consultations will be contained in an agreement to be concluded by the parties within three months of the exchange of the instruments of ratification of this treaty.

7. The parties undertake to work as a matter of priority, and as soon as possible in the context of the Multilateral Working Group on Arms Control and Regional Security, and jointly, towards the following:

(a) the creation in the Middle East of a region free from hostile alliances and coalitions;

(b) the creation of a Middle East free from weapons of mass destruction, both conventional and non-conventional, in the context of a comprehensive, lasting and stable peace, characterized by the renunciation of the use of force, reconciliation and goodwill.

Article 5: Diplomatic and Other Bilateral Relations

1. The parties agree to establish full diplomatic and consular relations and to exchange resident ambassadors within one month of the exchange of the instruments of ratification of this treaty.

2. The parties agree that the normal relationship between them will further include economic and cultural relations.

Article 6: Water

With the view to achieving a comprehensive and lasting settlement of all the water problems between them:

1. The parties agree mutually to recognize the rightful allocations of both of them in Jordan river and Yarmouk river waters and Araba/Arava ground water in accordance with the agreed acceptable principles, quantities and quality as set out in Annex II, which shall be fully respected and complied with.

2. The parties, recognizing the necessity to find a practical, just and agreed solution to their water problems and with the view that the subject of water can form the basis for the advancement of cooperation between them, jointly undertake to ensure that the management and development of their water resources do not, in any way, harm the water resources of the other party.

3. The parties recognize that their water resources are not sufficient to meet their needs. More water should be supplied for their use through various methods, including projects of regional and international cooperation.

4. In light of paragraph 3 of this article, with the understanding that cooperation in water-related subjects would be to the benefit of both parties, and will help alleviate their water shortages, and that water issues along their entire boundary must be dealt with in their totality, including the possibility of trans-boundary water transfers, the parties agree to search for ways to alleviate water shortages and to cooperate in the following fields:

(a) development of existing and new water resources, increasing the water availability, including cooperation on a regional basis as appropriate, and minimising wastage of water resources through the chain of their uses;

(b) prevention of contamination of water resources;

(c) mutual assistance in the alleviation of water shortages;

(d) transfer of information and joint research and development in water-related subjects, and review of the potentials for enhancement of water resources development and use.

5. The implementation of both parties' undertakings under this article is detailed in Annex II.

Article 7: Economic Relations

1. Viewing economic development and prosperity as pillars of peace, security and harmonious relations between states, peoples and individual human beings, the parties, taking note of understandings reached between them, affirm their mutual desire to promote economic cooperation between them, as well as within the framework of wider regional economic cooperation.

2. In order to accomplish this goal, the parties agree to the following:

(a) to remove all discriminatory barriers to normal economic relations, to terminate economic boycotts directed at each other, and to cooperate in terminating boycotts against either party by third parties;

(b) recognizing that the principle of free and unimpeded flow of goods and services should guide their relations, the parties will enter into negotiations with a view to concluding agreements on economic cooperation, including trade and the establishment of a free trade area or areas, investment, banking, industrial cooperation and labour, for the purpose of promoting beneficial economic relations, based on principles to be agreed upon, as well as on human development considerations on a regional basis. These negotiations will be concluded no later than six months from the exchange of the instruments of ratification of this treaty;

(c) to cooperate bilaterally, as well as in multilateral forums, towards the promotion of their respective economies and of their neighbourly economic relations with other regional parties.

Article 8: Refugees and Displaced Persons

1. Recognizing the massive human problems caused to both parties by the conflict in the Middle East, as well as the contribution made by them towards the alleviation of human suffering, the parties will seek to further alleviate those problems arising on a bilateral level.

2. Recognizing that the above human problems caused by the conflict in the Middle East cannot be fully resolved on the bilateral level, the parties will seek to resolve them in appropriate forums, in accordance with international law, including the following:

(a) in the case of displaced persons, in a quadripartite committee together with Egypt and the Palestinians;

(b) in the case of refugees, (i) in the framework of the Multilateral Working Group on Refugees; (ii) in negotiations, in a framework to be agreed, bilateral or otherwise, in conjunction with and at the same time as the permanent status negotiations pertaining to the territories referred to in Article 3 of this treaty;

(c) through the implementation of agreed United Nations programmes and other agreed international economic programmes concerning refugees and displaced persons, including assistance to their settlement.

Article 9: Places of Historical and Religious Significance and Inter-faith Relations

1. Each party will provide freedom of access to places of religious and historical significance.

2. In this regard, in accordance with the Washington Declaration, Israel respects the present social role of the Hashemite Kingdom of Jordan in Muslim holy shrines in Jerusalem. When negotiations on the permanent status will take place, Israel will give high priority to the Jordanian historic role in these shrines.

3. The parties will act together to promote inter-faith relations among the three monotheistic religions, with the aim of working towards religious understanding, moral commitment, freedom of religious worship, and tolerance and peace.

Article 10: Cultural and Scientific Exchanges

The parties, wishing to remove biases developed through periods of conflict, recognize the desirability of cultural and scientific exchanges in all fields, and agree to establish normal cultural relations between them. Thus, they shall, as soon as possible and not later than nine months from the exchange of instruments of ratification of this treaty, conclude the negotiations on cultural and scientific agreements.

Article 11: Mutual Understanding and Good Neighbourly Relations

1. The parties will seek to foster mutual understanding and tolerance based on shared historic values, and accordingly undertake:

(a) to abstain from hostile or discriminatory propaganda against each other, and to take all possible legal and administrative measures to prevent the dissemination of such propaganda by any organization or individual present in the territory of either party;

(b) as soon as possible, and not later than 3 months from the exchange of the instruments of ratification of this treaty, to repeal all adverse or discriminatory references and expressions of hostility in their respective legislation;

(c) to refrain in all government publications from any such references or expressions;

(d) to ensure mutual enjoyment by each other's citizens of due process of law within their respective legal systems and before their courts.

2. Paragraph 1(a) of this article is without prejudice to the right to freedom of expression as contained in the International Covenant on Civil and Political Rights.

3. A joint committee shall be formed to examine incidents where one party claims there has been a violation of this article.

Article 12: Combating Crime and Drugs

The parties will cooperate in combating crime, with an emphasis on smuggling, and will take all necessary measures to combat and prevent such activities as the production of, as well as the trafficking in illicit drugs, and will bring to trial perpetrators of such acts. In this regard, they take note of the understandings reached between them in the above spheres, in accordance with Annex III and undertake to conclude all relevant agreements not later than nine months from the date of the exchange of the instruments of ratification of this treaty.

Article 13: Transportation and Roads

Taking note of the progress already made in the area of transportation, the parties recognize the mutuality of interest in good neighbourly relations in the area of transportation and agree to the following means to promote relations between them in this sphere:

1. Each party will permit the free movement of nationals and vehicles of the other into and within its territory according to the general rules applicable to nationals and vehicles of other

states. Neither party will impose discriminatory taxes or restrictions on the free movement of persons and vehicles from its territory to the territory of the other.

2. The parties will open and maintain roads and border-crossings between their countries and will consider further road and rail links between them.

3. The parties will continue their negotiations concerning mutual transportation agreements in the above and other areas, such as joint projects, traffic safety, transport standards and norms, licensing of vehicles, land passages, shipment of goods and cargo, and meteorology, to be concluded not later than six months from the exchange of the instruments of ratification of this treaty.

4. The parties agree to continue their negotiations for a highway to be constructed and maintained between Egypt, Israel and Jordan near Eilat.

Article 14: Freedom of Navigation and Access to Ports

1. Without prejudice to the provisions of paragraph 3, each party recognizes the right of the vessels of the other party to innocent passage through its territorial waters in accordance with the rules of international law.

2. Each party will grant normal access to its ports for vessels and cargoes of the other, as well as vessels and cargoes destined for or coming from the other party. Such access will be granted on the same conditions as generally applicable to vessels and cargoes of other nations.

3. The parties consider the Strait of Tiran and the Gulf of Aqaba to be international waterways open to all nations for unimpeded and non-suspendable freedom of navigation and overflight. The parties will respect each other's right to navigation and overflight for access to either party through the Strait of Tiran and the Gulf of Aqaba.

Article 15: Civil Aviation

1. The parties recognize as applicable to each other the rights, privileges and obligations provided for by the multilateral aviation agreements to which they are both party, particularly by the 1944 Convention on International Civil Aviation (the Chicago Convention) and the 1944 International Air Services Transit Agreement.

2. Any declaration of national emergency by a party under Article 89 of the Chicago Convention will not be applied to the other party on a discriminatory basis.

3. The parties take note of the negotiations on the international air corridor to be opened between them in accordance with the Washington Declaration. In addition, the parties shall, upon ratification of this treaty, enter into negotiations for the purpose of concluding a Civil Aviation Agreement. All the above negotiations are to be concluded not later than six months from the exchange of the instruments of ratification of this treaty.

Article 16: Posts and Telecommunications

The parties take note of the opening between them, in accordance with the Washington Declaration, of direct telephone and facsimile lines. Postal links, the negotiations on which having been concluded, will be activated upon the signature of this treaty. The parties further agree that normal wireless and cable communications and television relay services by cable, radio and satellite, will be established between them, in accordance with all relevant international conventions and regulations. The negotiations on these subjects will be concluded not later than nine months from the exchange of the instruments of ratification of this treaty.

Article 17: Tourism

The parties affirm their mutual desire to promote cooperation between them in the field of tourism. In order to accomplish this goal, the parties—taking note of the understandings reached between them concerning tourism—agree to negotiate, as soon as possible, and to conclude not later than three months from the exchange of the instruments of ratification of this treaty, an agreement to facilitate and encourage mutual tourism and tourism from third countries.

Article 18: Environment

The parties will cooperate in matters relating to the environment, a sphere to which they attach great importance, including conservation of nature and prevention of pollution, as set forth in Annex IV. They will negotiate an agreement on the above, to be concluded not later than six months from the exchange of the instruments of ratification of this treaty.

Article 19: Energy

1. The parties will cooperate in the development of energy resources, including the development of energy-related projects such as the utilisation of solar energy.

2. The parties, having concluded their negotiations on the interconnecting of their electric grids in the Eilat-Aqaba area, will implement the interconnecting upon the signature of this treaty. The parties view this step as a part of a wider binational and regional concept. They agree to continue their negotiations as soon as possible to widen the scope of their inter-connected grids.

3. The parties will conclude the relevant agreements in the field of energy with six months from the date of exchange of the instruments of ratification of this treaty.

Article 20: Rift Valley Development

The parties attach great importance to the integrated development of the Jordan Rift Valley area, including joint projects in the economic, environmental, energy-related and tourism fields. Taking note of the terms of reference developed in the framework of the Trilateral Israel–Jordan–US Economic Committee towards the Jordan Rift Valley Development Master Plan, they will vigorously continue their efforts towards the completion of planning and towards implementation.

Article 21: Health

The parties will cooperate in the area of health and shall negotiate with a view to the conclusion of an agreement within nine months from the exchange of the instruments of ratification of this treaty.

Article 22: Agriculture

The parties will cooperate in the areas of agriculture, including veterinary services, plant protection, biotechnology and marketing, and shall negotiate with a view to the conclusion of an agreement within six months from the date of the exchange of instruments of ratification of this treaty.

Article 23: Aqaba and Eilat

The parties agree to enter into negotiations, as soon as possible, and not later than one month from the exchange of the instruments of ratification of this treaty, on arrangements that would enable the joint development of the towns of Aqaba and Eilat with regard to such matters, *inter alia*, as joint tourism development, joint customs posts, free trade zone, cooperation in aviation, prevention of pollution, maritime matters, police, customs and health cooperation. The parties will conclude all relevant agreements within nine months from the exchange of the instruments of ratification of the treaty.

Article 24: Claims

The parties agree to establish a claims commission for the mutual settlement of all financial claims.

Article 25: Rights and Obligations

1. This treaty does not affect and shall not be interpreted as affecting, in any way, the rights and obligations of the parties under the Charter of the United Nations.

2. The parties undertake to fulfil in good faith their obligations under this treaty, without regard to action or inaction of any other party and independently of any instrument inconsistent with this treaty. For the purposes of this paragraph each party represents to the other that in its opinion and interpretation there is no inconsistency between their existing treaty obligations and this treaty.

3. They further undertake to take all the necessary measures for the application in their relations of the provisions of the multilateral conventions to which they are parties, including the submission of appropriate notification to the Secretary-General of the United Nations and other depositories of such conventions.

4. Both parties will also take all the necessary steps to abolish all pejorative references to the other party, in multinational conventions to which they are parties, to the extent that such references exist.

5. The parties undertake not to enter into any obligation in conflict with this treaty.

6. Subject to Article 103 of the United Nations Charter, in the event of a conflict between the obligations of the parties under the present treaty and any of their other obligations, the obligations under this treaty will be binding and implemented.

Article 26: Legislation

Within three months of the exchange of ratifications of this treaty the parties undertake to enact any legislation necessary in order to implement the treaty, and to terminate any international commitments and to repeal any legislation that is inconsistent with the treaty.

Article 27: Ratification

1. This treaty shall be ratified by both parties in conformity with their respective national procedures. It shall enter into force on the exchange of the instruments of ratification.
2. The annexes, appendices, and other attachments to this treaty shall be considered integral parts thereof.

Article 28: Interim Measures

The parties will apply, in certain spheres, to be agreed upon, interim measures pending the conclusion of the relevant agreements in accordance with this treaty, as stipulated in Annex V.

Article 29: Settlement of Disputes

1. Disputes arising out of the application or interpretation of this treaty shall be resolved by negotiations.
2. Any such disputes which cannot be settled by negotiations shall be resolved by conciliation or submitted to arbitration.

Article 30: Registration

This treaty shall be transmitted to the Secretary-General of the United Nations for registration in accordance with the provisions of Article 102 of the Charter of the United Nations.

Done at the Arava/Araba Crossing Point this day Heshvan 21st, 5755, Jumada Al-Ula 21st, 1415 which corresponds to 26 October 1994 in the Hebrew, English and Arabic languages, all texts being equally authentic. In case of divergence of interpretation the English text shall prevail.

For the State of Israel	For the Hashemite Kingdom of Jordan
Yitzhak Rabin	Abdul Salam Majali
Prime Minister	Prime Minister

Witnessed by:

William J. Clinton
President of the United States of America

Agreed Minutes

A. Concerning Article 3(f) . . . the Parties recognize the practical questions connected with the deployment (such as demarcation, minefields, fences), and therefore would interpret the language to mean that the deployment would start immediately, continue uninterruptedly and expeditiously, and conclude no later than three months after the exchange of the instruments of ratification.

B. With regard to economic and monetary matters, pertaining specifically to the territories under Israeli military control, the two governments shall consult with each other with the aim of: 1. eliminating or mitigating adverse effects on their economies; 2. giving each other enough time to make the necessary adjustments.

The above is without prejudice to activities which are the results of relations with other states or to former obligations with regard to the territories referred to above, except to the extent that the implementation of such obligations may have adverse effects and to the extent that the implementation is within their control.

C. In the spirit of peace, the two parties attach high priority to the planned recreation joint venture project in the Naharayim/Baqura area, they favourably consider the partnership in peace to be created there, and will endeavor together to promote its implementation as soon as possible.

D. The parties will, upon the signature of this treaty, establish a joint committee headed by senior officials to monitor the implementation of this treaty and the conclusion of relevant agreements, in accordance with the treaty provisions.

5.   UNITED KINGDOM CONSERVATIVE CABINET

(as at 31 December 1994, following a reshuffle on 20 July)

Prime Minister, First Lord of the Treasury and Minister for the Civil Service	Rt. Hon. John Major, MP
Lord Chancellor	Rt. Hon. The Lord Mackay of Clashfern
Secretary of State for Foreign and Commonwealth Affairs	Rt. Hon. Douglas Hurd, CBE, MP
Chancellor of the Exchequer	Rt. Hon. Kenneth Clarke, QC, MP
Secretary of State for the Home Department	Rt. Hon. Michael Howard, QC, MP
President of the Board of Trade (Secretary of State for Trade and Industry)	Rt. Hon. Michael Heseltine, MP
Secretary of State for Defence	Rt. Hon. Malcolm Rifkind, QC, MP
Lord President of the Council and Leader of the House of Commons	Rt. Hon. Anthony Newton, OBE, MP
Secretary of State for the Environment	Rt. Hon. John Selwyn Gummer, MP
Chancellor of the Duchy of Lancaster (Minister of Public Service and Science)	Rt. Hon. David Hunt, MP
Secretary of State for Social Security	Rt. Hon. Peter Lilley, MP
Minister of Agriculture, Fisheries and Food	Rt. Hon. William Waldegrave, MP
Secretary of State for Scotland	Rt. Hon. Ian Lang, MP
Secretary of State for Northern Ireland	Rt. Hon. Sir Patrick Mayhew, QC, MP
Secretary of State for Health	Rt. Hon. Virginia Bottomley, MP
Secretary of State for Education	Rt. Hon. Gillian Shephard, MP
Secretary of State for Employment	Rt. Hon. Michael Portillo, MP
Secretary of State for Wales	Rt. Hon. John Redwood, MP
Secretary of State for Transport	Rt. Hon. Dr Brian Mawhinney, MP
Secretary of State for National Heritage	Rt. Hon. Stephen Dorrell, MP
Lord Privy Seal and Leader of the House of Lords	Rt. Hon. Viscount Cranborne
Chief Secretary to the Treasury	Rt. Hon. Jonathan Aitken, MP
Minister Without Portfolio	Rt. Hon. Jeremy Hanley, MP

6. UNITED STATES DEMOCRATIC ADMINISTRATION

(as at 31 December 1994)

Members of the Cabinet

President	Bill Clinton
Vice-President	Al Gore
Secretary of State	Warren M. Christopher
Secretary of the Treasury	Robert E. Rubin
Secretary of Defence	William J. Perry
Secretary of the Interior	Bruce Babbitt
Secretary of Agriculture	Dan Glickman
Secretary of Commerce	Ronald H. Brown
Secretary of Housing & Urban Development	Henry G. Cisneros
Secretary of Transportation	Frederico Pena
Secretary of Health & Human Services	Donna E. Shalala
Attorney-General	Janet Reno
Secretary of Labour	Robert R. Reich
Secretary of Energy	Hazel R. O'Leary
Secretary of Education	Richard W. Riley
Secretary of Veterans' Affairs	Jesse Brown

Other Leading Executive Branch Officials

White House Chief of Staff	Leon Panetta
Director of Office of Management & Budget	Alice Rivlin
Chairman of Council of Economic Advisers	Laura Tyson Jr
National Security Adviser	Anthony Lake
Head of Environmental Protection Agency	Carol Browner
Director of Central Intelligence Agency	(vacant)
Representative for Trade Negotiations	Mickey Kantor
Chairman of National Economic Council	(vacant)
Ambassador to United Nations	Madeleine K. Albright

XX OBITUARY

Abs, Hermann (b. 1901), German banker, became a director of Deutsche Bank in 1938 and from that base exerted a powerful influence on Germany's financial policies under both the Nazi regime and that of the Federal Republic. As head of the Kreditanstalt für Wiederaufbau from 1948 he used Marshall Aid to stabilize Germany's financial system, the prime condition of the subsequent 'economic miracle'. Died 6 February

Acton, Sir Harold (b. 1904), British author and aesthete, was the natural leader of any circle of culture that he adorned. It was so at Oxford in the 1920s, and admirers of that era still revered him at the ends of their lives—figures like Evelyn Waugh, Nancy Mitford, Lord David Cecil. Heir to a beautiful house, *La Pietra*, near Florence, and a magnificent art collection, he entertained there with generosity. His own literary output—art history, short stories, biography, travel—was of modest weight, but his *Memoirs of an Aesthete* (1948, 1970) delighted a wide readership. He was knighted in 1974 for his service to Anglo-Italian relations. Died 27 February

Afanasyev, Viktor (b. in the Tatar Republic 1922), was editor-in-chief (1976–89) of *Pravda*, the mouthpiece of the Soviet Communist Party's central committee, of which he was himself a member. He had been its deputy editor 1968–74, after heading the department of scientific socialism at the Moscow Academy of Sciences 1960–68, and was editor-in-chief of the monthly journal *Kommunist* 1974–76. Described as the most powerful single instrument of propaganda in the Soviet Union, he was an unregenerate hardliner to whom *glasnost* was anathema, and he was dismissed by President Gorbachev in 1989. Died 10 April

Armstrong, Sir Thomas (b. 1898), British organist and choral conductor, was principal of the Royal College of Music 1955–68, but his chief contribution to the musical world was his service as organist of Christ Church, Oxford, from 1933 and as Choragus of the University, lecturer in music and conductor of the Oxford Bach Choir from 1937; for he was a brilliant teacher, bringing out the best in his students and choirs, who included people of many nationalities and varied talent. Died 26 June

Ball, George (b. 1909), was US Under-Secretary of State 1961–66 and ambassador to the UN 1966–68. A practising lawyer, he was drawn into government service by his friendship with Adlai Stevenson, and caught the eye of President Kennedy, who made him Under-Secretary of State for Economic Afairs while asking his advice on wider questions of foreign policy. By the time of the Cuban missile crisis, when he recommended the high-risk policy that Kennedy adopted, he was effectively deputy Secretary of State. Died 26 May

Barrault, Jean-Louis (b. 1910), French actor-manager, married in 1940 the actress Madeleine Renaud (q.v.), ten years older than himself and already a star of the Comédie Française; thereafter their careers were inextricably entwined. In 1946 they launched the Renaud-Barrault company, which became world-famous for its productions both of classic drama and of the works of twentieth-century dramatists like Kafka and Claudel. By an incomprehensible irony, their theatre was destroyed by rioting students in 1968.

Undeterred, they continued to mount contemporary and other plays in a variety of theatres, with unsullied success. Barrault himself had been a fine actor who gained worldwide applause for his role in the famous film *Les Enfants du Paradis* (1944). Briefly survived by his wife, still brilliantly acting in her 90s, he died 22 January

Bich, Baron Marcel (b.1914), French businessman and yachtsman, made a fortune from selling, mostly under the brand-name Bic, such goods as throw-away razors and lighters, ballpoint and felt-tip pens, and ladies' tights, cheaply and on a mass scale. In 1971, and in three later contests, he challenged for the America's Cup, with his yacht *La France*, without success. Died 30 May

Blanch, Rt Rev Lord, PC (b. 1918), was Archbishop of York 1975–83. An airman in World War II, he graduated as a non-collegiate student at Oxford, and after five years in parish work returned to academic life as a teacher and head in theological colleges. From 1960 until his translation to York he was Bishop of Liverpool. As archbishop, friend of Dr Coggan, the Primate of England, and a fellow Evangelical, he enjoyed a high reputation for his preaching, his learning and his influence at home and abroad; but, disappointed of succeeding Dr Coggan at Canterbury, he suffered a breakdown in health and cut down his official commitments. On his retirement at the age of 65, he was given a temporal peerage. His influential works included *For All Mankind* (1975), *The Trumpet in the Morning* (1979) and *Living by Faith* 1983. Died 3 June

Borotra, Jean (b. 1898), Basque lawn-tennis player, won the Wimbledon title in 1924 and 1926. He and his fellow countrymen Cochet, Lacoste and Brugnon, popularly known as the Four Musketeers, raised French tennis to its highest peak in the 1920s. No great server, he won largely through his acute eye and his extraordinary speed and agility, which made his play most enjoyable to watch. His lapse in joining Marshal Pétain's Vichy government in 1940 was redeemed by his subsequent arrest and deportation by the Gestapo, and he never lost his Légion d'Honneur or his Croix de Guerre, earned in World War I. He went on playing high-class tennis into his 80s. Died 17 July

Boulle, Pierre (b. 1912), French author, wrote many worthy novels, many of which successfully bore translation into English; but, of them all, his worldwide reputation rested upon two which were scripted into popular films, *The Bridge on the River Kwai* (1954) and *Planet of the Apes* (1963). Died 30 January

Burnett, Most Rev Bill (b. 1917), was Archbishop of Cape Town and Metropolitan of South Africa 1974–81, after serving as Bishop of Bloemfontein 1959–67 and of Grahamstown 1967–74, and in the intervening two years as general secretary of the South African Council of Churches. At his first consecration as bishop he denounced the doctrine of race separation as 'repugnant to the word of God', and he continued vehemently to oppose apartheid; after conversion to evangelicanism in 1972 he led the South African Anglican Church away from political confrontation, while joining in protests against cases of oppression. Died 23 August

Busby, Sir Matt (b. 1909), British football player and manager, was a hero for addicts of a professional sport in which managers sometimes outshone players. Born in Scotland, Busby played for Manchester City and Liverpool in the 1930s. After World War II he joined Manchester United as manager (1945–69), general manager (1969–71) and thereafter the club's president. His pinnacle of achievement was United's victory in the European Cup in 1968, his greatest feat the rebuilding of his team after five top players had been killed in an aircraft crash in Munich; but his popularity owed most to his warm, equable and upright character. Died 20 January

Calloway, Cabell (Cab) (b.1907), black American singer, was one of the band leaders of the great age of jazz in the 1940s, succeeding Duke Ellington at the famous Cotton Club in Harlem, New York. Thereafter he combined intermittent band leadership with star singing on stage and screen, in such productions as *Porgy and Bess*, *The Cincinnati Kid* and *Hello Dolly*. He published a guide to Harlem language, *The Hepster's Dictionary*, and an autobiography with a title recalling one of his best-remembered jazz songs, *Minnie the Moocher and Me*. Died 18 November

Canetti, Elias (b. in Bulgaria 1905), was awarded the Nobel Prize for Literature in 1983. Of Spanish–Jewish Sephardic descent, he spent two of his early years in England, but most in Vienna, where he graduated and where German became his main language. After the 1938 Austro-German *Anschluss* he migrated to England, and remained British though writing in German and maintaining a second home in Zürich. His first major work was a novel, *Die Blendung* (1935, translated 1946 as *Auto da Fé* in Britain and *Tower of Babel* in the USA), followed by his most famous product, *Masse und Macht* (1960, translated 1962 as *Crowds and Power*), a huge historical study of mass action and psychology. Three volumes of memoirs published in German and English in the 1970s and '80s won him a more popular readership. In German-speaking Europe he was held in the highest esteem. Died 14 August

Cernik, Oldrich (b.1921), was Prime Minister of Czechoslovakia 1968–70. A member of the skilled working-class, he had steadily progressed in the Czechoslovak communist establishment and had joined the presidium of the party's central committee in 1966, in charge of economic planning. The reformist Dubcek appointed him Prime Minister, to become a key figure in the Prague Spring of 1968; but when it was suppressed by Soviet force he straddled the rift, stressing the economic and political dependence of his country upon the Soviet Union; continuing in office until demoted in 1970, he took a strong pro-Soviet stance. Died 14 October

Clavell, James (b. in Australia 1924), British author, made a fortune from a small number of long adventure stories selling millions of copies, notably *King Rat* (1962), *Tai-Pan* (1966) and *Shogun* (1975). Deeply researched, they drew realism from his appalling experiences as a prisoner of the Japanese, mostly in the notorious Changi gaol, for three years of World War II. His two later books did not have quite as great a popular success. Died 6 September

Curry, John (b. 1949), won the Olympic gold medal for ice skating in 1976, after winning the British championship five times in the previous six years and the world championship in 1973. He brought originality and grace to a previously rather dull sport, ushering in a new era of balletic figure skating. Died 15 April

Cushing, Peter (b. 1913), British actor, became the top star of the horror film industry from 1957, when he played the title role in Hammer Films' *The Curse of Frankenstein*. But a long career on the stage and in films and television demonstrated his acting talent in classical and modern parts of wide variety, of which the farthest-famed was Winston Smith in the 1950 television production of George Orwell's *1984*. Died 11 August

Dean, Sir Patrick, GCMG (b. 1909), was British ambassador in Washington 1965–69. Originally an academic lawyer and barrister, he joined the Foreign Office in 1939 and rose swiftly in its hierarchy, becoming the UK permanent representative at the UN 1960–64. In retirement, among other activities he was chairman of the English-Speaking Union. Died 5 November

Decoutray, HE Cardinal Albert (b. 1923), was Archbishop of Lyons from 1981, and from 1985 held from the Pope the honorific title of Primate of the Gauls. Though in Catholic faith and order he followed the conservative Vatican line, he was an ardent ecumenicalist, cultivating relations with Muslim and Jewish communities and denouncing the racist policies of Le Pen's National Front. Died 16 September

Del Portillo, Mgr Alvaro (b. in Spain 1914), was president-general of the conservative Roman Catholic organization Opus Dei from 1975 and was appointed by the Pope a titular bishop in 1991. As secretary of the conciliar commission for the clergy he had been active in the traditionalist cause at the Second Vatican Council in 1962. He had joined Opus Dei in 1935, and had led a hunted life during the Spanish Civil War before the victory of General Franco, with whom he stayed in sympathy. Died 23 March

Delvaux, Paul (b. 1897), French painter who followed De Chirico and Magritte on a surrealist path from the 1930s onwards, with his own charismatic images. Though best known in his own country, where he was rewarded with a gallery solely dedicated to his work, he was honoured abroad with many exhibitions and prizes, and gained still wider popular fame through the surrealist film *Le Monde de Paul Delvaux*, which won a major prize at the Venice Biennale in 1948. Died 20 July

Dissanayake, Gamini (b. 1942), confidently hoped, as candidate of Sri Lanka's United National Party, to win the 1994 election for the nation's presidency. In ministerial office under President Jayawardene in the 1980s, he had won applause for carrying out the country's largest development project, a series of dams and canals to use the waters of the Mahaweli river for irrigation and hydro-electricity, and had played a key part in bringing Indian troops to help suppress the Tamil separatists. Assassinated 23 October

Ellison, Ralph (b. 1914), black American author, wrote one novel, *Invisible Man* (1952), which was not only lauded by literary critics and became a best-seller, but also did more to enlighten the US majority on the plight and frustration of black people than all the propaganda of radical activists. Ellison spurned polemics and declined to endorse the 'black revolution'. He received high academic and public honours, but wrote nothing more of the quality and influence of his 1952 novel. Died 16 April

Enrique y Tarançon, HE Cardinal Vicente (b.1907), was Archbishop of Oviedo 1964–69, of Toledo 1969–71 (with the status of Primate of Spain) and of Madrid 1971–83. As head of the Spanish Episcopal Conference 1971–81 he led the Catholic Church in its relations with the state during the Franco regime and the transition to democracy. Throughout, he held stoutly to two principles, that the Church was champion of the poor and weak, and that it must keep itself independent of the structure of the state. Thus, in face of intense opposition, he rejected any plan to identify it with a Christian democratic party in the new political system. Died 28 November

Erikson, Professor Erik (b. in Germany 1902), of Danish, part-Jewish descent, exerted a strong influence on psychoanalytic studies with his theory of stage-by-stage progress of emotional life and his diagnosis of the 'identity crisis'. From the mid-1930s he had worked in the USA, becoming eventually professor of human development at Harvard. His most revolutionary book, *Childhood and Society*, developing and partly contradicting the theories of his former friend and mentor Sigmund Freud, was published in 1950. Died 12 May

Fisher, Sandra (b. in New York 1947), American painter and draughtsman, in 1971 moved to London, where in 1983 she married her long-time lover, the painter R.B. Kitaj. Her work, mainly portraits, illustrations and photos, drew inspiration from opera and literature, culminating in an unfinished series of paintings for the reconstructed Shakespeare Globe Theatre, and was represented in top American as well as British public and private collections. Died 19 September

Ghika, Nikos, hon. RA (b.1906), Greek artist, was reckoned his country's most renowned and influential painter. He was, besides, a sculptor, professor of architecture, town planner, author, translator, stage designer (famously, for Stravinsky's *Persephone* at Covent Garden), *bon viveur* and host to literary and artistic friends, many from England and from Paris, where he had studied in his youth and had started his artistic career in the 1920s. Died 3 September

Gilliat, Sydney (b. 1908), British film director and script-writer, enjoyed most of his success in partnership with Frank Launder. They began with thrillers, writing scripts for such films as Hitchcock's *The Lady Vanishes* (1938) and Carole Reed's *Night Train to Munich* (1943). The partners then progressed to direction, sharing credit for cheerful films like *The Happiest Days of Your Life* (1950) and *The Belles of St Trinian's* (1954). Gilliat directed, among other films, *Only Two Can Play* (with Peter Sellers, 1962) and *Endless Night* (by Agatha Christie, 1971). His

partnership with Launder ended only with their retirement. Died 31 May

Goren, Rabbi Shlomo (b. in Poland 1917), was Chief Rabbi (Ashkenazi) of Israel 1972–82. As head chaplain of the Israeli armed forces he had tasted the realities both of war and of religious observance in hard conditions. An utterly devoted Zionist, he equally opposed Israeli claims to non-biblical territory and softness towards Palestinian advances in any part of the Promised Land. Died 29 October

Grès, Madame (b. 1903), was one of the great Parisian couturiers of the century. Although she did not ignore the new waves of fashion launched by such masters as Jacques Fath or Christian Dior, she never swerved from her ideal of grace and natural line; for her, the cut mattered above all else. Died 24 November 1993, a fact not revealed until late in 1994

Harkness, Jack (b. 1918), British rose grower, produced world-famous hybrids, including *Marjorie Fair*, which won the gold medal of the City of Rome in 1977 and first prize in the Paris Concours of 1988, and *Fellowship*, which won the gold medals of the Royal National and All American Rose Societies. His books, articles and lectures spread his creative influence. Died 18 June

Healey, Geoffrey (b. 1922), British automobile engineer, designed a succession of racing and sports cars bearing his name: the Anglo-American Nash Healey of the early 1950s, and the Healey 100, which shone at Le Mans and Sebring and was popular on both sides of the Atlantic. After the Austin marque disappeared, Healey continued to design cars for British Leyland, and shared in the development of the Rovers of the 1980s. Died 29 April

Herron, Ron (b. 1930), British architect, was famous more for his inspired teaching and innovative genius than for the actual buildings he designed. His contribution was summed up in the title of his partnership (1969): Herron Associates of Imagination, the name he had given to the building in London which best realised his inventive ideas—tent-like structures, fabric cladding, slender materials giving maximum light and space. For 14 years from 1968 he taught in a number of prestigious American universities while keeping up his practice and teaching in London. Died 1 October

Hoad, Lew (b. 1934), Australian lawn-tennis player, won the Wimbledon title in 1956 and 1957, on the former occasion beating his fellow-countryman Ken Rosewall whom he partnered in doubles in a triumphant Davis Cup career. He also won the Italian and French singles titles in 1956, but the US title eluded him. After his amateur successes he turned professional. Died 3 July

Hodgkin, Professor Dorothy, OM (b. Crowfoot 1910), British molecular biologist, Nobel laureate for chemistry (1964), was recognized as one of the most brilliant scientists of her time. Her discovery of the structure of penicillin, insulin and Vitamin B12, which counters pernicious anaemia, opened a new era for medicine and drug manufacture worldwide. From Somerville College, Oxford, she had gone to work under the pioneer crystallographer J.D. Bernal in Cambridge. In 1934 she married the scholar and Africanist Thomas Hodgkin. Returning to Oxford, she progressed from tutor to university lecturer (1946), reader (1956) and Wolfson Research Professor (1960–77). In 1970 she had been elected chancellor of Bristol University, where she continued her research and her work for scientific liaison across the Iron Curtain. She had won the Royal Society's gold medal in 1956 and membership of the Order of Merit in 1965, and was honoured

by many scientific institutions around the world. Despite crippling arthritis, she went on working to the end. Died 29 July

Honecker, Erich (b. 1912), was general secretary of East Germany's Communist Party 1971–89 and its head of state 1976–89. An unswerving communist from childhood, Moscow-trained, he spent 10 years in gaol under the Nazi regime until liberation by the Soviet army in 1945. Ten years later he had advanced to candidate membership of the East German politburo. A full member from 1958, he steadily gathered authority until, with Soviet backing, in 1971 he was elected to succeed Walter Ulbricht at the head of the party. Meanwhile, as chairman of the National Security Council, he had been involved in building the infamous Berlin Wall in 1961. In supreme office, his policies hinged upon a view of East Germany as a distinct communist national state, not identified with the Soviet Union but establishing balanced relations with its brother Germany to the West. His relatively independent economic policies did make his country the most prosperous in the communist bloc, though still impoverished by the socialist system, and his foreign policy was crowned by his symbolic handshake with the Federal Chancellor in Bonn in 1984. As Honecker aged, his domestic line grew harder, contrary to the changes proceeding in the Soviet Union under President Gorbachev, and in 1989 he was overthrown by a reformist faction. Charged with multiple murder of escapers across the Berlin Wall, he found temporary sanctuary in Moscow, then sought permanent refuge in Chile, but was obliged to return to Berlin to stand trial. Only his extreme illness—he was dying of cancer—saved him from sentence in this world. Died 29 May

Ionesco, Eugène (b. in Romania 1912), French author and playwright, after a varied literary career cast himself as the fearless revolutionary of the modern theatre. His irreverent play *The Bald Prima Donna* (1950), which had an extraordinary vogue, launched the so-called Theatre of the Absurd. This was followed by a succession of brilliant plays, produced worldwide, of which *The Lesson* and *Amédée* were perhaps the best. Later, avant-garde admirers thought him stifled by the approbation of the French establishment: he was elected to the Académie Française in 1971 and showered with cultural honours. Died 28 March

Jerne, Professor Niels, FRS (b.1911), shared the 1984 Nobel Prize for Medicine with two other medical biologists for their work on antibodies of the immune system. Though born in England of Danish parentage, he spent most of his life in continental Europe, culminating in his directorship of the Hoffmann-La Roche Institute for Immunology in Basel 1969–87. His highly innovative contribution to theory and practice had begun with a study of 'the natural selection theory of antibody formation' in 1955, which revolutionized scientific thought on immunology, and he had subsequently held leading posts in the WHO, the University of Pittsburgh and the Paul Ehrlich Institute in Frankfurt. Died 7 October

Joseph, Lord, CH, PC (b.1918), as Sir Keith Joseph, Bt, held key offices in the Macmillan, Heath and Thatcher governments (Housing and Local Government 1962–64, Health and Social Security 1970–74, Industry 1979–81, Education 1981–87) after a rapid climb up the junior ministerial ladder. A scion of one of the most respected and wealthy families of British Jewry, he was a scholar of brilliant academic record, and his political career displayed both the merits and the defects of a highly intellectual personality—sharp rational conviction sometimes followed by doubt and self-criticism. An influential theorist of the

post-1979 'Thatcherite revolution', he was made a life peer in 1987. Died 10 December

Kaplan, Jacob (b. 1895), was Chief Rabbi of France 1955–80. Of Polish-Jewish ancestry, educated at the Sorbonne, he became a rabbi after heroic army service in World War I. Deputy Chief Rabbi from 1939, he filled his arrested chief's place after the German occupation, and won a second Croix de Guerre for his implacable resistance to the Nazis. He became Chief Rabbi of Paris in 1950, and of France in 1955. In office he was equally courageous in defending his faith and world Jewry, not fearing to clash with such giants as General de Gaulle. In 1987 he was awarded the Grand Cross of the Légion d'Honneur. Died 8 December

Kelly, Felix (b. in New Zealand 1914), British artist, was famous above all for his paintings, at once romantic and architecturally authentic, of country houses and their interiors in Britain and North America, which reached a summit in his mural for the wing of Castle Howard rebuilt after a calamitous fire. His subjects, however, extended to Nash's urban villas and the architecture of St Petersburg and the Nile valley, and to stage sets and book illustrations. Died 3 July

Kennedy, Jacqueline: *see* Onassis, Jacqueline Bouvier Kennedy

Kim Il Sung, (b. Kim Song Ju, 1912), was President and party leader of North Korea from 1948 until his death. His rule was personal, dictatorial and absolute. To the mass of his people he assumed the likeness of a god. So intense was the cult of personality that 50,000 statues of himself were believed to have been set up for his worship: no dissidence was tolerated, no contact with the outside world permitted for the masses. His fundamental theme was nationalist and patriotic: though accepting communism from the Soviet

Union and military aid from China, his regime was no satellite of either. Seeking to unite all Korea under his mastery, he launched the war of 1950–53 against the South, to be defeated by American power under the UN banner, and saved in the North only by Chinese support. An anti-imperialist agitator from his youth, he joined the Communist Party in 1931, led the Korean People's Revolutionary Army in revolt against Japanese occupation in the 1930s and World War II, and proclaimed the Democratic People's Republic of Korea, with himself as its head, in 1948. Domestically, he conducted an energetic economic policy based on self-sufficiency and hard-working devotion to the nation-state, which succeeded in raising the standard of living but faltered for lack of capital and competitive strategy. The collapse of Soviet communism and the opening of China after the death of Mao Zedong left North Korea more isolated than ever, but Kim Il Sung's nationalism was unshaken until the end. Died 8 July

Lancaster, Burt (b. 1913), American actor, became the supreme player of 'good, tough guy' parts in the Hollywood cinema. Much more than a bruiser and and acrobatic athlete, he was a brilliant character actor. Among the best films in which he starred were *From Here to Eternity* (1953), *Sweet Smell of Success* (1957), *Elmer Gantry* (1960) which won him an Oscar waward, *Birdman of Alcatraz* (1962), Visconti's *The Leopard* (1963 and *Airport* 1970. Died 20 October

Leonov, Leonid (b. 1899), was reckoned the top among Russian novelists who escaped suppression or exile to labour camps under Stalin. Indeed he won two Stalin prizes. Whether he conformed to communist correctness from conviction of for the defence of his literary art remained an enigma. His most craven trimming was to rewrite his finest novel, *Vor*

(1927, translated as *The Thief* 1931), but as early as 1953 he wrote *Russkiy les* (translated as *The Russian Forest* 1966) an allegorical attack on the system so devastatingly depicted by Solzhenitsyn. Died 8 August

Louis Ferdinand, Prince, of Prussia (b.1907), would have become Emperor of Germany, had not that empire been defeated in 1918 and the hereditary throne of Prussia and of Germany been abandoned. As it was, the son of the Crown Prince ('Little Willy' of Great War lampoons) became a commercial air pilot, and after World War II returned to such family estates as remained in East Germany, a patriotic, paternalistic Prussian *Junker* to the end. Died 25 September

Lutoslawski, Witold (b. 1913), Polish composer and conductor, was best known for his four symphonies, the last of which was premièred by the Los Angeles Philharmonic Orchestra in 1993, to be honoured by a Classical Music Award for the best new work of the year; but many others of his compositions from the 1960s onwards reached the international repertoire. Died 7 February

Lwoff, André (b. 1902), French microbiologist, shared the 1965 Nobel Prize for Medicine with two younger colleagues for their researches in molecular biology, which significantly advanced the study of cancer. With doctorates from the University of Paris he joined the Pasteur Institute in 1925, becoming head of its department of microbiology and physiology in 1938; he was professor of microbiology at the Sorbonne 1959–68, and director of the Cancer Reseach Institute at Villejuif 1968–72. In retirement he was proactive in international scientific causes, not least UNESCO. Died 30 September

McCann, HE Cardinal Owen (b.1907), Archbishop of Cape Town 1951–84, was given the red hat in

1965 in recognition of his strong contribution to Vatican II and his condemnation of apartheid, which he countered by working closely with people of other creeds and all races in the cause of peace and justice. Died 26 March

Maczek, General Stanislaw, CB, DSO (b. 1892), commanded the 1st Polish Armoured Division in the fighting from Normandy to Wilhelmshaven, where he hoisted the Polish flag after Germany's unconditional surrender. When Germany invaded Poland in 1939, and Russia followed suit, he had escaped to Hungary with his motorized brigade, thence to France to join General Sikorski's forces, and eventually to the UK. After the communists took over Poland in 1946, he made his home in Scotland and never returned to his native land, from which he received its highest honour, the Order of the White Eagle. Died 11 December

Marty, HE Cardinal François (b. 1904), Archbishop of Paris 1968–81, was more a man of the people than an ecclesiastical magnate. He sought advice from ordinary men and women, and his own was often sought by prime ministers, as well as by Pope John Paul II over Vatican II and other issues. He retired to a Dominican community in 1981 and died in a car accident, 16 February

Maung Maung (b. 1925), was briefly President of Burma in 1988 before being ousted by the army in a bloody coup. To rapturous public applause he had lifted martial law and promised political reform, a programme hateful to the military. A lawyer, trained in London and the Netherlands, he had joined Gen. Ne Win's socialist, army-controlled dictatorial administration in 1962, rising to become attorney-general. Died 2 July

May, Peter (b.1929), English cricketer, was one of the finest batsmen of his era, and a successful captain of the England team 1955–61. He scored 85 centuries in first-class matches, 13 of them in Tests, including 285 not out against the West Indies in 1954. Died 27 December

Mercouri, Melina (b. 1925), Greek Minister of Culture 1981– 89 and again 1993–94, brought the glamour of a beautiful woman and the glitter of a film star to the drabber world of politics. Born to a political family, she had enjoyed a distinguished career in Greece's theatre and cinema before gaining international fame in such films as *Never on Sunday* (1960), *Phaedra* (1961) and *Topkapi* (1964). Reacting fiercely to the 'regime of the colonels' (1967–74), she was stripped of Greek citizenship, but returned from abroad to join Andreas Papandreou's Pasok movement and was elected to parliament in 1977. As Minister of Culture she travelled the world, and became specially well-known in Britain for her persistent but unsuccessful demand for return of the Elgin Marbles. Died 6 March

Millar, Professor Thomas, AO (b. 1925), Australian academic, author and administrator, fully earned his country's Order of Merit. He founded in 1966 the Strategic and Defence Studies Centre at Canberra University, was director of the Australian Institute of International Affairs 1969–76, and headed the Sir Robert Menzies Centre for Australian Studies in London 1985–90. His greatly-valued books reflected the interests expressed in those posts, and his own combination of idealims and pragmatic analysis of hard facts in defence and international politics. Died 5 June

Nixon, Richard Milhous (b.1913), was President of the USA from 1969 until 1974, when he resigned, facing impeachment for his part in initiating and trying to cover up an attempted burglary at the Watergate headquarters of the Democratic Party. Contrasting this slimy conduct with

Nixon's political successes and his standing as a world statesman, many perceived a conflict of two opposed characters in one man; but Nixon's whole life-story displayed a combination of huge drive for power with unscrupulousness in its pursuit—traits of an insecure ego. Born to a poor Quaker family, he worked his way into a career as a lawyer, and in 1946, after a brief spell of war service, was elected to the House of Representatives for a Californian district. A right-wing Republican, he was a member of the House's infamous committee on un-American activities. In 1950 he was elected to the US Senate, and in 1952 was chosen by Gen. Eisenhower as his vice-presidential candidate. After eight years as Vice-President, Nixon won the Republican nomination for the presidency, to be narrowly beaten by John F. Kennedy in 1960. Failing in 1962 to win the governorship of California, he opened a law practice in New York, but maintained a high political profile by speeches and publicized visits abroad. Still high in Republican esteem, he beat Hubert Humphrey in the 1968 contest for the White House, on a ticket of reconciliation for a divided nation. Making little progress domestically in face of a hostile Congress, he concentrated on foreign policy, with Henry Kissinger as his Secretary of State. His achievements included progress towards an Arab-Israeli settlement, relaxation of tension between Washington and Moscow, the SALT talks on mutual limitation of nuclear arms, and the opening of relations with communist China, which led to a Vietnam detente and the withdrawal of US forces. In 1972 he won a second term in a landslide, but before long the Watergate affair exposed his darker side. Exiled from the Washington scene, he returned to law practice but kept his international image alive by elder-statesmanlike visits to China, Europe and Russia. His devoted wife died in 1993, and he on 22 April

Odinga, J. A. Oginga (b.1911), was for more than 30 years the odd-man-out of politics in Kenya. Unlike his Kikuyu leader, Jomo Kenyatta, he, a Luo, remained at liberty in the Emergency that followed the Mau Mau rebellion and he took part in constitutional talks in London in 1959. When independence followed in 1963, he became Minister of Home Affairs and in 1965 Vice-President, but he quarrelled with Kenyatta and in 1966 resigned. In the political wilderness thereafter he and his small radical-socialist party were virtually the sole parliamentary opposition to one-party rule. In 1979 President Moi took him into government, but his habit of critical opposition continued in office and in 1982 he was expelled from the ruling party. Died 20 January

Ogarkov, Marshal Nikolai (b. 1917), was Chief of the General Staff of the USSR 1977–84, and after an interval was appointed by Gorbachev to command the ground forces of the Warsaw Pact. A military reformist and strategic thinker, he was dedicated to the defence of the Soviet empire against threats from the West. Died 23 January

Ogimura, Ichiro (b.1932), Japanese table tennis player, not only was undisputed champion in the 1950s but also revolutionized the game and was foremost in its worldwide structuring. He became president of the International Table Tennis Federation from 1987, at the head of the sport when it first entered the Olympic lists in 1990. Died 4 December

Onassis, Jacqueline Bouvier Kennedy (b. Bouvier 1929), had been wife of J.F. Kennedy, President of the USA, from 1953 until his assassination in 1963, and of Aristotle Onassis, Greek millionaire shipowner, from 1968 until he died in 1975. Unlike her husbands, she came from a high social background; her beauty, grace and gift for foreign languages offset the President's very different qualities, and were of great value in his dynamic political career and her own role as First Lady in the White House. Despite his notorious infidelities she stayed loyal to him, and her conduct when he fell bleeding to death at her side endeared her further to an adulatory American public. Her second marriage, to a rich foreigner, divorced and 23 years her senior, lowered her popularity, but sympathy rose again through two quiet decades spent largely in care for her family, and her death from cancer awakened memories of her brilliant days and restored her status as a legend of glamour and charm. Died 19 May

O'Neill, Thomas Philip (Tip) (b. 1912), Speaker of the US House of Representatives 1977–86, as a dyed-in-the-wool Boston Democrat exerted a fierce counter-balance of power against Republican Presidents Nixon and Reagan. He had been elected to President Kennedy's old seat in Congress in 1962 and ten years later became majority leader. Died 6 January

Onetti, Juan Carlos (b. in Uruguay 1909), was reckoned to be one of the great Latin American writers of his time; but English translations of his novels and stories were delayed, and his genius was recognized more in Spain, Italy and France than in Britain or the US. Among the best of them were *The Well* (1939) and *Brief Life* (1950). Onetti spent most of his life in Chile and Argentina, but ended it in Spain, where in 1980 he was awarded the coveted Cervantes Prize. Died 30 May

Osborne, John (b.1929), British playwright, actor, and stage and television producer, after an unimpressive decade on the stage sprang to fame with a play, *Look Back in Anger*, which caught the mood of disillusionment affecting many of his generation and evoked the catch-phrase 'angry young man'. This was closely followed by another mordant drama for stage and television, *The Entertainer*, in which Sir Laurence Olivier played the role of a failed music-hall comedian. Osborne excelled at writing parts for brilliant actors: Olivier, Albert Finney in *Luther* (1961) and an Oscar-winning screen-play of *Tom Jones* (1963), George Devine (his discoverer and patron at the Royal Court Theatre) in *A Patriot for Me* (1965), Paul Scofield in *The Hotel in Amsterdam* (1968), Ralph Richardson in *West of Suez* (1971). Later plays were less successful, but Osborne found ample vents for his spleen in journalism, autobiography and other channels. Died 24 December

Pauling, Linus (b. 1901), American scientist and anti-nuclear activist, had the unique distinction of winning two Nobel prizes, for chemistry in 1954 and for peace in 1963. His university education was at the California Institute of Technology (Caltech) where he became a full professor in 1930 and chairman of the chemistry faculty in 1936, retiring in 1963. Among other distinctions he was George Eastman Professor at Oxford in 1948. His seminal research into chemical structures, through the mode of wave mechanics, was presented in his book *The Nature of the Chemical Bond* (1939), which became a classic of contemporary science. Although in World War II he worked on atomic weaponry for the National Defense Research Commission, thereafter he gave more and more of his time to opposing nuclear armament—a cause which made him a pariah in the McCarthy era—and his scientific output declined. Died 19 August

Pinay, Antoine (b. 1891), was Prime Minister of France for a period in 1952, and Finance Minister under the Fifth Republic 1958–60, having been the first major politician to call for Gen. de Gaulle's return in the crisis over Algeria. Dismissed, and never again accepting office, he remained popular and influential in the penumbra of centre-right French politics. Died 13 December

Pope-Hennessy, Sir John (b.1913), British art historian, was director of the Victoria and Albert Museum 1967–73 and of the British Museum 1974–76. On the staff of the V&A from 1938, he specialized in the art of the Italian Renaissance, on which he wrote a number of monographs and lectured both in Britain and in the USA. He was Slade Professor of Fine Art at Oxford 1956–57 and at Cambridge 1964–65. Died in Florence 31 October

Popper, Sir Karl, FRS, CH (b. in Austria 1902), British philosopher, was professor of logic and scientific method at the London School of Economics and Political Science 1949–69, but his most innovative work, which made him a decisive influence upon Western thought, was done much earlier. His first major book, *Logik der Forschung*, was published in 1934; translated in 1959 and later much enlarged, it reappeared in 1982 as *The Logic of Scientific Discovery*. His still more impressive *The Open Society and Its Enemies*, begun in 1939, was published in 1945. Meanwhile he had fled the Nazi menace to become a senior lecturer in philosophy at a New Zealand university 1937–45, before enlistment to LSE. In retirement he continued to write and teach. Died 17 September

Porritt, Lord, GCMG, GCVO, FRCS, Bt (b. 1900), was Governor-General of New Zealand, his native country, 1967–72; but his early fame, as Arthur Porritt, was that of an Olympic athlete (a bronze sprint medal, 1924), and his main career that of a surgeon and leader of the medical profession. A Rhodes Scholar, after Oxford he studied, taught and practised at St Mary's Hospital, London, with an interval of war service in the RAMC. He was a fellow of the Royal College of Surgeons from 1928, on its council 1960–66 and its president 1960–63 and was also president of the British Medical Association in 1960. Meanwhile he had become surgeon to the royal household and had gathered high honours from the USA and France as well as the Commonwealth. Knighted in 1950, a baronet from 1963, he became a peer in 1972. Died 1 January

Renaud, Madeleine (b. 1900), French actress and theatre director, married Jean-Louis Barrault (q.v.) in 1940 and shared with him a supremely creative and happy partnership until his death in January 1994. She herself was one of the finest actresses of her time. As a member of the Comédie Française 1927–46 she had won high praise, as she did for her acting on film (*Marie Chapdelaine*, 1921), but her greatest performances were in her middle and old age in plays such as Claudel's *Partage du Midi*, Genet's *Les Paravents*, Beckett's *Oh! les Beaux Jours!* and Marguerite Duras's *L'Amant Anglaise*, in a new version of which she played her original old-lady role, at the age of 82, in what critics called the finest performance of her career. She had been rewarded with the highest honours that France could bestow. Died 23 September

Rusk, Dean (b. 1909), as US Secretary of State 1961–69, shared responsibility for the international policies of Presidents Kennedy and Johnson, including the Vietnam War and the confrontation with Khrushchev in the 1962 Cuban missile crisis. In the waging of the Cold War he was effectively America's tough chief of general staff. A Rhodes Scholar and academic teacher from a poor Presbyterian background in Georgia, he displayed his powers in military intelligence in World

War II, and in 1946 he joined the State Department, but broke off in 1952 to become president of the Rockefeller Foundation for eight years before Kennedy enlisted him to his cabinet. From 1971 he was professor of international law at the State University of Georgia. Died 20 December

Sallal, Abdullah (b. 1922), was President of the Yemen Arab Republic (North Yemen) 1962–67. By nature and action treacherous and subversive, he led the revolt which threw out Imam Badr a week after the Imam had made him Chief of the General Staff. As an instrument of Egyptian ambition in North Yemen he lost his power base when Egypt withdrew its forces after its defeat by Israel in 1967, and was bloodlessly deposed. Died 12 March

Schneerson, Rabbi Menachem (b. in Ukraine 1902), was leader of the Lubavich branch of Hasidic Orthodox Judaism from 1950. Fleeing the Nazi menace, he had settled in the USA in 1941, and never travelled to Israel, but from afar he exerted great influence on Israeli governments dependent on marginal Orthodox votes, opposing peace settlements with Arab neighbours and espousing the aim of Greater Israel. Died 12 January

Schweitzer, Pierre Paul (b. 1912), French banker, was managing director of the International Monetary Fund 1963–73, a period which saw a succession of monetary crises and devaluations, culminating in the so-called Smithsonian agreement on currency realignment in 1971. Between World War II, when he was consigned to Buchenwald as a man of the Resistance, and his appointment to the IMF, Schweitzer had risen swiftly in France's financial administration to become a deputy governor of the Banque de France. At the IMF his quest for order in the world monetary system brought him into conflict with President Nixon, who opposed devaluation of the dollar, but his creation of special drawing rights enhanced international liquidity and was of much value to the UK in the 1960s. Died 2 January

Schwinger, Professor Julian (b. 1918), American scientist, shared the Nobel Prize for Physics in 1965 with two others for their independent, parallel researches into the electro-dynamic structure of the atom, which opened the way to the development of ultra-high-energy physics. Schwinger held a professorial chair at Harvard University 1947–72, then worked at UCLA for the rest of his life. Died 16 July

Senna, Ayrton (b. 1960), was world champion in Formula One motor racing in 1988, 1990 and 1991. Universally regarded as the most brilliant driver of his time, as well as one of the toughest and most daring, he became a national hero in his native country, Brazil. Graduating through championships for less powerful cars, he entered the Grand Prix circuit in 1984, but supreme success did not come until, three years later, he joined the McLaren-Honda team, which already included his fierce rival Alain Prost. Finally in 1993 he achieved his ambition of driving for Williams-Renault, but it proved fatal. Meanwhile he had amassed 41 race victories (still fewer than Prost's record) and an unrivalled 64 poll-position starts. In a crash on the San Marino circuit, he died 1 May

Sharkey, Jack (b. 1902), British boxer, became world heavyweight champion when he defeated Max Schmeling on points in 1932, but lost the title to Primo Carnera a year later, knocked out in the sixth round. Died 17 August

Singh, Giani Zail (b. 1916), was President of India 1982–87. A man of modest ability, whose previous political experience had been almost entirely provincial, he was chosen by Prime Minister Indira Gandhi, as a pliant Sikh figure, for election to the presidency, and in office he was putty in her hands. He was reviled by his own community for acquiescing in the rape of the Golden Temple at Amritsar in 1984, which led to the assassination of Mrs Gandhi and the consequent massacre of Sikhs in Delhi. With her son Rajiv, who succeeded her, he fought a running battle of words and political tactics, not without small victories, and he was not re-elected after his five-year term as President. Died 25 December

Smith, Arnold, CH, OC (b. 1915), Canadian diplomat, had been ambassador to Cairo and Moscow before being appointed first secretary-general of the Commonwealth (1965–75). For the new institution that succeeded the British Empire, it was a troubled and divisive period, especially in regard to turmoil in southern Africa and elsewhere on that continent; and Smith, with his wide experience and his fortunate base in Canada, did more than anyone else to hold it together. The subsequently regular informal meetings of Commonwealth heads of government were his initiative. Died 7 February

Smith, Rt Hon John, QC, MP (b.1938), Leader of the Opposition in the UK parliament, had led the Labour Party since 1992, and was held chiefly responsible for a notable upturn in its fortunes. A brilliant student and a successful barrister on the Edinburgh circuit, he entered politics at an early age, and was first elected to parliament for a Scottish seat in 1970. In junior office in the Wilson government from 1975, at the age of 40 he was appointed, by Prime Minister Callaghan, Secretary of State for Trade and Industry, the youngest member of the cabinet. In opposition from 1979, he joined the front bench as shadow chancellor of the exchequer in 1987, and was at once recognized by the Conservative leadership as a formidable opponent. In 1992 he won the party's election to replace Neil Kinnock, an old friend and rival, as its leader. A severe cardiac warning in 1988 did not deter him from untiring labour in the House and in the country. Tributes to him from many supporters after his death confirmed that he was respected and admired by all ranks in all political parties for his honesty, integrity, openness and energy and his unstinted devotion to vital causes that he adopted—democracy within his party, British integration into Europe, and a socialist economic policy tempered by financial realism. Died 12 May

Somes, Michael (b. 1917), British ballet dancer, partnered Margot Fonteyn at the Sadlers Wells Ballet in the 1940s and '50s, his grace and technical skill as *premier danseur noble* matching her unique talent, both in classical productions and in ballets created for them by Frederick Ashton. Later he played character roles and assisted Ashton in direction of the Royal Ballet. Died 19 November

Spadolini, Giovanni (b. 1925), was Prime Minister of Italy from July 1981 to January 1983. Although his Republican Party had won only 3 per cent of the national vote, it held a key position in the midst of a political scandal of which it was clean. Spadolini, a journalist by profession, had been editor of Milan's *Corriere della Sera* for four years before entering the Senate in 1972; from 1974 he had served as minister for the environment and then for education in Christian Democrat-led coalitions. Becoming, after the 1983 elections, Defence Minister in Bettino Craxi's administration, he earned the respect of Western governments for his steadfastness in face of terrorism, notably over the hijacked cruise liner *Achille Lauro*, when Craxi's weak tactics brought his resignation. Later he served as Speaker of the Senate and enjoyed the status of an uncorrupt elder statesman. Died 5 August

Springer, Sir Hugh, GCMG, GCVO (b.1913), was Governor-General of Barbados 1984–90. He had entered Barbadian politics in 1940 as general secretary of the (Labour) Progressive League, but resigned in 1947 to become registrar of the University of the West Indies, and later director of its Institute of Education. In 1966 he was appointed assistant secretary-general (education) of the Commonwealth Secretariat, a base which established him as the leader of university development in the ex-colonial nations of the Commonwealth. Died 14 April

Steegmuller, Francis (b. 1906), American author and translator, had a love affair with the literature of France. His finest monument was his masterly translation of Flaubert (*Madame Bovary*, 1957, the *Letters*, 1981 and 1983, and the *Flaubert-Sand Correspondence*, with Barbara Bray 1993), but he also wrote novels, short stories, biographies (*Apollinaire* 1963, *Cocteau* 1970) and other works. Died 20 October

Synge, Professor Richard, FRS (b. 1914), British biochemist, won the Nobel Prize for Chemistry in 1952 for his development of the technique of partition chromatography in the separation of components of complex biological material. His whole professional career was devoted to research rather than teaching or the direction of institutes, but he also became a multi-linguist and an activist for world peace and against nuclear arms. Died 18 August

Talhouni, Bahjat (b. 1913), was three times Prime Minister of Jordan for short periods in the 1960s. A protégé of King Husain, who in 1954 appointed him head of the Royal Diwan (the King's personal secretariat), he suffered fluctuations of royal favour. Dismissed in 1970, he retreated to Jordan's upper house of parliament. Died 30 January

Tandy, Jessica (b. in England 1909), American actress, was one of the few leading stage actresses who never made a star career in films. Her grounding in England was primarily in Shakespeare, including seasons at the Old Vic and Ophelia to Gielgud's Hamlet in 1934. Migrating to the US in 1940, she was a Broadway sensation as Blanche DuBois in Tennessee Williams's *A Streetcar Named Desire* in 1947, and thereafter never looked back, playing in both Shakespeare and contemporary plays, often with her second husband Hume Cronyn, and winning three Tony awards. She became an American citizen in 1954 and was elected to the American Theatre Hall of Fame in 1979. Died 11 September

Teillac, Jean (b.1920), French nuclear physicist, was head of the Commissariat à l'Energie Atomique (CEA) 1975–93 and the all-powerful leader of France's huge nuclear energy programme. He had previously been a professor of nuclear physics, head of the nuclear physics institute at Orsay, and of the newly-created National Institute for Nuclear and Particle Physics (1971–75). Died 10 March

Thorneycroft, Lord, CH (b. 1909), as Peter Thorneycroft, MP, was Chancellor of the Exchequer in the Macmillan cabinet 1957–58, until resigning, with other Treasury ministers, on failure to get cabinet approval of the full cuts in defence spending they wanted. Barrister by profession and Royal Artilleryman in World War II, he had been President of the Board of Trade 1951–57 and was regarded as in line for the Conservative leadership, but he never again approached that status after his resignation. After accepting the Ministries of Aviation (1960–62) and Defence (1962–64) and becoming a life peer in 1967, he was chosen by Mrs Thatcher as chairman of the

Conservative Party, and served for six years from 1975, while maintaining his large business interests. Died 4 June

Vazgen I, Catholicos (b. L.K.Baljian in Romania 1908), was Patriarch of Echmiazdin and Catholicos of All Armenians from 1955 until his death. As head of the Armenian Orthodox Church the world over he travelled far and wide, meeting the political leaders and heads of the Roman Catholic and Anglican churches, and restoring the fortunes and prestige of a church persecuted by Soviet and other communist regimes. Died 18 August

Viola, General Roberto (b.1924), was President of Argentina for eight months in 1981 until ousted by General Galtieri. In 1985 he was tried for the gravest offences against human rights and sentenced to 17 years' imprisonment, which he served for five years before a general amnesty. Died 30 September

Wain, John (b. 1925), was professor of poetry at Oxford 1973–78, but he was renowned more for his novels—of which *Hurry On Down* (1953) was the first and most praised—and other prose work, such as his biography of Samuel Johnson (1974), and for his lecturing and literary criticism. He held a number of academic posts in England, the USA and elsewhere. Died 24 May

Walcott, 'Jersey' Joe (b.1914), American boxer, became world heavy-weight champion in 1951 at the record age of 37. After failing to beat Joe Louis on a split decision in 1947, he successfully defended his title against Ezzard Charles, but surrendered it to Rocky Marciano in 1952. Died 26 February

Weill-Hallé, Dr Marie-Andrée (b. 1916), was a determined French champion of women's rights to contraception and abortion in face of the Catholic Church and other conservative forces, including the Communist Party. Her book *La Maternité Heureuse* aroused public opinion and was followed by her founding of the Family Planning Association: reforms of the law in 1967 and 1975 bore witness to her success, which had turned her into an establishment figure. Died 13 January

White, Terence de Vere, LLD (b. 1912), Irish man of letters, displayed his writing talent while pursuing a successful career as a solicitor. Abandoning the law, from 1962 until 1974 he was literary editor of the *Irish Times*. His output included biography, history, novels—of which the most acclaimed were *Prenez Garde* (1962) and *Johnnie Cross* (1983)—and countless ephemera. He was also a keen supporter of the Irish theatre, a collector of Irish paintings, a wit in the Dublin tradition, and a man of many friends in the cultivated circles of Ireland and England. He married, secondly, the biographer and novelist Victoria Glendinning. Died 17 June

Wörner, Manfred (b.1934), German lawyer, airman, politician and admin-istrator, was secretary-general of NATO from 1988 until his death. With a doctorate in international law, a gift for languages and a high reputation as a sportsman and reserve air-force pilot, he was elected to the Bundestag on the Christian Democrat ticket in 1965, and quickly rose in the policy-making apparatus of the CDU/CSU alliance, especially in regard to defence and foreign policy, before becoming federal Minister of Defence in 1982. Strong in defensive policy, ardent for the US military presence in Europe, he was a natural choice for all the Western powers as the key civilian head of NATO. Arriving in the era of *glasnost* and eventually the collapse of the Soviet Union, he saw the end of the Cold War as a reason not for running down NATO but for giving it a new and more positive role: its adoption of a European peacekeeping duty owed much to his energetic advocacy, though for his last two years he was in the grip of cancer. Died 13 August

Youskevitch, Igor (b. in Ukraine 1912), ballet dancer who took US nationality in 1944, was renowned for the cool elegance and pure nobility of his support for such star ballerinas as Alicia Markova, with whom he first danced *Giselle*, his most famous classical role, and Alicia Alonso; it was for him and Alonso that Balanchine created his *Theme and Variations*. Dancing with Massine's Ballet Russe de Monte Carlo in 1939, when it was stranded in the US, Youskevitch served in the American Navy, and after World War II danced for Ballet Russe, American Ballet Theater and Alonso's Ballet Nacional de Cuba. Died 13 June

Zail Singh, Giani: *see* Singh, Giani Zail

Zetterling, Mai (b. in Sweden 1925), actress, film director and author, after a brilliant start in her native country, moved in 1951 to England, where she acted in many films and on the stage with success but little international fame. Her one venture into Hollywood was in the lead role opposite Danny Kaye in *Knock on Wood* in 1954. In 1961 she turned to film direction, with some distinction, and later to writing fiction. Her artistic attitude was as austere as her chosen life-style. Died 17 March

XXI CHRONICLE OF PRINCIPAL EVENTS IN 1994

JANUARY

1 European Economic Area (EEA), linking EU and EFTA in world's largest free trade market, came into existence.

North American Free Trade Agreement (NAFTA) entered into force.

In Mexico, peasants in state of Chiapas staged armed rebellion, demanding social and economic change.

3 In Russia, 120 died when TU154 airliner crashed in Siberia.

7 In Australia, areas around Sydney suffered worst bush fires for 50 years, fires burning within 15km of city centre.

10 Two-day NATO summit conference opened in Brussels; communique said Alliance wanted Partnership for Peace with newly-democratized East European countries and with neutral states.

11 Russia's new parliament (Duma) opened, following Dec. 1993 elections.

President Clinton visited Prague and, on 12 Jan. Kiev, where talks were held on scrapping of Ukraine's nuclear warheads.

12 Ratu Sir Kamisese Mara appointed President of Fiji in succession to late Ratu Sir Penaia Ganilau.

13 President Clinton in Moscow for two days of summit talks with President Yeltsin; a tripartite agreement was signed for dismantling of Ukraine's nuclear weapons inherited from former Soviet Union (see 5 Dec.)

Italian PM Carlo Azeglio Ciampi tendered his resignation; parliament was dissolved and an election called for 27 March.

Cyprien Ntaryamira (a Hutu) elected President of Burundi in succession to Melchior Ndadaye, who died in abortive coup in Oct. 1993 (see 6 April).

16 President Clinton held summit talks in Geneva with President Asad of Syria to discuss Middle East peace (see 27 Oct.)

18 In USA, 57 died in a severe earthquake which caused an estimated $30,000 million damage in Los Angeles.

20 Russia's PM Viktor Chernomyrdin named a new cabinet containing mostly conservatives, several radical reformers having refused to serve.

25 In State of Union address, President Clinton promised strong new measures against violent crime and radical reform of welfare system.

26 In Australia, Prince of Wales unharmed when a man fired shots at him during concert in Sydney.

27 Carlos Roberto Reina sworn in as President of Honduras.

30 Defence Minister Gen. Liamine Zéroual appointed President of Algeria, replacing five-man presidency which had ruled since cancellation of 1992 elections.

31 Rover, Britain's last mass car manufacturer, sold to German company BMW for £800 million.

FEBRUARY

1 Sinn Féin leader Gerry Adams visited New York, visa restrictions against him having been waived for first time in 20 years.

In Spain, Barcelona's 147–year-old Gran Teatro del Liceo destroyed by fire.

2 Rafael Caldera Rodríguez inaugurated as President of Venezuela, post he had held 20 years earlier.

3 President Clinton announced lifting of 19–year economic embargo against Vietnam.

5 In Bosnia, 68 died when mortar bomb hit Sarajevo market-place.
6 In presidential elections in Finland Martii Ahtisaari (Social Democratic Party) defeated Elisabeth Rehn (Swedish People's Party).
   José María Figueres (National Liberatioin Party) defeated Miguel Angel Rodríguez (ruling Social-Christian Party) in presidential election in Costa Rica; he was sworn in on 8 May.
9 NATO governments, meeting in Brussels to discuss possible military intervention in Bosnia, issued ultimatum to Serbs to withdraw heavy weapons around Sarajevo or face air strikes.
   In Bosnia, Britain's UN commander Gen. Sir Michael Rose negotiated ceasefire between warring sides in Sarajevo.
   Israeli and PLO leaders, meeting in Cairo, signed agreement overcoming some of obstacles preventing implementation of declaration on Palestinian self-rule signed in Washington in September 1993.
11 President Clinton and Japanese PM Hosokawa held talks in Washington but failed to reach agreement to correct imbalance in bilateral trade.
   Bosnian Serbs handed over first batch of heavy guns to UNPROFOR.
12 Winter Olympic Games opened at Lillehammer, Norway.
15 British Prime Minister Major in Moscow for talks with President Yeltsin.
17 Large-scale withdrawal of Serb artillery around Sarajevo commenced following Russian intervention.
18 HM Queen Elizabeth II began three-week tour of eight Caribbean states.
21 In UK, House of Commons voted to reduce age of consent for homosexuals to 18; it also voted against reintroduction of death penalty by largest majority since abolition.
22 Church of England General Synod met to promulgate canon changing ecclesiastical law in England to permit ordination of women to priesthood (see 12 March).
   In USA, former head of CIA's Soviet counter-intelligence section, Aldrich Ames, charged with espionage for USSR and Russia.
23 Russian parliament voted overwhelmingly for amnesty for those detained for their part in Aug. 1991 coup and Oct. 1993 armed rebellion; Aleksandr Rutskoi and Ruslan Khasbulatov and other rebels released on 26 Feb.
   Bosnian government and Croat forces signed a general ceasefire.
24 Malaysia severed trade relations with Britain following media criticism of abuse of grant aid in Pergau Dam hydroelectric project and dispute over arms sales.
   Hong Kong Legislative Council approved first part of political reform package.
25 In Israel, 29 died when Jewish fanatic fired on Arab Muslims at prayer in mosque at Hebron on West Bank.
27 British PM Major on two-day official visit to USA.
28 NATO fighters shot down four Serb warplanes defying no-fly zone over Bosnia, first offensive action in NATO's 45–year history.

MARCH

1 Sweden, Finland and Austria agreed terms for admission to EU on 1 Jan. 1995.
9 Five IRA mortar bombs landed on runway at London's Heathrow airport but failed to explode; further mortar attacks in subsequent days also failed.
11 Eduardo Frei Ruiz-Tagle inaugurated as President of Chile in succession to President Aylwin Azócar.
12 In UK, 32 women were the first to be ordained to priesthood at service in Bristol.
13 South Africa took direct control of black homeland Bophuthatswana following week of bloodshed there, deposing President Mangope who was refusing to take part in April elections.

UN observers entered besieged Muslim enclave of Maglaj, northern Bosnia, where some 20,000 were on verge of starvation.

Indian PM P.V. Narasimha Rao on five-day visit to UK.

14 In Slovakia, PM Vladimir Mečiar resigned and was replaced by Jozef Moravčik, chosen to lead five-party coalition (see 2 Oct.).

16 Israeli PM Rabin in Washington for talks with President Clinton on stalled Middle East peace negotiations; 18 March, Secretary of State Warren Christopher announced resumption of 'senior level' peace talks.

17 Bosnian Muslims and Serbs signed agreement allowing civilians freedom of movement into and out of Sarajevo for first time in two years.

18 PM Major visited British troops in Sarajevo.

Representatives from Bosnia-Hercegovina and Croatia signed accord on creation of federation of Bosnian Muslims and Croats at ceremony in Washington.

20 In Bosnia 20,000 people watched a football match in Sarajevo stadium, until recently battered by mortar fire.

El Salvador held first general elections following 12–year civil war (see 24 April).

21 In Tunisia, President Ben Ali re-elected with 99.99 per cent of vote.

22 In Bosnia, Tuzla airport reopened after nearly two years of war.

23 In Russia, 75 died when Aeroflot airbus crashed in remote area of Siberia.

In Mexico, presidential candidate of ruling PRI, Luis Donaldo Colosio, assassinated at election rally (see 21 Aug.).

25 Last US troops left Somalia, handing command of Mogadishu airport to Eyptian UN troops; 20,000 UN troops remained in country.

27 Italian general election won by right-wing Freedom Alliance led by media tycoon Silvio Berlusconi, leader of Forza Italia; he took office as PM at head of new coalition government on 11 May (see 22 Dec.)

28 In S. Africa, 60 died in violence in Johannesburg as Zulu demonstrators attempted to March on ANC HQ.

30 In Bosnia, Serb troops began major offensive against Muslim safe haven Goražde.

31 Israel and PLO agreed to stationing of armed foreign observers in West Bank town of Hebron following Feb. massacre.

APRIL

3 Ugo Mifsud Bonnici elected President of Malta in succession to Vincent Tabone.

6 Presidents Habyarimana of Rwanda and Ntaryamira of Burundi died when their plane was apparently shot down over Kigali, Rwanda.

In Israel, nine died in suicide car-bomb attack on school bus in Afula in reprisal for Hebron massacre.

Anglican Church in Wales voted against ordination of women.

7 Rwandan PM murdered and ten Belgian UN soldiers died in violence in Kigali, Rwanda.

9 In UK, Grand National won by Miinnehoma at 16–1.

10 NATO planes launched air strikes against Serb forces on besieged UN-designated safe haven of Goražde in defiance of UN and NATO warnings; further air strikes took place on 11 April.

12 In Rwanda, newly-appointed government fled from Kigali as rebel troops advanced on city.

13 In Israel, six died in bus bomb in Hadera, believed to be work of Hamas suicide bomber.

Greek parliament voted to strip ex-King Constantine of his property in Greece.

14 26 died when US warplanes accidentally shot down two UN helicopters in 'no-fly' zone over northern Iraq.

15 A new government, led by Mokdad Sifi, was formed in Algeria.

17 UN and NATO forces were unable to prevent Serb tanks entering centre of Goražde as Bosnian army defences collapsed.

In UK, London marathon won by Dionicio Ceron (Mexico) in 2 hrs 8 min 51 sec.

18 Brian Lara scored 375 runs against England in Antigua, highest individual score in 116 years of Test cricket.

19 In S. Africa, leaders of Inkatha Freedom Party, ANC and S. African government signed agreement enabling Inkatha, which had threatened boycott, to participate in forthcoming elections.

In France, former French militiaman and Nazi collaborator Paul Touvier (79) gaoled for life for crimes against humanity.

22 UN Security Council voted to withdraw all but token force from Rwanda (see 17 May).

NATO issued ultimatum to Bosnian Serbs to withdraw from Goražde.

24 International Red Cross reported 100,000 dead in tribal violence in Rwanda since 6 April.

In S. Africa, nine died in car-bomb explosion near ANC HQ in Johannesburg; white extremists believed responsible.

Serb forces began withdrawal from Goražde as convoy of UN peace-keepers entered city.

In El Salvador, Armando Calderón Sol (ruling Arena party) defeated Rubén Zamora Rivas in second round of presidential election; he was sworn in on 1 June.

25 In Japan, Tsutomu Hata elected PM in succession to Morihiro Hosokawa, who had resigned amid allegations of corruption (see 29 June).

S. Africa's white minority parliament met for last time to vote itself out of existence, ending 342 years of white rule.

France, Russia, UK and USA, newly-formed Contact Group, met in London to launch new initiative to bring ceasefire to Bosnia (see 5 July).

26 Voting commenced in S. Africa's first multi-racial elections; final results declared on 6 May gave ANC 62.6 per cent of vote against 20.4 per cent for National Party and 10.5 per cent for Inkatha.

261 died when China Airlines airbus A300 crashed at Nagoya airport, Japan.

27 S. Africa's new constitution, providing for multi-racial government, came into effect and country's new flag was raised.

29 More than 250,000 refugees fled from Rwanda to Tanzania in 24 hours amid fears of attacks by majority Hutu armed forces; death toll reported to have risen to 200,000.

MAY

3 At general election in Netherlands, Labour Party led by Wim Kok defeated ruling Christian Democrats led by PM Ruud Lubbers (see 18 Aug.).

4 Israel and PLO signed peace accord in Cairo ending 27 years of military rule in Jericho and Gaza Strip.

5 In UK, Conservative Party suffered worst losses of recent times, taking only 27 per cent of vote in local elections.

Civil war erupted in Yemen (unified in 1990) as northern troops, loyal to President Saleh, attempted to seize Aden in south (see 7 July).

6 Channel Tunnel officially opened by HM Queen Elizabeth II and President Mitterrand.

8 Panama held first elections since overthrow of military dictatorship of Gen. Manuel Noriega; Ernesto Pérez Balladares (Democratic Revolutionary Party) won presidential election.

10 Nelson Mandela sworn in as first black President of S. Africa in ceremonies attended by delegations from all around world.
11 In Haiti, Emile Jonassint appointed provisional President by Congress in move denounced as illegal by USA (see 15 Oct.).
12 In UK, Labour leader John Smith died suddenly of heart attack (see XX: Obituary); deputy leader Margaret Beckett assumed leadership pending party election for Smith's successor.
16 Massive fraud was alleged in presidential elections in Dominican Republic; President Balaguer (87) sworn in for reduced seventh term on 16 Aug.
17 UN Security Council unanimously passed resolution 918 agreeing to expansion of peace-keeping force in Rwanda.
   In first multi-party elections in Malawi since independence, ruling Malawi Congress led by President Hastings Banda defeated by United Democratic Front led by Bakili Muluzi, who was inaugurated as President on 21 May.
   President Mugabe of Zimbabwe on four-day state visit to UK.
   In UK, archaeologists reported discovery at Boxgrove, Sussex, of a limb fragment dated to about half-a-million years ago—the oldest human remains yet found in Europe.
22 Forces of Rwandan Patriotic Front took capital Kigali after four-day battle; 500,000 had died in slaughter since 6 April.
27 Nobel laureate Alexander Solzhenitsyn returned to Russia 20 years after being exiled by Soviet authorities.
29 In parliamentary elections in Hungary, ex-communist Socialist Party won landslide victory, defeating ruling Hungarian Democratic Forum; a government led by Gyula Horn was sworn in on 14 July.
   In Iraq, Saddam Husain assumed role of PM in addition to presidency.
30 In USA, Dan Rostenkowski, chairman of House ways and means committee, indicted on fraud and corruption charges.
31 In Bosnia, parliament in Sarajevo elected Krešimir Zubak President of new (Croat-Muslim) Bosnian Federation.
   Libya completed withdrawal from Aouzou Strip in Chad after 20 years' occupation, in compliance with International Court of Justice ruling.

JUNE

1 S. Africa rejoined Commonwealth after 33–year absence; it also joined Non-Aligned Movement.
   In UK, Derby won by Erhaab at 7–2.
2 UN Security Council unanimously adopted resolution 924 calling for immediate ceasefire in civil war in Yemen.
   President Clinton in Rome at start of European tour.
   29 died, mostly senior counter-terrorism experts in N. Ireland, when RAF Chinook helicopter crashed in western Scotland.
5 In elections for Ethiopia's Constituent Assembly, ruling Ethiopian People's Revolutionary Democratic Front and its allies gained overwhelming majority.
6 Ceremonies in Normandy, France, to commemorate 50th anniversary of World War II D-Day landings, were attended by world leaders and thousands of veterans from 14 allied countries.
9 Voting commenced in elections to European Parliament; results declared on 13 June gave Labour 62 of UK's 87 seats, leaving Tories with only 18 seats, a drop of 50 per cent.
15 USA proposed arms embargo and other sanctions against North Korea which was refusing to allow UN inspection of its nuclear facilities; former US President Jimmy Carter began four-day visit to N. Korea.

15th World Cup football championship opened in Chicago; in final at Pasadena on 17 July Brazil defeated Italy on penalties, no goal having been scored by either side.

18 In N. Ireland, loyalist UVF gunmen shot dead six Catholics watching Ireland's opening World Cup match in a bar.

19 In presidential election in Colombia, Ernesto Samper Pizano (ruling Liberal Party) defeated Andrés Pastrana (Conservative); he was inaugurated on 7 Aug.

In France, Michel Rocard (a former PM) resigned as leader of Socialist Party following its poor showing in elections for European Parliament.

22 President Kim Il Sung of North Korea agreed to freeze his country's nuclear programme in return for suspension of threatened US sanctions.

UN Security Council approved resolution 929, permitting French humanitarian intervention in Rwanda; first French troops arrived in country at at start of Operation Turquoise on 23 June (see 21 Aug.).

Twin parliaments of Bosnian republic and newly-formed Muslim-Croat Federation met in Sarajevo to form government and discuss international peace plan; Haris Silajzdić appointed PM on 23 June.

23 In UK, it was announced that the royal yacht *Britannia* would be decommissioned in 1997.

In Nigeria, Moshood Kashimawo Olawale Abiola, presumed winner of annulled 1993 elections, arrested.

24 Two-day EU summit meeting opened in Corfu (Greece); UK vetoed nomination of Belgian PM Jean-Luc Dehaene as Commission president (see 15 July).

25 US halted all commercial flights to Haiti under tighter sanctions against military regime.

29 In Japan, Tomiichi Murayama elected PM in succession to Tsutomu Hata who had resigned; heading a coalition government with Liberal Democrats, he was country's first Socialist leader since 1948.

In UK, Prince of Wales appeared in lengthy TV documentary in which he admitted adultery but said he did not think divorce would bar him from the throne.

Hong Kong's Legislative Council (Legco) approved Governor Patten's constitutional reform bill which included increasing number of directly-elected Legco members.

JULY

1 PLO leader Yassir Arafat paid first visit to Gaza for 27 years; on 12 July he returned to take up permanent residence.

Roman Herzog succeeded Richard von Weizsäcker as President of Germany.

2 Andrés Escobar, member of Colombia's World Cup football team who had put his side out with own goal, shot dead in Medellín.

4 President Mitterrand of France, making state visit to S. Africa, was first Western statesman to address its parliament since Harold Macmillan in 1960.

5 Contact Group of world powers, meeting in Geneva, agreed new plan for division of Bosnia-Hercegovina.

6 Rwandan Patriotic Front, now in control of Kigali and 75 per cent of country, declared itself legitimate government of Rwanda and agreed to allow French troops to police refugee zone in south of country.

In UK, government published White Paper, *The Future of the BBC: Serving the Nation, Competing Worldwide*, guaranteeing survival of licence-funded BBC into 21st century.

7 Two-month civil war in Yemen ended as northern forces took control of southern city of Aden.

8 G-7 summit opened in Naples; conference unanimously backed Geneva plan for Bosnia-Hercegovina but made little progress on economic issues.

North Korea's leader Kim Il Sung, the twentieth century's longest-surviving dictator, died (see XX: Obituary); he was apparently succeeded by his son Kim Jong Il, although no official announcement was made.

10 At presidential elections in Ukraine, former PM Leonid Kuchma defeated incumbent Leonid Kravchuk; Kuchma was sworn in on 19 July.

At elections in Belorussia, pro-Russian candidate Alyaksandr Lukashenka elected President.

11 President Clinton on two-day visit to Germany; addressing Berliners on 12 July, he pledged loyalty to that city 'now and forever'.

12 Germany's Constitutional Court ruled that German armed forces would be able to fight outside NATO region (under UN authority) for first time since World War II.

14 In UK, Defence Secretary Malcolm Rifkind announced £750 million cuts for armed forces, axing 18,700 jobs over three years and closing bases abroad.

15 EU leaders, at emergency summit in Brussels, named Luxembourg PM Jacques Santer to succeed Jacques Delors as Commission president in Jan. 1995.

Up to one million Rwandan (mostly Hutu) refugees poured into Zaïre, fleeing advance of Tutsi-dominated Rwanda Patriotic Front; it was described as possibly the biggest exodus in African history.

18 Bosnian Assembly approved Geneva partition plan; Bosnian Serb legislature rejected proposals.

Two days of peace talks between Israel and Jordan opened at the Arava/Araba border location.

Rwandan Patriotic Front claimed victory after four-month civil war possibly costing over half a million lives; a new government was installed on 19 July.

In Argentina, nearly 100 died in bomb blast at Jewish centre in Buenos Aires; Iranian-backed Muslim militants blamed by Israel.

20 In UK reshuffle, four ministers left cabinet; Michael Portillo moved to employment, Gillian Shephard to education.

21 In UK, Tony Blair elected leader of Labour Party in succession to late John Smith; John Prescott elected deputy leader.

22 President Clinton announced massive airlift of supplies to Rwanda; UN launched $434 million appeal; 2.5 million refugees reported to have fled Rwanda since 8 April.

23 In Gambia, government of Sir Dawda Jawara overthrown in military coup; Lt. Yahya Jammeh proclaimed leader of provisional military government.

24 Sinn Féin announced its objections to key parts of the Dec. 1993 Downing Street Declaration as basis for talks on future of N. Ireland (see 31 Aug.).

25 In Washington, King Husain of Jordan and Israeli PM Yitzhak Rabin signed declaration ending 46–year-old state of war between Israel and Jordan (see 8 Aug., 26 Oct.)

26 Fourteen injured when car bomb severely damaged Israeli embassy in London.

31 UN Security Council adopted resolution 940, authorizing 'all necessary means' to topple military regime in Haiti.

AUGUST

1 Ceremonies were held in Poland to mark fiftieth anniversary of Warsaw Uprising against Nazi occupation.

2 British troops flew to Rwanda to join international humanitarian mission, Operation Gabriel, to save victims of war.

5 In Cuba, many injured in violent demonstrations in Havana, the first such reported riots since 1959 revolution.

NATO planes attacked Serb target in Bosnia after Serbs had defied UN orders on deployment of heavy weapons.

8   Jordan and Israel opened border crossing between Aqaba and Eilat which had been closed for 46 years.

10 Bangladeshi author Taslima Nasreen threatened with death by Muslim fundamentalists for alleged blasphemy, given refuge in Sweden.

14 Illich Ramírez Sánchez, known as Carlos the Jackal, wanted in connexion with numerous terrorist atrocities around world in last 20 years, captured in Khartoum and transferred to gaol in Paris.

16 At general elections in Sri Lanka, United National Party defeated after 17 years in office; leader of opposition People's Alliance Chandrika Bandaranaike Kumaratunga sworn in as PM on 19 Aug. (see 9 Nov.).

17 In Lesotho, King Letsie III dismissed government and named provisional council to run country (see 14 Sept.).

18 In Netherlands, Wim Kok, leader of Labour Party, formed coalition government.

    In USA, governor of Florida declared state of emergency as thousands of Cuban refugees fled their country in boats.

    XV Commonwealth Games opened in Victoria, Canada; S. Africa participated for first time following its readmission to Commonwealth.

19 President Clinton ended 30–year US policy of right to asylum for Cuban refugees, who would now be held in detention centres.

21 In Mexico's presidential elections, Ernesto Zedillo, candidate of ruling Party of the Institutionalized Revolution, won with party's lowest-ever vote share.

    Thousands of Hutu refugees, seeking to follow French troops departing from Rwanda, forced back by Zaïrean troops at closed river border crossing.

28 Bosnian Serbs voted in referendum to reject Geneva peace plan.

31 IRA announced a ceasefire from midnight after 25 years of violence and bloodshed in Ireland and mainland Britain in which 3,168 had died (see 13 Oct.).

    The last Russian troops left Germany after a nearly 50–year presence.

SEPTEMBER

2   Chinese President Jiang Zemin in Moscow for four-day summit with President Yeltsin.

5   UN Conference on Population and Development opened in Cairo, ending 13 Sept.; agreement reached on 20–year action programme to promote family planning and improve education of women.

8   Western Allied leaders attended ceremonies to mark withdrawal of last troops from Berlin which they had protected since end of World War II.

    Government of Bulgaria resigned; caretaker government appointed on 18 Oct. (see 18 Dec.).

11 Thousands attended Mass celebrated by Pope John Paul II in Zagreb, Croatia; a visit to Sarajevo, Bosnia, was cancelled on security grounds.

12 In Canada, separatist Parti Québécois, led by Jacques Parizeau, gained sweeping victory in provincial elections in Quebec.

    In USA, pilot died when he crashed his light plane on White House lawn in Washington.

14 In Lesotho, government led by Ntsu Mokhele reinstated following S. African-brokered deal with King Letsie III who would abdicate in favour of his father King Moshoeshoe II.

15 British PM Major promised people of Ulster a referendum on their constitutional future and lifted broadcasting ban on Sinn Féin.

18 At general election in Sweden, Social Democrats defeated Conservative-led coalition of Carl Bildt; a minority government led by Ingvar Carlsson was sworn in on 7 Oct.

19 US troops landed in Haiti to begin mission to restore democracy; an agreement had

been reached for resignation of military junta and return of President Aristide (see 15 Oct.)

20 John Major on first official visit to S. Africa by a British PM since Harold Macmillan in 1960.

21 A general election was held in Denmark; a three-party coalition led by PM Poul Nyrup Rasmussen was sworn in on 26 Sept.

24 President Yeltsin of Russia held two days of talks with British PM Major at Chequers.

26 President Yeltsin began four-day tour of USA, including talks with President Clinton and address to UN General Assembly.

President Clinton announced lifting of US sanctions against Haiti.

In India, thousands reported to have fled from Surat, Gujarat, where an epidemic of pneumonic plague had broken out.

In USA, amid unprecedented media attention, trial opened in Los Angeles of black American football star O.J. Simpson on counts of murdering his former wife and her friend, both whites.

28 More than 900 died when ferry *Estonia* sank in Baltic Sea; only 140 survived.

29 Willy Claes, former Belgian Foreign Minister, named secretary-general of NATO in succession to late Manfred Wörner (see XX: Obituary).

OCTOBER

1 Two-day general elections in Slovakia gave substantial relative majority to ex-communist Movement for a Democratic Slovakia led by former PM Vladimir Mečiar (see 13 Dec.).

3 In Brazil, Fernando Henrique Cardoso of Social Democratic Party gained decisive victory in presidential election; he would take office on 1 Jan. 1995.

4 President Mandela of S. Africa on first official visit to Washington where he obtained pledges of $700 million aid.

5 In Switzerland, 48 members of a religious cult found dead at two separate locations; remains of their leader, Luc Jouret, suspected of engineering mass suicide and murder, were later identified among the bodies.

8 US, UK and France sent forces and/or warships to Gulf region amid renewed fears of Iraqi invasion of Kuwait; 13 Oct. President Clinton ordered cut in forces as Iraqi troops withdrew from border area.

9 In Austria, Chancellor Vrantizky's ruling centre-left coalition suffered severe setback in general election; right-wing Freedom Party gained 23 per cent of poll; a new cabinet, led by Vranitzky, was sworn in on 30 Nov.

11 Russian rouble suffered a record one-day fall of 20 per cent against US dollar.

13 Gen. Raoul Cédras, leader of Haiti's military junta, resigned and went into exile in Panama.

The three main loyalist paramilitary organizations in Northern Ireland declared a ceasefire from midnight.

14 Nobel Peace Prize awarded jointly to Israeli PM Rabin, Foreign Minister Peres and PLO leader Arafat for role as architects of Israeli-Palestinian peace agreement.

15 Fr Jean-Bertrand Aristide returned to Haiti after three years' exile in USA and was reinstalled as President.

16 At elections in Germany, ruling CDU/FDP coalition, led by Chancellor Kohl, returned with greatly reduced majority.

Finland voted in a referendum in favour of joining EU in Jan. 1995.

17 HM Queen Elizabeth II began historic four-day state visit to Russia.

19 In Israel, 22 died when Muslim suicide bomber blew up a bus in Tel Aviv.

21 British PM Major lifted exclusion orders against Sinn Féin leaders and announced reopening of all border crossings between N. Ireland and Republic; talks with Sinn

Féin would begin by Christmas on assumption that IRA ceasefire was intended to be permanent (see 7 Dec.).

24 In Sri Lanka, opposition presidential candidate Gamini Dissanayake assassinated (see XX: Obituary); 56 others died in bomb attack.

26 Israel-Jordan peace agreement at signed at Araba/Arava desert border area in presence of President Clinton.

In UK, Royal Commission report recommended a halt to road-building programme and improved public transport.

27 Polling began in Mozambique's first multi-party elections; final results released on 19 Nov. gave decisive victory to incumbent President Chissano and his Frelimo party.

President Clinton held talks in Damascus with President Asad, first visit to Syria by a US President for 20 years.

30 Middle East-North Africa economic summit conference opened in Casablanca.

31 Angolan government and Unita rebels agreed peace accord, again declaring an end to long civil war (see 20 Nov.).

NOVEMBER

2 Some 400 died in floods and fire when lightning struck a fuel depot in southern Egypt.

4 Bosnian Serbs announced a general military call-up following fall of town of Kupres to Bosnian Croat forces.

5 In US, George Foreman (45) became oldest man to win a world heavyweight boxing championship.

More than 60 people died in severe flooding in northern Italy.

A new post-communist constitution was rejected in a referendum in Albania.

Imamoli Rakhmanov gained decisive victory in Tajikistan's first presidential election; he was sworn in on 16 Nov.

7 Francophone summit conference opened in Biarritz.

8 At mid-term elections in USA, Republicans gained control of Senate and also, for the first time for 40 years, of House of Representatives.

9 Chandrika Bandaranaike Kumaratunga gained overwhelming victory in presidential election in Sri Lanka; she was sworn in on 12 November and appointed her mother, Sirima Bandaranaike, as PM.

10 Iraq formally recognized sovereignty of Kuwait and its borders.

King Husain of Jordan paid first visit to Israel for opening of new bridge across River Jordan (old one having been blown up in 1948).

13 Sweden voted in a referendum in favour of joining EU in Jan. 1995.

16 In UK, state opening of parliament; Queen's Speech foreshadowed 13 bills including one to increase Britain's contribution to EU.

17 Albert Reynolds (Fianna Fáil) resigned as PM of Republic of Ireland following withdrawal of Labour Party from his coalition (see 15 Dec.).

18 Fourteen killed, 200 injured in street battles in Gaza Strip betwen Palestinian police and Islamic militants.

An Anglo-French summit conference at Chartres signalled a new era in defence and security cooperation.

19 The first draw was held in Britain's new national lottery: the total pay-out was £22,004,123.

20 Angolan peace agreement was signed in Lusaka, Zambia, despite absence of President dos Santos and Unita leader Jonas Savimbi.

21 NATO carried out biggest raid in its 45–year history; 39 aircraft attacked Serb-held airfield in Croatia which had been used as base for Serb attacks on UN safe area of Bihać.

27 A former President, Julio María Sanguinetti (Colorado Party), won presidential election in Uruguay; he would take office in March 1995.
28 In Norwegian referendum, voters again rejected membership of European Union.
29 In UK, budget day; central government spending in 1995/96 financial year projected at £305,000 million, up nearly £10,000 million on 1994/95; measures announced to help get unemployed back to work; planned rise in VAT on domestic fuel rejected by House of Commons on 6 Dec., forcing Chancellor to announce further increases in excise duty on 8 Dec.
Two-day Franco-German summit opened in Bonn: leaders appealed for political rather than military settlement in Bosnia.
30 More than 1,000 passengers and crew rescued from burning cruise liner *Achille Lauro* (see AR 1985, pp.137–8), which later sank off coast of Somalia; two died.

DECEMBER

3 In Taiwan, local elections confirmed dominance of ruling Kuomintang but opposition gained ground.
5 More than 50 world leaders attended CSCE summit in Budapest; at a special ceremony, Ukraine signed Non-Proliferation Treaty clearing way for its accession to START I treaty.
7 Sinn Féin leaders began exploratory talks in Belfast with British government officials, first such negotiations for 23 years.
8 In Namibia's first elections since independence in 1990, ruling SWAPO party led by President Nujoma gained increased majority.
9 European Union held two-day summit in Essen, Germany; leaders recorded support for efforts of Contact Group to achieve peace in Bosnia and offered six E. European states eventual membership.
11 Russian forces invaded southern republic of Chechenya, which had declared independence from Moscow in 1991.
12 In Brazil, former President Fernando Collor de Mello acquitted of corruption charges.
13 In Ethiopia, trial opened in Addis Ababa of six men from former marxist regime charged with genocide.
In Slovakia, Vladimir Mečiar of the ex-communist Movement for a Democratic Slovakia returned to office heading coalition with two other parties.
14 President Dudayev, rebel leader of Chechenya, vowed his people would fight to the death following breakdown of talks with Russia.
15 In UK, Labour gained an unparalleled post-war by-election victory in Dudley West, which they took from the Tories with a 29 per cent swing.
In Republic of Ireland, John Bruton (Fine Gael) elected PM to head new coalition with Labour Party and Democratic Left.
18 At elections in Bulgaria, Bulgarian Socialist Party (comprising many former communists) gained majority of parliamentary seats.
19 Russian planes bombed Grozny, capital of rebel Chechenya, causing many civilian casualties; a sustained ground attack commenced on 22 Dec.
22 In Italy, PM Berlusconi tendered his resignation following collapse of coalition; a new government had not been formed at year end.
25 Uzbekistan held first parliamentary elections since independence; regionally-backed candidates did well, leaving ruling Democratic Party with only about one-third of seats.
26 In Marseilles, French anti-terrorist police stormed Air France Airbus, which had been hijacked in Algiers, killing all four Algerian Islamic hijackers and rescuing 170 passengers; three passengers had been killed by the terrorists at Algiers.
30 In UK, ownership of the coal industry passed back into private hands nearly 50 years after nationalization; only 7,000 miners remained compared with 700,000 in 1946.

INDEX

Page references in bold indicate location of main coverage.

AALAND ISLANDS, 82
AAMODT, Kjehil Andre, 539
ABACHA, Gen. Sani, Head of State of
    Nigeria, 271–3, 419
ABDALLAH, Ahmed Ould, 280
ABDIĆ, Fihret, 131
ABDOU, Mohamed, 348
ABDOULAYE, Souley, 283
ABDULLAH TUANKU ABDUL RAHMAN, Tunku,
    357
ABDULLOZHONOV, Abdumalik, 325
ABIOLA, Moshood Kashimawo Olawale,
    272–3, 611
ABKHAZIA, 152, 435
ABS, Hermann, obit., 589
ABSE, Dannie, 534, 537
ABU DHABI, 239, 243
ABURTO MARTÍNEZ, Mario, 200
ACOSA COLOMA, Francisco, 188
ACKROYD, Peter, 532, 537
ACTON, Sir Harold, obit., 589
ADAMI, Dr Eddie Fenech, Prime Minister of
    Malta, 100
ADAMS, Gerry, 22, 35, 43, 45, 69, 175, 606
ADAMS, John, 507
ADHIKARI, Man Mohan, Prime Minister of
    Nepal, 340–1
AFANASYEV, Viktor, obit., 589
AFGHANISTAN, **322–3**, 336–7, 416, 431
AFRICA WATCH, 263
AFRICAN CONFERENCES & ORGANIZATIONS,
    442–5
AFRICAN COUNTRIES OF OFFICIAL PORTUGUESE
    LANGUAGE (PALOP), 97
AGASSI, André, 547
AHERN, Bertie, 70
AHLBERG, Allan, 535, 537
AHLBERG, Janet, death, 535
AHMAR, Sheikh Abdullah bin Hussein al-,
    238
AHMED, Ahmed Dini, 263
AHO, Esko, Prime Minister of Finland, 82
AHTISAARI, Martii, President of Finland, 81,
    607
AIDS (acquired immune deficiency
    syndrome), 54, 265, 268, 290, 417, 476,
    511
AISIN GIORRO PU JIE, death, 373
AITCHISON, Craigie, 526
AITKEN, Jonathan, MP, 20, 27, 587
AITKENHEAD CASTILLO, Richard, 197
AJELLO, Aldo, 297, 410
AJODHIA, Jules, 213
AKASHI, Yasushi, 136, 414
AKAYEV, Askar, President of Kyrgyzstan,
    324, 326
AKIHITO, Emperor of Japan, 386
ALAGNA, Roberto, 503
ALATAS, Ali, 353
ALBANIA, 100, 101, **138–40**, 434, 435, 439,
    518, 551, 570

ALBEE, Edward, 513
ALBERO, Vicente, 92
ALBERT, Prince, of Monaco, 90
ALBRIGHT, Madeleine, 588
ALEKSI II, Patriarch, 466
ALEXANDER, Peter F., 538
ALFONSÍN FOULKES, Raúl, 181
ALGERIA, 56–7, 220, 250, **252–5**, 257, 258,
    281, 283, 425, 468, 488
ALI, Abdelrahman Abdel, 262
ALI, Maj.-Gen. Mohammed Chris, 273
ALIA, Ramiz, 138–9
ALLEYNE, Brian, 211
ALSOP, Will, 530
ALSTON, Richard, 509
ALTMAN, Robert, 514
ALTMAN, Roger, 164
AMELIO, Gianni, 518
AMERICAN ORGANIZATIONS, 177, 198–9, 207,
    449–52
AMERICAS, Summit of the, 177, 450, 452
AMES, Aldrich, 170, 173, 607
AMES, Maria del Rosario Casa, 170, 173
AMIN, Idi, 268
AMIS, Sir Kingsley, 537
AMNESTY INTERNATIONAL, 224, 227, 230, 255,
    288
AMOUR, Salmin, 267
ANCRAM, Michael, MP, 45
ANDEAN PACT, 450
ANDERSON, Lindsay, death, 520
ANDERSSON, Sten, 441
ANDERTON, Jim, 401
ANDORRA, **88, 89–90**, 438–9
ANDREJEVS, Georgs, 153
ANDREW, Rob, 546–7
ANDRIAMANJATO, Richard, 350
ANDRIANOPOULOS, Andreas, 102
ANDRIESSEN, Louis, 507
ANGOLA, 1, 97, 292, 296, 297, **298–300**, 317,
    410, 443, 444
ANTIGUA & BARBUDA, **210, 211**
ANTONACCI, Anna Caterina, 502–3
ANWAR IBRAHIM, Datuk Seri, 356
ANYAOKU, Chief Emeka, 338, 418–9
APTIDON, Hassan Gouled, President of
    Djibouti, 263
ARAB LEAGUE, 239, 248, 487
ARAB MAGHREB UNION (AMU), 225, 252
ARAB STATES OF THE GULF, **239–45**
ARAB WORLD, **200–3**
ARAFAT, Yassir, 1, 176, 217–8, 221–3, 225–6,
    251–2, 315, 572, 611, 614
ARAKI, Grand Ayatollah, 320
ARCHER, Lord (Jeffrey), 5, 533, 535, 537
ARCHER, Kenneth, 511
ARCHITECTURE, 42, **529–31**
ARCTIC, 81, 441
ARDANZA, José Antonio, 92
ARGENTINA, 37, **181–2**, 189, 409, 449, 450,
    451, 454, 552

315, 412; Sudan, 246, 247; Switzerland, 87; Trusteeship Council, 417; Western Sahara, 257–8, 412; women, 417–8; World Population Conference, 90, 224, 237, 321, 336, 417, 465, 485–6; Yemen, 239, 416; Yugoslavia (former), 1, 2–3, 34–5, 36, 129, 132, 135–8, 140, 176, 414–5, 455–5, 489–90

UNITED STATES OF AMERICA (USA), **157–77**
  EXTERNAL RELATIONS & DEFENCE (*see also* Arms Control & Disarmament, Conference on Security & Cooperation in Europe, North American Free Trade Agreement, North Atlantic Treaty Organization, Organization of American States, Partnership for Peace): Africa, 246, 267, 291, 315, 317; Arab-Israeli issues, 172, 175–6, 216, 218, 221, 223, 224, 228, 572, 579, 586; arms control, 151, 173, 453–4; Asia/Pacific, 172, 173–4, 320, 329, 336, 337, 352–3, 354, 355, 358–9, 361, 363, 375, 378, 382, 383–4, 386, 387–8, 389, 402, 406, 413, 417, 446, 458–60; Canada, 180; Caribbean, 451–2; Cuba, 174, 177, 193–4, 451, 452; Europe, Central/East, 115, 116, 127, 172; Europe, West, 35, 74, 100, 102, 110, 174; European Union, 426, 427, 452, 493; GATT, 177; Haiti, 173, 174–5, 195, 413, 449; Iraq/Kuwait, 175, 226, 233, 240–41, 244, 415; Japan, 173, 382, 383–4, 386; Korea, North, 173, 387–8, 389, 413, 458–60; Kurds, 234; Latin America, 174, 177, 183, 186, 188, 193–4, 198, 449, 450, 451; Libya, 225, 248, 410; Middle East, 225, 236; NAFTA, 200, 205, 450; Northern Ireland, 35, 43, 69, 175; Russia, 36, 148, 172, 173, 453–4; Somalia, 174, 262, 412; Summit of the Americas, 177, 450, 452; transnational crime, 462–3; UN arrears, 408; Yugoslavia (former), 1, 35, 101, 134, 136, 137, 138, 176, 414, 456
  HOME AFFAIRS: abortion issue, 171–2; Ames/CIA affair, 168, 170–71, 173; arts, 516–18, 524, 527; crime & punishment, 159, 160–61, 164–5, 171, 172;; disasters, 159, 473; economy, 34, 168, 169–70, 429, 551–2, 563–5; elections, 157, 165–8, 176; environmental issues, 483, 485; government appointments, 160, 161, 163, 168; health care, 162, 165; information technology, 477; Iran-Contra affair, 160; legal affairs, 171, **499–500**; O.J. Simpson case, 158; race relations, 158, 170, 171; religion, 90, 464, 465, 467–8; science, 471–2, 474; security, 157, 158, 171; social issues, 170–1; space exploration, 471–2; sport, 158, 541, **549**; welfare reform, 163; Whitewater affair, 157, 159–60, 161–3, 168
UNWIN, Sir Brian, 40
UPDIKE, John, 533, 537
URBIZO PANTING, Delmer, 198
URUGUAY, 189, **191**, 450
US VIRGIN ISLANDS, 451

UWILINGIYIMANA, Agathe, 293
UZBEKISTAN, 323, **324**, 325, **327–8**, 570

VĂCĂRIOU, Nicolae, Prime Minister of Romania, 124–5
VALLA, Ambra, 510
VAN DAMME, Johannes, 359
VAN DEN BROEK, Hans, 423
VAN DER STOEL, Max, 434
VANDE LANOTTE, Johan, 64
VANDENBROUCKE, Frank, 64
VANUATU, 398, **403**, **405**, 448, 449
VARENNIKOV, Gen. Valentin, 144
VATANA ASAVAHAME, 354
VATICAN, **88**, **90–1**, 133, 195, 219, 348, 417, 465, 485
VÄYRYNEN, Paavo, 81
VAZGEN I, Catholicos, obit., 604
VELÁSQUEZ, José Ramón, 191
VELAYATI, Ali Akbar, 321
VENDA, 311
VENETIAAN, Ronald, President of Suriname, 213
VENEZUELA, **191–2**, 449, 451, 452, 552
VERSTAPEN, Jos, 546
VICK, Graham, 502
VIDENOV, Zhan, 127
VIETNAM, 172, **363–4**, 384, 392, 396, 446
VIERA, João, President of Guinea-Bissau, 295
VILJOEN, Gen. Constand, 312, 314
VILLELA, Edward, 508
VILLIGER, Kaspar, 88
VINOGRADOV, Oleg, 508
VIOLA, Gen. Roberto, obit., 604
VISEGRAD GROUP, 115, 116, 154, 172
VO VAN KIET, Prime Minister of Vietnam, 364
VOJVODINA, 434
VRANITZKY, Dr Fred, Chancellor of Austria, 84–5, 614
VRANOPOULOS, Mikhail, 103
VU NGOC HAI, 364

WACHTMEISTER, Count Ian, 79
WADE, Abdoulaye, 278
WAIN, John, obit., 604
WAKEHAM, Lord (John), 20
WALCOTT, 'Jersey' Joe, obit., 604
WALDEGRAVE, William, MP, 20, 587
WALES, 12, **40–2**, 524
WALES, HRH Prince of, 19, 28, 42, 531, 536, 606, 611
WALES, HRH Princess of, 19, 28, 537
WALESA, Lech, President of Poland, 111–4, 116, 388
WALKER, Alexander, 538
WALLIS & FUTUNA ISLANDS, 404, 406
WALTER, Harriet, 514
WALVIS BAY, 306
WANAMAKER, Zoe, 511
WARNER, Deborah, 502, 515
WARNER, Marina, 538
WASMEIER, Marcus, 540